INSIGHT GUIDES

East Asia

Directed and Designed by Hans Höfer
Produced and Edited by Geoffrey Eu

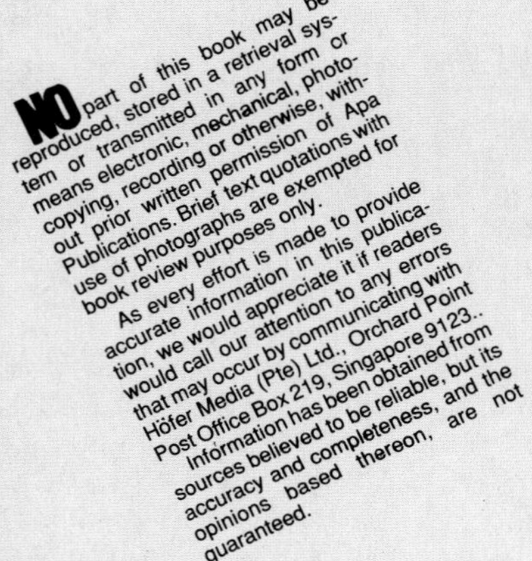

East Asia

First Edition (3rd Reprint)

Printed in Singapore by Höfer Press Pte. Ltd

About This Book

Asia is where it all began for Apa's *Insight Guides.* Going back over familiar territory while producing *Insight Guide: East Asia* was both a sentimental journey and an eye-opener: writing about the eternal time-tested attractions invoked memories of previous *Insight Guides*, while several newer but equally stunning locations and attractions have recently emerged.

Because nine of the 10 destinations featured are also individually available in existing Apa guides, *East Asia* represents a sort of highlight guide.

East Asia is geared for the first-time traveler or those who intend to visit several countries during a single regional trip. Space constraints dictated that only the more established and well-known destinations within each country be included in the guide.

Apa boss Hans Höfer has a special attachment to Asia, having first arrived in Indonesia in 1969, where he developed the *Guide to Bali*. This was only the first of the popular *Insight Guides* series. He later founded Apa Publications in Singapore and under his creative direction, the *Insight Guides* series has won worldwide acclaim.

Seasoned Writers

Apa editor **Geoffrey Eu** was entrusted with the task of seeing the project through to completion. Eu's first contacts with the travel business came from his undergraduate days in the School of Travel Industry Management at the University of Hawaii. He later went on to complete his Master's at Northeastern University's Medhill School of Journalism before finally returning to Singapore.

Wilhelm Klein, whose association with Apa dates back to *Insight Guide: Burma* and the photo album *Burma the Golden*, furnished text and some photographs for the Burma portion of the guide. Klein has traveled to Asia on a regular basis for over 20 years. He has long been drawn to the fascinating blend of Buddhism and Socialism found in Burma.

Saul Lockhart drew from his experience with *Insight Guide: Hong Kong* to provide the text for East Asia's Hong Kong segment. Lockhart is a respected freelance editor, writer and photographer who has been based in the Orient since 1966. From his home in Repulse Bay, Lockhart has also authored or co-authored the following: *Complete Guide to the Philippines*, the *Hong Kong Good Food Guide* and *A Diver's Guide to Asian Waters*.

Eric Oey is Apa's former marketing manager and editor of *Insight Guide: Indonesia*. Oey holds a Master's degree in Indonesian philosophy and linguistics and is nearing completion on doctoral work in the same field. His impeccable qualifications made him the perfect choice for writing the Indonesia section.

Jordan Sand has a degree in Japanese history and literature from Columbia University. Sand spends his spare time translating and writing on architecture and urban culture in Japan. His pet project involves the restoration of an old house in a downtown backstreet, just behind the Kasamori shrine.

To help us understand the strength of traditional Korea in the face of her galloping modernization, writers **Kim RonYong** and **Melanie Hahn** have distilled for us the wealth of information contained in *Insight Guide: Korea*. Novelist Kim RonYong's latest work,

Eu

Klein

Lockhart

Oey

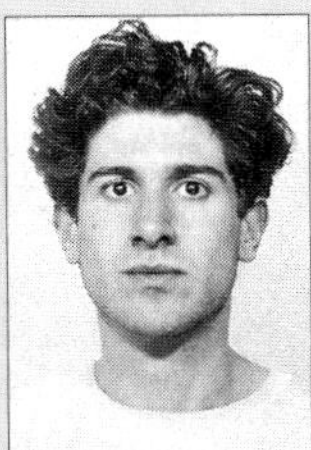

Sand

Clay Walls (1986), concerns the struggles of Korean-Americans in the 1930s and 1940s. Hahn directs a student writing program at UC Berkeley and has studied and taught in South Korea. Ardent travelers and residents there, both have had extensive experience in interpreting the complexities and contradictions of this burgeoning nation.

Manila-born **Alfred A. Yuson** is contributing editor and film critic for that city's Observer magazine. He was also a major contributor to *Insight Guide: Philippines*. Yuson has received numerous awards for his fiction writing and poetry.

Singaporean **N. Balakrishnan** represents some of the new blood in East Asia. Armed with a Master's degree from Columbia University's Graduate School of Journalism, he traveled widely in Asia, Europe and the US before returning home. Bala is currently a journalist at *The Straits Times*, Singapore's English daily newspaper, where between deadlines, he succeeded in producing the section on Singapore.

For the Taiwan section, we again turned to old Apa hand, **Daniel P. Reid**, whose manuscript on the Republic of China formed the backbone of *Insight Guide: Taiwan*. He holds a Master's degree in Chinese language and civilization from the Monterey Institute of International Studies and is proficient in both spoken and written Mandarin. After more than a decade in Taiwan, Reid's expertise and intimate knowledge of the land enabled him to produce a concise yet informative piece for *East Asia*.

Steve Van Beek is a transplanted American who has been living in Thailand since 1969. After graduating with a history degree from the University of Oregon, he served with the Peace Corps in Nepal, before finding his way to Bangkok. He edited three local magazines, then turned freelance in 1977. He has written *The Arts of Thailand*, *Bangkok Only Yesterday*, the *Guide to Pattaya and Southeastern Thailand*, among others and most recently authored Apa Publication's latest offering, the *What To Do In Bangkok* guide. Van Beek has also turned his attention to films and audiovisual equipment.

Skilled Photographers

The pictures selected for *East Asia* represent the work of many different photographers, underlining the international nature of collaboration on the book. Most have been long-time contributors to Apa. Included among them are **Gunter Pfannmuller**, **Manfred Gottschalk**, **Max Lawrence**, **Kal Muller**, **Jean Kugler**, **D & J Heaton**, **Bill Wassman**, **Bill Rubinstein**, **Alain Evrard**, Wilhelm Klein, Hans Höfer, **David Ryan**, **Ray Cranbourne**, **R. Ian Lloyd**, **Alain Compost**, **Paul Van Riel**, **Nik Wheeler**, **Rene Dorel**, **Ben Nakayama**, Eric Oey, **Peter Friedrich**, **Allen F. Grazer**, **Peter Bruchmann**, **Thomas Schoelhammer**, **Leonard Lueras**, **Michel Hetier**, **Lyle Lawson**, **Tony Joyce**, **Philip Little**, **Blair Seitz**, **Noli Yamsuan, Jr.**, **Frank Salmoiraghi**, **Luca Invernizzi**, **Ingo Jezierski**, **Heidrun Guether**, **G.P. Reichelt**, **Paul Von Stroheim**, **Dan Rocovits**, **Jill Gocher**, **Rendo Yap** and **Yap Piang Kian**, **"Wah"** provided several historical shots.

Thanks go to **Ronald Harris**, president of Hemphill/Harris Travel Corporation in California. His personal input helped turn *East Asia* into reality.

—Apa Publications

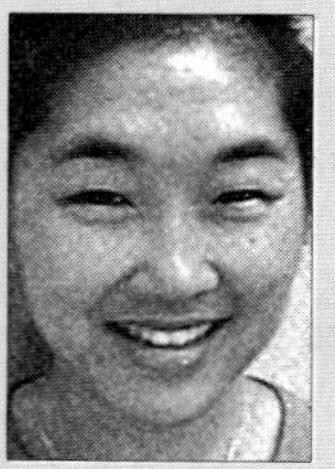

Hahn

Yuson

Balakrishnan

Reid

Van Beek

BURMA

—by Wilhelm Klein

HONG KONG

—by Wilhelm Klein

INDONESIA

—by Eric Oey

JAPAN

—by Jordan Sand

SOUTH KOREA

—by Melanie Hahn/Kim RonYong

MALAYSIA

—by Geoffrey Eu

TRAVEL TIPS

林少
佛

Terre de la Compagnie
T. des Etats
I. de Yeso
Amur R
Nerzinskoi
L. Baikal
Selinginskoi
Houmari
Kulon L.
Teitcicar
CHINOIS
Mingousta
Fourdan
Kerlon R
Loulco
Goncher
TARTARIE
Nayman
Leabting
Eke Aral
Ourat
Hami
cobi
Muraille
Pekin
Tayven
Golfe de Petcheli
COREE
Pinian
Kingkitao
Kinghing
Jedo
Meaco
JAPON
Ximo
GRANDE
Ortous
Petcheli
Tayyuen
Tsinan
Contgchang
Hohan Ho
Changi
Potrao
Sigan
Caifong
Hohan Ho
Siau
Nankin
CHINE
Mtratico
Hongtchou
Nangcheou
Lekio I.
Longugam
Tchintu
Vutchan
Telekiang
Tropique du Cancer
Nantchou
Koeijan
Futcheu
Keilin
Tingtekou
Canton
Yunan
I. Formose
MER
Kaoutcheou
Macao
Hai tanchan
Hayman I.
Golfe de Cochinchine
Cochinchine
I. des Luzon
Pres. de l'Inde au dela du Gange
Pegu
Siam
Judia
Samar
Manille
PHILIPINES
Camboja
Ciampa
ISLES
I. Mindanao
gale
Tanasserim
I. de Condor
G. de Siam
Malacca
LES MOLUQUES
Mt. St. Pedro
Borneo
I. Gilolo
Achem
I. de Legor
BORNEO
Detroit de Malacca
Poncian
I. Cocos
Lava
Celebes I.
I. de Sumatra
Succadana
I. Nias
I. Ceram
I. Nassaw
Macassar
Dt. de la Sonde
I. Maduro
Bali
I. de Cumbava
I. de Java
Batavia
Mataran
Ende I.
Timor

An Asian Snapshot

Traveling to the fabled East isn't what it used to be. Gone is the Romantic Age when one had to set aside days; or even weeks, for journeys to distant lands on ocean steamers, trans-continental railways and the China Clipper. Travel patterns have changed, and most places on earth are now within physical and financial reach.

Much of the not-so-mysterious East is now only a plane hop, skip or jump away. Balinese dances, pagodas at Pagan, "wild men" of Borneo and the rice terraces of Luzon can ball be experienced without a hint of discomfort. Cities like Hong Kong, Seoul, Tokyo, and Singapore are as modern as any in the Western world, so the luxuries of the urban lifestyle are never far away.

Although change is very much in evidence, some things never change. Like the spectacular architecture of ancient civilizations, the cultural impact of the great religions, the sounds of the forest and the work in the paddy fields. Rice, the lifeblood of Asia, is the Great Unifier, from Japan to Indonesia, Burma to the Philippines. Outside the cities, the unceasing sight of men, women and animals working the fields is the one image that will remain with visitors.

It would be an injustice, not to mention a near-impossibility, to include all the marvels of the East in a single volume. *Insight Guide: East Asia* brings the area to manageable proportions by highlighting attractions in 10 destinations: Burma, Hong Kong, Indonesia, Japan, South Korea, Malaysia, the Philippines, Singapore, Taiwan and Thailand. China has been left for a future *Insight Guide*. Nevertheless, *East Asia* gives the reader a clear and comprehensive picture of the region and its peoples. It's just like modern-day travel: short and satisfying.

Preceding pages: Kimono-clad Japanese child; all set for the lion dance in Singapore; Korean fisherman; northern Thai hill tribe girl and baby; graceful Filipina beauties; merry Muslim portrait; Javanese dance master; expressive Balinese dancer; young monk near the Thai-Burma border and left, old map of East Asia.

BURMA: BUDDHIST SPLENDOR

"When the system of economic relations of a given age can no longer serve the interest of his society, man thinks of, and endeavors to establish new systems which can better serve his interest."

The System Of Correlation Of Man And His Environment

Burma is, first and foremost, a Buddhist country. Revolutionary as the philosophy of the Burma Socialist Program Party appears, it is essentially the same as that preached by Gautama the last Buddha, 2,500 years ago and on which a new religion was founded to uproot Brahmin haughtiness and caste oppression.

To an open-minded visitor, Burma is enthralling. Enthralling because of the unpretentious, almost otherworldly life of its people; and because of a 20th-century realism in its political outlook. Anyone who has visited the Shwedagon Pagoda during the candle-studded full moon night of the *Thadingyut* and who has also noticed the pride and prowess in the eyes of the cadres marching through Rangoon's streets on Union Day, will instantly realize that Burma is one of the few remaining places where diverse cultural expression is still impressively present. The country mirrors human development from its animist origins to its socialist present in such a riot of colors, forms and ideas, that the first-time visitor can only be stunned. Philosophy has always been a part of daily life in this country of torrential rain and arid plains, of rivers and rice fields, of jungle warfare and meditative calm. The ideas which govern Burma are millennia old. The people who live them try cautiously to align with the encroaching forces of our time; cautiously, because that is innately Burmese.

With 261,789 square miles (678,033 square km), Burma is the largest mainland country in Southeast Asia. The borders with Bangladesh, India, China, Laos and Thailand are closed to ground transport and are to a large extent controlled by federalist insurgents who struggle against the central government in Rangoon.

The last census recorded more than 35 million inhabitants, 80 percent of which still live in small rural hamlets.

Rangoon may by now be a Third World-type metropolis with all its drawbacks. But just outside the city limits, a few miles from the Sule Pagoda, in small villages shaded by tamarind and mango trees, life goes on as it always did; in a perennial rhythm dictated only by the planting, growing and harvesting of paddy. The well-preserved edifices of bygone eras and the vestiges of glorious Buddhist times radiate the strength and grace this religion has instilled in its devout disciples.

The Burmese live within their heritage; they are a flourishing part of it. A visitor to Burma has no need for sterile cultural shows. For if the senses are receptive, the whole country becomes a stage and the show spans the lifetime of a nation.

Preceding pages: The temple-studded plain of Pagan is one of Asia's most stunning sights. Left, a minister at the 19th-century Burmese court.

THE PAST IN THE PRESENT

In prehistoric times, a hunting and food gathering people, unacquainted with the cultivation of paddy and similar agricultural techniques, lived in caves and shelters along the eastern hill ranges of Burma and in its fertile valleys. In the Padah-Lin Caves in Shan State, neolithic paintings and stone axe chips of a forgotten people have been discovered. These proto-Australoids have long since vanished. They moved on towards Malaysia, Indonesia and the Andaman islands.

Much later, yet long before the Burmans occupied the Irrawaddy valley, the Mons had come to the lush, inviting southern coastline. Anthropologists call them the Mon-Khmer, a people who centuries before our time emigrated from Central Asia. They inhabited an area extending from the shores of the Andaman Sea, in the west, to what is today Kampuchea in Indochina. They propagated the Buddhist creed in Burma, and so became the progenitors of what eventually developed into today's specific Burmese culture.

Their kingdom, Suvannabhumi, the Golden Land, was for centuries the heartland of Southeast Asia. We know from Indian sources that they traded with Asoka's empire during the third century B.C. According to legend, it was during their time that the foundation of the Shwedagon Pagoda was laid.

Another tribe, the Pyu, Tibeto-Burman as is the present-day majority, settled at a later period along the middle reaches of the Irrawaddy. Artifacts uncovered at their flourishing capital Sri Ksetra show that Theravada Buddhism was already practiced in their mature city-states.

It was during the ninth century, an era of migration in Southeast Asia, that the Mrâmmâ, whom we know today as Burmans, entered the Irrawaddy valley and settled in the Kyaukse plain. Their original home was along the China-Tibet border, but the migratory impulse that originated in Yunnan's Nan-ch'ao kingdom unsettled them too; it made them search for a new, less troublesome homeland.

The rice-growing Kyaukse plain and in particular the city of Pagan, which they fortified, became the core of the kingdom. It is still of vital importance. Though chronicles tell us that Pagan was already founded in A.D. 108, the First Burmese Empire emerged only after King Anawrahta conquered the Mon capital of Thaton. The prisoners of war which he brought to Pagan, craftsmen, artisans, musicians, monks and paddy cultivators with a thousand-year-old tradition of agriculture, transformed the headquarters of a tribe into the capital of a thriving nation.

The meeting of the Mons, highly cultivated and devout people, with the Burmans, a sturdy, courageous tribe accustomed to hardship and trials, became an instant blueprint for success.

Four Million Pagodas: For 250 years, until its subsequent fall to Kublai Khan's army, Pagan was the jewel in the crown of Buddhist cities. Most of the surplus of the land was transformed into sacred buildings. The outstanding workmanship, combined with the fact that Pagan is only marginally affected by the southwest monsoon, has helped preserve many of the edifices.

Every king and nobleman had his temple or pagoda constructed, each more beautiful and imposing than the other. During the 12th century Pagan became known as the "city of four million pagodas." Some two thousand of them are still scattered over the Pagan plain.

Once Pagan was defeated, the hegemony

which the Burmans had established over the region, crumbled. The Mons founded their own kingdom in Pegu, the Arakanese revived theirs and the Shans governed from Ava.

The center of Burmese culture shifted to Pegu. It became a city of Buddhist learning. Several Caucasians, too, reached there by the 15th century. Stories about the wealth of the Pegu court had spread all over Europe after Nicolo di Conti, a Venetian merchant, returned from his four-month stay in the city. It was the Portuguese, who, a few years after establishing themselves in Goa and Malacca, opened trading posts along the coast.

Splendor at the Court: Alaungpaya, a Burman from Shwebo in Upper Burma, laid the foundation for what became Burma's most splendid historical period. After conquering Ayutthaya, the Siamese capital, in 1767, a successor, Hsinbyushin, did what Anawrahta had done 710 years earlier. He brought Siamese artisans and craftsmen to Ava, where a revival and regeneration of cultural values and expressions took place. The Mons, who, until this reemergence of Burmese power were still nurturing the idea of their own kingdom, were once and for all subdued. Since 1755, after Alaungpaya's entry into Rangoon, then was called Yangon, meaning "end of strife," the Mons have absorbed into the mainstream of Burmese life.

British Dominance: The European dominance in South and Southeast Asia did not bypass Burma. In 1824 British interests brought the East Indian Company into conflict with Burmese hegemonial aspirations. The ensuing war and the consequent treaty of Yandabo (1826) made the Burmese cede Arakan and Tenasserim to the British. Then again in 1852, after the unfair treatment of a British sea captain in Rangoon, the Second Anglo-Burmese War took place, leading to the occupation of Lower Burma.

A year later, Mindon Min, a pious and progressive king, ascended the throne in Amarapura. He advocated the idea of a nation that should be open to western industrial achievements but remain Buddhist in its outlook. In conformity with ancient traditions he shifted the capital and founded Mandalay to commemorate the

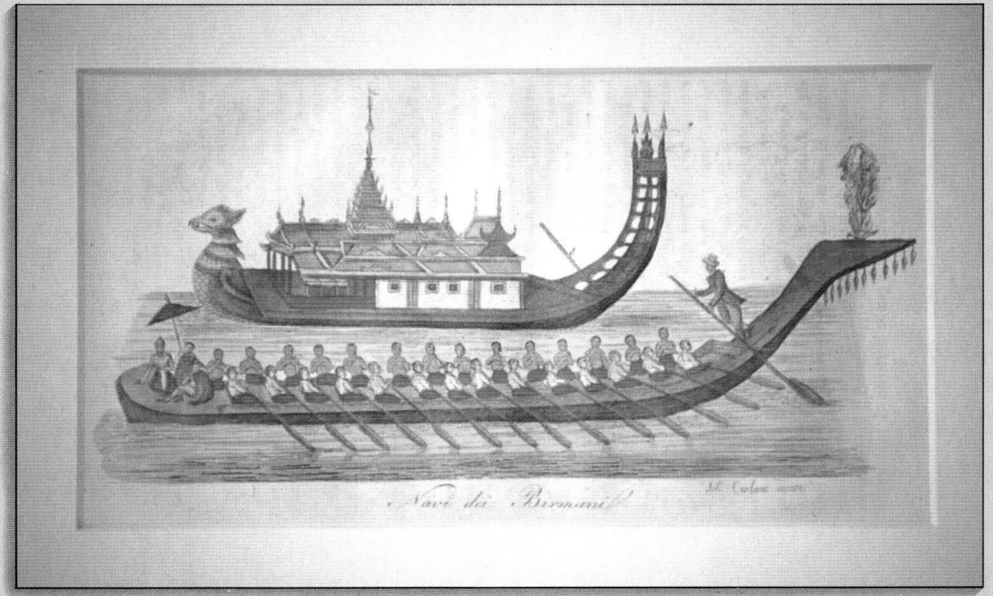

Left, 19th-century print of a Burmese noble. Above, royal barge escorted by Burmese navy vessel.

2,400th anniversary of the establishment of the Buddhist faith.

Attempts initiated by Mindon to come to grips with the permanent confrontation with British interests foundered during the reign of his successor Thibaw. In 1885, the Third Anglo-Burmese War brought defeat and ended Burmese sovereignty for the ensuing 63 years.

The first decade of British administration was characterized by an anti-guerrilla war in which the British used Indian, Chin, Kachin and Shan troops to fight the resistance in Upper Burma. By the turn of the century, however, that resistance abated in the face of an economic upswing and the modernization of some aspects of the society. London-trained Burmese lawyers founded the Young Men's Buddhist Association in 1906 and set a fast-developing nationalism into motion. In 1923 the "dyarchy reform," which finally extended to Burma, brought a certain degree of self-government.

Then, in the 1930s, the Thakin idea emerged out of the All Burma Student Movement. The group's leaders, Thakin (which means Master or *Sahib*) Aung San and Thakin Nu, were to become the post-war leaders of the country.

War and Independence: The Japanese landed in Lower Burma in December 1941 and within a few months the Allied troops were driven out of the country. With the Japanese were a group of 30 Thakins. They had received leadership training in Hainan and immediately organized the Burmese Liberation Army. This group fought on the Japanese side until 1945, when it suddenly switched to the Allies, and, renamed as the Patriotic Burmese Forces, helped to defeat the Imperial Army.

The British Labour Party government was set to get rid of its colonial burdens. At a conference in January 1947, the date for independence was set for January 4, 1948. Aung San, who led the country to freedom and who was to become its first prime minister, did not live to see that day. On July 19, he was assassinated while still drafting the new constitution. Thakin Nu, better known as U Nu, became independent Burma's post-war leader.

From the beginning the new nation had to cope with armed revolts and civil war. Most of the non-Burman minority groups took up arms together with two rival communist organizations and splinter military factions.

In economic terms, the first years of independence were disastrous for Burma. Income from rice exports plummeted and tax revenue diminished, yet the expenditure needed to maintain the oversized military machine grew out of control.

U Nu's consequent political steering, making Buddhism the state religion and promising autonomy to some of Burma's non-Burman people, culminated in Ne Win's nearly bloodless coup in 1962.

Ne Win, who first was commander in chief of the armed forces, then minister of defence and from 1958 leader of a caretaker government, initiated "The Burmese Way to Socialism," which is still the country's guiding ideology.

The manifesto declared that man would not "be set free from social evils as long as pernicious economic systems exist in which man exploits man and lives on the fat of such appropriation. The Council believes it to be possible only when exploitation of man by man is brought to an end and a socialist economy based on justice is established . . . for an empty stomach is not conducive to wholesome morality . . . "

For the next 12 years, Ne Win ruled by decree. Foreign businesses were nationalized, and the state took control of everything including banks. The army was put in charge of commerce and industry. A foreign policy of self-imposed isolation and neutrality was pursued. Tourist visas were limited to 24 hours. Throughout this entire period, farmers and workers in all parts of the country participated in seminars, where they were educated in "The Burmese Way to Socialism" and made aware of their rights and duties.

Left, the British inflict defeat at Rangoon in 1824. Above, General Ne Win, president from 1962 to 1981.

Then, in 1974, after the introduction of a new constitution and nationwide elections, the "Socialist Republic of the Union of Burma" came into being.

After years of decline and stagnation, Burma's economic situation has recently shown some signs of improvement. Since 1974, more foreign investment has been permitted, and privately owned businesses are now allowed in certain fields. Tourist visas have been extended to seven days, and tourist dollars now provide an additional source of income for the nation. A series of "Four Year Plans" have been introduced to stimulate agricultural production. The growth rate of the gross national product (GNP) since the mid-1970s has averaged five to six percent a year, as opposed to about two percent per annum in the preceding decade. The per capita GNP is estimated by the World Bank as $180 a year, but there is sufficient rice, and the population isn't starving.

Burma shocked much of the world in September 1979 when it became the first country to withdraw from the 88-member Non-Aligned Movement. Impatience with "big powers engaged in a behind-the-scene struggle for exerting their influence on the movement" was the official government explanation for the decision to pull out.

In spite of internal reforms that gave semi-autonomy to the non-Burman regions, the civil war along the northern and eastern frontiers has not abated. Ne Win retired from the presidency in 1981 and was succeeded by U San Yu, one of his staunch followers. In his seventies and in frail health, he remains the chairman of the Burma Socialist Program Party.

There are differing opinions on the relative successes or failures of the Ne Win regime. Burmese socialism is not built strictly on Marxist lines, as Marxism and Buddhism are not sufficiently compatible. The Revolutionary Council sought to plot a middle course, one that would steer the country away from hunger and exploitation, but would have a real chance of being accepted in a deeply Buddhist land.

Burma's course into the future is set. It will remain non-aligned and strictly neutral in its foreign policy. On the domestic level it pursues its own brand of socialist development, based on large organizations in agriculture and industry. The turmoil of the Indochina wars has bypassed Burma; so does the debt crisis which has hit nearly all the other countries in the region. And while the cultural heritage of surrounding countries is either commercialized or vanishing, it is alive and thriving in Burma.

RANGOON: THE ORIENTAL CITY

Of all Southeast Asian capitals, **Rangoon** is the least known. A city with so little international coverage that it seems not to exist in most publications. Rangoon emits no news. Everything still is as it was, 40 years ago.

The cars which run alongside the gray and mildewed Victorian buildings of downtown Rangoon are more often than not vintage models of 1948 or earlier. Men still wear *longyis* (sarongs) instead of jeans, women adorn their faces with ocher-colored concentric circles, made of *thanaka* paste and old ladies still puff their huge white cheroots with the same self-possessed pride as during Kipling's time. Meanwhile, *pongyis* (monks) seem to float in the crowds like specks of saffron in a polychrome sea.

Burmese love *pwes*, local festivals which last all night. And somewhere in Rangoon, there is always a *pwe* in progress. It might be on one of the many pagoda grounds or at the revered shrine of a neighborhood *nat* (spirit). Rangoon is a lively city because Rangoonans know how to live cheerfully with simple means. There are no nightclubs and there is little alcohol, but there is gaiety galore. Rangoon is the prototypical "Oriental City." A mixture of ancient and modern, Indian and Chinese, Buddhist and Socialist, with a sweet-scented air heavy with the fragrance of the tropics.

Preceding pages: Kaunghmudaw Pagoda near Sagaing, built in 1636. Left, Bangkok's famed Shwedagon Pagoda by starlight. Right, Buddha in Sule Pagoda achieves a neon-like effect.

We know from Ceylonese chronicles that a village called Okkala existed here 2,500 years ago. But it was the Shwedagon Pagoda, whose foundation was laid at that time, which made it known far and wide. The history of Rangoon has always been the history of its famous pagoda. The city as such only came into existence in 1755 when King Alaungpaya, after defeating the Mons, named it Yagon, meaning end of strife.

The British stormed the city for the first time in 1824 during the First Anglo-Burmese War and again in 1852, whence they remained until 1948.

A Pagoda at the Center: Modern Rangoon is built around the **Sule Pagoda**. With a height of 157 feet (48 meters) it is still the tallest building in downtown Rangoon. Its legend goes back to the Third Buddhist Synod in 230 B.C., which sent the two monks Sona and Uttara to Suvannabhumi to preach the Buddhist gospel. There, at Okkala, they enshrined a hair of the Buddha. For centuries it was known as the *Kyaik Athok*, the "pagoda with Buddha's hair," but was later renamed after the "Sule Nat," guardian spirit of Singguttara Hill.

Strand Road, where the colonial-style **Strand Hotel** charms visitors with its atmosphere of the 30s, leads to the **Botataung Pagoda**, which can also offer a 2,000-year-old history. When it was hit by an Allied bomb in 1943 a casket containing a hair of the Buddha was found. Reconstructed, the Botataung is now a novelty in pagoda architecture. Also in downtown Rangoon is the **National Museum** with the **Lion's Throne** from the Mandalay Palace which was moved to London after the Third Anglo-Burmese War and returned to Burma in 1964. The **Independence Monument**, close to the Sule Pagoda and the **Tourist Burma Office**, symbolizes the harmony between the different peoples of the nation.

The **Bogyoke Aung San Market** is Rangoon's largest market. Close to the **Rangoon Railway Station**, it ensnares the visitor with its labyrinth of alleys and its multitude of stalls that cater not only to the daily needs of the population but offer everything from smuggled foreign goods to handicrafts. But there are also the **Thein Gyi Zei**, **(Indian Market)** and the **Chinese Market** which sell specific goods and have their specific smells. The **Diplomatic Store** on **Sule Pagoda Road** is where Tourist Burma would like the foreign visitor to shop for his needs. Spare rolls of film are available. But here, he also has to pay in foreign currency.

The **Royal Lake** in **Bogyoke Aung San Park** is the jewel in the center of Greater Rangoon. It mirrors the Shwedagon Pagoda and is the pleasure ground for Rangoon's families. There, the brick-built **Karaweik Restaurant**, constructed in the form of the mythological Burmese water bird, seems to float on the lake. The **Zoological Garden** which once housed a White Elephant, and the **Horticultural Gardens** are in its vicinity.

On the way to Inya Lake one passes the **Kyauk Htat Gyi Pagoda** which houses a 230-foot (70-meter) long reclining Buddha and 600 monks who come here to study the sacred scriptures. The **Nga Htat Gyi**, the "five-story Buddha" is in the **Ashay Tawya Kyaung** on **Campbell Road**.

Passing by the huge artificial **Inya Lake** and the Russian-built **Inya Lake Hotel**, one arrives at the **Kaba Aye Pagoda**, modern Burma's foremost Buddhist monument. U Nu, the pious first prime minister of independent Burma, had it built between 1950 and 1952. It contains the relics of two of the Buddha's disciples.

U Nu convened the Sixth Buddhist Synod in the capital of this young nation to commemorate the 2,500th anniversary of the birth of Buddhism. For that purpose he had the **Maha Pasan Guha**, the "Great Cave," constructed, where 10,000 people could assemble. The Synod, which lasted for two years, read, interpreted, amended and sanctioned the current version of the *Tripitaka*. The **Institute for Advanced Buddhistic Studies** was founded and now has its seat next to the Maha Pasan Guha.

Vestiges of the colonial past can be found at the Strand Hotel.

Buddha and the 37 Nats

Burmese Buddhism is far from being a uniform religion, being based on Theravada, the conservative "Way of the Elders" which finds its inspiration in the ancient Pali scriptures. It is the creed propagated by the *Sangha*, the brotherhood of monks, and by deeply involved individuals. The average layman, however, follows a combination that is sometimes called Pagoda Buddhism. It is this blend of the Theravada doctrine and the local belief in spirits that adds color and soul to an otherwise scientific philosophy.

A common scene at a pagoda is of a devotee on the platform, prostrating himself toward the *stupa*. At such occasions he is murmuring the Buddhist prayer: "I take refuge in Buddha, I take refuge in the *Dharma*, I take refuge in the *Sangha*." Known as *Triratna*, the Three Jewels, it is the ritual which Buddhism asks its disciples to perform thrice daily.

Spirit deity in banyan tree.

For the monks, called *pongy* or "great glory," the situation is different. They are bound by the 227 rules of the order found in the *vinaya*, the second book of the *Tripitaka*, the Buddhist Bible. A *pongy* has to beg for his meals, but must never thank the donor. He must live in celibacy; a woman should not touch him, or his begging bowl, nor tread on his mat. His aim is to attain *nibbana* (the Pali word for nirvana) which will release him from the perpetual rounds of *samsara* or rebirths.

According to Gautama Buddha, life consists mainly of suffering. Desire is the cause of suffering and to overcome desire one should give up all attachments and follow the "Noble Eightfold Path." This teaches the right views, the right intent, the right speech, the right conduct, the right means of livelihood, the right endeavor, the right mindfulness and the right meditation.

Every young Burman is supposed to become a novice for at least a few weeks in his life. At the initiation ceremony, called *shin-pyu*, he becomes a "son of Buddha" and receives a Pali name. Only if he stays past his 20th birthday can he join the *Sangha* in a renewed ordination. If he remains a member he will devote the rest of his life to the study of the scriptures, to meditation and to teaching in the monastery schools.

Ancient animistic beliefs of spirits inhabiting trees, rivers and hills have been streamlined in Burma. The *Glass Palace Chronicle*, a historical treatise from the Konbaung Dynasty, tells about a national assembly of *nats* (spirits) on Mount Popa. Since then many more have been added at different periods until with *Thagyamin*, the king of the *nats*, they numbered

The 37 Nats evoke the same response as do the saints in Catholicism. People turn to them in times of need. In a small shack behind the Shwezigon Pagoda in Pagan, the images of all the 37 have been conserved. Mount Popa, not far from the erstwhile capital, is the living center of their worship. Every year in June the Spirit Festival takes place on this magical, cylindrical outcrop.

SHWEDAGON: RANGOON'S GOLDEN GLORY

The **Shwedagon Pagoda** is the most lively place of worship in the entire Buddhist world. It is also the most serene. Though not the tallest, its 330-foot (100-meter) gold-plated *stupa* rises above **Singuttara Hill** and dominates Rangoon and its environs. The Shwedagon is also a treasure chest. A huge emerald, set with more than two thousand other precious stones, adorns its *hti* (umbrella). With every movement of the wind, 1500 gold and silver bells ring in unison.

According to legend it was during the time of King Okkalapa, a contemporary of Buddha Gautama, that the original structure was built. Okkalapa prayed, and when Gautama was enlightened he gave eight of his hairs to Tapussa and Bhallika, two merchants from Suvannabhumi, who delivered them to their king. The hairs were enshrined in a 65-foot (20-meter) tall golden *stupa* that covered smaller ones in silver, lead, tin, copper, marble and iron.

Four stairways lead to the main platform. At the southern and eastern ones are colorful bazaars that sell pagoda art, flowers, banners and antiques. Using one of them and ascending the hundred-odd steps is like an overture to a *concerto*. The rich colors, multiform structures and mythological images, reflected on the main marble platform, are beyond compare.

Burmese Buddhism, the popular version of it, calls this platform home. A devotee who comes here will circle the *stupa* clockwise and thereby receive all the instructions of the religion. Incidents and stations of Buddha's life are depicted in various forms, along with Buddhist cosmoogy's *chinthes*, *hamsas* (mythological figures), ogres, *nats*, and planetary posts.

The structures on the opposite side are called *tazaungs*, praying or resting halls. On the southern side is the **Chinese Community Tazaung**. On the west, with its many wood carvings, is the **Arakan Tazaung** followed by the **Chinese Merchant's Tazaung** and the **Two Pice Tazaung** which receives its

Young Burmese girls use pale yellow thanaka bark powder as makeup.

name from voluntary tributes of a *pice*, a small coin, for the reconstruction of the Western Stairway. To the north are the **Sandawdwin**, the **Kannaze** and the **Shin Itzagone Tazaung**. Beneath the Sandawdwin is the spring where Buddha's hairs were washed. At the Kannaze is the "wish-granting stone" and the Shin Itzagone recalls a story from early Pagan times, of a *zawgyi*, an alchemist, who searched for the Philosopher's Stone. On the east is the **U Nyo Tazaung** with stories from Buddha's life carved in wood.

There are two famous bells on the platform. The 23-ton **Maha Gandha Bell** on the west is part of national history. The British were removing it in 1825 when it fell into the **Rangoon River**, from where they could not salvage it. The Burmese volunteered to do so on the condition that it remain in Burma. They succeeded, and gained national pride. The **Maha Tissada Bell** on the north weighs 42 tons and was cast during the time of King Tharrawaddy in 1842.

Next to the Arakan Tazaung, encased in glass, is the ethereal image of **Bo Bo Gyi**, the guardian *nat* of the Shwedagon. The statue of its legendary founder **Okkalapa** is to the left of the **Temple of Buddha Kassapa**, opposite the western landing. To its right are the statues of **Sakka**, the king of the *nats* and **Mai La Mu**, his mystical parents.

Behind the **Assembly Hall** to the northwest of the platform, where venerated *sayadaws*, Buddhist abbots, expound the scriptures to *pongyis* and the laity, is the **Wonder Working Buddha Image**. Together with the **Wish Granting Stone** in the Kannaze Tazaung they are the meeting place for superstitious Buddhists. At the latter, a subjective assessment of the stone's weight determines if the wish will come true. The octagonal **Eight Weekdays Pagoda** in front of the Assembly Hall demonstrates perfectly the integral components of Buddhist astrology. Behind the Wonder Working Buddha, in the northwest corner, stands a sapling of the original Bodhi tree in Bodhgaya. U Nu, who convened the Sixth Buddhist Synod in 1954, brought and planted it personally.

Above the main platform of the pagoda, accessible by a small, ladder-like staircase, is the meditator's platform. Theravadins sit here for hours, bathed in the luminous light of the gilded spires. They are at an advanced stage in their religious pursuit, and able to meditate, undisturbed by the hustle and bustle below. This level is not open to women. According to Buddhist belief women are still one step away from "entering the stream," from those destined to reach nirvana. They will first have to accumulate more karma to be reborn as men before they can reach the Buddhist objective.

There are specific hours in which the Shwedagon is incomparably beautiful. There is the hour before sunrise. Then, it is quiet and calm on the platform and the powerful feeling prevails that this is the one place where the law of the universe has been transformed into simple human proportions.

It is different in the early hours of the evening. Then, the warmth of the sun-baked marble slabs below one's feet, and the rising mountain of gold, like the yearned-for Buddhist heavens above, encompass the people in a feeling of peace and happiness. One does not have to be a Buddhist to indulge in it. The Shwedagon delights everyone.

Shwedagon's golden stupa dwarfs everything around it.

MANDALAY

Though **Mandalay** is not the capital, it is, nevertheless, the core of the country, the pounding pulse of the nation. As the commercial and cultural hub of central and northern Burma, it is the city to which the many races and tribes of the frontier area come to trade and treat themselves to taste of the big city. With only 600,000 inhabitants, it is neither a metropolis nor an ancient city.

Mandalay is a planned city, like New Delhi, Chandigarh or Brasilia. Its grid street plan, which surrounds the erstwhile "Golden City" of King Mindon, stands witness to that.

To shift capitals according to auspicious signs or prophecies is an old Brahman custom. The kings of Burma who had Manipuri Brahmans at their court to explain the multiform phenomena of the universe were always eager to follow their advice.

During the Konbaung Dynasty the capital was repeatedly shifted between Ava and Amarapura, but when Mindon ascended the throne in 1852 he planned an entirely new capital. It was a move which complied with an ancient prophecy, but was also to help him accumulate the required karma for his definite entry into nirvana.

Buddha himself is said to have visited **Mandalay Hill** and there he told his favorite pupil Ananda that 2,400 years after the establishment of his religion, a Buddhist city of learning would exist beneath the slopes of the hill. This anniversary was to be celebrated in 1857 and Mindon had the city built in time for the Fifth Buddhist Synod to convene there.

The history of Mandalay is short and tragic. Some 26 years after its formal completion, the British ousted Thibaw, Mindon's son and the last king of the Konbaung Dynasty.

In 1945 tragedy struck again. During the battle for Mandalay, British shells destroyed what was once the heart of the city: the famous **Royal Palace** of Mandalay.

Except for a scale model of the "Golden City" within the walls of what is today **Mandalay Fort**, and can only

Preceding pages: On the boulevard: strolling in front of Kuthodaw Pagoda at Mandalay. Left, chugging up the Irrawaddy River by steamer.

be visited with special permission, nothing is left of what once constituted the splendor of Mandalay.

Mandalay Hill is the beauty spot of the city. Entering at the base, between two huge white *chinthes*, the mythological figures who function as temple guardians, one climbs up covered stairways which keep the sun away but not the wind. Soothsayers, palmists, astrologers, begging nuns and soft drink peddlers line the path. Halfway up stands the huge gold-plated **Shweyattaw Buddha**. His outstretched arm points toward Mandalay Fort.

It was the monk U Khanti, who, in the second half of last century, transformed this outcrop on the dry plain of Upper Burma into a place of pilgrimage. The view from the top makes climbing the 1,729 steps worthwhile. To the west flows the broad and lazy **Irrawaddy River**, framed by the Sagaing and Mingun hills which are covered with pagodas. To the north the fertile rice growing area of Upper Burma stretches toward a green horizon, while to the east, visible on clear days, rise the distant Shan hills. The bustling city of Mandalay lies in the plain to the south, surrounded by a multitude of small, individually-built white pagodas.

Descending the southeast stairway, one arrives at the **Kuthodaw Pagoda**, Mandalay's "stone book." It has the whole Buddhist canon, the *Tripitaka*, recorded on 729 marble slabs, each one protected by a small *pitaka* pagoda. They are to carry Buddha's message for posterity. This was Mindon's gift to the Fifth Synod and painstakingly created by 2,400 monks.

From the center of the square rises the **Maha Lawka Marazein Pagoda**. It is a replica of Pagan's famous Shwezigon Pagoda. Not far from it is the **Sandamuni Pagoda**, where commentaries to the *Tripitaka* have been chiseled on another 1,774 stone plates.

The **Nandaw Kyaung** is the one wooden structure of the "Golden City" which survived the holocaust that swept over Mandalay in 1945. Mindon died in this palace and his son removed it from the palace grounds. The intricate wood carvings make a visit worthwhile. Next to it are the remnants of foundation walls of what was once Mandalay's fabulous **Atumashi**

Ox-powered transport at Kuthodaw.

Kyaung, the "Incomparable Monastery." It held four sets of ancient *Tripitaka* scripts and protected a huge Buddha image with an enormous gem in its forehead. In 1890 it burned to ashes. Burmese from all over the country and Buddhists from around the world come to Mandalay just to touch once in their life the sacred **Maha Muni**, the only image of Buddha that is said to have been produced during his lifetime.

The Maha Muni is impressive. At 12 feet 7 inches (3.8 meters) tall, it is covered with a several-inch-thick layer of gold leaf which the devotees have applied over the centuries. Within the pagoda are other historical objects, such as an image of Bodawpaya and his collection of ancient stone inscriptions which are invaluable aids for historical research.

There are also six bronze sculptures whose origin is known. During the 15th century, they stood in the Khmer capital of Angkor Wat, and were then shifted to Ayutthaya, Pegu and Arakan in the course of successive wars. From there they were brought to Amarapura, together with the Maha Muni.

Zegyo Market: Mandalay is not only pagodas and sacred buildings. Mandalay is a living place, conducive to studying the Burmese way of life. Behind the Maha Muni are the quarters of the pagoda-craft artisans. Buddha images in all sizes, forms and material, as well as many other Buddhist paraphernalia are produced here on the sidewalks of the bustling streets.

Zegyo Market in downtown Mandalay is the meeting place for shoppers looking for western goods which have not entered the country through official channels. In the evening when the night market opens, all the races of northern and central Burma can be seen here. Zegyo Market is what is understood by an "oriental bazaar," with all its smells, colors, jostling crowds and seemingly endless variety of goods.

Mandalay Environs: Mandalay was not constructed in the wilderness. The area around Mandalay is where the first Burmans who came to the Irrawaddy valley, settled. The royal cities of different historical epochs are in its vicinity.

On the outskirts of Mandalay, a few miles beyond the Maha Muni, are the

The Royal Palace at Mandalay.

remains of **Amarapura**. Constructed in 1782, it was a brainchild of King Bodawpaya. He moved there from Ava when his court astrologers reported inauspicious signs for the kingdom. The walled Royal City was the center, as in Mandalay, and around it were the orderly quarters of different traders and different nationalities. Amarapura still has many overgrown and ruined structures which cast a nostalgic spell over the visitor.

Before the construction of Mandalay, the Burmese kingdom was referred to as the Court of Ava, even when it actually resided in Amarapura. Ava was dismantled to build Amarapura, but many of its stone buildings, including the huge **Aungmye Bonzan Kyaung**, a rare example of a monastery built in stone, have weathered the times. Here is also the **Adoniram Judson Memorial**, erected for the American missionary who compiled the first Anglo-Burmese dictionary and who was incarcerated here during the First Anglo-Burmese War.

Across the **Ava Bridge**, the only bridge spanning the Irrawaddy, lies **Sagaing**. It was also a capital city during the 14th century when the Shans controlled the area. But the charms of Sagaing are neither mundane nor material. There are 600 monasteries, *kyaungs*, as the Burmese call them, spread over the Sagaing hills and valleys. They are all interconnected by covered stairways and tranquil, tree-lined paths. An average of 5,000 *pongyis* live, meditate, chant, preach and teach here.

About six miles (10 km) north of Mandalay, accessible by riverboat, lies the small village of **Mingun**. There, like a natural mountain, rises the remains of the **Mantara Gyi**, the Mingun Pagoda. King Bodawpaya meant it to be the world's tallest pagoda, but he never saw it finished. He died in 1813 and none of his successors completed the job. In 1838, however, as if decreed by the heavens, the existing structure stood at the epicenter of an earthquake.

Today it is the largest mound of bricks in the world. Mingun also houses the world's largest unbroken (87 tons) bell. It was meant to be placed in front of the Mantara Gyi. Now it hangs in a shack, forgotten by the world, treasured by the Burmese.

Room with a view at Mingun.

PAGAN: PAGODAS AND PALACES

Pagan is unique. A total of 2,217 brick-and-stone structures, most of them aesthetically pleasing temples and pagodas, are strewn over this small plain on the Irrawaddy. Dating from the 10th century to the 13th century, they are reminders of another age.

Pagan is fortunate. Not only does the **Arakan Yoma** mountain range shield it from the monsoon, its secluded location has also deterred large groups of package tourists. Pagan is for the initiated.

It all started with the monk Shin Arahan who converted King Anawrahta to the Theravada creed. Anawrahta waged war against Thaton in order to seize the *Tripitaka*, the holy scriptures. The Mons whom he brought as prisoners of war soon changed this walled city of a belligerent tribe into a thriving and flourishing kingdom.

The chronicles tell us of 11 kings between 1044, when Anawrahta ascended the throne, and 1287, when Narathihapate was defeated by Kublai Khan's forces. All profane structures of the era, including the kings' palaces, were built in wood. However, in conforming with the Buddha's teaching that everything is transitory except his word, each of the kings constructed religious buildings, which now tell the fascinating story of their time.

The most impressive of all the Pagan temples is the **Ananda**. Kyanzittha, Pagan's most virtuous and pious king, constructed it to represent the imaginary Himalayan Nandamula Caves. The Ananda Temple is whitewashed, reminding one, in the midst of this hot and arid plain, of craggy mountain peaks and the eternal snows. Its interior, a perfect Greek Cross, houses four 31-foot (9.5-meter)-tall images of the last four Buddhas: Kakusandha, Konagamana, Kassapa and Gautama.

The Ananda is a typical Mon structure. The many-tiered roof with *sikharas* (crowns) rising gracefully at every corner of its ascending levels, signals from the outside a celestial otherworldliness, while inside it is dark and cave-like. It was built for medita-

Burmese girl surveys the Pagan plain.

tion by a people with a thousand years of experience in religious architecture.

In the vicinity of Pagan village, within easy reach by horse-drawn *tongas*, are all the huge Burman-style, two-story temples.

The **Thatbyinnyu**, not far from the Ananda, was built during the 12th century by Alaungsithu, Kyanzittha's grandson. It is a two-story temple, 201 feet (61 meters) tall, with large, flamboyant pediments around two-tiered windows which brighten the interior and cool it with a constant current of air. Only when climbing to the topmost terrace of this tallest of the Pagan temples, with a view that encompasses the whole plain, can one fully grasp the number of preserved structures and the splendor of that bygone age.

On the outskirts of Pagan village is the **Gawdawpalin Temple**, built during the 12th century by King Narapatisithu. Typical also for its Burman-style architecture, it was the most severely affected structure during a 1975 earthquake. Though it was feared to be beyond repair, the Burmese Directorate of Archaeology has restored it to its former greatness. Its upper terrace is the place to be, to see the most dramatic sunsets east of the pyramids.

Within the village is the most ancient of the Burman-style temples, the **Shweguyi Temple**, also erected during Alaungsithu's reign. At the age of 81 he was smothered to death here by his son Narathu. To atone for this patricide, Narathu built Pagan's most colossal temple, the **Dhammayangyi**. It was meant to resemble the Ananda but misses its serene lightness and harmony. It is, however, Pagan's best-preserved structure. Narathu had masons put to death if the blade of a knife could enter the space between two bricks.

On the road to **Nyaung U**, beyond the city gate, stands the **Thilominlo Temple**. Built in 1211 by King Nantaungmya, it is the birthplace of the **Pyithu Hluttaw**, the unicameral Burmese parliament. Nantaungmya, who was not the crown prince, became king because of auspicious signs that were in his favor. He established a council named *hluttaw* in which his brothers could share the responsibilities of the state.

There is one more great temple in

A typically sensational Pagan evening.

the vicinity, about half-way between Pagan and **Minnanthu** village. Named **Sulamani**, after the god Indra's splendid residence on Mount Meru, it is designed along the plans of the Thatbyinnyu. After the rainy season, a small lake forms nearby in which this red brick structure is reflected in all its wondrous glory.

Each one of Pagan's two-story temples can be ascended by intricate stairways, built both inside and outside. To find them, one just has to follow the smell of bats which have made the stairways their home.

Pagodas: Buddhist structures are erected to remind the believer of the eternal truth his religion preaches. Apart from temples, which were built for meditation and to house monks, there are also the *stupas*, or pagodas. They are found in different forms and styles all over Asia. The Burmese *stupa* has a distinct shape. Its prototype can be found on the banks of the Irrawaddy. The **Bupaya Pagoda** was built a thousand years before Pagan's heyday, at the time, when, according to the chronicles, Pagan was founded. Since it has also served as a navigational aid for the boatmen of the river, a small shrine for **Mondaing**, the *nat* of the storms, was erected next to it.

Burma's most important pagoda, the **Shwezigon Pagoda**, stands in Nyaung U. Anawrahta had it built to slowly convert his animistic compatriots to Buddhism. The 37 *Nats* were once standing on its lower terrace to draw people toward the *stupa* and the new religion. They are still there, at the rear of the pagoda in a small hut. The Shwezigon became the model for all large *stupas* in Burma. Anawrahta also had other pagodas built in Pagan. The most beautiful of these is the whitewashed **Shwesandaw Pagoda** which was erected to commemorate his victorious return from Thaton. Next to it is the **Shinbintalaung**, which houses a cramped, reclining Buddha. The other two *stupas* built by him are the **Lokananda**, in **Thiripyitsaya** and the **Myinkaba Pagoda** in the village of the same name. The **Minglazedi Pagoda** is the last and the most beautiful of all Pagan pagodas. The *stupa* rises on top of three terraces which again have small *stupas* at each corner. Narathihapate, Pagan's last king, was not willing to pay tribute to the growing Mongol Empire in the north. So Kublai Khan invaded Pagan, signaling the end of the kingdom.

Myinkaba: Manuha, the defeated king of Thaton was brought to Pagan and settled in **Myinkaba**. He was afraid of dying a temple slave, so he had the **Manuha Temple** built to improve his karma. Though it is clearly in the Mon style, its upper story is unusual. It houses three large Buddha images in a very narrow space. Next to it is the **Nanpaya Temple** which was once Manuha's residence. Most of the Mon temples in Myinkaba show a strong Indian influence, such as the **Abeyadana Temple**, which was built by Kyanzittha's first wife, and the **Nagayon Temple** which was also constructed by Kyanzittha, whose fascination with Mon culture is well-documented. The **Kubyaukkyi Temple**, built by Rajakumar, Kyanzittha's oldest son, is home to Burma's "**Rosetta Stone**." Rajakumar had it inscribed in Burman, Mon, Pali and Pyu and so gave us the key to the otherwise lost Pyu language.

Today, Myinkaba has a highly-developed lacquerware industry and a museum which displays ancient examples of this typical Pagan art.

Pagan Village: Without tourists, Pagan would be one in a thousand Burmese villages. People in the area lead very simple lives, since the dry plains of Upper Burma yield no abundant crop.

Pagan houses a small but very pleasant **museum** where salvaged Buddha images, inscription plates and glazed tiles with Buddhist pictograms of the *Jataka* tales are kept.

Around the **Sarabha Gate**, which is flanked by the two images of the **Mahagiri Nats**, there is a small market. At the time of the Ananda festival in January it develops into a frolicsome fair. Along the main road, near the **Tourist Burma** and **Burma Airways** offices are many small shops which sell authentic lacquerware and, sometimes, not-so-authentic rubies.

Pagan can be reached either by a daily airplane from Rangoon and Mandalay or by bus from Mandalay. The Nyaung U Mann takes about 10 hours. A scheduled bus service from Rangoon comes via Kyaukpadaung and takes about 16 hours. Another way is by boat from Mandalay. However, until new ships are available, it is only recommended for resolute travelers.

Right, another busy day at Taunggyi market.

HONG KONG: "ONE COUNTRY, TWO SYSTEMS"

". . . a barren rock with hardly a house upon it."
Lord Palmerston, 19th century
". . . on borrowed time in a borrowed place."
Han Su-yin, 20th century

The most famous descriptions of Hong Kong, one of the most frantic and vibrant, yet anachronistic, destinations on this earth.

Other places may take their passage in time at a gentle, barely discernible pace. But not Hong Kong. Its movements in modern history and life are in very discernible, almost daily, steps, pushed and pulled by a refuge-minded population which seems to be permanently on the run. Of course, what they'll do or what will happen if they ever abruptly reach their destiny one fine day is a moot point . . . always conveniently ignored in the present.

Queen Victoria's Foreign Secretary Lord Palmerston, whose venomous outburst at being told of the latest colonial acquisition in Her Majesty's name, has earned his infamous place in every history of Hong Kong.

Of course, the China traders assessment of Hong Kong's naturally protected harbor, and the "barren rock's" potential as an entrepôt, a free trading port, proved correct, as any passenger crossing Hong Kong's "fragrant harbor" (for that is what the name means) on the Star Ferry can attest.

But Han Su-yin's description in a *Life* magazine article published in 1959 still holds true to this very day.

She, of course, was referring to a deadline of June 30, 1997 when the 99-year lease on the New Territories expires. That "future" has now been settled through the 1984 Sino-British Joint Declaration guaranteeing the capitalist entrepôt of Hong Kong life for another 50 years until 2147, as a Special Administrative Region of the People's Republic of China. "One country, two systems" is the current battle cry to lead the territory into the 21st century.

The local population was not consulted by either government as to their wishes for a post-1977 future—a proviso of the Chinese, not the British, it should be said. Yet, with stoic resignation, Hong Kong's six million accept the half-century extension of their horizon.

Who knows what the future really foretells? Only one thing is certain: The "place" may have been returned, but the "time" is still borrowed.

Preceding pages: A 19th-century print of old Hong Kong. Left, the typhoon shelter in evening light.

EXIT THE LION, ENTER THE DRAGON

When Britain hauls down the Union Jack at midnight June 30, 1997, Hong Kong's colonial status will have lasted 156 years, five months and 10 days.

There cannot be many places where you can pinpoint the future as accurately as the past. One has visions of some bowler-hatted mandarin in deepest, darkest Whitehall, toting up the cost the morning after like a nightclub tab after an all-night bash.

If the truth be known, Hong Kong has always been a rather pesky, yet virtually self-governing, colonial possession to the British, and a problem only solved by the inscrutable oriental patience of the Chinese.

If Hong Kong was fiction instead of fact, its birth would have been an accident of history. In fact it certainly was not. But its founding was controversial and unpopular with the mandarins back in London from the start. So distasteful did they find the affair that the man who did the deed was called back, censured and eventually sent to the 19th-century version of English diplomatic purgatory, the consulate in Texas, bereft of the honors usually bestowed by grateful monarchs on those who add to the realm. And he is not honored in Hong Kong either, though other lesser souls more in favor live on as street names.

It all began on January 20, 1841, when Britain's sole remaining plenipotentiary in China—Trade Superintendant Captain Charles Elliot, RN, annexed Hong Kong Island on his own volition, and by force of arms, to obtain trade concessions, to recover compensation for thousands of chests of British opium confiscated earlier at Canton, and to redeem a bent British pride.

The opium traders—for whom Elliot blockaded Canton and occupied three forts in order to secure "one of the islands . . . conveniently situated for commerce intercourse"—attacked Elliot after the fact because in their opinion his Convention of Chuen Pi was too conciliatory; indeed, the "foreign mud" (opium) merchants still had to pay customs charges to the Chinese, even though trading from desolate Hong Kong was less convenient than trading at Whampoa (their traditional entrepôt at Canton).

London was livid. Lord Palmerston, Queen Victoria's Foreign Secretary, dismissed Hong Kong by calling it a "barren island with hardly a house upon it." It would never become a trading center, he harrumphed.

The dubious honor of being the first governor of this backwater Victorian White Elephant fell to Sir Henry Pottinger (1843-1844).

In spite of the fact that London had been a bit lax in declaring sovereignty over its newest acquisition, Pottinger felt so strongly about Hong Kong's potential future that he encouraged permanent building and awarded land grants. These

practices he ordered stopped when he went north to take part in renewed hostilities against the stubborn Chinese. A long round of fighting ended at Nanking—on August 29, 1842 with the signing of a Treaty of Nanking—when the Chinese capitulated just as Pottinger's forces were preparing to attack that city. At the time, Pottinger was being politically chastized for spending too much public money on "useless" Hong Kong development projects.

With the Treaty of Nanking, however, those arguments ended and London gladly accepted the Island of Hong Kong in perpetuity, so that Britain could have "a Port whereat they may careen and refit their Ships, when required, and keep Stores for that purpose . . . "

Previous to this time, Macau and Whampoa were the major China trading ports. But with the eventual silting of Macau's harbor—located adjacent to the Pearl River Estuary—and the weakening of Portuguese power in Asia (and the growing strength of England), British traders wanted a place of their own to build godowns and process and sell profitable "foreign mud," as opium was nicknamed by the Chinese.

By fortuitous accident, Hong Kong Island became England's China port, and became, almost from the beginning, both a swashbuckling embarrassment and lucrative money machine for England. Hong Kong was founded for trade and continues to exist only for that commercial reason.

The Treaty of Nanking was only the first of three "bites" the British Lion took out of the Chinese Dragon's rear.

During the six months Pottinger had been away from the colony fighting, much progress had been made in settling this barren island. Though there was confusion over land sales, astute British traders instantly recognized that if Hong Kong did indeed become a prosperous colony, the key to success here would be land. And of course, the local Chinese were way ahead. They readily sold land whether they had title to it or not. Good *joss* (luck) apparently was with the traders, because on June 26, 1843, Hong Kong was officially declared a British Crown Colony.

The second of Britain's three bites occurred as a result of the Arrow War (also called the Second Opium War) when a Hong Kong-registered *lorcha* (a junk-rigged schooner with a foreign hull) named the *Arrow* was boarded off Canton in October 1856 by Chinese sailors. The *Arrow's* crew was detained, and this impropriety irritated the British.

Hong Kong's Consul-General, Harry Parkes, retaliated in force, hoping to use this *casus belli* to force the Chinese to allow foreigners back into Canton. (Entrance into Canton was guaranteed by the 1842 Treaty of Nanking, but had never been asserted.) The British fleet sailed up the Pearl River, breached Canton's city walls and forced their way to the Chinese Viceroy. Immediate British demands inspired by the *Arrow* incident were quickly met, but the key question of access to Canton was not. The

Left, illustration of a Chinese junk. Above, postcard showing coolies at mealtime.

Viceroy said he could not guarantee the safety of foreigners if they were allowed in the city.

Shortly thereafter, guerilla warfare broke out and foreign-held factories in Canton were attacked. Until that time, Hong Kong had been only a minor commercial dependence of Canton. The *hongs* (the original trading houses, some of which still do business in Hong Kong today) at this time transferred their headquarters to the security of the new British colony at Hong Kong and that trading situation was reversed. Hong Kong took its first step forward towards becoming a full-fledged entrepôt.

Local acts of terrorism continued to occur in Hong Kong, Canton and along the vital Pearl River. British forces, this time joined by French allies, fought back and in December 1857 captured Canton yet again. By the summer of 1858, allied forces had moved to the far north, where they eventually forced another Chinese capitulation and negotiated stronger concessions known as the Treaties of Tientsin. Under the terms of these agreements, foreigners now gained the rights to station diplomats in Peking and travel at will throughout China. On March 26, 1860, under a subsequent Convention of Peking, Kowloon Point (Tsimshatsui) was leased in perpetuity from the Chinese. In October of that same year, another battle took place in the north and the Emperor's Summer Palace in Peking was sacked by the allies. Lord Elgin, the British plenipotentiary who negotiated for the British this time, secured the cession of an additional 3.75 square miles of new territory consisting of Kowloon Point (on which the British had built a harbor defence fort in 1842) and Stonecutters Island (in the harbor) with the signing of two Conventions of Peking.

With that second British "bite," Hong Kong now consisted of nearly 36 square miles (94 square km) of "sovereign" territory. The colony's harbor could now be defended on both sides and the colony's British residents had a convenient haven across the water where they could engage in nefarious—mostly sexual—intercourse with Kowloon's natives.

England's third and last "nibble" of the Middle Kingdom occurred in 1898—and it is this final morsel which now keeps Hong Kong nourished and economically alive. By the mid 1880s, the colony's powers were concerned about the territory's security. What pushed Britain to force China's hand was a coaling station grant to France on the South China Coast opposite Hainan Island. After expressing Her Majesty's displeasure regarding this grant, Britain duly informed Peking that for defence purposes (nothing was said about "balance of power" with France), the colony would require additional territory. Eventually a demarcation line was drawn from Deep Bay to Mirs Bay and Britain forced China to lease New

Territories for 99 years from July 1, 1898.

In that third bite, the Crown Colony gained about 350 square miles (930 square km) spread over the mainland and 234 outlying islands. It also inherited a late 20th-century headache—an uncertain future.

For most of its history, and certainly the entire 20th century part, Hong Kong's historical path has never deviated from the self-imposed limits of this real estate lease. The year 1997 was well over the horizon in 1898. And it still seemed far, far away through the war-filled years up to the middle of this century. The date was blotted out of the collective psyche . . . a non-thing to be never spoken of . . . in the economically fat years of the sixties and seventies. Then instead of exploding into the open, it slowly bubbled to the surface in mid-1982 with the lead up to Prime Minister Margaret Thatcher's visit to Peking

The British and the Chinese signed on the dotted line in December 1984 after two years of at times quite acrimonious discussions. During this period, the Chinese bombarded the world, and particularly Hong Kong, with propaganda whilst the British kept a stiff upper lip with a self-imposed rule of silence. It is no secret that the British wanted to continue on after the magic date, and that the local population wanted Hong Kong to remain in the status quo.

Left, modern girls take to the promenade at Kowloon's New World complex. Above, early morning tai chi in Victoria Park.

That was not to be. The British entered the negotiations with their mind set only on the rented area of the New Territories, the other parts having been signed over to Her Britannic Majesty in perpetuity by treaty. The Chinese threw that out in the first minutes with a claim of sovereignty over the entire colony stating, as they had many times in history, the treaties were "unequal," meaning they were forced down their 19th-century throats with gunboat diplomacy.

The British fought a rear-guard action from the outset. The joint declaration as it stands does provide a guarantee for the freedoms, including private ownership of businesses and land, already enjoyed. Though a colony, Hong Kong enjoys—and has enjoyed—just about all the freedoms of a Western democracy and one of the freest places in Asian.

Ironically, while finally answering the "1997 question," it sets up another deadline a half-century in the future.

Until 2047, the Chinese are designating all of Hong Kong as a Special Administrative Region, where the lifestyle, economy, freedoms and laws can be and will be different from the rest of China. Beyond 2047, the picture becomes ever fuzzier. But there are some encourging signs.

Busy at work behind the scenes is a joint Hong Kong-Chinese group which is doing no less than writing the basic law—a mini-constitution—for the 21st century.

China's turbulent history is not very reassuring, at least on the surface. But China-watchers point out that even with the destructive force of, say, the decade-long Cultural Revolution, China kept its international treaties—particularly with Hong Kong—in spite of shrill and hysterical cries to the contrary.

Also, the average observer would point out that it would be foolish of China to close its foreign exchange window on the world. (Hong Kong provides China with an estimated US$5 billion to $6 billion annually, 35 percent to 40 percent of its foreign earnings.)

Finally, Chinese leaders believe the Hong Kong agreement is the first step in bringing Taiwan back into the fold. It comes down to this: If China can set up a special Administrative Region for capitalist Hong Kong, and keep it working as the efficient money machine it always has been, then something could be worked out with Taiwan. (One country, three systems?)

ASEA
瑞典電器有限公司
泰華電機器材行
華僑日報
偉達電動機械水泵行
國醫
趙文傑
專科
耳鼻喉
中醫
趙文傑
專科
耳鼻喉
男女專科
虛弱皮膚尿毒
C.A.NORGREN
ENOTS

中山醫務所
樓婦科
二李麗萍
皮膚
陳永熙
陳永陸
李麗萍
驗孕即知
特效通經
通宵營業 歡迎外賣 313860
理髮廳
國產專營
金顯康樂總會
大押

RADO
WATCH
HYF

HONG KONG ISLE: CENTRAL, WESTERN

Central: Everyone always starts a written Hong Kong travelogue in Hong Kong Island's **Central District**, even though most of the visitors stay in the Tsimshatsui tourist district of Kowloon for the simple reason there are more hotels there.

Nonetheless, Central is good place to start because most people end up there, regardless of where they are resting their heads. Central, as she is known, is quite simply the hub of the colony. As the name implies, it is the business, commercial, financial and political center.

Yet for all its urban pull, this Central vortex serves the same purpose it did nearly 150 years ago. The port, with its 15,000 ocean-going vessels a year, was the colony's *raison d'être.*

To see the north side of Hong Kong island (the side facing Kowloon) at its best costs not even a dollar (HK) aboard one of the ancient double-decker trams—certainly one of the great travel bargains in the world.

When one exits from the **Star Ferry** underpass, looking ahead at the great concrete vista to the south, he or she sees the ultra modern US$1 billion **Hongkong and Shanghai Bank**, reputedly the most expensive building in the world. Those lions guarding the front entrance on **Des Voeux Road** protect the bank's *fung shui,* the balance of the forces acting on life, the *Yin* and *Yang,* thus creating good *joss* (luck).

There are few truly historic buildings to give Central real character.

The blue-and-white Hong Kong Club was demolished in 1981 and has been replaced by a modern skyscraper. But the colonial-style **Supreme Court Building**, once evacuated in mid-session because its foundations were undermined by the construction of the MTR (the underground railway), is now repaired and renovated, and houses the Legislative Council. One colonial building left that has been saved, at the eastern end of Central, is **Flagstaff House**, built in 1845. Not used by the army any longer, Flagstaff House has been saved and converted into the **Museum of Tea Ware**.

Preceding pages: Chock-a-block street scene in Kowloon, and that's before the crowds arrive. Left, the world's most famous harbor view. Right, Hongkong Bank's expensive high-tech headquarters.

Another superb old building, **St. John's Cathedral**, is behind the **Hilton Hotel** on **Garden Road**. It was built between 1847 and 1849 and reflects early Victorian-Gothic elegance.

More to the Central style is **The Landmark** (they don't even call it a building), a structure opened in 1980 on Des Voeux Road. Five floors surround a vast 20,000-square-foot (1,860-square-meter) atrium with 100 shops.

The best place to begin a Central tour is at the **Star Ferry Terminal.** (The ferry provides passenger service across the harbor to Kowloon.)

At the right of the Hong Kong piers is the unmistakable polka-dotted **Connaught Centre** with its distinctive round windows. Just in front of this holey wonder is the **General Post Office** inside of which is the **Government Bookshop**.

Across the street and to the west of the G.P.O. and Connaught Centre are the shiny towers of **Exchange Square**, one of the most modern office buildings in the world and the home of the Stock Exchange of Hong Kong.

Blake Pier, from whence many tours

leave, is between the G.P.O. and Exchange Square. Even farther west is the **Outlying Districts Ferry Pier** where Hongkongians hop a ferry to escape to one of the more peaceful outer islands. A covered walkway extends from the G.P.O./Connaught Centre/Exchange Square west to the Outlying Districts Pier and south to, and through, **Swire House** and **Alexandra House**, finally ending in The Landmark. A good thing to keep in mind when it's raining.

To the left is **Queen's Pier** and **City Hall**. This complex's **Low Block** houses a concert hall and theater, and most important, billboards which advertize cultural programs.

City Hall's **High Block** is in the same compound. inside this block are the **Museum of Art**, with its excellent collection of ceramics, plus a library.

Across **Connaught Road Central** is an open space full of fountains and things that look like benches for bus stops. This is **Statue Square**, Central's "concrete" green lung and gathering place for thousands of Filipina maids on Sundays. Bordering the square to the east is the **Hong Kong Club Building** with its tiny balcony overlooking everything.

Adjacent to the east is **Sutherland House**, easily spotted by its blue coloring, and beyond, the **Furama Hotel**. Opposite those buildings is **Chater Garden** and beyond is **Hutchison House** and **Bank of America Tower**, which were in the Eastern edge of Central until the advent of the **Admiralty Complex**, across the street from which is the **Supreme Court Building**, moved the mental border farther east.

On the western side of Statue Square, is the swank **Mandarin Hotel** and **Prince's Building**.

Heading west on Queen's Road Central, you find **Lane Crawford**, the singlemost famous luxury department store in Hong Kong. Founded in the mid 1950s by a sea captain who wanted to outfit visiting ships, Lane Crawford today hardly poses as a ship chandlery.

While in "lower" Central, explore some of the side streets between **Queen's Road** and Des Voeux Road. Just west of the **Queen's Theatre** are two interesting little streets—**Li Yuen Street East** and **Li Yuen Street West**—

Shooting the breeze in the park.

which have stalls and shops that sell clothing, look-alike high fashion accessories and fabrics galore. Bargaining is expected here. Another popular "cloth alley" is on **Wing On Street** just west of the **Central Market**.

On Queen's Road looking south, one realizes why Hong Kong was considered basically "worthless" when first taken over. The original island, before reclamation, was simply a huge mountain. Behind Queen's Road, the old waterfront road, is a hill which rises precipitously from sea level. Climb up **Ice House** or **Wyndham streets** till they meet. That old, triangular-shaped ice storage building (circa 1911) now houses the **Foreign Correspondents** and the **Fringe Clubs**.

Another worthwhile Climb is **D'Aguilar Street** with its fascinating boutiques. Continuing up D'Aguilar, cross **Wellington Street** and continue up. On the right is **Wo On Lane** with its fun shops. Farther along, lanes open off at both sides. The one on the left, **Lan Kwai Fong**, with its trendy restaurants, is Hong Kong's most modest version of London's Covent Garden.

Follow Wellington Street to the west, past all the frame-makers, to **Lyndhurst Terrace**, a pretty little place with shops that sell Chinese opera costumes. Lyndhurst Terrace leads to **Hollywood Road** with its plethora of antique, furniture, rattan and used books shops.

Following Hollywood Road west, one eventually reaches **Possession Street** which marks the border between Central and the down-to-earth old Chinese section of Hong Kong called **Western**.

Western: Western was the very first district to be settled by the British. They soon moved out, however, after malaria epidemics decimated their numbers. Its mosquitos were left ot Chinese immigrants who came pouring into the colony after 1848. Today, there is virually nothing British about this area. It is now traditional Chinese urban society at its purest: not especially pretty, perhaps, but undeniably colorful.

For one thing, Western is known as a last refuge of the Hong Kong Chinese artisan. One intriguing artisan is the chop-maker who carves name stamps along **Man Wa Lane**. Perhaps only the

Streetside foodstalls in Central.

Arabs have as much respect for calligraphy as the Chinese. And watching a Man Wan chop-carver sculpt a man's name out of stone, ivory, jade or wood is a fascinating experience.

Western is also a home to jade-carvers, opera costumers, fan-makers, pottery-shapers and eggroll-bakers. There are Chinese surprises on every corner.

At the harbor is a "temporary" pier for ferries heading to China. (Temporary is an interesting word since it was the "temporary" Macau Pier for more than two decades.) At night, the parking lot in front of the "temporary" pier is converted into a popular "**Poor Man's Nightclub**," where outdoor stalls sell Chinese food, shirts, watches, cassette tapes, and virtually anything else made of plastic, imitation gold, silver, leather and ivory et al.

At right angles to Man Wa Lane, between the continuation of Queen's Road (**Bonham Strand**) and Des Voeux Road, is colorful **Wing Lok Street** with its shops selling herbs, odd medicines, preserved seafoods and tea.

One now reaches Possession Street. Here, too, are fortunetellers, and on **Fat Hing Street** is a line of shops which specialize only in traditional baby goods.

Just one block above Bonham Strand is **Jervois Street**, another "speciality" street, this one devoted entirely to snake restaurants and Chinese wineshops.

While returning to Central, don't miss a trip down one of the most fascinating of all local shopping areas: the wildly steep **Ladder Street**.

Where Ladder Street meets Hollywood Road is the area's so-called "**Thieves Market**." The lanes here are filled with incredible bric-a-brac, fake and real antiques, and more stalls than one can ever browse through. Bargaining is the rule here—whether for the safety pin, shoelace or (if you should be so lucky) a Tang dynasty horse.

At the corner of Hollywood Road and Ladder Street is **Man Mo Temple**, built around 1842 on what must have been a little dirt track leading up from Central. Tourists regularly throng through Man Mo—but this doesn't inhibit its regular worshippers who animatedly create thick and redolent clouds with their burning joss offerings.

Business as usual at the Poor Man's Night Club.

"SOMETHING FOR EVERYONE"

Hong Kong is a giant marketplace. An intrepid visitor, with a penchant for modest adventure and having an abundance of energy, can find bargains in Hong Kong that never fail to amaze long-time residents. For the less energetic, who prefer air-conditioning within or close to the hotel compared to street markets and forays in out-of-the-way areas, the prices are still very competitive. In short, the trite cliche, "something for everyone" applies.

Hong Kong is justly famous for its ladies and gents tailored clothes. If tailored clothing, as distinct from off-the–peg, ready-to-wear clothes (no matter how expensive or chic) is anywhere on your shopping list, move it right up to the number one spot even before you arrive.

Apart from clothes, there are many other items to buy here. Photographic and hi-fi equipment, calculators, televisions, electronic gear, electrical appliances, watches, etc. are relatively easy to find because, once again, there are thousands of shops.

Do not miss a meander down the miles of corridor, lined with hundreds of shops, in the interconnected Ocean Terminal/Hong Kong Hotel/Ocean Centre/Harbour City in the tourist district of Tsimshatsui in Kowloon, near the Star Ferry Concourse.

Across the harbor on Hong Kong Island, in Central District is The Landmark, a four-story shoppping complex surrounding a beautiful atrium which probably houses the poshest shops in the territory. Similar shops occupy several surrounding buildings. The best known of the local department stores is Lane Crawford, a very posh, up-market and European-oriented department store.

On Hong Kong Island, the big market is Stanley Village on the south side. The main street of the village is chock-a-block with shops selling overruns or designer seconds.

The Causeway Bay area of Hong Kong, just around the Daimaru Department Store, is also a marvellous place to shop.

Shopping in the factories is one way to find bargains, particularly with designer clothes. Kaiser Estate in the Hung Hom area of Kowloon has the largest concentration of designer clothing outlets and many tour companies include a stop there on their tour. Whether you're just fishing for souvenirs or looking for something specific, Hong Kong is one town where you can truly say "hello to good buys."

Jade Market in Canton Road.

THE PEAK, WANCHAI, HAPPY VALLEY, CAUSEWAY BAY

The Peak: Victoria Peak—**The Peak** to those who have made it to society's top—wasn't always regarded with such awe. "Although beautiful in the distance," wrote an early travel writer, "it is sterile and unpromising upon more close examination." Indeed, for the first six years of the colony, hardly anybody traveled to those inhospitable heights.

It wasn't until 1888, when the **Peak Tramway** (actually a funicular railway) was opened, that the Peak became *The* Peak. Everybody who was anybody longed to live on The Peak. Before the tramway, sedan chairs transported lucky colonials to the top.

The Peak is as beautiful now as it has always been. And it's a cooling refuge even in the hottest season.

The best way to see The Peak in all its bucolic glory is by walking around **Lugard Road**, which begins just opposite the Peak Tram's upper terminus, 1,305 feet (395 meters) above sea level. Just to the right is the **Peak Tower Restaurant**, which offers magnificent views, if clouds haven't smothered them.

Going around Lugard Road to where it intersects with **Harlech Road**, one sees first the harbor, then Green Island and Peng Chau to the north, Lantau and Macau to the west, Cheung Chau farther west, Lamma Island to the southwest, and finally the great masses of junks and *sampans* at Aberdeen to the south. This hike takes about two hours from the Peak Tramway and back again.

For the really energetic, **Mount Austin Road** leads one to the gardens of a building which was once the summer residence of the Governor. This building was destroyed during World War II by the Japanese, but the walk about its former grounds is still stupendous.

While descending on the tram, stop at **Macdonnell Road** or **Kennedy Road**. Each leads to the entrance of the colony's **Botanical Gardens** and **Zoological Gardens**, which house good collections of flora and fauna. An aviary here has about 1,000 birds of 300 species. The best time to visit is dawn, when locals are engrossed in *tai chi* chuan excercises.

This rather curious exercise, which looks like a slow-motion ballet, is a shadow-boxing exercise which dates to the time of Confucius, utilizing movements and breathing inspired by Buddhist meditation forms.

Wanchai: Once upon a time, **Wanchai**, home of the fictitious Suzie Wong, was larger than life. As far back as the late 1940s, the "Wanch's" bars and brothels were well-known hangouts for sailors.

During the 1960s and 1970s, Wanchai helped give rest, recreation and succor to thousands of American, Australian and New Zealand soldiers and sailors on R & R from Vietnam, as well as hundreds of thousands of merchant marines from hundreds of countries. Then, as now, Hong Kong was a popular port-of-call.

Today, though, the "Wanch" lives on its reputation. Like an old prostitute, Wanchai now slouches more than she slinks. She's a bit shabbier these days, seen it all, and has good stories to tell, but it takes a special event (like a naval ship dropping anchor) to put life into the old girl.

Tramming up the Peak is a moving experience.

The Wanchai girls still stand around bar-doors and give a perfunctory "pssst" to potential customers. But these days they're sadly overwhelmed by newer and more palatable delights.

Wanchai's "red light district" now plays second fiddle to more liberated nightlife venues; gaudy big hostess clubs (ornate and expensive, with huge bands and pushy women who sit at your table for a dollar a minute); dozens of topless bars (if nipples could yawn, those here would); discos (which have all the electronic, stroboscopic and psychedelic audio-visual gadgetry that Hong Kong money can buy); and raucous English-style pubs (where the dartboards usually get more action than the women across the street) and trendy eateries.

There are also peculiarly Eastern forms of entertainment, like Chinese ballrooms, which foreigners rarely see.

Nobody thinks about Wanchai for culture, but it does harbor an up-market image on **Harbour Road**, adjacent to the **Wanchai Ferry**.

The **Hong Kong Arts Centre** opened in 1977. On any given night, it may be presenting a Shakespearian play, a Japanese *Kabuki* ensemble or a Humphrey Bogart film. Across the street is the **Academy for Performing Arts**, the territory's newest cultural addition.

Untamed colors run riot at the Tiger Balm Gardens.

Happy Valley: Western District was the first Hong Kong suburb occupied by Europeans, but they soon deserted it and moved to a spot which seemed healthier. They optimistically named this second living area **Happy Valley**. Happy Valley was relatively distant from the sea, was somewhat deserted and, most important, didn't have "unhealthy" and malaria-ridden rice farms in its vicinity. By 1850, anti-malaria laws had been passed, banning farming on the land.

In 1841, shortly after Happy Valley was settled, the colony's happy-go-lucky residents created the edifice which has made Happy Valley world famous: the Royal Hong Kong Jockey Club's **Happy Valley Racecourse**. Until a few years ago, this horse-racing oval was the only one in the colony. It's less than one mile long, but during the October-to-May racing season, it attracts thousands of race-goers (about 35,000 a running).

Outside of its racecourse, Happy Valley's second most well-known attraction is a place which looks like a hallucinogenic vision of a Chinese Disneyland. This is the **Aw Boon Haw** (formerly Tiger Balm) **Gardens** on **Tai Hang Road**. The 150,000-square-foot (13,900-square-meter) amusement park stands in celestially kitchy splendor. This zany site has terraced grottos which are profligate with bizarre stone sculptures and reliefs from the most awesome and awful tales of Chinese mythology.

Causeway Bay: Cruising down from Tai Hang Road to **King's Road**, opposite **Victoria Park**, one enters a fascinating modern sector of the island: **Causeway Bay**. (The area can also be reached by public transport.) It really was a bay until the 1950s when the bay disappeared into a great land reclamation project.

The present-day "bay" is occupied by the **Royal Hong Kong Yacht Club** and the **Typhoon Shelter**. To get there, cross **Victoria Park Road** in front of the **Excelsior Hotel**. At sunset hour, you will immediately be besieged by a gaggle of women, offering a ride in one of their "floating restaurant" *sampans.*

The deck is filled from beam to

boom with tables and chairs. Bargain before you get on—the price should come to around HK$100, depending on vessel's size.

Your *sampan* will weave its way through the crowded sea lanes of the typhoon basin by paddle power, a-bobbing while dodging other restaurant *sampans,* fishing junks, pleasure yachts, and large passenger ferries. The place is alive with water traffic. Bring your own wine, if you wish, because the bar *sampans* (which buzz your craft moments after it clears land) add offshore markups to the price of their booze. Cold beer, however, is reasonably priced.

Kitchen *sampans* pull up next, vying for orders and showing off their fresh prawns, crabs and fish. Seafood, noodles, congee, omelettes—just about anything edible—can be prepared before you in these precarious floating kitchens.

Music is provided by a live-band-*sampan*. A song list is passed over for your consideration, but be warned that by popular colonial consensus, this floating combo is considered to be the worst, most out-of-tune band in Hong Kong, or perhaps the world. The "song menu" usually includes two selections. No other music is played, and the band's favorite and standard tune is—would you believe—"*The Yellow Rose of Texas*." This floating musical repertoire has not changed in a decade.

Though they hardly serve Chinese *haute cuisine*, restaurant *sampans* are a fun experience, and the food is fresh, tasty and filling. Be warned, though, that the penalty for over-indulgence is a visit to the "washroom" (a euphemism if ever there was one).

Causeway Bay's "modern" history began in 1973 when the **Cross-Harbour Tunnel** was opened. This underwater freeway is one of the largest tunnels in Asia, and its four lanes cross one mile of water between Hong Kong and Kowloon.

With this tunnel came the inevitable: Causeway Bay was transformed into a thriving little city. Three deluxe hotels opened—the **Park Lane**, the **Lee Gardens** and the Excelsior. Next door to the Excelsior is the **World Trade Center**, a 42-story complex with plush offices, restaurants and nightclubs.

Street blocks behind the Excelsior have shopping outlets which sell goods at prices cheaper than similar stores located in Central or Kowloon.

One block to the east of **Paterson Street**, is **Food Street**. In its two blocks and 80,000 square feet (7,400 square meters) of space are 28 diverse dining places, more than 200 chefs and menus listing some 2,000 dishes. More than 100,000 people gorge themselves here each week on Peking duck, Punjabi *dahl*, American beefsteak, Cantonese congee, Japanese *teppanyaki*, and garlicky Szechuan eggplant—among innumerable other dishes. The quality varies, but Food Street is good fun.

Due east two blocks is the aforementioned Victoria Park, which is busy about 20 hours a day. Around 4 a.m. *tai chi chuan* and jogging exercises begin. Later, tennis players on 14 different courts begin playing. And by mid-morning, football players, kite-fliers and swimmers are exercising.

During the Chinese New Year and the Autumn Lantern Festival, the park is aglow with flower displays—of peach, orange and narcissus blossoms—and hundreds of candlelit lanterns; it's one of the colony's most beautiful annual sights.

Left, waiting for a fare. Right, traditional Chinese opera performance.

SHEK O, STANLEY, REPULSE BAY

The south side of Hong Kong Island is a totally different world. It is a region of rocky coasts and smooth white beaches; of little fishing villages and unhurried markets. Outside of Aberdeen, neither an office building nor factory is anywhere in sight. But on summer weekends, every office, factory and farm worker in the colony seems to descend on the south side's shores.

Shek O: Of Hong Kong's 36 gazetted beaches, the south side of the island has 14. A few, like **Rocky Bay** on the road to **Shek O**, have virtually no facilities, save an unparalleled view and an uncrowded beach. Others, like **Repulse Bay**, feature busloads of tourists, restaurants, shops and bars, and about as much peace and quiet as a carnival.

Shek O Beach is somewhere at middle ground. The road from **Chaiwan** skirts **Mount Collinson** on the left and **Tai Tam Harbour** on the right. At a fork in the road, one can go left about four miles (six km) to **Big Wave Bay.** The Shek O beach and village, about the same distance from the fork, can be reached by public bus and Big Wave Bay's beach is a 30-minute walk from Shek O.

Following paths at right angles to the beach, one can wander through lane after lane of high-walled mansions owned by some of Hong Kong's most affluent citizens.

After the turn-off to Shek O, the road from Chaiwan continues in a curve to one of the most well-trodden hiking spots on the island: **Tai Tam Reservoir**. This was the first reservoir erected in Hong Kong, its earliest section completed in 1899. The two-hour trail walk in lovely areas surrounded by mountains, begins on **Tai Tam Road**, skirts around the different reservoirs, and ends at the top of **Wongneichong Gap Road** near the **Hong Kong Cricket Club**.

Stanley: Next stop is **Stanley Village**. Despite its English name (it was named after Lord Stanley, the 19th-century Secretary of State for the Colonies), Stanley was a thriving Chinese capital long before the British set foot here. In fact, the village's **Tin Hau Temple** documents that the town was founded in 1770 by a pirate, Chang Po Chai, who captured the island.

Once one of the colony's best-kept shopping secrets, today **Stanley Market** attracts thousands of visitors. Here, down a few steps from **New Street**, is a large area with shops selling fashionable clothes, rattan, fresh food, ceramic jugs, budget art, brass objects and other Chinese products.

From Stanley, one may travel to the "capital" of the south side, Repulse Bay, directly on **Repulse Bay Road**.

Repulse Bay: Repulse Bay has everything, except peace and quiet. It had one of the finest resort hotels in the East—the Repulse Bay Hotel, and a castle called Eucliff, but they are both gone. It does have, in addition to a nice beach and a fine bay, a giant statue of *Tin Hau*, goddess of the sea and, by extension, protector of swimmers, set in a small Chinese garden. In spite of the holiday and weekend beach crowds, Repulse Bay (and environs) is still one of the nicest places to live in the colony, as can be readily seen from the high-rises surrounding the beautiful bay.

Sampan by the bay.

DEEP WATER BAY AND ABERDEEN

Deep Water Bay: From Repulse Bay, the coast road curves westward over some of the colony's most beautiful scenery. **Deep Water Bay** has some very beautiful mansions (including the house where *Love is a Many-Splendoured Thing* was filmed). The turn before you get to the beach is the boat landing and the place to go water-skiing. Opposite the beach is a nine-hole golf course managed by the **Royal Hong Kong Golf Club**. Farther along is the more exclusive **Hong Kong Country Club**.

Two of Hong Kong's biggest tourist attractions, **Ocean Park** and the adjacent **Water World** are a bit farther along, just opposite the **Aberdeen Tunnel** entrance.

Opened in 1977, Ocean Park cost HK$ 150 million. Located on 170 acres of land, it is the world's largest oceanarium. The park actually consists of two sections: a **Lowland** site with 40 acres, and a **Headland** site of 130 acres. The two sectors are linked by cable car.

On the Lowland are a number of gardens, parks and a children's zoo. But it's the Headland, overlooking the South China Sea, at the end of a spectacular cable car ride which has the most interesting exhibits. These include the largest marine mammal theater in the world, with a seating capacity of 4,000. **Wave Cove** nearby, simulates a rocky coastline with a special wave-generating machine. At two different levels, sea lions, seals, penguins and sea birds may be seen diving or skimming along the cove's surface. Finally, there is an **Atoll Reef** with more than 300 different fish species and about 30,000 swimming specimens. It is the largest aquarium in the world, containing half-a-million gallons (two-million liters) of seawater. The aquarium can be viewed from three different levels.

In 1984, the adjacent Water World section was opened. This is a water play-park with a dozen different activities including water slides and a lovely beach. It is only open from May through October.

The main road, **Wong Chuk Hang**,

Crowd doing a sardine impression on a busy summer day.

proceeds towards **Aberdeen**. On the way in, at the first stoplights, turn left following the signs to Hong Kong's famous **Aberdeen Floating Restaurants**. There are three all lit up in the middle of this small section of the harbor where weekend admirals moor their yachts and junks. The road is **Shum Wan Road**. Located on it are the **Aberdeen Boat Club** and the very, very posh **Marina Club**. Farther along is another entrance to Ocean Park, via the world's longest escalator direct to the headland.

Aberdeen: Aberdeen has a character unlike any other town in the colony. Its charm, though, is questionable because this natural typhoon anchorage is home to about 20,000 of Hong Kong's 70,000 "boat people" and their 3,000-odd junks and *sampans*. It was named after the Scottish Earl of Aberdeen, the 1848 Secretary of State for the Colonies. The Cantonese name is *Heung Keung Tsai*, "little Hong Kong."

The term "boat people" has two meanings: one refers to Vietnamese refugees who came pouring into Hong Kong during the late 1970s. The more traditional boat people are those who have been living on local waters for thousands of years.

The latter group of these boat people consists of two main tribes: the *Tanka* (literally the "egg people," because they used to pay taxes in eggs rather than cash) and the *Hoklo*.

Other Chinese have never accepted them (pre-Communist China wouldn't even permit them to settle on land) but Hong Kong is encouraging them to leave their boats. Schools for their children are opening up, housing estates are being constructed for them, and as land is gradually reclaimed from the harbor, the fishing people are being lured to work in factories. Tourists are still seduced by the colorful 30-minute *sampan* ride through **Aberdeen Harbour**. They still enjoy the chaotic atmosphere, the incredible collection of sea life and the dynamism of this city upon the water.

Through Aberdeen and up the hill towards **Pokfulam** is **Chi Fu Fa Yean**, another huge housing development with its own shopping center including a "traditional" Chinese village. Pokfulam completes the circle for Hong Kong Island.

Bright lights and seafood at the Aberdeen floating restaurant.

KOWLOON: TSIMSHATSUI

Up to the aptly-named **Boundary Street**, **Kowloon** was ceded to Britain in 1860 under the Treaty of Peking which was negotiated as a Chinese concession at the time of the so-called Opium Wars. This was the second of three treaties that created the present British Crown Colony of Hong Kong.

Like Hong Kong Island itself, it was supposed to be British in perpetuity. As is evident from the 1984 Sino-British Declaration, it was not.

The name Kowloon is made up of two Chinese words, *gau*, meaning nine, and *lung*, meaning dragon. Tradition says that a boy emperor in the Sung Dynasty who once fled here noticed there were eight hills so he called them the "Eight Dragons." A servant pointed out that an emperor is considered to be a dragon also; therefore, with the eight hills plus the boy emperor there were really nine dragons,—*gaulung*. This was transliterated to English as Kowloon.

Several dragons have since been flattened, victims of government bulldozers and the shortage of usable land.

In area, official Kowloon is a mere 3.75 square miles (9.75 square km) but it is this small area that most people remember after a visit to Hong Kong. Kowloon is the "shoppers' paradise" most visitors aim for, and also the site of most of the colony's big hotels.

Tsimshatsui: The **Star Ferry** is no longer the only starting point when exploring **Tsimshatsui**, because you can now drive through the **Cross Harbour Tunnel** from Hong Kong Island, or whiz under the harbor on the **Mass Transit Railway (MTR)**. But for a century, the only way from the island was the faithful Star Ferry, and the reason for going there was to catch the train to Europe. Where the old clock tower stands was "this end" of the Orient Express, the Far East terminus of the rail journey to and from London.

Across from what was the old terminus, but is now a **Space Museum** and, in time, will be another cultural complex, is Hong Kong's most famous "railway hotel," the **Peninsula**. The tradition of tea in the famous lobby was begun by those waiting for trains.

Kowloon's Nathan Road is a shopper's paradise.

Next to the Star Ferry wharves is **Star House**, which contains the first of the shopping arcades. There is the large **Chinese Arts and Crafts** store, where everything from garments to expensive porcelain may be purchased.

Adjoining the Star House is the **Hong Kong Hotel/Ocean Terminal/Ocean Centre/Harbour City** complex, the largest shopping center in Asia.

A short walk from the Star Ferry takes you past the **YMCA** and the venerable (1928) Peninsula Hotel.

Across **Nathan Road**—the start of Hong Kong's famous **Golden Mile** tourist belt—is the **Sheraton Hotel**, new compared to The Pen but now a part of the scene. Across **Chatham Road** from the Sheraton is the **Regent Hotel**, a relative newcomer (opened in 1980) but already famous for its 40-foot high, glassed-in lobby.

Next to it is the giant shopping complex, **New World Centre**, which houses the **New World Hotel**. Continue in this direction and one comes to the new tourist area **East Tsimshatsui**.

Nathan Road is lined with an unending number of glittering jewelry shops, camera stores and hi-fi outlets, thousands of them. Indeed those technological playpens and numerous Oriental crafts shops which crowd Nathan Road and its cross-streets are what most visitors to Hong Kong remember when they return home.

Kowloon's Tsimshatsui is also the heart of Hong Kong nightlife. Most of the vintage servicemen's bars have been overshadowed by the more recent "topless bars" which line **Peking Road**. But be warned, tabs tend to skyrocket and before you know it, big no-neck bouncers are intimidating you into paying several hundred dollars for beer "plus services." The most famous topless establishment is the **Bottom's Up** on **Hankow Road**, but it is not a girlie bar in the aforementioned sense. This is a "socially acceptable" place and one even finds people with dates and wives in tow because it is a pleasant place in which to bend an elbow.

Discos abound, of course. The "hottest" ones are on **Canton Road** . . . **Canton** and **Hot Gossip** are in **Harbour City** while **Apollo 18** is in **Silvercord**, another shopping center. **Hollywood East** in the **Regal Meridien Hotel** also packs them in.

Rolls' at the Regent Hotel are a common sight.

NEW TERRITORIES

A visitor to Hong Kong is short-changing himself if he doesn't spend at least some time exploring the colony's **New Territories**.

Officially, the New Territories include the area right down to Boundary Street in Kowloon, but most people here say you're not really in the New Territories until you've traveled beyond **Lion Rock Tunnel**.

You can start your New Territories tour by heading out toward **Castle Peak** or towards Shatin and Tai Po. Alternatively, you can travel on **Clearwater Bay Road** which leads to the **Sai Kung Peninsula**.

On the Castle Peak side of the Kowloon peninsula is the Han Dynasty **Li Cheng Uk Tomb** and the **Laichikok Amusement Park**, which has been entertaining people for decades and is one of the world's few places where you can enjoy Chinese opera and ice skating in the same compound. Something new has been added, a **Sung Dynasty Village**. It's a recreation of a part of a village that existed in China 1,000 years ago.

A must on any trip around the New Territories is **Lau Fau Shan**, a huge fishmarket near **Yuen Long**. Here you'll find a "street" with dozens of restaurants, both small, open-air affairs and smart, air-conditioned places. Look at the live fish swimming around in the tanks, pick one out, pay for it, then take it to one of the nearby restaurants and have it cooked.

Near Yuen Long is the walled village of **Kam Tin**, the most popular for visitors. There are 400 people living at **Kat Hing Wai** (its real name), all with the same surname, Tang. Built in the 1600s, it is a fortified village with walls one foot thick, guardhouses on its four corners, arrow slits for fighting off attackers, and a moat. The "authenticity" may seem spoiled by some of the modern buildings inside, complete with television aerials peeping over the old-time fortifications, but there is still only one entrance, guarded by a heavy wrought iron gate. Unknown to most residents and visitors, Kam Tin also has a small SuzieWong-type bar scene.

Authentic costumes at the Sung Dynasty Village.

An exciting next stop is near the **Lok Ma Chau Police Station**. There, you can stand on a hilltop and gaze at a lot of flat land parted by a meandering river. That river is the **Shum Chun**, and it marks the Chinese border.

Driving through the New Territories, you'll see graves, shaped like concrete armchairs, which are sometimes huge. You can see them on hillsides, and if you stand by one you can usually view the sea or a pleasant valley.

One route back to the city is via **Shek Kong**, which is the big British military garrison and airfield. From Shek Kong village **Route Twisk** begins, and takes you on one of the best scenic drives in Hong Kong. Within minutes you are high in forested mountains, apparently far from all human habitation. Route Twisk twists and turns for miles and then suddenly plunges you right back into the techno-industrial age of modern **Tsuen Wan**.

Before turning into Route Twisk, you can continue on Lam Kam Road to **Paak Ngau Shek** in the **Lam Tsuen Valley**, where the **Kadoorie Experimental and Extension Farm** is located. Aside from the farming, this area is much like a manicured garden in a rural setting.

Another scenic rural route takes you from Shek Kong to **Fanling**, where there are three fine golf courses.

Tai Po is a place name meaning "buying place," and the town certainly lives up to its name, serving as it has for many years as a place for farmers and fishermen to meet and exchange goods. It too is being redeveloped.

The old town lies at the northeastern end of Tolo Harbour where the highway crosses the Lam Tsuen River.

Just to the east of Tai Po on **Ting Kok Road** is the famous **Tai Ping Carpet Factory**, a must on most visitor tours, where you can see all phases of Chinese carpet-making.

Whether you enter **Shatin** by road or rail, there's no doubt you'll be amazed to find a bustling metropolis in the middle of the agricultural New Territories. Massive housing projects occupy fields where just a few years ago the greatest activity was water buffalos pulling plows in rice paddies. The **New Town Plaza** is a massive shopping and entertainment complex, while **Riverside Plaza Hotel** along the banks of the Shing Mun River is another modern addition.

The Shatin Valley has several places of worship, of which three are worthy of note.

First is the **Temple of Ten Thousand Buddhas**, which can be reached by climbing 431 steps up the hillside above the old **Shatin Railway Station**. There you will find a main altar room with 12,000 small Buddha statues on its walls.

A further 69 steps up the hill is the **Temple of Man Fat**, where you can meet the man who created this temple and pagoda complex—even though he died years ago. His name was Yuet Kai and his body is preserved in gold leaf for posterity.

From either of these two places of worship you can look down on a third place of worship, one much more in tune with the present day spirit of Hong Kong. This shrine is dedicated to Instant Wealth, or The Fast Buck, and is called **Shatin Racecourse**. Thousands of punters go every October through May horseracing season to bet money on the ponies and then pray for good fortune.

Shan Tai Sin Temple in the New Territories.

THE OUTLYING ISLANDS

It is something of a minor tragedy that so few visitors make time to go to the outlying islands, for it is here that the real magic of Hong Kong is uncovered.

The three main islands—Lantau, Lamma and Cheung Chau—are easily accessible by scheduled ferry services which depart frequently from the Outlying Districts Ferry Pier on Hong Kong Island.

Lantau: Of all the outlying islands, the greatest in size is **Lantau**, which has a land area twice that of Hong Kong Island.

In Cantonese *lantau* means "Broken Head," perhaps because its rugged dignity is dominated by the ragged and two-part **Lantau Peak** that rises 3,100 feet (945 meters) high at the heart of lizard-shaped Lantau.

The island is cobwebbed with little wandering pathways and dusty trails which spiral up, down and around her scenic mountains.

Bun Festival on Cheung Chau Island.

For those who land at **Silver Mine Bay**, Lantau's main visitor point, regular buses travel from there along Lantau's southern resort coast to the brightly painted red-and-gold **Po Lin Monastery**. Here, in a large visitors' dining house, you can enjoy a good vegetarian lunch served by Po Lin's resident monks. The monastery is set on a hill north of **Shek Pik Reservoir**.

On the northern side of Lantau, try to visit **Tung Chung**, an old fortress (1817) and bay that curves around the pointed southern tip of little **Chek Lap Kok Island**.

Expansive Lantau is also understandably famed for its many long, smooth and often empty beaches. The finest sandy sweeps are on the southeast coastline that arcs from **Cheung Sha** south of Silver Mine Bay to **Tung Fuk**.

Lamma Island: The third largest of the outlying islands, and somehow less well-known both to visitors and to local people, is **Lamma Island**.

Though it is only just over five square miles in area, Lamma is rich in green hills and beautiful bays. And—because it's mountainous—there is a very small area of cultivation. Eroded mountain tops dominate the island's grassy lower slopes.

The village of **Sok Kwu Wan** is Lamma's most famous destination because its quay is lined with excellent fresh seafood restaurants.

Cheung Chau: Cheung Chau is different because it is urbanized in a rather charming "Old China" way.

Indeed, if it weren't for the distinctly Chinese junks and *sampans* which crowd Cheung Chau's curving little harbor, one would be deceived into believing that this is an Old World Mediterranean port—a neat little place with pastel homes set into pine-studded hills.

This dumbbell-shaped isle—with hills at its either end and a village nestled in a connecting isthmus of land—is narrow enough that you can walk from **Cheung Chau Harbour** on its west side to **Tung Wan Beach** on the east in a few minutes.

Once a year the whole island community comes together for a big **Bun Festival**, a celebration held to exorcise wandering and malicious ghosts who have been unable to find rest in this world.

MACAU: THE "LATIN ORIENT"

Macau is Hong Kong's 400-year-old Portuguese neighbor, some 40 miles (64 km) to the southeast across the **Pearl River Estuary**. It changed from a colony to a "Chinese territory under Portuguese administration" in 1974 after Portugal's own revolution and, like Hong Kong, will also become some sort of special territory in the future.

Macau tends always to be lumped in with Hong Kong—unfairly, because the two destinations are not mirror images.

For foreign visitors, particularly Westerners, Macau is a day tour or part of a day *en route* to China, both of which are an adjunct to their Hong Kong trip. Sad, because Macau is in itself a unique enclave.

Today, Macau is known as the "Latin Orient" or the "Las Vegas (or Monte Carlo) of the East." The former sobriquet refers to the relaxed Latin attitude which prevails in contrast to the perpetual hustle and bustle of Hong Kong, and also the Mediterranean-style architecture, admittedly fighting for survival these days with urban redevelopment.

Macau's second tag refers to its never-ending gambling. The territory's five casinos and various race tracks will relieve you of your cash, or reward you if lady luck is smiling in your direction, at any time round the clock.

Macau is small and compact enough to tour the 2.1-square-mile peninsula by car in less than two hours.

The first stop is usually **Penha Hill**, on which stands the magnificent **Bishop's Palace**, unoccupied for many years now. From one vantage point there, you can see across the Old City to Macau's **Inner Harbour**, and less than a mile farther, China. From another point, you can see **Outer Harbour** approaches and the island of **Taipa** which is connected to the peninsula by a bridge.

The most striking Macau church is the towering facade of **St. Paul's** with its impressive grand staircase. Historians call it the finest monument to Christianity in the Far East and it has come to symbolize Macau.

Tours here always include the Chinese temples of **A-Ma**, for which Macau is named and the **Kun Iam Temple**, famous for its fortune-telling.

The Temple of the Goddess A-Ma squats beneath **Barra Hill**, at the entrance to Macau's Inner Harbour.

It is the oldest temple in this Portuguese Territory, and is said to date back 600 years to the Ming dynasty. It certainly was there in 1557 when Macau was ceded to Portugal. The original temple was said to have been erected by Fukinese fishermen and dedicated to Tin Hua, the patron goddess of fishermen.

The temple complex of Kun Iam, which in Cantonese is pronounced *Kuan Yin*, is dedicated to the Goddess of Mercy. The present temple dates back to 1627 and was built on the site of an earlier 14th-century temple.

The ornate **Portas do Cerco**, Macau's main border gate (with China), was built in 1870. Today the gate is open to accommodate those going into China to resorts across the border.

Most tours make a quick visit to the **Dr. Sun Yat-sen Memorial House**. Dr. Sun—the "Father of Modern China" who is revered in both Peking and Taipei—lived here when he practiced medicine at nearby **Kiang Vu Hospital**.

A real "classic" worth a visit is the **Leal Senado** ("Loyal Senate") building on Macau's main square. This building was dedicated in 1784 and its facade was completed in 1876. It was restored in 1939 and more internal restoration was recently completed.

The **Camoes Gardens and Museum** is often missed by busy visitors. It is named after Portugal's most famous poet, Luis de Camoes (1524-1580) and is now completely renovated.

Don't miss seeing Macau's old churches because most of the intrigue and history of this colony's past 400-plus years took place behind their sanctified walls.

The church of **St. Dominic** is one of the oldest and most famous, dating from the 17th century. Once inside, note that many of the Christian motifs are of an Oriental style.

The baroque-style church of **St. Augustine** is the largest in the region. The present structure dates from 1814, and its ornate facade from 1875, but Spanish Augustinians founded a first church there in 1586.

St. Lawrence is another church

which dates from the 16th century, but which was rebuilt in 1803, 1846 and 1892. It is one of the most elegant of Macau's religious edifices. Its double staircase, iron gates, towers, and crystal chandeliers are European, but the roof is made of Chinese tiles.

For Macau's five million visitors each year—80 percent of them Hong Kong Chinese—gambling is the name of the game. Lady Luck—who lurks in five casinos, dog-racing and trotting tracks, and in a *jai alai fronton* here—thieves on the gambling-mad Chinese.

The latest running attraction in Macau's varied gambling world is Asia's only trotting track, the **Macau Trotting Club's Raceway** on Taipa Island, which is connected by bridge to the peninsula.

Though suspiciously foreign to most local gamblers, the sleek **Palacia de Pelota Basca** (Jai Alai Palace) by the Ferry Terminal in the Outer Harbour, is Macau's biggest and best-appointed focus for profitable sport. It offers a daily slate of contests among an agile squad of wicker-armed and plastic helmeted professionals.

Asia's Monaco wouldn't be complete without an annual Grand Prix. So, in the same manner as its glittering Mediterranean sister, Macau each year (in November) cordons off a twisting street circuit that starts and finishes on **Avenida de Amizade** across from the **Oriental Hotel**.

Screeching tires, sunshine and gaming tables, excellent restaurants and inexpensive Portuguese wine, draw a well-heeled, thoroughly hedonistic crowd to Macau's Grand Prix Weekend. Macau is inundated with some 50,000 racing *aficionados*, and this otherwise quiet territory swings with pre- and post-race parties. If you don't make hotel reservations well in advance it is next to impossible to find a room in Macau at this time.

The "Other Macau" is not on the peninsula that is generally regarded as Macau, but consists of the two islands of Taipa and **Coloane**.

Their cobble-stoned villages have grown a bit, but they are still tiny rural and charming—a cross between out-of-the-way Iberian villages built around a central plaza and typical old structures found in Chinese farming communities.

View of Macau and ruins of Sao Paulo from Monte Fortress.

EATING—CHINESE STYLE

Eating for the Chinese is not just a bit of necessary metabolic bother, to be consummated as quickly as possible with great globs of starch three times a day. Even though there has been a sad increase in Western or Western-style "fast food" outlets in Hong Kong, when eating here, one is still expected to enjoy a measure of entertainment and, most important, a proper and tasty titillation of the palate.

The Chinese concept of a meal is very much a communal affair and one that provides a strong sensory impact. Dishes are chosen with both taste and texture in mind—a stomach-pleasing succession of sweet-sour, sharp-bland, hot-cool, and crunchy and smooth.

Chinese nearly always insist on fresh food. It is only recently that frozen food has been accepted by Hong Kong's Cantonese chefs and housewives. Most traditional Chinese still shop three times a day for fresh fish, meat and vegetables. A Chinese cook does not start a dish like a stew or roast; rather, he or she goes to the market to buy what is fresh and in season, and then creates the dish.

Most Westerners experience difficulty in eating with chopsticks, which are thought to have been adopted because of a Confucian distaste for knives—potentially dangerous weapons—on the dining table.

Chinese cooking in Hong Kong is the world's finest—that includes the sizeable chunk of real estate north of the border. Judging by popular demand, Cantonese cuisine is the premier regional food of China.

The Cantonese live to eat and, at its most refined level, Cantonese gastronomy achieves a finicky discrimination that borders on cultism.

Visitors to Hong Kong who think they are familiar with Cantonese food soon learn to their surprise that this discipline has little to do with sweet 'n sour pork or chop suey.

In the Cantonese method of preparation, food is cooked quickly and lightly —stir fried— in a shallow water or oil base, usually in a *wok*. The flavor of the foods is thus preserved, not lost, in preparation. Many dishes, particularly vegetables or fish, are steamed. This discourages overcooking and preserves a food's delicate and "natural" flavors, not destroy them. The sauce usually contains contrasting ingredients like vinegar and sugar or ginger and onion.

A Cantonese restaurant is the place to eat fish, steamed whole with fresh ginger and spring onions and sprinkled with a little soy and sesame oil. Cantonese, unlike picky Western eaters, consider a fish's eyes and lips a delicacy. However, in keeping with a traditional superstition among fishing families, you will seldom see a Chinese diner turn over a fish to reach the meat underneath (He doesn't want a capsized boat and have the drowned crew on his conscience).

Prawns and crabs in various styles, steamed, or in a black-bean sauce, are popular Cantonese seafood dishes. If you hear the term "jumping prawns," this signifies that they are alive (and therefore fresh), but doesn't mean you are expected to eat them that way! Shark's fin soup, golden threads of gelatinous-like shark's fin in a broth, is the centerpiece of Cantonese banquets.

Cantonese barbecuing methods are also unrivaled. Try goose, duck or, best of all, tender slices of pork with a gold and honeyed skin served on a bed of anise-flavored preserved beans.

Also experience the taste sensation of double-boiled soups with duck, mushroom and tangerine peel, and a winter speciality called Monk Jumping Over the Wall. This is a blend of abalone, chicken, ham, mushrooms, and herbs that is so irresistible that monks are said to break their vows of vegetarianism if its fragrance is within smelling distance.

Take advantage of a stay in Hong Kong to try some other Chinese regional cuisines. The Peking duck rivals anything in the Chinese capital. Spicy food from the far west province of Szechuan (Sichuan) rounds out the big three of China's cuisines and there are more than enough restaurants to choose from.

Right, Dim Sum, food that "touches the heart."

INDONESIA: ISLANDS OF DISCOVERY

When embarking on a visit to the fabled "Spice Islands" of Indonesia, be sure to bring along a healthy sense of adventure—for found among these 13,677 tropical isles is the singlemost extraordinary collection of peoples, places, sights, sounds, smells, tastes and natural wonders on earth.

Known to naturalists and anthropologists as the fabulous Malay Archipelago, and remembered by many from the history books as the long-sought "East Indies" in an European "Age of Discovery," these islands still today encompass an incomparable treasure trove of biological wonders and ethnological curiosities.

And with over 165 million people, Indonesia also ranks now as the world's fifth most populous nation. Here, hundreds of distinct ethnic groups speak more than 350 mutually unintelligible languages, producing a cultural diversity of kaleidoscopic proportions.

Today's visitor to Indonesia follows in the footsteps of a long line of distinguished voyagers. One travelogue, penned by the Chinese monk Fa Hsien after having been shipwrecked off the coast of Java, dates from the early fifth century A.D. Marco Polo later sojourned along the eastern shores of Sumatra, in 1292. And in the 17th century, Ferdinand Magellan plotted his historic round-the-world voyage in search of valuable cargoes of Indonesian cloves, nutmegs, pepper and mace.

In 1770, Captain Cook cruised into Batavia (Jakarta) bay for repairs after charting the coasts of Australia and New Guinea. And then, of course, Joseph Conrad plied these waters as a young sea captain in the late-19th century, and later used several of the islands as settings for his gripping tales of trial and survival in the East.

The modern visitor is faced with truly limitless opportunities for exploration in Indonesia, as literally hundreds of islands await your very own personal discovery. And the journey is relatively easy and comfortable—good accommodation and transportation facilities are now available throughout the archipelago.

Partly as a result, the number of visitors has been growing steadily. Total tourist arrivals topped 600,000 in 1986, and the Indonesian government has recently stepped up its efforts to promote tourism in order to boost foreign exchange revenues. Despite the inevitable changes that this will bring, Indonesia is well-prepared to receive these modern-day Magellans. Not only is this a proud and cosmopolitan nation, but Indonesians in all walks of life possess a growing self-confidence and a strong cultural identity.

More seldom-visited corners of the archipelago still remain relatively uncharted, leaving the door wide open to some truly adventurous travel. More and more visitors are straying from the traditional Jakarta-Yogyakarta-Bali trail to explore some of Indonesia's remoter reaches—like Tanah Toraja in southern Sulawesi, northern Sumatra's Lake Toba, Bali's neighboring island of Lombok and Kalimantan's Mahakam River.

So whether your particular interest is hiking through dramatic volcanic landscapes, diving amidst colorful coral reefs, seeking out obscure antiquities or simply relaxing on the beach, remember that Indonesia is out there waiting to be "discovered."

Preceding pages: The Eka Dasa Rudra rite is held every hundred years at Bali's Pura Bersakih temple. Left, a Legong dancer.

THE WORLD'S LARGEST ARCHIPELAGO

The Indonesian archipelago is by far the world's largest — 13,677 islands strewn across 3,200 miles (5,160 km) of tropical seas. Superimposed on a map of Europe, it extends from Ireland to the Caspian Sea. On a map of North America, it stretches from Oregon all the way to Bermuda. Many of these islands are tiny, populated perhaps by a few seabirds, but a thousand of them are large enough to be inhabited. And Java, Borneo and Sumatra are as large as England, France and California, while New Guinea ranks as the world's second largest island (after Greenland). With a total land area of 780,000 square miles (2 million square km), Indonesia is the world's 14th largest political unit.

Unique geologic and climatic conditions have created incredibly diverse environments. An amazing variety of flora and fauna are found here, including rare animal species, exquisite plumage birds and beautiful butterflies.

Born out of many millennia of violent tectonic activity, it is no surprise that many islands periodically experience the death and destruction of volcanic eruptions. In areas where the volcanic ash is basic rather than acidic, spectacularly fertile soils have been produced. Through the construction of elaborate irrigation networks, man has achieved rice yields among the highest in the world here.

Lying within the tropical zone, the islands enjoy consistent temperatures (with a mean of 78 F–82 F/25 C–28 C) and plentiful rainfall year round. From November to May, rainfall and humidity increase markedly, while for much of the rest of the year, desiccating winds blow up from Australia bringing drier weather.

Vegetation is conditioned by rainfall, soils and altitude—and varies greatly. Lowland rainforests may contain up to 3,000 different tree species, hundreds of varieties of fruit-bearing palms, and many exotic orchids. At altitudes above 2,000 feet (600 meters), temperatures drop and species like chestnuts, laurels and oaks are found. Higher still, one encounters rhododendrons, edelweiss and alpine meadows more reminiscent of Switzerland than of the tropics.

Indonesian Melting-Pot: The broad range of physical types found in the Indonesian archipelago has often been explained in terms of a "wave theory" of successive migrations. The original inhabitants of these islands were probably the so-called "Australoids" who today inhabit New Guinea and Melanesia. They have dark skin, kinky hair, pronounced brow ridges and broad, flat noses—much resembling the peoples of Africa, who evolved in a similar environment.

Later Malayo-Polynesian (or "Austronesian") settlers are thought to have sailed to these islands via Taiwan and the Philippines beginning about six thousand years ago. Originally from southern China, and essentially "Mongolian" in appearance, with light skin and almond-shaped eyes, many groups later intermixed and acquired certain Australoid features, such as curly hair and brown skin—traits that are far more prevalent in the eastern islands.

Linguistic diversity also increases dramatically as one moves eastward in the archipelago. Over a hundred distinct languages are spoken in Irian Jaya alone by just over a million people! This indicates that these areas have remained relatively stable for many thousands of years, and indeed some New Guinean tribes have been headhunting and producing stone tools well into this century.

Two major styles of agriculture are found here. *Ladang* or "slash and burn" cultivation is practiced mainly in outlying or marginal areas, and consists of burning a plot prior to the onset of rains to fertilize the soils. The *ladang* method will not support large populations and requires its practitioners to be semi-nomadic, hence it is generally associated with more "primitive" tribal groups, though in actuality this is not always the case.

Sawah or wet-rice cultivation, on the other hand, requires and supports large populations to work the soils and maintain the elaborate irrigation system. It also requires a high degree of cooperation among members of the community, and often rewards them with an agricultural bounty.

Religious practices and beliefs in Indonesia are everywhere strongly tinged by local traditions—the body of public rites, private rituals, communal knowledge and customary laws that is passed from generation to generation and forms the distinctive fabric of each society. This is known throughout Indonesia as the *adat* (custom) of an ethnic group. And instead of strict adherence to any of the four major religions practiced in the archipelago (Islam, Christianity, Hinduism and Buddhism) one generally finds a remarkable eclecticism.

Left, Indonesian native. Above, Borobudur, ancient monument patterned on Indian models, was "rediscovered" in the 19th century and restored more recently.

Many ritual events here can be said to rank among the more extraordinary and dramatic spectacles in the traditional world. Central to most *adat* observances is the ritual sacrifice and communal feast, in which ceremonial foods are offered up to the spirits and then publicly consumed to ensure the well-being of the participants.

The Javanese *selamatan* (literally "safeguarding"), for example, is held on a wide variety of occasions: births, marriages, circumcisions, anniversaries, deaths and dedications of anything new.

In Bali an *odalan* or communal feast is held every 210 days to celebrate the anniversary of a village temple. Elaborate offerings, processions, symbolic ablutions (with specially-prepared holy water) and feasting characterize these ceremonies.

Such festivals are commonly thought to enhance the fertility and prosperity of the participants by strengthening their *semangat*, or life force. Considered by many groups to be concentrated in the head of humans, *semangat* was once "accumulated" by headhunting. Even today, locks of hair are exchanged in marriage rituals and human hair is applied to dance costumes in order to promote *semangat.*

This life force is found elsewhere, too. Pillars and weapons are often smeared with sacrificial blood to strengthen them. The cultivation of rice abounds with ritual observances designed to nurture the grain and guarantee a successful harvest. Souls of the deceased are treated with extreme care in elaborate funerary rites and shamanistic practices throughout Indonesia.

A Proud Heritage: Indonesia's earliest hominid inhabitant is popularly referred to today as "Java Man"—a member of the species *Homo erectus* who inhabited the Old World from about 1.7 million years ago. A direct ancestor of *Homo sapiens*, "Java Man" was an omnivore and food-gatherer who lived in caves and open campsites, and was the first creature to know the use of fire. He also produced an elaborate stone tool kit composed of choppers, axes and adzes.

During the Neolithic period, the first agriculturalists must have grown taro before rice, and seafarers engaged in inter-island trade long before the dawn of written history. Megalithic stone monuments were erected on many islands to honor the ancestral spirits.

In the second century A.D., highly sophisticated civilizations emerged whose cosmology, architecture and political organization were closely patterned on Indian models. Best known for the wondrous monuments they created, their rulers apparently "Indianized" these kingdoms to enhance an already complex economic and social order.

At the end of the seventh century, a Buddhist kingdom based in eastern Sumatra took control of the strategic Malacca and Sunda straits. Srivijaya ruled these seas for 600 years, developing the largest ships on the seas, and sailing them regularly to India and China.

Java, meanwhile, was the site of great inland empires, for here it was possible to support large populations with intensive

wet-rice rice cultivation. A Hindu ruler, Sanjaya, was the first great temple-builder whom we know of. But the later Sailendra line of Buddhist kings replaced him, and erected the magnificent monuments of Borobodur, Mendut, Kalasan and Sewu.

Rakai Pikatan, a descendant of Sanjaya, ousted the Sailendras in 856 A.D., and celebrated his victory by constructing the splendid Loro Jonggrang temple at Prambanan. Suddenly and mysteriously, however, the capital was shifted to East Java in about 930 A.D. Under the subsequent rule of King Airlangga, the Sanşkrit classics were translated into Javanese, thereby marking the flowering of an indigenous literature. A succession of East Javan rulers was able thereafter to combine the benefits of a strong agricultural economy with income from the growing and lucrative overseas trade. And in the process, the Javanese became the master mariners of Southeast Asia.

The East Javanese empire of Majapahit was the first to embrace the entire Indonesian archipelago—numbering all ports around the Java Sea among its vassals. Majapahit reached the zenith of its power in the middle of the 14th century under King Hayam Wuruk and *Patih* Gajah Mada, after whose death the kingdom rapidly went into a decline. Control of the vital coastal areas soon passed to a number of new Muslim trading states, and when the central Javanese ricelands were subsequently conquered by Islamic forces, much of the Hindu-Javanese aristocracy fled to Bali.

Muslim traders from India and the Middle East had already visited Indonesia for centuries when the trading ports of northeastern Sumatra began to convert to the new Islamic faith in the late-13th century. The dominant sect of these traders was Sufism—teachings of esoteric revelation, asceticism, dance, and poetry that were highly compatible with the earlier traditions of the Indianized courts.

The adoption of Islam seems not, therefore, to have disturbed the existing order. Moreover, conversion afforded many Indonesian rulers a certain economic advantage as well as protection from encroaching Thai and Javanese interests. Today, Islam continues to be a growing force throughout the archipelago, with over 80 percent of Indonesians declaring themselves disciples of Mohammed.

Arrival of the Europeans: The Portuguese arrived in Indonesian waters in 1509, just 12 years after Vasco da Gama rounded the tip of Africa, but were refused access to the Islamic-controlled spice trade.

Though never able to dominate the region, the Portuguese left a lasting imprint. Mixed Portuguese-Indonesian communities are to be found today in many coastal areas, and numerous words of Portuguese origin have found their way into the Malay/Indonesian language. Even more significant, perhaps, was the conversion by Portuguese missionaries of some 20,000 Indonesians to Catholicism during the 16th century. Though many later switched to Protestantism under Dutch rule, Christianity today retains a dominant presence in these areas of the archipelago.

The first Dutch expedition to Indonesia in 1596 met largely with disease and dissension, and returned to Holland after a year with only a third of its original crew and a meager cargo of spices. It nevertheless

Left, slave trading in Timor. Above, Dutch officials pay a visit to Bali in the 1930s.

touched off a fever of speculation in Dutch commercial circles, and in the following year 22 more ships were dispatched to the Indies.

Zealous Dutch traders pooled their resources to form the United Dutch East India Company, or VOC, in 1602, and it was soon empowered by the Dutch government to negotiate treaties, raise armies, build fortresses, and wage war on behalf of the Netherlands in Asia. The Dutch at this time dreamed of securing absolute control of the spice trade, and under the leadership of empire-builder Jan Pieterszoon Coen, they soon established a base at the pepper-port of Jayakarta (now Jakarta), and secured the tiny eastern Banda Islands which produced valuable nutmeg and mace.

reforms and rebuilt Batavia (Jakarta).

Then in 1811, a brilliant Englishman named Sir Thomas Stamford Raffles planned and led an invasion of Java and was appointed Lieutenant Governor at the tender age of 31. While in control, he attempted to replace the old mercantilist system with one deriving its income from taxes—but with Napoleon's defeat at Waterloo, Java was returned to the Dutch.

Raffles' taxation plan was adopted and modified, however, and thereafter resulted in a century of windfall profits from the sale of Indonesian coffee, tea, sugar, quinine, rubber, palm oil, tin, petroleum and other vital commodities—profits that retrieved the Dutch from bankruptcy and financed new waterways, dikes, roads and a national

railway system in Holland.

For Indonesians, however, the 19th-century "Cultivation System" (*Cultuurstelsel*) of land-use taxes and forced labor was oppressive, leaving them virtually slaves on their own land. Its injustices were exposed in novels such as *Max Havelaar*, written by a disillusioned colonial administrator, and liberal reforms were instituted. The Dutch also embarked on a series of bloody military campaigns that succeeded in imposing colonial rule throughout the Indonesian archipelago by the end of the first decade of this century—largely at the expense of the indigenous rulers.

During the 1640s and 50s, the Dutch tightened their grip on the eastern spice trade in a series of annual sweeps through the Moluccan islands, where clove trees grew in profusion. In other areas, they took military action to subdue rival European and Indonesian traders. So successful were these efforts, that by the end of the 17th century the Dutch had achieved effective control of the eastern archipelago and its lucrative spice trade.

On Java, however, official VOC corruption and a lengthy and costly series of wars bankrupted the company by the end of the 18th century. Iron-fisted Governor General Marshall Daendels, a follower of Napoleon, subsequently wrought numerous

Nationalism and Independence: Ironically, Dutch efforts at educational and political reform in Indonesia provided both an opportunity and an intellectual basis for Indonesian nationalism. Indonesians attending Dutch schools began to form organizations dedicated to the betterment of their fellows, while Islamic labor unions formed to offer some hope of relief from the oppressive economic conditions.

Strikes often erupted into violence during the 1910s and 20s, and severe crackdowns ensued in which many union leaders were jailed or killed. The leadership of the anti-colonial movement thereafter reverted to the student elite. The first political party with independence as its goal was formed by a young engineer by the name of Sukarno. His gifted oratory soon resulted in his imprisonment for "treasonous statements against the state"—and by 1935 the flower of secular nationalism would seem to have been effectively nipped in the bud.

The Japanese suddenly invaded Java in 1942, however, and were welcome by many Indonesians as liberators from Dutch rule. But it soon became apparent that the Japanese were there to exploit the Indies, not to free them. Still, they unwittingly contributed to an ever-growing sense of Indonesian nationhood, while training and equipping a sizable Indonesian militia.

Left, 19th-century map of the Dutch East Indies. Above, Jakarta monument commemorating the "liberation" of Irian Jaya.

On August 9, 1945—as the second atomic bomb was dropped—the Japanese Commander for Southeast Asia promised independence for all former Dutch possessions in Asia. Sukarno was appointed chairman of a preparatory committee, with Mohammed Hatta as vice-chairman. After Japan surrendered to the allies, two days later, Sukarno and Hatta proclaimed independence. The Dutch attempted to regain their colony, but heroic sacrifices on the battlefield by thousands of Indonesian youths resulted in a military stalemate. Finally, in 1949, the United Nation's Security Council ordered the Dutch to sue for peace and a year later the new Republic was secured.

While independence brought in its wake a wave of euphoria, massive social and economic problems beset the new nation. Factories and plantations were shut, capital and skilled personnel were scarce, rice production was insufficient to meet demand, and the population was expanding rapidly.

With more than 30 rival parties vying for power, the political situation gradually deteriorated during the 1950s. Sukarno finally declared martial law in 1959 and proceeded to lay the blame for Indonesia's problems at the feet of foreign imperialism and the West. Meanwhile, foreign investments fled, deficits left the government bankrupt, and inflation skyrocketed.

Six leading generals were kidnapped and executed by a group of young radicals in 1965, causing General Suharto, then head of the elite Army Strategic Reserve, to move in and take command. Months of bloodletting ensued, as old scores were settled between rival Communist, army and Muslim elements. In 1967, Suharto consolidated his power and restored order.

The new Suharto administration set about immediately to re-integrate Indonesia into the world economy, by attracting foreign investments in copper, tin, timber, and oil production facilities. Japanese and local investors established a manufacturing base, and with the rapid rise in oil prices in the 1970s, the economy boomed.

The past decade has been marked by stability and significant economic advances. But Indonesians continue to struggle for social and economic improvements against difficult odds, and the recent drop in oil prices has not helped. It is hoped, however, that the government's strategy of promoting self-sufficiency and stimulating exports will build a lasting prosperity for the nation.

JAKARTA

Capital to the world's fifth most populous nation and home to eight million Indonesians, **Jakarta** is a metropolis by any measure.

Yet apart from several skyscrapers and monuments in and around the city center, it is made up almost entirely of small one- and two-story structures. Most of these have sprung up rather haphazardly over the past few decades: shops, offices and factories are found in residential districts; market gardens and makeshift *kampung* dwellings impart something of a village atmosphere to many back alleys, and the people live just about everywhere.

Though not particularly popular among tourists (due to its oppressive heat and snarled traffic), the city nevertheless boasts good museums and many interesting examples of colonial architecture, as well as an excellent array of shops, restaurants and performing arts venues. The people of Jakarta, however, are her greatest asset, so give the city a chance.

Jakarta is located at the mouth of the **Ciliwung River**, on the site of a pepper-trading port that flourished here in the 16th century. In 1619, Dutch empire-builder J.P. Coen ordered construction of a new headquarters, and the town was subsequently dubbed "Batavia."

Under the Dutch East Indian Company (VOC), Batavia first prospered and then declined, as official corruption, declining market prices and frequent epidemics of malaria, cholera and typhoid took their toll.

Under Governor General Willem Daendels (1808-1811), the old city was demolished to provide building materials for a new one to the south, around what is **Medan Merdeka** (Freedom Square). French Empire and Neo-Classical styles blended with tree-lined boulevards and extensive gardens to impart an atmosphere of grace and elegance, and by the turn of the 19th century, Batavia was once again prosperous.

During the brief Japanese occupation (1942-45), Batavia was re-named Jakarta and quickly transformed from a tidy Dutch colonial town of 200,000 to an Indonesian city of more than one million. Since then it has rapidly blossomed to become the unrivaled political, cultural and economic hub of the new nation.

City Tour: Much of old Batavia has been destroyed over the years, with the notable exception of the old town square, which has been recently restored and renamed **Taman Fatahillah**. Three of the surrounding colonial edifices are now museums.

The **Jakarta History Museum** on the south side of the square was formerly the city hall, and now houses 18th-century furnishings and portraits of the VOC governors as well as many Hindu and Portuguese period artifacts. The **Wayang Museum** on the western side of the square displays puppets and masks from all over Indonesia.

There are buffalo-hide shadow puppets (*wayang kulit*), round-stick puppets (*wayang golek*), flat-stick puppets (*wayang klithik*), Chinese hand puppets (*potehi*), Thai shadow puppets (*wayang siam*), patriotic shadow puppets (*wayang Suluh*), Biblical shadow puppets (*wayang wahyu*), and even a puppet of Batavia's founder, J.P.Coen. Interesting, too, are the simple puppets

'receding ages: The ver-opular ayang ulit shadow lay. Left, resent-day akarta kyline. ight, akarta lso suffers rom big ity traffic roblems.

made of rice straw and bamboo. There is also a collection of *topeng* masks, and tombstones of several early Dutch governors are on display. The **Fine Arts Museum** to the east is located in the former Court of Justice building, and houses collections of paintings and sculptures by modern Indonesian artists, as well as an exhibit of rare porcelains.

Walk behind the Wayang Museum to view two Dutch houses dating from the 18th century. Across the canal and to the left stands a solid red-brick townshouse that was built around 1730 by the then soon-to-be Governor General Van Imhoff. The design and particularly the fine Chinese-style woodwork are typical of old Batavian residences. Three doors to the left stands the only other house from the same period, now the offices of the **Chartered Bank**.

To the north lies the old harbor, **Sunda Kelapa**, with its mile-long wharf that has been in continuous use since 1817. Moored here are scores of sailing vessels from Kalimantan and Sulawesi, and a leisurely morning or evening walk amidst this nautical bustle to the sea is one of Jakarta's unforgettable experiences.

Just opposite the port stands a 19th-century Dutch lookout tower and an old warehouse dating from 1652, now the **Maritime Museum**, housing traditional sailing craft from all corners of the archipelago. Down a narrow lane and around a corner lies the **Jakarta Fish Market** (*Pasar Ikan*), beyond numerous stalls selling nautical gear.

At the very center of Jakarta towers the **National Monument** (*Monas*), a 450-foot (137-meter) marble obelisk surmounted by an observation deck and a bronze flame sheathed in 73 pounds (33 kg) of gold. It was commissioned by Sukarno and completed in 1961—a combination Olympic Flame/Washington Monument.

The **Presidential Palace** facing the northern side of Medan Merdeka is made up of two 19th-century Neo–Classical–style mansions and adjoining executive office buildings. Farther eastward, the **Istiqlal Mosque** is said to be the largest in East Asia, and boasts a massive white dome with rakish minarets.

Lapangan Banteng (Wild-Ox Field)

Courtyard at the National Museum.

lies just to the east, bounded on the north by the neo-Gothic **National Cathedral** (completed in 1901), on the east by the **Supreme Court** (1848) and the **Department of Finance** (1982), and on the south by the monstrous **Borobudur Hotel**. In the center of the square stands a muscle-bound giant bursting from his shackles. This is the **Irian Jaya Freedom Memorial**—placed here in 1963 by Sukarno to commemorate the annexation of Irian Jaya (West New Guinea).

On the western border of Medan Merdeka lies the **National Museum**, housing valuable collections of antiquities, books and ethnographic artifacts. The exquisite **Treasure Room** upstairs—containing a plundered hoard of royal heirlooms—is open only on Sunday mornings.

To get quite a different view of Jakarta, hail a cab and brace yourself for the high-speed cruise down **Jalan Thamrin** to the **Blok M** shopping district in **Kebayoran**. Along the way, you'll pass the monuments to Indonesia's recent economic development—banks, shopping centers and gleaming office blocks.

In Kebayoran, which is an upper-class suburb of the city, visit the **Sarinah Jaya Department Store** for a look at their extensive handicraft selection, then browse the shops around Blok M and have a meal in one of the chic restaurants—to get a feel for the standard of living to which many Jakartans have become accustomed.

If you have the time, a visit to **Taman Mini**, the "Indonesia in Miniature Park," should not be missed. Located about six miles (10 km) south of Jakarta and encompassing 247 acres (100 hectares), this park has 27 main pavilions, one for each of Indonesia's provinces, employing authentic materials and workmanship to exhibit a traditional style of architecture representative of the province. Inside are displays of handicrafts, costumes, musical instruments and other artifacts. There are at least 30 other attractions here as well, including a Tropical Bird Park, an Orchid Garden, a model of Borobodur and the magnificent new **Museum Indonesia**—a three-story Balinese palace filled with traditional textiles, houses, boats, puppets, jewelry and wedding costumes.

Vessels parked at the picturesque port of Sunda Kelapa.

SIDE-TRIPS FROM JAKARTA

Little do most visitors suspect that within a few hours of Jakarta, the western third of Java offers beaches and landscapes as attractive as any in the more heavily-touristed areas of Indonesia. The Sundanese of West Java are known for their mellifluous language, hardy individualism and staunch adherence to Islam. The rugged highlands they inhabit (the so-called "Sunda Lands") are famous for their cool climate, stunning vistas and excellent travel facilities.

This part of the island has been inhabited for many millennia, despite its relative impenetrability, and during the early-16th century, the coastal port of Banten was one of Asia's largest and most cosmopolitan trading emporiums. Having settled in Jakarta in the early-17th century, the Dutch were later ceded much of the so-called Priangan Highlands, and these tangled uplands were finally opened up when Governor General Daendels ordered the construction of a great trans-Java post road linking Jakarta with other cities.

After 1830, the Dutch operated tea, quinine and rubber estates here, and modern industry has followed, so that the area is now a cornerstone of the Indonesian economy. The highland towns of Bogor and Bandung were originally established as Dutch administrative centers and continue to attract new residents at a disproportionate rate, together with many textile, pharmaceutical and aircraft plants.

Escape From Jakarta: The easiest "escape" from Jakarta is actually northward—hop a boat or plane to one of the 600 islands clustered offshore, known collectively as the **Thousand Islands** (*Pulau Seribu*). Several of the closer ones were used by the East India Company as depots and drydocks. Others are privately owned, like **Pulau Putri**, which is now a tourist resort with air-conditioned bungalows and an airstrip. Encircled by coral reefs, all the islands are excellent for diving, water skiing, wind surfing and relaxing.

The infamous volcanic islands of **Krakatau** lie just 94 miles (152 km) to the southwest of Jakarta. The nearby beach resorts of **Anyer** and **Carita** have comfortable accommodations bordering palm-fringed shores. From the port of **Labuan**, charter a boat for the smooth two-hour journey out to the volcanoes. Though dormant for centuries, Krakatau achieved instant infamy in 1883 when it erupted with cataclysmic force, ripping out a huge chunk of the earth's crust and forming a monstrous submarine caldera. The sea rushed in, creating tidal waves that claimed more than 35,000 lives. Undersea activity continued for decades thereafter, producing a new cone with a gaping half-crater: **Anak Krakatau** ("Son of Krakatau").

Also available from Labuan are boats to **Ujung Kulon National Park** at Java's southwesternmost tip. Here are found pristine tropical rainforests and many near-extinct Javan wildlife species, like the *badak* or rhinoceros. If you wish to visit the park, make arrangements first through a travel agent or at the PPA (Conservation Dept) offices in Labuan.

Perhaps the most scenic of West Java's excursions is the ascent into

An angry Anak Krakatau in West Java.

the dramatic Parahyangan highlands ("Abode of the Gods") to the south of Jakarta. The town of **Bogor** is only an hour's drive from the capital via the new **Jagorawi Expressway**. Here are the glorious **Botanical Gardens** (*Kebun Raya*) housing over 15,000 species of tropical trees and plants, orchid nurseries, a zoological museum and a vast botanical library. Next to the park stands the imposing **Presidential Summer Palace**, once the colonial governor general's residence.

A good road over dramatic **Puncak Pass** (altitude: 4863 feet/1474 meters) leads down to the cool mountain resort of **Cipanas**, where many Jakartans maintain fashionable villas. In the nearby **Cibodas Botanical Gardens** is a famous collection of montane and temperate-climate flora. From here, a six-hour climb takes you to the summit of **Mount Gede** or **Mount Pangrango**—with their superb views, waterfalls and fascinating wildlife.

Only three-and-a-half hours from Jakarta by train, four or more by road, the highland city of **Bandung** offers a cool alternative to the capital's oppressive heat. The population and cultural center of the Sunda Lands, Bandung sits in a basin 2300 feet (700 meters) above sea level and is surrounded by lofty peaks. Known as the "Paris of Java" before the war, it was then a small Dutch administrative and university town with broad boulevards and elegant homes.

Still beautiful today, even with a population of over 1.5 million, it offers several interesting sights. The **Geological Museum** on **Jalan Diponegoro** contains an array of rocks, maps and fossils, including replicas of the famous "Java Man" skulls. Bandung's **Institute of Technology** (ITB) is Indonesia's oldest and finest university. And the area around **Jalan Braga** contains many colonial art-deco buildings.

The breathtaking peaks surrounding Bandung are easily visited. **Tangkuban Prahu** the "Upturned Boat" volcano, lies only 20 miles (32 km) to the north of the city and has a road leading right up to the crater's rim. Here, cold mountain mists and sulfurous fumes swirl about jagged ridges. Visit the **Ciater** hot springs beyond the Tangkuban Prahu exit for a meal and a soothing soak in their piping-hot pools.

The Presidential Palace at Bogor.

YOGYAKARTA

The noble city of **Yogyakarta** (Yogya) sits astride a broad, green crescent of fertile ricelands on the southern flanks of towering **Mount Merapi**, where average population densities soar as high as 3,000 persons per square mile. Cultural attractions abound as well—for this was the site of Central Java's two great Mataram empires (one ancient and one modern). Yogyakarta is today a bastion of Javanese traditional life, as well as the jumping-off point for visits to the fabled monuments of Borobudur and Prambanan.

Ruled by a succession of Hindu-Buddhist kings from the eighth century until the early-10th century, the courts of Central Java suddenly and inexplicably shifted to the east after 928. The region then remained relatively deserted until the end of the 16th century when Muslim ruler Panembahan Senapati founded a New or Second Mataram Dynasty.

His grandson, Sultan Agung (1613-45), greatly expanded the empire, but their descendants became embroiled in an endless series of bitter and bloody disputes involving rival courts, the Dutch and the Madurese. In 1755, the Dutch finally imposed a treaty which divided the empire in half. Sultan Hamengkubuwana I of Yogya then proceeded to build a new palace and an elaborate pleasure garden.

The subsequent history of the Yogyakarta sultanate is notably one of resistance to ever-increasing Dutch colonial influence in Central Java. Invaded by the Dutch and the British in 1810 and 1812, and swept up in the great Java War of 1825-30, Yogya later served as provisional capital for the new nation during the Revolution (1946-9).

The "Navel" of the Universe: Despite all the changes of the past few decades, it is still Yogya's traditional attractions that most visitors come to see. The royal **Kraton**, a 200-year-old palace complex in the heart of the city, exemplifies the Javanese belief that the ruler is the "navel" of the universe. The palace is thus both the center of

Two reflective Javanese men.

the kingdom and the hub of the cosmos. It contains private chambers for the sultan, his family and the dynastic regalia, as well as a magnificent throne hall, meditational chambers, performance pavilions, a mosque, stables, barracks, an armaments foundry and two expansive parade grounds—all within a walled compound measuring a mile on every side.

The interior of the Kraton was remodeled in the 19th century along European lines, incorporating Italian marble, cast-iron columns, crystal chandeliers and rococo furnishings into an otherwise classically Javanese setting. The throne hall, an ancient *gamelan* set and two great *kala* head gateways all contribute to the visual effect.

The **Taman Sari** royal pleasure gardens lie just to the west and south of the Kraton. An opulent and architecturally ingenious complex consisting of an artificial lake, underground and underwater passages, meditational retreats, sunken bathing pools, and a two-story European-style mansion (known as the "Water Castle"), Taman Sari was constructed over a period of many years in the late-18th century and then abruptly abandoned. It was once fortified, and was originally surrounded on all sides by a man-made lake. Today the complex borders on a crowded bird market and a colony of young *batik* painters.

An underground passageway behind the Water Castle leads to a series of partially–restored bathing pools. Designed for the use of queens, concubines and princesses, it is overlooked by a tower where the sultan "rested" during the day. The **Pesarean Pertapaan**, farther to the south through an ornate archway, is a small Chinese-style temple with galleries and a forecourt where the sultan and his sons are said to have meditated for seven days and nights at a time.

The **Sumur Gumuling** ("circular well"), often referred to by locals as a mosque, is a fascinating underground gallery (to one side of the Water Castle). It was likely intended as a trysting place for the sultan and Nyai Loro Kidul, the powerful Goddess of the South Seas to whom all Mataram rulers were promised in marriage by the dynasty's founder (and from whom

'uppet heater ncorporates ales from ndian and ld avanese pics.

they are said to derive their mystical powers).

A stroll down Yogya's main street, **Jalan Malioboro**, begins in front of the royal audience pavilion at the central town square (north of the Kraton), and ends one mile away at a phallic *lingga* dedicated to the local guardian spirit, Kyai Jaga. Once a processional boulevard, this thoroughfare today bustles with cars, pedicabs and people. Both sides of the street are lined with shops selling *batik* textiles, leather goods, baskets, tortoise-shell jewelry and endless knick-knacks.

The **Sana Budaya Museum** on the northwestern side of the square was established in 1935 by the Java Institute, a cultural foundation composed of wealthy Javanese and Dutch art patrons. Today it houses prehistoric artifacts, Hindu-Buddhist bronzes, *wayang* puppets, dance costumes and traditional Javanese weapons.

Yogya is known for its sophisticated performing arts. The *wayang kulit* shadow play undoubtedly lies closest to the heart of the Javanese. The *dalang* or puppeteer is the key to the performance—breathing new life into each retelling of familiar tales from the Indian *Mahabarata* epic. Performances for *selamatan* feasts, weddings, or circumcisions occur regularly, beginning around 9 p.m. and continuing until dawn. A full eight-hour presentation is held on the second Saturday of every month at the *Sasana Inggil* south of the Kraton, and mini-performances are held daily at 3 p.m. for the benefit of tourists at the **Agastya Art Institute** *dalang* school.

Classical Javanese Dance is another highlight of Yogya's cultural scene. The weekly rehearsal within the Kraton should not be missed.

Yogya is also justly famous for its *batik*. Visit the **Batik Research Center** (*Balai Penelitian Batik*) at **Jalan Kusumanegara** No. 2 for an introduction to the wax-resist dyeing process, and to the staggering variety of patterns and colors to be found throughout Java. **Jalan Tirtodipuran** in the south of Yogya also has over 25 factories and showrooms, where you can see the cloth being drawn and dyed. **Toko Terang Bulan** shop on Jalan Malioboro sells finished *sarung, kain,* tablecloths, shirts and dresses at fixed prices. *Batik*

Dusty Yogya street scene.

paintings designed for framing and hanging are produced by a number of well-known artists.

Monumental Java: A visit to one of the hundred-odd *candi* or ancient stone monuments that lie scattered about the dramatic volcanic landscapes of Central Java is an unforgettable experience. Since 1900, a great deal of effort has been expended to excavate and restore them, but we still know little about their function within ancient Javanese society. There is no denying, though, that these awe-inspiring structures are among the most technically–accomplished edifices of ancient times.

The legendary *stupa* of **Borobudur**, located 26 miles (42 km) to the northwest of Yogya, is the world's largest Buddhist monument. Built sometime between 778 and 856, but then inexplicably deserted within a century of its completion, Borobudur has undergone a long process of "rediscovery" and restoration.

[B]orobudur [i]s the [w]orld's [l]argest [B]uddhist [m]onument, [b]uilt 300 [y]ears before [A]ngkor [W]at.

In 1814, English Lieutenant Governor Thomas Stamford Raffles dispatched his military engineer to investigate what was rumored to be a "mountain of Buddhist sculptures." The uncovering of the monument, however, led to years of plunder and abuse by local villagers and Dutch officials.

A cry of outrage from within the colonial government in 1900 resulted in a massive campaign to reconstruct and preserve the monument. But the restorers subsequently realized that internal erosion was slowing eating away at Borobudur's foundation and would eventually destroy it.

Two world wars, the Depression and several earthquakes left Borobudur in a sorry state by 1967, when UNESCO finally sponsored a fund-raising drive and feasibility study. In 1973, the massive project finally got underway.

It took 700 men working six days a week fully 10 years to dismantle, chemically treat and reassemble Borobudur's 1.3 million andesite blocks. And this was accomplished only with the use of power cranes and computers! The final cost of the project amounted to US$25 million.

It is estimated that it originally took 30,000 stonecutters, 15,000 carriers and thousands of masons 50 to 75

years to build Borobudur. This represents a commitment of about 10 percent of the entire population of Central Java at the time. Was it spiritual faith or coercive force that made possible this remarkable achievement? We shall never know.

Seen from the air, Borobudur forms a *mandala* or geometric meditational aid. From a distance, it is a *stupa* or reliquary—a model of the cosmos in three vertical parts. The base, now covered, has reliefs depicting *khamadhatu*, the lower sphere of bodily human desires.

The middle terraces and galleries teach of *rupadhatu* or the sphere of "form," and contain reliefs depicting the life of Prince Siddharta on his way to becoming the Gautama Buddha. Statues of the meditating Buddha at the monument's highest levels symbolize *arupadhatu*, the realm of formlessness and total abstraction represented by the central dagoba.

Borobudur was thus erected for the glorification of the Ultimate Reality, the serene realm of the Lord Buddha—and as a tangible lesson for priests and pilgrims. It was also likely a massive mausoleum, and may have once housed the relics of a Buddhist ruler or saint.

Two smaller temples lie just to the east of Borobudur. **Pawon** (the "kitchen" or "crematorium") is decorated with heavenly money trees and celestial musicians. **Candi Mendut**, now missing its crown, depicts scenes from moralistic fables and folktales, *bodhisattvas* and Buddhist goddesses. Inside are three Buddhist sculptures reputed to be the finest found anywhere—a seated Sakyamuni Buddha flanked by the *Bodhisattvas* Vajrapani and Avalokitesvara.

"Valley of Kings": Ten miles (16 km) to the east of Yogyakarta, in the center of a plain that is literally littered with ancient ruins (known by natives as the "Valley of the Kings"), lies the small town of **Prambanan**, beside a temple complex by the same name. Completed in 856 A.D. to commemorate the victory of Hindu Rakai Pikatan over the last Buddhist Sailendran king of Central Java, Prambanan is thought by many to be Indonesia's most elegant monument.

The complex consists of eight structures. The three main temples are arrayed north-to-south, with the large **Loro Jonggrang** ("Slender Maiden") Siva shrine in the middle, flanked on either side by slightly smaller shrines dedicated to Vishnu and Brahma.

Local legend has it that Loro Jonggrang was a princess wooed by an unwanted suitor. She commanded him to build a temple in one night, and then frustrated his efforts by prematurely announcing the dawn. Enraged, he turned her to stone, and she now resides in the northern chamber of the temple—as a statue of Siva's consort, Durga.

Loro Jonggrang is graced with a glorious symmetry and a wealth of sculptural detail. Celestial beings, animals, illustrations of the classical Indian dance manual or *Natyasastra*, and vivid depictions of the *Ramayana* are all carved in *bas-relief* on the temple's balustrades. The movement within these carvings is free-flowing and filled with fascinating detail.

Not to be missed is the **Ramayana Ballet**, held under a full moon over four consecutive nights during the dry season (May-October) in front of Loro Jonggrang.

Left, country road leads to temple complex near Yogya. Right, the Prambanan Temple complex.

EXPLORING JAVA

Though most visitors make a beeline for Bali, the island of Java has much to offer the intrepid traveler. All that is needed is a bit of time and a desire to stray from the beaten track.

The quiet, old court city of **Surakarta** (also known as "**Solo**"), for example, lies just an hour east of Yogya by car. Here, the main attraction is a still-functioning 18th-century palace.

Solo's **Kraton Kasusuhunan** was constructed between 1743 and 1746 on the banks of the mighty **Bengawan Solo River**. Like the Yogyakarta palace, its outer walls enclose a labyrinthine network of narrow lanes and smaller compounds, two large squares, a mosque and an inner palace complex. Unfortunately, the elegant throne hall recently burned to the ground and has yet to be rebuilt. But the area around the palace is well worth visiting.

The **Palace Museum** was established in 1963 and contains ancient Hindu-Javanese bronzes, traditional weapons and coaches dating back to the 1740s. Be sure also to visit **Sasana Mulya**, a music and dance pavilion belonging to ASKI, the Indonesian Performing Arts Academy, just to the west of the main palace gate. Here you may witness *gamelan* rehearsals, dance performances and *wayang kulit* shows.

Another branch of the royal family has constructed their own *kraton* about half-a-mile to the northwest of the main palace. Completed in 1866, the **Pura Mangkunegaran** boasts the largest *pendopo*, or audience pavilion, in Java. Built of solid teak wood, jointed and fitted in the traditional manner without nails, it features a brightly-painted ceiling bordered by Javanese zodiacal symbols. Register at the east gate and ask for a tour of the inner sanctum, containing the exquisite private collection of Mangkunegara IV—dance costumes, *topeng* masks, jewelry and *kris* blades.

Solo is also an excellent place for the unhurried shopper who likes to explore out-of-the-way places in the hopes of finding hidden treasures. A sizable antique market, **Pasar Triwindu**, lies just to the south of the Mangkunegaran Palace. *Batik* shops line the main streets, and you should also visit the huge textile market, **Pasar Klewar**, near the Grand Mosque and the town square.

North Coast: The north coast, once the site of Java's busiest and richest trading ports, is now one of the finest areas for handicrafts and the scene of eccentric palaces, holy graves, ancient mosques, bustling markets and colorful Chinese temples.

The town of **Cirebon** is famous both for its seafood and its colorful past. At one time the seat of a powerful sultanate, it has two major palaces. The **Kraton Kasepuhan** displays a fascinating blend of Javanese, Chinese, Islamic and European influences. The **Mesjid Ageng** (Grand Mosque) next door was erected around 1500, making it one of the oldest Islamic landmarks on Java. The **Kraton Kanoman** behind the market has European furnishings and walls studded with Delft tiles and Chinese porcelains.

Farther to the east is the bustling city of **Semarang,** a commercial hub and provincial capital. Visit the old **Dutch Church** on **Jalan Suprapto**, and the **Chinatown District**, with its temples

Almost all fertile land is cultivated.

and very distinctive Nanyang-style townhouses.

The road south from Semarang climbs up into the foothills of **Mount Ungaran**. If you have time, make a detour to the cool mountain resort of **Bandungan** to visit the **Gedung Songo** temples—several of the oldest, and certainly the most spectacularly situated antiquities on Java.

East Java: East Java is a paradise for rugged individualists who relish the search for ancient temples or the breathtaking views from the rims of desolate volcanoes. For five centuries after 930 A.D., the **Brantas River** valley of East Java was the locus of power and civilization on the island, and the kingdoms of this period have left a rich heritage of temple art, literature, music and drama. The volcanic peaks of the eastern salient, moreover, contain many secluded nature reserves and an unparalleled scenic beauty.

The city of **Surabaya** was the largest seaport in the archipelago before the turn of the century—today a sprawling city of four million. The old Arab, Chinese and Dutch quarters lie to the north of the city. At the **Hong Tik Hian Temple** on **Jalan Dukuh II/2,** daily Chinese hand-puppet shows can be seen. From here, cross over the "**Red Bridge**" to see the old Dutch commercial district.

Tretes, 34 miles (55 km) south of Surabaya, is a delightful mountain resort where you can walk or ride horseback to one of three lovely waterfalls in the vicinity. A hike up **Mount Arjuna**, 11,000 feet (3,340 meters) through lush casuarina forests or across the **Lalijiwa Plateau** to neighboring **Mount Welirang** will appeal to hardier souls. Ancient temples (*candi*) are scattered throughout the area. **Candi Jawi** is on the main road, four miles (seven km) below Tretes—a slender shrine dedicated to King Kertanegara. It overlooks **Mount Penanggungan**, site of 81 sanctuaries, grottoes and sacred pools. Many more *candi* are found around **Trowulan** and **Malang**.

Nature lovers will revel in the moonscapes of **Mount Bromo**, the **Yang Plateau** and the **Ijen Crater**. And at the reserves lining the eastern and southern coasts, one can witness everything from wild deer to giant sea turtles laying eggs in the sand at midnight.

romo andscape is tark and pectacular.

BALI: "PARADISE ON EARTH"

In so many ways, Bali is the star jewel in the treasure chest of marvels that comprise the Indonesian archipelago. Formed by an east-west volcanic range, drenched by tropical showers and bathed with radiant sunshine, the island is first and foremost a verdant masterpiece of nature. The people of Bali have done much to turn such natural blessings to their advantage, achieving great agricultural success through a fruitful cooperation with the land, the gods and with each other—in a culture that is both materially efficient and spiritually satisfying. For this reason, Bali has long been referred to as a "paradise on earth."

Settled thousands of years ago by a people closely related to the Javanese, Bali became a vassal of the great Indianized empires of East Java a millennium ago. Then, at the turn of the 16th century, as Islamic forces advanced across Java, the entire Hinduized aristocracy is said to have taken refuge on Bali.

The subsequent unification of Bali under an independent ruler, Batu Renggong, in 1550, led to a cultural "golden age" in which an elaborate ceremonial life and its associated arts flourished. Nine great temples were built at this time, and a complex schedule of island-wide ritual observances was developed. For 300 years, between 1600 and 1900, the Balinese lived in virtual isolation from the rest of the world, refining their elaborate artistic traditions for the benefit of court and temple.

Although Bali was largely spared the colonial ravages of the 19th century, it became the scene of mass suicide battles (*puputan*) at the beginning of this century, in which Balinese kings and courtiers threw themselves on their *keris* or ran headlong into Dutch gunfire rather than face the humiliation of surrender. The Dutch conquest of Bali was complete by 1908, and has since been followed by a succession of more peaceful assaults on the island and her unique culture.

Balinese aristocrats today command a good deal of respect in their role as *pengamong*, guardians of the island's 5,000 or more major temples.

The tourist invasion of Bali since the 1960s has left many people wondering whether the island's fabled culture is losing much of its glitter. Fortunately this is not so, for history shows that the Balinese are incredibly adept at integrating and adapting foreign elements into their own flexible and resilient living traditions.

The polyglot nature of Balinese art, with Indian, Hindu-Javanese, Chinese, European and indigenous elements all in evidence, is a striking example of the the Balinese ability to digest and absorb—a fan here, a gold arabesque there, new deities everywhere—and to reject those elements not compatible with their sophisticated, conservative way of life.

Each person on Bali finds himself born into a complex web of social bonds. Children are privileged, for it is believed that their souls are closer to heaven. Babies are carried everywhere, never permitted to touch the impure earth and always comforted by warm hands and soothing voices. Ceremonies are held at prescribed intervals, notably on the child's first birthday, when offerings are made by a priest. Thus begins the complex cycle of rites-of-passage which ushers the Balinese from cradle to grave.

On a larger scale, too, the society is elaborately defined in terms of groups bound together through ritual observances. Communal activities revolve around the three village temples, each of which has a separate calendar of local events, as well as participating in a schedule of regional and island-wide festivities. Within each *desa*, or village, are smaller cooperative units (*banjar*) whose members assist each other in marriages, festivals and funeral cremations. The *banjar* controls community property—usually including a *gamelan* orchestra and dance costumes—and has a kitchen for preparing banquets, a signal drum tower (*kulkul*), an open meeting pavilion, or *bale*, and a communal temple. Every Balinese is thus at once a member of his family, his *banjar*, his *desa* and the island-wide culture. This strong sense of community fosters an equally strong sense of personal identity, allowing each generation to be as fresh and dynamic as the one before it. The same can be said of each visit to beautiful Bali.

eft, ance is n all- mportant lement of ultural life. his egong ancer is rom Bali.

SOUTH BALI

As the focus for Bali's tourism, commerce and government, the south is by far the busiest region. Bali's three famous beach resorts are all here, along with the international airport and the capital city of **Denpasar**. The entire area has experienced unprecedented economic and population growth during the last decades as a result of the tourist boom.

Yet beyond the hotels, shops and blaring discotheques, a traditional village culture manages to thrive on much as it did before. The south's temple festivals are legendary for the intensity of their trance dances and the earthiness of their rituals. Many village troupes now put on highly professional dance performances nightly.

Tiny **Sanur**, six miles (10 km) to the southeast of Denpasar, used to be a quiet fishing village. During the 1930s, its peaceful shores attracted Western intellectuals and artists, like anthropologist Margaret Mead and painter Walter Spies. Mass tourism followed in the early 1960s, when several hotels were built along the edge of the lagoon.

Today, these hotels host thousands of visitors from Australia, Europe, Japan and the U.S., while still managing to preserve a sense of charm and quiet dignity. There are now three large hotels in Sanur and a number of smaller bungalow establishments. The beach and the main road are lined with souvenir shops, restaurants and money changers—but a quick, half-hour's walk inland will lead one down village lanes and through verdant ricefields.

Sanur's main attraction is leisure—a facet of life not unknown to those who live here. Strolls up and down the beach can easily occupy your day, capped by a fine meal and an evening dance performance.

With Sanur's beachfront all but used up, a new tourist development has been created with help from the World Bank at **Nusa Dua**, on the secluded **Bukit Peninsula** south of the airport. Five luxury hotels have been licensed, the first of which opened in late 1982. All have magnificent beachfronts and extensive sports facilities, and are set in a vast expanse of manicured lawns owned and maintained by the Bali Tourist Development Corporation. As a result, Nusa Dua is blissfully free of souvenir sellers and garish billboards—offering all the advantages (and disadvantages) of a "total" hotel environment.

Nearby **Puru Uluwatu**, precariously perched on a cliff 330 feet (100 metres) over the ocean, is a sublime place to watch the sunset.

Kuta Beach on South Bali's western shore has blossomed recently into a bargain basement beach party. Discovered by surfers in the early 1970s, Kuta's chief natural attractions are a broad, sloping beach, a pounding surf and technicolor sunsets. Informal accommodations line the beach and byways, along with a staggering array of restaurants, cafes, pubs, boutiques, discos, bike rentals, artshops and tour agencies. Thankfully, serene rice paddies and long stretches of sandy beach are never more than a few minutes away. Kuta is, incidentally, one of the best places to shop and eat on Bali—found here are some fine antique and clothing boutiques, as well as a wide variety of restaurants serving Asian

eft, amayana cene from a 930s ainting, rtist nknown. ight, waters round ali provide lenty of ood fishing.

and Western fare.

To the north lies **Legian**, an extension of Kuta and now a tourist resort in its own right, though considerably quieter. Farther on is **Seminak**, and then empty space. The important estuary temple of **Peti Tenget** at the northern end of the beach is said to be where the first Hindu-Javanese priest and the first Dutchman both set foot on Bali.

Kerobokan lies even farther north along the main road, an outpost of rural charm and as instant a trip into the "real" Bali as one could hope to find. The main road is lined by a series of shrines and leads to a richly-carved palace. The "art nouveau" temple in nearby **Kaji** is also worth a visit, on the road back to **Sempidi**—itself a haven of mossy gulleys, streams, dams and waterfalls.

Denpasar has grown tenfold since 1945, to a bustling mini-metropolis of 200,000 today. But within the suburban sprawl are to be found a number of attractions. The main square was the scene of a *puputan* suicide in 1906, and successive governments have erected monuments in commemoration of this event. A 16-foot (5-meter) **statue of Bhatara Guru**, teacher and lord-protector of the realm, stands at the middle of an intersection, and in the square is a triple life-size **bronze statue** symbolizing the role of peasants in the nation's struggle for independence.

The **Bali Museum** on the eastern edge of the square houses a fine collection of archaeological artifacts and Balinese crafts. In the morning, visit **Kokar/SMKI** on **Jalan Ratna**, the influential conservatory of dance, music and puppet theater—to see the island's graceful and handsome teenage stars rehearsing. The tertiary level of the school, ASTI, is located inside the new performing arts center, **Werdi Budaya**, at **Abian Kapas**. Visitors are welcome to observe dance and music classes in progress. Evening performances are held regularly in the center's open-air stage. An Arts Festival is also held here annually in June and July, with an extensive program of *gamelan* competitions, art contests, dance and theater revivals, and craft exhibitions. This has become a draw for thousands of art lovers and Baliphiles the world over.

Anything and everything goes (off) at Kuta Beach.

THE SPLENDOR OF BALINESE DANCE

The traditional Balinese polity has been described as a "theater state." And while a culture as vital and as lively as Bali's has certainly not remained immutable, there are clear indications that dance and drama have played a central role in Balinese life since time immemorial.

A good deal of Indian influence is evident. In fact the Balinese dancers of today more resemble those depicted in the classical Hindu-Javanese temple reliefs than do the court dancers of Java. And like his Javanese counterpart, the Balinese dancer adopts the basic "Indian" stance—knees bent, legs turned-out , body straight, head tilted—with highly expressive hand and finger gestures.

In other respects, though, Balinese dance imparts a very different feeling. While the Javanese have developed slow, controlled, continuous movements performed with eyes downcast, and limbs held close to the body (in keeping with their aesthetic of refinement), the Balinese dancer is charged with energy—eyes agape, darting this way and that, high-stepping, arms up, moving with quick, cat-like bursts that would startle a Javanese.

All dances are connected in some way with rituals. Temple festivals always require a theatrical performance of some kind as entertainment for the gods (as well as for the participants). The Balinese, nevertheless, distinguish between those dances that are sacred (*wali*), ceremonial (*bebali*) and secular (*bali-balihan*).

The *Legong Keraton*, for example, has been the most popular dance in Bali since it was first performed in the villages in the 1920s. It is now seen frequently at village temple festivals and has become a big hit with tourists. Traditionally, the *Legong* is performed by two very young girls, introduced by a court attendant who first sweeps the stage and presents the dancers with fans. Sheathed in glittering costumes, with headdresses crowned by frangipani blossoms, the two dancers then enact one of a dozen or so stories.

The best-known Balinese dance is undoubtedly the *Barong*—immortalized in the Margaret Mead film of the 1950s, *Trance and Dance in Bali*. It is a contest between the opposing forces of good and evil in the universe, embodied in the good beast Barong and the evil witch Rangda.

The powerful *Kecak* dance was adapted from the *Sanghyang Dedari* trance dance in 1928, by isolating the chorus of the latter and treating it as Hanuman's monkey army in the *Ramayana*. Now performed by as many as a hundred chanting and swaying men dressed in loincloths, the *Kecak* is by far Bali's most popular tourist spectacle.

And in the 1930s, the legendary I Nyoman Mario introduced several new creations, such as the *Kebyar* and the *Oleg Tambulilingan*. The former is a solo virtuoso dance performed with the upper body only while in a sitting position. The latter depicts two bumblebees making love in a garden of flowers!

Classic Bali mask, old man of the Topeng dance.

EXPLORING BALI

When embarking from the southern beach resorts on a tour of the island, the central district of **Gianyar** is your first stop. Easily the island's most exotic and artistic region, these villages have been patronized by Bali's rajas ever since the 17th century, as a source for everything from carvings to jewelry to dancers.

Northeast of Denpasar is the village of **Batubulan**, where *barong* and *kecak* dancers entertain busloads of tourists daily. Also an area of beautiful temples, this is the source for the soft soapstone used to smother most Balinese shrines with ornate carvings. Batubulan's **Pura Puseh** temple has a massive temple gate with the Hindu pantheon on one side and a meditating Buddha on the other.

Celuk is the center for gold and silver work. Here you will find fine filigree produced by craftsmen who learn the trade from a young age. The nearby village of **Sukawati** was once a center for Chinese traders, and is now home to Bali's greatest puppet masters. **Batuan** residents are best known for their painting and dance. Under the patronage of Walter Spies, the Batuan School of the 1930s was the first to produce secular paintings on Bali. The dancers of this village often win island-wide competitions, and may be seen during the *odalan* anniversary rites for the village temples.

Mas is a village of master carvers, who originally produced only religious or court pieces, but today make decorative and expressionistic works for export. The famous Ida Bagus Nyana, whose visionary modernist sculptures of the 1940s are now on display in the gallery of his son, Ida Bagus Tilem, lived here. **Peliatan** is the home of an especially active dance troupe which presents excellent performances year-round.

Ubud has become a mecca for foreign and local artists who enjoy the quiet and creative atmosphere of this peaceful village. A local artistocrat, Cokorda Sukawati, joined forces with German painter Walter Spies in the 1930s to form the Pita Maha art

Woodcarver at Ubud, where artists abound.

society. Many fine works from those years are exhibited in the **Puri Lukisan Museum** and **Neka Gallery**.

Among the Pita Maha artists, I Gusti Nyoman Lempad was probably the greatest. His ink drawings, cremation towers and temple stone carvings are greatly admired—a few are on display in the gallery now operated by his children. Other well-known artists include American Antonio Blanco, Dutchman Hans Snel and Javanese Abdul Azziz.

Ubud's greatest work of art, however, is the surrounding countryside. Take some time to wander the back lanes—with a visit, for example, to the "**Monkey Forest**" temple about a mile to the south.

To the east of Ubud lies **Goa Gajah** (the "Elephant Cave"), whose carved opening was thought to portray the image of an elephant. Probably once a hermitage for Buddhist monks, the cave and its adjacent bathing pools were discovered and excavated in 1923. The nearby ruins of **Yeh Pulu** date to the 14th century and feature a unique frieze said to have been etched by the thumbnail of a giant.

ntrance ɔ Goa ɩajah.

North of **Bedulu**, on the main road, is the **Archeological Museum**, which houses a collection of Neolithic axe heads, sarcophagi, weapons, bronze jewelry and Chinese ceramics. Several temples nearby contain objects of interest. Most famous of these is the **Pura Penataran Sasih**, containing the beautiful 2,000-year-old Moon of Pejeng **bronze drum** which is shaped like an hourglass and cast in one piece.

Two of Bali's holiest spots are found along the road up to **Mount Batur**. **Gunung Kawi** is a spectacular ancient royal tomb reached by descending a stairway through a stone arch into a watery canyon. The **Pura Tirta Empul** spring at **Tampaksiring** was supposedly created when the god Indra pierced a stone to produce *amrta* holy water with which to revive his poisoned army. The waters of Tampaksiring are still believed to have magic curative powers.

North Bali Round-Trip: Volcanic **Lake Batur**, viewed from the main road north of Tampaksiring, is Bali's most dramatic sight. The village of **Penelokan** perches on the lip of this 12–mile (20–km) wide caldera and you may hire motorized canoes at the lake's edge to visit the Bali Aga (pre-Hindu) community of **Trunyan** and the hot sulfur springs at **Toya Bungkah**.

The village of **Kintamani** crouches along the western rim of the caldera. Bali's highest temple is just nearby, atop **Mount Penulisan** and believed to have been the sanctuary of the ancient kings of Pejeng.

Roads leading over the mountains to the north of Bali were constructed by the Dutch only in the 1920s, and the cultures of the two regions are quite different. The language of the north is more rapid and less refined. The music is also more *allegro*, and the temple ornamentation more fanciful. The carvings at **Pura Maduwe Karang** temple in **Kubutambahan**, for example, depict domestic scenes, ghouls, lovers and even a Dutch official riding a bicycle. The temple at **Jagaraga** is decorated with reliefs depicting Europeans in a Model-T, a propeller plane diving into the sea, and a steamship attacked by sea monsters.

The port of **Singaraja** was once a bustling center of commerce and government under the Dutch, but is today a quiet backwater. The **Gedung**

Kertya on **Jalan Veteran** houses a vast collection of palm-leaf *lontar* manuscripts, and at the harbor you can see sailing vessels loading coffee, corn and rice.

Lovina Beach on Bali's northern shore is the ideal hideaway for travelers in search of quiet. Located seven miles (11 km) to the west of Singaraja, it was originally the site of a retreat built by the ruler for his wife.

An alternate, western road winds over the mountains, skirting the southern shores of peaceful **Lake Bratan**, where there is a government-run guesthouse and restaurant. Children fish for minnows here, while canoes carry firewood to villages on the other side. Just below the lake is the village of **Bedugul** where orchids and tree ferns are sold at the market.

The road down from Bedugul passes through the village of **Mengwi**, the site of magnificent **Pura Taman Ayun** with its moat, lotus pond and pagoda-like wooden shrines. Northeast of Mengwi is the famed Monkey Forest at **Sangeh**. Tall nutmeg trees, a moss-covered temple and a mischievous monkey tribe are to be found here.

The remarkable temple of **Tanah Lot**, founded by the Hindu saint, Naratha, perches on a large rock in the ocean at Bali's southwestern shore. At low tide, it is possible to cross over and ascend to the temple. And on the shore opposite, tables and chairs have been set up for visitors to witness the tropical sunset through the temple's twin towers.

Excursion to East Bali: Coming from the south, all roads pass through Gianyar, the center for Bali's weaving industry. Beautiful hand-woven and hand-dyed textiles are still produced here, though the use of machine-spun thread, quick chemical dyes and tinsel foil is now commonplace. Facing the town square, Gianyar's **palace** still houses the royal family and boasts intricately carved wooden pillars and stone-work exemplary of the opulence once enjoyed by Bali's rulers.

Nearby **Klungkung** was also once the site of a royal palace, and at its center stands the 18th-century **Kerta Gosa** hall of justice and the **Bale Kambang** "floating pavilion." On the ceiling of the former are depicted scenes from the *Bima Suarga*, Bali's answer to Dan-

Kechak dance in the shadow of Tanah Lot.

te's *Inferno.* In the nearby central market, you may purchase a great variety of baskets and traditional housewares while the main street of Klungkung has several good antique shops.

The mountain road north from Klungkung winds up through spectacular rice-fields to **Pura Besakih**, Bali's "mother temple." Regarded as a holy place for centuries, this is the meeting place for all deities in the extensive Balinese pantheon. Each of Bali's many caste groups also has its own shrine here, with its own *odalan* anniversary celebrations. At every full moon the *turun kabeh* ("all descend") ceremony is held to mark Besakih's consecration.

East of Klungkung on the coastal road is **Goa Lawah**, considered one of the nine great temples of Bali and the home of thousands of small, black bats. The cave is also believed to be the terminus of an underground passageway up to Besakih—as well as the abode of Naga Basuki, the sacred dragon of **Mount Agung**.

About nine miles (15 km) past Goa Lawah is the picturesque harbor of **Padang Bai**, where the Lombok ferry departs and cruise ships anchor. Just east of this natural bay lies **Candi Dasa**, a newly-developed beach resort for the island's *cognoscenti.* Inland, in a hilly area of lush bamboo forests and banyan trees is **Tenganan**, home of a pre-Hindu Bali Aga tribe which still retains distinctive traditions of government, art and kinship. The sacred *geringsing* fabric is woven here—used in temple rituals throughout Bali and thought to immunize the wearer against evil influences and diseases.

The easternmost town of **Amlapura**, once known as Karangasem, is the home of the only Balinese raja allowed to retain his title and powers after the Dutch conquest. The palace, **Puri Kanginan**, is an eclectic creation of European and Chinese design. Five miles (eight km) to the south lies **Ujung**, site of the ruins of an elaborate royal retreat. Just north of Amlapura, the **Tirta Gangga** pools were acclaimed as a masterwork of hydraulic engineering when first built in 1946. Today they may still be used for swimming, and a number of inexpensive accommodations have sprung up here.

…king a …vig of …freshing …conut …ater.

"OUTER ISLANDS"

A distinction is commonly drawn between the "Inner" and "Outer" islands of Indonesia. The "Inner Islands"—Java and Bali—are extremely densely-populated, wet-rice growing areas that were under the direct influence of Indianized kingdoms from a very early period. Today they support over two-thirds of Indonesia's population on less than 10 percent of the nation's total land area. The other islands of Indonesia, the so-called "Outer Islands," by contrast, are sparsely-populated and extremely heterogeneous—containing a startling array of different peoples, customs and material lifestyles.

Though a majority of visitors still come primarily to see Central Java and Bali, there is no reason to stop here. Recent improvements in the transportation and accommodation facilities now make convenient and comfortable travel throughout the Indonesian archipelago a reality.

Sumatra: The great island of **Sumatra**—third largest in the archipelago and fifth largest in the world (roughly the size of California)—has always formed a kind of pivotal "backbone" for Indonesia, due to its strategic, economic and political importance. Second among the islands in population (with 30 million inhabitants) but first in exports (oil, natural gas, rubber, palm oil, tobacco, tea and timber), Sumatra stands at the crossroads of Asia—heir to an illustrious past and home to a broad spectrum of dynamic and fiercely independent peoples.

Sumatra's primary gateway is the city of **Medan** in the northeast. Once the site of a small sultanate, this area was later developed by Dutch and British planters in the late-19th century and is now the most densely-populated region in Sumatra. The discovery of oil here in 1883, and subsequent finds all along the east coast of the island, have made this the source of 75 percent of the nation's crude, as well as a range of petrochemical products.

Modern Medan has retained many architectural anachronisms from its

Traditional Minangkaba style house in West Sumatra.

colonial days. The largest concentration of rococo and art-deco buildings is found along **Jalan Jend. A.Yani** and around **Merdeka Square**—the **Post Office**, the former Witte Societeit (now **Bank Negara**) and several hotels. Chinese shops line the main streets, and four large markets are located in the busy downtown area. At the southern end of town stands the imposing **Grand Mosque**—built in a rococo style in 1906 just opposite the **Istana Maimun** (Sultan's Palace). The palace, designed by an Italian architect in 1888, still houses the royal family and may be visited during the day.

Sumatra's finest sight is the blue-green **Lake Toba**, a vast crater lake 110 miles (176 km) south of Medan. Along the way, stop at **Brastagi**, a hill resort and market town with colonial guest-houses and a cool climate. Nearby *Karo Batak* villages, with their massive wooden clan houses, are easily visited from here.

The *Bataks* inhabit a fertile volcanic plateau that covers much of northern central Sumatra. They are sophisticated agriculturalists who possess elaborate crafts, calendars and cosmological texts written in an Indic alphabet. Their reputation for aggressiveness dates back to a time in the not-so-distant past when many tribes were engaged in perpetual ritual warfare, and headhunting and cannibalism were common. Most *Bataks* are now Christians, due to a century of missionary activities.

Lake Toba lies in the very heart of the *Batak* lands. This is the largest lake in Southeast Asia, as well as one of the highest (3,000 feet/900 meters) and deepest (1,500 feet/450 meters) in the world. Geologists tell us that it was formed eons ago by the largest volcanic explosion the earth has ever known.

From the town of **Prapat** on the lake's eastern shore, cross over by boat to the picturesque island of **Samosir**. The island's main landing is at **Tomok**, site of the stone tomb of King Sidabuta. In an enclosure opposite the boat-shaped tomb are ritual statues of a buffalo sacrifice.

Another landing at nearby **Tuk Tuk**, on a tiny peninsula, is now the site of many small hotels. **Ambarita**, an hour's walk north of Tuk Tuk, has three megalithic complexes that were once

Aerial view of Lombok landscape.

used for cannibalistic rituals. At the village of **Simanindo** at Samosir's northern tip, a large royal clan house has been restored and transformed into a museum.

Travelers with more time on their hands can continue on from Lake Toba to the spectacular Minangkabau highlands around **Bukit Tinggi** (in the province of West Sumatra) or to the island of **Nias** off Sumatra's west coast—home of a unique, megalithic tribal group.

Kalimantan: Rich in oil, natural gas, timber and diamonds, **Kalimantan** comprises about three-fourths of Borneo, the world's third largest island. Yet it is very sparsely populated—covered by swamps and tropical rainforests which make cultivation and communication difficult. The interior is inhabited by a great number of different tribes, known collectively as the *Dyaks*, while the coastal ports are settled by Malay, Javanese, Chinese and expatriate traders and oil workers.

Balikpapan is East Kalimantan's oil town, with an airport and a luxury hotel. But most travelers don't stay long, preferring instead to head inland in search of remote trading posts, steamy jungles and fascinating *Dyak* villages.

Rivers are Kalimantan's roads, and a leisurely cruise aboard an *African Queen*-style riverboat up the **Mahakam River** is an unforgettable adventure. The jumping-off point is **Tenggarong**, about 155 miles (250 km) from Balikpapan and the site of a museum housing an amazing collection of ceramics and tribal crafts. From here, book passage to the lakeside village of **Tanjung Isuy**, where you will be welcomed by the hospitable *Banuaq Dyaks*, famous for their weavings and dances. Continue on to **Melak** and **Sekolak Darat**, home of rare black orchids and huge totem poles adorned with fiendish images—used to ward off evil spirits.

The Eastern Islands: Centrally located within the archipelago, the rugged island of **Sulawesi** ("The Celebes") has been a focus for inter-island migrations and trading operations since pre-historic times and is now inhabited by over 40 different ethnic groups. The most developed area is South Sulawesi, where Bugis traders inhabit the coastal town. The upland *Torajan* peoples of south-central Sulawesi are famed for their boat-shaped houses and elaborate burial rites.

The capital, **Ujung Pandang**, is a rich blend of Dutch, Chinese, Portuguese and indigenous influences, with a harbor full of sailing ships and a Dutch fort that is now a museum. From here take a bus up to **Rantepao** in the heart of **Tanah Toraja** country, 200 miles (325 km) away, to see traditional villages, weavings, folk dances and unique cliff-face cave tombs lined with carved ancestral figures.

Bali's neighboring island of **Lombok** was invaded at various times by the Balinese, Muslim traders and the Dutch. What remains is an interesting spectrum of contrasting customs and architecture. The island is dominated by towering **Mount Rinjani** (12,300 feet/3,888 meters) and the majority of her population occupy a narrow 16-mile (25-km) strip of land in a central east-west corridor.

The most interesting of the island's three towns, **Cakranegara** was the royal capital until the turn of the century. Today it is a major market town. **Pura Meru**, the central temple for Lombok's Hindus, and **Puri Mayura**, the royal pleasure garden, are located here.

A temple atop **Mount Pengsong** offers exquisite views of the island, while skin-diving enthusiasts will surely wish to visit **Pemenang Beach** and **Gili Air** island on Lombok's northwestern shore, to investigate the spectacular coral formations and marine life.

Narmada, six miles (10 km) east of Cakranegara, is the site of regal complex of tiered gardens, ponds, fountains and arbors constructed in the 19th century. The temple at nearby **Suranadi** is a pilgrimage point for Hindus, for its holy springwater.

The tiny island of **Komodo** between **Sumbawa** and **Flores** is the home of the world's largest reptile—the "Komodo Dragon." This giant monitor lizard (*Varanus komodoensis*) is a relative of the dinosaurs which roamed the earth 100 million years ago and can reach 10 feet (three meters) in length, 330 pounds (150 kg) in weight. The Indonesian Nature Conservation Directorate (PPA) arranges tours and will even bring along a goat for slaughter. You can then witness the lizards from the safety of a raised platform, but be sure to stay clear—the lizards' tails are lethal weapons.

Right, women wearing traditional ikat fabric.

JAPAN: A YEN FOR SUCCESS

We are so inundated with literature of the genre, "What is Japan?", "How the Japanese do it," "The riddle of Japan unraveled," and so on that the one thing that can be said with certainty of Japan today is that it is Asia's most self-conscious nation. Pride in the country's long history and traditions as well as in its modern economic success, and a sense of the unity of the Japanese people and nation play an important role in the thinking of many modern Japanese. At the same time, admiration of the products of Europe and America, even envy of Westerners, is emitted from every organ of the mass media, which are without doubt reflecting the values of the younger audience.

The foreign visitor will repeatedly hear "*gaijin*" (foreigner) or *gaijin-san* (Mr./Ms. Foreigner)—terms that enforce the impression of Japan's "us and them" view of the world. In the face of this vast cultural simplification, observant travelers may also be surprised with the human and cultural diversity among different regions of Japan. The most immediate evidence of this is a striking variety of facial types.

Urban Japan has developed tremendously in the past two decades. And yet, in Japanese homes and workplaces, lifestyles and customs of pre-modern vintage persist.

Japan's total population stood at 120.7 million in 1985. Of that number, close to 70 million live in cities with populations over 100,000. Although Japan's economy no longer rests on agrarian foundations, the majority of inhabitable rural areas continue to be made up of small farms, using every arable inch for intensive rice cultivation.

Prosperity, reaching almost every corner of the country, is the greatest single factor that has distinguished Japan today from its recent past—or for that matter from many other Asian nations. One by-product of prosperity is a nation of tourists, as the Japanese now have the leisure time to travel. Domestic tourism has left no stone unturned. The fact may be discouraging to the traveler with a romantic yearning for the "undiscovered" Asia. But seen in a more positive light, Japan is a country with something worth finding everywhere. It would be only slight hyperbole to say that every stone turned reveals either something of cultural interest —or a hot spring. In both cultural and natural terms, Japan is that rich.

Preceding pages: Mount Fuji looms over Lake Ashino. Left, woodblock print of a Japanese lady.

SHOGUNS AND SAMURAI

Prehistory: The earliest Japanese records describe the creation of the Japanese archipelago by the gods Izanagi and Izanami, who accomplished the task by dancing around a heavenly pillar and meeting in conjugal embrace. On the first attempt, Izanagi gave birth to a "leech-child." The second go-round produced a string of islands. The source of the story is late, from the eighth century, by which time there had already been considerable cultural influx from Korea and China, but the myth itself bears remarkable similarity to Polynesian creation myths. This, along with linguistic and architectural evidence, suggests some prehistoric connection between the cultures of Japan and the South Pacific.

Archeological remains of the neolithic period include pieces of pottery more than 10,000 years old. The entry of continental culture is evidenced in the appearance of wheel-thrown pottery and bronze implements during the Yayoi Period (ca. 300 B.C. to 300 A.D.).

It is difficult to say how much of a Bronze Age Japan had, for the iron culture of Han China seems to have arrived fast on the heels of bronze. In the first centuries A.D., powerful kings and a hierarchical military society arose in central and western Japan. The aristocracy of this time were buried in immense tumuli with stores of helmets, swords, mirrors and jewels. The sword, mirror and "curved jewel" (*magatama*) which are the regalia of Japan's historical emperors probably have their origin in this prehistoric culture. The largest of the tombs, called the tomb of Emperor Nintoku, is near the city of Sakai (Kansai), a keyhole-shaped island surrounded by three moats. In terms of area it is the largest funerary construction in the world.

Nara Period: Beginning in the seventh century with the active importation of Chinese culture and learning, the construction of Buddhist temples and the establishment of a state with a written code of government in the Yamato valley (present-day Nara Prefecture), Japan at last entered recorded history. No writing system seems to have existed before the fifth century, when Chinese ideographic characters (which had already been in existence for at least two thousand years) were brought into use. Matters were later improved by means of simplified syllabic characters. A page of Japanese today is typically about 50 percent Chinese characters.

Buddhist icons had arrived in Japan from Korea during the sixth century, rousing debate in court and a brief civil war between advocates of the new religion and adherents to the native Shinto. The primacy of Buddhism was firmly established by Prince Shotoku Taishi, Imperial Regent from 593, who promulgated a Buddhist moral code and built numerous temples. Shotoku never condemned Shinto, but he devoted himself to Buddhism, lecturing personally on the Lotus Sutra, and also promoting all forms of Chinese art and scholarship.

Under Chinese tutelage, Nara witnessed a great cultural flowering. The Japanese court sent envoys across the Japan Sea at great risk, instructing them to bring back books and scholars of government, philosophy and religion. The sight of Chang-an, the Chinese capital, and the scale on which the Chinese did things must have overwhelmed the Japanese. The Sui Emperor is reported to have gone on outings on the Yellow River in a fleet of pleasure boats drawn by 80,000 men. This splendor could not be emulated, but Japan's first permanent capital was planned to match in every way possible the model of Chang-an. In 710, the capital Heijo-kyo was established at Nara. Palaces, government offices, storehouses and great temples were erected. The Buddhist temples of the city, by far the greatest buildings ever to have been built in Japan, held center stage, and miraculously remain today as a legacy of the first era of the Japanese state.

Heian Period: In 794 the capital was moved to present-day Kyōto and named Heian-kyōto, Capital of Peace and Tranquility. The move seems to have been made this time to give the government a fresh start away from the great temples like Tōdai-ji, which had come to dominate Nara politics. The new capital was also built on the Chinese model. A century later official contact with China was halted. During the period that followed, heavily Chinese-influenced court culture incubated in the Heian capital, cut off from the outside world, even from the Japanese provinces. The Heian Period (794-1185) represents on one hand the stagnation and inevitable decline of institutions begun in Nara, but on the other, a time of brilliance at court—within its tiny, cloistered society, a kind of classical age of Japanese aesthetics. The major poetry anthologies and literary diaries date from this period. Women were the revolutionary force in Heian literature, writing in a new Japanese vernacular liberated from the stodginess of academic Chinese. The undisputed masterpiece of Heian literature, and all Japanese prose, is the *Tale of Genji*, written around the year 1000 by Murasaki Shikibu, a lady-in-waiting to the empress. It is a narrative of over a thousand pages termed by some the world's first novel. The pages of *Genji* give a vivid sense of the rarified air of the author's environment. Daily life was taken up entirely by ceremony. An infinitesimal error of taste could cause a stir and social alienation. Women wore up to 12 layers of carefully-matched kimono, color and pattern dictated by rank, season and occasion. They grew their hair down to the floor and hid themselves from the sun and the eyes of others with standing screens and blinds.

In the eyes of residents of the capital, the countryside just a few hours journey away was a barren and forbidding place of exile. Military clans were entrusted with the subjugation of the distant provinces. In the 10th century, these clans consolidated

Kamakura period: Taira clan absconds with the emperor in a 12th-century insurrection.

power, making inroads in the administration of the country. In 1156, the Taira clan came into domination in Kyōto. In a series of bloody confrontations the Taira subdued their rivals the Minamoto and established themselves as the first military family to control the throne and the empire. The following 700 years would see almost uninterrupted *samurai* rule.

The Taira's day of glory was short. The Minamoto returned in 1180 under the brilliant general Minamoto Yoritomo and routed them in a war of five years that extended across Honshu.

Kamakura Period: *Samurai* means "one who serves." In the regime established at Kamakura by Yoritomo, and in the ranks of the *samurai* caste throughout the country, loyal service to one's lord was the single ethic governing all individual conduct. The *samurai* served with his sword, and there developed a cult of the sword, as well as a cult of the god of war, Hachiman. The custom of ritual sucide, *seppuku* or *harakiri* (meaning "belly-slitting") also has its roots in this period.

The warrior nation under the Kamakura Shogunate was mobilized twice to defend Japan, in 1274 and 1281, when forces of the Mongol ruler Kublai Khan, who was then sovereign of the world's largest empire, attacked the shores of Kyushu. But both battles were decided by fateful typhoons which shipwrecked and scattered the invading fleet. The storms that had saved the day were called *kamikaze*, "divine winds," a word which was revived the next time Japan encountered the threat of a foreign invasion, in World War Two.

In 1332, Emperor Godaigo attempted a restoration of direct imperial rule. With strong military support and treachery on the part of several key men at Kamakura, the shogunate was toppled. But the barons who had fought for Godaigo controlled the armies and could continue to call the shots. Soon Godaigo was forced to flee the capital by the very general who had brought about his victory over Kamakura. A new emperor was set up in Kyoto, but Godaigo still had a following who continued to maintain his right to the throne. The years from 1336 to 1392 are called the Northern and Southern Courts Period. Civil wars were waged, ostensibly in dispute over the throne, but more often than not actually for territorial gain.

Ashikaga (Muromachi) Period: The family of Ashikaga Takauji, who had turned on Kamakura to support Godaigo and then banished Godaigo himself, managed to hold on to a position of relative strength based in Kyōto during 56 years of anarchy. The Ashikaga Period, from 1392 to 1573, was not characterized by good government, as the shoguns pursued a sweet life of aesthetic pastimes and left administration to ministers who pursued personal gain.

The arts flourished in Kyōto. Trade opened up again with China, bringing in pottery and monochrome paintings of a style which would have great influence in Japan. Tea drinking, a custom first practiced by zen monks in the Kamakura Period, became the center of a cult in which art objects, teas and tea wares were admired and compared.

The "tea ceremony," called *chanoyu*, has since become the greatest single influence on the applied arts and Japanese tastes in general. It is the most popularly-studied avocation in Japan today. A tea ceremony is a gathering in a small room decorated with a few carefully chosen objects of beauty, in which tea is served and received according to a fixed etiquette, and the tea utensils are admired and perhaps discussed. Rustic simplicity is emphasized, and the bareness of the environment allows concentration of each of the senses on aesthetic experience.

TYPES AND COSTUMES OF CITIZENS OF TOKIO.

While Shogun Yoshimasa practiced tea in his suburban-Kyoto retreat, the Onin War, another large-scale regrouping of feudal estates, raged in the streets of Kyoto. Ten years of fighting, from 1467 to 1477, led to no satisfactory resolution, but caused destruction on a scale previously unseen and ushered in another century of disorder, usually referred to as the Warring States Period. The actors in this period of turmoil were not only local *samurai* forces but included armies of monks from the powerful temples around Kyoto.

Left, various modes of Japanese dress. Above, the costumes worn by Tokyo citizens.

Three great generals finally distinguished themselves from the fray, and their campaigns unified Japan under a single government. Oda Nobunaga, Toyotomi Hideyoshi and Tokugawa Ieyasu were allies in the 1560s and 1570s, when Nobunaga led them in a series of victories over the other military families.

Nobunaga had particular venom for the Buddhist monasteries, and saw to the brutal eradication of several of them. At the same time, he courted Christian missionaries, who had come from Portugal and were collecting Japanese converts. Nobunaga, like many others of the military class, was more interested in the material aspects of European civilization, in particular the Portuguese *arquebus*, the first gun seen in Japan. Later missionaries did not meet with such hospitality, for Christianity was outlawed by Nobunaga's successor, Hideyoshi, and persecuted into oblivion under the first Tokugawa *shoguns*.

Momoyama Period: Nobunaga was assassinated by one of his retainers at the height of his power, and control of one third of Japan was left to his general, Toyotomi Hideyoshi. Through generous bribes and prolonged sieges, Hideyoshi subjugated the remaining clans and brought a tenuous peace to Japan for the first time in 100 years.

Hideyoshi surrounded himself with opulence, his tastes reflecting a paradox in Momoyama culture. He was the patron of Sen no Rikyu, Japan's greatest tea master, who brought the art to the extreme of aesthetic severity, but for himself, Hideyoshi wanted a tea room made entirely of gold (Hideyoshi's gold tea room can be seen at the Nagoya Museum).

Hideyoshi laid the groundwork for a more centralized feudal society. One of his edicts forbade farmers to bear arms and *samurai* to farm. The resulting "sword hunt" of 1587 served to separate the *samurai* class from the peasantry and make the sword an emblem of rank. It also reduced the possibility of peasant uprisings, which were a constantly recurring problem for the medieval *daimyo* (powerful land-owners).

Tokugawa (Edo) Period: Hideyoshi spent his life in empire-building campaigns, and died in 1598 without leaving an able heir. In the battle over succession that followed, Tokugawa Ieyasu developed the strongest backing, winning a decisive victory at the battle of Sekigahara in 1600. The following year, he obliged the other *daimyo* to sign an oath of loyalty to his newly-established shogunate and juggled the apportionment of fiefs to discourage alliances. The 258 years of Tokugawa rule were the most peaceful period in Japanese history. With time the shogunate located in Ieyasu's castle-town of Edo (present-day Tokyo) developed into an immense administrative institution regulating in every detail the strictly hierarchical four-class society of *samurai*, farmers, artisans and merchants. This social order was derived from the moral philosophy of Neo-confucianism, which served as the state creed. The shogunate kept the *daimyo* in check by a system of "alternate attendance" which compelled them to live half of each year on estates in Edo and leave their families there year-round, effectively as hostages. Travel to and from their home provinces, public works they were required to support in Edo, and the expense of keeping their estates conspired to financially drain them.

After the final ban on Christianity, the Tokugawa severed all connections between Japan and the rest of the world, regulating the size of sea-going vessels, executing any Japanese who went abroad and returned, and limiting trade contact to a handful of Dutchmen and Chinese in the port of Nagasaki. This law, like all enacted by the shogunate, was a strategy to guarantee their static and absolute rule. But Japan in the Tokugawa Period was far from unchanging. Peace meant prosperity, and the alternate attendance system brought commercial development. Ironically, the ones to benefit most were the merchants, who sat on the bottom rung of the Confucian social ladder. Commercial empires were built, several of which survive today. The Mitsui company, for example, began as Edo's first off-the-rack clothier in the late 17th century. The *samurai*, on the other hand, were soldiers without wars to fight.

A striking development during the Tokugawa Period was the appearance of a popular culture of theater, literature, music and art catering to the bourgeois tastes of the merchant townspeople. The locus of this artistic activity was in the licensed prostitution and entertainment districts, referred to as the *Ukiyo*, or "floating world." It's idols were *geisha* and *Kabuki* actors, who were immortalized in *ukiyoe*, "pictures of the floating world." The *ukiyoe* woodblock prints were originally produced as no more than theater advertisements. *Samurai* too were drawn into the decadent life of the "gay quarter" despite repeated edicts forbidding them to mix in the fun, closing theaters and condemning frivolity. The arts of the floating world show a radically new outlook, in which philosophical depth is replaced by this-worldly materialism and sensuousness. Edo printmakers not only produced portraits of beauties but also unexpurgated pornography. The *Kabuki* theater, in contrast to aristocratic *Nō*, (or *Noh*), was flamboyant and raucous. Fights were frequent in the audience.

Meiji Period: In 1853, American ship captain Commodore Perry anchored in Uraga Bay and announced America's demand that Japan open its ports to trade.

The shogunate, in financial straits and militarily unable to repel the foreigners, was forced into concessions. The ever-weakening shogunate signed unequal treaties with America and European nations. Eventually, *samurai* of the provinces of Satsuma and Choshu, which were far from the seat of power and had always remained aloof from the Tokugawa, rose in rebellion. With nowhere to turn, Shogun Tokugawa Yoshinobu resigned in 1867.

In 1868, the imperial capital was moved to Edo, which was renamed Tokyo, and monarchy was restored under Emperor Meiji, a vivacious if less-than-brilliant ruler. But it was not Meiji himself who had brought it about, and the group of former *samurai* who had initiated the political revolution became the moving force of the new government. In the first two years, the *samurai* class was abolished and *daimyo* estates were repossessed. Ports were opened and a policy of across-the-board Europeanization was embarked upon in Japanese institutions. It was, however, 21 years before the promulgation of a constitution and the formation of a Diet on the Prussian model.

Meiji was a time of frenetic change and experimentation. Much of the population followed the government in trying on a western suit of clothes, giving rise to the adjective "*hai-kara*" (from "high collar"), meaning up-to-date, dandy or Occidental.

Victory at war with China in 1895 and with Russia in 1905 changed Japan's image of itself among world nations and surprised the West. The defeat of the Russian navy in particular announced that Japan was a power to be reckoned with. Japan had learned its lessons well watching the imperial expansion of Western nations. The Sino-Japanese War yielded the island of Taiwan, and Russia yielded the southern half of Sakhalin. In 1910, Japan annexed Korea.

Taisho Period: Emperor Meiji died in 1912, marking the end of Japan's first era as a modern nation. His son had none of Meiji's charisma, and reigned for 24 years (1912-1926), removed from politics and the public eye. The present emperor (whose name is Hirohito, but this name is seldom used) functioned as regent from 1920. With the death of the Taisho emperor in 1926, Hirohito succeeded to the throne, beginning the Showa Period.

Taisho does not represent a distinct era in Japanese history, but there are trends and events of the 1910s and 1920s which are associated with the reign. The nation continued to pursue a policy of military expansion, but at home Japan saw a brief flush of liberalism in parliamentary politics and in society at large. The daring youth of Japan's Roaring '20s, weaned on jazz and Chaplin, Marxism, milk and waffles (at the "milk hall," precursor of the coffee shop), were called "*mobo*" and "*moga*" (modern boy, modern girl).

Political reality contrasted starkly with the carefree young society of Taisho. Harsh reality overshadows the memory of the early Showa Period (1930s). Military extremists led the nation deeper into a war for Asian domination. In 1932, Manchuria was made a Japanese protectorate under martial rule. The following year, Japan withdrew from the League of Nations, isolating itself from European critics. In 1937, lower army officers stationed in Manchuria staged an incident with Chinese forces. Japan lurched into an all-out invasion southward into China. Although direct involvement of Western nations apart from Russia would not come for another four years, the Second World War in Asia was in full swing. One day after the bombing of Pearl Harbor on December 7, 1941, the U.S. and Britain declared war on Japan.

The history of the Pacific War is well-known and documented. Upon surrender in September 1945, Japan was reduced to its borders as they had stood at the beginning of Meiji. On the following New Year's Day, the emperor made a radio broadcast renouncing his divinity. A new constitution was written under direction of Allied Occupation leaders. The Occupation continued until 1952.

The early 60s saw a skyrocketing Japanese economy and an Olympics in Tokyo, representing for the Japanese people a moment of pride and redeemed respectability. Since then, Japan has been on an accelerating course of modernization (it might be more accurate to say "futurization") and economic development, leaving other countries in its wake.

Left, lavish costume at a Japanese festival. Above, the tea ceremony is elaborate and painstakingly exacting.

バーゲン
ステレオ
ビデオ
テレビ
冷暖房エアコン
ファンヒーター
ロケット1号店
テレビ・ビデオ キャンペーン実施中
ファッション テレコ 安い
ロケット1号店
maxell
ファッションテレコ
ラジオ

TOKYO

By some counts the largest city in the world, by many accounts the most perplexing and contradictory. **Tokyo** is a megalopolis woven of a thousand small towns, each with a station, a shopping arcade and a tangle of residential streets. The surface is a nondescript high-tech but inside, neighborhoods are suburban in quality, even villagey. And the sprawl goes on and on—the adjacent cities of **Kawasaki** and **Yokohama** are part of an unbroken continuum.

Tokyo has some 83,000 streets. Only the largest of these bear names. An address is rarely sufficient to get even the experienced Tokyoite to his destination—one wonders, how does the mailman do it? With difficulty. And cab drivers? Most cab rides involve intermediate goals, stations, hotels, major intersections or landmarks. Driver and passenger proceed like captain and navigator. If you are not equipped for this dialogue, and have only a residential address to show your driver, he will probably stop a couple of times in the neighborhood for directions or look for a policeman. Police boxes have complete local maps. Most people draw maps and send them to visitors in advance to save them the hunt. In almost all cases one starts at a station. In fact, what might otherwise be an unbearable chaos is made a very efficient and manageable city by the network of superbly punctual trains and subways. The trains have gained notoriety for overcrowding. The men hired to push people aboard are particularly renowned. There are few in evidence today, and people say the crowds have gotten lighter, but the morning rush is still an ordeal, the bodies packed in "like *sushi*" (the Japanese equivalent of sardines). At least the morning crowd is an extremely civil one. Some of the same blue-suited company professionals ("*sararii-man*") are sure to be found on the 11:30 p.m. on their way home, sloppy drunk. The party-worn crowd on the last trains of the evening (most lines stop running just after midnight) can be a lot more trying than a morning train with twice the number of people, but all sober.

receding ages: hinjuku kyline in okyo. eft, not-so-ubtle ignage the kihabara istrict. ight, okyo's nperial alace.

Imperial Palace: Tokyo became Tokyo in 1868, when the emperor, ensconced in Kyōto for over one thousand years, was moved here to set up shop on the site of the former shogun's castle. "Tokyo" means eastern capital; the second character "kyo," meaning capital, is the same as the first character in "Kyōto." The city of Edo (Tokyo before 1868) was the castle town of the Tokugawa shoguns, and left behind the castle site with its gates and moats, some large *daimyo* lords' estates and temples, and a low congested merchant city. More than half of Tokyo was leveled in an earthquake in 1923, and over 70 percent of the city was destroyed by firebombing during the war, but the legacy of Edo is still subtly apparent. The castle area, now the **Imperial Palace**, is where it was, preserving its gates and inner moat. Most of the main *daimyo* estates have become public land, containing most of the government buildings and **Hibiya Park**. **Tokyo University** still sports the massive red gate of the Maeda clan mansion. Temple land is largely as it was, although few temple buildings

predate this century, and the congested merchant city is just that, only more so, and a little taller.

The Imperial Palace occupies a huge area in the heart of Tokyo. There are a couple of roads cutting through the palace grounds, but most traffic goes around. In fact, traffic patterns throughout the city are said to revolve around the circuit along the inner moat of the palace. An island of lush green slopes and expanses of gravel with low trees, the palace grounds are a strange hollow in the middle of dense urban surroundings. The **National Museum of Modern Art**, the **Science Museum**, and the **Budokan Concert Hall** are here, and portions of the grounds are open as public park space, but the majority of the Imperial Palace is seen only by the quiet, reclusive Imperial family. The emperor is less of a public figure than most European royalty. People see him in the flesh on New Year's and his birthday, April 29, when crowds charge through the gates into the palace courtyard and greet him with shouts of "*banzai*!"

Nijū-bashi, the "Double Bridge," is a good place to start a visit to the palace. The Nijū-bashi stop on the Chiyoda subway line will let you off across the street. There are actually two bridges; the taller one is Nijū-bashi, leading into the palace courtyard. It is an imperial symbol, and people are invariably seen having their pictures taken in front by the photographers who make their livings on this spot.

The **Ōtemon Gate** to the Imperial Palace **East Garden** (Higashi Gyōen) is a short walk northeast along the moat. Entering the first gate here, you will be in a walled square space with a two-story gate on your right. The garden within has the merit of being free, large and relaxing, but essentially unremarkable. Part of it is laid out in traditional Japanese style. Elsewhere inside, the foundation stones of Edo Castle's central keep survive: a platform of carefully hewn stones several feet tall.

From the **Idemitsu Museum**, on top of the building housing the **Imperial Theater** near **Hibiya Station**, a good view of the palace area can be obtained along with a cup of tea in the museum's self-service lounge. The museum also has an excellent collection of Japanese

Tokyo street, abou[t] 200 years ago.

STREET IN YEDO.

and Chinese art and ceramics.

Ginza: It is not far from Hibiya and the southeast corner of the Imperial Palace to **Ginza**, Tokyo's Fifth Avenue/Champs Elysées shopping and entertainment district. If you walk up **Harumi-dōri** from Hibiya, you will see the train overpass (the Bullet passes every few minutes) and the **Seibu-Hankyū** building ahead. On the right side of the street, with the question mark sign, is a Japan National Tourist Organization (JNTO) Information Center. They provide English maps of Tokyo, as well as excellent pamphlets on travel in Japan. The JNTO is the best source of travel information and any other assistance short of hotel reservations.

The heart of the Ginza is the **Ginza-Yonchōme** intersection, with the stately **Wako Building** (mostly watches) on the left side and the futuristic round **San-ai Building** (mostly young women's fashion) on the right. The main outlets of the **Mitsukoshi**, **Matsuya** and **Matsuzakaya** department stores are along this strip. Browsing can be a cultural education as well as being good fun. The department stores have moderately priced restaurants on the top floors, but even if you aren't looking for a meal, be sure to ride the elevator a few floors just to hear the elevator girl's patter.

There are many famous shops catering to the well-to-do along **Chūō-dōri**. The **Koyanagi** shop on Chūō-dōri at **Ginza 1-chōme** has been selling ceramic wares since the Ginza's birth as Tokyo's cosmopolitan shopping street 100 years ago. The **Kyūkyōdō** is of similar vintage, and a good place to pick up small gifts, stocking a beautiful variety of over a thousand papers and paper products, calligraphy brushes and incense. The Ginza area has close to 500 art galleries, but most of them are off the ground level and a little tricky to find. You can see *ukiyoe* woodblock prints at the **Riccar Museum**, located on the seventh floor of the **Riccar Building** behind the **Imperial Hotel**. Or wander and see what you find—the sidestreets offer a lot. Eating and drinking spots are also plentiful on the sidestreets between **Ginza 4-chōme** and **Yurakucho**.

If you find you've had a sufficient dose of the ritzy Ginza by the end of

he Ginza n a aturday fternoon.

the afternoon and feel like a little safe and sanitary slumming (Tokyo offers no other kind), cross Harumi-dōri in front of the Seibu-Hankyū Building and head down the back street along the railroad overpass. In immediate proximity and striking contrast to the area you have just come from is a back-alley cluster of *yakitori* bars, most of them built right under the tracks with the overpass itself as their roof. Naturally they are cheap, and popular with businessmen after work. The atmosphere is more like parts of Hong Kong or the Tokyo of 30 years ago than other Tokyo eating places.

Tsukiji Market: The people of Tokyo consume thousands of pounds of tuna every day, almost all of it raw. Ninety percent of this fish comes during the first hours of the day into the **Tsukiji Market** on **Tokyo Bay**. Tuna is the largest item, but every variety of seafood comes here, including lots of octopi, sea urchins and seaweed. Tuna are frozen aboard ship immediately after being caught, as tuna fishermen stay at sea for months. The Tsukiji Market is not exclusively for restaurateurs, and many housewives come here too to buy from the source. By 8:30 all important business has been transacted, and it's time to join the rubber-booted crowd for a *sushi* breakfast at one of the local "susheries."

Meiji Shrine: Meiji Jingū (*"jingū,"* like *"jinia"* refers to a Shinto shrine) is Tokyo's grandest shrine. It is dedicated to Emperor Meiji, who reigned until 1912. The broad and shady gravel paths and beautiful woods of the shrine precincts give an impressive sense of procession as well as making this one of the most relaxing places in Tokyo. The Meiji Empress loved irises and so the shrine has a garden with particularly spectacular irises. Certain days of the year bring out three-quarters of the population of Tokyo at Meiji Shrine. On New Year's, more than two million come in one day to pray, and it takes several hours to go from the entrance to within sight of the shrine. January 15, "Coming-of-Age Day" and November 15, "Three-Five-Seven Festival" are also big and colorful events, the former for women turned 20 and the the latter for children. The display of *kimono* on these days is more dazzling than the flowers in June.

Harajuku: Step out of the north exit of **Harajuku**, cross the street and look down the slight hill ahead of you. A sea of little heads—this is **Takeshita Dōri**, Mecca for all of teenage Japan. On a Saturday it is unbelievable. What attracts them is fashion (junk to *haute*), ice cream, and other teenagers. Harajuku is the haunt of the *takenoko-zoku*, outlandishly dressed dance squads who gained notoriety doing their choreographed thing on Sundays in nearby **Yoyogi Park**.

In a different vein, there is an excellent antique flea market on the grounds of **Togo Shrine** five minutes from Harajuku Station on the first Sunday of every month. Go in the morning before things sell out.

Shibuya: Another youth magnet, **Shibuya** is a larger scale Harajuku, with fashion department stores and scores of restaurant alleys. The crowd is a little older, but equally carefree and chic. The older generation may keep it in the bank, but kids here are wearing modern Japan's affluence on their backs. Every date in Shibuya starts next to **Hachiko**, an unremarkable little statue of a dog in front of the station. Hachiko waited in front of

Certain Western elements are evident in this girl's hairdo

Shibuya Station to welcome his master home every day, until the day the man went off to war and never returned. The dog stayed in front of the station until his death. After the statue was erected to commemorate his loyalty it became Tokyo's number one meeting place.

Let's go to the 'Rop': Roppongi is the heart of Tokyo's nightlife. Discos, rock and jazz clubs and bars keep the area hopping all night, despite the fact that the trains most people need to get home stop running between midnight and 5 a.m. The scene is Japan's most international, and there are several restaurants and clubs catering to or managed by Westerners. A look around at the foreign crowd out to play in Roppongi offers some clues as to why the Japanese tend to consider all foreigners eccentrics.

Shinjuku: The 1981 American film *Blade Runner*, depicting a decadent space-city of the future, was a big hit in Japan. Perhaps it was the familiarity of home that appealed to Tokyo viewers; parts of **Shinjuku** are uncannily similar to the science-fiction sets used in the film. The visual impact of this is strongest at night; exit east from **Shinjuku Station** (exiting the station itself is no mean feat) and cross the **East Exit Plaza** with the giant television screen, and walk down the shopping street on the far side, until you come out at a major avenue. This is the **Kabuki-chō** entertainment district. Until legal restrictions were imposed in 1985, sex was the commodity, in every imaginable form. Things have been cleaned up a bit, but the industry still flourishes. Drinking spots, generally inexpensive, clubs and "love hotels" attract a real cross-section of Tokyo.

During the day, Shinjuku offers a number of department stores and a couple of the biggest discount camera shops. This is probably the best place to buy a duty-free camera, or compact electronic and audio equipment.

The majority of Tokyo's skyscrapers are located on the west side of Shinjuku Station. This area is believed to be more geologically stable. The top of the **Sumitomo Building** is a good place from which to see the city.

The underground maze of Shinjuku Station can take a few weeks off a

elling it
ike it isn't:
gay bar
n Roppongi.

person's life. It is said to be not only Japan's busiest station, but the busiest place on the planet, in terms of the number of human beings passing through in a day.

Ueno: Ueno Park was Tokyo's first public park, opened in 1868 with the new era of government. It has the city zoo and aquarium, museums of art and science, a boat pond and very popular cherry trees. **Ueno Tōshōgū Shrine** is tucked away in a corner of the park, surviving from the 17th century. It was built as a memorial to Shogun Ieyasu, in the gaudy style that is the earmark of the Tokugawa shoguns, and is a designated important national property. From the shrine one can see a five-story pagoda nearby. This building, a relic of the same period, has found itself situated in the middle of the zoo.

Tokyo National Museum: Japan's foremost art collection is housed here. The museum collection is divided between three buildings, the **Honkan** (Main Building), the **Hyōkeikan** (Japanese Archaeological Collection) and the **Tōyōkan** (Oriental Collection). The Honkan is by far the largest, and contains the Japanese art collection. Displays rotate three to six times in a year. Poor lighting and a lack of English explanations make this a sometimes frustrating way to view the greatest of Japanese art. The Hyōkeikan, housing archaeological artifacts, is friendlier to the English-speaking visitor, if less colorful in content. The Tōyōkan contains art works from China and other far eastern countries outside of Japan.

Asakusa: From the mid-19th to the mid-20th century **Asakusa** was Tokyo's theater and entertainment district, the heart of *"shitamachi"* (downtown, the "common people's city"). After destruction in the war, it never regained its former status. The rest of Tokyo raced on ahead of it. There lies its charm today. Small shops, inexpensive food, and a different breed of Tokyoite, more open and informal, make the Asakusa-*shitamachi* atmosphere a pleasure not to be found elsewhere. The center of Asakusa life and culture is the **Asakusa Kannon (Sensō-ji Temple)**.

The history of Sensō-ji begins in 628, making it Tokyo's oldest temple. It is also Tokyo's most popular temple. Crowds of pilgrims and tourists pour through the **Kaminarimon** (Thunder Gate) with its famous red lantern, and down the **Nakamise Shopping Arcade** to the temple. "Pilgrim" and "tourist" are not distinct groups: Japanese visitors combine recreations, souvenir shopping and prayer, as they have from centuries.

The temple's main building received a new coat of vermilion lacquer in 1985-86, and glistens handsomely. The smoke rising from the large incense pot in front is supposed to make you wiser. A 15-minute walk west from Sensō-ji brings you to **Kappabashi-dori**, location of the restaurant supply district. There might seem to be little reason for travelers to come here, but recently it has become quite popular. Several shops here make and sell the plastic food models ubiquitous in Japanese restaurant windows. According to the vendors here the number one market is the restaurants (of course) and the number two market is *gaijin* (foreigners). The models are terrific pop-art, and some are very cleverly made. There is also a shop here selling *noren*, Japanese shop curtains with *"soba"* or *"sushi"* etc. printed on them.

Asakusa Kannon Temple.

SUMO!

Sumo, Japan's national sport, is simplicity itself in form and rules but carries the imprint of a rich tradition.

The style of modern sumo dates largely from the Edo Period (17th to 19th century). While ritual sumo continued as a part of Shinto festivals, the sport was adopted by *samurai* after the Heian Period as a method of developing skills for hand-to-hand combat. The majority of techniques involve grappling, tripping and striking with open hands.

The Edo authorities discouraged street-corner sumo, and restricted performances to within the precincts of Shinto shrines. As a result, entertainment sumo took on Shinto trappings, producing its modern incarnation, which is a combination of ritual and sport. The 15-foot ring is regarded as sacred ground, and into it the wrestlers throw salt, common in Shinto rites of purification. Hand-clapping and foot-stamping (the curious movement called *shiko*, in which each leg is lifted high in the air to one side) is performed before the bout.

The bout begins with the two wrestlers in a squatting position. There are usually several face-offs, interrupted by the wrestlers themselves, who return to their corners, toss more salt and otherwise delay action to maximize the tension for their opponent and audience.

It is often only a few seconds of tussling from the initial clash to the end of the fight. The most common winning technique, called *yori-kiri*, involves getting a grip on the opponent and forcing him out of the ring. Once he has touched outside of the ring he is defeated.

Wrestlers wear only a loincloth, the belt of which is key in all grappling techniques. The loincloth, *mawashi*, is a band of silk or cotton close to 30 feet (9 meters) in length which is wrapped three to eight times, depending on the wrestler's girth.

What's his beef?

Why are sumo wrestlers so fat? There are no weight or height limits or divisions, and a wrestler may find himself pitted against someone literally twice his size. When the wrestlers find themselves in a position of deadlock as often happens, the man with greater body weight and a lower center of gravity has an obvious advantage. So, many wrestlers develop huge bellies, which are cultivated on a diet of fish and vegetable stew, called *chanko-nabe*, and bowl after bowl of rice.

Though they all come in one size—extra large—sumo wrestlers come in a number of shapes. The contemporary *yokozuna* (grand champion) Chiyonofuji, has a weight-lifter's chest and shoulders and a comparatively lean figure, while the Hawaiian-Sāmoan Konishiki stands 6 feet 2 inches (1.86 meters) tall at a staggering 504 pounds (229 kg).

Tournaments, called *basho*, run 15 days and are held six times a year in the cities of Tokyo, Osaka, Nagoya and Fukuoka. The center of Japanese sumo is in Tokyo, in a district called Ryogoku. Here are located the Kokugikan National Sumo Stadium and the majority of the "stables" where the wrestlers live and train. And eat.

KAMAKURA

One hour from Tokyo by train, **Kamakura** is an historical treasure—a window on Japan's first feudal era. In 1185, Shogun Minamoto Yoritomo set up a military government in this coast town far from the imperial capital. The Kamakura shogunate lasted until the mid-14th century, and under its rule the town became a political and cultural center. More recently, it has been a home to artists and writers and a popular resort. The town is spotted with temples and set in wooded hills ideal for hiking.

Tsurugaoka Hachimangū: Appropriate to the capital of a military regime, Kamakura is built around a shrine to the god of war. Hachimangū was established on this site against **Tsurugaoka** (Crane Hill) in 1191 and a broad avenue was laid out on axis from the shrine entrance to the sea, with three *torii* gates along the way. This avenue, **Wakamiya Ōji**, functions as the main street today. In front of the shrine, traffic is divided in two with a cherry-tree and lantern-lined path down the middle. On the way into the shrine is a small bridge, the **Taiko Bashi**, which is too steep to cross without a running start. Locals make a pastime of watching visitors trying to cope with this.

Kamakura Buddha.

After you cross the bridge, there are ponds to either side of the path. The **Genji** and **Heike ponds** are named for the *samurai* clans who fought in the Genpei War. The Genji (also called Minamoto) having won, are represented by the larger pond, with a shrine to Benzaiten on an island in the middle. In later summer large pink and white lotus flowers are in bloom. The main shrine is at the top of steep stone steps. A thousand-year-old gingko tree stands to the left of the steps, with a rope around it indicating its sacredness.

To the left inside the shrine is a small museum displaying shrine possessions. There is another excellent museum in the eastern area of the shrine grounds: the **Kamakura City Museum**, housing important works possessed by Kamakura's temples and shrines. The most expressive and naturalistic Japanese sculpture was produced in the Kamakura period. The one-room museum, in a handsome traditional-style building, is well worth a look.

Kenchō-ji: This Zen monastery is Kamakura's greatest temple complex. Established by a monk from Sung China in the 13th century, the temple has the axial arrangement of buildings found also in Chinese Zen temples. Enter the main gate and approach the **Sanmon Gate**. This gate was rebuilt in 1775 in the style of the 13th-century original. The upper story conceals sculptures of 500 Buddhist ascetics. To the right, under a small thatched roof, is Kenchō-ji's bell, one of the few things surviving from the time of the temple's founding. Between the Sanmon and the **Buddha Hall** are juniper trees imported from China at the same time. Where the abbot's residence would normally be located, in back of the Buddha Hall and **Dharma Hall** (used for lectures), are a guest hall and garden.

If you walk to Kenchō-ji from the Hachimangū Shrine, you will pass the **modern art museum** and **Ennōji Temple** on the left, and on your right a parking lot/shrine where people come to pray for the recovery of ailing cars.

Daibutsu and Hase-dera: Kamakura's most famous sight is the bronze **Daibutsu** (Great Buddha) seated in the woods at **Kotōku-ji** south of the city.

The statue is of Amida, the Buddha of Salvation, and is 39 feet (11.9 meters) high on a stone base. Originally it was gold lacquered and kept in a temple hall, but the building was washed away by a tidal wave in 1495, leaving the statue expose. It has aged admirably, and sits today august and beatific, oblivious to the waves of tourists who come by the bus-load.

A couple of minutes' walk downhill from the Daibutsu and to the right toward **Hase Station** is **Hase-dera Temple** (or Hase Kannon). Hase-dera has a nice view of the coast, an ancient bell, and a tall though not very beautiful statue of Kannon. More interesting are the thousands of statues of the *bodhisattva* Jizō donated by people for the souls of dead or aborted babies. They cover the hillside along the temple path. Many have little toys, pinwheels and teething rings. A mood of haunting black comedy pervades.

The Enoden: A local train called the **Enoden** or E.E.R. runs between Kamakura Station and the town of **Fujisawa**, taking 27 minutes. The stop at Hase is convenient to Hase-dera and the Daibutsu. The line also goes right down a shopping street, leaving no room for cars to pass when it comes, through some backyards and along the beach. The stop at **Enoshima** will leave you close to the beach.

Shrines and Temples: Zeni-arai Benten is a cave shrine to goddess of luck Benten. Money washed in a pool at the shrine will return three times its value. There are also tunnels of *torii* gates here and the setting is pretty.

Hokoku-ji temple is known less for its buildings than for its garden and bamboo grove. Bamboo, the quintessential oriental tree, grows in profusion in many parts of the countryside but a stroll in a well-tended bamboo grove is actually a rare opportunity.

Zuisen-ji Temple, surrounded by a wood filled with maple trees, is popular for its flora. The temple gardens have such a variety of flowers that something is in bloom at any time of year. Autumn is particularly beautiful, with the maples turning color and bush clover in bloom.

ovice ionks take art in oundation eremony.

NIKKO

The **Nikko Tōshōgū Shrine**, a mausoleum for Tokugawa Ieyasu and his grandson Iemitsu, is one of Japan's most spectacular and popular sights, and most visitors to Tokyo make the day trip, about two hours in each direction by train.

Set in a forest of towering cryptomeria cedars, the shrine presents a series of dramatically unfolding vistas in a carefully orchestrated approach. In layout and in ornamentation Nikko Tōshōgū is Japan's baroque masterpiece. It is without question one of the gaudiest buildings in the world. The main gate, the **Yomeimon**, is also known as the **Hisgurashi no Mon**, or Until-Day's-End Gate, referring to the time one could spend examining the polychromatic dragons and other mythical beasts carved in relief on every inch of its surface.

Before entering the main processional way (*Omotesando*) to the shrine, stop to see the sacred bridge (*Shinkūo*). Legend has it that two holy snakes spanned the **Daiya River** at this spot 1200 years ago for the shrine's founding priest to cross. The bridge was built in 1636 and rebuilt in the same style after a flood in 1907.

The cryptomeria trees, a relieving element of natural beauty setting off the shrine buildings, were planted by the *daimyo* Matsudaira in honor of Ieyasu. They line the road to the shrine for over 19 miles (30 km). This beautiful stretch of road can be seen on the bus from **Imaichi**, but traffic crawls sometimes on the weekend.

Pass through the front gate (**Omotemon**), and you will see an unpainted building on your left. This is a sacred stable. Frieze panels on the building depict monkeys, believed to protect horses. Among these panels are the famous "see-no-evil, hear-no-evil, speak-no-evil" monkeys.

If it has not grown dark while you were viewing the bestiary on the Yomeimon, progress into the sanctuary proper, with the Chinese Gate (**Karamon**, usually closed) ahead of you. The **Honden** main hall within can be entered. The spirit of Tokugawa Ieyasu is enshrined and worshipped as a Shinto god here.

The tomb in which Ieyasu's ashes are interred, at the top of 200 stone steps behind the shrine, is a memorial of severe simplicity, sharply contrasting with the main shrine. Under the dark canopy of trees, often shrouded in mist, the bronze-covered shrine building, pagoda and urns make a very mysterious atmosphere.

Taiyūinbyō Shrine: On the hill west of Tōshōgū, about 1300 feet (400 meters) away from his grandfather's tomb, Shogun Iemitsu is entombed. Iemitsu was the central actor in the project to create the Tōshōgū mausoleum, and for his effort he was duly entombed in similar grandeur, on a slightly smaller scale.

The Nikko area is known for its waterfalls and forests, and for **Chūzen-ji-ko**, a popular resort lake. **Kegon Falls**, the best known waterfall in the area, spills over a 330-foot (100-meter) drop and can be viewed from a platform built over the basin it fills. Rain and mist are copious in Nikko, and often you have to settle for the roaring sound of the falls, completely invisible just a few yards away.

eft, the ist-hrouded ōshōgū hrine omplex in ikko. ight, print f a Nikko uddhist hrine.

Mount Fuji, Hakone and Izu

The Fuji-Five Lakes-Hakone-Izu Peninsula region extends into three prefectures, but it forms a single large national park district and vacation area. Besides Fuji, it includes countless hot springs and the best beaches within easy reach of Tokyo.

Mount Fuji has been worshipped by the Japanese for as long as they have inhabited the island, and is worshipped by not a few today. It is also a favorite subject of poetry and art. Japanese art has a genius for improving on nature—one need only look at what they have done with so many humble trees and flowers never given a second glance in the west. Fuji is one certain exception; the sight of this mountain simply cannot be improved upon. No matter how many pictures one has seen, the real thing is breathtaking (when it's visible—three-quarters of the time it is obscured by clouds). Since a view of Fuji is the special pleasure of staying at resort towns near the mountain, wise travelers check weather reports or phone ahead and inquire about conditions. Of course, some will not be satisfied until they have set foot on the summit.

Mount Fuji is not a difficult slope by climber's standards, but it's no casual stroll. Weather conditions can take sudden and menacing turns at any time of year. The official climbing season is from July 1 to August 31. The main event of a Fuji climb is the sunrise (*goraikō*) seen from the summit or near it. Many people start late in the evening and climb all night. The entire ascent takes between five and nine hours.

Five Lakes (Fuji Goku): Yamanaka-ko, Kawaguchi-ko, Sai-ko, Shōji-ko and Motosu-ko (*ko* means lake) form an arc north of Fuji. They are popular vacationing and camping places, with beautiful reflections of the peak.

Yamanaka-ko and **Kawaguchi-ko** are the largest and the first on the way from Tokyo and Hakone. Naturally, they are also the most built up. Clusters of *ryokan* inns, hotels and entertainment places line the shores.

Lakes **Sai-ko**, **Shōji-ko** and **Motosu-ko** are comparatively wild, although

19th-century view of Mount Fuji from the Gohyaku Rakan Temple, Tokyo.

they are accessible by road and there are *minshuku* inns and youth hostels in the vicinity. A short distance from Sai-ko are two volcanic caves, the **Narusawa Ice Cave** and the **Fugaku Wind Cave**. Both are icy cold inside year round. Sai-ko provides a superb view of Mount Fuji. Shōji-ko is small and picturesque. Motosu-ko is the most out of the way and the deepest. Between Shōji-ko and Mount Fuji lies **Aoki-gahara**, a tall forest of ominous beauty and a favored suicide spot. Farther along the road toward the city of **Fujinomiya** is **Shiraito Falls**, an unusual and pretty waterfall.

Hakone has been the number one place of retreat from Tokyo since the 19th century. There are several hot spring resorts and the environment is very beautiful, particularly around October when fall colors often combine with clear skies and an unobstructed view of the peak. From **Odawara**, a tiny and antiquated train climbs through the spa towns **Hakon-Yumoto**, **Dogashima** and **Miyanoshita**, passes the **Chōkoku no Mori** open-air museum and terminates in the town of **Gora**. From Gora, a ropeway continues up via **Owakudani**, an area of volcanic activity and sulfur spouts, and **Ubako**, a smaller spa, to **Togendai** on the northern tip of **Lake Ashi**. From Togendai, buses run around the lake and boats leave for **Hakone Park** and the town of Hakone.

Izu Peninsula: This 37-mile (60-km) projection into the Pacific has a long-standing association with foreigners. Englishman William Adams, the model for the hero of James Clavell's novel *Shogun*, lived in the town of **Ito** on Izu's east coast at the beginning of the 17th century. Townsend Harris, the first American consul to Japan, waited out two years of treaty negotiations, between 1856 and 1858, in the town of **Shimoda** near the southern tip. Modern Izu has some attractive coastline and hot springs, but it probably still has more appeal to natives than to travelers. It is a good place to go if you need to get away from Tokyo and relax. In Shimoda you can see the temple which Townsend Harris called home, and another associated with the unhappy *geisha* who was made his consort for a short time. This latter temple is filled with erotic sculpture.

wo much-photographed apanese andmarks, Mount uji and the ullet rain.

KYŌTO AND ENVIRONS

Kyōto, once called Heian-kyō or "Capital of Peace and Tranquility," was the imperial capital from 794 to 1868 and Japan's cultural hub for the better part of that millennium. Spared the ravages of war in this century, Kyōto's temples, palaces, gardens and houses offer views of every period of its long and variegated history. However, the "Capital of Peace and Tranquility" was hardly true to its name in previous centuries, as warring *samurai* sacked Kyōto repeatedly, leveling it with the ease that one might expect to have in a town made largely of wood and paper. And although it hasn't been bombed, Kyōto has not escaped the fate of all Japanese cities since the war, being rebuilt in a modern style without much distinction. Visitors expecting the city itself to be a monument of old Japan, or a preserved village, will be surprised to find instead a burgeoning metropolis with a population of 2.5 million, a subway system, McDonald's, and any number of rivals and a cluster of eight-story department stores.

The Golden Pavilion in Kyōto.

Central Kyōto is laid out on a grid of deceptively large square blocks broken up by smaller intersecting streets, a survival of the uniform block plan borrowed from eighth-century China. In the east, shallow waterways are threaded into the street system here and there, and although not always clean, they are a cooling sight in the oppressive summer heat. Largest of these is the **Kamo River**, the embankment of which is a favorite spot for strolling, picnicking, and festival-time fireworks.

Kinkaku-ji and Ryoan-ji: Here are two of the most famous sights in Kyōto, standing in fairly close proximity to one another in the northeast of the city, and they could hardly stand in greater contrast.

Kinkaku-ji, the Gold Pavilion, was originally built as the mountain retreat of Shogun Ashikaga Yoshimitsu in 1397. Yoshimitsu was a devotee of Zen and directed that upon his death the building be made a Zen temple. Its three stories, incorporating elements of Chinese Zen style, are covered entirely in gold leaf. The present structure is a faithful reconstruction completed in 1955 after the old pavilion was destroyed by a fire lit by a deranged monk. A psychological portrait of the arsonist became the central theme of Yukio Mishima's novel *Temple of the Gold Pavilion*.

Ryoan-ji, a few hundred yards down the road, is a another Zen temple, founded in the 15th century. Temple buildings were destroyed in the 1790s and rebuilt on a smaller scale. Ryoan-ji sat quietly undistinguished among the thousands of Kyōto temples until the 1930s, when its rock garden, a simple array of 15 stones in a sea of raked sand, suddenly attracted public attention and droves of photographers, who spread the garden's fame around the world. Numerous interpretations of the stone configuration have developed ("a tigress and her cubs," "dragons," "the Chinese character for 'mind'," etc.). Scholars still speculate about the person responsible for its creation, some suggesting Soami, a painter and aesthete of the Ashikaga circle. But approached as just what it is, the garden can be a beautiful and meditative experience.

Palace Agency: The Kyōto **Imperial Palace**, **Katsura Rikyu Palace**, the gardens of **Shugakuin Villa** and **Sendoin** are managed by the Imperial Household Agency, whose offices are on the Kyōto Palace grounds. You have to obtain permission and make an appointment at this office before seeing these sights. The seldom-used Imperial Palace (built after the emperor moved to Tokyo) has handsome interiors, but the gardens are disappointing and the tour lacks particular charm. The gardens of the other three are outstanding.

Katsura Rikyu is the most famous. The palace has been acclaimed by Western architects more than any other Japanese building. However, visitors are allowed to see only the outside. Tours are conducted (in Japanese and English) through the gardens, along a circuit of tea pavilions around a pond. Every view in the garden is choreographed, every tree bears some meaning or makes a poetic allusions. Far removed from the politics of the nation and a half-day trip from the palace in town, 17th-century Kyōto aristocrats retreated here to enjoy moon-viewing parties, celebrate the first tea of the season, and compose poetry while boating on the pond.

Shugakuin is in the northeast hills of the city—a pretty, somewhat rural district worth a wander around. The gardens are the feature of a guided tour here too, but the whole is more spread out and the pace more relaxed than at the other imperial sites. The Shugakuin gardens are renowned for their incorporation of distant views, and for their fall foliage. One teahouse also contains a famous set of shelves called "Bank of Clouds." If you have a day to spare and want to get out of the heart of the city (strongly recommended), Shugakuin combines nicely with visits to **Manshuin** (a *shōin* building) and Sendoin (a secluded and beautiful garden).

Nishi-Honganji: This enormous temple, headquarters of the Jōdō Shinshū ("True Teaching of the Pure Land") Sect, is a short distance northwest of **Kyōto Station**. With over 10,000 temples elsewhere in the country, Jōdō Shinshū is one of the most popular sects of Japanese Buddhism. Genuine

**n
arden at
yoan-ji.**

pilgrims as well as tourists come to Nishi-Honganji in droves. Architecture in the temple compound includes halls of worship, a *shōin*-style palace, famous *Nō* theater stage and a garden pavilion. Most of these date from the 17th century. After taking in the gigantic and sumptuous Main Gate and temple halls (**Gōei-dō** and **Amida-dō**) join the guided tour through the *shōin* pavilions.

Ni jō Castle (Ni jō-jō): The name "Ni jō Castle" is misleading, as there is no longer a castle here. The castle built by Shogun Tokugawa Ieyasu was lost to fire in the 18th century. What remains is the **Ninomaru Palace**, built by Ieyasu's grandson Iemitsu for formal receptions, in particular for the reception of Emperor Gomizunōō in 1626.

The building is a series of pavilions which reflect in every detail the strict hierarchy governing society around the *shogun*. In function and design, the rooms become progressively more intimate as you pass through the building. The first pavilion contains rooms for the reception of "outer" *samurai*, whose low rank forbade them entry deeper into the palace. These rooms are decorated with paintings of tigers and leopards, calculated to intimidate the visitor with the power of his august host. In the middle pavilions, for the reception of *daimyo* lords close to the *shogun*, the style of painting remains powerful but the subject matter becomes more subdued. In the innermost apartments, where only the *shogun*, his wife and ladies-in-waiting ever set foot, the monochrome paintings of Chinese landscapes are so quiet they are hard to make out.

A classic of the *shōin* style of architecture, the Ninomaru displays elements which became standard not only in feudal buildings, but in Japanese homes down to the present day. The decorative alcove and shelves seen in so many restaurants, inns and houses, for example, are humble descendants of this style. Even the *tatami*-mat floor and the paper sliding-doors (*shōji* and *fusuma*) have their origin in the *shōin* room.

One thing everyone remembers about Ni jō-jō is the "Nightingale floor." The floorboards in the hallways have been designed to squeak when walked on, to alert occupants of intruders. A diagram on the left-hand wall inside the entrance explains this mechanism. It might be a greater wonder if, after 350 years, the floorboards didn't creak.

Ni jō Jinya: Ni jō Jinya is an eccentric building—a fortified inn full of false-bottomed closets and hidden staircases. It was built in the 17th century by a *samurai*-turned-innkeeper named Ogawa, who received *daimyo* visiting Kyōto. Every one of the 24 rooms has some feature designed to foil assassins or conceal bodyguards.

Sanjū-sangendō (The Hall of Thirty-three Bays): If you have seen a few Buddhist temples, you will recognize that this one, built in 1266, is an odd one. The building is a long box—400 feet (120 meters) long—with 1001 statues of Kannon, the goddess of mercy, standing in tiers like a choir. Reigning in their midst is one twice the size of the rest. Each has a distinct facial expression, and some visitors make donations to decorate a statue to which they bear a resemblance. In the passage behind this eerie array are 28 more statues also from the Kamakura period (Japan's sculptural Renaissance), including the gods of thunder

Fine example of Japanese craftsmanship at Ni jō Castle.

and wind and several bizarre human-animal combinations.

In the Edo period an archery contest was held on the long verandah here. The event still takes place every year in January, but off of the verandah to avoid damaging the building.

Kiyomizu-dera: Dramatically set in the forest of the **Higashiyama** mountain district, **Kiyomizu Temple** has been one of the most popular places to visit in Kyōto for centuries. The Japanese come here to anoint themselves at the temple's sacred waterfall ("*Kiyomizu*" means "pure water"), to pray to the image of Kannon, to enjoy the view from the temple's famous balcony, built on wooden pylons out over the valley, and to visit shops and entertainment establishments along the roads leading up to the temple. The short but somewhat arduous walk up the winding streets and steps from **Yasaka Shrine** and **Maruyama Park** is an integral part of a visit to Kiyomizu. Shops offering Kyōto confections, fans, dolls, bamboo products and pottery line the narrow and well-trodden lanes. There are also a number of nice teahouses and coffee shops and some restaurants offering Kyōto cuisine, which is generally characterized by a preponderance of *tofu*, extreme refinement and daunting prices.

The city of Kyōto, despite its size, is a small and conservative social community. In the annual events of Kyōto society Yasaka Shrine is the community shrine. It is the focus in particular of the Gion Festival in July, Kyōto's biggest festival.

Also in the area is the temple **Chion-in**, with the largest temple gate and bell in Japan. Chion-in is busier with religious activity than sightseers, and you are likely to find robed priests chanting *sutras* and performing funerary rites. The enormous temple structures date chiefly from the early 17th century. You may hear about "nightingale floors" here too.

The "floating world" of the *geisha* conducts itself in exclusive secrecy behind the wooden latticed fronts of the entertainment houses in the **Gion District**, extending north and south from **Shijo-dōri** halfway between **Shijō Ōhashi Bridge** and Yasaka Shrine. Although their services are not available to most of us, the area is intriguing

Gion Corner dance by geisha and maiko.

to explore. Keep one eye peeled for *maiko* (apprentice *geisha*), who are the most extravagantly adorned and wear wooden sandals that lift them six inches (15 cm) from the ground. A section of Gion has been made an historic preservation district.

Ponto-chō is also an entertainment district, but a lot more accessible. It is a narrow alley running parallel to the Kamo River, lined with restaurants and drinking spots. To avoid being taken for a lot of money, stay away from places with hostesses and no indication of prices.

Daitoku-ji: This sprawling Zen temple complex contains more than two dozen sub-temples, with some of the most excellent examples of the intimate Zen garden in the country. Only certain of the sub-temples and their gardens are open to the public, and among these a few are particularly famous. Try the gardens of **Daisen-in**, **Ryōgen-in**, **Kōtō-in** and **Zuihō-in**. The rocks in the rear garden of the Zuihō-in are arranged in the form of a cross; the original owner was one of the few medieval lords converted to Christianity by Portuguese missionaries.

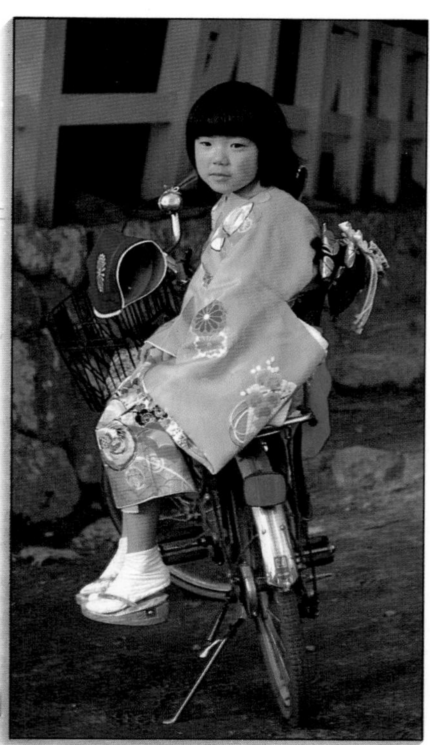

Posing on a pedal pusher in Kyōto.

Daisen-in is famous for the ship-like rock around which its garden was designed. The rock is said to have been the prize possession of Shogun Yoshimasa. Handsomely shaped rocks were so esteemed in Medieval Japan that when General Nobunaga occupied Kyōto and became *de facto shogun* in 1568, he demonstrated his military and political might by removing his favorite rocks from the gardens of Kyōto's nobility and placing them in his own. Daisen-in and Ryōgen-in are of the "dry landscape" variety, entirely rocks and sand. Kōtō-in has some green and shade, and a lot of charm.

Ginkaku-ji (The Silver Pavilion): Shogun Ashikaga Yoshimasa built this retreat in the northeastern hills of the city in 1483, as his grandfather Yoshimitsu had built the Gold Pavilion in the northwest almost a century before. Here, however, the original main buildings are intact. The pavilion is similar in appearance to its predecessor, but smaller and more subdued, reflecting the aesthetics of Yoshimasa's age. Despite its name, the building was never silver-plated. The pond and garden have undergone careful restoration from the 17th century to the present, and are strikingly beautiful against the background of the Higashiyama hills.

Although there is no shortage of things to do in the city, the visitor with more than a couple of days should venture farther. Some of Kyōto's most splendid buildings and gardens are outside the city proper, and in settings of great natural beauty.

Ohara: The principal places to visit in this rural area northeast of the city are the temples **Jakkō-in** and **Sanzen-in**.

Jakkō-in is a nunnery, known for its connection with the tragic story of Kenrei-mon, mother of Japan's shortest-lived emperor. Her son, the Emperor Antoku, leapt to his death with his grandmother at the straits of Dan-no-ura, where the last battle of the Genpei War was fought and lost by their clan. Kenrei-mon followed them, but was dragged from the water and brought back to Kyōto as the last surviving member of the Taira clan. She became a nun, eventually retiring to this lonely temple to live out the remaining 30 years of her life.

Sanzen-in also dates from the Heian period. As one of five Tendai sect temples associated with the imperial line, Sanzen-in has a number of art objects by or associated with past emperors. It also has some unusually old sculpture and gardens. A place of quintessential Kyōto elegance.

Uji, Daigo-ji and Sambō-in: The town of **Uji**, about 40 minutes south of Kyōto by local train, is known for its green tea, said to be the best in the country. It is also the home of one of Japan's most beautiful buildings, the **Phoenix Hall** at **Byōdō-in**. The site was originally the villa of a Heian minister but was converted into a temple upon his death. The Phoenix Hall survives from the time of the conversion (1052), in style half a palace and half a temple. It was made the Hall of Amida, Buddha of the Western Paradise, and the garden and the building together were intended as an earthly realization of paradise. An immense and serene Amida which practically fills the room, and 52 tiny attendants in full relief on the walls, are the work of master-sculptor Jōchō, and are considered the triumph of Heian sculpture. The little images of Amida's attendants, carrying musical instruments and sitting on wisps of cloud, convey more vividly than the great Amida in their midst the role of Buddha in Amidist religion. It was believed by the Heian aristocrats that when approaching death they should lie with their heads to the west, and holding a silken cord, repeat Amida's name. The Buddha would then come surfing down on a bank of clouds accompanied by a heavenly retinue, and sweep the soul off to the Western Paradise.

In the same day or half-day excursion, you can also see **Daigo-ji** temple and the **Sambō-in**, a mansion and garden planned by Hideyoshi, principal figure of the late-16th century. Hideyoshi had lavish tastes, and a fondness for parties. At the height of his power he invited everyone in the cities of Kyōto and Osaka to a tea party *al fresco* which lasted for 10 days. For parties on a more intimate scale, he made tea houses of gold, and passed trays of money among his guests. The Sambō-in complex was built explicitly for one of these events, a cherry-blossom viewing party. Along with the artificial natural beauty of the garden, the screen paintings in the *shōin*, by

The Jidai Matsuri procession in Kyōto.

Kano Sanraku and others, are also very fine.

Hideyoshi found the Daigo-ji temple in ruins and restored all of the temple buildings. The five-story pagoda survives from the mid-10th century, making it the oldest building in Kyōto-fu (Kyōto Prefecture). The **Yakushi Hall** and other structures in the upper temple precincts are on a hilltop, reached by one mile of steps.

Closer to Kyōto city in the same area is **Fushimi Inari Shrine**. Inari shrines dedicated to the god of the rice plant and flanked by images of his fox emissaries, are the most ubiquitous Shinto shrine type. The main building of the shrine and a nearby tea pavilion date from the 15th century. But the most remarkable thing at the Fushimi Inari are the tunnels of red *torii* gates enclosing the paths to the inner shrine. These have been erected with private donations, and currently number between twenty and thirty thousand.

Temple On A Mount: Enryaku-ji temple has stood atop **Mount Hiei** as a protector of the northeastern quarter since the founding of the capital of Heian-kyō. As the headquarters of the largest branch of Tendai Buddhism, the Enryaku-ji complex grew in size and political power to formidable proportions, at one time possessing some three thousand sub-temples and an army of warrior monks powerful enough to be the deciding factor in many battles. These monks took their pleasure, when the court refused to grant it, by picking up the portable Shinto shrine housed in their precincts and carrying it down to the capital, where they threatened the court and marauded about the city. Heian-kyō's residents were powerless to respond, confronted not only with an imposing military force but a holy procession. Enryaku-ji's salad days came to an end in 1571, when General Nobunaga, not to be held by propriety or precedent, surrounded the mountain, torched its temples and killed the fleeing occupants. Thanks to renewed patronage under subsequent *shoguns*, the mountains today has 130 temple structures, but nothing predates 1571. From some spots, there is a terrific view of **Lake Biwa**, Japan's largest lake. There is also a cable-car down the east side of the mountain to **Hiyoshi Shrine**.

Some of the 100,000 toriis of Fushimi Inari Shrine.

ALL STEAMED UP

The Victorian visitor to Japan Edward Morse commented, "if cleanliness is next to godliness then verily the Japanese are a godly people." Ordinary workmen, he noted, bathed two or three times a day. That's a lot of baths. In England or America at the time, immersion as much as once in a week was the height of hygenic diligence. Even today, with frequent washing of the body a norm through much of the world, the Japanese distinguish themselves with their assiduity. And despite the spread of that equalizer, the shower, they still have unique practices and attitudes regarding bathing. Native Japanese fastidiousness does play a role, but Morse missed the real reason that everyone here bathes so much: it is not mere eagerness to get clean, it is a love of the bath itself.

The relaxation and sensual satisfaction of a good soak in hot water is an affordable luxury prized by all Japanese. The soak is usually in water considerably hotter than Westerners are accustomed to, in a tub deep enough to sit in up to the neck. The getting clean is done first so that no soap or dirt gets into the water, which is generally re-used. Families with young children bathe all together. Most bathe in the evening before dinner. This practice is followed at inns too, where *yukata* bathing gowns are provided to change into after an evening soak.

Japan's situation on the Pacific volcanic belt has brought the curse of countless natural disasters, but at the same time it has blessed the country with close to 20,000 hot springs. Many springs were discovered by wandering priests in the early years of Japanese Buddhism, establishing a connection between springs and temples. Springs are also known for the healing properties of minerals they contain. While some springs boast cures for everything from bad eyesight to financial failure, modern medicine has confirmed the benefits of mineral baths for various muscular and digestive ailments, as well as for the skin.

Part of the appeal of hot springs today is their natural settings. Boiling sulphurous springs, referred to as "hells," are found in bleak volcanic landscapes that seem to belong to another planet. Springs of milder composition nourish small oases of tropical or semi-tropical verdure. The very remotest mountain enclaves very often conceal a hot spring with a handful of inns and perhaps a temple. At the other end of the spectrum are the sprawling hot spring resorts that mix bathing with all kinds of entertainment facilities, including some morally dubious ones. All *onsen-machi* (hot spring towns) have in common a peculiar *onsen* atmosphere. It is not only the fact that the town's *raison d'etre* is recreation, which is evident in the faces of visitors and residents. To really appreciate the special quality of *onsen-machi*, one must first know the feeling of complacency combined with mild euphoria which follows a bath hot enough to warm the body through.

Sandbather at Ibuseki hot springs.

NARA AND OSAKA

Nara is a place of beginnings—Japan's first permanent capital and earliest historical records, the roots of Japanese Buddhism and the country's oldest buildings. The city has many of Japan's greatest historical treasures, including the oldest and the largest wooden buildings in the world. After its cultural flowering, Nara relinquished the spotlight to the new capital of Kyōto, but its temples lived on, and still do. Kyōto as capital and cultural center for the millenium after Nara's decline has left a diverse legacy. Nara, by contrast, stands as a testament to the Buddhist religion.

The modern city is expanding, and **Yamato** region around Nara, the Tigris-Euphrates Valley of Japanese civilization, is being uglified by industry. But the temples are secure; they are maintained by the government as national treasures.

Nara Park, Kōfuku-ji and Tōdai-ji: The park covers 1,300 acres (525 hectares) and includes two major temples, a Shinto shrine and Nara's **National Museum**.

Kōfuku-ji has Japan's second tallest five-story pagoda, a structure of about 165 feet (50 meters), dating from 1426. A three-story pagoda here dates from 1143. The temple museum, a modern concrete building, contains one of the greatest collections of Buddhist sculpture in the world.

Tōdai-ji temple is vast in every dimension. **Nandaimon** (The Great South Gate), through which you enter the temple is a reconstruction completed in 1199, using technological and stylistic devices imported from Sung Period China. The austere and massive gate was a symbol of the power of Minamoto Yoritomo and the Kamakura shogunate which funded its construction. It was one of the first great structures of medieval Japan.

The **Great Buddha Hall**, which is said to be the largest wooden building in the world and contains the largest cast-bronze statue, stands from 1709, having been rebuilt several times. Scroll paintings from the Medieval Period indicate that it was actually one-third larger at that time. The bronze Buddha (*Daibutsu*) has been damaged by fire and replaced in sections several times too since its casting in 749. It remains an awesome sight, although not an object of grace and beauty. One of the immense columns supporting the hall has a hole cut through it, and crawling through the hole is supposed to bring good luck.

The **Sangatsu-dō** stands in the eastern part of the Tōdai-ji compound. It is the only original building from Tōdai-ji's construction in the early-eighth century. The central structure (built in 733) is filled with sculpture, creating an environment that no museum exhibit can. Seven of the sculptures are national treasures and more than 1,200 years old.

Walking east from Kōfuku-ji, past **Sarusawa Pond**, brings you to the path into **Kasuga Shrine**, lined with tall straight cryptomeria trees and thousands of stone lanterns. The lanterns are lit twice a year on the festivals of the first day of spring by the old calendar (in February), and midsummer (in August). *Bugaku* classical dances are performed at the inner shrine on these nights. The shrine is believed to have been established in the 730s, and was rebuilt every 20 years, until the late-19th century, when the present structure was built.

Yakushi-ji and Tōshōdai-ji: These two eighth-century temples stand about half-a-mile apart in the **Nishino-kyō** section of the city.

Yakushi-ji's main landmark is its eastern pagoda, built in 730. The identical west pagoda was destroyed in 1528, and until 1980 only its foundation stones occupied the site. Now, a replica has been built.

The Yakushi-ji **Kondō** (Golden Hall) was reconstructed in 1976. It contains a statue of Yakushi, the Buddha of Healing, escorted by Gākkō and Nikkō, the *bodhisattvas* of the moon and sun. The bronze and gold cast statues survived a fire which has left them a glossy black. All three statues are probably from the eighth century. Elsewhere on the temple grounds is the **Buddha's Foot Hall**, containing an impression in stone of the Buddha's foot made from a tracing imported from India. The characters on this stone are the earliest surviving texts of Japanese poetry.

Tōshōdai-ji is ostensibly just one

Left, a school of carp flags flutters in the wind.

more temple, and many people pass it up. However, it is actually the most complete surviving temple complex of the Nara Period, and possibly the most beautiful. The temple was founded by Ganjin, a Chinese monk who devoted his life to the propagation of Buddhism in Japan. He was invited to come to Japan and teach in 733, but it took him 20 years and five attempts, foiled by pirates, shipwrecks and his own country's authorities, before he finally arrived in Kyushu. He was brought haggard and blind to Nara, where he ordained four hundred monks in a ceremony at Tōdai-ji and settled at Tōshodai-ji to live out his remaining years. Along with orthodox Buddhism, he is credited with the introduction of medicines, sculpture and building techniques, and *miso* paste.

Hōryū-ji: Located about six miles (10 km) southwest of the center of Nara City, **Hōryū-ji** temple is the oldest wooden structure in the world and the most important single landmark of Japanese architecture and ancient art. The monastery was founded under the reign of Empress Suiko in 607, but it is most often associated with the name of Prince Shotoku Taishi, an enlightened statesman and devout Buddhist. He was responsible for the dissemination of Buddhist principles and the creation of the first Japanese state's system of government.

Records indicate that temple buildings were destroyed by fire in 670 and reconstructed in 708. Sculptures survive from the seventh century.

Hōryū-ji's Kondō is almost square and houses cast-bronze and wooden sculptures in the so-called *Asuka* Style, showing a formal abstraction and simplicity carried over from Chinese stonework. The pagoda contains four sculptural portrayals of the life and death of Gautama Buddha (the historical Buddha), but they are hidden in almost total darkness.

The main point of interest in the eastern section of the temple is the **Yumedono**, or Hall of Dreams. According to legend an angel visited Shotoku Taishi in a dream here. The octagonal building houses a delicate and elongated figure of Kannon, which is in such excellent condition (it has not lost its lacquer veneer over almost 1,300 years) that it is only shown a few weeks of the

Tōdaiji Temple, the largest wooden temple in the world.

year, between April 11 and May 5 and between October 22 and November 3.

Within walking distance of Hōryū-ji are the nunnery **Chūgū-ji** and the temples **Hōrin-ji** and **Hokki-ji**. Hokki-ji has a beautiful three-story pagoda of similar vintage to Hōryū-ji.

Osaka: Japan's number two industrial city consists mostly of bleak modern buildings. Its history is long and illustrious, but not much evidence of it remains. Many foreigners come here on business, but those sightseeing generally skip Osaka and go to Kyōto, which is a bare 15 minutes away by bullet train. Should you find yourself in Osaka, do not lament it—Osaka was once called "the kitchen of the empire," and deservedly maintains a high reputation for dining and drinking.

The biggest place to go out on the town is the **Shinsaibashi** area. If you have experienced the sensory bombardment of Shinjuku at night, get ready for Shinsaibashi, one step beyond. The number of restaurants and bars, the number of signs (some of them are terrific too), and the volume of people, all just out to play, is overwhelming. A crescendo is reached at the bridge over the **Dotonbori River**, where a youthful mixture makes the scene. During the day, Shinsaibashi is a shopping arcade, Japan's largest, but otherwise indistinguishable from that of any major city.

The original **Osaka Castle** was built by Toyotomi Hideyoshi in 1586, and was Japan's greatest castle at the time. The Tokugawa sieged and destroyed it in 1615, but rebuilt it as a symbol of their own power. It was again destroyed in 1867 by Tokugawa forces in retreat during one of the last battles of the Meiji Restoration. The present building was constructed in 1931 and retains only the external appearance of its predecessor.

The structures of the Shinto shrine **Sumiyoshi Taisha** date from 1810, having survived the war by fluke. It consists of four identical buildings brightly painted in auspicious red and white, roofed with layers of cypress bark. Sumiyoshi sits in the middle of an urban neighborhood today, but originally the shrine faced the sea. The god enshrined is the patron of sea voyages, vital to Osaka, which was Japan's largest pre-modern port.

aka's
isu Shrine
ring the
stival of
God
Business.

HIMEJI CASTLE

Japan's finest surviving castle is in **Himeji City**, Hyogo Prefecture. **Himeji Castle**, also called **Hakuraku-jō** (White Egret Castle) for its white plaster walls, was built between 1601 and 1609 by the son-in-law of Shogun Ieyasu. Hideyoshi had earlier built a castle here, and pieces of it were used in the reconstruction. It was further added to later in the Edo Period. Today the castle consists of 78 buildings linked by labyrinthine passages around a five-story central keep. It was made intentionally confusing in plan for defensive purposes. But it was built as much to impress the eye with its exquisiteness. Decorative details like the cusped arch windows, and the dolphin-like finials mounted on the roof ridges reflect the aesthetic of the age of castle building, a combination of subtle elegance and mythic grandeur.

The castle sits on a 50-foot (15-meter) foundation of carefully hewn stones, but it is constructed entirely of wood, earth and plaster.

About Castles: Japan's period of castle-building was brief. In the 16th century, the Portuguese brought the first firearms into a Japan torn by internecine wars. General Oda Nobunaga demonstrated their potential in crushing victories over conventional forces in the 1570's, and recognizing that the new weapons also called for a new quality of fortification, constructed Japan's first multi-story stronghold. Nobunaga's **Azuchi Castle** stood on a ridge over Lake Biwa, six stories of scarlet, blue and gold plaster walls, wooden in construction but thickly reinforced for fireproofing. Every interior surface was decorated with gold leaf and paintings. Azuchi set the standard for opulence and defense, and later castles were built in a similar manner. But none were indestructible. Twelve castles have survived to the present. Of these, Himeji is by far the grandest in scale. **Matsumoto Castle**, in Nagano Prefecture (Chūbu) is a handsome red, black and white structure set against the scenic Japan Alps. **Hikone Castle**, in Shiga Prefecture (Chūbu) is small but admired for its gold trim and elegant details.

White Egret Castl at Himeji.

Hiroshima and Miyajima

In one instant on the morning of August 6, 1945, most of the city of Hiroshima was turned to vapor, making it the first victim of the atomic age. Since the war, the city has risen miraculously from radioactive rubble, becoming once again a booming industrial port, with trees and flowers that people had speculated might never grow again, and a population in the neighborhood of 200,000. But Hiroshima has not forgotten. The people of the city and of the nation wish Hiroshima to stand as a memorial attesting to the horror of nuclear war and as a "beacon of peace" in the Pacific. As may be imagined, the city proper does not have the appeal of antiquity claimed by most of the famous spots to visit in Japan, but people come here from all over the world anyway, and no one can be unaffected by the experience.

The **Peace Memorial Park**, in which 2 million people gather every August 6 for a day of prayer and protest, is otherwise a sedate municipal park with boating and picnic spots. It contains the skeletal remains of the dome of the **Industrial Promotion Hall**, which stood at ground zero and by a caprice of nature remained standing. The only ruin left intact, this fragile-looking miracle has become a symbol of the park and of the bomb's destruction. South of the dome is a cenotaph to the memory of the bomb victims, shaped like an ancient tomb. Farther south is the **Peace Memorial Museum**. The museum contains statistical information, photos and films about the bomb.

Miyajima: A 10-minute ferry ride from **Miyajima-guchi** near Hiroshima brings you to this four-mile-long island. It has been sacred since the sixth century, and is one of the traditional three places of outstanding scenic beauty in Japan. The other two are **Matsushima** near the city of **Sendai** (Tohoku), and **Amanohashidate** on the Japan Sea coast in Kyōto Prefecture (Chugoku). These designations are based in some measure on allusions in poetry and nostalgic value.

Number one on the agenda is **Itsukushima Shrine**, built out over the water of the bay so that it appears to float at high tide, with its *torii* gate (the largest wooden one in the country) standing farther out, up to its ankles, or knees. The *torii* dates from 1895, and most of the shrine buildings are also comparatively recent reconstructions, but the famous *Nō* stage is from the Edo Period. An evening performance on this floating stage is unequalled for the quality of mystery which is an essential part of *Nō*. There are also occasional performances of *Kagura* and *Bugaku* ancient dances on a stage at the shrine.

The **Inner Shrine** is closed to the public, and so you will have to content yourself with the view from the shore, but the **Asazaya Hall**, built on the water, is open and displays masks and costumes.

The museum **(Hōmotsu-kan)** on shore has a large collection of art and important historical artifacts. There is also a folkcrafts museum **(mingeika)**.

Miyajima is so holy that traditionally no birth or death was allowed to defile it. Pregnant women and the aged and ailing were rushed to the mainland, and their families waited out a period of purification before returning.

iyajima orii.

KANAZAWA AND TAKAYAMA

Kanazawa was a provincial capital during the Edo Period, and has been comparatively well-preserved in this century. It is sometimes referred to as a little Kyōto. The Maeda clan, whose castle was here, had the largest revenue (measured in bushels of rice, the official unit of exchange under the Tokugawa system) of all *daimyo* houses, and promoted culture and the arts in their capital. Modernization rapidly encroaches today, but one can still get something of the flavor of each of the districts of the Edo period castle town.

Kanazawa Castle was destroyed by fire in 1881, leaving one gate, the **Ishikawa-mon**, and an armory building inside. The castle walls now contain the campus of **Kanazawa University**. In one corner of the campus is **Ōyama Jinja**, a very unusual Shinto shrine. The shrine gate is a three-story brick structure called the **Shinmon**. It was designed in 1870 by a Dutchman, and served as a lighthouse as well. The crest carved on each story is a plum blossom, crest of the Maeda family.

Across the street from the castle gate is **Kenroku-en Garden**, completed as the castle garden in 1837. Kenroku-en is designated as one of the three most beautiful gardens in Japan, but of course the designation is as arbitrary as the designation of the city of **Hakodate** (in Hokkaido) as the world's third most beautiful night view. The Japanese have a penchant for ranking things. There is, however, no question that Kenroku-en is a lovely garden. Its name means "combination of six," and refers to the six elements desirable in a garden: spaciousness, depth, artistry, an antiquated appearance, flowing water and good vistas.

Seisonkaku, a *shōin*-style mansion built by the last Maeda *daimyo* for his mother, stands in the southern part of the garden. Despite the fact that it was built in the very last days of waning *samurai* power, the building still displays the lavish traditional style and the ingenious defenses of a military ruler's house.

Kanazawa has its own style of *Nō* theater, the Hōshō School. Long-term residents are very proud of this tradition, and keep alive one of the most active *Nō* performance halls in the country, the **Kanazawa Nōgaku Bunka Kaikan**. *Nō* is a very stylized combination of dance and drama developed in the Medieval Period, with dazzling costumes, haunting music, and a galactically slow pace.

The *daimyo* lords maintained social order in their castle towns by practicing a simple sort of urban planning. *Samurai* were placed in one quarter close to the castle walls, merchants and artisans were placed in another, temples in another, and finally, in a place as inconspicuous as possible without being out of reach, the *geisha* quarter was designated. Something remains of each of these in Kanazawa.

The legendary black-clad *samurai* assassins called *ninja* have been popularized outside of Japan through novels and films. **Myōryū-ji**, with the benign exterior of the Maeda family temple, served also as a secret encampment in the event of an attack or intrigue at the castle. It has gained the name **Ninja-dera** (*Ninja* Temple).

Kanazawa is an excellent place to buy traditional crafts. The local pottery, Kutani ware, is brightly colored and distinctive. Other famous Kanazawa crafts are *Kaga Yūzen*, a dyed kimono fabric, and lacquerware.

Takayama (Hida-Takayama): This small city whose name means "High Mountain" is situated deep in the hills of Gifu Prefecture. Getting there is half the fun. It is reached by some of the most scenic train lines and scenic but treacherous roads in Japan. Yet despite its remote location, Takayama has had an exceptional cultural development. The city produced and continues to produce excellent crafts, especially lacquerware and woodwork. The charm of Takayama is in its houses. The city is made for strolling, with blocks of narrow lanes lined with wooden houses and small shops selling local products.

There are several small museums, including the **Hida Fubutsu-kan**, the **Kusakabe Mingei-kan** and the **Takayama Kyōdō-kan** (all essentially museums of local artifacts from daily life), and the **Kyōdō Gengō-kan**, a doll and toy museum. **Hachiman Shrine**, the city's main shrine, is the terminus of festival parades.

Right, participant in the Jidai Matsuri Festival.

蕙園

SOUTH KOREA: THE "HERMIT KINGDOM" EMERGES

The small, ruggedly beautiful Korean peninsula, site of the fastest-growing economy in the world today, was long known as the "Hermit Kingdom" of East Asia. Invaded by Japanese warlord Hideyoshi in 1597 and then overrun by Manchu hordes, Korea was ravaged and plundered by foreigners during the 17th century. The country responded by withdrawing from the outside world, cultivating a self-sufficient economy and an autonomous way of life.

Korea remained in isolation until 1876, when the port of Inch'ōn was forced open by the Japanese and foreign ships began arriving in ever-increasing numbers. The yoke of Japanese domination rapidly tightened, however, after Korea futilely sought neutrality in the Russo-Japanese War of 1898-9. And with the establishment of a colonial Japanese government in 1906, Koreans found themselves little better than slaves in their own country.

Foreign domination brought with it a growing familiarity with the modern world. But nothing thrust Korea into the 20th century with the speed and impact of General Douglas MacArthur's landing at Inch'ōn on September 15, 1950. The bloody Korean War pitted communist against non-communist, North Korean against South Korean, and ultimately left the country divided in half along the 38th parallel—where to this day periodic talks are held between American, Chinese and Korean negotiators. Meanwhile, dramatic economic growth and an unprecedented prosperity have bolstered South Korea's confidence to meet any challenge.

Since the 1960s, a number of aggressive Korean industrial firms have launched the nation pell-mell onto the world economic stage—as producers of automobiles, computers, textiles and a host of other export items. Currently, South Korea is the world's largest importer of foreign industrial technology and the fourth largest buyer of foreign farm products. South Koreans are also investing heavily abroad—in a television plant in New Jersey, a coal mine in Pennsylvania, and a steel-sheet manufacturing plant in California.

The Korean economy is expected to develop at an annual rate of 7 percent throughout the rest of this century. By the year 2000, South Koreans expect to enjoy a standard of living on a par with that of Western nations. Plans call for evolutionary changes in the nation's political structure, and for rapid development in the fields of science, technology, arts and culture, education and social welfare.

The acceptance of South Korea as a member of the international community is symbolized by her role as host for the 1988 Olympic Games. With lavish new sports facilities and meticulous planning, Koreans are staking their reputation and resources on the success of the games. Among the many projects undertaken, the most impressive is Seoul's new 73-mile (117-km) subway system.

Sports Minister Yong-ho Lee justifies the high cost of these projects as an investment in Korea's future. "You must consider," he says, "that it is traditional in this country to over-entertain guests. Koreans often are willing to go into debt to prepare a great feast." Whether arriving in Korea for the Olympic Games or at any other time, we are constantly made aware of this generous spirit of hospitality and openness.

Preceding pages: Peeping toms and bathing ladies are the subject of this Korean painting. Left, honoring Confucius at the Sōkchōn ceremony.

KOREAN HISTORY: WINDS OF CHANGE

The Korean peninsula is relatively small (northern Korea is about 49,000 square miles 126,900 square km and southern Korea is about 40,000 square miles 103,600 square km), but it appears even smaller because only 20 percent of its total land area is flatland. The entire country is ribbed by low rising, sharp and often bare mountain ridges. This scenic "chain of hills" reaches like a jagged adze toward Japan and the vast Pacific. The peaks never rise above 9,000 feet (2,800 meters) which suggests a young land. Korea is, in fact, one of the world's oldest land areas, dating back to the pre-Cambrian period (1,600 to 2,700 million years ago).

The peninsula's compactness, 600 miles (1,000 km) long and 134 miles (216 km) at its narrowest point, makes possible a drive over the entire length of the country in about 12 hours. Seoul, the capital of South Korea, is approximately 680 miles (1,100 km) from Peking and 870 miles (1,400 km) from Tokyo, a geographic fact that influenced the course of history.

Korean history invariably begins with an account of the mythical founder of the nation, Tan'gun. The story goes that on hearing the prayers of a bear and tiger who wished to become human beings, Hwanung, son of the Divine Creator, descended to earth and proclaimed himself king. He gave each of the animals 20 pieces of garlic and a piece of artemisia and told them they would be transformed after eating the plants and withdrawing from sunlight for a hundred days. The animals ate the offering and retired to their caves. The tiger's restlessness drove him out before the required time, but the bear remained the full one hundred days and emerged as a woman.

The first wish of the bear woman was to have a son. She prayed under a sandalwood tree and her wish was granted in the form of Tan'gun, who became the first human king. Whatever one may wish to make of the myth, evidence of human life on the Korean peninsula has been dated to 4270 B.C.

Located geographically at the crossroads of northern Asia, the Korean peninsula has been trampled on by armies of Chinese, Japanese, Mongols, Manchus, Russians and Americans, each incursion leaving its mark. Despite these onslaughts, Koreans have maintained a distinct political and cultural identity.

Three Kingdoms period: The southern part of the peninsula was peopled by a number of distinctive but related tribes that had, by the third century A.D., formed three weak tribal confederations: Mahan, Chinhan, and Pyōnhan. It was in this area—during the third and fourth centuries—that the Paekche and Silla tribes arose, who, with Koguryō, dominated the so-called Three Kingdoms period in Korea.

Paekche emerged among the Mahan tribes of the southwest. Led by a royal clan

that may have been related to the Koguryō peoples, Paekche occupied the area south of the Han River and initially placed its capital in the vicinity of modern Kwangju. In subsequent years Paekche expanded its territory, organized a bureaucratic government along Chinese lines, and established relations with the Eastern Chin state of south China.

Last to develop as a major kingdom was Silla, whose origins consisted of a loose federation of tribes in the Kyōngju plain in the southeastern corner of Korea, the region farthest from the reaches of Chinese influence. Silla's transition from tribal league to kingdom took place in the late-fourth and early-fifth centuries.

The Sillan conquest of the peninsula often is taken as the beginning of a unified Korean state and that state continued to exist until the division of north and south Korea in 1945.

Chinese civilization flowed into Korea during the Three Kingdoms period, in the form of Buddhism, Confucianism, arts, architecture, and the written language of China. The internal institutions of *hwarang* and the *kolp'um,* the former a training by austere discipline fostered by Buddhist and Confucian precepts, the latter a highly stratified hierarchy of rank by birth, contributed to the cohesiveness of the Sillan state.

The 10th century saw the rise to power of Wang Kōn, son of a merchant family who subdued a Paekche threat and named his new state Koryō, a contraction of Koguryō.

The Mongols were the most formidable foes during the Koryō period. In 1213 the Mongols overran most of northern Korea and forced the government to surrender. When the Mongols relaxed their grip the following year, the Koryō government fled from the capital Kaesōng and took refuge on Kangwha Island. The ensuing years saw treaties made and broken. Although the Mongols allowed the Koryō government to remain in control, large annual tributes, especially when the Mongols established the Yuan Dynasty in China, were required. Koryō crown princes were sent to Peking as children, compelled to marry Mongol princesses, who often wielded more power as queens.

The burden on the lower classes depleted the farmers. The demand to furnish ships for ill-fated Mongol invasions of Japan burdened the Korean government. Yet under the Mongols, the Koreans gained knowledge of astrology, medicine, artistic skills and cotton cultivation.

Yi Dynasty: With the fall of the Yuan Dynasty in China, Korea underwent a revival of her independence. Factions advocating loyalty to the Mongols and those loyal to the Ming Chinese with a third faction seeking the favor of both led to internal struggles. Yi Sōng-gye, descended from a military family, seized Kaesōng and replaced the Koryō king with the king's son. In 1392, after replacing the king's own son with another royal descendant, Yi took the throne and founded his own dynasty,

Left, statues of Admiral Yi Sun-sin are found all over Korea. Above, residents in a Korean village.

restoring the ancient Chinese name of Korea, Chosōn. Tributary relations with China were resumed and Confucian norms were woven into the fabric of Korean society.

The Yi Dynasty survived for more than 500 years and was the last ruling house in Korean history. Yi kings ranged from the intelligent and scholarly Sejong (1418-1450) who presided over the conception of the remarkable Korean alphabet, *hangul*, to the despotic Sejo, who seized the throne in 1456 and ruled by purges, executions, banishments and seizure of property.

Contributing to the decline of the Yi Dynasty was the Japanese invasion of Toyotomi Hideyoshi in 1592. Determined to conquer China, Hideyoshi invited Chosōn to join his campaign. The Yi government declined. The Japanese government overran most of Korea within a month. At sea, however, the story was different. General Yi Sun-sin and his naval force, including Korea's famous 'turtle ships,' broke the back of the Japanese invasion by cutting off their flow of supplies and troop reinforcements. In January, 1597, Hideyoshi renewed the war. Yi Sun-sin was again called to duty. With a smaller fleet, Yi's brilliant tactics prevailed. At the height of victory, Yi was shot and killed while standing at the bow of his flagship. Hideyoshi died in September, 1598 and the war ended.

Capture of Heijo Korla by the Japanese Army

The Manchus had had designs on Korea since the late 1500s. By the early-17th century, they had captured Pyōng-yang in the north and the Yi capital at Seoul. The Manchus demanded, and got, a Confucius-style elder-younger brother relationship from Chosōn and aid for use against the Ming Dynasty. In 1632 they declared Korea to be a vassal state and demanded annual tribute. The Koreans declared war, but the Manchus prevailed and went on to conquer China and establish the Ch'ing Dynasty.

In the 18th century, the Yi Dynasty recovered some of its earlier vitality. Financial problems had been resolved with improvements in the tax system.

The 19th century was a century of crisis for Korea. Despite its longevity and its occasional brilliance, the Yi Dynasty did not give Korea an efficient administration. Decades of social unrest and popular agitation in the early-19th century, including major rebellions in 1811 and 1862, made the conservative ruling class reactionary and inward-looking. And that was a time when Korea, along with the rest of Asia, faced the challenge of an expansive and technologically superior West.

Although Korea had never been as isolated as might be suggested by the popular nickname, "Hermit Kingdom," her contacts with her two main neighbors, China and Japan, had been closely regulated.

Apart from clandestine missionaries, direct contacts with the West continued to be limited until the 1860s. Korean officials, however, were well-informed about contemporary affairs in China and they were badly shaken by the news that British and French troops had occupied Peking in 1860. This strengthened their determination that foreigners should be excluded from the peninsula.

It was not until 1882 that exclusionism was finally cast aside, beginning with a treaty with the U.S.

Korea had now become an international battleground for contending powers. The rise of Japanese influence after 1876 spurred the Chinese to redouble their efforts to preserve their traditional influence. This led to a series of confrontations, culminating in the Sino-Japanese War, in which the Japanese emerged victorious.

When the Russians tried to exert some influence, Japan again moved in and had resumed total control by the end of the Russo-Japanese War of 1904-1905.

Despite the efforts of an independence movement, Japan retained her colonial grip on Korea until her defeat by the Allies in World War II.

The subsequent Cold War between the U.S. and the Russians led to the establishment of the 38th parallel as the official demarcation line between the communist north and the south of the peninsula.

Left, lithograph of 19th-century attack by Japanese troops. Above, monument to a 20th-century war.

In rapid succession, Yi Sŭng-man was sworn in as the first president of the Republic of Korea on August 15, 1948 while up north, Kim Il-Sŏng's provisional government became the government of the Democratic People's Republic of Korea on September 9, 1948.

The stage was set for civil war, and North Korean troops crossed the 38th parallel in strength on June 25, 1950. The Americans moved in to help the south and the Korean War, including eventual intervention by the Chinese, dragged on until a truce was signed on July 27, 1953.

The war dealt a fatal blow to any hopes of a speedy, peaceful reunification of Korea. The creation of the demilitarized zone made the border between the two Korean states one of the most effective artificial barriers in the world, and the fighting had inevitably hardened the hostility on both sides.

In the south, the period following the war was one of stagnation and slow recovery. President Yi's government collapsed in 1960, following widespread student demonstrations and violent intervention by the authorities.

The subsequent government proved incapable of retaining power and fell to a military coup in 1961. Major General Park Chung-Hee emerged as the strongman and with a return to civilian government, was elected President in 1963.

Park's rule came to an end on October 26, 1979, when he was shot to death by the chief of his Central Intelligence Agency, Kim Chae-Kyu, who claimed he had assassinated Park in order to end dictatorship and restore democracy. Kim was convicted, along with six accomplices, and was executed.

The long-term legacy of Park's 18 years in office comprised two trends: Park's idea of Korean-style democracy placed a strong emphasis on administrative efficiency, and he presided over a series of development programs that made Korea one of the most remarkable economic successes of the 1960s and 1970s.

Following a period of uncertainty, after Park's sudden death, another military man, Major General Chun Doo-Hwan became President. Under him, South Korea has continued to enjoy economic growth. Opposition to his regime remains outspoken, but the general outlook for the future in the Land of Morning Calm is an optimistic one.

SEOUL PLAZA HOTEL

LOTTE

SEOUL

Seoul, the capital for more than five hundred years, is the heart of the nation, home to one quarter of the country's population of 40 million.

Topographically, the center of the city is wooded **Nam-san** (South Mountain), a 900-foot (273 meter) elevation that gazes across mid-town at conically-shaped **Peagak-san** (North Mountain). Between these peaks sprawled the old walled city. The original wall of earth is gone except for a few crumbling stretches and restored patches that were rebuilt for tourist visibility. Five of the nine gates that once pierced the wall still stand. The two largest—**Namdaemun** (Great South Gate) and **Tongdaemun** (Great East Gate)—are reminders of the capital as it was originally laid out.

Some consider the **City Hall Plaza** the center of the city. This fountained square is bounded on the north by **City Hall**, on the south by the **Plaza Hotel**, on the east by the entrance to **Ulchi-ro** (one of the main east-west streets), and on the west by **Tōksu Palace** (a remnant of the old dynasty that founded the city).

Other centrists claim that the **Kwanghwa-mun** (Gate of Transformation by Light) intersection is Seoul's center. People who believe this probably think so because it is the entrance to **Chongno**, the city's original main street.

The governmental heart of the old walled city was **Kyōngbok Palace** (Palace of Shining Happiness). A plaque hangs from the gate's roof and proclaims its name in a script by Korea's late President Park Chung-hee in *han'gūl*, the Korean alphabet.

Many people think Seoul's real center today is modern **Myōng-dong**, an area of narrow alleys that starts a 10-minute walk southeast from City Hall Plaza directly across from **Midop'a Department Store**. Myōng-dong's main thoroughfare is lined on both sides by swanky shops that sell chic clothes and accessories, and it ends at the top of a low hill before **Myōng-dong Cathedral**. Myōng-dong alleyways come alive in the evening when they are crowded with after-work strollers window-shopping past the various fancy displays of shoes, handbags and clothes. Tiny drinking houses that serve cheap liquor are already jammed with happy, noisy customers. Since Koreans always eat when they drink, many of these drinking houses display their *anju (hors d'oeuvres)* in the window.

Soul of Seoul: A good place to start a tour of Seoul is at the central and historical Tōksu Palace (Palace of Virtuous Longevity), whose gate faces City Hall Plaza. Among the most conspicuous structures on the palace grounds is a **statue of Sejong**, the great 15th-century king who commissioned scholars to develop a distinctive Korean writing system (different from the traditional Chinese characters) and officially promulgated it in 1446. There are also two European-style stone buildings with Ionic and Corinthian columns designed by an Englishman in 1909 (housing the **National Museum of Modern Art**).

The **National Museum** dominates a corner of the nearby Kyōngbok Palace grounds. The museum showcases a panorama of Korean culture. At the rear of the palace grounds stands a **Folk Museum** which houses artifacts of

[P]receding [p]ages: Seoul [s]kyline. [L]eft, mother [a]nd child at [t]he Bamboo [m]arket in [D]amyang. [R]ight, the [N]ational [M]useum is [i]n the heart [o]f Seoul.

everyday use and dioramas showing how they are used.

About a block east of Kyōngbok lies **Ch'angdōk Palace** (Palace of Illustration Virtue). The well-preserved Ch'angdōk has a throneroom hall surrounded by long drafty corridors leading past reception rooms furnished with heavy European chairs and sofas. In private living quarters, the furnishings are those of traditional Korea: low, slatted beds, lacquered chests and tables.

Naksōn-jae, a small complex of buildings within Ch'angdōk's grounds, is still the residence of descendants of the royal family. Behind Ch'angdōk lies the extensive acreage of **Piwōn**, the Secret Garden, so called because it was formerly a private park for the royal family. The most picturesque of these sites is **Pando-ji**, (peninsula pond) shaped like the outline of the Korean peninsula. From its shore extending out over the water stands an exquisite fan-shaped pavilion.

One block east from Ch'angdōk lies **Ch'anggyongwōn**, another ancient palace grounds now open to the public. Across the street from Ch'anggyongwōn lies **Ch'ongmyo**, the Royal Ancestral Shrine. This walled complex includes two long pillared buildings housing ancestral tablets listing the names and accomplishments of the 27 Yi kings and their queens. Once a year on the first Sunday in May, a traditional ceremony honoring the spirits of the kings and queens is held here.

The similar Sōkchōn ceremony is held biennially at the **Sōnggyun'gwan shrine** located on the grounds of **Sōnggyun'gwan University** to the northeast of Piwōn. The Sōkchōn honors the spirit of Kongja, the great Sage Confucius, the man whose principles formed the basis of government and code of behavior in Yi Korea.

Sōnngyun'gwan University is a modern transformation of the old Sōnngyun'gwan, a national institute sponsored and supported by the Yi court where Korea's best scholars pursued the Confucian Classics and instructed those who aspired to pass government examinations in order to receive official appointments.

The Confucian Yi court tried hard to extinguish the spirit of the Buddha throughout the country but it failed

Prince Yi Kyu and descendants in Confucian rites at Ch'ongmyo shrine.

miserably. Buddhist temples abound. **Chogye-sa**, founded in 1910 and the headquarters of the official sect of Buddhism in Korea, is right downtown off **An'guk-dong-no**. As the center of Buddhism in the country, it hums with activity, and on the occasion of the Buddha's birthday, it becomes the hub of Buddhist festivities in Korea.

Cruising 'It': It'aewōn is an urban area that runs down from the southern flank of Nam-san and eastward from the fenced edge of **Yongsan Garrison**, the site of the headquarters of the Eighth U.S. Army.

It'aewōn merchants attract shoppers and visitors from all over the world. By day, bargain-hunters swarm through the hundreds of clothing, eelskin, brassware, shoe and antique stores where they stock up on Korean-made goods. By night, It'aewōn attracts as many young Koreans as it does foreigners. The neons light up and the music begins—this mile-long strip is now home to literally hundreds of bars and discotheques which rock until the break of dawn. Alcohol pours freely here and cross-cultural marriages often get their starts in the packed It'aewōn clubs. Older Koreans blame It'aewōn for the westernization of Korea's youth, particularly of the young ladies who now partake of beer and tobacco without hesitation. But the Koreans hold their own against the foreigners. It'aewōn is a place where many foreigners learn to appreciate the Korean temperament.

Chinatown: For years there was a special secton of the city for the Chinese. This "Chinatown" was behind the Plaza Hotel, but the construction of that hotel and other forms of city renovation razed much of the old area and scattered the Chinese around the city.

Once a year on a spring day determined by the lunar calendar, Chinese residents offer an all-day performance of Chinese opera here in a temple in a Myōng-dong side alley. The day celebrates the birth of the Chinese goddess of progeny. The performers are amateurs who practice for weeks to produce the high-pitched voices required by this kind of music. Of course, there are Chinese restaurants everywhere in Seoul—with fare ranging from awful to delicious, usually depending upon

chool's ut for ese Seoul enagers.

the cheap to very expensive prices.

Shopping: Any foreign visitor to Seoul should venture into a proper market. If not one of the neighborhood markets, then certainly into one or both of the great central markets downtown: **Namdae-mun Sijang** (Great South Gate Market), located east of the gate itself and **Tongdae-mun Sijang** (Great East Gate Market), a large area that stretches south of **Chong-no 5-ka** and **6-ka**.

The city offers other somewhat more convenient (if less colorful) shopping places: modern department stores; the above-ground shopping arcades and the luxury hotel shopping arcades in the hotels all just off City Hall Plaza.

Underground labyrinthine shopping arcades lie invisibly beneath some of the city streets: the **Sogong Arcade** runs from under the corner of the Plaza Hotel, turns left at the **Chosun Hotel** and continues as far as the basement of the **Cosmos Department Store** in Myōng-dong; the **Hoehyon Arcade** starts in front of the **Central Post Office** and runs up to **T'oegye-re**; and other mini-arcades exist where pedestrian underpasses allow room for a few stores.

Silk merchant at the East Gate Market.

The time-honored location for the antique dealers is **Insa-dong** along a narrow street called by foreigners "**Mary's Alley**" that leads south from **An'guk-dong Rotary** to **Pagoda Park**. Some good shops offering fine Koryō celadon, Silla pottery and Yi furniture are still flourishing there, but many have fled to other sections of the city, notably to **Ch'onggyech'on 8-ka**.

Sports: Most Korean men and boys are sports buffs, and to further stress the point, Seoul has three sports arenas to satisfy their lust for organized athletic competitions: **Seoul Stadium** for baseball and soccer, **Ch'angch'ung Field House** for volleyball and boxing, and the new **Olympic Sports Complex** in **Chamsil**, south of the river.

Sports has gained in popularity recently, due in no small part to the 1986 Asian Games and the forthcoming 1988 Olympic Games.

Age-old Korean martial arts such as **t'aekwōn-do**, **hapki-do** and **yu-do** are taught in schools and centers nationally, and around the world. A favorite **t'aekwōn-do** viewing spot is the **Yuksamdong World T'aekwōn-do Headquarters** across the **Third Han River Bridge**.

Korea's unofficial sport for young and old alike is hiking and trekking year-round, probably because 70 percent of the country is mountainous. In the fall, weekend hikers wearing alpine gear can be seen lining up to board buses out of the city to assault the nearby mountain peaks. A favorite and easy peak to scale among Seoulites is **Tobong-san**, which is just northeast of Seoul. Once on top, hikers let loose with not-so-alpine-like haloos and yahoos.

Seoul After Dark: Concert-goers can see performances held in either of two luxurious concert and theater halls: the **National Theater** on the slopes of Nam-san or the **Sejong Cultural Center** in the middle of the city opposite the **American Embassy** on **Sejong-no**.

All of the first-class hotels in Seoul have discos, the best of which are at the Chosun Hotel (**Xanadu**) and the **Hilton** (**Rainforest**). It'aewōn, of course, is the main area for nighttime romping. For a chic, private atmosphere, It'aewōn regulars go to **Rumors**, located next to the **Crown Hotel** but by far the most popular everyman's club is **Sportman's** smack in the middle of It'aewōn.

SEOUL EXCURSIONS

Beyond Seoul's secure city walls there are numerous day outings one can go on to get away from the bustle of urban life. Stroll down to any bus, subway or train terminal, set off in virtually any direction from Seoul, and classical intrigues await you only minutes outside this sprawling city.

Namhansansōng: The South Han Mountain Fortress is a popular weekend hiking area about 19 miles (30 km) southeast of Seoul proper. This grand highland redoubt was originally built about 2,000 years ago during Korea's Paekche Dynasty. Most of the fort's now visible structures, however, date to the 17th and 18th centuries, when the fortress served Yi kings of that period as a retreat from invading Chinese armies. This spectacular place is located just east of **Sōngnam**.

Pukhansansōng: The North Han Mountain Fortress. This one, which is similar in design and setting to Namhansansōng, is located above the sprawling northeast suburbs of Seoul along the high ridges of **Pukhan Mountain**. These same walls were partially destroyed during the Korean War, but have since been restored to honor their historic importance. On the road back to Seoul, if you take the northern access highway, look carefully to your left and right. You may see shamanistic spirit posts (a rarity these days) peeking out at you through the brush and pines.

Walker Hill Resort: This nightlife area of Las Vegas-style revues, gambling (in the **Sheraton-Walker Hill Casino**), and resort amenities is located above Seoul's eastern suburbs, the swank **Seoul Country Club**, and a picturesque bend in the **Han River**. Walker Hill was named after Gen. Walton H.Walker, former Commanding General of the U.S. Eighth Army, who was killed in action during a major Korean War campaign in this area.

Kwangnūng: The impressive Confucian-style burial tombs of King Sejo (r. 1456-1468), the 7th Yi king, and his wife, Queen Yun Chōn-hi, are probably the most aesthetically and idyllically-located tombs in the Seoul area.

'egas-style evue at the Valker Hill heraton.

These monumental mounds are about 17 miles (28 km) northeast of Seoul and just past Ŭijŏngbu.

Hŏninnŭng: These tombs of the 3rd and 24th Yi kings lie in the southeast skirts of Seoul in **Naekok-dong** and near a green belt area. If you are in Korea on May 8, you may want to attend a formal *chesa* (ancestor worship) ceremony conducted annually at Hŏninnŭng by Yi Dynasty descendants.

Yong-in Farmland: An African safari, American zoo and Korean amusements come improbably together at Yong-in Farmland, a recreation complex on the north side of **National Highway 4** about 21 miles (34 km) southeast of Seoul. Hidden behind a 1,634-acre (660-hectare) curtain of pine, chestnut, walnut, paulownia and other hardy trees is a Korean-style lion safari; a 163-acre (65-hectare) nursery with 1,200 kinds of rare plants; tree park of apples, plums, pears, peaches, grapes and 14 other fruits; and the advertised "fancy performances of wild pigs and flamingoes."

Ich'ŏn: The pottery kilns of two of Korea's finest potters are about 43 miles (70 km) south of Seoul near Ich'ŏn (also just north of National Highway 4). In **Sukwang-ni, Sindŭng-myŏn**, north of Ich'ŏn proper, you can observe Koryŏ celadons being created by a ceramics master, or you can marvel at Yi Dynasty whiteware as it's pulled hot from traditional kilns. At the other end of the potting spectrum, you will find row upon row of the ubiquitous shiny, brown, tall and oblong *kimch'i* pots. These utilitarian wares are hand-thrown and fired in adobe huts. After a day of pot-shopping, languish in the hot springwaters that burble into the **Ich'ŏn Spa Hotel** before returning to Seoul.

Yangju: The Yangju *pyŏlsandae* masked dance drama is performed in this small village just north of Ŭijŏngbu. Traditional performance times are during *Tano* (a spring festival), on *Ch'usŏk* (an autumn festival), and sometimes for the convenience of visiting cultural groups. The performance begins with a parade around the village by the various characters dressed in full costume and mask (made of paper or gourd).

Korean Folk Village: A morning excursion 28 miles (45 km) south of Seoul will give you a full day to tour the 240 homes, shops and other attractions in this authentically-rendered Yi Dynasty village. Visit ceramic and bamboo shops, drink rice wines in a wayside tavern, then join the daily staged wedding procession of a traditionally-costumed bride and groom who are trailed by a colorful, whirling farmers' dance band.

Suwŏn: The easy-going capital of Kyŏnggi Province is an old fortress city about 32 miles (51 km) south of Seoul in the vicinity of **Mount Paltal**. These days Suwŏn is renowned for its recently-restored castle walls and support structures. The first thing you'll notice about the city are its massive fortress walls, gates, and other historic architectural facilities which meander around the old city proper.

Yongju-sa: A Buddhist temple which, like the Suwŏn fortress, was also built by King Chŏnjo in his father's memory. Yongju-sa, "The Dragon Jewel," rests in a rural, pinery area about a 20-minute bus ride south of Suwŏn's midtown South Gate. Built in 1790 on the site of an earlier Silla Dynasty temple (dating from 854), Yongju-sa's grounds boast, among other attrac-

The Sogni-san National Park is a favorite family spot.

tions, a seven-story pagoda, a 3,300-pound (1,500-kg) Koryŏ-era brass bell, and in its main hall, a superb Buddhist painting by the Yi genre painting master Danwŏn Kim Hong-do.

Sogni-san National Park: This mountain retreat in North Ch'ungch'ŏng Province is superb any time of the year, but is most favored by discriminating Korea weekenders in the autumn when its trees are burning with color. Indeed, since ancient times Sogni has been a preferred resort area, and appropriately, *Sogni* means "escape from the vulgar." You can "escape from the vulgar" by motoring directly from Seoul via **Ch'ŏngju City**. It's about a three-hour ride each way.

Seoulites who know try to arrive in Sogni village at lunchtime, when they can enjoy a fabled Sogni mushroom lunch. Such a lunch can feature as many as six completely different mushroom dishes served with a dizzying array of side dishes, *kimch'i* and rice.

Following this mushroom overdose, proceed uphill to Sogni-san's biggest attraction, **Pŏpju-sa**, a large temple complex dominated by a massive **Mirŭk Buddha of the Future** fashioned of modern poured cement. This 88-foot (27-meter) image, completed in 1964, is often identified by tour guides as "the biggest Buddha in Korea."

Remnants of this favored temple's days of spiritual grandeur can be found on all parts of the compound. Consider the famed **Ch'ŏlhwak**, a massive iron rice pot which was cast in 720. Perhaps the most celebrated historical treasure at Pŏpju-sa is the five-story **P'alsang-jŏn**, or Eight Image Hall, which rises in symmetrical splendor above the complex's roomy main courtyard.

Sambuyŏn: Due south of the **Sinch'ŏl-wŏn** area—in a deep canyon and off a steep dirt road—is the little known Sambuyŏn or "Dragon Waterfall." You'll see local villagers fishing for carp in pools above the falls. The carp is regarded by Koreans as a symbol of strength and perseverance.

On your way back to Seoul, you may want to picnic and recuperate at **San-jŏng Lake**, an artificial lake resort built by Japanese engineers during Japan's colonial occupation of Korea. The lake is a popular skating spot in the winter-time, and most of the year it's a fine area for hiking and relaxation.

he prawling 'ŏpju-sa emple omplex is ogni-san's iggest ttraction.

INCH' ŌN, KANGHWA-DO, P'ANMUNJŌM

In the old days most travelers put in at Seoul's chief seaport, **Inch'ōn**. Up to the 1880s, Inch'ōn was a sleepy fishing village called Chemulp'o—for a long time the only Korean place foreigners were allowed to visit. Today Inch'ōn is a booming harbor and Korea's fourth largest city. The number of trading ships calling at Inch'ōn has increased each year, and consequently the 24-mile (39-km) stretch between Seoul proper and the Port of Inch'ōn has become the most important sea, road and rail supply route in Korea.

Once you arrive at **Inch'ōn-dong station**, take a cab or hike up to **Freedom Hill** above this town of steep streets and endless ocean terminals. The ocean view from up there is overtly industrial, but sea breezes are crisp, and beside the **statue of Gen. Douglas MacArthur**, you'll find a whitewashed replica of America's **Statue of Liberty** and a charming moon-watching **pavilion**.

The walk down from Freedom Hill through old Inch'ōn is a pleasant one down cobble- and flag-stoned byways and stairs past some of Korea's most distinctive verandahs and storefronts.

There is only one deluxe hotel in Inch'ōn. If your budget yearns for a more Korean experience, there are several *yōgwan* (inns) to choose from.

Popular nearby diversions include seafood dining on one of the area's landlinked islands, either **Wōlmi-do** (Moon Tail Island) or **Sōwōlmi-do**. During the summer, various offshore islands become favored Korean resort destinations. Once you reach one of these isles you can bake on white sand beaches or wallow in lovely man-made lagoons rimmed by colorful cabanas.

Travelers also enjoy visiting the big public seafood market on the southern side of Inch'ōn's tidal basin. Ask for the **Yonan Pudu O-sijang** (fish market).

Kanghwa-do is an island about 31 miles (50 km) northwest of Seoul and across the narrow **Yōmha Strait**. Kanghwa town proper is small and easy-going—just the right size for pedestrian tourists who like to putter around marketplaces and in handicraft shops. Korea's finest rushcraft weaving is meticulously done in Kanghwa-do, so in local shops you'll find numerous baskets, woven into fun shapes, colors and sizes. You'll also discover fine floor mats and doorway hangings which are woven so tightly they let summer breezes in while filtering out pesky warm-weather mosquitos.

Off the main street on the road opposite the bridge fronting the marketplace is the restored **Koryō Palace**. From there, catch a taxi up to the neatly restored North Gate, **Pungmun**, for a view of the distant blue mountains of North Korea. On a clear day you can see for several miles across the **Han-Imjin Estuary** and into the forbidden and Communist north.

On the way back down to town, ask your driver to stop along the road and send you down a narrow footpath which leads to Korea's oldest and most unique Episcopal Church, **Kam Tok Kyohwe**. This Christian structure, built in 1900 by Bishop Charles Corfe about 10 years after his arrival in Korea, harmoniously combines Christian, Taoist and Buddhist elements in its overall design.

Northwest of Kanghwa town is one

Mending fishing nets at Inch'ōn.

of the most mysterious sculptures in Korea. The scenery along the way is dominated mostly by fields of ginseng protected by low thatched lean-tos, and typical Kanghwa farmhouses and grain silos decorated with contemporary folk art.

About two miles outside of town, down a dirt path behind a chicken farm, is a primitive stone sculpture constructed of three large, flat boulders. Archaeologists have identified this as a northern-style **dolmen** (in Korean, *chisong-myo* or *koin-dol*)—a sacred tomb or altar—which dates back to paleolithic times. Life goes on around it as it stands undisturbed in the midst of peppers, tobacco and ginseng.

Further down the road, in **Hajŏn-myŏn**, there is another old but less-visited stone sculpture. It is a five-story pagoda (*sŏk t'ap*) that was once a part of Koryŏ temple. The pagoda is about a half-mile walk from the main road past farmhouses. You might also wish to scale **Pongch'on-san**, the high hill behind it.

Military presence at P'anmunjŏm.

On the southern end of Kanghwa-do about 10 miles (16 km) south of Kanghwa town, is one of the oldest temples in Korea, **Chŏndŭng-sa**, the "Temple of the Inherited Lamp." Chŏndŭng-sa was named for a jade lamp presented to the temple by a Koryŏ queen.

On the temple grounds is an iron bell about six feet tall. It was cast in 1097 during the Northern Sung Dynasty in a typical Chinese style. Despite its foreign origin, the bell has been designated a national treasure.

One significant excursion that takes the better part of a day is a trip to the **"Eyebrow Rock" Buddha** at **Pomun-sa** on the neighboring island of **Songmodo**. This pilgrimage starts with a quick bus ride to **Ŭip'o**, a small fishing village on the west coast.

Pomun-sa is a neatly-restored 1,400-year-old temple. It overlooks the light blue **Yellow Sea** and strangely-shaped islands that dissolve into the horizon. Behind the temple, carved into the mountain, is a stone chamber with 22 small niches behind an altar. Steps lead further above this stone chamber through junipers. At the end of a steep, heart-thumping hike is the massive concave "Eyebrow Rock" Buddha intricately sculpted into the granite mountainside.

About 35 miles (56 km) north of Seoul is **P'anmunjŏm**, the historic place at Korea's **38th parallel** where a cease-fire truce was signed here between Allied and Communist forces on July 27, 1953. The truce agreement formally divided Korea into north and south political sectors and put an uneasy end to the bloody Korean War.

The area is the only point of official contact between North Korea and the free world. You can book a tour to P'anmunjŏm and the demilitarized zone ("DMZ") by contacting the Korea Tourist Bureau or by making arrangements for the same tour through agents stationed at most of Seoul's luxury hotels.

Once at P'anmunjŏm, you will be escorted around a heavily-guarded sector formally called the **Joint Security Area**. You will be taken on a tour of the **Conference Room** where the on-going truce talks take place, and from atop **Freedom House**, an ornate Korean-style pavilion, you'll be treated to a rare, panoramic view of North Korea, a place often referred to as "the world's most sealed-off society."

SŌRAK-SAN

Sōrak-san, the "Snow Peak Mountain," more formally known as the **Sōrak-san National Park**, is a much-touted resort area highlighted by a series of peaks in the mid-section of the spectacular **Taebaek Sanmaek**, or "Great White Range," Korea's most prominent geographical region.

Inje, the renowned "Gateway to Inner Sōrak," is a good place to begin. But even in Inje town you'll have to decide which of two scenic ways you'll take to traverse the Sōrak range. The **Southern Route**, goes through the **Han'gye-ryong Pass** while the **Northern Route** winds through two back mountain passes, before descending in to **Sokch'o** on the **East Sea**. Most travelers prefer the Southern Route, both for the comfort and scenery. But, for a bit of "roughing it," head north.

The Southern Route from Inje winds its way through "Inner Sōrak," **Naesōrak**, through the southern fringes of "Outer Sōrak," **Wesōrak**, until you emerge at lovely **Yangyang** town on the turquoise blue East Sea.

En route you'll encounter numerous nature trails. Some travelers like to pause at **Chang Su Dae** and hike up to the **Taesung** waterfalls, then course onward and upward to **Paekdam-sa**, a charming Buddhist temple in the interior of Inner Sōrak.

The 15-minute bus ride from the sandy East Coast into **Sōrak Village** is a grand transition from beach cabana chic to mountain resort cool.

A large and detailed information sign just below the charming **Sōrak-san Tourist Hotel** offers a few suggestions for excursions, including the following:

Stroll up the main flagstone and fir-lined path which leads to **Sinhung-sa**, an ancient *Sōn* (or Zen) temple originally built near its present location in 652. Just before you reach the temple compound proper, you'll pass a neatly-kept cemetery full of unusual bell-shaped tombstones erected to honor formerly illustrious Zen monks.

Kejo Hermitage, a subsidiary of the mother Sinhung Temple, is partially built into a granite cave at the base of **Ulsan-bawi**, a spectacular granite formation that dominates this part of the Sōrak area.

The hermitage is identified by a bright red Buddhist swastika carved and painted over an entrance arch. A narrow and cool corridor leads to the cave interior where you'll find a superb altar where candles burn before a small but exquisite golden Buddha.

Fronting the Kejo Hermitage and Ulsan-bawi is another geologic curiosity which has become a major tourist attraction over the years. This is the famed **Rocking Rock**, a massive boulder which rocks back and forth in its secure place when given a solid nudge.

The hike to **Pison-dae** (Flying Fairy Peak), a vertical rock that juts heavenward at the entrance to an extremely picturesque gorge, is easy enough. From this restful camp at the base of Pison-dae, serious Buddhist pilgrims head up a smaller path to **Kumgang Cave**, which is located near the top of Pison-dae. After negotiating 649 steps to reach this charming cave-shrine, there's usually a young fellow at the cave entrance who makes a living selling Buddha medals to which he adds your name and the date you conquered the Flying Fairy Peak.

Flying Fairy Peak at Sōrak-san National Park.

THE COASTS

East Coast: Korea's East Coast with its ski resorts and highland hot springs is a land of contrasts. At the southern end are **Pokang** and **Ulsan**, recently-created industrial cities. To the north are seaside retreats.

A central pivot point for travel is **Kangnūng,** the major city in Kangwōn Province. About 25 miles (40 km) west of Kangnūng, a little beyond **Chinbu** village lies **Mount Odae National Park**, location of two of Korea's most well-known temple complexes, **Wōljōng-sa** and **Sangwōn-sa**. The road to Odae-san is dotted with small hermitages, Zen meditation niches, and other impressive remnants of Buddhism which date to the seventh century and Korea's Silla Dynasty.

Wōljōng-sa, which sits on the southern fringe of Odae-san, is a sprawling temple complex distinguished by a superb nine-story octagonal pagoda and an unusual kneeling sculpture of the Buddha.

Even higher up, just east of Odae-san's main peak, is Sangwōn-sa, a temple which features a large bronze bell, the oldest known one in Korea and cast in 725 during the reign of the Silla King Sōngdōk.

Another seven miles (11 km) east is the **Taekwallyōng** mountain region, where Korea's most modern and well-equipped ski resort is located. Most slopes are located in the vicinity of a small town called **Hwoeng-gye**, but the newest and favorite runs have been developed in a place called **Yongpyōng**, or the Dragon Valley.

About two-and-a-half miles north of Kangnūng is **Ojuk-hōn** (Black Bamboo Shrine), birthplace of the prominent Confucian scholar-statesman-poet Yi I (1536-1584).

Proceed north towards Yangyang, **Naksan**, Sokch'o, **Hwanjinp'o**, and, at the northernmost reaches of **Highway 7**, the sleepy fishing village of **Taejin**. Just above Yangyang, on the southern skirts of Sokch'o, you'll find what is probably the most charming and impressive religious site in this part of Korea. This is **Naksan-sa**, a Buddhist temple complex originally established

olorful ofs of an ast coast llage.

DISCOVERING KOREAN ART

In Korean art can be found the aesthetics born of indigenous tastes and those imported as other cultures made their impact upon Korea. Through native art and the modifications of foreign art, we find the Korean expression.

In the early sixth century, in the southeastern and relatively remote regions of Silla, Shaman kings ruled. The people's belief in spirits, coupled with the custom of cairn-type tomb burial in which shaman royalty went to their graves in full religious regalia, made the Silla capital, Kyŏngju, Asia's single most spectacular archaeological site.

Breathtaking crowns of hammered, beaten gold with saw-tooth or wave designs representing the nether world have been unearthed. Curved pieces of jade symbolizing human fertility, male virility and the power to destroy evil forces formed a major part of crown design.When the ruler, who symbolized the power of the sun, as well as other forms of nature's energy, moved his head ever so slightly, he created a dazzling sight and vibrating sounds, making an unforgettable impression upon his audience. The rich crowns proclaim the divine power of old Silla rulers and their right to the wealth of the country.

When Buddhism reached Korea, the iconography of Buddhist art had swept from India to Central and Eastern Asia and China, having gone through changes with time and locale.

Korea's earliest bronzes appear relatively flat and linear, inspired by the calligraphic line as in Chinese Buddhist figures; but soon her natural genius in metallurgy and her skilled stone chiselers initiated their own directions. By the seventh century, Korean Buddhist art attained a peak of spiritual expession. The '*Miruk*' figure in the Seoul National Museum and the cave grotto at Kyŏngju represent this artistic peak.

Paintings from the Yi Dynasty (1392-1910) reflect the life, customs and beliefs of the Korean people. Though not technically superior, they symbolize the religious and philosophical concepts of the times.

Perhaps what distinguishes Korean taste from any other culture is found in the art of her ceramics. Artisans shaped pots to resemble melon, small animals as well as large jars decorated sparsely with subjects of nature. Celedon glazes of shades of blue and green of the Koryŏ period are treasured. Most desirable is the color described as 'sky blue after the rain' and 'sea water washed by rain and wind.'

Around 1150 A.D. Korean potters began using inlay techniques. White porcelains were developed for upper-class use. Unlike the Chinese who often used the pot's surface as though it were an easel for painting, Korean design was casual rather than pretentious, suggesting an early Korean spirit. Sixteenth–century Japanese tea masters came to value Korean peasant rice bowls for their "refined pottery aesthetic."

In the end, one needs only to examine closely works of Korean art to know it is distinctive and individual.

Going potty at Kyŏngju.

at this site by the Silla high priest Ulsang in 671.

Sokch'o, an important northeast coast fishing port, has long been a hopping off point for seaside resorts to the north. A favorite spot is **Hwajinp'o Beach** about halfway between Sokch'o and the DMZ. Korea's presidents have traditionally maintained summer villas here.

Most travel beyond Sokch'o is on dirt road. End of the line—and as far north as you can go in Southern Korea—is Taejin, a friendly little town of tiny streets with one of the most colorful fishmarket docks in Korea.

Among sights and sites along the southeast coast are the strangely beautiful **Songnyu Cave**, just south and then inland from **Uljin** town.

Approximately 19 miles (30 km) south of Uljin is **P'yōnghae**, a quiet farming town where you can book a taxi or take a bus to Korea's picturesque **Paegam Mountain and Hot Springs**.

In the foothills of **Naeyon-san**, about nine miles (15 km) north of **Pohang**, is **Pogyōng-sa**, a temple that offers a long history and a hike to a nearby pool and waterfall.

West Coast: Korea's jagged West Coast, cut by the Yellow Sea, is dotted with peninsular islets floating offshore, and bordered by sandy beaches overlooked by quiet pine glens.

Onyang, about 11 miles (18 km) west of **Ch'ōn-an** on **Highway 21**, is a refreshing stop. A hot spring and **Hyōnch'ungsa Shrine** have long attracted visitors, together with the **Onyang Folk Museum** in **Kōngok-ni**. Considered the best all-round collection of Korean folk art in the world, the privately-owned museum has more than 7,000 traditional Korean folk articles on display.

Veteran Westerners in Korea have long favored the West Coast's **Taech'ōn Beach** about nine miles (14 km) from the town of Taech'ōn, as a spring through fall resort haven.

Farther inland lie the ancient towns of **Kongju** and **Puyō**. In Kongju, a national museum houses relics excavated from King Muryong's (r. 501-532) tomb.

Paekche historical remains also abound in Puyō. There is in a park near the entrance to town a seated stone Buddha and a five-story stone pagoda—one of three left from the Three Kingdoms Period. Other relics attesting to the excellence of Paekche craftsmen are in the **Puyō National Museum**.

Chōnju, which is 58 miles (93 km) south of Seoul, is the provincial capital of Chōllapuk-do. It is the ancestral home of the descendants of Yi Sōnggye, founder of the Yi Dynasty, and is famous for paper products, *pi pim pap*, (a savory rice dish) and food in general.

Just five minutes outside of Chōnju, you will see a series of hills covered with hundreds of traditional Korean grave mounds. This is an unusually crowded pre-Christian-style cemetery. A few miles farther, a splendid Buddha can be seen enshrined in a large granite bluff.

Kwangju, the ancient provincial capital of Chōllanam-do, is a low-key city. **Mudūng** (Peerless) **Mountain** hovers like a guardian over Kwangju City. A splendid resort area has been created at its base.

The two-story **Kwangju Museum** was built specially to house Yuan Dynasty booty that was discovered in a sunken 600-year-old Chinese ship in the Yellow sea in 1976.

he ousand-ear-old njin Mirūk tatue is the rgest tanding tone Buddha the ountry.

KYŌNGJU AND PUSAN

Kyōngju, the capital city of North Kyōngsang Province, was well known to Asia's ancients as Kūmsōng, the home of powerful and opulent Shaman kings. This 86-square mile (214-square km) valley is literally dotted with first-to-eighth-century burial tombs, tiered pagodas, fortress ruins, granite standing and relief sculptures, palace grounds and other remnants of the rich Three Kingdoms Era.

The Sillan Tombs at Tumuli Park: In this unique 1.7 million-square-foot (158,000-square-meter) "park" on the southeast side of Kyōngju are some 20 tombs. The largest of the tombs, that of King Mich'u (r. 262-285), has been identified in ancient chronicles as the "**Great Tomb**." However, a secondary tomb, the so-called **Ch'ōnma-ch'ong**, "Heavenly Horse" or "Flying Horse" tomb, is probably the most well-known gravesite in Tumuli Park.

More than ten thousand objects were discovered in this unknown king's tomb, but the most celebrated find was a painting of a galloping, winged horse. Many of the most important treasures are safely displayed in larger national museum structures at Seoul and at nearby **Kyōngju Museum**.

In the museum's vast and modern compound on the eastern skirts of Kyōngju you can see some of the finest of more than 80,000 items unearthed during recent and oldtime digs in this area.

The sprawling temple complex of **Pulguk-sa**, (Temple of the Buddha-land) about 10 miles (16 km) east of Kyōngju on the western slopes of **Mount T'oham** is one of the oldest surviving Buddhist monasteries in Korea and is Korea's most famous temple. First built in the early sixth century, it is flawlessly restored as a splendid example of Silla-era architecture. It also enshrines some of the country's and Korean Buddhism's most important national treasures.

Sōkkuram, the Stone Cave Hermitage, is a Pulguk-sa annex several miles northeast of Pulguk-sa proper. It is a grotto temple, set among pines and maples, which enshrines a white gran-

The Sōkkuram Grotto at Kyōngju.

ite Sōkkamoni Buddha image considered by some art historians to be the most perfect Buddha image of its kind anywhere. Unlike grotto temples in other parts of Asia, Sōkkuram was not carved out of granite hillside or built inside an existing cave. Rather, it's an artificial chapel built of large granite bricks placed on a summit.

The government has created what is probably the most complete resort complex in Korea—the **Bomun Lake Resort**, a sprawling playland about four miles east of Kyōngju proper. Deluxe-class hotels, a 900-seat convention hall, 18-hole golf course, a folk arts amphitheater and a lakeside marina with a posh clubhouse are but a few of the amenities which await Kyōngju tourists who stay at Bomun Lake.

Also high on the Kyōngju must-do list is the impressive **tomb of General Kim Su-yin**, which is rimmed by superbly-carved stone zodiac figures; the **Punhang** (Famous Emperor) temple with the oldest datable pagoda in Korea; and **O-nūng**, the serene five mounds memorial park on the south side of Kyōngju.

Pusan: Wedged between a range of mountains and the sea is the big port of **Pusan**, about 60 miles (100 km) south of Kyōngju. For those willing to dare the murky waters of **Pusan Harbor**, **Songdo Beach** is just a stone's throw southwest of **City Hall**. Somewhat cleaner waters are available at three sandy beaches to the east of the city. The most popular is **Haeun-dae**, which has good hotels and a properly bustling resort town.

A few small Buddhist temples are scattered around town and two large, important ones are within easy reach by bus or taxi. **Pomo-sa**, the closer of the two and the headquarters of the Dyana sect, is a mountain temple a few miles from **Tongrae Hot Springs**.

T'ongdo-sa is about half an hour to the north along the highway to **Taegu**. With a total of 65 buildings, T'ongdo-sa is Korea's largest temple. Virtually every major Buddhist deity is honored in a separate shrine in the central cluster of buildings. The buildings themselves comprise an unusual variety of exceptional architecture, some of which are left pleasantly unpainted or faded to the muted brown of weathered pine.

he ntrance to 'ongdo-sa.

CHEJU-DO

The egg-shaped isle of **Cheju-do** lies about 93 miles (150 km) south of Pusan in the channel between Korea and Japan.

Cheju can boast to be home of the world's longest known lava tubes—the **Snake** and **Manjang caverns** located at **Kim Nyōng** between **Cheju City** and **Sōngsanp'o**. The Manjang cavern, the longer of the two tubes, is over four miles long with a diameter that ranges from 10 feet to 66 feet.

Cheju-do is one of Asia's great vacation idylls. She can be easily reached—either by ferries from Pusan or **Mokp'o**, or by regular flights from Seoul or Pusan.

It was during the reign of Koryō King Kojong (1214-1260) that Cheju received its present name. *Che* means "across' or "over there." And *ju* in earlier times referred to an administrative district. Therefore, Cheju is the *do*, island, in the "district over there."

In the 13th century, Cheju-do became a Mongol possession for about 100 years (from 1276 to 1375). These Mongol conquerors permanently altered Cheju ways. The present-day dialect (unlike the languages spoken on the Korean mainland) is a direct result of the Mongol influence. Through them, Cheju became a stock-raising area and a famous breeding area for horses. Buddhism was also brought to Cheju by the Mongols along with temples and statues.

The first Westerners to visit and tell the outside world about Cheju-do (and Korea proper) were Dutch sailors who were shipwrecked at **Mosūlp'o** on Cheju's south shore in 1653. Cheju-do didn't become a tourist destination until about two decades ago.

The idyllic Cheju-do situation has changed considerably. The island is now crisscrossed and circled with paved streets and highways and dotted by hotels and *yogwan* (inns). And at the **KAL Hotel** in Cheju City you can even retire to a proper casino for high-stakes games of chance.

Among the island's attractions are Cheju-do's superb beaches. Favorite crescents of sand are located at **Hyōpje**, **Kwakji**, **Hamdōk** and **Sōngsan** along Cheju's upper half, and at **Hwasun**, **Chungmun** and **P'yōson** in the south sector. Most of these spots feature superb seafood restaurants.

At the **Hallim weavers village** on the northwest shore you'll find the **Hallim Handweavers** complex where Koreans trained by Columban Roman Catholic priests and nuns are creating some of the finest Irish woolens outside of Ireland. This village's unusual cottage industry was begun in the 1960s by an Irish priest who imported about 500 Japanese and New Zealand sheep to this natural grazing spot.

At the Handweavers factory you can watch Koreans shear sheep, then wash, card, spin, warp, thread, weave, check, tenter and steam raw wool into a weavable product. Only traditional Irish patterns are created by Hallim's industrious "Irish of the Orient."

The series of waterfalls on both the east and west sides of lovely **Sōgwip'o Town** are unique. The strong **Chōngbang Falls** right in Sōgwip'o town is often referred to as "the only waterfall in Asia that plunges directly into the sea."

The *tol-harubang*, or grandfather stones, are carved lava rock statues, 52 in all, which can be seen on all parts of Cheju-do. Good places to study these images up close are at the entrance to the **Samsonghyōl Museum** in Cheju City or in front of **Kwandok-jōk-jōng** (a 15th-century pavilion, and the oldest standing building on Cheju-do, which faces Cheju City's main square).

Koreans also suggest a visit to **Yongdu-am**, or "Dragon's Head Rock," on the sea in Cheju City's western suburbs near Cheju's main airport.

Probably the most dominant memories one will have of this island after a proper tour will be of its famous diving women, awesome **Mount Halla** (the highest in the country), and if you visit in the springtime, brilliant fields of mustard blossoms that paint broad yellow splotches across Cheju-do's pasturelands. Cheju-do's diving women, called *haenyo*, have long been a symbol of this island and its purported matriarchal culture.

When sea and weather conditions are favorable, scores of the *haenyo*, who range from teenagers to wrinkled grandmothers, can be seen bobbing offshore between free dives for seaweed, shellfish and sea urchins.

Right, masking one's emotions is an Asian trait.

MALAYSIA: THE PERFECT TRAVEL CURE

The tourist brochures modestly claim that "only Malaysia . . . has it all." And so it does. Picturesque fishing villages, cozy hill resorts, unexplored tropical forests and miles of empty white sand beaches. Mix into these scenes the cultural pastiche that is the Malaysian people, and the result is an irresistible combination of rural charm, intriguing lifestyles and a slight but ever-so-appealing hint of adventure that's guaranteed to send expectant visitors to travel heaven.

And that's just the tip of the coconut tree. Malaysia's multitudinous attractions also include traditional arts and crafts, colorful religious festivals and copious amounts of comestibles to pacify even the most epicurean tastes. In fact, sampling some mouth-watering Malaysian food comes close to being a religious experience in itself.

Situated smack in the middle of Southeast Asia, with a total land area of 132,000 square miles (342,000 square km), Malaysia is about the size of Japan, but with only a fraction of the population (about 15 million compared to Japan's 121 million). Peninsular Malaysia accounts for 40 percent of the land area, and 86 percent of the population. The East Malaysian states of Sabah and Sarawak are separated from the peninsula by 400 miles (640 km) of the South China Sea, but each of the 13 states has a charm and character of its own. Malay and indigenous tribes make up over half the population while Chinese, Indians and others also come under the broad spectrum that is covered by the term "Malaysian."

The country's economy is based mainly on agricultural commodities, and it is one of the world's major suppliers of tin, palm oil and rubber. Since achieving independence from colonial rule in 1957, Malaysia has faced a series of internal and external economic and political pitfalls. It has emerged each time with the same clear-eyed determination to succeed.

Despite some physical changes, the inevitable outcome of living in an age of rapid development and high technology, Malaysia is still very much a land of *kampungs* (villages), jungles, beaches and rice fields, made that much more appealing by a friendly, deeply religious and uniquely diverse group of peoples. Malaysia really does have it all.

Preceding pages: Main gasing (top spinning) is a popular Malaysian sport. Left, Muslim girl reflects the face of Malaysian youth.

THE LONG ROAD TO "MERDEKA"

Mula-mula. In the beginning. Traditional Malay tales of the country's origins always began with the words "*Mula-mula . . .*," and if archaeological findings are to be believed, it all started back in 35,000 B.C. That's when the skull of possibly the first *Homo Sapiens* in the East was found in Sarawak's Niah Caves. In the Malay peninsula, stone implements found in the limestone hills of Perak provided further evidence, although these date back only 10,000 years. Without doubt, though, Malaysia's strategic position, its abundant natural resources and ability to support human communities helped to make it an easy and logical place to settle.

Of present-day inhabitants, the earliest are the *Orang Asli* in the peninsula and similar tribes in Sabah and Sarawak, who still pursue a nomadic way of life. Their ancestors wandered down the peninsula from Yunnan in Southwest China, going through the mainland to the Indonesian archipelago and beyond. They were followed by the more sophisticated Proto-Malays, who probably established themselves around 2,000 B.C. Along the way, considerable seafaring and navigational skills were acquired. The next wave of immigrants (Deutero-Malays) came equipped with knowledge of new agrarian skills, settling into the small, self-contained communities which have developed into the complex ethnic pattern of Malaysia and Indonesia today. The Malays of the peninsula had practically indivisible links with their counterparts in Sumatra, just across the Straits of Malacca.

Today, the peninsular Malays, along with the *Orang Asli* ("original people"), make up the indigenous peoples of Malaysia, and are collectivelly called *bumiputera*, or "sons of the soil." While differences do exist in the makeup of the various *bumi* groups, certain characteristics are shared, especially those rooted in the agricultural-seafaring economy and the village society that are even now so much a part of Malaysia.

Around the first century B.C., initial trading contacts were made between the peninsula and more established trading powers, particularly China and India. Over the next thousand years, Hindu and Buddhist elements of the Indian culture left their mark on the region, especially in the areas of language and social customs. These influences began to fade around the 14th century with the introduction of Islam into the area by Indian and Arab traders.

Islamic conversion in the peninsula centered around Malacca, a coastal village which had risen to prominence as a strategic trading post. Malacca was founded in 1403 by the Sumatran prince Parameswara, and his settlement blossomed into a prosperous and widely-respected port. Among its admirers was Admiral Cheng Ho, the famous "Three-Jewel Eunuch," envoy for the emperor of China. Parameswara paid a

reciprocal visit to China, where the emperor extended him his protection and proclaimed him to be king of Malacca and beyond. Parameswara's successors later extended the Kingdom to include the entire south of the peninsula. Malacca's status increased dramatically, while Parameswara and his heirs also ensured that Islam would be the religion of the realm. The Kingdom of Malacca dominated the Straits of Malacca for 100 years, a period which marks the classical age of Malay culture. Indeed, most of the peninsular states can trace their beginnings back to the Malacca sultanate.

In 1511, colonialism arrived in the form of a large Portuguese fleet led by Alfonso de Albuquerque, the architect of Portugal's expansion plans in Asia. Malacca fell to a Portuguese assault, forcing the reigning sultan and his family to flee and establish themselves in other states. The Portuguese administrators lasted until 1641, when Dutch forces stormed the Portuguese-built *A Famosa* (The Famous) fort and turned Malacca into an ordinary outpost of the Dutch empire. The Dutch government had already decided that Batavia (now Jakarta) was to be their capital. Malacca's halcyon days were over.

After the Dutch, it was Britain's turn to show the flag out East. This they succeeded in doing in 1786, when Captain Francis Light of the British East India Company secured trading rights on the island of Penang, off the peninsula's northwest coast. Meanwhile, Malacca was also transferred to the British in 1795, at the time of the Napoleonic Wars, part of a Dutch attempt to forestall the French from taking over.

The Dutch formally ceded Malacca to Britain under the Anglo-Dutch Treaty of 1824. According to the terms of the treaty, the Dutch gave up all their territory on the Malayan peninsula and the British gave up theirs in the East Indies, promising not to interfere in each other's domain.

In 1826, British domination of the peninsula became apparent when Penang joined Singapore and Malacca as part of the newly-established Straits Settlements, a Crown Colony headed by a British governor. Six years later, the seat of British administration was transferred from Penang to Singapore, which by 1860 succeeded Penang and Malacca to become the area's premier port.

In 1874, the governor, Sir Andrew Clarke, arranged for the appointment of British Advisers to Perak, Selangor and Sungei Ujong, although it was not until 1891 before the system became acceptable. This led to the formation of the Federated Malay States of Selangor, Perak, Negri Sembilan and Pahang in 1896. The remaining four northern states of Kedah, Perlis, Kelantan and Trengganu, along with the southernmost state of Johore, became the Unfederated States of Malaya.

While affairs on the Malay peninsula were taking shape, the territories on the island of Borneo were themselves in a state

Left, Alfonso de Albuquerque led the wave of colonizers. Above, Malacca was once a bustling trading port.

of flux. Locals in Sarawak, a province of the Brunei sultanate, were voicing dissent against misrule by the governor there. Enter James Brooke, an English adventurer who happened to be sailing around the region. He first landed in Sarawak in 1839 and within two years, found himself installed as the Rajah of Sarawak, his reward for helping to put down a local rebellion. Brooke and his successors ruled Sarawak for over a hundred years, bringing it out of the dark ages by clamping down on the activities of head-hunting natives and expanding trading ties.

In North Borneo, the British North Borneo Company had a rebellion of its own to deal with. Achieving local acceptance of white rule was not as easy, and recurring resistance was encountered until the Company finally gained full control with the death of local rebel chief Mat Salleh in 1900.

The British spent the next 40 years consolidating their already formidable position in Malaya. One of their better experiments had been the planting of nine Brazilian rubber trees in 1878, an action which attracted little attention until John Dunlop invented the pneumatic tire and Henry Ford put the automobile on the assembly line. The man responsible for the crop that would take up three-quarters of all developed land in the nation was Henry Ridley, Director of the Botanic Gardens in Singapore. Tin mining, the province of the Chinese community, was already in full tilt.

Colonial supremacy suffered a rude awakening in 1941 with the invasion of Japanese forces. For three-and-a-half years, British, Malay and Chinese guerrilla fought World War II from their jungle bases. In September 1945, colonial authority was re-established by the British Military Administration. However, the Japanese experience had unleashed the potent and determined forces of nationalism. The British were faced with a totally new political environment, and a change became inevitable.

The Straits Settlements were dissolved, with Penang and Malacca joining the Malay states of the peninsula to form a new Malayan Union, which was intended to have a central government and a governor. Sovereignty was to shift from the sultans to the Crown, in effect turning the whole country into a colony. The idea did not go down well with the Malays, and in March 1941, delegates from 41 Malay associations met in the capital, Kuala Lumpur, to oppose the Union. The United Malay National Organisation (UMNO) was born. As a consequence, the British abandoned the Union scheme and established instead the Federation of Malaya in 1948, which provided for the sovereignty of the sultans. The Federation consisted of all nine peninsular Malay states, plus Malacca and Penang, to be united under a federal government and headed by a British High

Commissioner. Singapore remained a colony and was later joined by North Borneo and Sarawak, which did not have the resources to continue being run by the North Borneo Company and the Brooke family, respectively.

By agreement, the Federation was the first step on the road to independence. Apart from nationalist pressure, the threat of communism also served to accelerate the independence process. Jungle-based guerrillas attacked colonial estates and harassed villages in a 12-year "war of nerves" against British security forces. Known as the Emergency, this period lasted until 1960, by which time most of the communists had been wiped out. In fact, the threat had sufficiently diminished by 1955 that the

first federal elections could be held. UMNO and the Malayan Chinese Association (MCA), the two principal communal parties, formed an alliance with the Malayan Indian Congress (MIC), winning 51 out of the 52 seats contested. The Alliance, led by Tunku Abdul Rahman, successfully pressed for independence and *Merdeka* ("freedom") was attained on August 31, 1957. The Tunku became the Federation of Malaya's first prime minister. Two days later, the *Yang di-Pertuan Agong*, "King and Ruler of the Federation of Malaya," performed a symbolic ceremony of acceptance of office by unsheathing his gold Kris of State and kissing its blade.

Left, Merdeka! Tungku Abdul Rahman at the proclamation of independence, 1957. Above, modern-day religious architecture.

By 1961, after a sustained period of progress and reform, Tunku mooted the idea of a new political entity called Malaysia, to include Malaya, Singapore, North Borneo, Sarawak and Brunei. Apart from Brunei, which opted out, the other territories voiced their enthusiasm for the plan. Considerable opposition, however, came from Indonesia, which denounced the scheme as a "neo-colonialist" plot and the Philippines, which staked a claim to North Borneo. In 1963, Indonesia embarked on a policy of "Confrontation," which included armed incursions across the borders of North Borneo (renamed Sabah) and Sarawak from Indonesian Kalimantan. A United Nations survey confirming the desire to join the Federation was rejected by both Indonesia and the Philippines. Nevertheless, the Federation of Malaysia was inaugurated on September 16, 1963. By 1966, a new Indonesian government had dropped its aggressive stance, as did the Philippines in 1977. Singapore, meanwhile, had left the Federation in 1965, becoming a sovereign state in its own right.

In 1970, the widely-revered "Father of Malaysia," Tunku Abdul Rahman, retired, handing over the reins to Tun Abdul Razak. He in turn was followed by Datuk Hussein Onn in 1976 and in 1981 by the current prime minister, Datuk Seri Dr. Mahathir Mohamad. They have steered Malaysia on a course of continued progress and economic development to the stage where its people now enjoy one of the highest standards of living in Southeast Asia. The country's New Economic Policy (NEP) was introduced to encourage a fairer distribution of wealth among racial groups. Under the NEP, development corporations and share ownership schemes were set up to ensure greater *bumiputera* involvement in all areas of the economy. Recent declines in major commodity prices have hindered progress, and along with many other developing nations, Malaysia has adopted a program of austerity to help weather the bumpy seas ahead. It has taken many centuries to cultivate a national identity, emerging from the yoke of colonialism and the trauma of invasion. Armed with the knowledge of times gone by, and fostered by a strong nationalistic spirit, Malaysians can look ahead to the 21st century with the realization that as a nation, Malaysia has really come of age.

BELL

KUALA LUMPUR

"In the beginning, there was nothing but a lot of mud . . . " Thus might begin an accurate but deceptively unappealing chronicle of **Kuala Lumpur's** origins. Returning to its roots might seem redundant, as the federal capital, situated in the heart of the peninsula, has never really left its past behind.

Despite the proliferation in recent years of highways, high-rises and high society, 'KL' is still very much a 'down home' kind of town. Somehow, the seemingly incongruous blend of past and present, eastern mysticism and western technology, are able to gel into a unique entity, and one that works to boot.

On narrow city streets and six-lane super highways, expensive European cars and more modest Japanese makes rub hubcaps (often quite literally, given the Malaysian drivers' natural affinity for bumper-bashing) daily with a growing rash of Proton Sagas, Malaysia's national car since 1985, the product of a joint M$230 million (US$88 million) project between the government and its Japanese partners.

Meanwhile, concrete, steel and glass high-rises of every conceivable design sprout up almost indiscriminately amongst the older, more sedate buildings of the colonial past. And at night, as roadside hawkers enjoy a brisk business, royalty and the jet set hobnob with mere mortals in chic meeting spots like the Tin Mine nightclub, its name a somewhat ironic reminder of the city's humble beginnings.

About 130 years ago, Kuala Lumpur was a precise representation of what its name means in Malay: muddy river mouth. At that time, a group of tin prospectors, financed by the local Malay chief, journeyed upriver to the confluence of the less-than-crystal-clear waters of the **Klang** and **Gombak rivers**. Things eventually "panned" out for them and those that followed, having discovered an abundance of tin slightly inland at **Ampang**.

eceding ges: Old d new erge as e in ala mpur. ft, local ungster. ght, Mesjid me and conut lms.

Under Yap Ah Loy, the tough, astute administrator appointed by the local sultan to keep the peace among unruly Chinese miners, and later Frank Swettenham, the British Resident of Selangor, Kuala Lumpur blossomed into a Southeast Asian boom town. Supported by a rapidly-expanding infrastructure and growing lines of communication, then nourished by the tin and rubber bonanzas, KL quickly achieved capital city status.

In 1974, the 98 square miles (244 square km) encompassing the city and its population (currently one million) was formally declared the Federal Territory, separate from its mother state of Selangor.

The Old City: Visitors today to the still-muddied confluence of the Klang and Gombak rivers will find the magnificent **Mesjid Jame**. Built in 1909 and nestled in a picturesque grove of coconut palms, Mesjid Jame is adapted from a Moghul mosque of North India, although it was designed by an Englishman, A.B. Hubbock. Accessible from **Jalan Tun Perak**, the mosque features a walled courtyard, or *sahn*, and a three-domed prayer hall flanked by two minarets rising above the height of the palms.

Behind the mosque, starting from the corner of **Jalan Tuanku Abdul**

Rahman and **Jalan Raya**, sits a line of former colonial-built public buildings, all designed in the distinctive Moorish style deemed appropriate for an Islamic country. Each was the creation of A.C. Norman, a colleague of Hubbock's in the Public Works Department. The **Information Department**, old **City Hall**, **High Court**, the **Secretariat** (now the Sultan Abdul Samad Building which houses the Supreme Court) and the former **General Post Office** were all completed around the turn of the century. They remain impervious to the changing times, functional and visually stunning monuments to an elegant past.

Across from these buildings is another product of Norman's fertile mind, the **Royal Selangor Club**, a mock-Tudor sports and social club that became the center of colonial society after its construction in 1890. Fronting the club is an expanse of green known as the **Padang**, on which some of the more notable social virtues, such as drinking tea and playing cricket, were practiced, and still are to this day. The Padang is also the venue for Independence Day celebrations, held on August 31 each year.

Festivities of a different kind are held each night at the Padang, as local transvestites and transsexuals make the rounds, like models on a catwalk, adding some local color (literally!) to the neighborhood.

Not to be outdone by the prolific Mr. Norman, Hubbock produced the twin Moorish wonders of the **Malaya Railway Administration Building** and the **Kuala Lumpur Railway Station**, which together give new meaning to the word grandoise. The station, in particular, with its profusion of turrets, spires, minarets and domes, resembles nothing so much as the Eastern prototype of Disney's Fantasyland.

Opposite the station, on **Jalan Sultan Hishamuddin**, is the former Majestic Hotel, KL's contribution to grand colonial hostelries. Rescued from the wrecking ball in 1983, it has been converted into the **National Art Gallery**, housing a permanent collection of works by Malaysian artists.

The milky-white **Dayabumi Complex** on **Jalan Raya**, next to the old post office, is an interesting combination of Arabic and modern high-rise archi-

More Moorish: the KL Railway Administration Building.

tecture. This government office-cum-shopping center also houses the new **Central Post Office**. For an elevated view of the city, take a ride to the building's 30th floor.

A pedestrian bridge across the Klang River links the complex with the **Central Market**, a 1936 Art Deco-style former produce market which has been spruced up in an effort to become KL's answer to London's Covent Garden and Boston's Quincy Market. The high-ceilinged, block-long structure now sports a pastel pink and baby-blue facade, central airconditioning and a trendy wine bar. Although it contains the usual souvenir shops and fast food outlets, Central Market is also a cultural showcase for Malaysian arts and crafts. On weekends especially, artists and artisans can be found demonstrating such skills as woodcarving, painting and jewelry-making.

The spiritual center of Kuala Lumpur, and indeed the symbol of Islam for the whole country, is the **Masjid Negara**, or National Mosque. Built in 1965 and occupying a 13-acre (5.2-hectare) landscaped site on Jalan Sultan Himshamuddin, the complex is dominated by a jagged, star-shaped dome, and a single minaret rising 240 feet (73 meters) from the center of a fountain area. The 18-point dome represents Malaysia's 13 states and the five pillars of Islam. One of the largest in the region, the mosque blends traditional Muslim decorative art with modern-day interpretations of Islam. The **Grand Hall** can accommodate 8,000 people and is busiest on Fridays, the Muslim holy day.

Situated on an incline overlooking **Jalan Travers**, about a 15-minute walk away, is **Muzium Negara** (National Museum). It features a traditional Malay-style roof and two large murals of Italian mosaic which flank the main entrance. Among the museum's varied collection of "Malaysiana" is a life-size exhibit depicting a royal wedding and the circumcision ceremony of a prince.

Near the museum is the southern entrance to the **Lake Gardens**, a gently-undulating, flower-carpeted and tree-lined 173-acre (70-hectare) oasis that also holds the **Parliament House**, **National Monument** and a sizable lake.

Chinatown marks a distinct shift from the tranquil splendor of the Lake

Padang fronts the Sultan Abdul Samad Building.

Gardens. A concentrated area of frenetic activity near the Central Market, Chinatown is bounded roughly by **Jalan Bandar**, **Jalan Petaling** and **Jalan Sultan**. Along these and adjoining side streets, a dazzling array of textiles, fruits, flowers, live animals, herbal medicines and other exotic delicacies are available at all hours of the day, it seems. Organized chaos, more commonly known as shopping, reaches a frenzied peak at dusk, when the middle section of Jalan Petaling is cordoned off and transformed into an open-air night market (*pasar malam*). Here, skills in the noble art of sidestepping pedestrian traffic while keeping an eye out for useful bargains are honed to perfection.

Lining the streets and sidewalks around Chinatown after dark are a variety of mobile kitchens, manned by hawkers who set up shop in narrow alleyways and along the walls of commercial buildings. The quality of fare offered by these itinerant food vendors is almost uniformly excellent. The Malay equivalent of these sidewalk cafes can be found several blocks north at the **Munshi Abdullah** stalls on **Jalan Dang Wangi** and the **Campbell** stalls that appear at night in the nearby parking lot.

Fine examples of religious architecture can also be digested in this section of town. The elaborate, wildly decorative **Sri Mahamariamman Temple** on Jalan Bandar was built in 1873. Here, Hindu worshippers offer prayers to the four-armed Lord Murugan, his two wives and a six-armed goddess.

Two prominent illustrations of Chinese temples are the typically ornate **Chan See Shu Yuen Temple** at the southern end of Jalan Petaling, and the historic Taoist **Sze Ya Temple**, opposite Central Market off **Jalan Hang Kasturi**, built by Yap Ah Loy in the 1880s.

Shopping for local goods is concentrated around Jalan Tuanku Abdul Rahman, **Jalan Tun Perak** and **Jalan Masjid India**. All the trappings of big city life, meanwhile, can be found around **Jalan Ampang** and **Jalan Bukit Bintang**. They are major arteries of the **Golden Triangle**, a district cluttered with tall office blocks, shopping centers, five-star hotels and enough nightlife to satisfy even the most discriminating insomniacs.

The Sri Mahamariamman Temple is a riot of design and color.

OUTSIDE KUALA LUMPUR

Petaling Jaya (PJ), the country's first satellite town just six miles (10 km) from KL on the southbound **Federal Highway**, is typical suburbia, with a dose of 'modern industrial' thrown in as an afterthought. The town of 250,000 is fully self-contained, and while offering little by way of tourist sights, has become something of a drawing card for baby boomers from the big city (KLuppies?) who come to seek respite from the upscale, up-market amusements available in the Golden Triangle. PJ's more laid-back style, from its open-air hawker centers to its smoke-filled jazz-and-gin joints, is a welcome and attractive entertainment alternative.

Some eight miles (13 km) north of the capital on the **Ipoh Highway**, meanwhile, lie the **Batu Caves**, an imposing limestone outcrop dotted with numerous huge caverns. Discovered a hundred years ago, the caves themselves date back about 400 million years. The caverns are a mine of scientific information, but are better known as the site of the Hindu community's *Thaipusam* Festival, held early each year in honor of the deity Lord Murugan. Chanting devotees carry a statue of the deity up the 272 steps that lead to a shrine within the caves. To seek penance, the entranced worshippers each carry a *kavadi*, an elaborately-decorated wooden frame supported by piercing the bearer's flesh with a variety of skewers and hooks, to no apparent discomfort. Accompanied by the incessant beat of Indian drums and shouts of encouragement from thousands of followers and spectators, the procession to the **Cathedral Cave** is visual testimony to the power of religious conviction.

If, after a visit to Batu Caves the desire for wide-open spaces becomes overwhelming, head for **Templer Park**, a 3,000-acre (1,200-hectare) nature reserve located several miles farther north. Within its luxuriant green boundaries are numerous waterfalls, pools and jungle walks, all designed to remove stress induced by city life. **Mimaland**, a similar distance from Batu Caves, but on the old **Pahang Highway** heading northeast, is a 300-acre (120-hectare) recreational park featuring more lush gardens, a lake for fishing and boating, an enormous free-form pool and a mini-zoo to keep the children occupied. It's popular with the locals, so avoid going on weekends.

Hill Stations: Genting Highlands, a modern hill resort boasting Malaysia's only casino, claims to meet the needs of the non-gamblers as well, but don't bet on it. True, the excellent golf course, other man-made attractions and cool temperatures near the top of the 5,600-foot (1,700-meter) summit are inviting enough, but there's no doubt that roulette, blackjack, baccarat and other games of chance are the prime time events. Everything else is strictly loose change. Genting is about 30 miles (50 km) from KL.

Chances are that low-rollers in search of a mountain retreat will instead head another 30 miles north to **Fraser's Hill**, slightly lower than Genting at 5,000 feet (1,500 meters), but sporting a more tranquil, relaxed atmosphere. Activity centers around the golf course and the highlight of the day is likely to be a jungle walk or a

avadi-arrying evotee eels little iscomfort.

swim at the base of **Jerlau Waterfall**. The resort is named after a British adventurer of the late-19th century, Louis James Fraser, who alledgedly operated a few questionable businesses from a shack hidden in the hills. The shack is gone, but a series of colonial bungalows, complete with neat little rose gardens, have taken its place, completing the cool, clean, countryside charm of the place.

Cameron Highlands, the largest and most extensive of the hill stations, lies in Pahang state, some 136 miles (220 km) north of Kuala Lumpur. After turning off the main Ipoh trunk road at **Tapah**, it's another 29 miles (46 km) along a narrow, twisting road hewn from the mountainside before reaching **Ringlet**, first of the area's three one-horse-townships. The main town of **Tanah Rata** is eight miles (13 km) farther on, and **Brinchang** lies another two miles (three km) up the road. Along the way, you're likely to encounter some *Orang Asli* (Original Man), indigenous blowpipe-toting aboriginal tribesmen who live in Malaysia's jungles. They sell fruits and carvings to passing motorists.

Ranging in altitude between 5,000 feet (1,500 meters) and 6,000 feet (1,800 meters), the highlands were discovered in 1885 by a government surveyor named William Cameron, who mapped the area and found "a fine plateau with gentle slopes shut in by lofty mountains." He was followed by a steady stream of tea planters, vegetable farmers and wealthy colonials seeking relief from the lowland heat and humidity. The colonials successfully sculpted Camerons into a tropical cousin of the English countryside, lining the main valley between Tanah Rata and Brinchang with Tudor-style homes overlooking a magnificent golf course. They added attractive rose and orchid gardens which have since blossomed into a budding horticultural industry, and strawberry patches a-plenty.

The unbeatable combination of its natural beauty, calm disposition and the soothing effect of its benign temperatures (between 70 F/21 C and 50 F/10 C) makes the Cameron Highlands a place for solitude and quiet reflection. It is one of Malaysia's most desirable destinations.

Panorama of the Cameron Highlands.

MALACCA

Strategically located on the **Straits of Malacca**, about 95 miles (150 km) south of Kuala Lumpur, **Malacca** (Melaka) is a town with a proud past. The Malay Prince Parameswara first established Malacca in the early-15th century, naming it after a tree he was standing near. It developed into a trading post and was visited in 1409 by the Ming emperor's envoy, Admiral Cheng Ho (the Three-Jewel Eunuch), who forged formal links with Malacca's rulers and built the port into a powerful trading center.

Chinese settlers from this period came to be known as *Babas* (Straits-born Chinese), representing a unique fusion of their traditional Chinese origins and the Malay environment. The Chinese were followed by a succession of European colonizers—the Portuguese in 1511, the Dutch in 1641 and the British in 1824. Architectural and cultural reminders of their time in Malacca are easily apparent, and this is what makes the place a historical gold mine, despite the recent appearance of modern buildings and hotels.

The richest vein is centered around the town's own version of red square, otherwise known as **Malacca Dutch Square**, which is flanked by the tell-tale salmon pink brick-and-laterite buildings constructed by the Dutch. The **Stadhuys** (Town Hall), which originally housed Dutch officials, was completed in the 1650s and is the oldest still-functioning Dutch building in the East. It has been converted into the Malacca Historical Museum, whose exhibits trace the city's history from the time of the ancient Malay kingdoms. Next door is **Christ Church** (1753), also unmistakably Dutch in origin. It was started in 1741 to commemorate the centenary of Dutch occupation.

On the south end of the square is **St. Paul's Hill**, with the ruins of **St. Paul's Church** at the summit. It was built by the Portuguese around 1590 on the site of a former chapel built in 1521. St. Francis Xavier first preached here in 1545, and was temporarily buried here

'iew of the 1alacca ₹iver has hanged ttle in ecent years.

in 1553. The ruins contain several large tombstones in Latin, Dutch and Portuguese. The hill itself was subsequently turned into a burial ground for Dutch notables in 1753. At the base of the hill is **Porta de Santiago** (Gateway of St. James), the only remaining relic of the Portuguese fortress **A Famosa** (circa 1512).

At one time, A Famosa encompassed the entire hill, its walls enclosing the European settlement, including a castle, two palaces and five churches. Later, Dutch colonialist restored the fort, but the British destroyed the fortifications in the early-19th century. Not far from the gateway is the **Melaka Sultanate Palace**, a recently-completed, artifact-filled replica of the 15th-century palace of Sultan Mansur Shah.

A short distance away on a hill overlooking the town are the ruins of **St. John's Fort**, a Dutch construction of the 1770s. Its appearance has been undermined somewhat by the 20th-century water treatment plant and high-rise apartment block on either side of it.

Near the back of town is **Bukit China**, "China Hill," an old Chinese cemetery which holds graves dating back to the Ming Dynasty. These are some of the oldest Chinese relics in the country.

A concrete bridge across the west side of Dutch Square leads to the old trading section of Malacca, known today as **Chinatown**. The area's most prominent landmark is the **Cheng Hoon Teng** (Green Cloud Temple) on **Jalan Tekong**, the oldest Chinese temple in the country. It was founded in 1645, with additions being made to the original structure in 1704 and again in 1804. Figures from Chinese mythology adorn the temple roof, ridges and eaves, made from broken porcelain and colored glass, which blend the three doctrinal systems of Taoism, Confucianism and Buddhism. The temple covers some 50,000 square feet (4,500 square meters) of land, an impressive size considering the close proximity of all the buildings in this part of town.

The **Kampong Keling Mosque** (1868) just up the road is of typical Sumatran design and features a three-tiered roof and beautiful carved wooded ceiling. Next door is the **Sri Poyyatha Vinayagar**

Baba architecture interior of the Tun Tan Cheng Lock house.

Moorthi Temple, built by the Hindu community in the 1780s. The deity Vinayagar is represented by a human body with four hands and an elephant's head.

One of the most well-known Malaccan streets is nearby **Jalan Tun Tan Cheng Lock**, named after a leading *Baba* who helped bring independence to Malaysia. The road is lined with ancestral homes of the *Babas*, whose narrow, long houses offer an insight into local architectural styles of two hundred years ago. Many houses have intricately-carved doors and interesting interiors, containing generations of family heirlooms and antiques.

A parallel street is **Jalan Hang Jebat** (formerly Jonkers Street and Jalan Gelanggang), featuring an assortment of antique shops. Anything from Victorian brass beds to Chinese rosewood furniture to vintage phonographs are waiting to be discovered, but don't expect to find anything rare unless you're ready to pay for it. The merchants here have long been sharpening their sales pitches and the real challenge is in bargaining them down to a mutually agreeable price. Local handicrafts and souvenirs can be found at the various beachfront bazaars.

The narrow streets and overall compactness of Malacca make it ideal to travel by pedal-powered trishaws. More in-depth exploration can easily be made on foot.

About a mile from the town square, descendants of the early Portuguese live in a seaside community known as the **Portuguese (Eurasian) Settlement**. Established in 1930, the settlement consists of a small number of *kampung*-style dwellings inhabited by residents who still speak *Cristao*, an Iberian-influenced dialect from which many Malay words are derived.

The main attraction of the settlement is a yearly festival based on the Feast of St. Peter (*Festa de San Pedro*), in which fishermen decorate their boats to be blessed by the parish priest.

A new structure, the government-built **Portuguese Square**, has several restaurants and shops that cater to visitors, but the settlement's charm remains in the older, well-established buildings. Similarly, the trappings of a bygone age are what make Malacca such an attractive place to visit.

olorful iles haracterize ypical Malaccan- tyle esign.

PENANG

Take one tropical island, add a luxurious beach resort, augment with a significant amount of history and toss in a liberal dose of superb local food. The result would be **Penang**, the "Pearl of the Orient." Pulau Pinang (Island of the Betelnut Palm), as it is also called, lies just off the northwest coast of the peninsula and is indeed a gem, touted as a veritable heaven on earth. Visitors will be hard pressed to deny it.

Originally a territory of the Sultan of Kedah, Penang was largely uninhabited until 1786, when the ubiquitous British East India Company decided to turn it into a commercial outpost, being as it was favorably located on the eastern end of the Indian Ocean. The island thus became the first British settlement in Malaysia, predating the other two "Straits Settlements" of Malacca and Singapore.

Since September 1985, the island's 114 square miles (285 square km) of territory have been linked to the peninsula by the five-mile (13-km)–long **Penang Bridge**. Previously, travelers had to fly in or come over on older but equally picturesque cross-channel ferries.

Apart from the bridge, and several new hotels, one of the few other visible signs of present-day influences on Penang is the **Komtar** government complex, a cylindrical skyscraper that dominates the island's main city of **Georgetown** (Bandaraya Tanjung).

Reminders of the past are much more evident. **Fort Cornwallis**, on the northeastern tip of the island, was the site of the first British camp. Built by convict labor at the turn of the 19th century, only its outer walls still stand. A stone's throw away are more colonial-style buildings. The **Supreme Court** and **Penang Museum** on **Leboh Farquhar** merit a visit.

A short stroll around old Georgetown is a fascinating cross-cultural education in religious diversity. Near the museum on **Leboh Pitt** is the **Kuan Yin Temple**, one of the oldest and most revered sites in Penang. Built over 150 years ago, it is crowded all year round, but especially so during Chinese New

Bridges from different ages: the Penang Bridge is brand new, the wooden bridge has been around a while.

Year, when good luck is at a premium.

In stark contrast nearby is the Indian-influenced **Kapitan Kling Mosque**, built by the island's first Indian Muslim settlers around 1800. Christian churches like **St. George's** (1818) on Leboh Farquhar are also in evidence.

Possibly the most well-known religious buildings in town, however, is the **Khoo Kongsi** at the junction of Leboh Pitt and **Leboh Acheh**. A *kongsi* is a clan house, part-temple and part-meeting place for Chinese of the same clan or surname. Built at the end of the 19th century and immediately re-done after a fire destroyed the original roof, Khoo Kongsi features an elaborate mixture of paintings, woodcarving and stonework.

The best way to shop in Georgetown requires a lot of poking around the narrow streets and alleyways by **Penang Road**, where there are a string of handicraft and antique shops. Nearby is **Leboh Campbell**, where it is possible to haggle with street vendors over the prices of nylon shirts, fake alligator-skin shoes and precious stones. The dusty streets in the area, with intriguing names like **Rope Walk** and **Love Lane**, are lined with a variety of shops hawking just about every imaginable type of paraphernalia, some of which might less charitably be described as junk. Still, the prospect of uncovering a memento or two to take home is always there. Any interests in *mahjong* sets, Chinese name seals, joss sticks and medicinal items are likely to be satisfied here.

A few miles out of Georgetown on a hill at **Air Itam**, the towering pagoda of the **Kek Lok Si Temple** can be spotted some distance away. This is the largest Buddhist temple in Malaysia and houses a large number of Buddha statuettes from different countries. Apart from the seven-story pagoda, the site also holds a three-tiered, multi-cultural temple, a turtle pond, souvenir shops and a giant statue of Kuan Yin, the Goddess of Mercy.

A short distance north of Kek Lok Si is the vintage funicular railway that leads up to the resort of **Penang Hill**. The half-hour ride (including a train change halfway up) to the cooler temperatures of the 2,700-foot (830-meter) hill will reward you with

omtar
mplex
wers over
eorgetown.

spectacular views of the island and across to the peninsula. With its pleasant gardens, a small hotel, temple, mosque and police station, life at the top is redolent of a more romantic age.

The dreamy-sounding **Temple of Azure Cloud** might turn out to be more of a nightmare for those with an aversion to snakes. At one time, this ordinary-looking temple about eight miles (13 km) south of Georgetown was a must on the tourist agenda. It's not everyday that green and yellow pit vipers can be found sliding up and down every altar, shrine and incense burner in a temple. Nowadays though, the serpentine slitherers are so few in number that a sleepy snake or two is about the most excitement one can hope for. In one of the rooms, two decidely non-aggressive-looking vipers spend their time posing for pictures with out-of-towners.

Where the sight-seeing ceases, the beach-bumming begins. Several luxury hotels are clustered at the **Batu Ferringhi** beach resort on the island's north coast. Here, the more tedious activities include sailing, riding, hiking or just lying around on sun-baked stretches of white sand beaches. The usual assortment of restaurants and art galleries offer some pleasing diversions. At nearby **Telok Bahang** is a charming fishing village while a mile further on is what is billed as the "world's largest butterfly farm," a large caged enclosure featuring many species of butterflies and plants.

Finally, no visit to Penang would be complete without tucking in to the taste-tempting, lip-smacking delights of local food. It is no exaggeration to say that Penangites enjoy some of the finest fare in the region. Despite appearances to the contrary, much of the best food is found at unfashionable roadside stalls and cramped coffee shops in the old section of town. Anything from Indian curry to Malay *nasi* (rice) to Chinese *Bah Kut Teh* (pork ribs in herbal soup) and Penang *laksa* (fish-based soup dish) should be willingly sampled at all hours of the day. At night, an even wider range is available. The hawker stalls and centers around Georgetown and especially along **Gurney Drive** and **Jalan Burma** are good spots for an initiation into some of the finer points of Penang gastronomy.

Shop shades protect from rain and help to advertise, too.

LAUGHING WITH LAT

Hanging in the bar of the Coliseum Cafe, a Kuala Lumpur landmark for over 60 years, is a cartoon of a local couple. They are hiding matter-of-factly behind a tablecloth while a waiter serves the cafe's famous smoke-and-oil-splattering 'sizzling steak' specialty. Uncaptioned, the amusing illustration still speaks volumes about one of the oddities of Malaysian life: a love of food while going to great lengths to avoid any inconvenience associated with it.

The cartoonist, himself a semi-permanent fixture at the cafe, is also something of a Malaysian institution. Mohammad Nor Khalid, better known as Lat, describes himself as "a midget approaching forty," which is typical of his self-deprecating style. His frank, humorous and highly perceptive pokes at Malaysian norms and life-styles have endeared him to his countrymen since 1973, when a depiction of his own circumcision ceremony appeared in *Asia Magazine.* His editorial drawings for a national daily and his ever-increasing collection of cartoon books are all eagerly digested by an adoring public. One former editor calls him a "folk hero and minor genius," a label Lat vigorously rejects.

Lat (for *bulat*, meaning round), was born and raised in a Malay *kampung*. It's no surprise that his most popular cartoons chronicle daily life in a typical village.

He appears in many of his drawings, either in the form of a mischievous *kampung* boy or a more grown-up, but equally recognizable version of himself. "You should look at yourself first rather than criticizing others," he maintains, adding that "once you draw yourself, you're safe . . . (in making fun of people)."

Much of his broad multi-racial appeal lies in the fact that he "cannot look at things the way a Malay looks. I have to look as it as a Malaysian." And while his characters speak both Malay and English, along with sprinklings of Tamil and Chinese, he avoids dialogue whenever possible, being a firm believer in the pictures-speak-louder-than-words school of thought.

On the other hand, Lat shuns being photographed in order to sketch his subjects and surroundings in relative annonymity, although he confesses that people still recognize him in the street. He relies mainly on personal experience, friends and his two young daughters for inspiration.

Despite his simple upbringing, Lat says he's no longer the innocent young man he was when he first started cartooning. In those early days, everything was fresh to him, including the time he saw people kissing in the street in London, something totally alien to his strict Muslim background.

Nowadays, the burdens of responsibility weigh more heavily on him, and he has gained the confidence to tackle the more serious issues of Malaysian life. He expresses a desire to produce animated cartoons and push public opinion to "a stage where people say, 'Don't take him seriously. It's only Lat and he's crazy.' " To Mohammad Nor Khalid, the best praises are undoubtedly those sung to music from a *Looney Tunes* cartoon.

EAST COAST

From **Butterworth** on the peninsula opposite Penang island, the **East-West Highway** runs a pleasant cross-country route some 224 miles (373 km) along the Thai-Malaysian border, offering scenes of rural Malaysia at its best. The highway ends at **Gerik**, after which the quality of the road tends to drop dramatically. About 60 miles (100 km) further on is **Kota Bahru**, capital of Kelantan and only a few miles from the Thai border. It is here that the charms of the **East Coast** becomes easily apparent. A big attraction here is the **Central Market**, a three-story complex where a mind-boggling selection of fish, fruits, vegetables, meats and dried goods is sold by women traders.

Slightly past the market is **Padang Merdeka**, site of the original state palace, **Istana Balai Besar**, built in 1844 and recently-restored. It is flanked by the state **mosque**, the state **parliament** and the state **museum**. The museum is a converted palace and offers a variety of cultural riches. Kelantan craftsmen are reputed to be the country's most skilled and the display of local pottery, silverware, costumes, kites (*wau*), giant tops (*gasing*), and antique birdcages is ample proof of that claim.

Kelantan is also the center of Malaysian batik and *sungkit* weaving. Young Malay girls turn balls of cotton and silk into yards of material with hand drawn, waxed-and-dyed designs. In addition to clothing, batik is used for many other aspects of the Malaysian lifestyle, from bedspreads to tablecloths and dish covers.

Just outside Kota Bahru is perhaps the most famous beach on the East Coast, **Pantai Cinta Berahi**, the romantically-named "Beach of Passionate Love." In actual fact, its white sands are little different from the miles of other beaches which line the coast.

South of Kota Bahru, the coast road runs beside a series of fishing villages and endless coconut palms before reaching **Kuala Trengganu**, capital of Trengganu. Boats can be hired from the jetty at the end of **Jalan Bandar** to journey along the **Trengganu River** .

East coast remedies: lots of beach and quiet.

The offshore islands of **Kapas** and **Redang** are also worthy sun spots, while postcard-perfect **Marang** gives a good idea of life in a coastal village.

About 30 miles (50 km) south of Kuala Trengganu, the beach at **Rantau Abang** is the scene of yearly migrations by giant leatherback turtles. They come back to this particular stretch of shore between May and September each year to lay their eggs. The slow-moving *penyu* (turtle in Malay), one of the country's prime attractions, has been adopted as Malaysia's tourism symbol. The sight of one of these benign giants laboring up the beach, digging a hole and depositing several dozen ping-pong-ball-sized eggs, then crawling its way back to sea, is an experience to treasure.

The government-run **Tanjong Jara Beach Hotel**, an attractive and comfortable resort built in traditional Malay style, is a pleasant base from which to conduct your turtle-watching activities.

Kuantan: Turtles can also be seen at the beaches around **Kuantan**, capital of Pahang. Here too, craftsmen are noted for their woodcarving and weaving skills. Off the coast lie several islands, each one a Mecca for the many swimming and diving enthusiasts who come between March and October each year (November to February being the monsoon season).

An excellent sidetrip from Kuantan is an unusual and mildly adventurous journey to **Lake Chini**. About 50 miles (80 km) from Kuantan towards Kuala Lumpur, an hour-long boat ride from **Kampung Tasek Chini** along the **Pahang and Chini rivers** leads to the lake, actually a series of 12 connecting bodies of water. Navigable all year (waterways are sometimes a little too shallow, and some pushing may be required), the lake is covered between June and September by a carpet of lotus blossoms. The shores around the lake are home to an *Orang Asli* village. While there are unmistakable signs of commercialism, Lake Chini remains a nature lover's sanctuary. Hundred-foot high trees are commonplace, as are many of Malaysia's numerous species of butterflies and birds. Stocked with an abundance of marine life, fishermen especially are apt to fall for the place hook, line and sinker.

'enyu vatching is lipping vonderful.

SABAH AND SARAWAK

Borneo. The name conjures up worlds-away images of primeval jungles, slow-winding rivers and primitive spear-wielding tribes. Occupying the north and northwest coasts of the world's third largest island, the East Malaysian states of **Sabah** and **Sarawak** combined are larger than peninsular Malaysia, although their populations account for only 14 percent of the country's 15 million people.

Sabah: Known as the Land Below the Wind because it lies below the typhoon belt, Sabah has a wealth of nature- and culture-related exotica to make any visit memorable. **Kota Kinabalu** (formerly Jesselton), the capital, is well-planned and relatively new, having being rebuilt after World War II. Taking pride of place is the gold-domed **State Mosque**, outside town on the way to the airport. Just south of the airport is a three-mile (five-km) stretch of beach at **Tanjung Aru**, which offers a resort hotel and glorious sunsets.

A two-hour drive away is the state's major attraction, the **Kinabalu National Park** and its centerpiece, the imposing **Mount Kinabalu** 13,330 feet (4,060 meters). It was named *Aki-Nabalu* ("home of the spirits of the departed") by the *Kadazans*, Sabah's indigenous population. The slopes leading to the summit are a botanical and ornithological paradise with over 800 varieties of orchids and 500 species of birds.

On Sabah's east coast about 240 miles (386 km) from Kota Kinabalu, is **Sandakan**, which serves as a loading point for the state's various commodities such as timber, rubber and rattan. Those wishing to chance a glimpse of the legendary "wild men of Borneo" should journey to **Sepilok Sanctuary**, 15 miles (24 km) from Sandakan, site of the world's largest *orang utan* reserve.

Sarawak: Once upon a time, a visit to the riverine state of Sarawak was likely to be a heady experience. Literally, that is. The *Ibans*, the state's largest indigenous group, were once belligerent headhunters, and even now, some *Iban* longhouses display the skulls of enemies taken from a long-ago encounter. For about a hundred years until the Japanese arrival on the island during World War II, Sarawak was also the private property of the White Rajahs, the family of British adventurer James Brooke, who was made Rajah after he helped to quell a local uprising.

The center of the White Rajah rule and gateway to a vast tropical hinterland is **Kuching**, perched on the banks of the **Sarawak River**. Although development has touched it in recent years, the town retains much of its steamy tropical charm, like something out of an *Indiana Jones* movie.

By far the best attraction in Kuching is the **Sarawak Museum**, which houses an amazing collection of archaeological and cultural artifacts, along with a huge variety of stuffed animals and birds from its jungle backyard.

Beyond Kuching, stay in an *Iban* longhouse, go on a safari up the **Skrang River**, hike in the primary forest of **Bako National Park**, and journey further to the **Niah Caves**. It's all part of an exhilarating education about this wonderfully diverse and ruggedly mysterious East Malaysian state.

Left, Mount Kinabalu. Right, Dayak woman is all ears in Sarawak.

THE PHILIPPINES: ASIAN FIESTA

The Philippines has long intrigued watchers of the Asian scene. The archipelago of some 7,000 islands continues to mystify with its curious turns of history and happenstance. "Discovered" in 1521 by a Spanish circumnavigating expedition led by Portuguese adventurer Ferdinand Magellan, the islands have since been referred to as having weathered colonization in the form of "four hundred years in a convent followed by fifty in Hollywood."

The long Spanish rule has left such an imprint on the Filipino that he is often called the Asian Latino. A sense of fiesta appears to be his hallmark of character, one that allows too for the imperative siesta—an indication of lassitude often traced to his legacy of tropical sun and lush nature setting.

It was said that the native could toss the remains of a meal out the window and expect to have a new crop beside him next season.

Fertile land was his birthright, together with the seas' munificence and a year broken simply into the rainy and the dry months.

No wonder then that when the Spanish arrived with Sword and Cross, they found a people unfamiliar with adversity, living gently off a collection of disunited islands ruled by small sultanates.

Proud regional differences have persisted to this day, having survived the waning Spanish empire as well as the second colonizing power that was the United States. The twin colonial experience certainly left its mark, but the result is uniquely Filipino.

The Philippines is the only predominantly Catholic country in Southeast Asia. Seventy years of English as the primary language of instruction makes it easier for the English-speaking visitor to strike up a conversation with a rural Filipino than any other Asian villager.

Long considered the least oriental of all Orientals, he enjoys a cuisine that is a sedate mixture of ascetic atoll diet, Chinese imagination and Spanish conservatism—with only a few areas where chillies come into their own.

The Filipino is also Asia's music man, marked by flair and friendliness, capriciousness and volatility, and an inordinate supply of unfailing good humor.

There is much contrariness, even contradiction, in the *Pinoy* (as the Filipino calls himself colloquially). But his innate Malay warmth and generosity, coupled with Latin temperament, allows for sudden shifts from Utopian optimism to moody fatalism. His odd mixture of brashness and grace, indeed, often makes the Filipino's fanciful act a hard one to follow.

Preceding pages: Rice-growing is big business in northern Luzon. Left, a sailor and seashells by the seashore.

A HISTORICAL QUILT

Lying between 21 degrees north latitude and 5 degrees north latitude on the westernmost rim of the Pacific Ocean, the Philippines is actually a series of half-drowned mountain ranges, part of a great cordillera extending from Indonesia to Japan. The country stretches 1,100 miles (1,770 km) from north to south, and spans 685 miles (1,102 km) at its widest point.

Of the total land area of 120,312 square miles (311,600 square km), 96 percent is taken up by 11 large islands, and less than one in 10 of the Philippines' 7,000-odd islands is inhabited. The two largest islands, Luzon and Mindanao, account for 65 percent of the total land area and contain 60 percent of the country's population of 56 million. The land mass of the archipelago, taken as a whole, is about the size of Italy, slightly smaller than Japan, and slightly larger than the British Isles. Yet with so many islands dotted across such a vast expanse of water, it is not surprising that the Philippines coastline is double that of the U.S.

The highest elevations in the Philippines are volcanic peaks. Twelve of these active and that many more either dormant or extinct, they are evidence of early linkage with that 'chain of fire' at the borders of the Pacific. The dramatic vulcanism of these island groups' first million years are recorded in the Philippines by present fracture lines running the length of the archipelago. Also along these fault lines is the Mindanao Trough (east of Mindanao island) whose recorded depth of 35,210 feet (10,705 meters) makes it the world's second deepest trench.

A full 60 species of Bornean plants are found in the southern islands of Mindoro, Palawan and Mindanao. Flora identified with Celebes and the Moluccas are widespread in the Philippines, mainly in the form of ferns, orchids, and a great wood, the *dipterocarp,* which makes up the country's primary forests as it does in Thailand, Indochina and Indonesia.

In the wilds of Palawan and Calamianes, the same mousedeer, weasel, mongoose, porcupine, skunk, anteater and otter are found as in Borneo's interior. Species of Palawan shrews, as well as a rare bat found in Mindanao, have kin in Celebes.

Fish in the waters of eastern Sumatra and western Borneo are much like those in southwestern Philippines, as are the fish between eastern Mindanao and New Guinea. Many Malaysian and Bornean birds make their home in Palawan.

The oldest human remains discovered in the country are the 1962 Tabon Cave find. High up a cliff facing the China Sea in Northern Palawan, the fossilized skullcap of a Tabon Woman was found with other human bones, flake tools and the fossilized bones of bats and birds. Carbon-dated at 22,000 B.C., Tabon Woman and her fellow cave dwellers have been tentatively identified as Australoid.

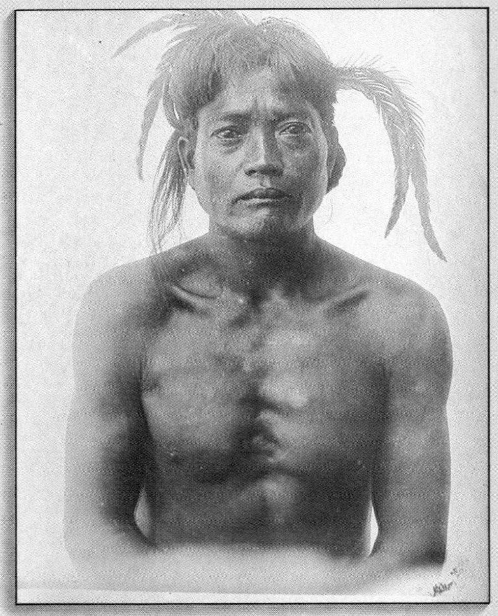

Should this identification be corroborated, the growing speculation that early man in the Philippines was part of a huge and fascinating family tree comes closer to proof. It was a tree that included, at its roots, the prehistoric progenitors of the Chinese and all the Asian races. According to this theory, the Filipino emerged from the same branch that brought forth the ancestors of all the Pacific Islands and Australia. Scientists suggest that the Austronesian civilization could be older than either the Chinese or the Indian, and that it had Southeast Asia as its hearth.

The Philippines joined this scenario around the third millennium B.C. when the

Austronesians came on outrigger canoes bearing pottery, wood carvings, barkcloth and the art of tattooing with a highly developed geometric art style. Today many cultural minorities, still living on the fringe of the predominantly Christian civilization of the country, utilize this style in their mats, hats, jewelry, weaponry, pots and cloth.

Ethnohistory weaves its dazzling colors into the Philippine cultural fabric. There are over three dozen major ethnic groups scattered in relative isolation about the islands, each keyed to unique warps and wefts of time and custom.

Close to 10 percent of the total population are designated cultural minorities. These five million people, eking out a living outside the cultural mainstream of Filipino Christian lowlanders, comprise the most diverse and exotic population of the country. Sixty percent of this ethnic minority are Muslim Filipinos, generally living in the southern islands of Mindanao and the Sulu Archipelago. The remaining peoples—native animists—color the most inaccessible mountain provinces of Northern and Central Luzon, and the highland plains, rainforests and isolated seashores of Mindanao and Palawan.

Considered as a whole, the Muslims—also called the Moslems or Moros, of old—constitute the largest cultural minority of the Philippines. They claim Mindanao and the Sulu Archipelago farther south as their own holy land, and until today they seek geographical and political autonomy from the national government far to the north. The Muslims, fiercely independent and pugnacious among themselves, are divided into five major groups: Tausug, Maranao, Maguindanao, Samal and Badjao.

Contact with the outside world had been minimal until about A.D. 1000, when Chinese, Indian, Arab and Indonesian traders brought in pottery, textiles, iron weapons, tools, jewelry and trinkets to barter for pearls, corals, gold and possibly rice, dried fish and handicrafts. They also introduced the first truly civilizing influences. By the 12th century the Chinese were supplying prestige wares which acquired ceremonial significance—pottery and metal objects, for example, which are now being recovered from ancient graves.

Early in the 14th century other traders introduced Islam, which swept through the

Left, Filipino native. Above, baptism scene from painting of the Magellan Cross.

Sulu Archipelago and farther north. The new faith served to consolidate and to invigorate little sultanates that were later very vigorously to resist the Spanish, the Americans and the Philippine national government.

The modern era in the Philippines dates from the arrival of Ferdinand Magellan on Samar Island (March 16, 1521). Magellan had set out on behalf of the King of Spain to find a route westward across the Pacific to tap the riches of the Indies. The "discovery" of the islands ended tragically when Magellan was killed shortly after in a skirmish with Lapulapu, petty chieftain of Mactan Island.

Four more Spanish expeditions failed to establish significant contact, and it was not until 1565 that Miguel Lopez de Legazpi, sailing from Mexico, gained a foothold in Cebu and claimed the islands of the archipelago in the name of King Philip II of Spain. Thus did the islands eventually gain the name *Filipinas*.

Bands of *conquistadores*, newly-arrived from Mexico, spread out to conquer Luzon and Visayas. They encountered little opposition, and soon entrenched themselves as lords of great estates worked by native peons. The accompanying friars quickly converted and civilized the population. The various religious orders competed vigorously with one another and with the civil and military authorities for prestige, privilege, power and wealth.

In the late-18th and early-19th centuries the Spanish effected important political, economic and social reforms, allowing some native participation in government, introducing sugar, tobacco, indigo and hemp as major cash crops, and ending the Manila Galleon monopoly on foreign commerce. But the reforms had been late in coming, and there was already an incipient nationalist movement led by the liberal clergy, professionals, and a clique of students in Spain.

Nationalist and revolutionary movements developed rapidly in the last two decades of the 19th century. Jose Rizal, Andres Bonifacio and Emilio Aguinaldo emerged as the leaders, respectively, of the Propaganda Movement (demanding Filipino equality with the Spaniards), the Katipunan (a secret society advocating armed insurrection), and the first declaration of a Philippine Republic (June 12, 1898).

In the meantime, Spain and America had gone to war on the question of Cuba. On May 1, 1898, while the Filipino revolutionaries marched on the capital, Commodore George Dewey sailed into Manila Bay and defeated the Spanish fleet. The Spanish commander surrendered the city after token resistance. With the end of the Spanish-American conflict, Spain ceded the Philippines, Puerto Rico and Guam to the U.S.

Filipinos had sided with the Americans against the Spanish, but were now angered because the Americans offered not independence but a new style of colonialism. The Philippine Insurrection against the Americans was not put down until 1902. The Americans, defining their role as one of trusteeship and tutelage, promoted rapid political, economic and social development. On November 15, 1935, the Philippines was constituted a Commonwealth with the promise of independence in 1945. But World War II intervened.

On December 10,1941, the Japanese landed an expeditionary force, which fought its way down the Bataan Peninsula (despite the heroic resistance of General Douglas MacArthur's American and Filipino troops), stormed the fortress island of Corregidor, occupied Manila, and overran the whole of the archipelago. As he made his escape from besieged Corregidor on May 6, 1941, General MacArthur pledged "I shall return"—and he did, on October 20, 1944, with a massive American invasion force.

With the aid of Fil-American troops who had campaigned as guerrillas during the three-year Japanese occupation, the Americans fought their way back into Manila in February 1945. The liberation of the Philippines cost the Filipinos enormous losses in lives and property, but it was greeted with jubilation.

Even after the granting of independence on July 4, 1946, Philippine-American relations have not been untroubled. The major conflicts have related to "parity" (special American business privileges), "bases" (American military installations), and what the Filipinos have perceived as an American conspiracy not just to develop but to dominate the local economy and to manipulate the nation's policies, politics and politicians.

Successive Philippine administrations have encountered staggering and monotonously recurrent problems. Ferdinand Marcos was elected President in 1965, declared Martial Law in 1972, and ruled with firm hand until political events coupled with long-standing social unrest conspired to end his 20-year rule. In 1986, a four-day bloodless revolution installed the popular Corazon Aquino, widow of an assassinated oppositionist, as President.

Current difficulties include a carry-over problematic economy and continuing insurgency. Among Filipinos long since impatient for efficient leadership, however, Mrs. Aquino enjoys tremendous support, and continues to raise much hope.

It speaks eloquently for the basic rationality and sobriety of the Philippines (despite the volatility that often comes to the surface) that the nation continues, in the face of awesome obstacles, to push bravely and optimistically forward.

Left, mural of country's national heroes. Above, Cory Aquino is all "dolled" up amongst her "people power" supporters.

P. CASTAÑEDA

P.CASTAÑEDA 1-77

Manila

The logical place to start on a tour of **Manila** would be **Fort Santiago**. It is easily reached by taxi from the **Ermita** district, the so-called "tourist belt" where most hotels are.

Manila is bisected by the **Pasig River**, so that most city areas are known to be either north or south of the Pasig. Fort Santiago is situated south, close to where the river empties itself into **Manila Bay**. On this site four centuries ago stood the bamboo fortress of Rajah Sulayman, a young warrior who ruled the palisaded city state of about two thousand inhabitants.

The Spanish conquistador Miguel Lopez de Legazpi arrived in 1571. He did battle and took over the ruins of Sulayman's fortress, which according to legend the recalcitrant chieftain razed to the ground upon sensing his impending defeat.

Legazpi founded Spanish Manila that same year, beginning construction of a medieval fortified town that was to become Spain's most durable monument in the East. The city fortress, an expanded version of the original Fort Santiago, and defended by moats and turreted walls 33 feet (10 meters) thick with well-positioned batteries, was called **Intramuros**, or "within the walls."

Four gates connected the Walled City to the outlying boroughs, where lived the *indios* (as the Spaniards called the natives), the *mestizos*, Chinese, Indians and other foreigners, including a number of Spanish commoners. Trade and commerce flourished to such an extent in these suburbs that they soon outstripped the city proper in area and population.

A tour through Intramuros should start from within the inner gate of Fort Santiago, where parapets allow one to walk around the well-preserved walls. A stately building houses the memorabilia of Dr. Jose Rizal, national hero. On another end of the quadrangle is **Rizal's Cell**, where he wrote his farewell poem to his people on the eve of his execution by the Spanish in 1896. The open-air courtyard beside it is now the **Raha Sulayman Theater**, where a theater group carries on a season of plays in Pilipino.

Across Fort Santiago is the **Manila Cathedral**, an imposing romanesque structure constructed of Philippine adobe.

Intramuros' perimeter measured some two-and-a-half miles (four km). Following Legazpi's blueprint for the capital, succeeding Spanish governors constructed 18 churches, several chapels, convents, schools, a hospital, a printing press, a university (as early as 1611), palaces for the governor general and the archbishop, soldiers' barracks and houses for the "in" community. These were laid out over a pattern of streets intersecting at right angles to form 64 blocks within an uneven pentagon served by seven gates.

The single structure spared (miraculously, say some) by the American bombing holocaust of 1945 is the **San** Agustin Church and Museum. Walk down **General Luna Street**, past the western side of the Cathedral, and after four short blocks you come upon the intersection of General Luna and **Calle Real**, the main street of Intramuros' fabled time. Here, incongruous Chinese lions carved of granite guard the

eceding
ges:
onkey-
ting eagle
an
dangered
ecies;
rnbill
ght) is
ore
undant.
ft, U.S.
luence is
parent in
games
ildren
ay. Right,
jeepney
a form of
nsport
d a work
modern
.

entrance to the church courtyard.

The original structure on this site, built of bamboo and *nipa* (a local palm), was the first church of Intramuros, constructed shortly after Legazpi defeated Sulayman in 1571. Another structure was started in 1599 and completed in 1606, and this is what remains to this day, surviving both natural and man-made calamities which have at one time or another leveled other old churches of Manila.

Adjoining the church is the monastery-museum containing a treasure trove of Philippine artifacts and religious art. Here on permanent exhibit are what remain of the vast collection amassed by the Augustinians in their 400 years' work in the islands.

Across the church courtyard is the **Plaza San Luis** complex, a block of reconstructed houses featuring antique galleries, restaurants, a cafe and **Casa Manila**, a museum replicating the aristocratic lifestyle at the turn of the century. Cultural presentations are performed in the courtyard as well as in the house proper, where costumed actors recreate a day in the life of old Intramuros.

From this area you have several options to continue your tour. You can turn eastward at Calle Real and prowl the remains of Intramuros till you reach **Muralla Street**. Here you can follow the walls or pass through one of the restored gates which will lead you back to the Pasig River or to a plaza called **Liwasang Bonifacio**. On this busy square is a statue of the revolutionary leader Andres Bonifacio. The plaza is bordered by the **Post Office Building** to the north, and to the east the newly-restored **Metropolitan Theater** with its original art deco appointments.

Between these two landmarks is a system of overpasses handling, at all hours, a great bulk of Manila traffic. The left lane leads to **Jones Bridge**, the center lane to **MacArthur Bridge**, and the right one to **Quezon Bridge**. These three bridges are the major passageways across the river, leading to the half of Manila known as "north of the Pasig."

If from San Agustin Church you turn left or westward at Calle Real, you wind up shortly at **Bonifacio Drive**, which leads southwards to **Roxas**

Manila's Roxas Boulevard is lined with impressive buildings.

Boulevard by the bay.

Bonifacio Drive ends where Roxas Boulevard begins, at the site of the vast **Rizal Park** formerly known as *Luneta* (or little moon, for its crescent shape), where Rizal was shot in 1896. Towards the right is the grand old **Manila Hotel**. At the central portion of the park is a monument to the hero, the object of much wreath-laying by visiting dignitaries the whole year round. It is under 24-hour guard, and the regular drill maneuvers of the sentries have become an attraction. This spot also has the distinction of being kilometer zero, or the point of reference in land travel throughout the island of Luzon.

Behind the **Rizal Monument** is a series of plaques on which are inscribed Rizal's poem *"Mi Ultimo Adios"* (My Last Farewell) in the original Spanish and in various translations. A marble slab marks the spot where Rizal met his martyr's death by musketry.

The central section where the monument stands is bordered by Roxas Boulevard to the west, **Kalaw Street** to the south, **Orosa Street** to the east, and **Padre Burgos Street** to the north. Close to the Burgos side are the **Japanese Garden** and **Chinese Garden**, which charge token fees for entrance. On this side too is the **City Planetarium**, where an audio-visual show is conducted twice daily.

On the Kalaw Street side of the park's central section is the **National Library**. The park's eastern section, across Orosa Street, is dominated by the **Ministry of Tourism Building**. Travelers may call upon the tourism staffers for guides, books, information and any such assistance. The eastern side is bounded by **Taft Avenue**, clearly the major artery cutting through the Manila "south of the river." Both Burgos and Kalaw streets end up at Taft Avenue. If you follow Burgos you reach the former **Legislative Building**, where the **National Museum** continues to be housed on a temporary basis. Proceeding northward through Taft Avenue, you pass the **Maharnilad** or Manila City Hall and end up at Liwasang Bonifacio, from where the three bridges give you options for further browsing north of the Pasig.

Directly across Taft Avenue from Rizal Park is the **Jai Alai Fronton**, the

Old postcard shows a Manila street scene.

first such establishment in Asia and one of the few outside Spain. Here, professional Spanish Basque and Filipino players perform a nightly treat for gambling *aficionados* and curious sightseers. The game, which is similar to squash except that the players use crescent-shaped wicker baskets called *cestas*, is fast and exciting, given to individual displays of high-leaping acrobatics, strength and agility.

From Taft, turn right at any of the perpendicular streets beginning with **United Nations Avenue**, where the **Manila Hilton** stands. This will lead to Ermita.

Ermita is an unusual district in many respects, its "tourist belt" reputation built on the strength of its proximity to Rizal Park and Manila Bay. Hotels and lodging houses are a dime a dozen in the area, in turn attracting a conglomeration of eateries, nightspots, beer gardens, boutiques, antique shops, handicraft and curio stalls, and travel agency offices. The two major streets, narrow enough to necessitate one-way traffic, are the southbound **M.H. del Pilar** and the northbound **A. Mabini**. On del Pilar Street is a gaudy bar strip where evenings find the ladies of the clubs airing themselves on the sidewalks to attract potential male customers. A-go-go bars featuring bikinied girls dancing onstage are the staple entertainment on the notorious del Pilar strip.

Scattered here and there within the area are more reputable nightspots featuring Filipino folk singers and rock and jazz groups. Here, still another facet of the Ermita spirit may be glimpsed—the bohemian character of its younger residents.

Also running parallel to the major Ermita streets is Roxas Boulevard by the bay.

Past the **Philippine Navy Headquarters** on the seaward side of Roxas Boulevard rises the Imelda-inspired **Cultural Center of the Philippines**, otherwise known as the CCP Complex. Manila Proper ends on **Buendia Avenue** past the CCP Complex.

MIA Avenue at boulevard's end leads to the **Manila International Airport** as well as the **Domestic Terminal**. Those hoping to meet lady luck may visit the casino here. Another is located at the **Silahis Hotel**

Blowing his horn: top local musician Eddie Katindig.

Close to the airport is another favorite tourist haunt, the *Nayong Pilipino* (**Philippine Village**), where the country's regions are represented in miniature in a landscaped village designed to allow short-term visitors a glimpse into the archipelago's attractions and diverse cultures. The **Philippine Museum of Ethnology** is found within the grounds. It showcases the arts and crafts of the minority groups, and is a good bet for purchases which otherwise may only be made by traveling the length and breadth of the country.

From MIA Avenue you can take a short bus or taxi ride to Makati via the **Epifanio de los Santos Highway** or EDSA. Makati's main street, **Ayala Avenue**, has been dubbed the Philippine Wall Street, being the financial hub of the metropolitan area. Off Ayala Avenue, on Makati Avenue is the **Ayala Museum and Aviary**. The museum has an outstanding archive and a permanent exhibit of dioramas portraying significant episodes in Philippine history, along with detailed replicas of boats and ships which have plied Philippine waters. The aviary features Philippine birds in a naturalistic setting enclosed within a giant net.

From Ayala Avenue's end at the EDSA, you can cross the highway to enter the plush residential village called **Forbes Park**, which continues to enjoy the highest status among the affluent burgher villages in the area. Forbes Park's **McKinley Road** leads to the **Manila Polo Club** and the **Manila American Memorial Cemetery**, where the remains of 17,000 Allied dead rest below row upon row of unmarked white crosses. The *Libingan ng Mga Bayani* (**Graveyard of Heroes**) is close by with its eternal flame burning by the **Tomb of the Unknown Soldier**.

The half of Manila north of the Pasig does not have as many attractions for the foreigner as the southern side, except for a few landmarks scattered around the residential districts. Manila's **Chinatown** may be reached by crossing over Jones Bridge from Liwasang Bonifacio. If Quezon Bridge is used you wind up immediately at **Quiapo**, an area long been considered the heart (some say the armpit) of downtown Manila. Beside the **Quiapo Church** you'll find sidewalk stalls

Religious paraphernalia sold by street vendor.

offering herbs and ointments of all persuasions, amulets, candles, religious calendars, local almanacs, flowers and lottery tickets.

Down **Quezon Boulevard** towards **Recto Avenue** is a mercantile strip of textile shops, army surplus stores, pawnshops, hole-in-the-wall palmists and astrologers, martial arts schools, bike shops, restaurants and moviehouses. You can turn right at Recto Avenue towards the "university belt," where several institutions disgorge thousands of students to add to downtown Manila's transport problems. Close to where Recto Avenue becomes **Mendiola Street** is the **San Sebastian Church**, reputedly the only pre-fabricated steel church in the world. Every single piece of its neo-gothic structure was fabricated in Belgium and shipped here for assembly in the closing years of the 19th century.

Mendiola Street leads past several private colleges to the **Malacañang Palace**, office-residence of Philippine Presidents. Since the end of the Marcos era, Malacañang has become the top tourist attraction in Manila. Tickets for the hour-long tour are distributed by the Ministry of Tourism. The tour takes you through the luxurious halls of the Palace, and includes a peek at former President Marcos' study and bedroom, as well as the more lavish accoutrements of the former First Lady. A high point of the tour, curiously enough, is the basement where Imelda Marcos kept much of her inordinate wardrobe, including the bulk of her now world-renowned collection of footwear.

Clock tower of the University of Santo Tomas.

Backtracking up Mendiola Street and Recto Avenue you turn at **Nicanor Reyes Street** and shortly find yourself on **España Street** where the large campus of the **University of Santo Tomas** is located. The university antedates Harvard by a good 25 years, having been founded by the Dominicans in 1611. It is the oldest university in Asia. The U.S.T., as it is more commonly called, also boasts a library with a rare manuscript collection of 12,000 volumes and a first-rate museum, the nucleus of which is as old as the university itself.

España Street leads straight to the boundary between Manila Proper and **Quezon City**, the country's official capital before its integration into Metro Manila. Where España ends, Quezon City's **Welcome Rotunda** marks the beginning of the former capital's two major thoroughfares. Forking right is **Rodriguez Avenue** which leads to **Cubao**, a commercial center whose endearing landmark is the **Armata Coliseum**, billed in the early 60s as the world's largest domed coliseum.

The other major street, **Quezon Avenue**, leads straight to the **Capitol Site Rotunda** or **Elliptical Circle**, off which are found a number of government buildings including the **Quezon City Hall** and the **Philippine Heart Center for Asia**. On the last stretch of Quezon Avenue before the circle are **Fr. Aguilar's Zoo** and the **National Parks and Wildlife Grounds**. Within the large rotunda area is the **Quezon Memorial Hall** which contains the memorabilia of Philippine Commonwealth President Manuel Luis Quezon as well as the modest beginnings of a projected Quezon City Museum.

Beyond this circle is **University Avenue** which leads to the sprawling main campus of the **University of the Philippines**. Here, the air is cooler and the atmosphere more laid-back.

A FILIPINO FOR ALL SEASONS

Traveling widely through the Philippines, one easily recognizes recurring landmarks. In town after town, the plaza has to include a basketball court, a small concrete stage for political and beauty contests, and a statue of a man revered as the national hero.

The man is Dr. Jose Rizal, born in 1861, whose execution by the Spanish 35 years later provoked the first war of independence launched by an Asian country against a foreign colonizer. In his short life Jose Rizal managed to earn himself such sobriquets as "The Great Malay" and "Pride of the Malay Race."

He was an artist, sculptor, poet, playwright, novelist, musician, naturalist, scientist, linguist, engineer, doctor, propagandist and above all, a social reformist.

His two novels written in Spanish, *Noli Me Tangere* (*Touch Me Not*, 1887) and *El Filibusterismo* (*Filibusterism*, 1891) were produced while he nearly starved in Europe spearheading the Filipino propaganda movement. The novels established his reputation as the leading spokesman of the Philippine reform movement. The books were printed with the help of friends in the continent, and were immediately declared seditious by the Spanish authorities. Satirizing abusive religious and political figures in Spanish officialdom, while also presenting an allegory of latent nationalism about to explode into revolution, the novels were cited as evidence in the mock trial that doomed Rizal.

There were truly many facets of the man, some of them in apparent contrariety. Rizal believed in peaceful reform and rejected the call of revolutionaries for an armed uprising. Against the advice of his parents and friends, he returned home in 1892. On exile in the lonely isle of Dapitan in the Southern Philippines, he turned down a plan to spirit him out. He was content with designing a waterworks system for the town, practicing as an eye doctor, and exploring the countryside for new species of lizards to send to Europe, one of which was named scientifically after him.

He was also quite keen on romance, having taken to heart and home Josephine Bracken, daughter of an Irish patient visiting from Hong Kong. Inspired by her perhaps, he composed lovely sonatas celebrating their idyllic life in exile. When the Cuban War broke out, he volunteered his services for the medical corps. The authorities allowed him to leave, but in mid-journey he was recalled to face trial for subversion.

On the eve of his execution, he wrote a long poem of farewell to his beloved country (*Ultimo Adios*), then concealed it in a gas lamp. He faced his death by musketry with calm and dignity. And when the volley was ordered, his last supreme effort was to twist his body around for a last glimpse of his country's sunrise. Such was the intense patriotism of the man, to whom generations of Filipinos owe a debt of genius, martyrdom, and inspiration.

**ne of
any
onuments
patriot
ose Rizal.**

Beyond Manila

The usual coach tour itinerary for the short-term Philippine visitor covers day excursions from Manila to **Tagaytay** to view the **Taal Lake and Volcano**, **Pagsanjan Falls** in **Laguna** to "shoot the rapids," and **Corregidor Island** at the entrance to **Manila Bay**.

Tagaytay is a leisurely hour's drive south on a fine highway traversing **Cavite** province's verdant countryside.

There are three ways to get to Tagaytay from Manila. One is by taking the new Cavite coastal road at the end of Roxas Boulevard which bypasses the traffic-prone suburbs from **Parañaque** onwards. Another is through **Quirino Avenue** from the airport area, but this is recommended only if one is determined to make a stop at the **Las Piñas Church** for the historic and unique **Bamboo Organ**. The third way is via the **South Superhighway** until the turn-off to **Carmona**, as pointed out by numerous signs.

You may view the lake and volcano from any of several sheds lining the **Tagaytay Ridge**, or from several resorts in the area. If you're traveling on your own, you may push farther south for the popular Batangas province's beaches of **Matabungkay** and **Nasugbu**, which offer moderately priced lodging. These are another hour's drive from Tagaytay.

At a junction before Tagaytay Ridge, a steep and very rough road descends to **Talisay**, a small Taal lakeside town where you can hire a boatman to take you across to **Volcano Island**.

On your way back to Manila, you can detour through the historic towns of Cavite, including **Kawit**, where the former residence of Philippine Revolutionary President Emilio Aguinaldo, who declared independence from Spain in 1896 at this site, has been turned into an interesting museum.

Fresh oysters and mussels sell cheaply on Cavite's roadsides. Beach resorts on a modest scale are plentiful in the area, the top of the line being **Puerto Azul** in **Ternate** town, which has a spectacular golf course, a hotel and beach cottages, and complete watersports facilities.

Pagsanjan is a two-hour drive southeast from Manila, or halfway round the Laguna Bay Loop. The route takes you past the southern lakeside towns, the first of which you'll hit after the South Superhighway from Makati.

Hot spring resorts are clustered in the towns of **Los Baños** and **Pansol**, halfway to Pagsanjan on the southern route. Private roman pools, cottages and picnic huts are the standard features of these resorts.

Some 25 miles (40 km) before Pagsanjan is **San Pablo City** with its seven miniature lakes, while in nearby Alaminos town is the popular **Hidden Valley** resort in a lush tropical setting with soda pools, waterfall and giant age-old trees. **Lake Caliraya**, a manmade lake fringed with plush country-club-type resorts, is close enough to Pagsanjan for a side trip.

A number of resorts and hotels in Pagsanjan offer boatmen's services for going upriver to the falls, behind which is a small cave reached by a rope-guided raft for the more adventurous at heart. Two boatmen skillfully navigate the *banca* (outrigger canoe) downriver past the rocky shallows. It is no whitewater experience really, but an

Rafting by the falls at Pagsanjan.

appreciation of the *bangkeros'* (boatmen's) dexterous moves could make your day.

On the way back to Manila, past Los Baños is **Calamba**, birthplace of Jose Rizal. The old Rizal house on the main street is now a national shrine landscaped with representative Philippine fruit trees. It is a treat to wander in this fragrant garden and then to go indoors to see the wealthy appointments of 19th-century Laguna gentry.

From Manila, hovercraft and ferry boats leave for **Corregidor Island** on a regular daily schedule from a pier off the CCP Complex. A strategic tadpole-shaped island commanding the approach to Manila Bay, the Rock, as Corregidor is fondly called, receives many nostalgic visits from World War II veterans and history buffs.

A memorial to the Filipino and American war dead stands in a lovely park at the heart of the fortress island. At a promontory called **Suicide Cliff**, where Japanese soldiers jumped off rather than accept the changing fortunes of war, a small Buddhist shrine has been set up by Japanese visitors.

A tour of the island will take you through **Malinta Tunnel**, where Fil-American troops mapped out their delaying tactics in the dark summer of 1942, **Battery Way** close to Suicide Cliff on the northwest coast, and the ruins of **Topside Barracks** on a plateau overlooking the Bataan coast across the channel. Elsewhere on the island are limestone caves where Japanese troops holed up in 1945 while the Allied forces mounted recapture operations.

Corregidor Inn, perched atop a hill right on the island's middle, provides panoramic views from its breezy terrace. North across the channel the rugged coast of **Bataan** is almost close enough to touch. Turning southward, you aim a curious squint at Cavite's shimmering white coves. Ships glide in and out of your timeless picture.

Farther Out: Popular beaches for a quick drive from Manila would include those of **Batangas** to the south and Bataan and Zambales provinces to the northwest. In the Batangas, a number of specialized resorts catering to diving and other watersports enthusiasts may be found in **Anilao** off **Batangas City**. Two hours to the northwest in **Bagac**, Bataan, a white-

easide versions 're entiful the hilippines.

sand beach and complete watersports facilities are available. Bagac and the town of **Mariveles** were the starting points of the infamous Death March, which took a heavier toll among the Allied prisoners than the actual fighting in Bataan. The route is traced by several markers along Bataan's east coast. On the approach to Bagac in the west coast, a **Friendship Tower** has been erected by a Japanese Buddhist Society, with a massive tree trunk serving as clapper to a great bronze bell.

Bataan is companion piece to Corregidor, hallowed ground for the war veteran making a touristic comeback to the scene of his early valor and patriotic anguish. Wreath-laying is a year-round affair, but the most important and lengthiest speeches are reserved for April 9, the date of Bataan's fall. On that day, the President leads a throng of ex-heroes up **Mount Samat**, site of the fiercest battle in 1942 before the Fil-American forces capitulated. Near the summit stands a great cross marking a memorial shrine to the war dead, known as *Dambana ng Kagitingan* (**Shrine of Valor**). An elevator takes visitors up the cross, some 30 stories high, for a fine commanding view of the surrounding mountain ranges, plains, the Manila Bay on one side and the China Sea on the other.

North of Bataan is **Zambales** province, a rugged strip of mountain ranges and picturesque coastline forming a western border to the Central Luzon provinces. The American naval base at **Subic** lies near **Olongapo City**. The bay area between the two, and the fine coastal stretch from **San Antonio** to **Iba** is filled with beach resorts catering to the ubiquitous American serviceman.

North of Zambales is **Pangasinan** province. The most famous of Pangasinan's tourist destinations is **Hundred Islands** off **Alaminos** town. Visitors are ferried by boat from the wharf at **Barrio Lucap** for the collection of isles strewn along the Lingayen Gulf. Only **Quezon Island** has drinking water and lodging facilities.

Pangasinan is also noted for its preponderance of faith healers. They are found mostly in the towns of **Villasis**, **Rosales**, **Asingan** and **Urdaneta** off the main highway from Manila, **MacArthur Highway**, which leads to Baguio City as well as the Ilocos region.

Ruins of the army barracks at Corregidor Island.

The Ilocos Region

Past the town of **Sison**, Pangasinan, the road forks right toward **Baguio City**, and left to **La Union**, the southernmost of the Ilocos provinces. The capital, **San Fernando**, can be reached in four hours from Manila. Before San Fernando is **Agoo** town at the entrance to La Union where the **Museo Iloko**, a repository of Ilocano artifacts, and the nearby *Agoo Minor Basilica* (**Our Lady of Charity Shrine**) are worth a stop.

Bauang town is 14 miles (23 km) north of Agoo, and from there a six-mile (10-km) coastal stretch to San Fernando is marked by a series of beach resorts frequented by Baguio visitors and American servicemen. The former **Marcos Highway** connects Agoo to Baguio, while **Naguillan Highway** does the same for Bauang. Both are an hour's drive up to the mountain resort city, with the former featuring a park and golf course lorded over by the controversial Marcos Bust, a large cement likeness of the former President.

Past San Fernando on the **Maharlika Highway** that hugs the Ilocos coastline, the old churches of **San Juan** and **Balaoan** are worthwhile stops. Remnants of old watchtowers are found in San Juan, **Luna** off Balaoan and at **Darigayo Pt.** off Luna. Fine woven blankets and handcrafted *boloes*, or machetes, the best in the region, are sold on the roadsides of **Bangar** town.

The next province, **Ilocos Sur**, has charming old churches in **Sta. Lucia**, **Candon**, **Sta. Maria**, **Santa** and **Bantay**.

From Bantay, a road veers left off the national highway to enter **Vigan**, provincial capital. Close to the imposing **Vigan Cathedral** is **Burgos House**. The birthplace of martyr-priest Father Jose Burgos, the colonial two-story house has a good antique collection, iconographic archives and library. A series of paintings depicting scenes from the Basi Revolt of 1807 titillates with its curious imagery set in folk perspective. Fronting the plaza is **St. Joseph's Antique Shop**, the most reliable of the capital's numerous dealers in antique items.

Follow the coastal highway passing the interesting baroque churches of

arvesting
ce near San
ernando in
gan.

San Vicente, **Magsingal**, and **Cabugao**. Two miles past Cabugao, a side road turns left towards **Pug-os Beach**, an undeveloped large cove with warm placid waters. A few more miles northward and you cross the provincial boundary to **Ilocos Norte**.

The first town is **Badoc** where the **Luna House** calls for a stopover. Exhibited in the reconstructed ancestral house are reproductions of the 19th-century Filipino painter Juan Luna. **Badoc Church** is also worth a visit. But the prime example of the centuries-old churches in the region is to be found in **Paoay**, two towns north. Here the **Paoay Church** is a real stunner, a successful hybrid creation wedding the strong features of "earthquake baroque" (such as massive lateral buttresses) with an exotic oriental quality reminiscent of Javanese temples. Built at the turn of the 18th century, restored and repaired in 1793, it is the most celebrated of all Ilocos churches.

Half-a-mile from the town proper is **Paoay Lake**, overlooking which is the *Malacañang Ti Amianan* or **Malacañang of the North**, Marcos' former resthouse which has now been converted into a highlight of the Ilocos tour attractions.

Farther north is **Laoag City**, the provincial capital, with the **Laoag International Airport**. The **Laoag Cathedral**, dating back to the 16th century, is another notable example of "earthquake baroque" architecture. A road leads east from Laoag to **Sarrat**, birthplace of Ferdinand Marcos, where the **Marcos Museum** houses family memorabilia, including the four-poster bed where the controversial Great Ilocano was born, the clock beside it set to the exact hour and minute of his birth. The **Sta. Monica Church and Convent** of Sarrat, connected by a massive bridge-staircase, are well-preserved specimens of colonial architecture.

Farther north, off Burgos town, the **Cape Bojeador Lighthouse** stands over a dramatic coastal expanse of jagged rocks. After **Bangui** town is **Pagudpud** with its little-known but spectacular **Saud Beach**, a long curving stretch of white sand. Shortly beyond you'll have reached the northern coast of Luzon, and the road now turns east towards **Cagayan** Province.

Paoay Church in Ilocos.

Baguio and the Northern Skyland

A favorite destination of short-term visitors to the Philippines is **Baguio**, the summer capital, a mountain resort city perched amid pine stands at some 5,000 feet (1,500 meters). It is a four-hour drive from Manila, or 40 minutes by plane. The last hour is a scenic drive up the zigzag course of **Kennon Road**, hewed out of the mountainsides by the Americans at the turn of the century. The first-timer in Baguio City may find a weekend all too brief for making the mandatory rounds of attractions. It is not so much the number of "tourist spots" that will induce you to prolong your stay, but the sense of leisure that comes inevitably with the first invigorating whiff of pine air. With an average temperature of 65 F (18 C), clean parks and lovely gardens, winding roads set against a backdrop of rugged mountain ranges, Baguio offers a fine respite from the lowland dust, heat and bustle. Not a few visitors have decried Baguio's commercialism, but most transients would agree that Baguio's charms easily offset such a gripe.

Long walks become the most popular form of recreation, the time-honored constitutional being up and down **Session Road** with its mainstreet gamut of commercial shops. At the lower, northern end of Session Road you can cross over to the bountiful **Baguio Market** for highland fruits and vegetables, seafood from the coastal towns an hour away, fresh mushrooms, jams, handicrafts and army surplus goods. Or you may fork left towards **Burnham Park**, where you can ponder on the relative fluff of life on a bench under a weeping willow, or watch the lovers boating in the lagoon.

Driving around in Baguio without a proper map can become a frustrating experience, unless you're casually airing your driving skills or are naturally predisposed to winding mazes. Getting somewhere seems easier by cab or any of the drab-looking jeepneys clustered on the side streets off Session Road. They follow regular routes, but are inclined to take you on a "short trip" to any part of the city for a set fee. Cabs can also take you to any point, even to

illtops erve as layground r these cal kids.

the relatively far reaches of the city proper like **San Carlos Heights** off **Naguillan Road** for a spectacular view of the sunset over the Pangasinan coastline, or **Mount Santo Tomas** where a radar station competes with the view of the China Sea in the distance.

Between these two points located west and southwest of the city center, respectively, may be found the **Lourdes Grotto** perched above 225 steps where devotees test their zeal and heart condition, and farther on, a woodcarving village on the way to **Asin Hot Springs**.

North of the city center down **Bokawkan Road** is the **Easter Weaving Room** where native cloth and curio items sell for bargain prices. Weavers at work are an attraction for camera bugs. Farther north down **Magsaysay Avenue**, some 10 minutes' drive from the downtown area is **Bell Temple**, an edifice of gracious lines bedecked with dragons and Chinese ornamentalia. It is open to visitors during certain hours. Its priests, who practice a blend of Buddhism, Taoism, Confucianism and Christianity, are inclined to cast fortunes for the curious.

In the northeast part of the city, down **Leonard Wood Road**, you'll find the former Botanical Garden now named **Chion Park**. A replica of an *Igorot* village (*Igorot* being the blanket term for the diverse ethnic groupings in the mountain provinces) has been structured with prototypes of native architecture representing the different mountain tribes. These are ringed by handicraft and silver jewelry shops.

Farther up is **Mansion House**, summer residence of Philippine presidents. Fronting it is **Wright Park**, featuring the **Pool of the Pines**, the end of which overlooks a riding field with horses for hire. Up **Gibraltar Road** and into **Torres Street** you come upon another cluster of souvenir shops across **Mines View Park**, a familiar image for having become *the* classic Baguio postcard. It is really nothing more than a viewdeck overlooking Baguio's mineral bowl. Children in a nearby gully have made it a tradition to call out for coins, which you toss over and they scamper in the brush for.

South of Mansion House is the **Baguio Country Club**, and past it the

Vegetable seller at Baguio Market.

John Hay Air Base with its scenic parks, golf course and restaurants. A cute stop within the rolling manicured grounds is the **Cemetery of Negativism**, a series of mock tombstones depicting characteristic loser types, with witty epitaphs suggesting that the visitor bury his negative vibes here.

Accommodation is no problem in Baguio City except during Holy Week, the high point of the summer excursion time when the city's population of some 200,000 is nearly quadrupled. A listing of lodging places, a map of the city, and other pertinent information are available at the local Tourism office at **Gov. Pack Road** connected to the southern end of Session Road.

Baguio also serves as the gateway to several points of interest in the Cordillera region. The most popular destinations are **Bontoc** which is six hours away, Banawe which is two hours farther, and **Sagada** which is just off Bontoc. All points north are reached through the **Halsema Highway**, a rugged but pleasantly scenic road carved out of mountainsides. An expansion of the old mountain trail, it offers vistas of the Grand Cordillera chain at every turn, reaching elevations of more than 7,000 feet (2,120 meters) at certain points.

Buses leave early in the morning. A hundred kilometers from Baguio the road ascends to **Mount Data**, a lumber town often enshrouded by mist and an eerie quiet faintly hinting at Olympian settings.

Some two hours farther are Bontoc and Sagada, the latter reached by forking off from the highway at a junction before Bontoc. Much of the charm and coziness lacking in Bontoc, the provincial capital, can be found in Sagada which is popular with foreign backpackers for its cool climate, pretty scenery, interesting hiking trails, caves, ponds and falls.

Nestling on a low valley by the **Chico River**, Bontoc is much warmer in the daytime, and has a somewhat harsh-looking trading post exterior. The **Bontoc Museum** is an interesting stop-over, however. From Bontoc, you can take the early morning bus to Banawe to view the famous **Banawe Rice Terraces**. From Banawe, you may travel directly back to Manila without passing the same route through Baguio.

ice rraces ovide an nazing mmetry the ndscape.

THE VISAYAN ISLANDS

A major destination in the Philippines is **Cebu City**, the "Queen City of the South," capital of **Cebu** province and second only to Manila in terms of trade and commerce. It is the hub of all activities in the Visayan region. Normally, one flies from Manila to Cebu, or takes a ship for a 14-hour sea trip. The **Mactan International Airport** also receives travelers directly from abroad. It is situated on the small island of **Mactan** which is connected by bridge to the Cebu mainland.

Mactan is of historical attraction, having been the site of Magellan's downfall at the hands of local chieftain Lapulapu in the Battle of Mactan in 1521. The **Magellan Monument** erected in 1886 marks the spot where he died on Mactan's shore, while the **Lapulapu Monument** stands at the plaza fronting the **Lapulapu City Hall** on the same island.

Beach resorts cater to hordes of Japanese visitors, specially during the peak season of July and August. Among the better ones are **Costabella** and **Tambuli**. **Olango Island**, across Mactan is a divers' destination.

Lazing around on Tambuli Beach in Cebu.

A large wooden cross left by Magellan commemorates the archipelago's first encounter with the west. **Magellan's Cross** is now Cebu's most important historical landmark, its remnants encased within a black cross of *tindalo* wood housed in a kiosk found at upper **Magallanes Street**.

Close by on **San Juan Street**, is **San Agustin Church**, built in 1565 to house the country's oldest religious relic, the Image of the Holy Child Jesus presented by Magellan to Queen Juana of Cebu upon her conversion to Christianity. One of Legazpi's men found that image intact some 40 years later when Spain resumed its colonization. The church is now known as the **Basilica Minore of Santo Niño**, its conversion ordered by the Pope in 1965 in recognition of its importance and that of Cebu City as the cradle of Christianity in the East.

Near the waterfront is **Fort San Pedro**, the construction of which was started by Legazpi in 1565. Finally completed in 1738, the triangular bastion stood close to the sea to serve as a lookout against Muslim marauders from Mindanao. The Ministry of Tourism office is found within the fort, which has become a favorite promenade ground.

Close to the fort is **Colon Street**, the oldest street in the country, situated within the Parian district which was Cebu's original Chinatown. The Chinese community is very much in evidence in Cebu, and is largely responsible for its continued growth as an industrial and commercial center.

Among the more interesting cultural attractions within the city are **Casa Gorordo** which replicates turn-of-the-century aristocratic lifestyles, the **University of San Carlos Museum**, **Jumalon's Family Cultural Project** which displays fascinating lepido-mosaic art utilizing butterfly wings as medium, and the **Medalle Collection of Old Cebu Photographs**.

Atop **Beverly Hills** in Lahug district is Cebu's **Taoist Temple**, while a short drive up north to **Manadaue City** leads to the **Chapel of the Last Supper** which features life-sized statues of Christ and the apostles handcarved during the

Spanish times.

Southeast of Cebu is **Bohol Island**, which for its relatively small size has much to offer in terms of historical and natural attractions. Legazpi anchored briefly off the island in 1563 and is recorded to have sealed a blood compact with a native chieftain named Sikatuna. The **Blood Compact Marker** commemorates this event on its original site a few miles from the capital, **Tagbilaran City**. A good road system traverses the entire island. Its coastline is marked by a fascinating array of picturesque coves and clean white-sand beaches, most of them a short ride from the city.

Four miles (seven km) from Tagbilaran is **Baclayon Church**, the oldest stone church in the country. Built in 1595, it has an interesting museum housing a rich collection of religious relics, vestments, icons, and old librettos of church music printed in Latin on animal skins.

Close by, a causeway leads to **Panglao Island**, where worthwhile stops include **Dauis Church**, the **Hinagdanan Cave** with an underground bathing pool and natural skylights, **Bikini Beach** and **Alona Beach**. Off Panglao Island is **Balicasag Island**, a marine reserve and favored dive spot.

North of Tagbilaran is the old **Punta Cruz Watchtower** in **Maribojoc**, and farther up, **Calape Church** with its reputedly miraculous image of the Virgin. A visit to the inland town of **Antequera** on an early Sunday morning will allow you a pick of the cheap handicrafts woven of vine, reed and grass.

But what remains Bohol's most famous attraction, with which in fact the island has become synonymous, is a unique panorama in the vicinity of **Carmen**, a town 34 miles (55 km) northeast of Tagbilaran. Here several hundred haycock hills formed by limestone, shale and sandstone rise some 100 feet (30 meters) above the flat terrain. These are the **Chocolate Hills** of Bohol, so-called for the confectionary spectacle they present at the height of summer when their sparse grass cover turns dry and brown.

It is a 20-minute flight from Tagbilaran to Mactan Airport. Buses hop over by ferry to Cebu and **Negros Island**, with **Bacolod City** as the final destination.

North of Bacolod City, the capital of Negros Occidental province, is charming **Silay City** with several quaint old houses recalling the Castilian past. The **Hofileña Art Collection** includes the works of Dr. Jose Rizal and turn-of-the-century Filipino masters Juan Luna and Felix Hidalgo, plus a few Picassos and Goyas.

Farther north is the **Chapel of the Angry Christ** within the Vicmico Compound, with its psychedelic mural and mosaic of pop bottles depicting an angry Christ with the saints as Filipinos in native dress.

From Bacolod it is a two-hour ferry boat ride to **Iloilo City** in **Panay Island**. The *Museo ng Iloilo* (**Iloilo Museum**) at **Bonifacio Drive** showcases prehistoric artifacts dug up from the many burial sites in Panay. The **Tiongco Antique Collection** in **Molo** town is a must for lovers of pottery. The churches in the towns around Iloilo City are all fascinating specimens of colonial architecture. The most celebrated is the **Miagao Fortress Church**. A squat, massive structure, it has a beautiful ornate facade featuring native flora in relief carving.

he eyes agerly igest the hocolate ills of ohol.

Mindanao and the Marginal Islands

South of the Visayas is **Mindanao**, the second largest island in the Philippines. Mindanao is a land of superlatives—the rarest eagle in the world (the Philippine monkey-eating eagle); the largest city in the world in terms of area (Davao); one of the most expensive shells in the world (Gloria Maris); the richest nickel deposits in the world (Surigao del Norte); and one of the most obscure tribes in the world (the Tasaday).

It is a pity, however, that a confederation of several armed guerrilla groups (the MNLF or Moro National Liberation Front), which appeared in the early 70s, is still a force whose avowed aim is the creation of an autonomous Muslim state under Filipino sovereignty. It is not exactly a dangerous island to visit except for a few particular areas, but its distance from Manila and news of frequent kidnappings often deter foreign visitors.

Zamboanga City is certainly a charming place to visit for its rich Castilian heritage and lovely parks and gardens. The colorful Muslim *vinta* or sailboat is also much in evidence in the bay, where resplendent pandanus mats and shell and coral items are sold directly from various watercraft. Just past the **Lantaka Hotel**, itself a landmark overlooking the bay, is **Fort de Pilar**, its three-foot thick coral walls overgrown with moss. A bronze plaque at the eastern gate tells not only its dramatic story, but much of the colorful history of Mindanao. A 25-minute boat ride from Lantaka Hotel takes you to **Santa Cruz Island** with its pinkish-white sands and Samal graveyard. A few hundred yards to the east is the Samal water village of **Rio Hondo**. Twelve miles (19 km) east of the city is **Taluksangay**, another picturesque Muslim village on stilts.

Davao City in the southeast portion of Mindanao is another popular destination, for its exotic fruits such as durian, mangosteen, rambutan and pomelo, as well as for a climb up the country's highest peak, **Mount Apo**. Called the "grandfather of Philippine mountains," Mount Apo is a dormant volcano with a gigantic verdant cap stretching to a height of 10,000 feet (3,000 meters) and covering 188,000 acres (76,000 hectares).

Other worthwhile places to visit in Mindanao are **Cagayan de Oro City** in the north coast, off which is enchanting **Camiguin Island** with the diminutive but violent **Hibok-Hibok Volcano**, **Iligan City** for the **Maria Cristina Falls**, and **Marawi City** for **Lake Lanao**, the second largest and deepest lake in the Philippines.

The Marginal Islands: Popular weekend destinations for the beach fancier include several out-of-the way places in marginal islands. Off the southeast corner of Panay Island in the Visayas is **Sicogon Island** which has been fully developed into a plush resort.

On the northwestern tip of Panay Island is **Boracay Island**, of pristine beauty. Its lovely stretches of powdery white sand and cheap tropical-style lodging continue to attract a good number of European budget travelers and Manila residents. Boracay is close to the town of **Malay** in the mainland, but is also accessible by pumpboat from **Nabas** and **Ibajay** towns. Small aircraft can be chartered from Manila to fly to the nearby Caticlan airstrip.

Another favorite among budget travelers and beach freaks is **Puerto Galera** in **Mindoro Island**, much closer to Manila. Word of mouth has made Puerto Galera such an "in" place in recent years that fears have risen it may soon be spoiled. Its proximity to Manila is another advantage. You can take a two-hour bus ride to **Batangas City** and then another two-hour ride by ferry to this trendy haunt among young Europeans.

Off the northwestern tip of the Palawan mainland (which is an attractive option for the rugged adventurer for its natural and wildlife riches) is **El Nido**, where towering black marble cliffs provide the swiftlet with enough nooks and crannies on which to build its edible nest that is much fancied by gourmets for *nido*, or bird's nest soup. On **Miniloc Island** nearby is **El Nido Resort**, possibly the classiest island paradise in the country. Charter flights from Manila will take you to this exquisite and exclusive playground of secluded coves, emerald lagoons leading to secret caves, untouched coral reefs, and exotic fish which will feed off your hand.

Right, lighting up at the Ati-Atihan festival, one more excuse to have a good time.

SINGAPORE: THE LION CITY

Visitors to Singapore wishing to sample some of the mystique associated with its founder Sir Stamford Raffles will find a choice awaiting them.

They can of course stay at the legendary Raffles Hotel, home of the Singapore Sling and the epitome of colonial charm, and where the suite that Somerset Maugham stayed in is still available for occupancy. Alternatively, they can walk next door to "Raffles City" where the 73-story Westin Stamford, the world's tallest hotel, (746 feet/226 meters), stands in all its ultra high-tech aluminum splendor.

The contrast between the two hotels brings out in tangible form what has been said about this 238-square-mile (616-square-km) island with 2.5 million people so many times it has become a cliche, but like many cliches remains largely true, that Singapore is an exciting amalgam of the East and West, old and new.

Though more than three-quarters of its population is Chinese, Singapore's official language is English and it is so widely understood that the visitor can use it to order snake soup in Chinatown or French cuisine at Maxim's.

Besides its Chinatown, Singapore also boasts a Little India, an Arab Street and Geylang, where Malay culture predominates.

Visitors from the West are pleasantly surprised to find super-clean taxis driven by cabbies who don't expect a tip and a gastronomical paradise that they can enjoy without ever having to worry about what may be in the water. The tree-lined roads are invariably the cleanest anywhere and the epithet "Garden City" is aptly-named for Singapore, whose well-planned public housing system and island-wide parks are justifiably lauded by urban planners around the world.

A few blinkered people from the developed countries, fed on wartime tales about an exotic, sin-filled Singapore, are surprised to find that trishaws are no longer that common, or that far from being filled with opium dens, Singapore actually has one of the toughest drug control laws in the world.

There are also some self-appointed *cognoscenti* of world travel, who on the basis of a few travel articles, have concluded that there is nothing to Singapore except sterile skyscrapers and shopping centers.

A more detailed look would reveal that the Singapore of today remains as interesting a place as it was in the past, if not more so. It is still very much an Asian society, one that represents the descendants of three great cultures from Asia.

Stone and concrete monuments have their appeal, as does going to mechanically-created theme parks that purport to show us what the future is likely to be. But nothing beats the lively and dynamic fusion of the past and the present in a living society. And nowhere is this global drama of old societies and values changing into the present and peeking into the future as easily or as comfortably viewed as from Singapore.

Preceding pages: 19th-century scene at the Singapore Padang. What a difference a hundred years makes! Rugby and Raffles City at the present-day Padang. Left, Singapore Harbour at sunset.

THE LITTLE ISLAND THAT COULD

When Sir Stamford Raffles, one of the few British colonial pioneers with both vision and a scholarly mind, set foot on Singapore in 1819, he did so with the conviction that the island, at the crossroads of the South China Sea, would one day become an important port.

But the history of Singapore does not begin with the arrival of Raffles. The Malay Annals record that Singapore derives its name from *Singa*, which means lion. Since the animal was not normally found in these parts, we can only conclude that the anecdote of a Malay prince naming the city after sighting the beast in the island belongs to that realm of history generously mixed with mythology.

The first written records of Singapore's history begin around the 13th century and chronicle the island passing through the hands of various regional empires. The Thai kings, the Javanese and even the Chola kings from far-away India seemed to have invaded and controlled Singapore for various periods.

The mighty Majapahit empire that was centered in what is modern-day Indonesia brought Singapore under its control in the early part of the 15th century. But they went on to develop Malacca, farther north in Malaya, into a big port and Singapore became an obscure fishing village until the landing of Raffles in January, 1819.

Raffles himself spent only a year in Singapore but he left his mark on the city with far-reaching ideas such as his action of declaring Singapore a free port.

Just six months after his arrival, Singapore's population had grown to five thousand and the first official census in 1824 showed an increase to 11,000.

Despite a lack of lions, there was no shortage of tigers. Records indicate that in the 1850s, when immigrants tried to clear the thick jungle covering the island to make way for commercial crops, as many as 300 people were killed by tigers. But under a combined onslaught by the multitudes of immigrants, the jungles were soon cleared and Singapore emerged as a thriving trading port, becoming one of the most important trading posts of the British empire before the end of the 19th century.

The main items of trade were tea and silk from China, timber from Malaya and spices from Indonesia. The colony also imported opium and fabrics from India as well as English-manufactured goods from Britain.

Singapore's free port status attracted many merchants and its development was accelerated to such a pace that it soon overtook much older British colonial ports in the region, such as Penang and Bencoolen in Sumatra.

Singapore's commerce and reputation grew by leaps and bounds with the arrival of thousands of Chinese and Indian immigrants in the later part of the 19th century.

World War I did not affect Singapore directly and in fact it was a time of great prosperity for the island as it was enjoying the fruits of the Malayan rubber boom.

The war did cause the German community in Singapore to be ostracized by the colony's British administration. There was also a revolt by some of the Indian soldiers stationed in Singapore, incited by an underground Indian independence movement and the German secret service.

But the British were able to suppress the revolt in a few days with the help of the Japanese, who were at that time allied with the British.

By 1911, the population of Singapore had grown to 250,000 and the census recorded 48 races speaking 54 languages in the island.

The Great Depression that gripped the West in the late 1920s had its reverberations in Singapore too as the prices of commodities such as rubber collapsed. But even in its relative poverty, Singapore was secure as the greatest naval base of the British empire, east of Suez.

That security was rudely shattered when the Japanese invaded Malaya in 1941. Rather than confront British naval might from the sea, the Japanese landed in north Malaya on December 8 of that year and advanced down the peninsula towards Singapore.

Despite an appeal by Winston Churchill to the local governor to fight to the "bitter end," the British administration in Singapore surrendered on February 8, 1942.

The Japanese renamed Singapore *Syonan*, "Light of the South." Under their occupation many civilians, particularly the Chinese, suffered unspeakable hardships.

The commerce of Singapore died down and the population had to cultivate tapioca in their backyards to survive. The Japanese rule that lasted about three-and-a-half years ended in August, 1945 with the landing of Allied troops.

The British then separated Singapore from Malaya and made it into a Crown Colony. The returning British also had to face problems from the Communist Party of Malaya in both Singapore and Malaya. With the assumption of emergency powers, however, the Communist challenge was contained.

But as older residents of Singapore, including many of its senior political leaders, have testified, the Japanese occupation taught Singaporeans the unreliability of depending on Britain or anyone else for their protection. That lesson was eventually to lead to an independent Singapore which was not willing to depend on any external powers for its protection.

Sensing the post-occupation mood, the British in 1948 allowed a limited form of elections to the legislative council. But it was only in 1955 that full elections were held and self-government was granted to Singapore.

As befitting the polyglot nature of Singapore, a descendant of Iraqi Jews and a

Left, Sir Thomas Stamford Raffles. Above, early 20th-century photograph of Raffles Place.

brilliant British-trained lawyer, David Marshall, became Singapore's first chief minister.

Marshall remained in power for less than a year and the chief minister who followed him, Lim Yew Hock, negotiated for full self-government under a new constitution in 1959.

The dramatic changes that propelled Singapore from a sleepy colonial port into the metropolis it is today are due largely to the party that came to power in the elections of 1959, the People's Action Party (PAP) and the man who led it, eventually becoming the country's prime minister, Lee Kuan Yew.

First, the PAP had to fight tooth and nail to convince Chinese Singaporeans, many of whom were under Communist influence in those days, that their destiny lay with joining the proposed Federation of Malaysia that would be dominated by the Malays.

The Communists too thought that the destiny of Singapore lay with Malaya but they denounced as an imperialist plot the British proposals to join not just Malaya and Singapore but also North Borneo and Sarawak into one federation to be known as Malaysia.

The PAP was able to persuade Singaporeans to overcome their primordial loyalties and in an historic referendum, they voted to join Malaysia in September, 1963.

But differences between the leaders of Malaysia and Singapore became serious enough for a separation and Singapore became an independent nation on August 9, 1965.

Few thought that Singapore had a chance to survive for long, let alone prosper. The skeptics had facts on their side. Singapore had a population that was booming and few natural resources. The British troops and their dependants, who at one time numbered 100,000 and provided employment to thousands of Singaporeans, were scheduled to leave for good.

But in the face of adversity, Singapore succeeded, even beyond the expectations of its well-wishers.

The only real resource Singapore has besides its people is the deepwater port that lies in one of the busiest trading routes of the world, at the entrance to the Straits of Malacca. Oil from the Middle East to Japan, minerals from Australia to Europe, manufactured goods from Europe and the US all find it convenient to pass through Singaporean waters.

But the leaders of Singapore felt that the port alone was not enough to employ a burgeoning labor force of about one million. They set out to scour the developed nations for industrial investment in the republic and cleared the formerly marshy land of Jurong in the island's west coast for ready-made factories that were leased to industrialists who arrived.

Labor laws were tightened, making strikes more difficult under the premise

that it is better to employ people, even under low wages, than to drive away foreign investment with demands for high wages.

The government also set about building affordable highrise apartments in one of the most ambitious public housing development programs ever undertaken. A compulsory savings scheme was also introduced. About one-quarter of every wage earner's salary is automatically deducted and individually credited by the government-sponsored pension fund, the Central Provident Fund (CPF).

The government considers Western-style welfare benefits as anti-work ethic and an anathema. You can, however, use your CPF funds to buy an apartment or a house. The government finds this a good way to house the population as well as to give citizens of immigrant origin a real stake in the future of the country.

Showing the flag during National Day celebrations.

As the prime minister once remarked, a population aware that riots in the streets makes property values go down is hardly likely to riot, if it is also a home-owning population. At present, more than 80 percent of Singaporeans live in government-built housing.

National service was introduced for all males over 18 and this more than anything else has been responsible for the development of the "Singaporean identity."

Trying to point out how difficult it was to have built a "Singaporean identity" at all, First Deputy Prime Minister Goh Chok Tong said there are Singaporeans alive today who have undergone four changes in nationality. Before the Japanese occupation they were British "subjects." They then became Japanese subjects under occupation, only to be British subjects again after liberation. They became Malaysians in 1963 and Singaporeans again in 1965. The minister added that he hoped Singaporeans would not have to change nationalities again.

Despite its recent turbulent history, Singaporeans bear very few emotional scars of the past. They generally look to the future rather than live with the bitter memories of the past. The Japanese, British, and most other nationalities are equally welcome in the Singapore of today, which, despite its free enterprise economy, maintains diplomatic relations with most Communist states and has a thriving trade with them.

The Singapore government does not believe there are things that cannot be planned for. With slogans such as "Two is Enough," "Speak Mandarin," "Keep Singapore Clean," and medical benefits that favor the less fecund, it has succeeded so well in controlling the population that this country, which once used to worry about how to provide employment to its people, now has to import foreign labor.

A nation that had to build in a frenzy to put a roof over the multitudes is now saddled with excess capacity in everything from luxury condominiums to highrise office space.

The fear that Singaporeans of various races would drift apart has receded into distant memory. The nation now confronts the problem of how to preserve the traces of old ethnic cultures for tourists who are disappointed to find a Singaporean who is not "native" or "colorful" enough to meet their pre-conceived notions.

Singaporeans of the next generation will confront a different set of problems. They will have to deal not with problems of overpopulation, shortages and poverty, but declining birth rates, excess capacity and maintaining a strict work ethic that has been softened by a comfortable and secure lifestyle.

There is no doubt, however, that more than a few developing nations would like to swap Singapore's problems of affluence with their own problems of poverty.

WELC

RH

THE CITY

You can see all of Singapore without getting out of an air-conditioned bus. Since the city is so compact, even one or two tours can in fact give a fairly good idea of this diverse and well-developed city-state.

But that would be a pity. The city is very safe and a cool drink is never far away. So you can also "do" the entire city on foot in a few days.

Perhaps the best combination would be to join a tour that covers important parts of the city and then return later to those areas that interest you most.

Most city tours of Singapore take about four hours from the comfort of coaches that pick you up at your hotel. Alternatively, you can also take an individualized tour with a qualified guide recommended by the Singapore Tourist Promotion Board (STPB). Most tours cost in the range of S$25 (US$12).

The old colonial heart of Singapore is located around the mouth of the **Singapore River** and the **Padang**—the town common where on weekends you can still watch a leisurely game of cricket.

The Padang is flanked on one side by **City Hall**, which houses important government ministries and the office of the prime minister. The area is also worth a visit at night when the neo-classical columns of City Hall, built by Indian convicts, takes on a majestic air under spotlights.

As you are facing City Hall, across a busy junction on your right, you can't fail to notice the world's tallest hotel. It is **Raffles City**, a "city-within-a-city."

Named after Singapore's founder, it contains two hotels and an office and shopping complex. Nestled next to this giant is the much smaller but still charming original **Raffles Hotel**, over a century old and still attractively fringed with traveler's palms.

Right across from Raffles City is another complex of three seafront hotels which were built on reclaimed land: **Marina Square**. If you walk along the edge of the Padang on the other side of City Hall you will find **Elizabeth Walk**, which skirts the waterfront and eventually leads to the statue of the **Merlion**, the half-lion, half-mermaid mythical creature that has become the national symbol of this newly-industrialized city-state.

An evening stroll along this walk is particularly rewarding, for you can stop to sample a few sticks of *satay*—the skewered Malay version of the *kebab*—at the **Satay Club** at the edge of Elizabeth Walk.

Just next to the Satay Club are two war memorials. One is a towering needle-like structure, nicknamed "**The Four Chopsticks**," which honors the civilian dead during the Japanese occupation. The other memorial, **The Cenotaph**, is a memorial to Lim Bo Seng, a young resistance leader who died under torture by the Japanese.

If you walk past the Padang towards the city instead of towards the sea, you will find **Parliament House**, and behind it the Singapore River, where the city began.

The bum boats are no longer there, displaced by the tunnels of the city's **Mass Rapid Transit (MRT)** system, which run under the river, but along its banks the charateristic hum of commerce is still evident.

ceding ges: Shop Little lia plays ificial wers. ft, orman at original ffles tel retains onial rb. Right, rlion is nbol of rism.

Just next to Parliament House are the other gems of colonial Singapore architecture, the **Victoria Memorial Hall** and the **Victoria Theater**, where the Singapore Symphony Orchestra plays regularly.

The **Cavenagh Bridge**, an elegant iron bridge built in Scotland, still has an old sign that forbids bullock carts from entering. It also connects Empress Place to **Raffles Place**.

Raffles Place is the financial hub of this third most important financial center in Asia. Here, you can feast your eyes on some of the most impressive skyscrapers in the East. Fronting Raffles place is **Clifford Pier**, where boats from Indonesia dock.

Also here is the aptly-named **Change Alley**, where you can change almost any currency of the world, usually at better rates than the banks housed in skyscrapers.

You can also buy all sorts of trinkets and electronic goods in Change Alley and the shops that dot the financial district. Don't forget to bargain though.

You can continue past Clifford Pier to **Shenton Way**, an extension of the financial district which eventually leads to the busy container port of **Tanjong Pagar**.

The Port: The shipping activity is largely shielded from the roads and those interested in a firsthand look at the bustling harbor and the enormous stacks of colorful containers may want to take a harbor cruise on a modern boat, or if you are more exotically inclined, on an old Chinese junk.

Although the Port of Singapore actually has seven gateways, its center remains in the Tanjong Pagar area exactly where Raffles envisioned it growing when he claimed Singapore island for the British Empire in 1819. The strategic Straits of Malacca flow north from the island toward the Indian Ocean while the South China Sea stretches east to Indochina, the Philippines, and beyond.

Raffles decreed the port open to all maritime nations. More than 300 international shipping lines still take advantage of that decree. At any one time, there are more than 400 ships in port. One arrives or weighs anchor every 10 minutes or less. One ton of cargo is handled in less than one

Singapore's business district with the port in the background.

second, every second, every day of the year.

Other aspects of the port have also taken on modern trappings. Harbor pilots, for instance, once climbed into slow-moving craft to get to vessels in need of aid in navigation. Now they jump into helicopters which cut their arrival time by at least four-fifths of what it once was. Warehouses have taken on new shapes. They hold a wider and more varied range of goods than those stored in the picturesque, but ramshackle old godowns along the Singapore River. They are automated and computerized.

Singapore's port, like its ever-changing skyscape, has charted a course for a future where there is no room for the past. The reasons are obvious. The old boats may bring in a few sightseeing tourists, but the increasingly sophisticated offerings of the port bring in much more business. In fact, so much business has flowed in since 1981 that Singapore has outstripped London, New York and Yokohama to become the world's second busiest port. Only Rotterdam still does more business than Singapore.

Today, giant 300,000-ton supertankers dominate the scene, leaving the bumboats and *tongkangs* bobbing in their wake as they sail across the shimmering waters of **Singapore Harbour**. The line of ships at their moorings once stretched so far it awed visiting 19th-century officials. Now it extends past the horizon.

Singapore remains a seatown as it was and always will be. It thrives on the trade, commerce and industry produced by shipping. But it has grown from a single city port to become the region's largest ship building and repair center, largest oil port and refining center, largest container port, major feeder port, and a financial center for shipping. It is also a major staging port for oil exploration and the base for a large regional and international fleet.

More History: If you are more interested in history than finance, proceed west from City Hall towards **Fort Canning Hill**—Singapore's oldest landmark. It is also a lovely and shady park.

The shortest way to Fort Canning from the Padang is via **Coleman Street** and on the way you will see two his-

affles still verlooks e ingapore iver and kyline, lmost 170 ears after e first tepped shore.

toric churches of Singapore.

Just between City Hall and the gigantic Raffles City is **St. Andrew's Cathedral**, built in the 1850s by Indian convicts and draftsmen who had never seen an English church before in their lives.

Even today, its interior, flushed with tropical sunlight filtered through stained glass, remains a quiet sanctuary not far from one of Singapore's busiest throughfares.

But St. Andrews is not the oldest church in Singapore. That distinction belongs to the **Armenian Church**, which is just before the entrance to Fort Canning.

The Armenians were once a thriving business community in Singapore and started, among other things, the Raffles Hotel. Their numbers have dwindled in recent years, however, as many have emigrated elsewhere.

Fort Canning, which was known as Forbidden Hill when Raffles arrived in Singapore, contains the reputed tomb of the last Malay ruler of Singapore, Sultan Iskandar Shah. The oldest settlements of Singapore were established here.

The hill also contains an old Christian cemetery which reveals that many Europeans in the topics died at an early age in those days. The park highlights some modern sculptures from neighboring Asian countries.

Cable Cars and Tiger Balms: Singapore is almost a flat island but there are other points besides the tops of skyscrapers from which one can get a panoramic view of the city. The well-situated **Mount Faber** is one of them. A winding five-minute ride takes you to the top from where cable cars depart for the offshore island of **Sentosa** (Tranquility).

The island features several resort-type facilities, including a golf course. There are museums with maritime artifacts, art, sea-shells and insects. The island also has a wax museum depicting scenes such as the Japanese surrender of Singapore and is a pleasant retreat from the bustle of town. A monorail circles the island, offering views of sandy beaches and cool forest.

One can return to the city via cable car or by boat to the **World Trade Center**. Boats for the other, smaller islands of Singapore also leave from the World Trade Center.

Kusu (Turtle) **Island**, a 30-minute ferry ride away, is an idyllic retreat for those wishing to "get away from it all." It features a Chinese temple and a Malay *keramat*, or "holy place."

Just west of the World Trade Center are the famous **Tiger Balm Gardens**, officially known as **Haw Par Villa**. Built in the 1950s by the Aw brothers who made millions selling Tiger Balm, a patent medicine that is supposed to cure most common ailments, the gardens depict scenes from Chinese folklore in a boisterous style.

It has already been called the "Confucian Disneyland" and it will soon really become one when the multi-million-dollar renovation project incorporating lasers and mystery rides are completed.

The Aw brothers also had a taste for more sedate objects of art and their fabulous jade collection is now housed at the **National Museum**. The museum, at **Stamford Road**, has undergone major renovations and houses realistic diaromas of local cultural rites. It also has a rich collection of artifacts from neighboring countries. Local works of art are regularly featured.

Left, the overhead route to Sentosa Island. Right, sexual miscreants at the Tiger Balm Gardens.

THE SPICE(S) OF LIFE

One can never overestimate the importance of eating to Asians. With such a diversity of ethnic backgrounds, it is not surprising that Singaporean taste buds have been honed to a highly refined and discriminating level.

It is possible to find much of what Singapore offers elsewhere, but nowhere else can one find in one place such a variety of food at such reasonable prices.

As visitors to China and India will tell you, you can get better Chinese and Indian food in Singapore than in the countries of origin themselves. After all, gourmet eating is a function of affluence and Singaporeans are certainly affluent by Asian standards.

But it is in the area of "informal" dining that Singapore really excels. Eating Singapore-style at "hawker stalls" is a must. The seats and cutlery may be basic but the food is clean and tasty. Among the more popular items are chicken rice (much more exciting than it sounds!), *satay*, *mee goreng* (fried noodles), *rojak* (a kind of local salad) and desserts like *ice kacang* (shaved ice with an assortment of fillings) and *goreng pisang* (banana fritters).

The most accessible hawker centers are the *Rasa Singapura*, just next to the Tourist Promotion Board office at Tanglin Road, and Cuppage Center, which is just behind the Centrepoint shopping complex on Orchard Road. The Newton Circus hawker stalls at the junction of Newton Road and Scotts Road are popular at night time, especially after midnight.

Seafood prepared the Singapore way, grilled or barbecued with spices, is usually an instant hit with the visitors. Chilli crab—fresh crabs on the shell, stirfried with garlic, sugar, soy sauce, tomato sauce, chillies and eggs—has already garnered a place in the Singapore foodhall of fame. Do not be afraid to ask for the dishes to be modified to your taste with less spices if that is way you prefer it.

Those who value air-conditioned comfort and proper cutlery over the native charm of hawker stalls will find that there is no shortage of upmarket restaurants serving Chinese food from the various regions, including Cantonese, Szechuan, Peking and Teochew cuisine.

One particular variation worth trying by those who prefer lighter meals is *dim sum* (literally "touching the heart"). Served at lunch and as a brunch during weekends, *dim sum* is a series of light snacks that is washed down with cups of Chinese tea.

Hawker food can be a fiery affair.

Shopping and Entertainment

Most tourists are aware that cameras and electronic goods are imported duty free into Singapore and are often cheaper than in Japan, where they are made. But not many are aware that a whole range of other items including carpets and electrical goods are also allowed in duty free and can be good buys.

Orchard Road, which lies northwest of the financial district, is the entertainment and shopping heart of Singapore and is a lovely road flanked by trees and wide pavements.

Numerous hotels, shopping complexes and department stores line this road and **Scotts Road** and **Tanglin Road** that join it.

Next to the STPB office in Tanglin Road is the **Singapore Handicraft Center**, where arts and crafts from Singapore and neighboring countries are sold. There is silverwork from Malaysia, woodcarving from Indonesia, silks from Thailand, dramatic hand-painted opera masks from China and shell lampshades from the Philippines. Next door is one of the best hawker centers in town (**Rasa Singapura**), where the delights of local food can be appreciated.

Among the more important names around this area are **Tang's**, the Chinese curio store of the old days that has been transformed into a multi-story department store but still selling a fascinating selection of Chinese silks and handicrafts.

Farther down at **Centrepoint** is **Robinsons**, which is no longer a store appealing just to the British but to anyone looking for good buys.

Most of Orchard Road is now steel and glass but just next to Centrepoint is something different. It is **Peranakan Place**, a charming converted pre-war shophouse—the kind of business and residential establishment that used to dot most of Singapore's shopping district just three decades ago.

Peranakans are the descendants of Chinese immigrants who absorbed some of the Malay influences in their language, cuisine and other aspects but also retained traditional Chinese customs and values.

'iendly
ces at
rchard
oad.

The corner and a street of adjoining shophouses are now preserved by law to remind future generations of what Singapore once looked like.

Other popular shopping areas are the **People's Park Complex** in **Chinatown**, the **Sim Lim Tower** at **Rochor Road** for electronic goods and **Arab Street** for batik and other Malay handicrafts.

Some believe that these less flashy shopping centers offer better bargains than Orchard Road. But there is an intense competition for retail business in Singapore and prices do not really vary very much.

Those who are not comfortable with bargaining are advised to stick with the better shops that have fixed prices.

Most shops are open from about 10 a.m. to 9 p.m and are generally also open on Saturdays and Sundays.

It is true that the "Sin" in Singapore, well known in its pre-independence days, has largely disappeared from modern Singapore and those looking for the pleasures of the flesh would do better in Manila or Bangkok. But the positive result of the cleanup is that there is no sleaziness or danger in enjoying the low-key, wholesome nightlife that is to be found in Singapore today.

Don't look for the legendary transvestite and transsexual beauties of **Bugis Street**. Bugis Street has been a victim of urban renewal but many of the "beauties" can now be seen wandering along Orchard Road itself during the later hours.

Orchard Road hotels and the many nightclubs in the area are the main source of nighttime entertainment in Singapore. The **Tropicana** nightclub near the **Royal Holiday Inn** at the junction of Orchard Road and Scotts Road has been part of the Singapore scene for many years. Even now, it usually provides the raciest nightlife in town, its well-worn stage featuring the occasional bare-breasted dancer. Niteclubs and discos of both the Chinese and Western variety are readily available in the Orchard Road area, so barhoppers will not have any great distance to travel. Several spots alternate between disc-jockeys and live bands. Those who venture away from the tourist belt will be rewarded with more ethnic-type amusements and generally lower prices.

Shopping, Singapore style: Far East Plaza in Scotts Road.

ETHNIC ENCLAVES

These are not be what they used to be but there is still plenty of life and color left in the older parts of Singapore where the main ethnic communities first started.

Chinatown: Though it may at first look odd to have one in a city where three-quarters of the population is of Chinese origin, the Chinatown in Singapore has that certain something the rest of the city does not.

The area bounded by **New Bridge Road** and **South Bridge Road** is known as Chinatown. It is a compact area but a slow stroll along its narrow lanes will reward the visitor with Chinese food stalls, temples, and on occasion, open-air operas.

You can also catch glimpses of Chinese medicine men and fortune tellers, particularly in the evening. If time permits, a day and night tour of Chinatown will show the very different activities that occur in this part of town. There are also excellent walking tours and trishaw tours that go through Chinatown.

A lot of the small businesses that dotted the streets and sidewalks of Chinatown have been relocated at the massive **Kereta Ayer Complex** at the street of the same name.

Little India: The beginning of **Serangoon Road** and its side streets are known as Little India and it is again worth both a day and nocturnal visit. It is filled with vegetarian restaurants, flower garland shops and of course spice shops.

Geylang: A Little farther away from town is **Geylang Serai** along **Geylang Road**, considered the heart of Malay culture in Singapore. There are also Malay *kampungs* (villages) even farther away in areas such as **Punggol** and **Changi**, but these are fast-disappearing as families are relocated to modern government-built apartments.

The **Geylang Market**, especially during Muslim festival seasons, teems with Malay food and decorative items. Various open-air cultural programs and open-air markets are also held during festivals celebrated by the various ethnic groups.

urning ss sets the ood in hinatown.

PARKS AND GARDENS

One of the most remarkable things about Singapore is that it has not just some of the highest buildings in this part of the world but also some of the best-kept urban parks.

Singaporeans are determined not to let concrete prevail. Parks, gardens and neatly shaved trees and bushes line the sidewalks of the busiest street. Ubiquitous employees and vehicles belonging to the Parks and Recreation Department of the Ministry of National Development ensure that even the smallest plant is well-manicured.

Besides Fort Canning, there are the **Botanic Gardens**, just off **Holland Road**. In bloom for over a century, the gardens are home to almost half-a-million species of plants and trees from around the world, thriving luxuriantly in Singapore's hot and wet climate.

If it is real jungle you want, you can go to **Bukit Timah Nature Reserve**, which is the only place in the island where the original foliage covering it has been retained. The reserve's 185 acres (75 hectares), lined with jungle walks, have enough birds and butterflies to give you a taste of jungle even if you don't have time to sample the real thing.

What the nature reserve lacks in animals, you can find at the **Singapore Zoological Gardens**—which bills itself the "Open Zoo." It is aptly named since few of its animals are caged and the visitor does not feel like a heartless voyeur. The animals, even some of the birds, roam free in what must be one of the best-landscaped zoos in the world.

In the mornings the zoo offers a rare treat—breakfast with Singapore's favorite *orangutan*, Ah Meng.

Flower lovers will find it worth their while to visit the **Mandai Orchid Gardens** which are very near the zoo. The gardens exports millions of flowers around the world. Situated at the edge of secondary jungle, the grounds are filled with a variety of orchids.

Singapore has also turned its water catchment areas into beautiful parks and many of them are worth visiting. **MacRitchie Reservoir** is the one that is

Picture-perfect at the Chinese Gardens.

nearest to the city and the most popular with young lovers. **Seletar Reservoir** is near the zoo while **Peirce Reservoir** is almost at the center of the island.

But if it is birds of the feathered variety that you are interested in, visit the **Jurong Bird Park**.

True to Singapore's flair for international personalities, the Bird Park population is globally oriented. If you've missed witnessing an Australian emu lay huge black-spotted eggs, or an Indian white-crested laughing thrush giggle, your chance to take in the view is here. Hillside aviaries shelter birds flown in from every direction: Taiwan magpies, Peking robins, Brazilian rheas, African koribusters, Japanese bantams.

After the bird park, catch a glimpse of Jurong's industrial estates, where large factories make everything from steel to small electronic products.

Two theme parks, devoted to the two great East Asian cultures, are also in Jurong: the **Chinese Gardens** and **Japanese Gardens**. Both are well landscaped and serve as a green oasis in this industrial area of Singapore. The **Singapore Science Centre**, halfway between Jurong and the city at **Jurong Town Hall Road**, should be of particular interest to youngsters.

Public Housing: After visiting all those parks you may want to visit the "real" Singapore: the concrete housing estates of the **Housing Development Board** (HDB) where more than 80 percent of Singapore's population lives.

Though large-scale and largely functional in design, the HDB estates have a lot of greenery amidst them and are well provided with amenities such as shops, theaters and community centers where working-class Singaporeans can learn everything from aerobics to French cooking.

Alert visitors will notice the bamboo poles jutting out from windows that are used for hanging laundry to dry. For some reason, dryers have never become popular among Singaporeans. Though many own washing machines, solar energy still seems to be the preferred mode for drying.

At one time, some local aesthetes regarded the drying of laundry as an eyesore but the tide has since turned and this style has become a particularly local characteristic.

…e ever-…anging …ce of …ingapore: …w HDB …partment …ocks.

TEMPLES AND MOSQUES

As to be expected in a multi-faith, multi-religious society, there are more places of worship in Singapore than even a dedicated tourist can visit. And not all of them are in places where you would expect them to be. For example, the oldest Hindu temple in Singapore is in Chinatown.

The **Sri Mariamman Hindu Temple** was built in 1862 and is of the South Indian variety, with a characteristic, colorful tower filled with the many gods from the Hindu pantheon.

Every evening it has a service to which visitors are usually admitted if they are dressed formally and are prepared to take off their shoes. The temple also has an annual fire walking festival during which devotees run across a pit filled with burning embers.

The other Indian temple of note is **Chettiar's Temple**, at the junction of **Tank Road** and **River Valley Road**. It was recently rebuilt on the site of an older temple.

Variety highlights the style of Singapore's Chinese temples. They range from tiny shrines in attap huts to ornately embellished monasteries of the old style.

The country's oldest Chinese temple, the "**Temple of Heavenly Happiness**," otherwise known as **Thian Hok Keng Temple**, is located at **Telok Ayer Street** not far from Chinatown. Once a refuge for fresh immigrants from the Fukien province of China, it still retains an old world charm that is not to be found in the bigger but more modern Chinese temples.

But the most popular Chinese temple is the **Goddess of Mercy Temple** at **Waterloo Street**. Known in Chinese as *Kuan Yin*, the Goddess of Mercy refers to a goddess who spurned the gates of paradise upon hearing a cry of anguish from the earth and returned to earth to work for the alleviation of human suffering.

This temple demonstrates the strength of faith people had in their religion, although the temple itself is not particularly ornate. For that, you have to go to the grand **Siong Lim See** Temple at **Kim Keat Road**. In translation, it is known as the "Twin Grove of the Lotus Mountain Buddhist Temple."

This lavish temple is guarded by imposing giant statues who are bodyguards at the gates of Heaven. But the inner sanctum is a serene place where the Laughing Buddha and merciful *Kuan Yin* reign. Built entirely in old Chinese style, the temple's sagging roofs, upturned eaves and twisting woodwork will appeal to architectural buffs.

Sakya Muni Buddha Gaya Temple on **Race Course Road** is a particularly fine and cosy example of a Thai Buddhist temple.

Built decades ago by a Thai monk, the temple recalls the grandoise aura of a Thai *wat* with picture postcards of Bangkok's famous temples to heighten the mood.

Islam, the faith of one fifth of mankind, came to Singapore early. The last king of ancient Singapura, Sultan Iskandar Shah, was an early convert to Islam in the 14th century. Raffles found a strong following among the Malay settlers on the island in 1819. During negotiations with Sultan Hussin Shah of Johore, he donated $3,000 to help build the first Masjid Sultan, or **Sultan Mosque** which is situated off **North Bridge Road**. A hundred years later, the three-tiered roof on the old mosque came tumbling down to make room for the opulent domes and spires of the present shrine. The current building has been renovated and enlarged.

The five tenets of Islam—to verify there is no god but Allah, to pray five times daily, to fast during the month of Ramadzan, to give alms and to go on a pilgrimage to Mecca—are closely followed by Muslims in Singapore. The soulful chant of the *muezzin* sounds above street corners form the minarets of many mosques. The oldest among them, built only a year after the founding of Singapore in 1819, lies in the heart of **Kampong Malacca**, an old quarter of the city that now belongs to Chinatown. An odd minaret, suggestive of a steeple, tops the lovely old **Fatimah's Mosque**, erected by a rich Malay lady who married a Bugis lord. In the smallest Malay kampong where dirt pathways weave among clap-board homes, a small dome rises from the center of the neighborhood sheltering the local *surau*, village mosque.

Right, time for quiet study in a Singapore mosque.

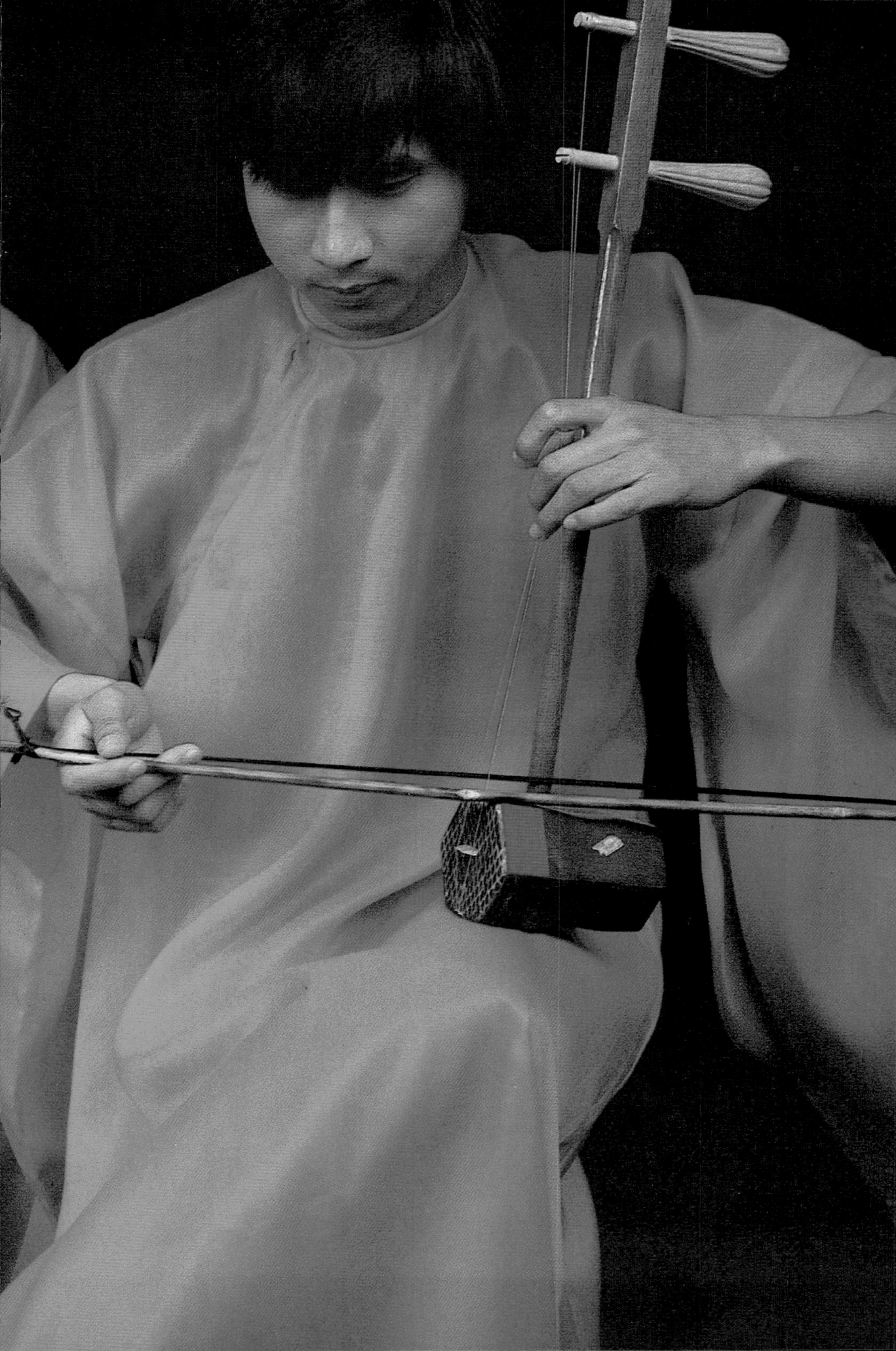

TAIWAN: THE "BEAUTIFUL ISLAND"

Ilha Formosa: the "Beautiful Island." That's what Portuguese mariners who first put Taiwan on European maps during the 1590s called this emerald isle. To the early waves of Chinese settlers who flooded Taiwan's shores half a century later it was *Bao-Dao*, "Treasure Island." Beauty and prosperity have been the island's hallmarks ever since.

For the practical yet highly aesthetic Chinese, Taiwan was a dream come true. What more could anyone desire of life than to live and work in peace and security in a place that's rich and beautiful? Today, Taiwan's small but devoted force of expatriates stays for precisely the same reasons: profit and pleasure. But don't be fooled into thinking that the island's attractions are merely skin-deep: Taiwan is a tireless champion of ancient Chinese traditions and culture.

One can neither fully appreciate the attractions, nor completely understand the significance, of contemporary Taiwan without constant reference to mainland China. Ever since the trauma of dynastic change on the mainland triggered mass migrations to Taiwan during the 17th century, the island has served as a haven for merchants and mandarins, fishermen and farmers, monks and millionaires. The early emigrés hailed from every corner and social stratum of China and brought with them traditional culture, life-styles and values. The seeds of classical Chinese civilization quickly took root and blossomed in Taiwan.

Taiwan today is an island of sharp contrasts: contrasts between ancient culture and modern economy, time-honored values and contemporary concerns, temples and skyscrapers, rice-paddies and freeways. Such contrasts are the real keys to appreciating and understanding Taiwan, for among the Chinese, "contrast" means "completion" rather than "contradiction," just as *Yin* completes rather than conflicts with *Yang*.

Nesting securely on the firm foundations of their 5,000-year-old heritage, the Chinese in Taiwan nurtured a fully developed modern economy in less than 30 years, a growth so healthy and rapid that foreign observers have dubbbed it to be nothing less than an "economic miracle."

To its people, however, there is nothing magical or miraculous about Taiwan's outstanding performance: it is the logical outcome of a strict work ethic, boundless energy and natural entrepreneurial talent.

In the opening line of *The Analects*, Confucius wrote, "When friends visit from afar, is this not indeed a pleasure?" The ebullient enthusiasm with which the people of Taiwan receive foreign visitors and the obvious pleasure they take in hosting "friends from afar" are perhaps the strongest impressions and most lasting souvenirs which travelers from all over the world take home with themfrom the "Beautiful Island."

Preceding pages: Fiddling around:—musicians in a Chinese band. Left, door knocker at the gate to the Chiang Kai-shek Memorial Hall.

"EL DORADO" OF THE ORIENT

Taiwan straddles the Tropic of Cancer about 120 miles (193 km) off the shores of mainland China's Fukien province. Sparkling like an emerald in the cobalt waters of the East China Sea, the island occupies a strategic pivotal position between Japan, Korea, Hong Kong, the Philippines, and mainland China.

Shaped like a tea leaf, Taiwan stretches 250 miles (402 km) from north to south and about 80 miles (129 km) across its widest point. That makes this island of 19 million people about the size of Holland. Included within Taiwan's domain are several offshore islands, such as the Pescadores, Orchid Island, Green Island, and the militarily strategic Kinmen (Quemoy) and Matsu.

Two-thirds of Taiwan is corrugated by rugged mountains pushed up from ocean depths by prehistoric volcanic action. Traces of coral from the island's ancient seabed can still be found in igneous rock formations as high as 2,000 feet (610 meters) above sea level. Taiwan's Central Range runs like a boney spine along the island's north-south axis and includes Jade Mountain (Mount Morrison), which at 13,114 feet (3,997 meters) boasts the tallest peak in all of Northeast Asia. The violent volcanic eruptions which formed these mountains left the island seamed from tip to toe with the sulfurous brimstones of over 100 major hot springs, whose bubbling thermal waters constitute one of Taiwan's greatest recreational attractions—soothing hot mineral baths.

The east coast of Taiwan drops abruptly from the mountains into the sea, forming some of the most spectacular scenery on the island. This coastline is strongly reminiscent of California's fabled Big Sur coast and Korea's equally scenic eastern shoreline. The western part of Taiwan consists of broad alluvial plains watered by short, swift rivers which wind down from the Central Range. East and west are linked by the fabulously scenic East-West Cross-Island Highway, which cuts a serpentine route for 120 dramatic, cliff-hanging miles through the peaks and gorges of the Central Range. Ten thousand retired servicemen spent four years and sacrificed 450 lives building this road, known locally as the "Rainbow of Treasure Island."

Generally speaking, there are two distinct seasons in Taiwan: hot (May-September) and cold (November-March). The most pleasant times of year to travel in Taiwan are April-May and October-November, when days are pleasantly warm but not steamy and nights refreshingly cool but not cold. But be forewarned: weather in Taiwan can change dramatically from day to day and hour to hour, any time of year. You might get soaked to the skin by a sudden thunderstorm in mid-July, or baked to the bone by an unseasonably hot day in January.

Long before the Chinese ever set foot on Taiwan, the island was inhabited by a colorful—and quarrelsome—array of primitive aborigine tribes, who came to Taiwan from Mongolia, the Malay peninsula, and the South pacific. Radiocarbon dating of ancient artifacts recently unearthed along Taiwan's rugged eastern coastline indicate that aboriginal man was well established on the island at least 10,000 years ago, and probably much longer. Today, there are still over 250,000 ethnic aborigines scattered across Taiwan, including remnants of 19 different tribes. Nine of these tribes still have sufficient numbers and interest in their own origins to maintain their traditional tribal lifestyles in specially designated homelands tucked in the steep mountains and deep valleys of the Central Range. The largest tribe is the *Ami*, who live in the mountains near the east coast town of Hualien and boast over 60,000 members. Their annual "Ami Harvest Festival," held in Hualien in August, remains one of the island's most colorful and popular events.

Perhaps the most interesting and authentic tribe of the bunch is the *Yami*, a seafaring tribe on offshore Orchid Island whose elegantly carved fishing boats give strong credence to claims of polynesian roots.

With their traditional costumes and feathered headgear, elaborately carved totem poles and other handicrafts, and their inherent love of music and dance, Taiwan's native tribes form some of the brightest, boldest threads in the colorful cultural tapestry of Taiwan. Among the most salient themes shared by all of these tribes is their veneration of the venomous "Hundred Pacer" snake as their "spiritual ancestor." This deadly serpent gets its name from the fact that its victims rarely make it more than a hundred paces before dropping dead. The other motif which appears with the snake on almost all aborigine carvings, paintings, and weaving is the dismembered human head, a thematic remnant of their heyday as headhunters.

Left, Taiwan native. Above, 17th-century print of the Dutch command at Fort Zeelandia.

In 239 A.D., the Chinese Kingdom of Wu launched a 10,000-man expedition to lay claim to the island but the mission disappeared without a trace. Then in 1430, the famous seafaring eunuch and Ming official Cheng Ho, whose armada sailed as far as India and Persia, "discovered" the island once again, claimed it on behalf of the Ming emperor, and gave it its present name, "Taiwan," which means "terraced bay."

The first Chinese to actually settle permanently on Taiwan were a refugee minority group called "Hakkas," a word which literally means "guests" or "strangers." For some unknown, or perhaps unexplained, reason the Hakkas had been severely persecuted in China since ancient times and were driven from their ancestral homeland in northern China's Honan province about 1,500 years ago. The Hakkas wandered far and wide, eventually settling down along the southern shores of Fukien and Kwangtung, where they engaged in fishing and trade. These activities soon brought them to the offshore Pescadores Islands and then to Taiwan itself, where by 1000 A.D. the Hakkas had begun to establish permanent settlements along the island's southern shores. To this day, the Hakkas remain a major dynamic force in Taiwan's booming economy, and they still command deep respect for their entrepreneurial and financial acumen.

Taiwan's wealth and beauty did not long remain a Hakka secret. During the 15th and 16th centuries, the island and its lucrative coastal trade became both target and haven for marauding pirates from China and Japan.

After failing to wrest Macao from Portuguese rivals, the Dutch established a colony in 1624 on Taiwan's southern coast, where they built three forts.

In 1644, the militant Manchus commenced their relentless campaign to conquer the tottering Ming Dynasty and claim the Dragon Throne as their own. The Ming emperor sought aid from a Taiwan-based pirate named Cheng Chi-lung and his son Cheng Cheng-kung, who nearly succeeded in driving the Manchu invaders out of China, but for superior Manchu numbers and resources. In 1661, the younger Cheng, known in Western chronicles as "Koxinga," led his army of 100,000 men and armada of 3,000 war junks across the Taiwan Straits to safe refuge on "Treasure Island."

Koxinga captured the island from the Dutch and established a civil administration based on Chinese laws and principles. When Koxinga died in 1662 at the age of 38, his mantle passed on to his son and then his grandson, who kept the island free of Manchu control until 1684, when the Manchus managed to impose nominal sovereignty over Taiwan.

Britain's "Opium Wars" with China in the 19th century brought Taiwan into the limelight once more. Dr. William Jardine, co-founder of Hong Kong's "Noble House" trading firm Jardine, Matheson, & Co., was profoundly alarmed by Peking's attempt to forcibly forbid trade in his firm's most profitable product—opium. In a letter to British Foreign Secretary Lord Palmerston, he wrote, "We must proceed to take possession of three or four islands, say Formosa, Quemoy, and Amoy, in order to secure new markets and new footholds in China." The Treaty of Tientsin, which ended the first Opium War in 1860, thus opened four ports in Taiwan to foreign trade: Keelung and Suao in the north, Taiwanfoo (Tainan) and Takao (Kaohsiung) in the south. By 1867, about three dozen foreign traders lived permanently on the island, mostly British, American, and German. Then, as a result of the Sino-Japanese war of 1894-95, Taiwan was ceded to Japan, marking the start of 50 years of harsh colonial rule.

At the end of World War II, the island was formally restored to Nationalist Chinese rule, an event still celebrated each year in Taiwan as "Retrocession Day."

Meanwhile, fighting continued on the mainland as Nationalist and Communist Chinese armies fought for control of China. Finally, Nationalist leader Chiang Kai-shek led his two best divisions, plus a rambling entourage of scholars and artists, merchants and magistrates, across the Taiwan Straits. On December 7, 1949, the Republic of China (ROC) formally transferred its government headquarters to the provisional capital of Taipei.

A thorough land reform program was immediately effected, landowners were paid well in cash for their holdings, then offered tax breaks and other generous incentives to invest their newfound wealth in launching a modern industrial revolution in Taiwan. With this single bold stroke of the brush, the Nationalist Chinese government in Taiwan at once defused longstanding and potentially explosive peasant grievances, while simultaneously creating an entrepreneurial elite of former landlords who now had the money and motivation, as well as the education and experience, to preside over Taiwan's upcoming "economic miracle."

According to a report prepared by the Stanford Research Institute in 1986, Taiwan accomplished in less than 30 years what it takes most developing countries over 100 years to achieve. The report cites Taiwan as the single most outstanding model for success in modern economic development for the Third World today, and it credits Taiwan's phenomenal growth directly to the enlightened *laissez-faire* and economic *savoir-faire* of the island's leaders.

Left, girls on parade with Sun Yat-sen posters during "Double Ten" festivities. Above, band instruments at Chiang Kai-shek Memorial Hall.

Today, 99.7 percent of Taiwan's homes enjoy electricity, with an average 103 televisions per 100 households and 55 cars and 250 telephones per 1,000 persons. The average economic growth rate for the past 30 years has stood at an incredible 9 percent, even during the height of the oil crises, and per capita income now stands at US $3,000—more than 10 times the per capita income on the mainland. Taiwan is currently America's seventh largest trading partner worldwide, and the island enjoys a highly profitable world trade of over US$50 billion per year. Taiwan ranks second only to West Germany as the world's biggest container shipper, and the economy has already successfully entered the age of technology-intensive industries. These impressive economic achievements have prompted envious rivals to dub the island with yet another nick-name: "Taiwan, Inc."

Nothing, however, is more relevant than that unique social trait known as *ren-ching-wei,* literally "the flavor of human feeling."

Ren-ching-wei is what Confucius was talking about 2,500 years ago when he established harmonious human relations as the prime focal point of Chinese social life, and this flavor still permeates every aspect of life in Taiwan today. In practice, it simply means that human considerations must always take precedence over legal rigamarole and that human feelings are more important than logic. It explains the prime importance of hospitality in Chinese culture, as well as the stubborn demands to "save face" in Chinese society. It remains the fountainhead of Chinese social and psychological resilience in this fast-paced age of science and technology, and it alone prevents basic human concerns from being swallowed up by commerce and industry, as they have been in so many other countries these days.

Classical Chinese culture thrives alongside a booming high-tech economy in contemporary Taiwan. When it comes to tasting the "flavor of human feeling" and discovering cherished customs, there is no better place than among the friendly people and scenic landscapes of *Ilha Formosa.*

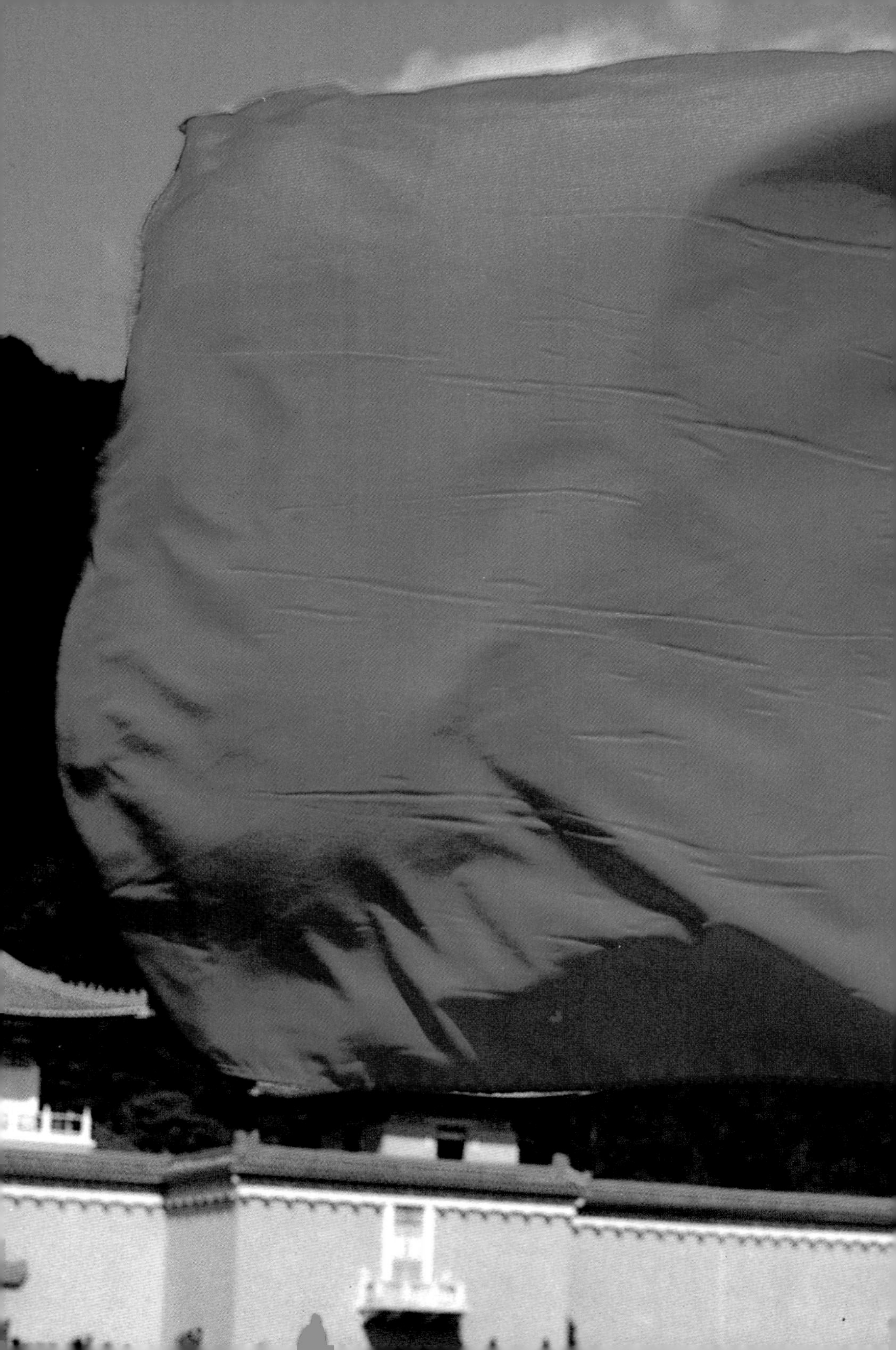

TAIPEI AND THE NORTHERN COAST

First-time visitors to **Taipei** are often confused by contradicting signals. As their jetliners float down through the island's cape of clouds to approach the airport, the first view they get is an endless patchwork panorama of green bamboo and banana groves, lush vegetable fields and fish ponds, punctuated here and there by red brick farmhouses and the bobbing straw hats of farmers wading knee-deep in shimmering rice paddies. This pastoral scene is abruptly cut short as the plane glides over the runway and lands on the tarmac of one of Asia's most modern airport facilities—**Chiang Kai-shek International Airport**, located in **Taoyuan**, about 40 miles (64 km) southwest of Taipei.

Speeding into town by bus or cab along the **Sun Yat-sen Memorial Freeway**, contrasts continue to assault the senses. Your driver, who treats you with respect and courtesy fit for a king, approaches other cars on the road as mortal enemies, frequently interrupting his polite dialogue with you to hurl dire curses at rival roadsters. The freeway, clean and nicely landscaped, is crowded with trucks and buses that engulf all other vehicles in odious clouds of noxious fumes. In the distance, beyond the tropical greenery that lines the freeway, power lines and factory chimneys loom on the horizon.

Some 45 minutes later, as you approach the exit into Taipei, your eyes behold a sight that distills the very essence of traditional Chinese spirit in modern-day Taiwan. Towering regally above the traffic and tumult of Taipei, aloof yet ever-present on its lofty perch on **Round Hill**, stands what appears to be an ancient but well-preserved Chinese palace. The eaves of this gargantuan, red-lacquered, gold-tiled, elaborately filigreed structure curve gracefully against the sky, framing the largest classical Chinese roof in the world. Could it be the President's Palace? Or the National Palace Museum? A huge temple perhaps? No, it's the **Grand Hotel**, one of Taipei's most imposing landmarks. Constructed in classical Chinese palace-style by contemporary architects using modern methods and materials, all under the personal supervision of Madame Chiang Kai-shek, the Grand symbolizes the fusion of tradition and technology, concrete and Confucius, classical style and contemporary function, *Yin* and *Yang*, in modern Taiwan.

You have arrived in Taipei (literally "Taiwan North")—provisional capital of the Republic of China, corporate headquarters of "Taiwan, Inc.," and one of the most staunchly Confucian Chinese cities in the world. Leave your cultural baggage at home, for it's best to approach Taipei with an open mind, uncluttered by preconceived notions of "China" or "Taiwan." Like a beautiful woman, Taipei resents comparisons: you must either accept her on her own terms, or not at all.

There are of course all sorts of different things to do and see in this sprawling metropolis of three million souls, but for the visitor with limited time who wishes to feel the Chinese heart that beats beneath the surface of the city's cosmetic facade, there are several sights which should not be overlooked.

First and foremost on any Taipei itinerary is the **National Palace Museum.**

receding ages: The OC flag, urce of ationalistic ride. Left, aborate none ooth in the ational useum of istory. ight, aiwan ancer.

This is more than just a museum—it is a graphic, mind-boggling journey into 5,000 years of Chinese creativity and an exquisite tribute to the Chinese love of beauty. First collected in 1924 from the vast stores of art treasures hoarded in Peking's fabulous Forbidden Ctiy by 20 consecutive Chinese emperors, the collection was subsequently sheperded to and fro across the face of war-torn China from 1931-1948 before making its way across to Taiwan with Chiang-Kai-shek in 1949. It is one of the most impressive collections on earth.

Near the Grand Hotel, which in itself is a monument worth visiting, you'll find the **National Revolutionary Martyr's Shrine**, a self-contained complex of classical structures built entirely in the imperial style of the Ming Dynasty and dedicated to China's fallen war heroes. This used to be one of President Chiang Kai-shek's favorite haunts, and he often spent entire afternoons relaxing within its well-manicured grounds and hallowed halls. The changing of the guard, which occurs once every hour, is at least as impressive as its counterpart at Buckingham Palace in London.

For an altogether different perspective of Taipei, proceed to "**Snake Alley**" and the **Lung-Shan** ("Dragon Mountain") **Temple**, preferably after dark. Located in the heart of Taipei's oldest district, Snake Alley gets its name from the various snake shops which line this funky little lane. The serpents are caught in the mountains by professional snake-catchers and sold as potent tonics for lower back pain, poor eyesight, and, inevitably, sexual debility. For the equivalent of about US$3 to $10, depending on the type, a hawker high on betel-nut will kill the snake of your choice and concoct a "Serpentine Cocktail" from the freshly squeezed blood and bile and some potent herbal spirits. Some adventurous customers even request a drop or two of venom to be added for an extra "kick." Does it work? Only the tippler knows for sure!

Other attractions in Snake Alley, officially known as **Hua-Hsi Street**, include excellent seafood eateries, fresh fruit stalls, fortune-tellers, vendors of medicinal herbs, and a lively assortment of revelers.

The famous Lung-Shan Temple,

Gateway to the National Palace Museum.

built about 250 years ago to commemorate the safe arrival in Taiwan of the first wave of Chinese settlers from the mainland, is located only two blocks from Snake Alley. Here, you'll see some of the world's best surviving Chinese temple carvings and other aspects of traditional architectural artistry. Pay especially close attention to the full-relief carvings in solid stone on the main supporting pillars and to the work on the ceilings and roofs. The chants and other rites you'll witness here have not changed a single syllable for many centuries.

Other spots in town worth visiting are the **Chiang Kai-shek Memorial**, the **Confucius Temple**, the shopping district called **Hsi-Men-Ding** (Taipei's own version of "Times Square"), the **Shin-Lin Night Market**, and the glittering gaggle of bars, clubs, and pubs clustered within the narrow lanes of "Sugar Daddy Row," near the **President** and **Imperial hotels**.

Standard organized group tours of Taipei by day or night may be readily arranged through any hotel in town.

Northern Diversions: Within easy reach of downtown Taipei are a number of diversions which provide a pleasant respite from the noise and traffic of the city, while also providing some scenic glimpses of the Beautiful Island's natural charms.

Due north of the Grand Hotel, for example, stand the lush green slopes of **Yangming Mountain**, the "Beverly Hills" of Taipei. Here you'll find the spacious villas and walled gardens of industrial tycoons, famous movie stars, and wealthy expatriate businessmen, as well as the "**White Cloud Villa**," the world's second largest supplier of orchids. Over one million orchids fill the greenhouses of this mountaintop nursery, and visitors are always welcome to browse and sniff around.

Farther up the mountain is **Yangming Mountain National Park**, site of the annual Taipei "Spring Flower Festival," which runs from mid-February till early April. A colorful complex of manicured gardens, flowering trees, bamboo groves, fragrant blossoms, and cosy little grottos, this park provides a quick "getaway" from the hustle and bustle of downtown Taipei. However, anyone in search of peace and quiet

ankow reet in the te ternoon.

should try to avoid visiting on Sundays and holidays, when it's more likely to get lost among forests of people rather than trees.

Less lofty but even farther removed from the urban sprawl of Taipei are the hills and valleys of **Peitou**, an old hot springs resort about 10 miles (16 km) north of town. Once a hotbed of "Rest and Recreation," first for the colonial Japanese officers who built it and then for visiting American GIs from Korea and Vietnam, Peitou today has matured into a pleasant, private mineral-bath spa for both local and foreign visitors. Among the several dozen inns which offer hot spring baths there, by far the best choice is the "**Whispering Pines Inn**," at 21 Yio-Ya Road. Built at the turn of the century in classical Japanese fashion, this elegant inn has been impeccably preserved and provides the wayfarer with a traditional style of service and comfort to which he will quickly grow accustomed, if not addicted.

If you have a full day to spare and the means to rent a car and driver, then a drive along Taiwan's northern coastline is an excellent way to spend it. The main freeway zips you out to the northern port of **Keelung** in about 25 minutes, and from there the **North Coast Highway** branches off in both directions to skirt the coastline. Keelung's natural harbor has 33 deep-water wharves and four mooring buoys that can handle vessels up to the 30,000-ton class. About 34 million tons of freight is handled here annually.

Egyptian queen's head at Yeh-Liu.

Near Keelung lies **Greenbay Beach**, one of the best beach resorts in northern Taiwan. A bit northwest of Keelung you'll find the popular sightseeing attraction called **Yeh-Liu** ("Wild Willows"), a coral promontory where aeons of wind and water have sculpted solid stone into all sorts of bizarre shapes and images. It looks more like the planet Mars than the northern coast of an earthly island. If you continue west along the highway it will eventually bring you around to the old fishing port and trading post of **Tan-Shui**, and from there it circles back to Taipei.

Traveling east along the North Coast Highway brings you first to **Pitouchiao**, a wave-washed stone bluff which juts dramatically out into the Pacific Ocean. Next stop is **Fulung**, another popular northern beach resort, with inexpensive beach bungalows available for overnight sojourns. There are also trains which run directly to Fulung from Taipei, servicing those who wish to make a bee-line for the beach.

The last and perhaps most interesting stop along the eastern branch of the North Coast Highway is the old port of **Suao**, an ancient fishing village which has also become a modern international seaport. Skip the new harbor and head straight for "Fisherman's Wharf," known as **Nanfang-Au** (Southside Suao). This salt-encrusted old marina is packed with vintage high-prowed fishing vessels and excellent dockside seafood restaurants which prepare the daily catch of fish, mollusks, and crustaceans with gourmet flair. Anyone with a taste for old boats and good seafood will love Southside Suao.

From Suao, you can either double back along the North Coast Highway to Keelung, then cut down the freeway to Taipei, or else wind your way back to town on **Route 9** which cuts a scenic route through the rolling hills between Taipei and the coast.

Portrait Of A Martial Artist

The 17 great martial artists were in agreement. Their young charge, Hung Yi-Hsiang, was undoubtedly a "Sleeping Dragon," an expression used to describe someone with enormous latent talent not yet fully matured. Under their expert tutelage though, and over the course of the next 35 years, he developed and perfected some eye-opening skills. Today, Hung-Yi-Hsiang, 50, is considered one of the greatest living exponents of the martial arts.

Master Hung has blended the various styles he learned to form his own unique school called "Tang-Shou-Tao." He defies the hackneyed image of a martial artist. Neither the wizened old greybeard in long flowing robes, nor the brash young tough of Bruce Lee ilk, Master Hung packs over 200 pounds of powerful bulk into a squat five-foot six-inch frame. His fist can pulverize two cinder blocks laid flat on a table, but those same fingers unfurl to gently heal the ailing with massage and acupuncture, execute exquisite Chinese painting and calligraphy, and cook gourmet Chinese food.

To watch Master Hung perform the cosmic dance of *Tai-Chi* or demonstrate the mesmerizing circles of *Ba-Kua* is a living lesson in the harmony of *Yin* and *Yang*. He glides effortlessly through seemingly impossible maneuvers—soft and fluid as water, swift and sudden as lightning. Asked to explain the fundamental secret of his style, he replies with a perfunctory monosyllabic grunt, "*Chee*!" In English, *chee* means "breath" and "air" as well as "energy." In other words, Master Hung follows the subtle "Internal Energy" school of martial arts.

Master Hung's style is directly rooted in *Tao*, which lies at the very heart of Chinese philosophy. "*Tao*" simply means "way" or "path," and it is the key to all things Chinese. To do things the "Chinese way" means to do things according to "Tao," the one and only "Way." Tao manifests itself in nature through the constant interplay of opposite but complementary cosmic forces called "*Yin*" and "*Yang*," i.e. male/female, hot/cold, light/dark, and so forth. It is these forces which the martial artist must manipulate and master.

"Properly applied," explains Master Hung, quoting the ancient sages, "four ounces of strength can topple 1,000 pounds." He advises his students to "concentrate on the inner meaning, not the outer strength."

Master Hung himself typifies the ancient Confucian ideal of a *jyun-dze*, which means "superior man" or "gentleman." A *jyun-dze* must be master of many talents, including *wen* (literary) and *wu* (martial) arts. He must cultivate his full potential while also contributing positively to family and society. Master Hung, for example, makes his living by day as a licensed physician of traditional Chinese medicine, while by night he transmits his precious heritage of martial arts to a handful of select students. He devotes much of his leisure time to the arts, and is also active in civic organizations.

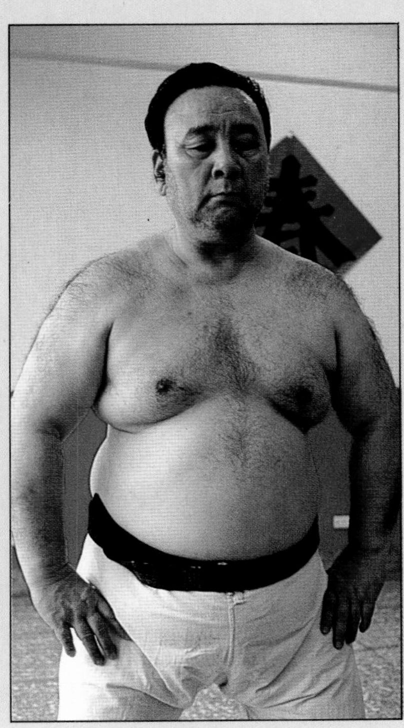

aster
ung
emonstrates
s "chi."

文武廟
忠昭日月義溥雲天
道貫古今德參造化

Taichung and Sun Moon Lake

About 60 miles (100 km) south of Taipei lies **Taichung** ("Taiwan Central"), the island's provincial capital and third largest city. Taichung was founded in 1721 by immigrants from China, and it still retains a distinctive aura of local color that has long since been washed from Taipei by modern urban development.

For most visitors, Taichung serves as a convenient springboard to the scenic attractions of central Taiwan. For example, only 13 miles (21 km) southwest of Taichung lies sleepy **Lukang** ("Deer Port"), which for over 200 years prior to the 20th century was the favorite port of entry for Chinese immigrants from the mainland. The town has changed very little since the turn of the century, but the harbor has long since been rendered useless by accumulations of silt and sand.

In Lukang are half a dozen 18th-century temples which clearly reflect the architectural and decorative styles brought to Taiwan from Ming China. Lukang remains the island's major center for production of incense, altar tables, oil lamps, wood carvings, icons, and other traditional temple accessories. You may watch craftsmen at work with traditional tools through the open fronts of their shops along Lukang's main street.

If forests and mountains appeal to you more than ports and temples, Taichung is only 14 miles (22 km) away from the **Hsitou Bamboo Forest**—a popular resort within a 6,150-acre (2,490-hectare) forest research station. At 3,800 feet (1,160 meters) above sea level, Hsitou is pleasantly cool even during the hottest months, and a complete ban on motor vehicles within the grounds keeps the air blessedly fresh and clean. Paved hiking trails criss-cross the entire forest, which boasts dense groves of over a dozen different varieties of bamboo, ranging in size from pencil-thin to thigh-thick. Along the pathways are ponds and pavilions, waterfalls and other scenic attractions. A chalet-style hotel and numerous private cabins provide comfortable accommodations.

Other scenic destinations within a convenient radius of Taichung include the hidden Shangrila of **Mount Lu** (a hot spring spa in the mountains due west), **Mount Ali** (famous for its magical sunrises), **Sungpoling** (a town renowned for its tea and its huge Taoist temple), and **Ku-Kuan** (first hill station on the west side of the East-West Cross-Island Highway). Taichung's most popular satellite, however, has always been **Sun Moon Lake** which is located about 25 miles (40 km) to the southwest.

Sun Moon Lake: The dreamy landscapes surrounding the tranquil turquoise waters of Sun Moon Lake, with their drifting mists and ever shifting moods, have made it Taiwan's most popular honeymoon resort. But it's also a major local tourist attraction, so it's best to either avoid weekends and holidays, or else rise at the crack of dawn while the tour groups are still snoring to commence your own private exploration of the lake and surrounding sights.

A paved road winds its way over hill and dale around the lake, offering various viewpoints and providing different perspectives. Highlights along the way include the magnificent **Wen-Wu Temple** (dedicated to the Martial and Literary Arts and their patron deities), and the simple but fascinating **Hsuan-Tsang Temple**, perched high on a hill overlooking the lake's southern shore.

Chiang Kai-shek—though himself a converted Christian—ordered the Hsuan-Tsang Temple built to house some of China's most precious Buddhist relics. Hsuan-Tsang was the Tang Dynasty monk who 1,500 years ago undertook a hazardous 17-year pilgrimage to India, an odyssey immortalized in the classical Chinese novel *Journey to the West*. A shard of his skullbone is housed in an ornate, jewel-encrusted reliquary on the third floor. On the ground floor stands another reliquary of solid gold in which are displayed half a dozen tiny nuggets known as *ssu-lee-dze* ("relic seeds"), collected from the cremated ashes of Sakyamuni Buddha 2,500 years ago and distributed among his disciples.

There are several good hotels and a number of inexpensive hotels at Sun Moon Lake. Buses to Sun Moon Lake depart Taichung every half hour between 7 a.m. and 2 p.m.

ɘft, group hoto at 'en Wu emple in un Moon ake.

TAROKO GORGE AND THE EASTERN COAST

Second only to the National Palace Museum in Taipei, Taiwan's greatest tourist attraction is the convoluted canyon of raw marble cliffs called **Taroko Gorge**. This gorgeous gorge covers the first 12 miles (20 km) of the East-West Cross-Island Highway from its eastern terminus near the coastal town of Hualien, headquarters of Taiwan's biggest aborigine tribe, the Ami. Taroko, which means "beautiful" in the Ami dialect, attracts about 5,000 visitors per day. There are daily one-day group tours to Taroko Gorge from Taipei, departing by air for Hualien early in the morning and returning late the same afternoon.

Taroko Gorge, which was carved through marble mountains by the waters of the **Li-wu** ("Foggy") **River**, is regarded by all who have been there as one of East Asia's greatest scenic wonders. The "Shrine of Eternal Spring," located a few miles from the entrance, is an elegant memorial dedicated to the 450 retired servicemen who died during constuction of the Cross-Island Highway or "Rainbow of Treasure Island." Other famous sights along the way include the "**Swallow's Grotto**," the sheer, mind-boggling marble walls of the "**Fuji Cliff**," the tortuous cliff-hugging stretch of road called "**Tunnel of Nine Turns**," the "**Bridge of Filial Devotion**," and the final stop on top called "**Tien Hsiang**" ("Celestial Blessing"), where an alpine lodge provides cosy accommodations.

All Taroko Gorge tours terminate and turn around at Tien Hsiang, but intrepid travelers with a taste for nature's more exotic surprises should venture another mile up the highway to the entrance of the **Wen Shan** ("Literary Mountain") hot springs, located next to the mouth of a tunnel. Steep steps and a swaying suspension bridge etch a winding trail down and across the gorge to the rocky banks of the Foggy River, where an open cave of raw marble has been walled off to form a delightful *alfresco* pool of piping hot mineral waters. The water seeps in through cracks in the cave and drains into the river through an outlet in the

The "gorge-ous" view at Taroko.

wall. Here bathers may enjoy the stimulating sensations of hot spring and cold river waters washing over their bodies by alternately dipping their limbs into the thermal pool and then the rumbling river.

Beyond Wen Shan Spa, the "Rainbow" road continues to twist across the Central Range to the western plains, a trip best taken by private car as an adventure in itself.

Hualien is the major urban center along Taiwan's eastern seaboard. Its greatest claims to fame are the Ami Harvest Festival, held in annually August, and the wide range of marble products it produces from raw marble mined in the mountains around Taroko Gorge. There are daily flights to Hualien from Taipei, but the most interesting way to get there is to take the new railway link between the capital and Hualien—a scenic 55 miles (90 km) of track that crosses 22 bridges and passes through 16 tunnels. The trip takes three hours and is usually heavily booked, so tickets should be arranged in advance.

Beyond Hualien, the East Coast Highway skirts south along the Pacific shoreline, with frothy breakers crashing on coral reefs on one side and the jade-green mountains of the Central Range tumbling down to the sea on the other. Along the way you'll pass the cliff-hanging "**Caves of the Eight Immortals**" and the coral-fringed "**Terrace of the Three Immortals**," before arriving in the sleepy coastal town of **Taitung** ("Taiwan East"). There is another road between Hualien and Taitung which runs parallel to the coastal highway, about 19 miles (30 km) inland, and a railway line runs along this inland route as well for those who prefer to travel by rail. Visitors may also fly directly to Taitung from Taipei.

Taitung is a quiet, unpretentious town, somewhat removed from Taiwan's international tourist trail. But like Taichung and Kaohsiung, Taitung is a convenient springboard to nearby attractions. For example, it provides direct access to the offshore resort on **Green Island** and to the Yami aborigine enclave on **Orchid Island**. Best of all, Taitung is right next door to what is arguably the island's most pleasant hot spring resort—**Chih Pen** and ("Source

Ami Harvest Festival near Hualien.

of Wisdom") **Spa**.

Tucked against a mountainside at the mouth of a lush canyon watered by the **Chih Pen River**, the Chih Pen Spa is one of Taiwan's oldest, most remote hot spring resorts. Located about 7.5 miles (12 km) south of Taitung, Chih Pen has about half a dozen hot spring inns, the most pleasant of which is the old **Chih Pen Hotel**, where you'll find the biggest and best outdoor mineral pools in Taiwan.

Nestled against the banyan-tangled cliff behind the hotel, the trio of pools are canopied by swaying palms and serenaded by tropical birds. The hottest pool is a steaming cauldron unbearable to all but the most seasoned hot spring bathers, but the medium pool is just right for long soothing soaks. Both hot pools are about 16 feet (5 meters) wide. The adjacent cool pool is fed by a cold mineral spring contrived to cascade down from a banyan tree, and it's long enough to swim laps. Bathers can spend all day (or night) here slithering across the smooth stones from hot to medium to cool pools and back again.

Beyond the spa village, the Chih Pen Valley offers a number of pleasant distractions, such as the **White Jade Falls** and the **Chih Pen Forest Recreation Area**. But the biggest treat of all in this verdant valley is the **Monastery of Clear Awakening**, a Buddhist monastery located on a steep hillside less than half a mile from the spa.

Inside the main hall sit two of the most precious, exquisitely crafted statues of Buddha in Taiwan. The big Brass Buddha is 10 feet (3 meters) tall, weighs 2,500 pounds (1,125 kg), and was cast in Thailand. Sitting right in front of it is the priceless White Jade Buddha, eight feet high and 10,000 pounds (4,500 kg) of solid white jade—a gift from Chinese Buddhists in Burma. To the left of the altar stands a small jewel-encrusted gold pagoda which houses two more of those mysterious "relic seeds" plucked from the ashes of Sakyamni Buddha over 2,500 years ago. The appeal of a few long soothing soaks in the Chih Pen Hotel's triple mineral pools plus a leisurely visit to the spiritually inspiring setting at the Monastery of Clear Awakening fully merits an excursion to this most unspoilt corner of Treasure Island.

Courtyard at the Temple of Confucius in Tainan.

TAINAN AND THE SOUTHERN COAST

From 1663 to 1885, the sunny southern city of **Tainan** ("Taiwan South") served as the island's administrative capital. While the provincial capital has since moved to Taichung, and the national capital to Taipei, Tainan still remains the island's undisputed capital of local color and culture.

It was on the shores of Tainan that early Hakka settlers first arrived, as did Dutch colonialists several centuries later, followed in 1661 by the Ming patriot Koxinga.

Today, temples remain the hallmark of Tainan, which is known as the "City of a Hundred Temples." In fact, this sobriquet is an understatement, for there are over 220 major temples scattered throughout Tainan and the surrounding country-side.

It would take an entire book to list and describe and several weeks to see the various Buddhist, Taoist, Confucian, and folk temples in and around Tainan. For travelers with only a few days to spend here, the following list briefly introduces the temples of most immediate interest:

Koxinga's Shrine: Built in 1875 in honor of Taiwan's greatest historical hero, this temple houses an impressive statue of Koxinga, flanked by his two most trusted generals and a phalanx of 114 loyal officers.

Confucius Temple: This is the oldest shrine to the Great Sage in all Taiwan. It was founded in 1665 by Koxinga's son and has since been restored 16 times. Set in a tranquil garden compound, with arched gates and corniced walls dividing the complex into a series of courtyards, this serene shrine contrasts markedly with the gaudiness of Buddhist and Taoist temples.

Kai-Yuan Monastery: Also built by Koxinga's son, this is one of Taiwan's oldest Buddhist monasteries. The main hall enshrines an icon of the smiling, pot-bellied Milofo (the "Happy Buddha"), guarded by four enormous celestial sentries striking awesome poses. This is more than a temple: it's a functioning monastery where visitors may witness freshly shaven monks and nuns in robes and

sandles bustle about the grounds attending to monastic duties in a fashion that has not changed for centuries.

Temple of the City God: This is one of the oldest and most original temples in Tainan, dedicated to Cheng Huang, the City God, whose duty it is to report the behavior of the city's residents to the Emperors of Heaven and Hell. Among the many ancient artifacts here are two giant abaci which hang from varnished, smoke-stained beams across the ceiling. The melon-sized beads of each abacus are used by the City God to tally the merits and demerits of each resident in his annual report to Heaven and Hell.

Temple of the Jade Emperor: An elaborate stone facade carved in deep relief marks the entrance to this ornate Taoist temple, one of the oldest of its kind on the island. The halls are full of paintings and statues of Taoist deities and the celestial animals associated with them. This is one of the few remaining places in Taiwan where visistors may still witness exorcisms and other occult rites performed in trance by Taoist mediums.

Deer Ear Gate: Located a bit north of Tainan, this is the shallow bay where Koxinga and his troops landed to oust the Dutch from their fortifications. The landing site itself is consecrated with an elaborate new **temple to Ma Tsu**, patron goddess of Taiwan, and here you'll find the 1,000-year-old camphor icon of the Goddess of the Sea (Ma Tsu) which Koxinga brought from the mainland. A few miles beyond the Ma Tsu Temple is what Tainan bills as the largest temple structure in East Asia: the gargantuan Temple of the Holy Mother.

In addition to temples, Tainan's historical sights include the remains of the old Dutch **Fort Zeelandia**, remnants of a former Chinese fort called the "**Eternal Castle**," the **Chin-Kan Towers** (site of the Dutch surrender to Koxinga), the **Antiques House of Tainan**, and the **Tainan Wax Museum**.

Sunny Southern Shores: Only a short hop south of Tainan lies **Kaohsiung**, Taiwan's second largest city and biggest international seaport, which can lay claim to being the world's foremost scrapper of old ships. Except for trade and industry, Kaohsiung offers relatively little of interest to the foreign traveler, but it is the gateway by boat to the offshore islands known as the **Pescadores** (Peng-Hu), or "Isles of the Fishermen," which makes an interest ing side-trip. Otherwise, besides Tainan itself, southern Taiwan's greatest attraction is its sun-kissed shoreline, which boasts the island's best swimming and sunbathing beaches.

Taiwan's southernmost coastline forms a crescent called the **Heng-Chun Peninsula**, where the four waters of the Pacific Ocean, Taiwan Straits, South China Sea, and Bashi Channel merge in an aquatic tapestry of green and blue. The eastern arm of this coastal crescent is called **Oluanpi** ("Goose Bell Beak") and the western arm is known as **Maopitau** ("Cat's Nose Cape"). The broad blue bay in between harbors the island's best beaches and some of its most scenic seascapes.

At **Kenting Botanical Gardens**, founded in 1906 by the Japanese, visitors may wander leisurely through 18.5 square miles (48 square km) of meticulously maintained botanical gardens where more than 1,200 varieties of tropical trees, vines, flowers, and other exotic plants gathered from all over the world flourish. A few hundred yards from the entrance lies **Kenting Beach**, which features a pristine white sand swimming beach that stretches for more than half a mile, with another mile or so of shoreline beyond for strolling. This beach, which is open from April through October, is generally regarded as the cleanest, warmest, and gentlest in Taiwan. Kenting was recently declared an official National Park.

A little south of Kenting stretches the long narrow cape of Oluanpi, famous for the landmark lighthouse at its southernmost tip and the fine beaches along its shores. Besides swimming and sunbathing, this cape is great for scuba diving, snorkeling, fishing, shell collecting, and sometimes even surfing.

There are daily local flights from Taipei to Tainan and Kaohsiung, and from there buses and cabs whisk visitors down to Kenting and Oluanpi in about an hour. Kaohsiung is also served by the only other international airport in Taiwan other than the one in Taipei. A pleasant alternative is to ride the train south—a scenic journey that takes about half a day—or else rent a car or cab and head south along the Sun Yat-sen Freeway.

Right, girl uses material to protect face from summer heat.

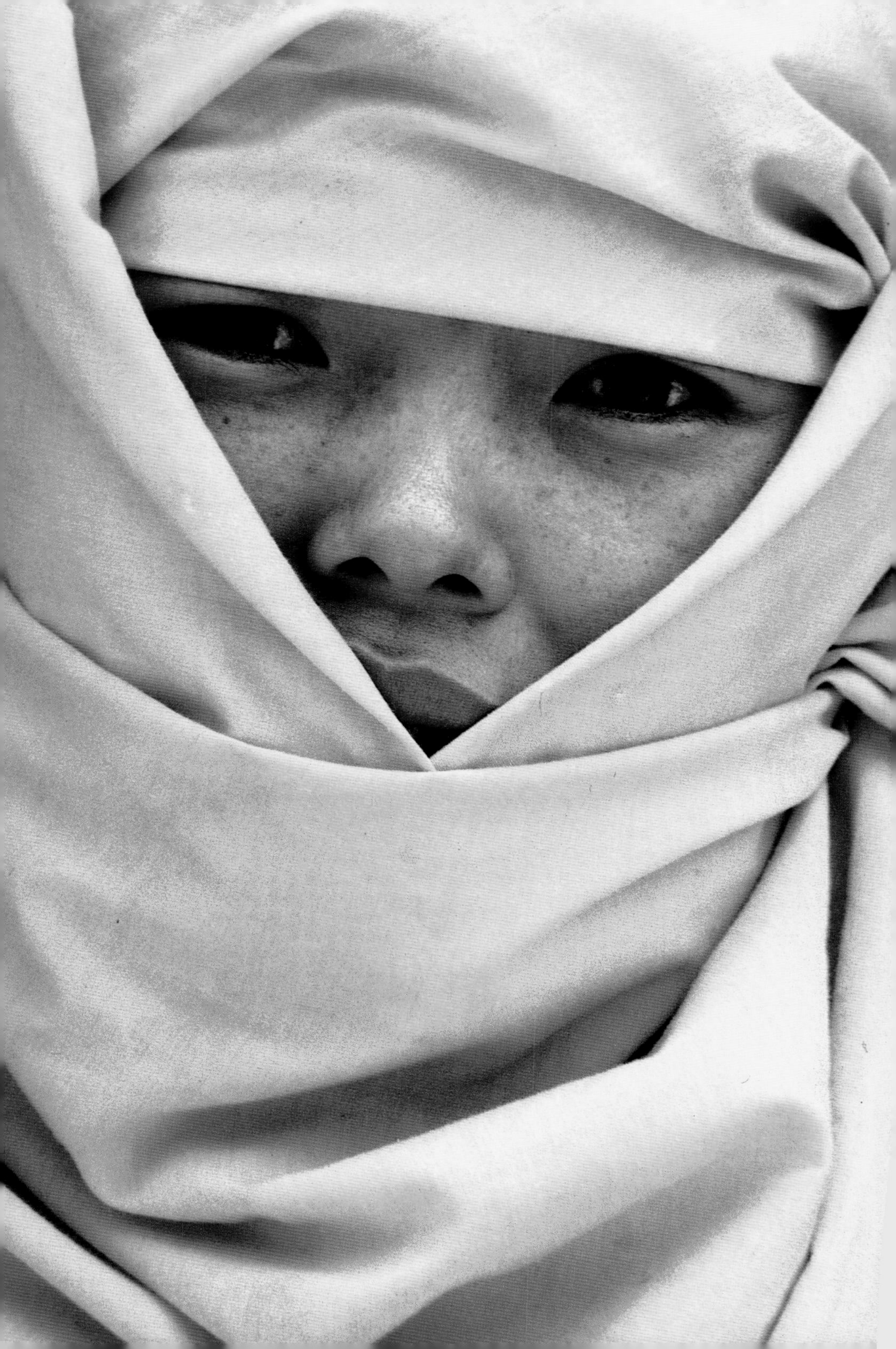

THAILAND: THE LAND OF SMILES

Imagine a land of infinite variety with high, tree-carpeted mountains; jungles rich with wildlife, orchids, and exotic plants; shining rivers tumbling to the plains on their way to a warm-water gulf rimmed by miles of golden sands. This is what the gods have given Thailand.

Picture orange temple roofs, golden spires glowing softly in the dusk light, silver canals crisscrossing the lowlands through a patchwork of fertile rice paddies; fragile arts of breathtaking beauty. This is what Thais have created from their exquisite land. Together, god-made and man-made Thailand has for eons served as a magnet of endless appeal for travelers, many of whom journeyed for a look and stayed a lifetime.

Land of the Free. Land of Smiles. The former is a literal translation of the name "Thailand"; the latter describes the cheerful demeanor of its people. Thais are proud of their ancestors' rejection of foreign domination, making their country the only one in Southeast Asia to escape the yoke of colonialism. This independent spirit is evident in everything they do. Beneath their graciousness is a strong sense of self, a humility without subservience, a willingness to suffer the consequences rather than to curry favor. It is this pride in themselves which underlies their sense of nationalism and their ability to smile at the vicissitudes of life.

But then, Thais have much to smile about: A sunny culture filled with color and brilliance, sparkling waterways that offer cooling comfort to the heat of the sun, food that is a match for any other cuisine in Asia, handsome men and beautiful women, a healthy economy, and a tolerance of religions and politicians. All these contribute to the Thais' natural warmth, hospitality, and genuine concern for the traveler.

Boasting a population of 50 million and a land area of 198,460 square miles (514,000 square km), Thailand is very nearly the size and shape of Central America. Its climate is tropical with three seasons: hot (March – June), monsoon (July – November) and cool (December – February). Its capital, Bangkok (population, five million) lies on the same latitude as Madras, Khartoum, Guatemala City, Guam, and Manila.

The country is commonly divided into four regions; the Central Plains which includes Bangkok, the North, the Northeast and the South. Each region has its own culture and appeal and must be explored thoroughly to gain a proper appreciation of Thailand's vast richness. Bangkok is but one small patch in the cultural quilt. When a Thai says "I'm heading up-country tomorrow," he could mean anywhere outside Bangkok's city limits; north, east, south or west. This is where the real Thailand begins. Up-country.

Preceding pages: Monks taking a leisurely stroll down a country road. Left, mural at Wat Suthat from the period of Rama III.

OF KINGS AND KINGDOMS

In 1966, in a small village on the Korat Plateau, a boy tripped over the root of a kapok tree and fell into the 36th century B.C. Surrounding him, exposed by erosion, were hard rings, rims of baked clay pots that would prove to be 5,600 years old. Beneath them were bronze tools, jewelry, and musical instruments. The boy walking through the village of Ban Chieng near the banks of the Mekong River that afternoon had literally stumbled onto one of the great archaeological finds of the century, the vast remains of what may well have been the world's first Bronze Age culture, the first civilized settlement in Thailand.

At an unknown date, these people of the high plains disappeared, likely scattered by invaders sweeping down from the north. These new people would later forge the great empires of Cambodia and create the fabulous stone cities of Angkor Wat and Angkor Thom as well as myriad temples and monuments, many of them scattered throughout Thailand's Northeast.

The next few millennia are blank pages in the history books. There may have been well-developed communities living in the Chao Phya Valley as early as the fourth century B.C. By the seventh and eighth centuries A.D., the towns of Nakhon Pathom and Lopburi to the west and north respectively of Bangkok were centers of learning and religion with famed monks traveling from as far away as India to preach Buddhism. In the South, there is evidence of Hindu settlement, merchants from southern India who established trading posts in the communities and minor chiefdoms which dominated the river-mouths. About the rest of the country, little is known.

In the 11th century, the power of the Khmers, the dominant tribe in Cambodia, extended into Thailand nearly to the border with Burma. Master builders, they erected monuments hewn from laterite or stone at sites in the Northeast and in Si Thep, Sukhothai, Lopburi and as far south as Petchburi. By the 13th century, however, the Khmer empire, beset by internal problems, began to wane and its former realms were taken over by a new race that would one day dominate the region.

For over a century, a new, more vigorous race of people had been filtering south out of China, crossing the misty mountains that form the eastern end of the Himalayas to establish small fiefdoms in the fertile valleys of northern Thailand. These people called themselves *Thai*, or "free." Growing more powerful steadily, they soon found themselves strong enough to challenge the hegemony of the Khmers. In 1238, King Intradit of Sukhothai bonded neighboring principalities into a federation and *Sukhothai*, translated as "The Dawn of Happiness," became Thailand's first capital. The date also marks the dawn of Thailand as a nation.

Sukhothai reigned as the capital of Thailand for only a century. Its greatest monarch, King Ramkamhaeng the Great (1279-1299) gave his people the Thai alphabet, codified laws, a peaceful kingdom and the respect of its neighbors. It was not to last. Later Sukhothai kings appear to have spent more time in religious devotion than in statecraft, leaving the mantle of power to pass to more aggressive Thais farther down-river at Ayutthaya.

Ayutthaya became the nation's capital in 1350. A succession of strong kings made it the most powerful kingdom in the region with one of the richest, most cultured civilizations in Asia.

At the height of its power in the 17th

century, Ayutthaya had a population of one million, more than contemporary London. In their journals, visitors marveled at its more than 2,000 gold spires and Buddha images, its wealth of architecture and the gorgeously decorated boats which plied its waters. Merchants came from far and wide to trade in its city. France, Britain, Portugal and Holland vied for favor, the Thais cleverly playing off each against the other to keep any one from becoming too influential. Foreign meddling in Thai politics led to the expulsion of all foreigners in 1688.

For centuries, the Burmese had cast covetous eyes on Thai wealth, sending expedition after expedition to attack Ayutthaya's ramparts. In 1767, they succeeded in storming the gates, and went on a rampage of looting and arson which razed the major buildings of the city.

Remnants of the Thai army succeeded in ejecting a Burmese garrison force from Ayutthaya but one look at the ruins told them that the once-glorious capital could never be re-built. They chose, instead, to relocate to a new, more easily-defended site further downriver at Thonburi, across the river from present-day Bangkok. For 15 years, Thonburi served principally as a staging area for continuous battles against the Burmese.

In 1780, a young general succeeded in driving the Burmese from the country and in 1782, he ascended the throne as King Rama I. The dynasty he founded, the *Chakri*, has lasted to the present day, the reigning king, Bhumibol Adulyadej, being the ninth in the line.

King Rama I was a visionary who foresaw a great future for his new realm now that peace had been restored. One of his first acts was to move his capital across the river to Bangkok, a small village (*bang*) located in a plantation of plum-olives (*kok*).

His next act was to build the beautiful *Wat Phra Kaew*, the "Temple of the Emerald Buddha," the glittering centerpiece holding the most revered Buddha image in the kingdom. With its transformation from a few motley merchant homes and plum-olive trees to a glittering city, its name was transformed from Bangkok to *Krung Thep*, "City of Angels."

Bangkok soon became a thriving metropolis. Early in the 19th century, foreign traders were welcomed back into the realm

Left, native Thai types. Above, general view of Bangkok.

but under the strict authority of the palace; the Thais were not about to repeat earlier mistakes. But by mid-century, foreign merchants, travelers and even Christian missionaries were being welcomed with open arms.

The initiator of this new policy was one of the most remarkable monarchs in Asia of that or any other time. King Mongkut is, unfortunately, known to the West as the foolish despot portrayed in the film still banned in Thailand, *The King and I*.

King Mongkut (1851-1868) ascended the throne armed with the wisdom gained from 27 years as a Buddhist monk. He also enlisted the aid of American missionaries to teach him English, using it to pursue an avid interest in science and technology.

Once on the throne, he applied his newfound knowledge and reforming zeal to modernizing his nation. Until his reign, transportation through Bangkok had been by elephant-back and canal boat. In 1863, Mongkut built Bangkok's first road, New Road, a macadamized street that wound through the heart of the city and then along the banks of the river, thereby facilitating communication and heralding a new era in trade and commerce. In 1868, he scientifically predicted a solar eclipse and took unbelieving Europeans to the site. As the moon covered the sun, he was hailed for his grasp of science. Tragically, he contracted malaria in the swampy area and died on his return to Bangkok.

Mongkut's son, Chulalongkorn (1868-1910) was no less impressive. Continuing his father's work, he established universities, developed the economy, sent the country's first rail lines snaking deep into the countryside, and sent his sons and nephews to study at universities in England, France, Germany and Russia thereby providing the country with skilled leadership. He made state visits to the capitals of Asia and Europe, his wife acting as regent in his absence, both acts diverging sharply from tradition. It was due to the innovativeness of these two monarchs and the execution of a very advanced foreign policy that, while neighboring countries were being colonized, Thais remained, as their name suggests, "free."

The 20th century saw Thailand emerge as one of the most developed, enlightened nations in Asia. The modernization did not come without a price to the monarchy that had conceived it. Thai students caught up in the revolutionary fervor that swept Europe during the 1920s returned home to foment rebellion. In 1932, they staged a *coup d'etat* and in one night overturned 700 years of Absolute Monarchy. They replaced it with a constitutional monarchy, with the king as titular head of a government run by a prime minister, a two-house parliament and an independent judiciary, the system which prevails today.

Since 1932, Thailand has been ruled

under a series of constitutions and by a series of governments, many of them installed by *coup d'etats* and functioning primarily as extensions of military power. Except for a brief period between 1973 and 1976 when the country experimented with true representative democracy, the military has been a pervasive force in the country, ruling either directly or from behind the scenes.

Throughout its history, Thailand has been characterized by its extreme tolerance for alien religions and beliefs. Although 92 percent of its populace professes Theravada Buddhism, the country has always extended religious freedom to its 6 percent Muslim subjects, its Hindu, Sikh and Christian minorities.

Though geographically closer to China, Thailand's principal cultural influences have come from the west. Buddhist missionaries were sent to the Chao Phya Valley by the Indian Emperor Asoka in the third century B.C.; 13th-century Theravada Buddhists from Sri Lanka arrived to give the religion more substantive form. The five-tone Thai language was enriched with polysyllabic Sanskrit and Pali words. This new infusion was introduced by Brahmin priests captured when Thai armies overran Angkor Wat in 1431. The same priests also introduced and oversaw the ceremonies of statecraft and the rites of passage for Thai royalty that are practiced today.

The monarchy is revered in Thailand. Left, the king at the investiture of the crown prince. Above, the royal couple preside over a ceremony.

In the arts, it is the Indian classical tale, the *Ramayana*, (*Ramakien*, in Thai) which forms the principal theme for literature, *khon* masked drama, *lakhon* dance-drama, and puppet and shadow puppet theater, all of which were once considered palace arts to be enjoyed by the nobility. Variations, often quite bawdy, appeared outside the palace walls and regional arts, notably folk dances, arose in the North and Northeast, *Manohra* drama in the South.

Architecture, sculpture and painting were, until the 20th century, devoted exclusively to religious themes. Architects created distinctive temples which held bronze, wooden, stone or stucco Buddha images. A walk through a temple is a visual trip through a religious work; scenes of the Buddha's life and past incarnations painted on the interior walls, each element in temple architecture rich with meaning.

A number of Thai festivals are directly associated with Buddhism. *Magha Puja*, *Visakha Puja*, and *Asalaha Puja*, falling on the full moon nights of February, May, and July, celebrate the birth, death, first sermon and enlightenment of Buddha in the sixth century B.C. Two of the most charming holidays, *Songkran* and *Loy Krathong*, are purely secular festivals. Though the day before *Songkran* is devoted to anointing the revered *Phra Buddha Sihing* image as it is paraded through the streets of Bangkok, the festival itself on April 13 is a riotous affair. Because *Songkran* is traditionally regarded as the start of the Thai New Year (though Thailand now follows the Western calendar), it is celebrated by sprinkling (and sometimes throwing) water on one's freinds to bless them for the coming year.

Though not an official holiday, *Loy Krathong*, Thailand's most beautiful festival, is celebrated on the full moon night of November and also centers on water. It is popular with lovers who launch tiny banana leaf boats laden with candles, incense sticks, and flowers onto rivers, ponds and canals in the hopes that their prayers will be answered.

At the Ploughing Ceremony held each May at the beginning of the rice planting season, bullocks led by Brahmin priests plough the *Sanam Luang* in the shadow of *Wat Phra Kaew*. The beasts are then offered a selection of grains; their choice of one over another determines the success of the coming year's crops.

Bangkok: Angel In Disguise

It is easy to forgive the first-time visitor for wondering if the angels of **Bangkok** have taken to their heels, driven away by the dust and din, heat and hullabaloo the city dishes out. How the angels could remain amid the chaotic traffic, noise, smoke-laden air and broken, heat-baked pavements is a mystery. There is no denying that Bangkok, or *Krung Thep* (City of Angels) as the Thais call it, is an assault on the senses, a city easy to dismiss and to wonder how one's friends, normally people of taste and discernment, could have made such a fuss about it.

What one soon discovers is that the angels are there. They can be found by doing what everyone must eventually do: delving beneath Bangkok's skin and searching for its hidden heart. The delights to be discovered are glittering temples, rich art, and cool canals; fragrant flowers and incense assailing the nostrils; tinkling chimes and monks' chants caressing the ears; succulently-prepared food tempting the palate. Most delightful of all are the warm and friendly people, the true angels of this vast city.

Bangkok began its life on the banks of the **Chao Phya River**, the "River of Kings," the "Mother of Waters." Though the city is some 400 years old, it became the nation's capital only in 1782 when the royal dynasty which now rules Thailand was established. The first king, Rama I (1782-1809) ordered that a canal be dug across the neck of an oxbow in the river, thereby creating an island which could be easily defended.

Bangkok's first major building was **Wat Phra Kaew**, the **Temple of the Emerald Buddha**, the holiest Buddha image in the realm. Wat Phra Kaew is a complex of sacred buildings erected over the course of Bangkok's first century in a seemingly random pattern and a delightful variety of styles. Walking through it, one's eyes are assaulted by twinkling pinpoints of sunlight reflected in hundreds of thousands of tiny colored mirrors that cover every jewel-like surface.

At the center of the complex is the *bot* or "ordination hall" that holds the Emerald Buddha. Gilded *garudas* (mythical birds) line its ramparts while *singhas* (mythical lions) protect the stairs and ferocious guardians carved on the doors see to it that evil spirits do not enter. The image they guard is rather small. Seated high on a pedestal, it is made of jasper and is clothed in the raiment of the season.

North of the *bot* are the pantheon holding the ashes of past kings and important royal personages; the library, repository for the Buddhist scriptures; and a tall golden-mosaic-tiled spire whose summit is clad in pure gold.

Surrounding the complex is a portico whose walls are covered, comic-strip fashion, with episodes from the Thai classic, the *Ramakien*, the story of the god-king Rama which is the principal work of Thai dance-drama, literature and puppet theater, and whose name the present dynasty's kings have assumed. A major part of the murals' charm lies in the off-stage areas which show the life, dress and pastimes of the common man, subjects the artists took particular relish in depicting.

Preceding pages: The magnificent Wat Phra Kaew Temple. Left, Buddha at Wat Phra Kaew. Right, Thai classical dancer.

The **Grand Palace** also evolved piecemeal, beginning with the **Dusit Mahaprasad Audience Hall** which sits on the west of the great courtyard. In front of it is perhaps the most charming structure, the jewel box-like **Aphon Phimok** pavilion where kings once dismounted from their royal elephants.

The most impressive building, the **Chakri Mahaprasad**, was in fact the last to be built. It sits at the center of the complex, fronted by a garden of sculpted trees. Built as a royal residence and audience hall in 1890, it was designed by British architects on an Italian Renaissance plan.

The original blueprints called for a rather plain roofline but, sensitive to Thai aesthetic sensibilities, King Chulalongkorn ordered that three spires crown it. The addition prompted wags to dub it "the *farang* (foreigner) wearing the *chada*," the headdress of a Thai classical dancer. The building is open to the public only on special days.

A stroll south of the Grand Palace leads to **Wat Chetupon** or, as it is popularly known, **Wat Po**.

Few statues are more impressive than Wat Po's mammoth **Reclining Buddha** which occupies the entirety of a long building in the northwestern corner. Regarded less for its artistic merit than its awesome size, the soles of the enormous image's feet are covered in 108 intricate mother-of-pearl signs by which a living Buddha can be recognized.

Wat Po is also a center of herbal medicine. Of special interest to visitors who have spent the day tramping through temples is the traditional massage hall where 120 *baht* acquires a soothing hour-long massage at the hands of expert practitioners.

Cross the street to the northeast of Wat Phra Kaew to **Lak Muang** which houses a tall *lingum* dedicated to Shiva and which demarcates the official center of the city. Here, devotees come to make wishes or to repay the spirits for wishes granted by hiring the resident *lakhon* dance-drama troupe to perform a small piece.

Wat Mahathat, the **Temple of the Great Relic**, although of little note architecturally, contains the **Buddhist University** where monks are trained. North of the *wat*, the **National Museum** houses some of the best sculptures the

The Royal Palace at Bangkok.

nation's artists have produced. It also contains the **Buddhaisawan Chapel** which holds the **Phra Buddha Sihing**, the kingdom's second most important Buddha image. Its murals are among the finest in Thailand.

Between Wat Mahathat and the riverbank is the **Amulet Market**. Thais are great believers in the power of clay amulets stamped with portraits of the Buddha to protect them from harm. Some amulets are said to be so powerful they will stop bullets or knives entering the wearer's body. The vendors may be willing to help you test the theory or you may prefer simply to take their word for it.

Although theoretically a profanation of Buddhism, having its roots in animism, amulets are worn by nearly every Buddhist. It is here and at a second amulet market next to **Wat Rajnadda**, that they flock, connoisseurs of the occult in search of talismans which will improve their lot in life.

Theves Flower Market, on the banks of **Klong Lawd**, is a plant lover's paradise. Orchids, shrubs, trees, line the sidewalks, a veritable jungle of exotic species. Walk a bit farther north to **Wat Indraviharn** with its colossal gilded **Standing Buddha**.

The core of nearby **Wat Rajabhopit** is a tall *chedi* or spire surrounded by a circular cloister. On the northern side is a beautiful jewel box *bot* on whose doors are beautiful mother-of-pearl depictions of royal decorations.

Wat Suthat was completed in the reign of King Rama II (1809-1824) to house a 28-foot (eight-meter)-tall Buddha image brought downriver from Sukhothai on a raft and then laboriously hauled on a chariot through the city streets. The doors, carved to a depth of two inches, are the creation of King Rama II himself, a talented artist who is said to have thrown his specially-designed tools into the river so no one could duplicate his feat. The interior murals depict fantastic sea creatures.

In front of Wat Suthat is one of the city's most famous landmarks, the **Giant Swing**. The tall structure was once the site for a ceremony now discontinued to honor the god Shiva. On a special day, a team of four athletic men would sit on a seat suspended from long ropes and at tempt to swing high enough to snatch a bag of gold set atop a long pole.

On the boundary of the original city is **Wat Saket** whose fame stems from the artificial mountain which rises beside it. The **Phu Kaew Thong** or **Golden Mount**, once the city's tallest structure, provides a superb panorama of the city for those with stamina to climb its many stairs.

Wat Trimitr near the **Hualampong Railway Station** is famed for its Buddha image. When moving the huge plaster image in 1957, a sling broke, cracking the plaster and revealing a second image hidden inside. When the plaster was stripped away, the inner image was found to be made of solid gold, 5.5 tons of it.

Near **Chitralada Palace** is **Wat Benchamabhopit** or the **Marble Temple** built in the year 1900. The last major temple to be constructed in Bangkok, it is clad in carrara marble imported from Italy.

The temple is a superb site to watch the candlelight procession that circles the temple three times on the nights of the three principal Buddhist holidays of *Visakha Puja*, *Magha Puja* and *Asalaha Puja*.

On the Thonburi bank of the Chao

Wat Arun, taken during an eclipse of the sun.

Phya River, **Wat Arun**, the **Temple of Dawn**, rises 284 feet (86 meters) into the air. Like the spire itself, many of its outer buildings are decorated in floral motifs fashioned from broken porcelain in the Chinese style.

Suan Pakaad on **Sri Ayutthaya Road** is a private palace comprised of old Thai houses and containing an excellent collection of lacquer and gold antique bookcases and Ban Chieng pottery and jewelry. The **Lacquer Pavilion** is regarded by some to be Asia's finest example of the art of gold and lacquer decoration.

Before he mysteriously disappeared in 1968, Jim Thompson, the American who made Thai silk famous, transported three wooden Thai-style houses from Ayutthaya, assembling them on the bank of a canal on **Soi Kasemsan II** and filling them with his superb antique collection. The **Jim Thompson House** and its lush gardens offer a unique look at the Thais' lifestyle before they discovered concrete.

While Bangkok's temples and palaces do form the core items of most visits, they are but a small part of the city's allure. Bangkok also has a **Chinatown**. Plunge into the small lanes that run either side of **New Road** and **Yaowarat Road** and discover a hidden world of shops selling six-foot tall incense sticks and Chinese violins, or chops, and of quiet Chinese temples unchanged for hundreds of years.

At the **Snake Farm** (the **Pasteur Institute**) on **Rama IV Road**, cobras are milked of their venom each morning at 11. The extract is used to produce anti-venom serums. For animal lovers, **Dusit Zoo** near Chitralada Palace provides an excellent introduction to the beasts of Thailand's jungles.

Sports fans can select from a menu including soccer matches at the **National Stadium** or horse racing during the dry season at the **Royal Bangkok Sports Club** (Saturday afternoons) or the **Army Race Track** (Sunday afternoons). At **Lumpini Stadium** on Rama IV Road and **Rajdamnern Stadium** Thai-style boxers pummel each other to pulp with fists, feet, knees and elbows, considered legitimate weapons in a fighter's arsenal.

In **Chatuchak Park's** famed **Weekend Market**, anything from second-hand clothes, live monitor lizards, and

Bangkok streets are always crowded, always dirty.

aphrodisiacs to old brass doorknobs, spiky durians, and shrimp paste can be found. Despite its name, the latter is not used to glue shrimp to walls but is a pungent, salty condiment made of pureed shrimps. Numerous other morning markets abound in the city and in the unlikeliest places: behind the facades of modern buildings, down lanes, just next to your hotel. Among the best known are **Pratunam** and **Bangrak**.

Even well into the 20th century, Bangkok streets meant a web of canals, overhung by palm trees and plied by tiny sampans paddling past houses built on rafts. A trip on the Chao Phya River or into the canals provides an educational glimpse of life on the water. Water buses called *Rua Duan* make regular stops at landings along the river. A seven-*baht* ticket will take you an hour upriver to the provincial market town of **Nonthaburi**.

To discover how rural life of the past century is still lived, head into the canals on the Thonburi side of the river. Long, low buses with propellers on long shafts (which gives them their name *rua hang yaow* or "long-tailed boats") take riders along narrow canals through coconut plantations, past quaint temples and stilt houses.

Bangkok's allure, and indeed much of its ill-earned reputation, is based on its nightlife. Travelers with a cultural bent will flock to restaurants that offer superb Thai cuisine and an evening of Thai classical dancing. Sooner or later, however, visitors find themselves gravitating towards one of Asia's most famous streets, **Patpong**, for a bit of harmless fun.

Patpong is known for its *a-go-go* bars and wealth of feminine pulchritude. Bar patrons are welcome to watch the girls dance, have a quiet chat with some of them, or simply to watch the anomalies of human behavior as men and women play ancient games of flirtation.

Patpong also offers massage parlors and gay bars. Touts and taxi drivers offer to transport those with jaded tastes to more lively entertainment located in the backstreets of town. **Soi Cowboy** off **Sukhumvit Soi 21** is a rowdier version of Patpong with a score of bars lining the street. Here, one will meet a different sort of angel.

Go-go girls on display at Patpong.

OUTSIDE BANGKOK

As night turns to dawn, tiny splashes can be heard along **Damnern Saduak** canal as women paddle sampans laden with vegetables and fruits to the **Floating Market**. For early risers, a tour to the market is one of the most fascinating experiences in Asia.

Later, go on to the **Phra Pathom Chedi**, 420 feet (127 meters) tall and clad in orange tiles. It's the largest Buddhist monument in Asia. The tour ends at the **Rose Garden**, a cultural/entertainment complex, for lunch by the river followed by a show of elephants at work, a Thai wedding ceremony, a bit of Thai boxing, sword fighting, cock fighting and other traditional village entertainments.

Fifty miles (80 km) north of Bangkok is the royal city of **Ayutthaya**, Thailand's capital from 1350 to 1767. Even in its ruined state, it evokes the grandeur of the people who conquered the kingdom of Angkor Wat, controlled most of Laos and a major portion of the Malay peninsula. Sit in the shadow of **Wat Rajburana** in whose vault a cache of intricately-fashioned gold ornaments was found in 1957. Wander among the giant stone Buddha heads at **Wat Mahathat** across the road, or stroll among the three spires of **Wat Si Sanphet**. Stop along the river for lunch at a floating restaurant.

Floating market at Damnern Saduak is especially famous for its fruits.

Bang Pa-in, once the royal summer palace, is closer to Bangkok and is usually visited on the same day as Ayutthaya. It features quaint architecture imitating 19th-century European styles. There is also a beautiful Chinese house and delicate pavilion.

The name **River Kwai** conjures up images of a bridge and Allied POWs made to work under horrendous conditions by their Japanese captors. In fact, the movie depicting the World War II incident was shot in Sri Lanka, the real bridge being a mundane iron trestle affair. Guaranteed to evoke emotion, however, is the **Allied Cemetery** with its rows and rows of gravestones honoring men who toiled to build the "Death Railway" between Thailand and Burma. The site can be reached by train which leaves Bangkok's Hualampong Station each morning and returns in the evening.

Up the Kwai are groups of rafthouses that serve as floating bungalows. These house explorers of bamboo forests, teak jungles, *Karen* hilltribe villages, the **Erawan Waterfalls**, caves and, for the hardy, a trek to **Three Pagodas Pass** through which Burmese armies mounted on elephants passed Hannibal-like on their way to do battle in the Chao Phya River Valley.

With 30,000 residents, the **Crocodile Farm** east of Bangkok at **Samut Prakan** claims to be the largest in the world. It is not out of humanitarian concern that it houses the beasts but for their skins which are made into shoes, belts, and other fashion accessories.

The **Ancient City** just down the road reflects a millionaire's passion to recreate in miniature all of Thailand's architectural masterpieces. On a 200-acre plot laid out in the shape of Thailand, are all of the major monuments plus villages of each of Thailand's principal regions, a task that required 10 years' work. Pick a cool morning to make the trip or you'll feel as though you have trekked the entire length of Thailand.

"FOOD, GLORIOUS FOOD!"

Thai cuisine is one of the delights of its culture. The ubiquity of fresh seafood, meats, fruits and vegetables, and the numerous ways the Thais combine them make dining one of the highlights of a stay in Thailand. Dishes are generally very spicy but some are only slightly spiced.

The base for Thai cuisine is rice, a long-grained variety that is among the tastiest in the world. On top of this, the Thai ladles a variety of meat and vegetable dishes. Thais have also adopted a number of Portuguese, Chinese and Indonesian dishes which use a minimal amount of hot spices.

As with butter in French food, and water in Japanese dishes, the base ingredient in much of Thai food is coconut milk, a rich, creamy liquid which provides a gentle flavor. The flavor is further enhanced by the addition of garlic, lemon grass, cumin, cardamon, tamarind, ginger, coriander, and laced with ample amounts of chillis, the hottest being the tiniest, the *prink kee noo*, the "mouse dropping" chillis. Additional flavor is achieved by splashing on a bit of *nam plaa*, a clear sauce made from the juices of salted, pressed baby shrimp.

Among the "must" dishes are soups like *Tom Yam Goong*, a spicy, sour shrimp-filled concoction, and *Po Taak*, a similar liquid containing a variety of seafoods.

Gai Tom Ka, a chicken dish, is often served as a soup but its delicious coconut milk gravy begs to be ladled over rice, rendering the long grains even tastier. There are dozens of curries but among the most popular are *Gaeng Karee*, a hot curry; *Penang Nua*, a dry beef curry; *Gaeng Gai*, chicken curry; *Gaeng Kiew Wan*, green beef curry.

Those with tender palates might prefer sweet and sour anything *Gai Pat Bai Krapao*, roasted sweet chicken pieces wrapped in a leaf; *Nua Phat Namman Hoi*, beef marinated in oyster sauce; *Kow Muu Dang*, slices of pork on plain rice and *Kow Phat*, fried rice.

Thais are great snackers and nibblers, and have created a wide number of tidbits to be eaten any hour of the day. Fried bananas dipped in honey; *salim*, a collection of multi-colored vermicelli noodles in sweetened coconut milk; make-it-yourself dishes with corn, lotus seeds, water chestnut, tapioca, lychees; almost all served with crushed ice, and dozens of others usually offered at market stalls.

Spicy Tom Yam soup is devilishly good.

PATTAYA

Two hours southeast of Bangkok, **Pattaya**, "Asia's Riviera," lies along a two-mile beachfront crescent lined with first-class hotels. Most of the action takes place along the beachfront where one can swim, ride water scooters, fly on a parasail, water ski, sail, or windsurf. Though the waters around Pattaya are somewhat murky, there is good diving off the outer islands, including a few shipwrecks. At **Bang Saray**, 12 miles (20 km) south, one can arrange to go deep sea fishing for mackerel, marlin and other game fish.

Ashore, there are motorcycles and jeeps for rent to explore the adjacent farm country. The local chapter of the cross-country running fraternity, the Hash House Harriers, runs through the countryside every Monday evening with ample beer afterwards. Air-conditioned sports emporiums offer snooker, bowling, and shooting ranges as well as outdoor archery and mini-golf ranges. Nearby is the world-class **Siam Country Club** golf course and the **Reo Ranch** with purebred Appaloosa-horses and acres of countryside to ride on.

Parasailing in Pattaya.

An adjacent beach, **Chomtien**, is not as developed as its bigger sister. Its special attractions are several complexes of thatched bungalows which offer rustic yet tranquil living. At Chomtien is **Pattaya Park** with water slides and other water recreation facilities for children. A new race track has been installed for weekend stock car races.

For culture, the **Elephant Kraal** in Pattaya offers daily shows during which elephants demonstrate their skills. **Nong Nooch**, nine miles (15 km) south of Pattaya has afternoon shows of Thai boxing, sword fighting, dancing, cockfighting, and elephants. It also has a unique cactus garden and orchid nursery.

Converted fishing trawlers travel to the outer island of **Koh Larn** whose prosaic name of "Bald Island" has somehow been transformed through tourist brochure hyperbole into "Coral Island" even though the coral has long since disappeared. Its waters are very clear and its beaches wide with white sand.

The same shopping items offered in Bangkok are found in Pattaya but at generally lower prices. Several shops have artists-in-residence who paint oil portraits from live sittings or from photographs.

Pattaya is known for its seafood. Succulent fish, shellfish, fresh vegetables and fruits are blended into mouth-watering dishes. Thai, Asian, and Continental cuisines are found in abundance. Wash it down with excellent Singha or Kloster beers or the local brew, Mehkong, a cane whiskey with a powerful, yet smooth-tasting punch.

South Pattaya comes into its element once the sun goes down. There are lounges with *a-go-go* girls but far more popular are the open air bars where you can nurse a beer and watch the girls, dressed in outlandish costumes, watching you.

Pattaya also has several discos that operate into the wee hours. Popular, especially among Asian travelers, are burlesque shows featuring male transvestites garbed in fabulous costumes mouthing the words to hit songs. Piano bars are also in abundance.

PHUKET

The island of **Phuket** calls itself the Pearl of the South, and for sheer natural beauty, few islands can match it. Tall jungled hills, an incomparable coastline, picturesque coconut plantations and rice farms, white sand beaches and azure waters—all the things that tourist brochures promise—are found in Phuket. Having made its fortune from tin and rubber, Phuket's beauty has become such a magnet for beach lovers that it is now rapidly developing as a major tourist resort.

The heaviest development has taken place at **Patong** and while planning has been somewhat haphazard, the beach offers a wide number of water sports along its wide, white sands. The major hotels are here, many of them built bungalow-style in deference to a building code stipulating that no hotel can rise higher than a palm tree.

To the north is **Surin Beach** with a bungalow complex set along a pretty hillside and a golf course where golfers compete with grazing water buffalo for the greens. South of Patong are **Kata** and **Kharon** beaches which are quickly becoming popular with visitors who have lots of time to while away. Kata's beauty has been appreciated by Club Med which has built its second Asian resort there.

Heavenly isle off Phuket.

Near Phuket's southern tip is the beautiful cove of **Nai Harn**, easily the prettiest spot on the island. Its natural beauty has been somewhat compromised by a large hotel which does not succeed in blending into the hillside.

Rawai at the southern extremity is a fishing village populated by *chao lay* or sea gypsies, and band of rovers who once roamed the oceans but have settled on several of the southern islands.

Just around the corner from Rawai is **Promthep Peninsula**, favored for its beautiful sunset views of the surrounding islands.

To the east of Phuket town is **Koh Siray**, another sea gypsy village, and the **Phuket Aquarium**. Near the intersection of the road to Kata and Kharon beaches is the Buddhist temple **Wat Chalong**. East of the intersection is **Ao Chalong**, a charming little seaside fishing village with excellent restaurants. Ao Chalong is also the departure point for **Loan Island** which is being developed as a tourist resort.

Divers will find few reefs as inviting as those off the **Similan Islands**, a few hours by boat to the northwest of Phuket. Coral reefs of astounding beauty hold a rich variety of sea life and make the Similans Thailand's premier scuba diving area.

Among the wonders of Asia is the island group of **Pang-nga**, two hours north of Phuket. Board a long-tailed boat to take a dawn trip down the bay among limestone monoliths seemingly lifted from Chinese brush paintings. One of them, **Ko Ping Gun**, served as the location for the James Bond movie, *The Man with the Golden Gun*. Another, **Koh Pannyi**, is a Muslim fishing village set entirely on stilts.

A few hours to the south of Phuket is **Pi Pi Island** with coves of remarkable beauty. Barely developed, its beautiful beaches are set among limestone monoliths that mark the southern end of the Pang-nga group and give the island the look of Bora Bora.

CHIANG MAI, THE NORTHEAST

"The Dawn of Happiness," as **Sukhothai's** name translates, marks the dawn of Thailand's existence as a nation. And for a city which started from a small federation of principalities of a people newly emerged, Sukhothai accomplished wonders in the 150 years of its short history.

The level of development is immediately evident in the ruins of its temples and palaces which are among the most impressive in Asia. Among the most important are **Wat Mahathat**, **Wat Phra Pai Luang**, and **Wat Si Chum** with its giant Buddha. The Museum contains numerous pieces of the gracefully-flowing bronze Sukhothai Buddha images, considered the zenith of Thai sculptors' skill.

Chiang Mai, The "Rose of the Northern Hills," is Thailand's second largest town. The years since it was founded in 1296 have laid a patina of antiquity on its temples and buildings that has enhanced its beauty.

Set in a valley ringed by low hills, Chiang Mai is encircled by a stout wall and defensive moat which today serves as a fishing and swimming pond for children. Once a town of quaint wooden buildings, its charm has been diminished somewhat by the introduction of concrete shophouses of no particular distinction. Yet, riding a *samlor* (pedicab) down a back lane or on an evening drive along the banks of the **Ping River**, its abundant charm is immediately evident.

Wat Phra Singh, Chiang Mai's most important temple, was founded in 1345 and contains a Buddha image said to have been created in Sri Lanka and transported to Chiang Mai. Of special note at Wat Phra Singh is the *ho trai* or library, a beautiful wooden structure set atop a high stucco base on which float carved *theps* (angles).

Wat Chedi Luang's original *stupa* or spire must have been an imposing structure before an earthquake destroyed it in 1545 reducing its height from 300 feet (90 meters) to 200 feet (60 meters). Its remains stand behind the present temple, which is richly decorated with mirror mosaics and

Sukhothai: Wat Mahath at sunset.

gilded vines and contains a large standing image of the Buddha.

Built in 1297, **Wat Chiang Man** is Chiang Mai's oldest temple. Behind it stands a *chedi* buttressed by rows of stucco elephants facing the four cardinal directions. Above them is a handsome spire sheathed in gilded bronze.

Located some distance from the center of town, **Chedi Si Liem** is a superb example of a style of architecture peculiar to the North. A steeply rising four-sided pyramid, it is divided into tiers with ranks of standing Buddha images set in niches surveying the large courtyard in which it stands.

Perhaps the most beautiful stucco carvings in the north are found at **Wat Chedi Chet Yot**. Wishing to honor the Buddha on the 2,000th year of his birth, King Trailoka in 1455 sent 30 architects and artisans to Bodhgaya, India where the Buddha is said to have reached enlightenment. They returned to build a rectangular block with a single spire (*yot*) surrounded by six smaller spires making a total of seven (*chet*). Its appeal lies in the 70 stucco figures who seem to float on the building's outer walls, their hands clasped in prayer.

Wat Ku Tao, a Burmese-style temple, is itself of little architectural note but its *chedi* is one of the most intriguing in Thailand. Five globes, like upturned monks' alms bowls, are stacked one atop the other in decreasing order of size. Like Wat Arun and many other *chedis*, its stuccoed surface is decorated with seashells and fragments of porcelain plates shaped into flowers.

While Chiang Mai celebrates the same holidays as Bangkok, it has one of its own which occurs during the cool month of February. The **Flower Festival** features a floral parade and cultural shows utilizing the blooms that flower in the crisp hill air. Chiang Mai celebrates *Songkran* a week later than Bangkok and in a much more boisterous fashion. Expect to be drenched several times if you venture into the streets, all in the spirit of fun.

The most popular of Chiang Mai's many markets is the **Night Market** on **Chiang Klan Road**. In the cool of the evening, shops selling local products are swamped with Thais and visitors looking for bargains. Sidewalk cafes

he lephant oundup is prime ourist ttraction.

offer drinks and snacks and the opportunity to watch the passing crowds.

Chiang Mai's most famous landmark sits atop a hill called **Doi Suthep** on the outskirts of the town. Legend says that when the 14th-century monk Sumana was looking for a site for a new temple, he placed a holy relic on the back of an elephant, instructing his disciples to erect the temple at the spot where the elephant rested. The elephant must have had a sadistic bent because it led the disciples up the steepest hill in the district, trumpeting three times at the summit before lying down.

To appreciate the disciples' zeal in following the elephant, drive the 10 miles (16 km) up the winding road to the base of the final hill and then trek up the stairs with its serpent balustrade to the temple itself. Survey the panorama of Chiang Mai in the distance or rest in the shadow of the tall golden spire and its beautiful brass umbrellas.

Many of Chiang Mai's attractions are found outside the city. To the west across the Ping River the 7.5-mile (12-km) road to **Borsang** is dotted with workshops creating the art objects for which the North is famed: silverwork, carved wood, gold and lacquer *objets d'art*, ceramics, celadon pottery, and woven silk.

At Borsang, the "Umbrella Village," women fashion Chiang Mai's famous umbrellas. The umbrellas are marvels of engineering: tiny bamboo pieces are intricately bound with thread and covered in oiled paper or silk and painted with bright designs. The umbrellas come in a variety of sizes with the largest sufficient to cover a substantial party.

North of Chiang Mai is the **Mae Sa Valley**, a new resort area of bungalows set in bucolic splendor along the banks of the burbling **Mae Sa River**. The area serves as a starting point for walks into the surrounding jungles.

In Mae Sa Valley, as in several other locales outside Chiang Mai, is a training school where elephants are taught the techniques of moving huge teak logs out of the forests. It is also possible to mount a *howdah* and ride for a short distance on elephant back, a bumpy experience not likely to convince the rider to trade in his car. Farther up the valley is picturesque **Mae Sa Waterfalls**, a series of cataracts that, depending on the season, crash or dribble over the rocks.

The northern hills are home to a half dozen hilltribes. Tour companies in Chiang Mai arrange treks lasting several days for visitors to observe the hilltribes close-up, staying overnight in *Yao*, *Hmong*, *Karen*, *E-kaw*, and other villages.

The Northeast: As the deep South is colored by the culture of Malaysia, the Northeast is tinted by the culture of its neighbors to the east. Its ruins show the imprint of the Khmer genius that created Angkor Wat. Its language, festivals and traditions have their genesis in Laotian culture.

Near **Sakhon Nakhon** is **Ban Chieng** which many archaeologists think may have been the birthplace of the Bronze Age. On display are skeletons unearthed from huge burial mounds as well as bronze artifacts and pottery with distinctive and highly original patterns.

Of the many Khmer ruins, those at **Phimai** northeast of **Korat** are the best known. Recently restored, the 12th-century sandstone temple and its extensive courtyard incorporates the key architectural components and decorations found at Angkor Wat, itself one of the most brilliant creations of ancient architects.

The most popular Northeastern festival is the **Elephant Round-up** which takes place in **Surin** each November. Years ago, elephants were trapped in the jungles and trained to work in teak forests, transport goods, and fight in wars. At Surin, visitors see how wild elephants are captured, demonstrate their dexterity, including their soccer skills and, as a grand finale, witness a mock war between two armies in which the elephants serve as the tank corps.

The **Rocket Festival** in **Yasothon** is a fertility rite, a time of riotous celebration before villagers get down to the hard work of planting rice. The rockets are homemade affairs of bamboo packed with gunpowder and launched with much singing and laughter. They are fired into the sky to persuade the Rain Goddess, *Mae Prasop*, to send sufficient supplies earthward to water the crops. The rites, on a Sunday in May, are preceded by day-long bacchanalian festivities with a distinct air of *Mardi Gras* bawdiness.

Right, Thai youngster and friend.

TRAVEL TIPS

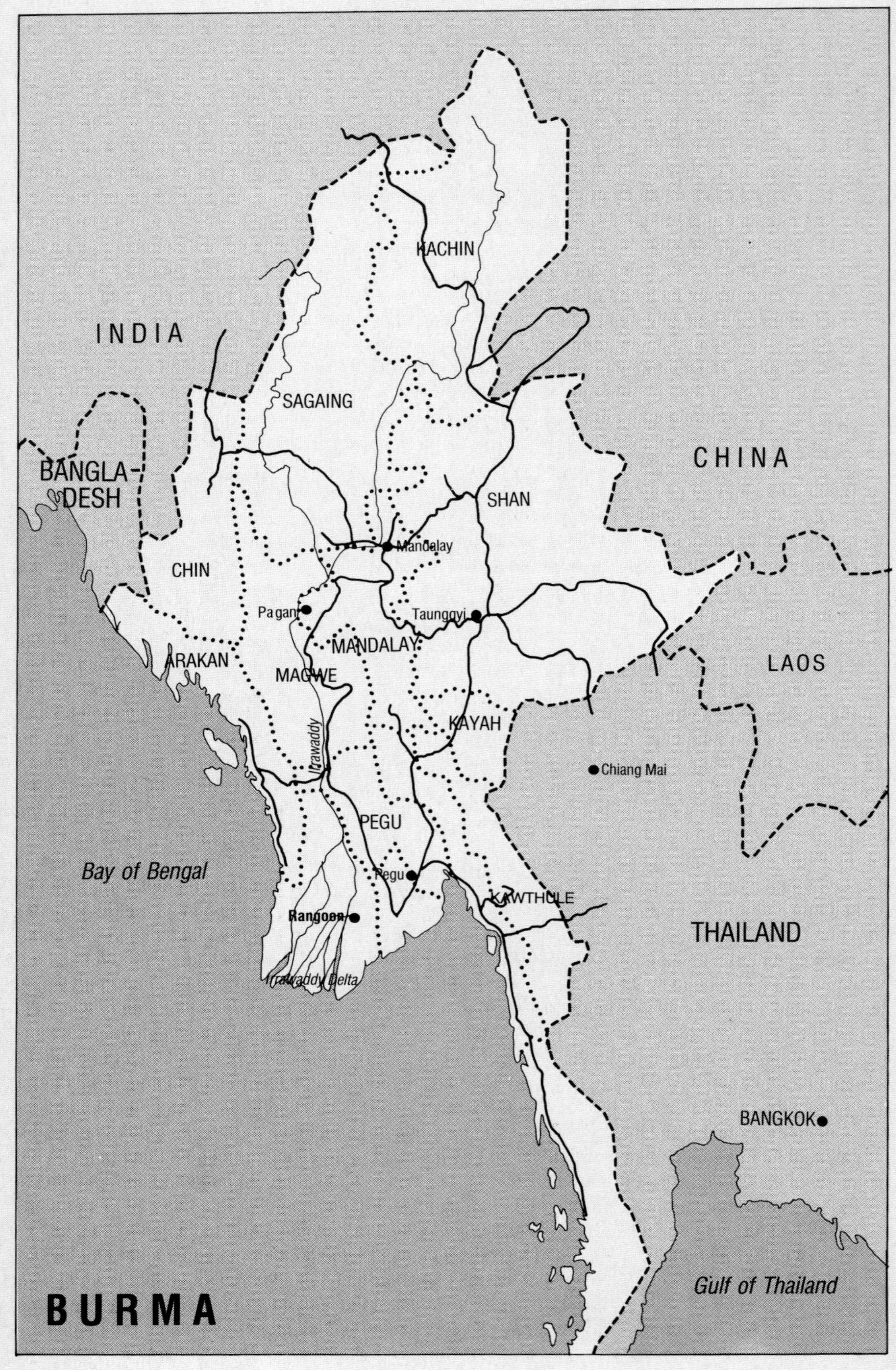
INDIA
BANGLA-DESH
CHINA
LAOS
THAILAND
KACHIN
SAGAING
CHIN
SHAN
ARAKAN
MAGWE
MANDALAY
KAYAH
PEGU
KAWTHULE
Mandalay
Pagan
Taunggyi
Irrawaddy
Pegu
Rangoon
Irrawaddy Delta
Chiang Mai
BANGKOK
Bay of Bengal
Gulf of Thailand
BURMA

Getting There

BY AIR

Rangoon's **Mingaladon** airport offers connections to Bangkok, Singapore, Calcutta, Dacca, Kathmandu, Kunming, Vientiane and Tbilisi. The route mostly used by tourists, Bangkok-Rangoon, is served daily by Burma Airways and thrice a week by Thai Airways. There is a 15 *kyat* **airport tax** at Mingaladon.

There is no officially sanctioned land route to Burma. Existing roads were closed in 1962. Visitors will have to arrive by air or by sea. Tourists who hold only a seven day visa may arrive only by air.

Travel Essentials

VISAS & PASSPORTS

To enter Burma you need a valid passport and a tourist visa which can be obtained at any Burmese embassy. Processing time is about two weeks except in Bangkok where a visa can be obtained within 24 hours.

Children above seven years of age, even if they are registered in the passports of their parents, need their own visa. Visa fee in Bangkok is 100 *baht*. Three passport photos must accompany the application. It is valid for three months from the date of issue.

Tourist visa permit a stay of seven days, i.e. you have to leave at latest on the same weekday you arrived in Rangoon.

Business visas for a longer sojourn can only be obtained with the assistance of a local sponsor.

MONEY MATTERS

When entering Burma, a Foreign Exchange Control Form must be filled, registering all forms of payment available, including currencies, checks, traveler's checks, credit cards, letters of credit and draft and payment orders. The import and export of *kyats*, the Burmese currency, is prohibited.

Whenever foreign currency is changed during the stay in Burma this form must be presented and the official exchange registered. Tourist Burma offices, the Diplomatic Store and the Foreign Trade Bank are licensed to exchange money. However only US$, British £, German marks, French francs, Swiss francs, Australian $, Malaysian $, Hong Kong $, Japanese yen and American Express cards are accepted.

On leaving the country one can re-exchange a quarter of the amount last changed. Hotels, flight tickets and all Tourist Burma services will have to be paid directly in foreign currency.

The Burmese currency comes in 1, 5, 10, 25, and 50 *pyas* and in 1, 10, 15, 35 and 75 *kyat* denominations, The official exchange rate at the time of going to press was 10.78 kyat to the US$, 10.78 to the British £ and 3.82 to the German mark.

HEALTH

Vaccination against cholera and yellow fever is necessary if visitors originate, or have transited from an affected area, within six days prior to arrival.

WHAT TO WEAR

Light and casual cotton clothes for hot weather are appropriate. If no official functions are attended, no tie is needed for men. Women should wear long skirts when entering temples or pagoda grounds. When traveling to the hills it is recommended to take some warm clothing. In winter the temperature can fall below freezing point during the night.

A visit to Burma will most probably include at least one visit to a pagoda, temple or *kyaung* per day. Since all religious buildings and their walled environs can only be visited barefoot it is advisable to wear sandals on such occasions. Many pathways and stairs on sacred grounds are hot and often thorny. Even there barefoot walking is mandatory.

CUSTOMS

The duty free import of 200 cigarettes, 50 cigars or eight ounces of pipe tobacco, one liter of alcoholic beverages and half a liter of cologne or perfume is permitted.

On a special customs form the visitor has to declare all personal items, i.e. cameras, tape recorders, radios, jewelry, etc. This form must again be presented at departure. If it is missing, considerable difficulties will arise.

Artifacts of archaeological value or precious stones can be exported only with an official export license.

GETTING ACQUAINTED

TIME ZONES

Burma Standard Time is 6½ hours ahead of GMT, i.e. coming from Bangkok one has to set the watch back half an hour.

CLIMATE

Burma is situated in the path of the southwest monsoon. The rains begin around the middle of May and last until October. The cool season which then starts is the best time to visit Burma. It is also the time when there are scarce means of transport and hotels are fully booked. March and April are the hot months in Burma with the temperature rising to 113°F (45°C).

GETTING AROUND

To get the most out of the seven days one should use the **Burma Airways** domestic flights. Tickets are not too expensive. Only Tourist Burma will arrange for them, they have to be paid for in foreign currency and need 24 hours to be issued.

The Union of Burma Railways: If there are no more seats available at Burma Airways, which happens more often than not during the peak season, there is always the **Union of Burma Railways**. It runs a 2,500-mile (4,000-km) network in the country. It is the Rangoon-Mandalay Line which most tourists use. Travel time is about 12 hours and the trains run at night. To reach Pagan one either has to detrain at Thazi and proceed by bus or continue to Mandalay and take a bus from there. Mandalay also offers a daily riverboat connection down the Irrawaddy to Pagan. It leaves in the early morning and if it does not hit a sandbank, will arrive late in the evening at Nyaung U. Thazi is also the point where one has to detrain for Taunggyi and Inle Lake. Though there is a train going up to Shwenyaung, taking the bus will save considerable time. There is also an early morning bus connection from Pagan to Taunggyi and vice versa.

Arrangements for planes, trains and buses should always be made at least a day in advance. During the travel season there is never enough transport available.

Where to Stay

Tourist Burma has licensed several hotels. They all have a marker on their entrance door and can only be paid for in foreign currency or with TB vouchers. Prices, according to category are between US$3.50 and US$30.00. There are three categories: Economy, Standard and Superior. Some of the hotels offer all three standards. They are listed here according to category, the most expensive first.

Rangoon:
Inya Lake Hotel /Strand Hotel /Thamada / Sakantha /Kandawgyi /Dagon and Garden Guest House/YMCA

Mandalay:
Mandalay Hotel /Mya Mandalay

Pagan:
Thiripyitsaya /Irra Inn

Taunggyi:
Taunggyi Hotel

Yaunghwe:
Inle Inn

Apart from the above-mentioned hotels there are other guest house available. If they are open to foreigners they carry the TB marker.

Things to Do

The Burmese government suggests four locations to be visited by foreign tourists: Rangoon, Mandalay, Pagan and Inle lake. The available time does not leave much choice, anyhow. Traveling to other areas, if not prohibited, is difficult. Tourist Burma will either have no suitable transport available or else no accommodation. Officially, one has to register when staying overnight. In the sponsored hotels this procedure is automatic.

Traveling without the assistance of Tourist Burma might be okay within the Irrawaddy Valley area south of Mandalay, but it is not recommended elsewhere. Most of the southeast, the east and the north of the country is controlled by armed insurgents and kidnappings have been reported.

TOUR OPERATORS

Within Burma all tourist activities are handled by **Tourist Burma** which has offices in all areas of tourist interest. Its main office is in Rangoon: Sule Pagoda Road 77-79. Hotel vouchers, airline, train and bus tickets, sightseeing and other travel arrangements, exchange of currency, tourist brochures and information can be obtained and processed there. If arriving with Thai Airways from Bangkok the return flight must be reconfirmed after arrival otherwise the seat might be given away. The office is next to Tourist Burma.

CHINA
Castle Peak
Tuen Mun Newtown
Tsuen Wan
Sung Dynasty Village
Lantau Island
Man Kok
Silver Mine Bay
Lantau Peak
Tong Fuk
Cheung Chau
Lamma

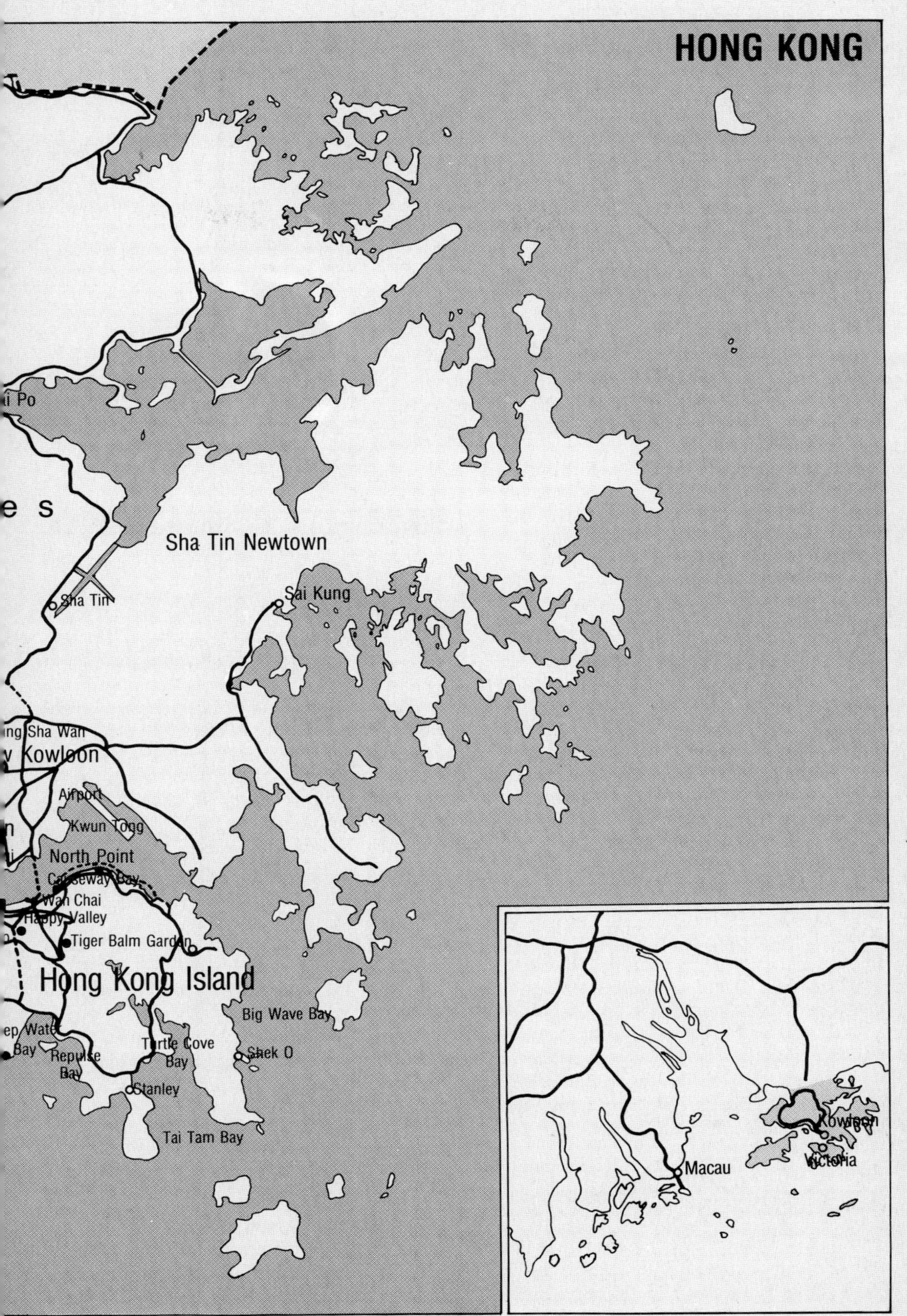
HONG KONG
Sha Tin Newtown
Sha Tin
Sai Kung
Kowloon
Airport
Kwun Tong
North Point
Wan Chai
Happy Valley
Tiger Balm Garden
Hong Kong Island
Big Wave Bay
Turtle Cove Bay
Shek O
Stanley
Tai Tam Bay
Macau
Victoria

GETTING THERE

BY AIR

The colony is served by more than 30 airline companies, plus another dozen charter and cargo airlines. Kai Tak has reached its air traffic saturation point by the mid-80s, but various expansion plans are in progress to extend the life of the airport.

Kai Tak is one of the few airports still located virtually within a city—less than three miles (five km) and about 10 minutes away from Kowloon's Tsimshatsui hotel district, 20 minutes from Causeway Bay and about 25 to 30 minutes from Central District (both on Hong Kong Island).

No airport handling more than 12 million passengers a year is fun. Kai Tak has been expanded—and expanded—but at times when a half-dozen 747s are arriving and departing at the same time, the runway and skies are like an airborne cattle yard. However, Hong Kong maintains one of the world's most efficient runway-to-hotel gauntlets.

The terminal building doesn't win architectural awards, but recent massive renovation efforts have eased many former traffic bottlenecks. Upon arrival, jumbo aircrafts park alongside modern passenger bridges. Immigration, customs and baggage check points are all within a short walking distance, and free baggage carts are available to assist travelers. Free phones are in the buffer hall immediately past customs. There are well-marked, but still confusing, exits: left is the greeting area if you are being met; straight ahead are hotel buses and city-bound tour coaches.

BY SEA

For those with plenty of time and very ample means, a half-dozen cruise lines include Hong Kong on their "Exotic East" or "Round-the-World" grand tours. Most have recently added a Chinese port—but few give enough time in any one place for more than a cursory view. Among the current fleet that tie up at Ocean Terminal are ships from **Norwegian America Line**, **Royal Viking Line**, **Holland-America Line**, **Cunard** and of course **P & O,** whose steamships once ruled the England-to-Far East run.

TRAVEL ESSENTIALS

VISAS & PASSPORTS

Most visitors need only a valid passport to enter Hong Kong. Also, in keeping with recent trends worldwide, vaccination certificates for cholera are waived *except* for arrivals from officially declared "infected areas."

Visitors are not allowed to take up employment, paid or unpaid, to establish or join any business, or to enter school as a student. And except in unusual circumstances, visitors are not allowed to change their citizenship status after arrival.

The maximum stay varies according to nationality: six months for British subjects (United Kingdom passport holders only); three months for other British passport holders (Commonwealth countries) and citizens of Andorra, Austria, Belgium, Brazil, Chile, Colombia, Denmark, Ecuador, Eire, France, Germany, Israel, Italy, Liechenstein, Luxembourg, the Maldives, Monaco, the Netherlands, Norway, Portugal, San Marino, Spain, Sweden, Switzerland, and Turkey; one month for citizens of Bolivia, Costa Rica, Dominican Republic, El Salvador, Finland, Mexico, Morocco, Nepal, Nicaragua, Pakistan, Panama, Greece, Guatemala, Honduras, Iceland. Paraguay, Peru, Tunisia, the U.S., Uruguay, and Venezuela; 14 days for citizens of Thailand and seven days for nationals of other countries, including the Vatican and the U.S. Trust Territory of The

Pacific Islands (American Micronesia), but excluding exceptions listed below.

Visitors from the categories listed below ALWAYS REQUIRE A VISA: (1) Nationals of Afghanistan, Albania, Argentina, Bulgaria, the People's Republic of China, Cuba, Czechoslovakia, Hungary, Kampuchea, Laos, Mongolia, North Korea, Poland, Rumania, the Soviet Union, Vietnam and (North) Yemen; (2) holders of Taiwan passports; (3) all "stateless" persons; and (4) holders of Iranian and Libyan passports.

Macau-China Trips: If admitted to Hong Kong with a multiple-entry visa, you will not need another Hong Kong visa to return from Macau or China. If you have a single-entry visa, you will need a re-entry visa (obtainable from the Immigration Department) to come back.

MONEY MATTERS

The financial arts are Hong Kong's stock-in-trade. Because it's a strategic center for international transactions, the colony has banks of every description and there are no local restrictions whatsoever on the import, export, purchase or sale of foreign currency.

Businessmen and tax fugitives notwithstanding, most visitors need not get too bogged down in the esoterica of floating exchange rates. Though the Hong Kong dollar fluctuates, its value is usually around HK$7.80 to the U.S. dollar. Hotel cashiers are handy, often open 24 hours, and as a rule they change either traveler's checks or major foreign currencies, usually at a slightly higher rate than financial institutions or money-changers.

The Hong Kong dollar has a singular distinction: it is the world's last major currency issued not by a government but by local private banks. With unflagging free enterprise, the two leading financial houses here—**The Hongkong and Shanghai Banking Corporation** and **The Standard Chartered**—issue all the colony's paper money, emblazoning notes with grandly stylized views of their own headquarters. The British Queen is confined to coins and one cent notes.

The Hong Kong dollar is divided into 100 cents. There are seven standard bills. Each bank uses a different motif, but all share similar denomination colors: $1000 (gold), $500 (brown), $100 (red), $50 (blue), $20 (orange) and $10 (green). (Note: Due to the changeover of the paper currency, you will find some notes in different sizes and colors.) There is also a small and rarely seen one cent (1¢) note that's only slightly larger than a subway ticket. They are blank on one side and make unique souvenirs. Coins include 5¢, 10¢, 20¢, 50¢, $1, $2, and $5.

Many licensed money-changers, usually open from 9 a.m. to late at night, will often accept more obscure foreign notes—at a substantial markdown. Nevertheless, their traveler's check and banknote rates are considerably better than those offered by hotels. For large transactions—US$250 or more—exchange rates often can be negotiated to even greater advantage.

They are sold here by foreign exchange dealers and banks. European or Japanese traveler's checks are as acceptable as U.S. dollar checks. Many small merchants here prefer traveler's checks to credit cards or hard currency, so hold out for more than the going bank rate during any negotiations involving traveler's checks. Personal checks will be of little use here, even at a local branch of the issuing bank back home unless prior arrangements have been made.

WHAT TO WEAR

Clothing should follow seasons not unlike those in the American Deep South. Dank winter months (January and February) require sweaters, heavy jackets or even a light topcoat. A fickle, cool-to-warm spring (March and April) is best handled with adaptable, all-purpose outfits. High, emphatically tropical summer (May through September) demands the lightest cloths, umbrellas (traditional local models are superb, raincoats a steamy washout) and some sort of protection against fanatic air-conditioning. Much favored and dry and temperate fall (October through December) is best suited by middle-weight clothes with perhaps a sweater for cool nights during the later months.

CUSTOMS

Though Hong Kong is a well-known duty-free port, arriving non-resident visitors still face the usual limitations on consumable luxuries: 200 cigarettes, 50 cigars or 250 grams of tobacco; a quart of liquor or spirits; and cosmetics "in reasonable quantities for personal use". The only import duties levied here are on petroleum products and alcohol products (both grog and perfumes). Everything else is duty-free. (The allowances for returning residents is half that of non-residents—100 cigarettes or 25 cigars or 125 grams of tobacco—plus one bottle of still wine—i.e. no liquor or spirits.)

Hong Kong is also a free money market, so there are no restrictions on the type or amount of money brought in or taken out.

Airport customs officers take a very active interest in drugs and firearms. The worst most tourists can expect is a very stern glance and a few pointed questions, but this interrogation frequently includes full-scale searches. Prescription medicines should always be carried in their original containers. Firearms, live ammunition, knives, spears, bows and arrows must be declared immediately and left in customs custody until departure.

EXTENSION OF STAY

It is extremely rare for a person on a visitor's visa to change his or her visa status category without first leaving the colony. However, visa extensions are usually given freely provided you have the means to stay here (without working) and onward ticketing. Address all queries to the Immigration Department, 7 Gloucester Road, Wanchai, Tel: 852-829-2332. (Visa extensions cost HK$115.)

ON DEPARTURE

Departure Transport: Hotels and travel agents offer regular airport transportation services. Any metered taxi will also gladly make the run to Kai Tak. An airport bus service stops every 10 to 20 minutes at major hotels in Central District and Causeway Bay (on Hong Kong Island) and at Tsimshatsui in Kowloon. On airport buses, however, there are no individual luggage racks (just a communal baggage bay) and the buses' steps are steep. Travelers with a lot of baggage would probably prefer a taxi or hotel service, because there is no porter service from the roadside bus stops. Route A1 serves Kowloon and the fare is HK$5. Route A2 and A3 serve Hong Kong Island and its fare is HK$7. Exact change only.

Check in: Though most airlines at Kai Tak Airport have computerized booking facilities, they still request check-in at least two hours before flight time because of the airport's burgeoning crowds. Most airlines begin their check-in three hours before flight time, but **Jardine Airways**, which handles quite a number of flights, allows a same day check-in at any time before the flight, which means you can drop your bags off and receive a boarding card any time during the day at your convenience. This system is especially popular with persons booking late-night long hauls to Europe, Africa or Australia.

Departure Tax: The airport's departure tax is HK$100 for adults and HK$50 for children two to 12 years of age. Travel agents may include this in your ticket price. If not, you pay at check-in and a receipt is attached to your ticket.

GETTING ACQUAINTED

GOVERNMENT

Law Enforcement: The British-administrated Royal Hong Kong Police wear light green uniforms in summer, blue ones in winter, and carry handguns. English speaking officers have a small red tab below their serial numbers.

In emergencies phone 999—and ask for the police, fire department, or ambulance, as required.

Identification Cards: In 1980, the Hong Kong government passed legislation requiring everyone to carry a Hong Kong identity card. If you are going to remain here for more than 180 days, you must register for a Hong Kong identity card within 30 days of arrival. Such ID cards are issued by the Immigration.

As the law is now written, visitors are required to have some form of identification. If you prefer to keep your passport in the hotel's safe deposit box, some other document with a photo (driver's licence or the like) will suffice. This is especially necessary if you are going out to the New Territories or one of the outlying islands.

CLIMATE

A historian recently noted that Hong Kong's weather is "trying for half the year." Foreign residents might agree, but few visitors stay long enough for the weather to become truly oppressive.

In meteorological terms, the climate is tropical (just barely) and monsoonal. Two seasons dominate the year—one consistently hot, wet and humid (the **Southwest Monsoon**, corresponding very roughly to spring/summer), and the other cool and dry (the **Northeast Monsoon**, corresponding to fall/winter). The colony can, however, experience great variations in this general pattern—notably in periods between successive monsoons—and dramatically during **typhoon season**.

TYPHOONS

If you are unlucky enough to be here when a full-scale **typhoon** or hurricane sweeps in from the South China Sea, you will find out first-hand why it was named *dai foo*, or "big wind," in Cantonese. There is not much you can do except slink back to your hotel and have a typhoon party, which is precisely what many Hong Kong residents do in their homes during these Asian hurricanes.

The **Royal Observatory** is modern enough to have early-warning computers and a weather satellite ground station, so no more does the weatherman stand out on the lawn to see which way the clouds are moving. When a typhoon or "**Severe Tropical Storm**" (which may escalate into a typhoon) comes within a 400-mile radius of the colony, storm signal #1 goes up. The populace is quite blase about a number one signal. A #1 signal can remain aloft for days—sometimes during beautiful pre-storm weather, or be quickly changed to the next important signal #3. Number three is the first real alert because it signifies that winds are reaching speeds of 22 to 33 knots with gusts up to 60 knots.

Never underestimate a typhoon: Too many visitors, mostly from the U.S. and the Caribbean, probably do because they have seen so many hurricanes. They tend to think typhoons are nothing more than severe rainstorms. A few statistics for the disbelievers. Typhoon Hope in 1979 left 12 dead and 260 injured. Severe Tropical Storm Agnes in 1978 left three dead and 126 injured, and Typhoon Rose, which left the harbor a shambles, claimed 130 lives, 80 on a capsized Hong Kong-Macau ferry. Typhoon Ruby in 1964 killed 120 and Typhoon Wanda in 1962 killed 138.

For information about a typhoon, call the **City & New Territories Department's Typhoon Emergency Number** (Tel: 3-692-255), but do not ring the Royal Observatory, the police or the first brigade, who all are on busy full alert. To find out if the airport is closed, phone 3-769-7531, but rest assured that individual airlines will regularly update you on the details of their own typhoon-disrupted flights.

DRY MONSOONS

The dry monsoon season begins sometime in September, and brings three months of warm (rather than hot) days and usually clear blue skies. Nights are cool, humidity low, and day-to-day temperature changes are slight. October and November are the best months to visit here, and the colony is predictably chock-a-block with visitors at that time. From December through early January, it is still sunny during the day and cool at night. This period signals a gradual shift to less predictable weather.

Beginning with Chinese New Year—late-January to mid-February—the temperature and clear and dry skies alternate with longer spells of cold wind and dank mist that can run unbroken for weeks. Mountaintops occasionally show night-time frost (the appearance of frost is always a headline story in local tabloids), and beaches at this time of the year are largely deserted.

Hong Kong's **rainy season** arrives in earnest about the middle of March, when the temperature rises, humidity thickens and trees grow green. Skies can be consistently gray, and heavy afternoon rainstorms become increasingly common. Though quite changeable, this "spring" season generally stays cool enough to be agreeable.

Mid May to September is high summer, and also the unpredictable typhoon season. Punctuated by cloudbursts, intense tropical sunshine scorches open land and broils even well-tanned skin.

BUSINESS HOURS

Local banking hours are now in the process of gradual extension, but 9:00 a.m. to 4:30 p.m. on weekdays, and 9 a.m. to noon Saturdays are normal business hours for foreign exchange services.

GETTING AROUND

FROM THE AIRPORT

There is a special airport bus service—both to and from the airport—to and from Tsimshatsui and Hong Kong Island. Route A1 to Tsimshatsui costs HK$5 and Route A2 and A3 to Hong Kong costs HK$7 (exact fare change only). Both bus routes stop at all major hotels.

Route A2 operates from 6:50 a.m. to 11:25 p.m. (11:14 p.m. Sundays) from the airport, and Route A3 begins at 6:55 a.m. to 10:40 p.m. from Hong Kong Island. Route A1 operates from 7 a.m. to 11 p.m. from the airport. For information call 3-745-4466.

Metered taxis are available and are somewhat cheaper on long runs. There is a HK$20 surcharge on any trip through the Cross-Harbor Tunnel, and HK$3 for the Aberdeen and Lion Rock Tunnels, plus a HK$2 charge on each piece of baggage. Taxi drivers are usually honest, but some try to overcharge on the very short trip (under HK$10) into Tsimshatsui so just pay whatever is on the meter. Avis self-drive cars are also available at HK$220-860 per day.

TRANSPORT TO SEZ

Shenzen: For tourist heading to Shenzhen (also called Shum Chun), China's first and largest and wealthiest Special Economic Zone (SEZ), and the adjacent oil port of Shekou, is dead easy because the travel agency does all the work.

For buses to Shenzhen, contact Citybus (China) Ltd., 3-722-4866. They run both double-decker buses and air-conditioned coaches (HK$30-45), depending on the day destination within the SEZ. Hong Kong's Kowloon Canton Railway runs to the border (Lo Wu) many times daily for HK$17.50 second class, HK$35 first class. (Call 0-606-9600 for information.) Here, you cross the border on foot. Be prepared for crowds pushing and shoving. The border is at Shenzhen and you take a bus or taxi to Shekou, about 19 miles away.

The resorts in the SEZ, which are well off the beaten track, often have their own buses direct from Hong Kong or which meet the public transport in the SEZ.

There is also a hovercraft service from Hong Kong departing from Kowloon's Taikoktsui Ferry Pier (three sailings, call-3-929345 for information) or the old Macau Ferry Terminal on Hong Kong Island (four sailings, call 5-448052 for information). The one-way fare from either terminal is HK$40.

Port of Zuhai: The Special Economic Zone of Zuhai is another oil exploration port, like the aforementioned Shekou, only this one is near Macau. There is a six-time daily "jetcat" service leaving from Hong Kong Island's old Macau Ferry Terminal, next to the Shun Tak Center, direct to this SEZ. The one-class fares are HK$70 on weekdays, HK$80 on weekends and public holidays. Day-light service only. Call 5-232136. It is only a 30-minute ride from Zuhai to Macau.

WATER TRANSPORT

There are 236 islands in the colony (Hong Kong Island of course is just one of them). A convenient **inter-island ferries** transportation system is in operation here to service many of them.

INTER-ISLAND FERRIES

At the **Outlying Districts Ferry Pier**, Connaught Road, Central, Hong Kong, you'll find double and triple-decker ferries—some with air-conditioning—that regularly travel to the outlying islands. The routes and times are too numerous to mention here, but there is regular service—quite crowded during weekends and holidays—to Lantau, Cheung Chau and Lamma islands (the big three) and many of the colony's smaller isles. Fares range from HK$4-11. Fare charges vary from children to adult, ordinary and deluxe.

The Hong Kong Tourist Association has a complete schedule of all ferry services and will answer telephone queries at 5-244-191 or 3-722-5555 or The **Hong Kong and Yaumatei Ferry Company's** enquiry number is 5-423081.

THE STAR FERRY

You can always tell the tourists from the residents on Hong Kong's most famous mode of transportation, the **Star Ferry**. The tourists are agog at the magnificent site of the world's third busiest harbor—and one of the best natural harbors in the world—as the double-bowed, green and white, double-decker ferries weave their way through the 0.8 nautical mile course between Hong Kong and Tsimshatsui (Kowloon).

The residents, on the other hand, are quite content to spend the seven minute sea voyage with their noses tucked into their newspapers or racing sheets. Upper deck, first class seats cost the princely sum of 70 Hong Kong cents and the view of the harbor from there will delight any shutterbug. A more exciting ride (because you are closer to the water racing past) is in second class seats on the lower deck; a ride there costs only 60 Hong Kong cents.

WALLAS-WALLAS

After the MTR closes at 1 a.m. and the Star Ferry at 11:30, you can still ride across the harbor in a small motorboat called a **walla-walla**. You can also take a taxi or bus through the cross-harbor tunnel, but if you are staying in Tsimshatsui and end up in Central—or vice versa—the direct cross-harbor water route by Star Ferry, MTR or walla-walla is the fastest and cheapest means of transportation. On Hong Kong Island, walla-wallas are located at Queen's Pier to the East of the Star Ferry concourse (to the right as you face the harbor, in front of City Hall) while in Kowloon, they are located at Kowloon Public Pier, (to the left of the Star Ferry as you face the water, opposite the Ocean Terminal). The cost is HK$4.50 per person or HK$45 for an entire boat if you are impatient.

PUBLIC TRANSPORT

Getting around Hong Kong is much easier than it seems. Though Cantonese is the language spoken by 98 percent of the population, English is also widely used (if only for English place names which differ from their Cantonese counterparts). It helps, however, to have an address or item written out in Chinese characters by a friend or hotel employee.

BUSES

Hong Kong has numerous scheduled buses and bus routes to just about every corner of the colony. **China Motor Buses** are blue whilst **Kowloon Motor Buses** are red. With the advent of the cross-harbor tunnel routes, however, they commute on each other's turf. Bus fares range from HK$1 to $5. The deluxe (no standing) buses to Repulse Bay Beach are numbers 260 and 262 and cost HK$4.80. (There is a convenient bus stop in front of the Hong Kong side Star Ferry Terminal.) The number six bus plies the same route for HK$3, but they are regular buses, usually packed like sardine cans during the summer.

MINIBUSES & MAXICABS

Yellow 14-seater vans with a red stripe—called minibuses here—ply all the main routes and make unscheduled stops and charge variable fares. There is a sign in the front indicating their destinations and fare charges. To complicate matters; other yellow 14-seater vans with a green stripe and roof—called **maxicabs**—run on fixed routes at fixed prices. There is a special maxicab to The Peak (HK$3) and another to

Ocean Park (HK$3). The maxi-bus terminal in Central is on the eastern side of the Star Ferry carpark.

TRAMS

On Hong Kong island there are trams running along the north shore from west to east (and vice versa) which pass through the main tourist areas of Central, Wanchai, Causeway Bay and Taikao Shingui Quarry Bay. The cost is 60 Hong Kong cents (exact change). Sit on the upper deck and watch the real Hong Kong bump and grind by.

THE PEAK TRAM

Hong Kong's other "tram" is the **Peak Tram**, which is not a tram at all but a funicular railway up to The Peak. It is a form of regular local commuter transport and a favorite "tourist attraction." The funicular rises 1,305 feet above sea level in about 10 minutes on a steep journey over 4,500 feet of track. The fare is HK$6 and travel hours are from 7 a.m. to midnight. The **Lower Peak Tram Station** in Central District is on Garden Road, up from the Hilton Hotel and across from the U.S. Consulate. A free topless double-decker shuttle bus service operates between the Lower Station and the Star Ferry from 9 a.m. to 7 p.m.daily at 20-minute intervals. There are five intermediate stations before you reach the **Upper Peak Tram Station** nestled underneath the **Peak Tower**, a futuristic building on stilts that houses a European restaurant and the Peak Tower Village with stalls full of Chinese handicrafts.

MASS TRANSIT RAILWAY (MTR)

The most dramatic change in Hong Kong's public transportation scene is the fully air-conditioned **Mass Transit Railway**, commonly called the **MTR**, which in other countries might be called an Underground, Tube, Metro or Subway. The 24-mile (38-km) system has three lines with 37 stations, stretching from industrial Kwun Tong (Kowloon) and Tsuen Wan (New Territories) through some of Kowloon's most populated areas, underneath Nathan Road to the Tsimshatsui tourist and entertainment district, and under the harbor to Central, the governmental and financial center of the colony and along the north shore of Hong Kong Island. (With the MTR, it is easy to reach many of the favorite tourist areas on the island, particularly Wanchai, Causeway Bay and Taikoo Shing.) The longest trip takes less than 60 minutes and fares range from HK$2.50-6. The four-minute cross-harbor trip is only HK$4.50. You can use the MTR for shopping or sight-seeing trips that previously could only be made on crowded and hot buses. The MTR is open 6 a.m. to 1 a.m. the following morning daily. See the *MTR Guide* for subway directions. For tourists really on the go, the HK$20 "Tourist Ticket" is good value.

A few points before you go charging underground. First, there are no toilets down there, and smoking, drinking and eating are prohibited. The ticket machines take exact change, but there are change booth where your can break notes. After placing money in a ticket machine, you receive a magnetic plastic card about the size of a credit card. This is placed in a slot by the turnstile for entry. Upon departure, the card is again placed in a turnstile. The amount you paid is electronically calculated, and if you paid enough, you are allowed to pass through the exit turnstile.

You will see signs warning about HK$1,000 fines for "ticket flickers" caught in the act. Ticket flickers are people who flick the plastic cards on their nails. "Ticket-flicking" is banned because the MTR found it damaged the fare cards. A last MTR warning: the MTR's shiny metal seats are slippery so be prepared to slide when the train starts up. The crossover with the railway is at Kowloon Tong Station.

KOWLOON-CANTON RAILWAY

The old **Kowloon-Canton Railway** is now a modern electrified commuter train because the trains to Canton are now Chinese-operated. There are nine stops on this 22 mile segment through Kowloon and the NT. Fares range from HK$2-10.80 second class, HK$35 for first class. Don't worry about inadvertently chug-chugging into China. Before the train enters the (Hong Kong) restricted zone after the Sheung Shui Station, police check to see if you have a China visa. Note: There are no toilets on the

Hong Kong trains, but there are such facilities on Chinese trains. The main railway station is Hung Hom, Kowloon, and there is direct passenger ferry service to that station from the Star Ferry in Central District. Tel: 0-606-9600 for information.

TAXIS

Metered taxis in urban areas are red with silver roofs and the dome atop the roof is lit at night when the taxis is unoccupied. (There are also green and white taxis restricted to the New Territories (NT) and these run on a different—and cheaper—fare system.)

If you have any trouble with a taxi—say you are victimized, overcharged or you have left your wallet in the back seat—contact the Royal Hong Kong Police special "taxi hotline" at Tel: 5-277-177. (Don't forget to record the taxi's number!) If a complaint is not resolved, you must be prepared to appear as a witness to the police prosecution. In most cases, the courts will push a tourist's case to the front of its judicial queues to make an example of the offender. The Hong Kong Tourist Association has a bilingual "Communication Card" to make life easier.

Some taxis are equipped with mobile telephones to phone anywhere in the colony. Charges are HK$2 per minute, in addition to the fare.

RICKSHAWS

Hong Kong still has a small number of **rickshaws** that congregate around Star Ferry concourses on both sides of the harbor. Tourists hire the rickshaws more to pose for pictures than as transportation, but the unofficial "official" rate is HK$50 for five minutes. However, because rickshaw-pullers refuse to budge without a round of bartering, the price extracted from visitors is usually more. The price for posing for a picture is between HK$20 to $30, depending on how hard you bargain.

PRIVATE TRANSPORT

Rental cars, self-Drive or chauffeured Cars, are also available. The familiar self-drive names of **Avis**, **Hertz** and **Budget** are here, along with a couple of dozen local firms. Those under 18 cannot hire any motor vehicles (including cycles and scooters). All visitors with a valid overseas driving license, however, can drive here for a year. Hotels, through their own transportation services, can usually handle requests for **chauffeur-driven cars**.

WHERE TO STAY

HOTELS

Luxury
Over HK$1,000 Per Day

Mandarin
5 Connaught Road, Central, Hong Kong
Tel: 5-220-111.

Peninsula
Salisbury Road, Tsimshatsui, Kowloon
Tel: 3-666-251.

Regent
Salisbury Road, Tsimshatsui, Kowloon
Tel: 3-721-211.

Shangri-La
64 Mody Road, Tsimshatsui East, Kowloon
Tel: 3-721-2111.

Expensive
Above HK$400 Per Day

Excelsior
Gloucester Road, Causeway Bay, Hong Kong
Tel: 5-767-365.

Furama Intercontinental
1 Connaught Road, Central, Hong Kong
Tel: 5-255-111.

Hilton
2 Queen's Road, Central, Hong Kong
Tel: 5-233-111.

Holiday Inn-Golden Mile
50 Nathan Road, Tsimshatsui East,
Kowloon
Tel: 3-693-111.

Holiday Inn Harbor View
10 Mody Road, Tsimshatsui East,
Kowloon
Tel: 3-721-5161.

Omni The Hongkong
3 Canton Road, Tsimshatsui, Kowloon
Tel: 3-676-011.

Hyatt-Regency
67 Nathan Road, Tsimshatsui, Kowloon
Tel: 3-662-321.

Kowloon
19-21 Nathan Road, Tsimshatsui,
Kowloon
Tel: 3-698-698.

Lee Gardens
Hysan Avenue, Causeway Bay,
Hong Kong
Tel: 5-767-211.

Omni Marco Polo
Harbor City, Canton Road, Tsimshatsui,
Kowloon
Tel: 3-721-5111.

Miramar
134 Nathan Road, Tsimshatsui, Kowloon
Tel: 3-681-111.

Omni Prince
Harbor City, Canton Road, Tsimshatsui,
Kowloon
Tel: 3-723-7788.

Regal Meridien
Mody Road, Tsimshatsui East, Kowloon
Tel: 3-722-1818.

Royal Meridien Airport
Sa Po Road, Kowloon
Tel: 3-718-0333.

Royal Garden
69 Mody Road, Tsimshatsui East
Kowloon
Tel: 3-721-5215, 3-681-111.

New World
22 Salisbury Road, Tsimshatsui
Kowloon
Tel: 3-694-111.

Park Lane
310 Gloucester Road, Causeway Bay,
Hong Kong
Tel: 5-790-1021.

Riverside Plaza
Tai Chung Kiu Road, Shatin,
New Territories
Tel: 0-649-7878.

Sheraton
20 Nathan Road, Tsimshatsui, Kowloon
Tel: 3-691-111.

Victoria
Shun Tak Center, Connaught Road,
Central, Hong Kong
Tel: 5-407-228.

Warwick
Cheung Chau Island
Tel: 5-981-0081.

Moderate
Above HK$300

Ambassador
4 Middle Road, Tsimshatsui, Kowloon
Tel: 3-666-321.

Astor
11 Carnarvon Road, Tsimshatsui,
Kowloon
Tel: 3-667-261.

Carlton
4½ Milestone, Tai Po Road,
North Kowloon
Tel: 3-866-222.

Empress
17-19 Chatham Road, Tsimshatsui,
Kowloon
Tel: 3-660-211.

Fortuna
355 Nathan Road, Yaumatei, Kowloon
Tel: 3-851-011.

Grand
14 Carnarvon Road, Tsimshatsui, Kowloon
Tel: 3-669-331.

Harbor View
4 Harbor Road, Hong Kong
Tel: 5-201-111.

Imperial
30-34 Nathan Road, Tsimshatsui, Kowloon
Tel: 3-662-201.

International
33 Cameron Road, Tsimshatsui, Kowloon
Tel: 3-663-381.

Luk Kwok
67 Gloucester Road, Hong Kong
Tel: 5-270-721.

Park
61-65 Chatham Road, Tsimshatsui Kowloon
Tel: 3-661-371.

Shamrock
223 Nathan Road, Yaumatei, Kowloon
Tel: 3-662-271.

Silvermine Bay Beach Hotel
Lantau Island
Tel: 5-984-8295.

Surf Hotel
Tai Mung Tsai Road, Sai Kung, New Territories
Tel: 3-281-4411.

Inexpensive Above HK$100

Bangkok
2-12 Pilkem Street, Tsimshatsui, Kowloon
Tel: 3-679-181.

Chung Hing
380 Nathan Road, Yaumatei, Kowloon
Tel: 3-887-001.

Galaxie
30 Pak Hoi Street, Yaumatei, Kowloon
Tel: 3-307-211.

King's
473-473A Nathan Road, Yaumatei, Kowloon
Tel: 3-301-281.

Under HK$100

The best bargains are Y's but they are usually quite full. Next come the guest houses especially those in **Chungking Mansions**.

Chungking House
Chungking Mansions, A Block 4th and 5th floors, 34-40 Nathan Road, Tsimshatsui, Kowloon
Tel: 3-665-362.

Green Jade House
29-31 Chatham Road, Tsimshatsui, Kowloon
Tel: 3-677-121.

International Guest House
Chungking Mansions, 9th-10th floors, 34-40 Nathan Road Tsimshatsui, Kowloon.
Tel: 3-664-256.

YMCA
Salisbury Road, Tsimshatsui, Kowloon
Tel: 3-692-211.

23 Waterloo Road, Yaumatei, Kowloon
Tel: 5-319-111.

1 Macdonnell Road, Hong Kong
Tel: 5-223-101.

5 Man Fuk Road, Waterloo Road Hill, Kowloon
Tel: 3-713-9211.

GETTING THERE

BY SEA

You will not believe the number of ways you can get from Hong Kong to Macau by sea. You could spend a little less than an hour crossing that 40 mile stretch of the Pearl River Estuary on a jetfoil or hoverferry, 70 minutes on a jetcat, 75 minutes on a hydrofoil, 90–100 minutes on a high-speed ferry, and 2½–3 hours by ferry. With all that sea transportation, you would reckon there would always be empty seats. Well, the old timers will tell you how drastically things have improved, but somehow Macau's over 4.5 million visitors annually usually manage to grab every seat, especially on weekends and public holidays. However, with the advent of computerized ticketing, there are less "full boats" sailing with empty seats. Another innovation is the night jetfoil service. Regardless of when you go, make certain you have your return tickets in your possession *before* you go. Just about all the Macau ferry sailings use the Macau Ferry Terminal in the Shun Tak Center, Connaught Road, Central, Hong Hong with the exception of the hoverferries (and a very, very limited jetfoil service) which sail regularly from the Shampuipo Ferry Pier in Kowloon.

Computer booking service: There is a computer booking service called Ticketmate with 11 outlets in Hong Kong (many of which are in the major Mass Transit Railway stations) and three in Macau where you can buy a passage up to 28 days in advance. Holders of American Express, Visa or Diners Club credit cards can book by phone up to 28 days in advance by dialing 5-859-3288 in Hong Kong. (The service is not offered in Macau).

JETFOILS

Jetfoils carry 240 people in two classes and leave either destination for the 55-minute journey at half-hourly intervals from 7 a.m. till 5 p.m. in the winter, 6 p.m. in summer, when the less frequent night jetfoils take over till 2 a.m. Upperdeck, first class fares (same airplane seats as lower deck passengers, but free coffee and newspapers, slightly better service, and first crack at exiting upon arrival) are HK$66 on weekday, daylight sailings, HK$72 on weekends and all public holidays, daylight hours, and HK$88 for the night service, any day. Lower deck economy fares are HK$57 for weekday, daylight trips, HK$63 on weekends and all public holidays, daylight hours, and HK$77 for all night sailings. Most departures are made from Hong Kong, and three from Kowloon's Shamshuipo Ferry Pier. For information on Hong Kong sailings call 5-859-3333; Kowloon sailings 3-866818.

JETCATS

These one-class, jet-propelled catamaran ferries carry up to 215 people and make ten 70-minute return trips daily (only daylight hours) for HK$46 one way on weekdays, and HK$58 on weekends and public holidays. American Express cardholders only can reserve and charge tickets by telephoning 5-232136, but must collect tickets within 24 hours of the booking. Ticketmate computer bookings available. For information, call 5-401882 (same day sailings only), 5-232136 (advanced sailing). Departure from Hong Kong.

HYDROFOILS

They depart half-hourly for the 75-minute crossing beginning at 8 a.m. with final departures at 5 p.m. in winter and 6 p.m. in summer. The one-class fares are HK$46 on weekdays, HK$58 on weekends and public holidays. American Express cardholders can reserve and charge tickets by calling 5-232136, but they must be collected within 24 hours of the booking. Ticketmate computer bookings are available. For information call 5-401822 (current sailings), 5-232136 (advanced sailings). All departures are from Hong Kong.

HIGH-SPEED FERRIES

These 690-passenger vessels make the 40-mile trip in 90–100 minutes, 5 roundtrips daily (an extra during the weekend) between 8 a.m. and 11 p.m. Tickets are HK$38 economy, HK$46 first class and HK$48 and HK$58 respectively on weekends. Same fares 7 days a week. The ferries are completely air-conditioned with aircraft seating, luggage racks, snack bars and slot machines. For information call 5-815-2789. Departures from Hong Kong. Ticketmate computer bookings available.

HOVERFERRIES

Eight 60-minute trips daily during the daylight hours for HK$45 one way on weekdays, HK$56 on weekends and public holidays. These 250-passenger vessels leave from the Shamshuipo Ferry Pier in Kowloon. For information call 3-862549.

FERRIES

For those who enjoy a more leisurely trip—the proverbial "slow boat to Macau"—try the old-fashioned regular ferries which chug along, twice daily, making the crossing in 2½ to 3 hours. Prices begin at HK$12 for a deck chair, dormitory bunk bed HK$23 (day) and HK$30 (night), aircraft seat HK$30, deluxe cabin for two HK$120 and VIP cabin for two HK$150. Children over 1 year HK$8. For information call 5-859-3333. Departures from Hong Kong.

TRAVEL ESSENTIALS

VISAS & PASSPORTS

Visas are NOT required by nationals of the U.S., Philippines, Japan, Australia, Canada, New Zealand, Malaysia, Thailand, Brazil, Austria, Belgium, Denmark, Spain, France, Greece, Italy, Norway, the Netherlands, the United Kingdom, Germany and Sweden (up to six months stay), or Hong Kong residents (British Commonwealth subjects for up to seven days, other nationalities for up to three days).

Getting a visa is usually painless. It is stamped into your passport upon arrival for HK$50. A family visa (HK$75) covers an individual or husband traveling with wife and children on the same passport, and is valid for a visit of 20 days or two visits within a 20-day period. (Group visas cost only HK$25 per person in bona fide groups of 10 or more).

Visas obtained from Portuguese consulates (including the one in Hong Kong which is located at 1001-1002, Two Exchange Square, Connaught Place, Central Hong Kong. Tel: 5-225789) cost HK$48.10 per person.

Nationals of countries which do not have diplomatic relations with Portugal must obtain their visas from Portuguese missions overseas. They cannot obtain them upon arrival in Macau.

MONEY MATTERS

Macau's *pataca* is a sort of shadow version of the Hong Kong dollar, the two normally differing in value by less than five percent. Hong Kong notes and coins traditionally enjoy a slight premium and (except at the post office and telecoms) circulate freely—with the spender thus taking a slight loss on *pataca*-denominated transactions. Changing money is the obvious solution, but to avoid double-costly reconversion—*pataca* are not acceptable in Hong Kong, except at banks or money-changers—the best policy is to change enough for basic expenses and cover any excess with HK dollars. (Note: in addition to being roughly equal, both currencies are usually symbolized by "$".) There are no restrictions on the amount of type of currency brought in or out.

The *pataca* is divided into 100 *avos* (¢), with coins and bills as follows: 5, 10 *avos* in brass, 1, 5 and 20 *patacas* in nickel, and 5, 10, 50, 100 and 500 *pataca* denominations in paper bank notes.

There are no restrictions on moving money in and out of the territory, but the *pataca* is rarely used outside of Macau, even in Hong Kong.

ON ARRIVAL

There is a HK$15 embarkation tax levied by the Hong Kong Government on all tickets to Macau.

LANGUAGE

Officially it's Portuguese. In practice it's Cantonese and English—though the latter is generally neither as common nor as fluent as in Hong Kong.

Given the difficulty of pronouncing correctly most Portuguese place names (which differ in Cantonese), taxi drivers will appreciate being shown a note in Chinese or the trilingual tourist map published by the Department of Tourism. Ask a tour agent or hotel clerk to help you with this. Restaurant and hotel reservations will similarly be streamlined by having a Cantonese or Portuguese speaker do the phoning for you.

GETTING AROUND

Buses: The islands—Taipa and Coloane—are a special case. With the demise of ferry runs from the Inner Harbor, the only other access is by public bus. Not all are the splendid, open-top double-deckers, but fairly frequent runs are scheduled from 7 a.m. to 11 p.m. The plaza opposite the **Lisboa Hotel** is the simplest place to wait. Fares are: Taipa, Ptc. 1, Coloane town, Ptc. 1.50, **Hac Sa beach**, Ptc. 2.

In-town Macau has five meandering bus routes, the most useful being perhaps the No. 5, which runs from the **Temple of A-Ma** out to the **Barrier Gate** via Avenida Almeida Ribeiro. The No 3 runs from the Macau Ferry Pier to the city center. Hours again are 7 a.m. to 11 p.m., fares a flat 50 avos.

Pedicabs: The greatest languor will certainly be encouraged by **pedicabs**, three-wheeled, two-passenger rickshaws that are pedalled rather than pulled. Still very much in day-to-day use (unlike Hong Kong's rickshaws), their drivers nevertheless—and with some justice—view tourists as walking gold mines. Firm, often largely non-verbal bargaining *beforehand* is the rule, about Ptc. 10 (for two) for a short ride (say, along the Praia Grande) or HK$25 to $30 an hour, usually enough to keep both sides happy.

Taxis: Taxis will of course go anywhere, at rates as cheap as any in the world (Ptc. 4 at flagfall, 50 avos each additional 1/5 mile—or a highly negotiable Ptc. 70 or so per hour). The driver's English abilities (or tourist Portuguese) vary enormously: a few can almost manage guided tours, while others will need to be shown notes in Chinese characters for destinations other than the major hotels. You will have to barter with them to go across to the islands, though the official surcharges are Ptc. 5 to Taipa and Ptc. 10 to Coloane.

Mini-Mokes: You will no doubt have a ball seeing Macau in these zippy four-seaters, the only rent-a-car service available. Rates range from HK$250 to HK$280 per day, depending on which day. Special hotel/moke rates are available with the Hyatt-Regency Hotel or Pousada de Coloane. Bookings can be made in Hong Kong at Macau Mokes Ltd., 1701 Hollywood Center, 233 Hollywood Rd., Hong Kong. Tel: 5-434190.

Bicycling: Off the main streets, a possibly more aesthetic choice is bicycling. Several places around the intersection of Rua do Campo and the Praia Grande, and on Avenida D. Joao IV alongside the **Sintra Hotel** rent out very basic models (and occasionally, motorcycles) or about Ptc. 3 to Ptc. 5 per hour, depending on the day of the week and time of day. Bikes can also be hired at the Hyatt-Regency and Oriental Hotels. Bicycles are not allowed to cross the bridge to Taipa.)

WHERE TO STAY

HOTELS

All rates listed below *exclude* the territory's 10 percent service charge and five percent tourism tax. An asterisk(*) indicates the Hong Kong phone number for booking rooms in that particular hotel.

Over HK$500

Hyatt-Regency
Taipa Island Resort
Taipa Island
Tel: 27000. *5-590-168.

Mandarin Oriental
Av. da Amizade
Tel: 567888, *5-487-676.

Pousada de Sao Tiago
Fortaleza da Barra,
Avenida Republica
Tel: 78111, *5-810-8332.

Royal
2 Estrade de Victoria
Tel: 552222, *5-422-033

Over HK$250

Estoril
Avenida Sidonio Pais
Tel: 5-72081.

Lisboa
Avenida de Amizade
Tel: 77666; *5-591-028.

Matsuya
5 Calcada de San Francisco
Tel: 75466, *3-686-181.

Metropole
63 Rua de Praia Grande
Tel: 88166. *5-406-333.

Pousada de Coloane
Praia de Cheoc Van,
Coloane Island
Tel: 28143, *3-696-922.

Presidente
Avenida de Amizade
Tel: 553888, *5-266-873.

Sintra
Avenida de Amizade
Tel: 85111; *5-408-208.

GETTING THERE

BY AIR

Coming from outside the Indonesian archipelago you have two main options: through Jakarta's new international airport at Cengkareng 12.5 miles (20 km) west of Jakarta or through Ngurah Rai Airport near Denpasar on the neighboring island of Bali with connecting flights to Yogyakarta. Airport tax on international flight departures is Rp. 11,000.

A new highway links Cengkareng with Jakarta and buses operate at regular intervals to Gambir Station in the city's center.

A majority of visitors arrive in Jakarta from Singapore. Garuda and Singapore Airlines have five to eight flights daily from Singapore to Jakarta at between US170 and $190 for round trip, one-month excursion fares.

BY SEA

If you're one of the lucky ones with plenty of time (and money), an ocean cruise to Indonesia should not be missed. Luxury cruise lines offer fly/cruise arrangements which allow you to fly to Bali and other ports where you can play in the sun, then catch your ship on the way home or vice versa.

Several other big shipping companies run ships both big and small, in and out of the hundreds of ports in Indonesia. However, most of them carry cargo with limited space for passengers. Check with the harbor master for prices. It's often cheaper to go to the captain himself and pay for your fare.

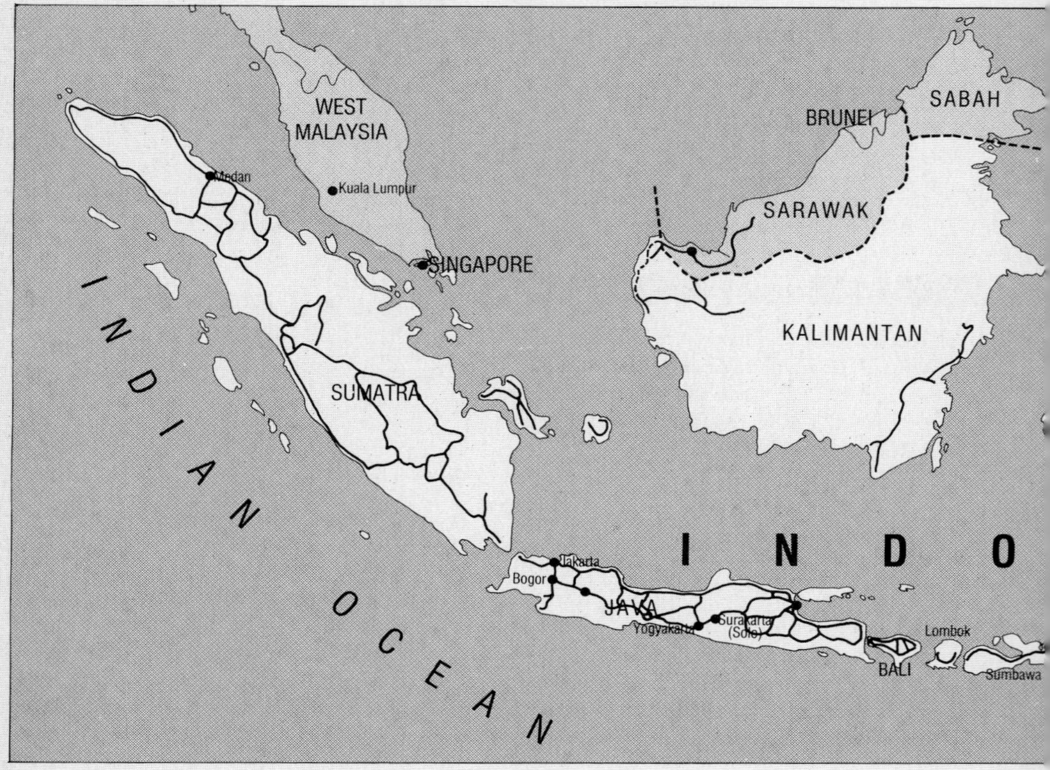

TRAVEL ESSENTIALS

VISAS & PASSPORTS

All travelers to Indonesia must be in possession of a passport valid for at least six months after arrival and with proof (tickets) of onward passages.

Visas have been waived for nationals of 28 countries for a visit not exceeding two months. Those countries are: Australia, Austria, Belgium, Brunei, Canada, Denmark, Finland, France, Germany, Greece, Iceland, Ireland, Italy, Japan, Luxembourg, Malaysia, Netherlands, New Zealand, Norway, Philippines, Singapore, South Korea, Spain, Sweden, Switzerland, Thailand, United Kingdom and United States of America.

Entry and exit must be through the air or seaports of Jakarta, Bali, Medan, Manado, Biak, Ambon, Batam, with the addition of Surabaya seaport only and the Pekanbaru airport.

For other ports of arrival and departure visas are required. Visas are free also for registered delegates attending a conference which has received official approval.

For citizens of countries other than the 28 listed above, tourist visas can be obtained from any Indonesian Embassy or consulate. Two photographs are required and a small fee is charged.

Business Visas for five weeks can be obtained on application and extensions at the discretion of the immigration authorities.

An airport tax of Rp. 3,000 per person is required on international departures from Jakarta, Medan and Denpasar.

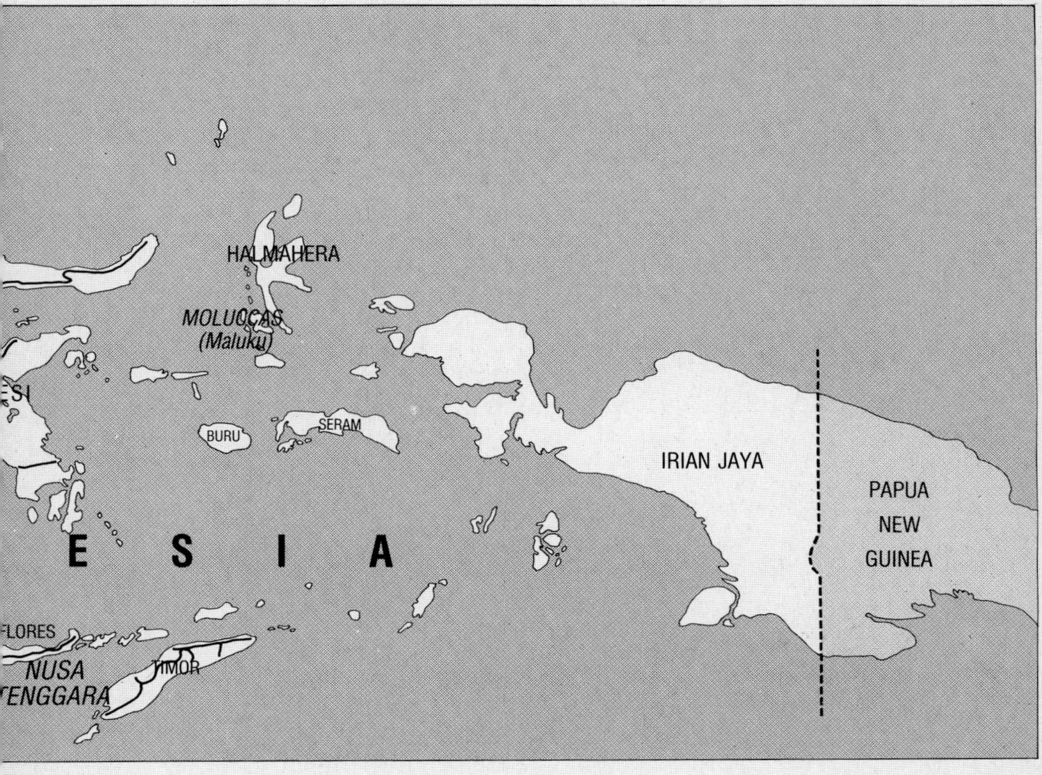

Surat Jalan: a *surat jalan* is a letter from the police permitting the bearer to go to certain places. It is advisable to carry one when traveling in some of the outer islands, but in Java only in such out-of-the-way places as the Ijen plateau. If in doubt check with a good travel agent. In Jakarta a *surat jalan* may be obtained in an hour or two at Police Headquarters (Markas Besar Kepolisian Republik Indonesia) in Jalan Trunojoyo (Kebayoran Baru).

MONEY MATTERS

The exchange rate for a US$1 was about Rp. 1791 at time of going to press. It is advisable not to exchange large sums of money if you plan to be in Indonesia for more than a month.

Foreign currency, in banknotes and travelers checks, is best exchanged at major banks. Banks in many smaller towns are not necessarily conversant with all foreign banknotes, so it is advisable to change currencies in the cities. Your *rupiah* may be freely converted to foreign currencies when you are leaving the country.

Traveler's checks are a mixed blessing. Major hotels, banks and some shops will accept them, but even in the cities it can take a long time to collect your money (in small towns, it is impossible). Credit cards are usable if you stay in the big hotels. International airline offices, a few big city restaurants and art shops will accept them, but they are useless elsewhere.

HEALTH

If you intend staying in Indonesia for some time, particularly outside of the big cities, gammaglobulin injections are recommended; they won't stop hepatitis, but many physicians believe that the risk of infection is greatly reduced. Diarrhea may be a problem: it can be prevented by a daily dose of Doxycycline, an antibiotic used to prevent 'traveler's diarrhea.' Obtain this from your doctor at home. At the first signs of stomach discomfort, try a diet of hot tea and a little patience. Stomach reactions are often due to a change in food and environment. Tablets such as Lomotil and Imodium are invaluable cures. A supply of malaria-suppressant tablets is also highly recommended. Make sure the suppressants are effective against all the strains of malaria. It was recently discovered that a malaria strain was resistant to the usual malarial prophylactic (chloroquine). Consult your physician.

All water, including well water, municipal water and water used for making ice, MUST be made safe before consumption. Bringing water to a rolling boil for 10 minutes is an effective method. Iodine (Globoline) and chlorine (Halazone) may also be used to make water potable. All fruit should be carefully peeled before eating and no raw vegetables should be eaten.

Last but not least, protect yourself against the sun. Tanning oils and creams are expensive in Indonesia, so bring your own.

GETTING AROUND

DOMESTIC TRAVEL

Indonesia, for those that can afford it, is aviation country. The national flag carrier, Garuda, serves both international as well as domestic routes. The only carrier using jet airplanes on domestic routes, it has several flights from Jakarta to all main provincial cities. Several flights daily run from Jakarta to Bali, Medan, Ujung Pandang, Manado, Balikpapan and other destinations. Shuttle flights run to Surabaya, Semarang, Bandung and Bandar Lampung.

Merpati also offers regular services to 100 destinations within Indonesia. Of special interest are the "pioneer flights" to remote areas not served by other airlines. Merpati is particularly active in eastern Indonesia, serving the small islands and interiors of Sulawesi, Kalimantan and Irian Jaya. Besides Garuda and Merpati, there are several privately owned airlines with both scheduled and charter services.

Garuda operates an air-travel pass. Called the "**Visit Indonesia Air Pass**," it allows for a number of flights for one payment:

Visit 1: flights between five cities of your choice as long as they are completed within no more than ten nights. Price: US$300.

Visit 2: flights between ten cities of your choice as long as they are completed within no more than 20 nights. Price: US$400.

Visit 3: flights between 33 cities of your choice as long as they are completed within no more than 60 nights.

The pass is operated only by Garuda and can be obtained in Japan, Australia, New Zealand, Europe and the United States. The pass is *not* for sale in Singapore. Airport tax must still be paid by the passenger.

Whether you have this air pass or not, you are likely to use the domestic air network in Indonesia. **Garuda**, **Merpati** and **Bouraq** are the principal carriers, between them covering a veritable labyrinth of destinations. The travel information under the regional listings that follow includes a box selecting just a few of the flights that might come in useful. Prices are rounded up to the nearest US dollar, *but should be treated as rough guidelines only* since the companies concerned change prices at short notice. Care has been taken to select routes that relate to the locations covered in this book. If you intend traveling by plane frequently you should get a copy of the timetables and latest fares from the respective company. A seemingly endless variety of itineraries can be planned. The three domestic airline offices are located at:

Garuda Indonesian Airways
Head Office, Jalan Ir. H. Juanda 15, Jakarta
Tel: 370709.

Merpati Nusantara Airlines
Jalan Angkasa 2, Jakarta
Tel: 411650.

Bouraq Indonesia Airlines
Jalan Angkasa 1–3, Jakarta
Tel: 655170.

JAKARTA

There are many "musts" in Jakarta, but be forewarned about trying to do too much. Two major sights or areas of the city a day are enough. Take a siesta or a swim in between to recover from the heat. Get an early start in the cool morning hours, do your errands and sightseeing, then get in out of the noonday sun. Venture out again in the late afternoon and early evening, when the weather has cooled off and the crowds are thinner.

City Orientation: At Jakarta's center lies **Medan Merdeka** (Freedom Square), a vast parade ground crisscrossed by broad ceremonial boulevards, with the National Monument towering in its midst. Going north, the major artery is Jl. Gajah Mada/Jl. Hayam Wuruk, two one-way roads with a canal separating them. This is the older, commercial area of town, horribly congested throughout much of the day and practically deserted at night. At the north end of this artery lies the old colonial city and the old harbor, now both major tourist sights. To the east along the coast are Ancol, a sprawling entertainment complex, and Tanjung Priok, the port. The "main street" of Jakarta is now **Jl. Thamrin/Jl. Jendral Sudirman**, which connects Medan Merdeka (the new satellite suburb). Many international hotels, office buildings, theaters, restaurants and nightclubs are on this street. To the east of Jl. Thamrin lie the older colonial residential areas of **Menteng**, **Cikini** and **Gondangdia**, with their luxurious mansions and tidy, tree-shaded streets. **Jl. Imam Bonjol/Jl. Diponegoro** is "Embassy Row," lined with many of the finest mansions in Jakarta and worth a quick drive or walk-through. Many shops, boutiques and restaurants are in this area, as is TIM, the arts center of Jakarta.

Public Transport: Taxis are by far the most practical way of getting around the city. Despite an increase, fares remain reasonable. It costs about US$2-5 for most cross-town journeys. Cabs are available at any hotel and easily hailed on major thoroughfares. President and Bluebird are the largest and generally the most reliable companies. Radio cabs may be summoned by phone. Be sure the meter is on when you get in, and that it stays on for the entire journey. Some cabbies will try and take you for a ride. Try to rent a cab by the hour if you intend making a lot of stops. Tipping is not customary, but drivers rarely have change, so carry some with you and even then be prepared to round off to the nearest Rp 500.

YOGYAKARTA

A majority of foreign visitors to Yogya arrive by air. **Garuda** has several daily flights from Jakarta's Cengkareng International Airport, and in fact it is often possible to bypass Jakarta completely—hopping on the first plane to Yogyakarta upon arrival from overseas.

The first-class **Bima Express** train that plies the Jakarta-Yogyakarta-Surabaya route nightly in either direction is Java's finest—comfortable air-conditioned sleeper cars with small two mattress bunk compartments, a sink and a table. The schedule is less than ideal, nonetheless. The Bima leaves Jakarta Kota Station at 4 p.m. and arrives in Yogya 10 hours later, which means that your sleep is interrupted and you travel by night. At US$25 one way, it's about half the price of an air-ticket. The second class **Senja Utama** and **Senja Yogya** trains from Jakarta cost much less (only US$8) but they are slower and not air-conditioned.

Inter-city buses always travel at night. The Jakarta-Yogyakarta run takes about nine hours and costs less than US$10. From Bandung it's only six hours and costs about US$6. The more expensive Mercedes buses are air-conditioned.

From Semarang or Solo or other nearby cities, you're better off taking a mini-bus, with services all day from dawn to dusk. Cost is only US$1.20 from Solo, US$2.50 from Semarang.

BALI

To the Balinese, the world is their living room and its travelers their guests. Do your best to respect their traditions and attitudes:

Settle all prices beforehand, otherwise you must pay the price demanded. Don't ask the price or make an offer unless you intend to buy.

Dress up rather than down. You are afforded special status as a foreigner, so don't abuse it. Old faded or torn clothes, bared thighs and excessively "native" dress are considered bad form.

Keep all valuables out of sight and preferably locked up. The Balinese have a strong sense of pride and consider temptation an affront, suspicion an insult.

Wear a temple sash whenever entering a temple, and expect to pay a token entrance fee to the custodian. Behave with reverence and deference.

Getting to Bali: Bali's Ngurah Rai International Airport, which straddles the narrow Tuban Isthmus in the south of the island, is served by many daily flights from Jakarta, Yogyakarta, Surabaya and various other cities in Indonesia.

Several weekly international flights arrive directly from Sydney, Melbourne, Perth and Darwin in Australia (Qantas and Garuda). Only Garuda and Singapore Airlines fly here from Europe and Singapore. Other international airlines fly only as far as Jakarta and you must then transfer to Garuda to reach Bali.

Flights to Bali from Jakarta's Cengkareng International Airport are frequent throughout the day, and you can generally catch a connection if you arrive before 6 p.m.

Getting Around: Balinese roads are a parade ground, used for escorting village deities to the sea, for funeral cremation processions, for filing to the local temple in Sunday best, or for performances of a trans-island *barong* dance. They are also now increasingly crowded. The volume of traffic has increased dramatically over the past two decades.

In the end, the best way to see Bali is on foot. Away from the heavily-traveled main roads, the island takes on an entirely different complexion.

Public Mini-Buses/Buses: The local system of pick-ups and mini-buses (collectively known as *bemos*) and intra-island buses is efficient and inexpensive. You can get from one end of the island to the other for less than US$2. In addition, almost every *bemo* on the road in Bali may be chartered by the trip or by the day, with the driver, by telling him where you want to go and then agreeing upon a price. Most drivers are willing to go anywhere on the island for US$25 to US$30 a day (which is what they normally make hauling passengers).

Guided Tours/Travel Agents: Expert daily bus tours, with well-informed multilingual guides are run by many travel agencies. They range in price from US$6 to US$7 for a half-day jaunt to Ubud or Sangeh/ Mengwi, up to US$15 to US$20 for a full-day cross-island trip up to Kintamani or Besakih, including a Barong Dance in Batubulan, lunch and several stops at shops and temples.

You can also design your own private guided tour, in an air-conditioned car with a chauffeur/guide, which allows you to establish the itinerary and the amount of time spent at each stop—US$30 up to US$60. The most experienced agents for the demanding traveler are **BIL** and **Pacto**. **Perama's** and many others in Kuta provide a decent service for budget group tours in mini-buses.

Taxis: There is a taxi service from the airport, with fares ranging from US$3 (to nearby Kuta Beach) on up to US$10 (to Ubud). To Sanur, Denpasar and Nusa Dua costs between US$5 and US$7.

Taxis and minibuses are for hire at every hotel (and in front of the Hyatt), just with a driver, or with an English-speaking driver/ guide. Rates are US$2 to US$4 per hour (two-hour minimum) and US$30 to US$40 per day, a bit more for air-conditioning, newer cars and long journeys. Often there is little different (other than the price) between simply renting a car for a day (many drivers speak good English) and going on a professionally guided tour.

The following is a sampling of rates for simple one-way drop offs (you will have to negotiate a bit more for roundtrip excursions with stops):

Sanur - Denpasar	US$3
Sanur - Kintamani	US$18
Sanur - Kuta	US$5
Sanur - Besakih	US$20
Sanur - Ubud	US$5
Sanur - Uluwatu	US$12

Car Rentals: The best way to get around the island independently is to rent a self-drive car, available in Kuta, Sanur or Denpasar. You must have a valid International Driving Permit. The most commonly rented vehicles are old beat-up **VW Safari** convertibles (US$30 per day/US$180 per week/US$240 for 10 days), although newer (sometimes air-conditioned) Suzuki Jimny's are also available for a bit more money (US$35 to US$40). You buy the gas. Buy the extra insurance also. Book a car through your hotel or from any of the companies listed below. Test-drive it before paying.

Bali Wisata
Jl. Imam Bonjol, Kuta
Tel: 4479.

Bali Car Rental
Jl. By-pass Ngurah Rai, Sanur
Tel: 8550, 8359.

Utama Motors
Jl. Imam Bonjol, Kuta
Tel: 22073.

Motorcycles: Convenient and inexpensive. Be aware that the roads are crowded and traffic is dangerous—your chances of an accident are uncomfortably high. Each year several tourists are killed in motorbike accidents, and many more injured. If you do rent a bike, ride slowly and defensively.

The cost of hiring a motorbike is usually a matter of bargaining, and varies greatly. The usual price of a 100cc or 125cc machine is US$3 to US$6 per day, or US$20 to US$30 per week (paid in advance).

WHERE TO STAY

ACCOMMODATIONS

JAKARTA

Luxury Class (above US$100 per night)

Jakarta now has three five-star hotels. Two have extensive grounds and sports facilities: the **Borobudur Intercontinental** and the **Jakarta Hilton**. In addition to Olympic-size swimming pools, tennis courts, squash courts, health clubs, jogging tracks and spacious gardens, they also boast discos and a full complement of European and Asian restaurants. The other hotel in the same category, the **Mandarin**, is a newer "city" hotel—providing a central location and emphasizing superior service and excellent food.

Borobudur Inter-Continental
(866 rooms)
Jl. Lapangan Banteng Selatan,
P.O. Box 329, Jakarta
Tel: 370108
Telex: 44150

Jakarta Hilton International
(396 rooms)
Jl. Jendral Gatot Subroto,
P.O. Box 3315, Jakarta.
Tel: 587981, 583051
Telex: JKT 46345, 46673, 46698

Jakarta Mandarin
(504 rooms)
Jl. M.H. Thamrin,
P.O. Box 3392, Jakarta.
Tel: 321307
Telex: 45755.

First Class (US$60 to US$100 per night)

There are another half-dozen or so first-class hotels in town. The **Sari Pacific** is centrally located and has a popular coffee shop and deli. The **Hyatt** boasts an excellent French restaurant. The **Horison** and the **Sahid Jaya** have restaurants specializing in seafood. The **President Hotel** is Japanese-operated with several Japanese restaurants. And the venerable **Hotel Indonesia** has a supper club with nightly floorshows and a swimming pool garden open to the public (US$4 admission).

Horizon Hotel
(350 rooms)
Jl. Pantai Indah,
Taman Impian Jaya Ancol,
P.O. Box 3340, Jakarta
Tel: 680008
Telex: 42824

Hotel Indonesia
(666 rooms)
Jl. M.H. Thamrin,
P.O. Box 54, Jakarta
Tel: 320008, 322008
Telex: 44233

Hyatt Aryaduta
(250 rooms)
Jl. Prapatan 44-46,
P.O. Box 3287, Jakarta
Tel: 376008
Telex: 46220

President Hotel
(354 rooms)
Jl. M.H. Thamrin 59
Tel: 320508
Telex: 46724

Sahid Jaya Hotel
(514 rooms)
Jl. Jendral Sudirman 86,
P.O. Box 41, Jakarta
Tel: 584151
Telex: 46331

Sari Pacific Hotel
(500 rooms)
Jl. M.H. Thamrin 6,
P. O. Box 3138, Jakarta
Tel: 323707
Telex: 44514

Intermediate Range (US$20 to US$60 per night)

At the upper end of the moderate price range, the most centrally-located hotels are the **Transaera**, the **Sabang Metropolitan**, the **Monas** and the **Asoka** (all are about US$35 and up for a double). The **Transaera** is particularly quiet, with older, spacious rooms and the **Monas** has a reputation for good service. The **Sabang Metropolitan** is convenient for business and shopping.

In Kebayoran Baru, you may choose between the **Kemang** and the **Kebayoran Inn**, both popular with frequent visitors for their reasonable prices and quiet, residential surroundings. Or try the **Interhouse**, centrally located by Kebayoran's shopping district, Blok M. There are several hotels in town providing small but clean, air-conditioned rooms for around US$25. These include the **Menteng Hotel** and the **Marco Polo**, both in Menteng.

Interhouse Hotel
(133 rooms)
Jl. Melawai Raya 18-20,
P.O. Box 128, Kebayoran Baru, Jakarta
Tel: 716408
Telex: 471811

Jayakarta Tower
(435 rooms)
Jl. Hayam Wuruk 126, Jakarta
Tel: 624408
Telex: 41113

Kartika Chandra
(200 rooms)
Jl. Gatot Subroto, Jakarta
Tel: 510808, 511008
Telex: 45843

Kartika Plaza
(331 rooms)
Jl. M.H. Thamrin 10,
P.O. Box 2081, Jakarta
Tel: 321008
Telex: 45843

Kebayoran Inn
(61 rooms)
Jl. Senayan 57,
Kebayoran Baru, Jakarta
Tel: 716208

Kemang Hotel
(100 rooms)
Jl. Kemang Raya,
P.O. Box 163, Kebayoran Baru, Jakarta
Tel: 793208
Telex: 47145

Menteng I
(82 rooms)
Jl. Gondangdia Lama, Jakarta
Tel: 352508

Menteng II
(70 rooms)
Jl. Cikini Raya 105, Jakarta
Tel: 326312, 325543, 326329

Putri Duyung Cottages
(102 cottages)
Taman Impian Jaya Ancol, Jakarta
Tel: 680611, 680108

Sabang Metropolitan (157 rooms)
Jl. H.A. Salim 11, P.O. Box 2725, Jakarta
Tel: 354031, 357621
Telex: 445555

Transaera Hotel
(50 rooms)
Jl. Merdeka Timur, 16,
P.O. Box 3380, Jakarta
Tel: 351373, 359336, 357059

Wisata International
(165 rooms)
Jl. M.H. Thamrin,
P.O. box 2457, Jakarta
Tel: 320308, 320408
Telex: 46787

Wisma Bumi Asih Guesthouse
Jl. Solo 4, Menteng, Jakarta
Tel: 35083

YOGYAKARTA

First Class (US$35 and up per night)

The 4-star **Ambarrukmo Hotel**, built by the Japanese in the early 1960s, is still the only international-class luxury hotel in Yogya, with rooms going for US$65 on up (plus 21 percent tax and service). It is symbolically situated some miles to the east of town near the airport upon the grounds of the old royal *pesanggrahan* or rest house once used to entertain visiting dignitaries to the court, and some of the old buildings survive, including the elegant *pendapa* and the *dalem agung* ceremonial chambers.

The old **Hotel Garuda** (US$35 to US$50 a night) right on Malioboro has just added a modern seven-storey wing at the back, and has up-graded their spacious colonial suites (huge rooms and bathrooms, with high ceilings and an outer sitting-room/balcony looking out onto a central courtyard). The hotel has quite a history, as it housed several government ministries during the Indonesian revolution (1946 to 1949).

Motel-style "cottage" hotels include the **Sahid Garden**, nice and thoroughly Javanese. Owned by an aristocratic Surakartan family (US$45 on up plus 21 per cent).

It's hard to beat the **Puri Artha's** friendly service and well-manicured surroundings

(US$35 a night). The nearby **Sri Manganti** and the **Sriwedari** (opposite the Ambarrukmo) are about the same price. All of these hotels have pools and quiet gardens, but none is within walking distance of Malioboro, so you'll have to think about transport.

Ambarrukmo Palace Hotel
(240 rooms)
Jl. Adisucipto,
P.O. Box 10, Yogyakarta
Tel: 88488, 88984
Telex: 12511

Hotel Garuda
Jl. Malioboro 72, Yogyakarta
Tel: 2113-4

Puri Artha
(60 rooms)
Jl. Cendrawasih 9, Yogyakarta
Tel: 5934-5
Telex: 25147

Sriwedari
(70 rooms)
Jl. Adisucipto,
P.O. Box 93, Yogyakarta
Tel: 88288

Sri Manganti
(46 rooms)
Jl. Urip Sumoharjo,
P.O. Box 46, Yogyakarta
Tel: 2881

Sahid Garden
(64 rooms)
Jl. Babarsari, Yogyakarta
Tel: 3697

Intermediate (US$15-35 a night)

The **Indraloka Homestay Service**, founded and run by Mrs. B. Moerdiyono, currently costs US$21 a night for a double (plus 21 per cent tax and service) including breakfast. Home-cooked lunch or dinner is an additional US$6. The families are mostly headed by Dutch-educated professionals (doctors and university lecturers), and the rooms have all the western amenities and a fan. Mrs Moerdiyono also arranges tours through Java to Bali, using her network of homestays in other cities.

Other choices depend largely on where you want to be and how much you want to pay. The **Arjuna Plaza** and the **New Batik Palace** hotels are both centrally located on Jl. Mangkubumi (US$25 to US$30 for a double, plus 21 percent). The **Gajah Mada Guesthouse**, with air-conditioned doubles for US$24 is a quiet place located on campus in the north of town.

Many other small hotels and guesthouses cluster along **Jalan Prawirotaman** in the south of Yogya. A few of these have air-conditioned rooms in the US$15-to-US$25 range (plus 21 per cent), including breakfast. Try the **Airlangga** or the **Duta**.

Airlangga
(25 rooms)
Jl. Prawirotaman 4, Yogyakarta
Tel: 3344

Arjuna Plaza
(25 rooms)
Jl. Mangkubumi 48, Yogyakarta
Tel: 3036, 86862

Batik Palace Hotel
(26 rooms)
Jl. Pasar Kembang 29,
P.O. Box 115, Yogyakarta
Tel: 2149

Duta Guest House
(15 rooms)
Jl. Prawirotaman 20, Yogyakarta
Tel: 5219.

Indraloka Homestay
(40 rooms)
Jl. Cik Ditiro 14, Yogyakarta
Tel: 0274, 3614.

Gajah Mada Guest House
(20 rooms)
Jl. Bulaksumur,
Kampus Universitas
Gajah Mada, Yogyakarta
Tel: 88461, 88688 ext. 625.

New Batik Palace Hotel
(22 rooms)
Jl. Mangkubumi 46, Yogyakarta
Tel: 2149.

Budget
(under US$15 a night)

The guest houses along **Jalan Prawirotaman** are all converted homes—generally quiet, clean and comfortable. Cheapest rate available here for a double is US$7.50, including tax, service and breakfast, but most are in the US$10-to-US$12 a night range. Some also have air-conditioned doubles for only US$15 a night.

The many small hotels around **Jalan Pasar Kembang** (also on Jl. Sorowijayan and down the small lanes in between), are substantially cheaper and more central, but this is not as pleasant an area. Many places here have rooms for US$3 to US$5 and even less. Try the **Kota** down at the end of Jl. Pasar Kembang—very clean.

SANUR

Sanur is for gracious living, peace and quiet—more international but far less cosmopolitan than frenetic Kuta. Foreigners have been staying in Sanur since the 1920s, and they know how to take care of you here. Strictly first-class. Seek out the lovely Sanur temples, particularly when they are having their anniversary ceremonies (*odalan*), every seven months.

There are so many excellent first-class hotels in Sanur, that you can scarcely go wrong. The main choice is between the convenience and luxury of a big four-star hotel (there are three: the **Bali Beach**, the **Bali Hyatt** and the **Sanur Beach**) or the quiet and personality of a private bungalow by the sea (at two-thirds to half the price). Reservations are advisable during the peak season: July to September and December to January. Prices quoted below do not include the obligatory 21 percent tax and service surcharge.

First Class
(above US$35 per night)

For such a large luxury hotel, the new **Bali Hyatt** offers a remarkably breezy, spacious Royal Hawaiian feeling, with striking public areas, clay tennis courts and hanging Babylonian gardens. The venerable **Hotel Bali Beach** (constructed by the Japanese in the early 1960s) looks more like a traditional Miami Beach luxury hotel—a 10-storey concrete block by the sea, set amidst a golf course, bowling alleys and swimming pools.

Last but not least of the three four-star establishments, the smaller **Sanur Beach Hotel**, owned by Garuda, claims to be the friendliest large hotel in Sanur.

Of the smaller cottage resorts, the **Tanjung Sari Hotel** is the hands down choice of frequent visitors. This was one of the island's first beach-bungalow establishments and is still its most charming and efficient. The latest addition (since the hotel's vintage Ford bus was attacked by a band of Balinese painters) is a nightclub, Rumors, which features backgammon and a well-stocked video loft.

The **Segara Village** deserves mention for its snazzy and congenial Indonesian atmosphere. **La Taverna** gets kudos for its Italian Balinesia and attractive beach-restaurant pizzeria. **Wisma Baruna**, the smallest and oldest first-class hotel in Sanur is also very cozy, with a superb breakfast pavilion overlooking the lagoon.

Alit's Beach Bungalow
(98 rooms)
Jl. Raya Sanur,
P.O. Box 102, Denpasar
Tel: 8567
Telex: 35165

Bali Hyatt Hotel
(387 rooms)
Sanur, P.O. Box 392, Denpasar
Tel: 8271-7
Telex: 35127

Bali Seaside Cottages
(111 rooms)
Jl. Segara, Sanur,
P.O. Box 217, Denpasar

Bali Sanur Besakih Bungalows
(50 rooms)
Jl. Tanjungsari, Sanur, Denpasar
Tel: 8423-4
Telex: 35178

Bali Sanur Penida View Bungalows
(44 rooms)
Jl. Bali Hyatt, Sanur, Denpasar
Tel: 8425-6
Telex: 35178

Bali Sanur Puri Dalem Bungalows
(44 rooms)
Jl. Raya Sanur,
P.O. Box 306, Denpasar
Tel: 8421-2
Telex: 35187

Gazebo Beach Cottages
(60 rooms)
Jl. Tanjung Sari, Sanur,
P.O. Box 134, Denpasar
Tel: 8300

Hotel Bali Beach Intercontinental
(605 rooms)
Sanur, P.O. Box 275, Denpasar
Tel: 8511-7
Telex: 35133, 35129

La Taverna Bungalows
(44 rooms)
Jl. Tanjungsari, Sanur, Denpasar
Tel: 8011-5
Telex: 35135

Respati Beach Bungalows
(25 rooms)
Sanur, P.O. Box 223, Denpasar
Tel: 8427

Santrian Beach Hotel
(80 rooms)
Jl. Tanjungsari, Sanur,
P.O. Box 55, Denpasar
Tel: 8181-3

Segara Village Hotel
(85 rooms)
Jl. Segara, Sanur,
P.O. Box 91, Denpasar
Tel: 8407-8, 8021-2
Telex: 35134

Sindhu Beach Hotel
(50 rooms)
Jl. Sindhu, Sanur,
P.O. Box 181, Denpasar
Tel: 8351-2
Telex: 35166

Tanjung Sari Hotel (24 rooms)
Jl Tanjungsari, Sanur,
P.O. Box 25, Denpasar
Tel: 8441
Telex: 35257

Wisma Baruna
(10 rooms)
Jl. Sindu, Sanur, Denpasar
Tel: 8546

Intermediate Range (US$15 to US$35 a night)

Bali Sanur Bungalows, at the upper end of the scale, are recommended. All of the other beach bungalow establishments in this category are excellent value and generally quite pleasant, the major consideration being whether you require air-conditioning or not (rooms at the lower end of the scale have only a fan).

Abian Irama Inn
Jl. Tanjungsari, Sanur, Denpasar.

Bali Sanur Irama Bungalows
(23 rooms)
Jl. Tanjungsari, Sanur, Denpasar
Tel: 8423-4

Diwangkara Beach Hotel
(36 rooms)
Jl. Pantai Sanur, Sanur,
P.O. Box 120, Denpasar
Tel: 8577, 8412

Hotel Ramayana
Jl. Tanjungsari, Sanur, Denpasar
Tel: 664359

Laghawa Beach Inn
(25 rooms)
Jl. Tanjung Sari, Sanur, Denpasar
Tel: 8494, 8214.

Mars Hotel
(14 rooms)
Jl. Raya Sanur, Sanur
P.O. Box 95, Denpasar.

Narmada Bali Inn
(17 rooms)
Jl. Sindhu, Sanur,
P.O. Box 119, Denpasar
Tel: 8054

Puri Mas Hotel
(16 rooms)
Jl. Raya Sanur,
Tanjung Bungakak, Denpasar.

Werdha Pura
(14 rooms)
Jl Tanjungsari, Sanur,
P.O. Box 24 Denpasar

Budget
(under US$15 a night)

Cheapest room in Sanur is US$7 a night. Your best bet is the **Tourist Beach Inn**, just 100 meters from the beach. Three bungalow establishments opposite the Post Office—**Sanur Indah**, **Taman Sari** and **Hotel Rani**—give you a bit more space, but are farther from the beach. The **Taman Agung** is the nicest budget place, with well-kept gardens and very quiet. True budget travelers get better value for money in Kuta, however.

Hotel Rani
Jl. Segara, Sanur, Denpasar.

Hotel Sanur Indah
Jl. Segara, Sanur, Denpasar.

Taman Agung Beach Inn
Jl. Tanjungsari, Sanur, Denpasar
Tel: 8549, 8006.

Tourist Beach Inn
Jl. Segara, Sanur,
P.O. Box 42, Denpasar
Tel: 8418.

KUTA BEACH

Kuta is like a malignant sea-side Carnaby Street of the 60s. Chaotic, noisy, lots of hype, but a great playground. Originally what drew visitors to Kuta was the wide beach and the surf, and it still has the best seafront on the island, now cluttered with hundreds of hotels, restaurants, bars, boutiques, travel agencies, antique shops, car and bike rentals, banks, cassette shops and wall-to-wall tourists. Though there are now many first-class hotels, the 3-mile (5-km) strip still caters best for the economy traveler who likes to be in the thick of things. The Legian end of the beach is the best place to stay for any period of time—much quieter and more relaxed.

Kuta Beach has so many bungalows, beach hotels and homestays (*losmen*) that no list could ever be complete, nor is it a really needed. Drop in and shop around. The difference between Kuta and Sanur is that one has far more choices in the lower price range here. Reservations are necessary for the larger hotels during July to September and December to January.

First Class
(above US$35 a night)

There are two luxury class hotels on the Kuta side, the **Bali Oberoi** and **Pertamina Cottages**. The Oberoi's restaurant, Kura Kura, is excellent, and breakfast *al fresco* at the Oberoi is one of Bali's great treats. Pertamina Cottages features tennis courts and convention facilities.

There are also several comfortable first-class bungalow resorts, notably the **Kuta Beach Palace**, the **Kuta Beach Hotel** and the **Kartika Plaza**. The **Legian Beach Hotel** offers air-conditioned rooms on the beach for under US$40 a night.

Bali Oberoi
(75 rooms)
Kayu Aya,
P.O. Box 351, Kuta
Tel: 25581-5

Beach Hotel Kartika Plaza
(120 rooms)
Kuta Beach,
P.O. Box 84, Denpasar
Tel: 22454, 25081-5.

Kuta Beach Club
(83 rooms)
Jl. Bakungsari,
P.O. Box 226, Kuta
Tel: 25056

Kuta Beach Palace
(107 rooms)
Legian, Kuta
Tel: 25858
Telex: 35234.

Legian Beach Hotel
(110 rooms)
Jl. Melasti, Legian,
P.O. Box 308, Denpasar
Tel: 26811-2
Telex: 35104.

Pertamina Cottages
(156 rooms)
Kuta Beach, P.O. Box 121 Kuta
Tel: 23061

Natour's Kuta Beach Hotel
(32 rooms)
Jl. Pantai Kuta,
P.O. Box 393, Kuta
Tel: 25791

Intermediate Range (US$15 to US$35 a night)

If you are willing to do without air-conditioning there are many beautiful bungalows in the US$20-to-US$30 range. **Poppies Cottages** is one of the most popular establishments, almost always fully booked. And the **Yasa Samudra** puts you right on the beach in Kuta. For more privacy and longer stays, the **Legian Sunset Beach**, the **Blue Ocean** (both in Legian) and **Nova Nova** (farther down, in Seminyak) are among the favorites (with many private bungalows renting for about US$10 to US$15 a night, less by the week or the month).

Kuta Cottages
(40 rooms)
Jl. Bakung Sari,
P.O. Box 300, Kuta
Tel: 24100

Sunset Beach Hotel
(16 rooms)
Legian, Kuta,
P.O. Box 346, Denpasar
Tel: 6721 ext. 60.

Mandara Cottages
(27 rooms)
Jl. Padma, Legian, Kuta
Tel: 25785

Poppies Cottages
(24 rooms)
Poppies Gang, Kuta
Tel: 23059.

Ramayana Seaside Cottages
(45 rooms)
Jl. Bakung Sari, Kuta,
P.O. Box 334, Denpasar
Tel: 6781-5, 5058

NUSA DUA

The newly-revamped **Hotel Bualu** offers a comprehensive water sports package, lush gardens and horse-drawn buggies (*dokar*) for romantic, tropical-evening rides up and down "hotel row." And the brand new **Nusa Dua Beach Hotel** offers the ultimate in opulence—a palatial Balinese setting, a health club, squash courts, three restaurants and a discotheque.

Hotel Bualu
(50 rooms)
Nusa Dua
Tel: 71310, 71320
Telex: 35231

Hotel Nusa Dua
(450 rooms)
Nusa Dua
Tel: 71210
Telex: 35206

FOOD DIGEST

WHAT TO EAT

Indonesian Food is of course the smart traveler's first choice in Jakarta, particularly as one may indulge in gastronomic island-hopping on consecutive nights.

The best Padang food is found at **Roda** and **Sari Bundo**. Here, as in all padang restaurants, between 10 and 15 spicy dishes are placed in front of you and you pay only for what you eat. For slightly more atmosphere and a view (at higher prices), try **The Pepper Pot**.

Javanese cuisine may be divided into three of four categories: Sundanese (West Javanese), Central Javanese, East Javanese and Madurese cooking. For an excellent Sundanese meal of grilled carp (*ikan mas bakar*), grilled chicken (*ayam bakar*), prawns (*undang pancet*), barbecued squid (*cumi-cumi bakar*) and a raw vegetable salad with shrimp-paste chili sauce (*lalap/ sambal cobek*), try the extremely popular **Sari Kuring**. This is, incidentally, one of the best seafood places in town, and serves a deliciously cooling cucumber- and lime-juice drink.

The Central Javanese delicacies are fried chicken and *gudeg*. Javanese chickens are farmyard chickens, allowed to run free in the village. As a result they are full of flavor but very tough in comparison with factory-feed chickens in the West. The Javanese boil their chickens first in a concoction of rich spices and coconut cream for several hours, finally deep frying them for about a minute at very high temperatures to crisp the outer coating. The two famous fried chicken places in Jakarta are both in Kebayoran: **Ayam Bulungan** and **Ayam Goreng Mbok Berek**.

Gudeg is the speciality of Yogyakarta, consisting of young jackfruit boiled in coconut cream and spices, served with buffalo hide boiled in chili sauce, chicken pieces, egg and gravy. The best *gudeg* is to be had at a branch of the Yogya restaurant, **Bu Tjitro's**.

East Java and Madura are known for their soups and their *sate*. For *soto madura* (spicy chicken broth with noodles or rice), the best place is **Pondok Jawa timur**. For chicken or mutton *sate* (barbecued meat skewers), the **Senayan Satay House** has a near monopoly on the Jakarta scene, with its three convenient locations.

JAKARTA

Dining in Jakarta can be a delightful experience, though on the whole restaurant meals are expensive here by Indonesian standards (about twice the price of a meal in the provinces), and the food is highly uneven in quality. Locals seek out obscure roadside stalls (*warung*) for a special *soto* or *sate* but too many visitors are hit with a stomach bug and this can ruin a week or more of your stay. It is possible to eat a good meal in a clean restaurant for US$2 and truly excellent Indonesian or Chinese food can be had for US$5 a head. With the exception of Western-style food and service, a meal at the best restaurants will rarely cost more than US$10 per person, all-inclusive. Seafood of any sort is excellent.

INDONESIAN FOOD

Ayam Bulungan
(Javanese Fried Chicken)
Jl. Bulungan I
No. 64, Kebayoran Baru
Tel: 772005.

Ayam Goreng Mbok Berek
(Javanese Fried Chicken)
Jl. Prof. Dro. Soepomo 2, Tebet
Tel: 825366.

Ayam Goreng Mbok Berek
(Javanese Fried Chicken)
Jl. Panglima Polim Raya No. 93
Tel: 770652.

Gudeg Bu Tjitro
Jl. Cikajang 80,
Blok Q2 Kebayoran Baru
Tel: 713202.

Gudeg Bu Tjitro
Jl. Senen Raya 25A
Tel: 371197.

Hotel Marunda Restaurant
Wisata International
Tel: 320408, 320308.

Natrabu Restaurant (Padang)
Jl. H. Agus Salim 29A
Tel: 371709.

The Pepper Pot (Padang and Javanese)
18th floor, Wisma Metropolitan,
Jl. Jendral Sudirman
Tel: 584736.

Pondok Jawa Timur (East Javanese)
Jl. Prapanca Raya, Kebayoran.

Ratu Sari (Sundanese)
Glodok Plaza,
Jl. Pinangsia Raya
Tel: 625999, 627701.

Roda (Padang)
Jl. Matraman Raya 65-67
Tel: 882879.

Sari Bundo (Padang)
Jl. Ir. H. Juanda 27
Tel: 358343.

Sari Kuring (Sundanese Seafood)
Jl. Batu Ceper No. 55A
Tel: 341542.

Senayan Satay House
Jl. Pakubuwono VI/No. 6,
Kebayoran Baru
Tel: 715821.

Senayan Satay House
Jl. Kebon Sirih 31A
Tel: 326238.

Senayan Satay House
Jl. Tanah Abang II/No. 76
Tel: 347720.

CHINESE FOOD

The premier banquet houses for **Chinese Food** are the **Cahaya Kota** and the **Istana Naga**.

For Szechuanese food, the only place is the pricey but delicious **Spice Garden** in the Mandarin Hotel.

While visiting the Chinatown/Kota area, or in fact for a light lunch anywhere, it is *de rigeur* to sample a bowl of Chinese noodles with chopped pickled vegetables and beefballs (*mee bakso*). The largest noodle house in Chinatown is **Bakmi Gajah Mada**.

Bakmi Gajah Mada
Jl. Gajah Mada 92.

Bakmi Gajah Maha
Jl. Melawai IV/25,
Blok M, Kebayoran Baru.

Cahaya Kota
Jl. Wahid Hasyim 9
Tel: 356331, 354362, 353015.

Istana Naga
Jl. Gatot Subroto
(Kav. 12, Case building)
Tel: 583081, 583087, 583089.

Spice Garden Restaurant
(Szechuanese)
Jakarta Mandarin Hotel.

WESTERN FOOD

If you insist on eating **European Food** in Jakarta, then the only acceptable excuse is to experience the colonial atmosphere (and cuisine) of Dutch Batavia. This is best done at the magnificent **Oasis Restaurant**, a turn-of-the-century mansion turned eatery. Specialities of the house include a flaming sword shishkebab and the traditional Dutch colonial *rijsttafel* ("rice table") consisting of 20 Indonesian dishes served by 16 attractive young ladies. *Rijsttafel* is also the speciality of the **Club Noordwijk**, which has a *tempo deoloe* "olden times") atmosphere in a somewhat less regal setting. Both establishments provide nightly musical entertainment. A less expensive place for *Indische* colonial food and atmosphere is the **Arts and Curios Restaurant** and Art Shop, conveniently located near TIM, the performing arts center of Jakarta.

Art and Curio Restaurant
(Dutch Colonial)
Jl. Kebon Binatang III/8A, Cikini
Tel: 322879.

Brasserie Le Parisien (French)
Aryaduta Hyatt Hotel,
Jl. Prapatan 44
Tel: 376008 ext. 141.

Club Noordwijk (Colonial/Dutch)
Jl. Ir. H. Juanda 5A
Tel: 353909.

The Club Room (French)
Jakarta Mandarin
Tel: 371208.

George & Dragon Pub & Restaurant
(English)
Jl. Telukbetung 32
Tel: 345625.

Jaya Pub (sandwiches & soups)
Jaya building, Jl. M.H. Thamrin 12
Tel: 327508 ext. 255.

Jayakarta Grill
Sari Pacific Hotel,
Jl. M.H. Thamrin 6
Tel: 359141 ext. 1481.

Le Bistro (French)
Jl.K.H. Wahid Hasyim 75
Tel: 347475.

Oasis Restaurant (Continental)
Jl. Raden Saleh 47
Tel: 326397, 327818.

YOGYAKARTA

The pilgrimage point for fried chicken lovers from all over Java (and all over the world now) is **Nyonya Suharti's** (also known as Ayam Goreng "Mbok Berek," after the women who invented this famous fried chicken recipe), located four miles (seven km) to the east of Yogya on the road to the airport (a short distance beyond the Ambarrukmo on the same side). The recipe is one of the best-kept culinary secrets in Indonesia—the chicken is first boiled and coated in spices and coconut, then fried crisp and served with a sweet chilli sauce and rice. Excellent when accompanied by pungent *petai* beans and raw cabbage. Indonesians patronize the place in droves, and you can see Jakartans in the airport lounge clutching their take-away boxes of Nyonya Suharti's chicken for friends and family back home.

Nasi Padang fanatics also rave about the fare at **Sinar Budi Restaurant**, at Jl. Mangkubumi 41, about 500 meters north of the railway tracks on the left (opposite the cinema). Muttons brain *opor*, beef *rendang* and *gulai ayam* (chicken curry) await you at a moment's notice. Be sure to ask for their spicy potato chips (*kentang goreng*)—Sinar Budi's answer to the barbecue flavored variety in the West.

The Yogya speciality is *gudeg*—a combination plate consisting of rice with boiled young jackfruit (*nangka muda*), a piece of chicken, egg, coconut cream gravy and spicy sauce with boiled buffalo hide (*sambal kulit*). The famous spot in Yogya for *gudeg* is **Juminten** at Jl. Asem Gede 22, Kranggan 69, just north of Jl. Diponegoro. The other *gudeg* restaurant of note is **Bu Citro's**, located just opposite the entrance to the airport out on Jl. Adisucipto (a good place to eat while waiting for a flight). Most restaurants in Yogya also serve the dish, and there is excellent *gudeg* just north of Taman Sari on the eastern side of Jl. Ngasem.

Western food is now readily available in Yogya, and not just in the large hotels. The **Legian Garden Restaurant** serves excellent steaks, chops, sautéed fish, avocado seafood cocktails, yoghurt and corn and crab soup. Everything is very reasonable, the beer is cold and the vegetables are not overcooked. Enter via a well-marked doorway around the corner from Jl. Malioboro—Jl. Perwakilan 9 (Tel: 87985). The Legian Garden now has a branch, called **The Rose**, on the southern side of Jl. Solo—the same menu and prices but more atmosphere. For more money, the **Gita Buana** offers air-conditioning and low lighting at two locations: Jl. Diponegoro 52 A and out at Jl. Adisucipto 169 by the Ambarrukmo hotel. The **French Grill** in the Arjuna Plaza hotel (Jl. Mangkubumi 48) is also good, and they have puppet and dance performances every other night.

There are several fine Chinese restaurants in town. The old standby and the favorite of the local Chinese community is the **Tiong San**, at Jl. Gandekan 29, a block west of Malioboro. The best seafood, however, and probably also the best Chinese food, is to be had at **Sintawang**, several doors north of Jl. Diponegoro at Jl. Mageland 9, on the west side of the street.

SANUR

The **Tanjung Sari Hotel Restaurant** has a formidable reputation for Indonesian *rijsttafel* and a sublime atmosphere. A bamboo *tingklink* orchestra provides the ideal accompaniment to dinner in a cosy, antique-filled dining area by the beach. The restaurant's new menu has a more creative nouveau-Bali slant, and the famous Bar, designed by Australian artist Donald Friend, is an elevated pavilion overlooking the sea.

At **Kuri Putih**, in the Bali Sanur Irama Bungalows, chef Nyoman Sana of Ubud has at last brought his kitchen to Sanur. Try the barbecued specials from the grill and help yourself to side dishes from a tempting buffet salad bar.

Telaga Naga, opposite the Bali Hyatt, is a spectacularly stylish Szechuanese restaurant in a lake, designed by Hyatt architect Kerry Hill. The food is good and the prices are non-hotel. Try the "Chicken With Dried Chilli Peppers," the king prawn and the duck dishes.

The best Italian food in Bali is available at **Trattoria Da Marco**, where Reno and Diddit da Marco have guarded their reputation and clientele for 15 years now. Try the grilled fish, *spaghetti carbonara*, bean salad and their steaks—truly the best in Bali.

La Taverna is part of a Hong Kong-based chain of Italian restaurants in Asia. The Sanur branch is a charming bar and open dining area on the beach, with a menu that features imported cheeses, French pepper steak, seafood and pizza from a real pizza oven.

For more local flavors, try the inexpensive **Beach Market** (on Jl. Segara right at the beach), a little outdoor restaurant run by Sanur's mayor. Great for lunch (*sate, nasi goreng* and fresh fried fish) or dinner (grilled lobster), with delicious Balinese desserts, all at unbeatable prices.

KUTA BEACH

New restaurants seem to open daily in Kuta, from small fruit salad and yoghurt stands by the beach to large Chinese, French or seafood establishments. The quality of the food goes up and down as cooks come and go, so we list here only a few old standbys where you can hardly ever go wrong. Ask around though for tips on the latest "in" restaurant.

Made's Warung on Jl. Pantai hasn't missed a beat in its metamorphosis from one of only two foodstalls on the main street of a sleepy fishing village, to a hip Cafe Voltaire in the St. Tropez of the East. It has great food (spare ribs, Thai salad, escargots, turtle steaks, home-made ice cream, chocolate mousse, capuccino, fresh squeezed orange and carrot juices, breakfast specials).

Poppies, down a narrow lane, is another Kuta fixture. Avocado seafood salads, pate, tacos, grilled lobster, steaks, shishkabob and tall mixed drinks pack this garden idyll to capacity during the peak tourist seasons. Get there early to get a table.

Bali Indah and Lenny's are both first-rate for Chinese cuisine and seafood. Try the crab-in-black-bean-sauce at Bali Indah. And for fresh lobster or fried tuna fish steaks, go over to the **Yasa Samudra Hotel** (at the end of Jl. Pantai Kuta) and dine under the stars by the sea.

In Legian, the **Blue Ocean Hotel's** beachside cafe is a popular gathering point for breakfast and lunch. And farther down, in Seminyak, **La Marmite** (also known as **Chez Gado-Gado**) serves Balinese "nouvelle cuisine" in a secluded open-air location by the beach. The after-dinner disco on Saturday nights is the happening thing.

The **Kura Kura** restaurant in the Bali Oberoi hotel, several miles beyond Legian, is perfect for that special occasion. A quiet pool-site terrace overlooking the ocean. Go there for the sunset, dinner and drinks. Very romantic. Try the pepper duck, or grilled lobster.

And Bali's only serious Japanese restaurant, **Shima**, is located in the Pertamina Cottage Hotel, several miles south of Kuta at Tuban. Two Japanese chefs prepare a full range of Japanese dishes.

CULTURE PLUS

YOGYAKARTA

Tourist performances are not necessarily any less authentic or in any way inferior (as some people insist), even though they are frequently shortened or excerpted versions of the originals, adapted for the benefit of foreign audiences.

What they do lack, of course, is a Javanese audience, and as the audience is as much a part of most performances as the players (especially in Java), you should try if at all possible to catch a village or *kampung* shadow play or dance drama. Being here at the right time to see one is just a matter of luck. Check with the **Tourist Information Office** (Jl. Malioboro 16) and travel agencies for up-to-date information.

GAMELAN

A *gamelan* orchestra is struck to accompany all of the dances and puppet shows listed below, and you can hardly avoid hearing recorded *gamelan* music everywhere you go in Yogya.

• Visit the **Kraton Gamelan Rehearsals** on Monday and Wednesday mornings.

• Concerts are also staged at the **Pakualaman Palace** on Jl. Sultan Agung every fifth Sunday Minggu Pahing beginning at 10. No admission charge.

• And if somehow you seem to be missing all the other performances, then you can always go over to the lobby of the Ambarrukmo Palace Hotel, where a small *gamelan* ensemble plays daily from 10:30 a.m. to 12:30 a.m., and then again from 3:30 p.m. No admission charge.

WAYANG KULIT

This is truly the most influential Javanese art form, the one that traditionally has provided the Javanese with a framework through which to see the world and themselves. Not surprisingly, many foreigners have become fascinated by the shadow play (even if very, very few of them are able to understand the dialogue), and there is quite a voluminous literature in Dutch and English on the subject. Traditional performances are always at night, beginning at 9 p.m. and running until dawn.

• **The Agastya Art Institute** (Jl. Gedong Kiwo MD III/237), a private *dalang* (puppeteer) school, stages "rehearsal" excerpt performances for the benefit of tourists every day except Saturday, 3 p.m. to 5 p.m. US$3 admission.

• Another tourist excerpt performance is at **Ambar Budaya** in the Yogyakarta Craft Center opposite the Ambarrukmo Palace Hotel every Monday, Wednesday and Friday from 9:30 p.m. to 10:30 p.m. of US$3 admission.

• On the second Saturday of each month, Radio Republik Indonesia broadcasts a live all-night performance from the pavilion to the south of the Kraton, **Sasono Hinggil Dwi Abad**. This is the best regular performance. Begins at 9 p.m. No admission charge.

• You can also try the **Habiranda Dalang School** at Pracimasono on the north-eastern side of the *alun-alun* town, square, where there are often informal training sessions or rehearsals in the evenings, 7 p.m. to 10 p.m., except Thursday and Sunday. No admission charge.

• *Wayang kulit* in an air-conditioned restaurant with dinner is the latest thing at the French Grill in the **Arjuna Plaza Hotel** (Jl. Mangkubumi 48) every Tuesday and Sunday night at 7 p.m.

JAVANESE DANCE

• There is a rehearsal of the **Kraton Dancers** every Sunday from 10:30 a.m. to 12 a.m. US$0.50 admission.

• The Mardawa Budaya School, one of the best in Yogya, now stages a wide selection of dance excerpts in an aristocratic **pendapa**, **Dalem Pujokusuman**, Jl. Brig. Jend. Katamso 45, every Monday, Wednesday and Friday evening from 8 p.m. to 10 p.m. US$3 admission.

• Of course, if you happen (or plan) to be here between May and October around the full moon, don't miss the **Ramayana Ballet** at Prambanan. This is a so-called *sendratari* spectacular with a cast of thousands but without any dialogue. Get a round-trip "package" ticket out to Prambanan and back, including the US$4 admission from any travel agent or from the Tourist Information Center on Jl. Malioboro, (about US$11).

• And if you prefer comfortable, hotel surroundings with dinner and refreshments, try the nightly "cultural show" at the **Ambarrukmo Palace Hotel**.

The regular performances listed above are all excellent. You should also visit some of the schools during the day to observe how Javanese dance is taught and studied. Most of them are situated in quite interesting surroundings—what are or used to be elegant homes of members of the royal family.

• **Krido bekso Wirama**, Dalem Tejokusuman, Jl. K.H. Wahid Hasyim. The first school to teach Javanese dance outside the Kraton.

• **Siswo Among Bekso**, Dalem Poerwodiningratan, Jl. Kadipaten Kidul 46. They have frequent student performances.

• **Mardawa Budaya**, Jl. Brig. Jen. Katamso 45. Regular tourist performances (see above).

• **Pamulangan Beksa Ngayoyakarta**.

• **Bagong Kussudiarjo**, Jl. Singosaren 9, off Jl. Wates. The best-known Javanese "modern" dancer and choreographer. He was one of the artists that helped to invent and develop the *sendratari* art-dance-drama in the 1950s. Still an energetic writer, teacher and choreographer.

• **Indonesian Dance Academy (ASTI)**. This is one of five government tertiary-level dance schools in the nation and they get all the most promising young dancers from the Yogya area. Visit the school out on Jl. Colombo. This is where the most innovative Javanese dancing is found.

BALI

The best way to see Balinese dances, *wayang kulit* puppet shows and *gamelan* orchestras is to attend a village temple festival. There is one going on somewhere on the island almost every day. Ask your hotel, or consult the **Bali Post Calendar**, available from most shops. In the fine print beneath are listed the names of villages having ceremonies and the type of celebration (it is not 100 percent accurate, however).

Public performances are also given at various central locations all over the island. These are mainly for the benefit of tourists only. Some of the best dancers and musicians in Bali participate in tourist performances, and for them it's a good source of income. The Bali Hyatt has a plush disco, the **Matahari** with deejays and music provided by Juliana's of London.

Also in Sanur, the **Karya Restaurant**, the **Purnama Terrace** (in the Bali Hyatt) and the **Kul Kul Restaurant** (book for the Frog Dance night) are the island's best venues for dinner and a show under the stars.

The **Nusa Dua Hotel** at night is a spectacle in its own right—go there for its Ramayana Night and dine in opera box-like seats surrounding an open-air stage.

For hot, pulsating nightlife with loud, gyrating crowds and ear-shattering music, make your way on over to the **Kuta Beach** side. This formerly somnambulant beach village is now on the go day and night.

A number of watering holes along Jalan Legian and Jalan Buni Sari stay open as long as there are people. **Casablanca** and **The Pub**, to mention just two, serve chilled Bintang beer in chilled mugs—a beer drinker's paradise.

SHOPPING

WHAT TO BUY

Jakarta: Jakarta is not known as a shopper's paradise—imported goods are heavily taxed and domestic manufactures can only rarely compete in quality, though they are cheap. The good buys are hence limited mainly to two categories: handicrafts and antiques, with certain exceptions—notably pirated cassette tapes and locally produced designer clothes.

BATIK

Batik Keris, with showrooms in Sarinah, has the largest selection of *batik* in Jakarta, particularly yard goods and inexpensive *kain*. Another big Solo-based batik maker, **Danar Hadi**, specializes in finer *tulis* work fabric and ready-made shirts and dresses. Connoisseurs will want to stop in at the shop of designer **Iwan Tirta**. For *batik* paintings, Yogya-based **Amri** is the best known artist. Smaller, quality boutiques selling a range of clothes and fabrics include **Srikandi** and several of the shops on Jl. Palatehan I (Blok M, Kebayoran) and in the **Hilton Bazaar**.

Amri Gallery
Jl. Utan Kayu 66E.

Batik Keris
Sarinah Jaya Department Store,
Kebayoran Baru.

Danar Hadi
Jl. Raden Saleh 1A
Tel: 342390, 343712.

Iwan Tirta
Jl. Panarukan 25
Tel: 349122

Iwan Tirta
Borobodur Intercontinental Hotel shopping arcade.

Srikandi
Jl. Melawai VI/6A
Tel: 775604.

Srikandi
Jl. Cikini Raya 90
Tel: 354446.

HANDICRAFTS

The first stop for handicrafts of every description is the **Handicraft Center** in the Sarinah Jaya Department Store in Kebayoran. Here you can get everything from baskets to cane chairs to leather sandals. Then for paintings, carvings, *wayang* puppet and other "art" items, spend an afternoon or evening at the **Art Market** (Pasar Seni) in Ancol, where you can observe craftsmen at work and chat with them.

The Indonesian Bazaar at the Hilton Hotel has a number of up-market boutiques selling quality *batik*, jewelry and *wayang* puppets. Many of the antique and art shops at Jl. Kebon Sirih Timur Dalam, Jl. Majapahit and Jl. Palatehan (Kebayoran) also sell handicrafts. A few shops, such as the **Irian Art and Gift Shop** specialize in tribal handicrafts and primitive art. (*See* below for shop listings.)

ANTIQUES & CURIOS

These are available throughout the city, but especially on **Jl. Kebon Sirih Timur Dalam**, where there are several tiny shops with names like **Bali**, **Bima**, **Djody** and **Nasrun**—all stocked with old furniture, weavings, masks, puppets and porcelains. Nearby **Johan Art** has one of the largest collections of old Chinese porcelains; they will refund your money if later dissatisfied, a rarity in Jakarta. Farther down Jl. Wahid Hasyim is a shop specializing in pewter ware: **The Banka Tin Shop**.

Several other shops are on Jl. Haji Agus Salim (Jl. Sabang). All the above are within walking distance of Sarinah or the Sari Pacific Hotel.

There are also concentrations of antique and art shops in other areas of the city:

• The **antique market** on Jl. Surabaya, near Embassy Row (Jl. Diponegoro) consists of about 20 stalls set in a row. Porcelains, puppets, tiles, brass and silver bric-a-brac, much of it new but made to look old, spill forth onto the sidewalk. Nearby, two homes houses a cache of antique Dutch furniture: Alex Papadimitriou's, and the Srirupa Shop.

• A new row of chic boutiques, galleries and studios catering to the foreign community and wealthy Jakartans is located in Kebayoran on **Jl. Papatehan I**. The new Sarinah Jaya Department Stote is next door, and Aldiron Plaza/Blok M is within walking distance.

Alex Papadimitrious (antiques)
Jl. Pasuruan 3.

Bali Art & Curio
Jl. Kebon Sirih Timur Dalam 42.

Bangka Tin Shop
Jl. Wahid Hasyim 178.

Bima Arts & Curios
Jl. Kebon Sirih Timur Dalam 257.

Djelita Art Shop
Jl. Palatehan I/137.

Djody Art & Curio
Jl. Kebon Sirih Timur Dalam 2.

Irian Art and Gift Shop
Jl. Pasar Baru 16A
Tel: 343422.

Johan Art
Jl. Wahid Hasyim 80.

Johan Art Curios
Jl. H. Agus Salim 59A.

Majapahit Arts & Curios
Jl. Melawai III/4, Blok M,
Kebayoran Baru.

Naini's Fine Arts
Jl. Palatehan I/20, Kebayoran Baru.

Pigura Art & Gift Shop
Jl. Palatehan I/41, Kebayoran Baru
Tel: 773599.

Tony's Gallery
Jl. Palatehan I/31, Kebayoran Baru.

Urip Store
Jl. Palatehan I/40, Kebayoran Baru.

BALI

Bali is a great place to shop. Hundreds of boutiques and roadside stalls have set up all over the island, and thousands of artisans, craftsmen, seamstresses, woodcarvers, painters, etc. are busy supplying the tourist demand.

WOODCARVINGS

You are sure to find good woodcarvings in the shops along the main roads in **Mas** (particularly well-known is Ida Bagus Tilem's Gallery and Museum). Also try the villages of **Pujung** (past Tegalalang north of Ubud), **Batuan** and **Jati**.

All types of indigenous wood, ranging from the butter-colored jackwood to inexpensive bespeckled coconut, are sculpted here in bold designs which set the standards for carvers elsewhere on the island. Woods imported from other islands—buff hibiscus, rich brown Javanese teak and black Sulawesian ebony are also hewn into delicate forms by Balinese craftsmen.

PAINTINGS

The artist's center is **Ubud**, including the surrounding villages of **Pengosekan**, **Penestanan**, **Sanggingan**, **Peliatan**, **Mas** and **Butuan**. The famous **Neka Gallery & Museum** and the **Puri Lukisan Museum**, both in Ubud, will give you an idea of the range of styles and the artistry achieved by the best painters. Then visit some of the other galleries in the area: **Gallery Munut**, **Gallery Agung** and the gallery of the **Pengosekan Community of Artists**. Examples from every school of painting active in Bali are found here as well as canvasses of young artists portraying festivals and dancers.

GOLD & SILVER

The centers for metal working are **Celuk** and **Kamasan**, where all such ornaments are on sale at reasonable prices. **Kuta** is another center for export gold and silver wares. For traditional Balinese jewelry, visit the shops on Jl. Sulawesi and Jl. Kartini in **Denpasar**.

HANDICRAFTS

Bamboo implements, *wayang kulit* figures and ornaments made of coconut shell and teakwood are sold at most souvenir shops. Bonecarvings can be had for good prices at **Tampak-siring**, while plaited hats and baskets are the specialty of the women of **Bedulu** and **Bona**. **Sukawati** market and the row of stands opposite **Goa Gajah** are the best places to buy baskets. **Klungkung** market also has some finely worked traditional wares.

The **Handicraft Center** (Sanggraha Karya Hasta) in Tohpati, Denpasar, has a collection of handicrafts from Bali and the other islands of Indonesia, such as baskets and weavings. Open 8 a.m. to 5 p.m. daily, closed Mondays.

The morning market at **Pasar Badung** in Denpasar is also an eye-opener. Coral-lined alleys will lead you to a ceremonial knick-knacks section selling baskets of every shape and size.

ANTIQUES

Try the shopping arcades of major hotels for truly outstanding pieces (at outstanding prices). In **Kuta**, Angang's and the East West Artshop have the best collection of antiques and primitive artifacts.

In **Denpasar**, there are several antique shops along Jl. Gajah Mada up near the town square end. Also on Jl. Arjuna, Jl. Dresna, Jl. Veteran and Jl. Gianyar. In **Sanur**, the shops are along Jl. Sanur.

The many antique shops adjacent to the Kerta Gosa in **Klungkung** house collections of rare Chinese porcelains, old Kamasan *wayang* style paintings, antique jewelry and Balinese weavings. Prices are reasonable. **Singaraja** has some of the best antique shops in Bali, too. They're all on the main roads of this northern city.

SPORTS

Bali: There are two golf courses on the island. The Hotel Bali Beach in Sanur has a small nine-hole course that can be used for a fee. But the serious golfer will want to visit the **Bali Handara Country Club** at Bedugal. This 18-hole championship course was designed by Peter Thompson and is perhaps the only course in the world set inside a volcano. Green fees are US$45 per day on the weekends, US$30 during the week.

For a fee ranging from US$1.50 to US$5 a per day, the **swimming** pools at most of the larger hotels may be used by non-guests.

Aquatic Sports—**surfing**, **diving**, **spearfishing**, **wind-surfing** and **deep-sea fishing**—have all become very popular in Bali.

Nusa Lembongan, the small island directly opposite Sanur has developed into a haven for surfers and divers alike. Group charters and safari tours are available, together with equipment and instruction if needed. A complete scuba outfit and a ride out to the reef at Sanur can be had for as little as US$20 a person for a group of five or more (US$40 for just one). Contact Nyoman at **Bali Aquatic Sports** in Kuta (in the La Barong Bar). Also in Kuta, try **Gloria Maris** (Jl. Airport) and **Nusa Lembongan Tours** (at the Happy Restaurant.)

For the best surfing, go down to **Ulu Watu** on the eastern side of the southern Bukit Peninsula.

LANGUAGE

Indonesia's motto , *Bhinneka Tunggal Ika* (unity in diversity) is seen in its most driving, potent form in the world of language. Although there are over 350 distinct languages and dialects spoken in the archipelago, the one national tongue, *Bahasa Indonesia*, will take you from the northernmost tip of Sumatra through Java and across the string of islands to Irian Jaya.

Bahasa Indonesia is both an old and new language. It is based on Malay, which has been the *lingua franca* throughout much of Southeast Asia for centuries, but it has changed rapidly in the past few decades to meet the needs of a modern nation.

Although formal Indonesian is a complex language demanding serious study, the construction of basic Indonesian sentences is relatively simple.

A compact and cheap book—*How to Master the Indonesian Language*, by Almatseier—is widely available in Indonesia and should prove invaluable in helping you say what you want to say. Indonesian is written in the Roman alphabet and, unlike some Asian languages, is not tonal.

Indonesians always use their language to show respect when addressing others, especially when a younger person speaks to his elders. The custom is to address an elder man as *bapak* or *pak* (father) and an elder woman as *ibu* (mother), and even in the case of slightly younger people who are obviously VIPs, this form is suitable and correct. *Bung* (in West Java) and *mas* (in Central and East Java) roughly translate as "brother" and are used with equals, people your own age whom you don't know all that well, and with hotel clerks, taxi drivers, tour guides and waiters (it's friendly, and a few notches above "buddy" or "mate").

GETTING THERE

BY AIR

There are four international airports on the main island of Honshu, in Tokyo, Osaka, Nagoya and Niigata. The majority of flights from Europe and America come into the New Tokyo International Airport at Narita. This airport is annoyingly far from the city—allow one-and-a-half to two hours to get into town.

Travelers with light luggage will do best to take the Skyliner Express train into town. Bus service provided by the city and by major hotels minimizes effort for people with a lot of bags, but can take a considerable amount of time in traffic. The cab ride is long and expensive.

Osaka airport is more conveniently located, and a good place to start a trip, as it is also close to Kyoto. Nagoya receives flights from Hong Kong, Seoul and Manila. The city is on the Shinkansen Super-express line, about an hour from Kyoto and two hours from Tokyo. Flights from the Soviet Union enter Niigata, which is four hours by express train from Tokyo.

BY SEA

Cruise ships stop mainly at Yokohama (an hour from Tokyo) and Kobe (less then an hour from Osaka and Kyoto). Ferries run between Pusan in Korea and Shimonoseki at the southern tip of Honshu three times a week. This is the cheapest route from Korea to Japan.

Ferries also run weekly between Shanghai

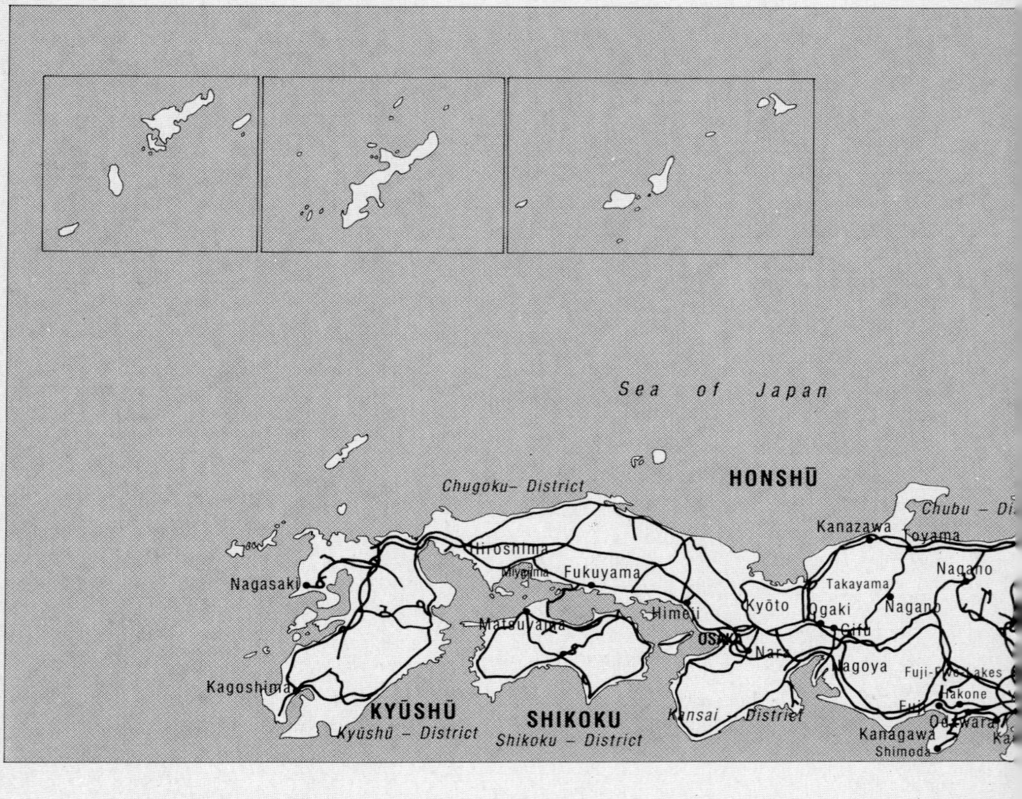

Sea of Japan
HONSHŪ
Chugoku– District
Kanazawa
Toyama
Hiroshima
Miyajima
Fukuyama
Nagasaki
Takayama
Nagano
Kyōto
Ogaki
Nagano
Himeji
Matsuyama
Gifu
OSAKA
Nara
Nagoya
Kagoshima
Hakone
Fuji
Odawara
KYŪSHŪ
Kyūshū – District
SHIKOKU
Shikoku – District
Kansai – District
Kanagawa
Shimoda

and Kobe/Osaka. Travelers should be sure to have visas and reservations taken care of well in advance if going from Japan to China.

TRAVEL ESSENTIALS

VISAS & PASSPORTS

The standard tourist visa is for 60-90 days. Some European countries have an arrangement with Japan whereby persons entering for purposes of tourism require no visa. Immigration inspectors sometimes require a visitor to show a return ticket, or evidence of adequate funds to leave.

Anyone staying longer than 90 days must get an Alien Registration Form at the Immigration Office. For further information consult your embassy or consulate, or a book called *Immigration—Guide to Alien Procedures in Japan*, which is available at the Kinokuniya and Maruzen bookstores in Tokyo and at Immigration offices.

MONEY MATTERS

Recent exchange rates places the yen at 145 yen = 1 US dollar range has made Japan extremely expensive for most foreign visitors. Although there is a seemingly infinite variety of goods available, Japan cannot be called Asia's bargain-hunting ground.

As rates are constantly in flux, it may be more meaningful to give some broad figures for the prices of things in yen. Inflation has been relatively slow since the late 70s.

Rooms at full-service hotels in Tokyo start around 10,000 yen; most are in the 15,000-

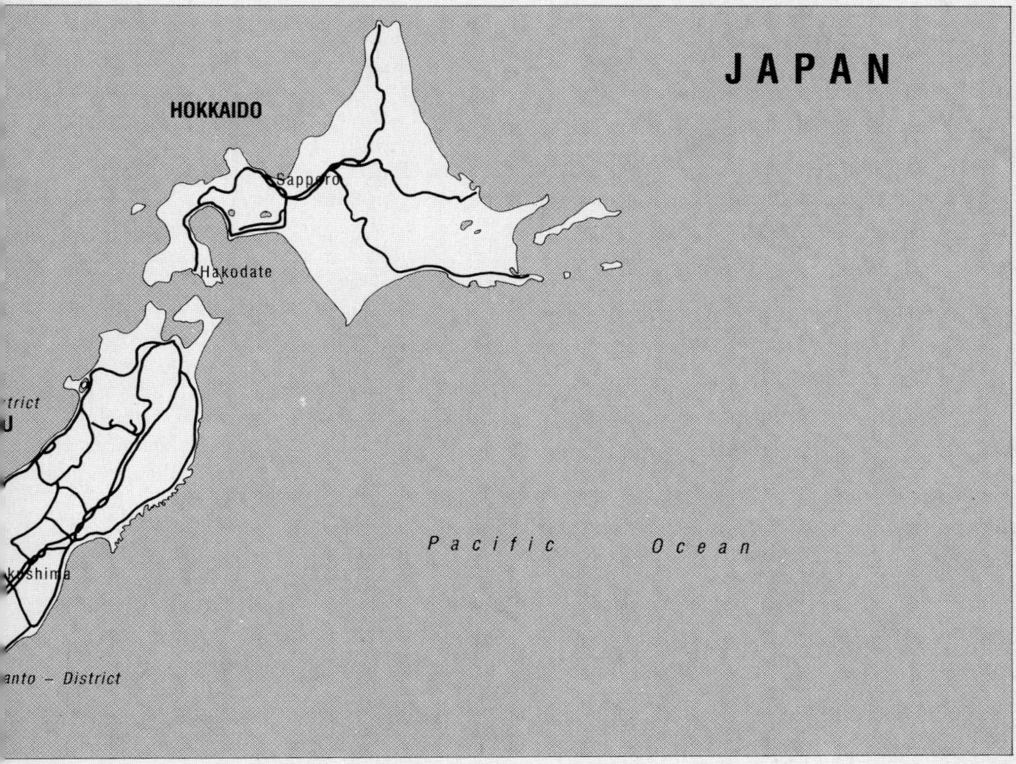

JAPAN

HOKKAIDO

Sapporo

Hakodate

Pacific Ocean

20,000 range. Restaurant prices vary of course, but a nice dinner can be had for 4,000-6,000 yen, good steak starts at about 5,000 yen (beef is a luxury), and cheap lunch (lunch is much more affordable as a rule) is available for 600-1,200 yen.

A taxi ride within central Tokyo will start at 470 yen and probably not exceed 3,000. Subway and inner-city train rides are between 120 and 280 yen, while the Shinkansen express train to Kyoto costs 12,800 yen.

Japanese yen is the only currency accepted in Japan. Many banks have foreign exchange counters, but these will not be found outside of major cities. Traveler's checks (better in dollars than in yen) are alright at these banks, but elsewhere, most people don't know what they are. There are no personal checks in Japan. The currencies of Taiwan and China are unexchangeable and therefore valueless in Japan. Diners Club, Visa, Mastercharge and American Express are fairly commonly accepted, but cannot be relied upon exclusively.

GETTING ACQUAINTED

GEOGRAPHY & CLIMATE

Japan is a belt of volcanic islands extending 1,730 miles (2,790 km) northeast to southwest. This is comparable to the extent of the east coast of the United States from Maine to Florida, which accounts in part for the wide climatic variation. The main islands of Japan are four: Hokkaido in the north, Honshu, central in the group, Kyushu in the southwest, and Shikoku, nestled between Honshu and Kyushu.

Hokkaido is spread out and more sparsely populated than the rest of Japan. The terrain is often compared with parts of North America. One can see a resemblance in the rolling hills and cow pastures, uncharacteristic of Japan. The Japanese began exploiting this island only in the last century, and when they found that the climate and soil were unsuitable for traditional rice cultivation, followed the advice of American agriculturists. However, unlike most of North America, Hokkaido is volcanically active, with many hot springs and a new mountain, Showa Shinzan, formed in 1943. Most of Hokkaido gets a lot of snow, but the annual climate (as seen in weather records for the capital city of Sapporo) is on the whole drier and sunnier than Honshu.

A mountain range cutting through central Honshu is responsible for the enormous climate differential between the northwestern side (Tohoku and Chubu along the Japan Sea coast) and the Pacific coast side in the southeast. Siberian winds sweep across the Japan Sea beginning in December, meet central Honshu's wall of mountains and dump snow on northwestern Japan daily through February. The huge accumulations made this an isolated hinterland until quite recently. It was referred to as the "back side of Japan," a term that has fallen into disfavor. It is still sometimes called "snow country." Barely two hours away by train, Tokyo and the "front side" of the Kanto and Chubu regions seldom see a substantial snowfall.

Western Honshu around the Inland Sea and Shikoku have a somewhat milder climate. Shikoku is the smallest of the four main islands, and the least visited. What was recently rustic, would now better be described as a suburban atmosphere here. There is quite a lot of National Park area, and a famous pilgrimage circuit of 88 temples, which many Japanese still follow. The Inland Sea is pretty, warm, and busy with every sort of craft, including ferries running from Kobe, Osaka, Wakayama and Hiroshima on Honshu, and Beppu on Kyushu.

Kyushu gets a lot of rain, but enjoys a mild climate through most of the year. The island has some striking contrasts of terrain, exemplified by Aso National Park, which contains dense forests as well as black-brown lava fields and Mount Ado, one of the world's largest calderas. One of Mount Aso's volcanic cones still belches ash, which is showered down onto the city of Kumamoto.

The group of islands forming Okinawa Prefecture lie far out in the Pacific Ocean south of Kyushu. The climate is sub-tropical, with summer temperatures from March to November and frequent typhoons in autumn. Historically, the islands were an autonomous kingdom which enjoyed the benefits of trade with and suffered suppression at the hands of both Japan and China. More recently, the imprint of America was left by the military occupation, which lasted until 1972, 20 years longer than in the rest of the country. These cultural factors, along with the southern climate and landscape, make Okinawa quite unlike other parts of Japan.

All of Japan experiences, in varying degrees, an early summer rainy season, called *tsuyu* or *baiyu* in Japanese. In central Honshu, this lasts for about three weeks in late June-July. Rain falls almost daily during this period, sometimes with intermittent sun and warm temperatures. Genuine summer heat and humidity follow. In the Kanto and Kansai areas, the temperature remains mild into October.

TIPPING

Very few situations require tipping in Japan. Station and airport porters usually receive one or two hundred yen per piece of luggage. There may be a sign indicating rates posted. Restaurants require no tip; they generally include a service charge. Taxi drivers also require no tip, but might appreciate one if they have done portering as well.

TOURIST INFORMATION

The main source of tourist information is the **JNTO**, Japan National Tourist Organization. The JNTO operates three Tourist Information Centers within Japan, in Narita Airport, in Yurakucho, Tokyo (near Yurakucho and Ginza stations) and in Kyoto (in the Kyoto Tower Building). They offer a wide variety of free publications and the assistance of an English-speaking staff. They do not make bookings and reservations. Although there are no centers apart from these three, the JNTO may be contacted by collect telephone call 9 a.m.-5 p.m. any day of the year from anywhere in the country. Dial 106 from a yellow, blue or green phone and say "collect call to TIC."

GETTING AROUND

DOMESTIC TRAVEL

By Air: There are domestic flights between most major cities. Flying is the easiest way to get to Okinawa, of course, and to Hokkaido and Kyushu from central Honshu if you are in a hurry.

RAIL TRANSPORT

Japan's excellent rail network will take you around Tokyo faster than a taxi, from Tokyo to Kyoto faster than the plane (including time to and fro airports), and into the farthest reaches of the countryside (but not always so quickly). The Japan National Railway, which also runs a number of bus lines, is in the process of splitting up, selling land to private enterprises, but most lines are still JNR. In Tokyo, there is also a subway system. One is never beyond easy walking distance of a station.

The **Shinkansen** ("New Trunk Line") Super Express, also called the Bullet, travels at speeds of up to 136 mph (220 kph) along three lines in Honshu and Kyushu. The Tohoku and Tokaido lines together extend from Morioka in the north to Hakata on Kyushu in the south. The Joetsu line travels northwest from Tokyo to the Japan Sea coast. This train has reduced to a fraction the travel-time between many Japanese cities. Tickets are bought separately from regular train tickets, at the green ticket windows in JNR stations. The express ticket is several thousand yen more than a local on the same line, but the time difference is five hours just between Tokyo and Kyoto.

Japan Rail Pass: The one-, two-and three-week passes offered by the JNR for foreign tourists, like the Eurorail Pass, is an excellent bargain. These must be purchased outside of the country, at a Japan Airlines, Japan Travel Bureau or Nippon Travel

Agency office. They are open-dated, so that you can validate them when you want to start traveling, and if you ride the Shinkansen more than two or three times you are almost sure to get your money's worth.

PUBLIC TRANSPORT

Taxis are freely available and on call. An empty taxi will have the tiny sign on the passenger side inside the windshield lit. A wave is sufficient to stop the driver. It is a good idea to carry the address (plus any explanatory information that may be necessary) written in Japanese. If you have a map, the driver will do his best to help you.

Buses are plentiful but offer no English and inadequate maps. In Kyoto, and in other parts of the country, the bus system can be quite useful. Make sure you have all of the bus numbers and transfer locations written down.

PRIVATE TRANSPORT

Licenses from most countries and International Driving permits can be used to drive in Japan for a short period of time. For a longer stay, it is not difficult to get one of these converted into a Japanese license. It is very difficult to get a new license in Japan. Numerous rent-a-car agencies offer their services. Driving is on the left-hand side and road conditions are generally good, but the roads are often narrow.

WHERE TO STAY

The following list of accommodations is intended only as a brief sample. More information is available at the Tourist Information Centers of the Japan National Tourist Organization and in publications like the *Tour Companion* (available at the JNTO and hotels). Whether you are looking for a youth hostel or a first-class hotel, no season is "quiet," and some telephoning around may be necessary if you are making your arrangements from within Japan. Listings below are for Tokyo and Kyoto, where most travelers begin. If you want the security of knowing you will have a roof over your head after nightfall, you are advised to arrange lodging in advance with the help of a JNTO office, travel agent or your hotel before setting out from either of these cities.

ACCOMMODATIONS IN TOKYO

HOTELS

Hotel Okura
2-10-4 Toranomon, Minato-ku
Tel: 582-0111.

New Otani Hotel
4-1 Kioi-cho, Chiyoda-ku.
Tel: 265-1111.

Akasaka Prince Hotel
1-2 Kioi-cho, Chiyoda-ku
Tel: 234-1111.

Keio Plaza Hotel
2-2-1 Nishi Shinjuku, Shinjuku-ku
Tel: 344-0111.

Meguro Gajoen Hotel
1-8 Shimo-Meguro, Meguro-ku
Tel: 491-0174.

BUSINESS HOTELS

These hotels are inexpensive and most of them provide only minimal services.

Tokyo Garden palace, Yushima Kaikan
Yushima 1-7-5, Bunkyo-ku
Tel: 813-6211.

Asia Center of Japan
8-10-32 Akasaka, Minato-ku
Tel: 402-611.

Kayabacho Pearl Hotel
1-2-5 Shinkawa, Chuo-ku
Tel: 553-2211.

Hotel Suigetsu
3-3-21 Ikenohata, Taitoku
Tel: 822-4611.

RYOKAN

Ryokan are Japanese inns. Rooms are usually floored with tatami mats, some are without bath.

Sawanoya
2-3-11 Yanaka, Taito-ku
Tel: 822-2251.

Mikawaya Bekkan
1-3-11 Asakusa, Taito-ku
Tel: 843-2345.

Inabaso
5-6-13 Shinjuku, Shinjuku-ku
Tel: 341-9581.

BUDGET

Cheap private lodgings (these are communal accommodations; safe but not very pretty):

Okubo House
In Shin-Okubo
Tel: 361-2348.

English House
Near Mejiro
Tel: 988-1743.

Yoshida House
On Seibu-Ikebukuro Line
Tel: 926-4563.

Toyama Houses
Tel: 948-2383.

ACCOMMODATIONS IN KYOTO

HOTELS

Miyako Hotel
Higashiyama area.
Tel: (075)771-7111.

Kyoto tower Hotel
Tel: (075)361-3211.

Hotel Fujita
Tel: (075)222-1511.

Holiday Inn Kyoto
Tel: (075)721-3131.

RYOKAN

Tawaraya Ryokan
Tel: (075)211-5566.

Kinta Ryokan
Tel: (075)351-1429.

Izumiya Ryokan
Tel: (075)371-2769.

Kitanoya Ryokan
Tel: (075)771-1488.

BUDGET

Kyoto has six youth hostels. They are inexpensive and reliable, but some travelers complain of restrictions (curfews etc.) Higashiyama (Tel: 761-8135) and Matsusan (221-5160) are near Kyoto Station. Kitayama (492-5345) and Ohara Youth Hostel (744-2721) are in the countryside north of the city.

Tani House
Tel: 492-5489.

English Guest House
Tel: 722-0495/6.

FOOD DIGEST

WHAT TO EAT

Tokyo is a complete compendium of modern Japan, with at least one of everything. In restaurants, this means a staggering variety of Japanese cuisine, along with representatives of just about every other nation on earth, and some amalgams unique to the city. There are so many little places with undecipherable facades, that restaurant hunting can be quite perplexing. Don't be afraid to follow your nose—no place is off-limits or unsafe. The plastic models displayed outside many establishments are a useful guide; they also inform you that the place does serve food, and probably won't be too expensive.

The following is a random sample of recommendable restaurants. Other suggestions may be found in JNTO publications, but if you have some time in Tokyo and a curious palate, you should not restrict yourself to places listed. Make your own discoveries.

WHERE TO EAT

Shabu-zen
Locations in Roppongi (Tel: 585-5388) and Ginza (Tel: 572-3806).
Serves shabu-shabu and sukiyaki, beef and vegetables stewed at the table.

Inakaya
In Roppongi (Tel: 405-9866). Ten-ichi-Tempura. Several locations: Ginza Sony Building (Tel: 571-3837), Akasaka Tokyu Plaza (Tel: 581-2166), Shinjuku Mitsui Building (Tel: 344-4706).
Traditional cooking at an open hearth. Lively atmosphere.

Tsunahachi
3-31-8 Shinjuku (Tel: 352-1012).
High quality, inexpensive tempura. Bust shop. A bit hard to find.

Toricho
Very near Inakaya, 10 minutes from Roppongi intersection. (Tel: 401-1827).
Good "up-scale" yakitori (grilled chicken etc. on skewers).

Jiro
In Ginza (Tel: 535-3600).
Haute sushi. Expensive but superb. Sushi is best in winter.

Kandagawa Honten
2-5-11 Soto Kanda (Tel: 251-5031).
Specializes in grilled eel. Traditional country-house interior.

Moti
Three locations, in Akasaka (Tel: 584-6640), Akasaka-mitsuke (582-3620), and Roppongi (479-1939).
Indian food has proliferated recently. The best is here.

Metropole
Near Roppongi. (Tel: 405-4400).
Very fashionable new sport with baroque-ish interior and "nouvelle" Chinese cuisine.

Shibuya Ju-ni kagetsu Building
1018 Jinnan, shibuya (Tel: 477-1200).
This building has seven restaurants offering various cuisines on top of one another. Including Hassan, which serves tea-ceremony cuisine, and Gotoh Steak House.

LANGUAGE

Everyone in Japan under about 50 has studied some English, but outside of hotels, travel agencies and international business circles, not many people are comfortable speaking it. Most Japanese comprehend more written than spoken English. Anyway, speaking slowly is a good idea. English Pronunciation is very troublesome for Japanese, as their own language has a very small syllable set.

By the same token, Japanese words are fairly easily to render intelligibly. There are five vowel sounds, short a, e, i, o and u, which are essentially unvarying, though they may appear in combination. They are similar in sound to the vowels in Italian or Spanish. "i" and "u" are sometimes pronounced very faintly, so that "basu", for example, actually sounds rather close to its English equivalent, "bus". All syllables in a word receive approximately equal stress.

A few phrases committed to memory will receive warm responses and certainly come in handy. You can go quite a long way on "domo" and "dozo" ("thank you" and "please") alone.

PHRASES

Good morning
Ohayo gozaimasu (*–masu* pronounced "mahs" with an unvoiced s)

good afternoon (hello)
konnichiwa

good evening
konbanwa

good night
oyasumi nasai ("ai" is pronounced as "Thailand")

How do you do
hajimemashite

I'm sorry, excuse me, thank you
sumimasen

Thank you
domo arigato gozaimasu, arigato, domo.

I'm sorry, forgive me
gomen nasai

Excuse me
shitsurei shimasu

Please (go ahead)
dozo

thank you (after a meal)
domo gochisosama

Please give me...
o kudasai

Hello (answering telephone, getting someone's attention)
moshi-moshi

Yes
hai

No
iie

Is that right? Oh, really?
so desu ka? honto?

No, that's not right, I disagree
iie, so dewa arimasen, chigaimasu

Goodbye
sayonara

Wait a moment
chotto matte

How much is it?
ikura desu ka?

I would like this please
kore o o-negai shimasu

No thank you
iie, kekko desu

Where is...?
...wa doko desu ka?

where is the station?
eki wa doko desu ka?

toilet
o-te-arai, toire

hotel
hoteru

bank
ginko

subway
chikatetsu

here, there (near you),
koko, soko

there (away from speaker and listener)
asoko

this, that, that over there
kore, sore, are

left, right
hidari, migi

straight
massugu

ahead, beyond
saki

next to...
...no tonari

north, south, east, west
kita, minami, higashi, nishi

yen
en

dollars
doru

29000 yen
ni-man-kyu-sen en

do you speak English?
Eigo ga hanasemasu ka?

NUMBERS

1	*ichi*
2	*ni*
3	*san*
4	*shi, yon*
5	*go*
6	*roku*
7	*shichi, nana*
8	*hachi*
9	*ku, kyu*
10	*ju*
20	*ni-ju*
100	*hyaku*
1000	*sen*
10000	*man, ichi-man*

Getting There

BY AIR

Kimp'o International Airport, 24 kilometers west of Seoul, receives more than 200 flights weekly from Japan, Taiwan, Hong Kong, the Philippines, Thailand, Singapore, and other world destinations. It is served from the United States by Korean Air Lines (Korea's national flag carrier), Japan Airlines, and Northwest Orient among a few others.

BY SEA

The overnight *Pukwan* ferry to Pusan disembarks from Shimonoseki, Japan, at 5 p.m. every day except Saturday. For more information, contact:

Tokyo Office: (03) 567-0971
Osaka Office: (06) 345-2245
Shimonoseki Office: (0832) 66-8211
Seoul Office: 752-9716
Pusan Office: 463-3161/8

Travel Essentials

VISAS & PASSPORTS

Visitors to Korea must present a valid passport or travel document. Except for those whose itineraries include cholera-infected areas, no certificate of vaccination is required. Tourists in transit with confirmed flights onward may stay five days without visa. For longer stays visas are required of all except: citizens of Austria, Chile, Greece, Mexico, and Switzerland, who are permitted 90 days; citizens of Belgium, Denmark, Finland, Iceland, Italy, Lesotho, Luxembourg, the Netherlands, Norway, Spain, Surinam, Sweden, Turkey, the United Kingdom, and West Germany, 60 days; and citizens of France and Tunisia, 30 days.

There is a 5,000 *won* airport tax payable on departure.

MONEY MATTERS

Procuring *won*, Korean currency, outside Korea is virtually impossible. In country, however, there are foreign exchange counters at the airport, major tourist hotels (which charge a few *won* per exchanged bill or traveler's check), major banks (some with branches in large hotels) and a few major department stores (e.g. Midopa and Lotte) in Seoul.

Banking hours are 9:30 a.m. to 4:30 p.m. Monday through Friday. 9:30 a.m. to 1:30 p.m. Saturday.

Credit cards like American Express Cards, Bank Americard-Visa, Master Charge, and Diners Club cards are popularly accepted in major hotels and restaurants.

HEALTH

Immunizations are administered at the International Clinic at Severance Hospital, which uses disposable needles, and also at

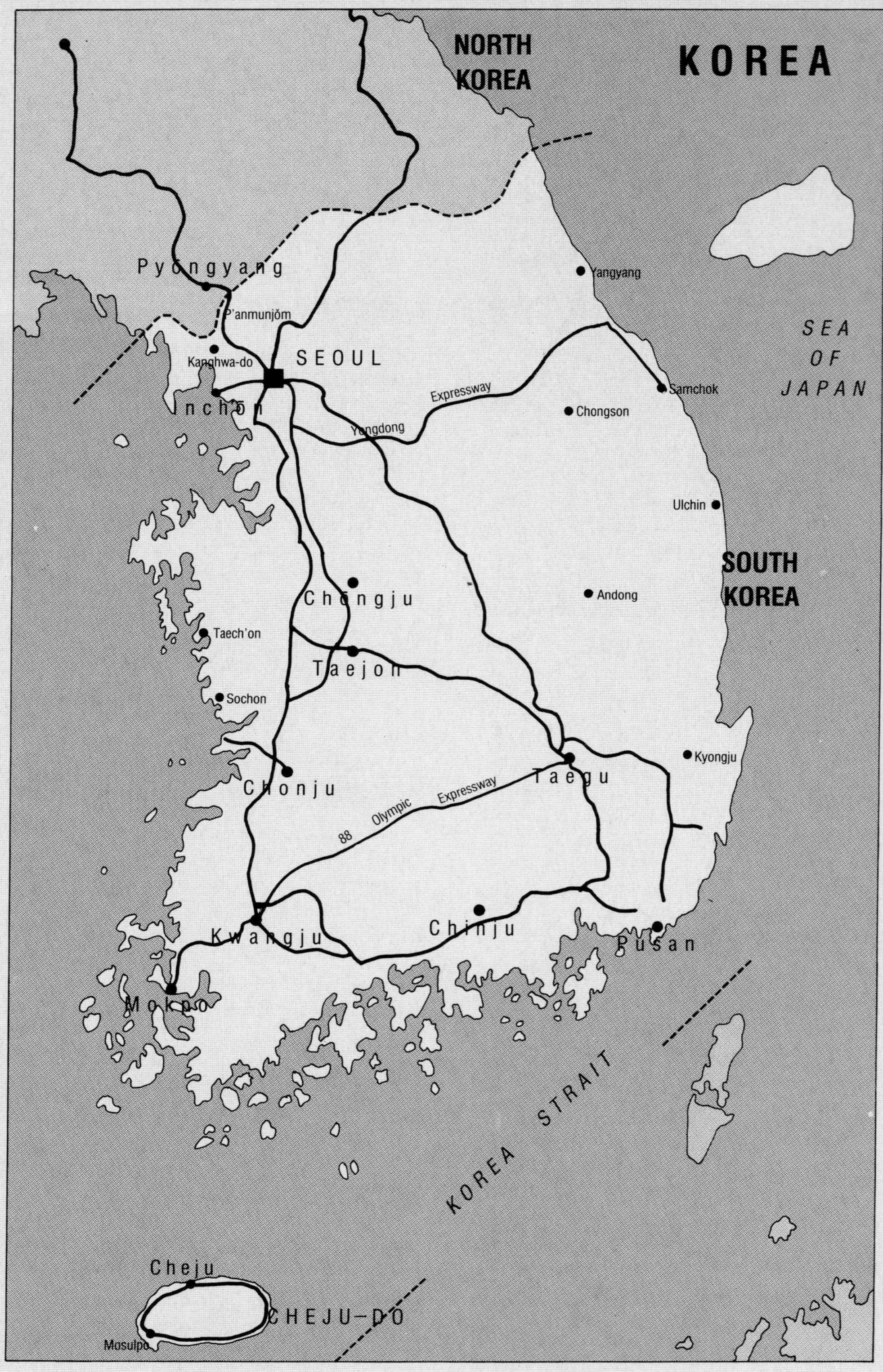
KOREA
NORTH KOREA
SOUTH KOREA
SEA OF JAPAN
KOREA STRAIT
Pyongyang
P'anmunjŏm
Kanghwa-do
SEOUL
Inchon
Yangyang
Samchok
Chongson
Expressway
Yongdong
Ulchin
Chongju
Andong
Taech'on
Taejon
Sochon
Kyongju
Chonju
Taegu
88 Olympic Expressway
Kwangju
Chinju
Pusan
Mokpo
Cheju
CHEJU-DO
Mosulpo

the Seoul Quarantine Office to the right of the USO compound in Kalwol-dong, Yongson-ku.

Many kinds of medicines and health care goods—from bottled sweetened vitamin tonics to contraceptives—are available at local pharmacies. Many drugs are imported. Except for the sales of narcotics and barbiturates, there is little government control over these businesses, and drugs are sometimes diluted or mixed, repackaged, and then sold. Placebos are not unheard of. Hospital pharmacies are more reliable drug outlets. Major hotels have house doctors.

WHAT TO WEAR

Influenced by climate and occasion, clothing in Korea follows function rather than style. Business suits are the proper mode, even in the summer, for metropolitan business activities. Otherwise, dress is casual. Backless and mini-dresses and shorts, though appropriate for muggy weather, are not acceptable wear in public. An umbrella, sunglasses, and rainy day footwear are practical accessories to pack.

CUSTOMS

Visitors may bring in 400 cigarettes, 50 cigars or 250 grams of pipe and 100 grams of powdered tobacco, two bottles of liquor and two ounces of perfume. Items needed for personal use (except certain exclusive goods such as vehicles, guns and musical instruments) may be brought into Korea duty free, but visitors must leave with these personal effects. Literature and items deemed "subversive" or "detrimental to public interest" are prohibited.

Korean antiques and cultural properties dating earlier than 1910 should be checked and appraised by the Cultural Property Preservation Bureau near the Capitol Building (tel: 725-3053) and a permit should be secured. For five or fewer antiques checking may be done at the Bureau's Kimp'o Airport office (tel: 66-0106). Even good imitations should be checked to prevent hassles at the airport. A limit of three kilograms of red ginseng with a sales receipt also may be taken out of the country.

GETTING ACQUAINTED

TIME ZONES

International time differences are staggered as follows:

Korea	12	noon today
Japan	12	noon today
Hawaii	5	p.m. yesterday
San Francisco	7	p.m. yesterday
New York	10	p.m. yesterday
London	3	a.m. today
Paris	4	a.m. today
Bonn	4	a.m. today
Bangkok	10	a.m. today

CLIMATE

Korea's location in the mid-latitudes and East-Asian Monsoon Belt means four distinct seasons with varying moods. A spring thaw comes in mid-April and lasts little more than two months. As summer approaches, humid southerlies vie for control and the spring drizzle will become an occasional downpour by summer (June–October).

July and August are the hottest, most humid months, especially in the inland basin around Taegu; the temperature there climbs into the upper 20°C to lower 30°C. Autumn comes in late October when the air currents shift back to the crisp northerlies. This climatic ideal intensifies by the end of November when the Siberian freeze whips down the peninsula for six months in a cycle of three consecutive cold days followed by four milder days. The northern inland region of the peninsula has a winter temperature mean of minus 20°C (Chungkangjin, north Korea, the peninsula's coldest spot, has a temperature mean in January of minus 20.8°C) while the southern provinces, in contrast, winter in less severe temperature (Chejudo's temperature mean for January is 4°C). The coldest months are January and February when the temperature drops to minus 12°C to 1.5°C. The favorable months in Korea are April (50°F or 10°C in Seoul). May (60°F or 16°C), June and September just before and after the summer rains (66°F or 19°C) and in October (54°F or 12°C).

GETTING AROUND

PUBLIC TRANSPORT

The majority of people living in Seoul depend on public transportation. The subway is the most convenient form of public transportation for visitors. It covers 116.5 kilometers with four lines and hooks up with the Korean National Railroad. Trains run from 5 a.m. to midnight at three-minute intervals during rush hours, and six-minute intervals at other times.

SUBWAY

Korea's subway system, which opened in August 1974, runs from Seoul Railway Station to six major destinations: Chongnyangni Train Station and Songbuk district to the north, and, connected with electrical tracks, to Inch'on, Suwon, Chamsil and Kuro. Trains come every five minutes. Smoking is prohibited in the cars. Following are points of interest within walking distance of each subway stop within the city walls:

1. **Seoul Train Station**
2. **City Hall (T'aepyõng-no)**
   City Hall
   Toksu Palace
   British Embassy
   Major hotels, banks, department stores
   Seoul Tourist Information Center
3. **Chonggak (Chong-no)**
   Posin-gak (city bell tower)
   Bookstores (with foreign-language sections)
   Korean National Tourism Corporation
   Ch'ogye-sa (Buddhist Temple)
   Communications Memorial Center
   Seoul Immigration Office
   Kyongbok Palace, National Museum, Folk Museum
   Embassies of U.S.A., Japan, Canada
   Sejong Cultural Center
   Yi Sun-sin statue at Kwanghwa-mun Intersection
4. **Chong-no 3-ka**
   Pagoda Park and shopping arcade
   Chongmyo (Royal Confucian Shrine)
   Insa-dong (Mary's Alley antique shops, art galleries, etc.)
5. **Chong-no 5-ka**
   East Gate marketplace
   Herb shops
6. **Tongdae-mum**
   Big East Gate
   Seoul Baseball Stadium

TRAINS

Today, five kinds of train services are available. Their classifications in order of increasing speed, comfort and punctuality and: *wanhaeng* (stops at each station along the way), *pot'ong kuphaeng* (ordinary express with berths, stops frequently and run at night), *tukkup* (limited express, reserved seats available, occasionally with diner car), *udung* (air-conditioned), and *Saemaul Ho* (luxury, air-conditioned super express with diner car. Try to purchase tickets in advance, especially during the summer vacation months. Round-trip tickets are not sold.

CITY BUSES

During less hectic commuting hours, getting around on the local city bus can be interesting, quick and cheap. The driver usually turns up his radio so all may listen to the local baseball game, a melodrama, or to the latest rock 'n roll or classical hits. Confucian ethics generally prevail on board the bus: student offer their seats to mothers toting babies and to grandfolk, and out of mutual consideration, those seated relieve those standing of their schoolbooks and shopping bags. Smoking is prohibited.

Buses run frequently from 5 a.m. to around 11:30 p.m. daily. Tokens available at most stops cost w120. Fares paid in cash cost an extra 10 won, payable upon entrance.

There are also express buses, which follow similar routes but with fewer stops and for a somewhat higher fare (w350). These are designed for commuter use and generally make few stops downtown.

A word of caution: beware of pickpockets on the bus and at crowded bus stops.

Destinations are written on the side of the bus in *han'gul* and on street signs at the bus stops. The routes are mapped out on a panel inside the bus, but destinations are again written only in *han'gul*.

The best way to get around the matter is to take the subway, and with directions from a hotel concierge or a business partner it is possible to brave the crowds. Two rules of thumb: when the bus comes, run to where it stops and leap on; at the other end, get to the exit before the bus stops and jump off just as fast.

INTER-CITY BUSES

Eight expressways cut across the farmlands and mountains of Korea: the Kyungjin (Seoul-Inch'on); Yongdong (Seoul–Kangnung); Tonghae (Kangnung–Pohang); Kuma (Taegu–Masan); Kyongbu (Seoul-Pusan); Namhae (Masan–Kwangju); Honam (Kwangju–Taejon); and the '88 Olympic (Taegu–Kwangju) Expressways.

There are three kinds of inter-city buses: *kosok* (highway express bus—the speediest, and therefore the most dangerous), *chikhaeng* (first class local and direct route), and *wanheang* (roundabout with frequent stops). Because of the high rate of inter-city bus accidents, trains are strongly recommended. Buy bus tickets in advance for a reserved seat. Listed below are eight main bus stations in Seoul and their more popular destinations:

1. **Kangnam Kosok Bus Terminal**
   Located across the Han River in Banpo-dong; provides the only express bus service to cities out of Seoul. (tel: 591-3402; 598-4151)
2. **Tongbu Bus Terminal**
   In Majang-dong; several meters away from city bus #41 stop; service to Ch'unch'on, Sorak, Sokch'o Yangyang, Yongmun-sa, Kangnung, Yoju, Chungju, Kwangju, Wonju, Andong. (tel: 966-6760)
3. **Nambu Bus Terminal**
   In south Yongsan along the main road; service to Kanghwa-do, Kosam, Taech'on Beach, Puyo, Kongju, Chonju, Songni-san, Ch'ongju, Taejon. (tel: 798-3355).
4. **Sinchon Bus Terminal**
   Service to Kanghwa-do: 6 a.m. to 8 p.m.; trip takes 1 hour 15 minutes. (tel: 324-0611)
5. **Miari Bus Terminal**
   Service to Soyo-san (north of Uijongbu, and Tongduch'on) for mountain climbing. (tel: 980-7638)
6. **Ch'onho-dong Bus Terminal**
   Located southeast of Seoul city limits; service to Namhan-sansong Fortress in southern Seoul, Kwangju. (tel: 478-1563)
7. **Yok Chon Terminal**
   Across the street from Seoul Train Station, to the left of the Daewoo building; service to Suwon, Inch'on, P'yongt'aek. (tel: 755-09888)
8. **Seoul Sobu Bus Terminal**
   In Pulang-dong (northern Sodaemun-gu); service to Haengju-sansong, Uijongbu. (tel: 388-5103)

TAXIS

By far the most expedient public transport, taxis are everywhere—weaving in and out of city traffic and darting along rural roads. Fare for regular cabs begins at w600 for the first two kilometers and w50 for each additional 300 meters. The meter also runs on time when movement is slower than 15 kilometers per hour. The special beige radio call taxis are more expensive: w1,000 for the first two kilometers and w100 for each additional 400 meters.

Cabs may be hailed to curbside and shared with other passengers bound in the same direction. Each passenger pays only for the distance he travels (two or more traveling as one party pay as one passenger). This taxi-sharing system is called *hapsong*.

After midnight, passengers are expected to pay a 20 percent surcharge on taxi fares. The driver should have a chart available listing officially calculated surcharge totals.

Long-distance rides can be bargained for.

Few drivers understand English, so try to have your destination written in *han'gul* before entering the cab.

U.S. military I.D. holders may also use Army-Air Force Exchange taxis, which charge slightly higher rates in dollars.

Kiamaster pick-up trucks transport bulky baggage and packages at metered and negotiated rates.

PRIVATE TRANSPORT

Car Rentals: Thus far there is only one car rental service in business—Korea Rent-a-Car, affiliated with the American Hertz Rent-a-Car Service operation. They have four Seoul offices: one at Kimp'o Airport, one in the Chosun Hotel, one in the Lotte Hotel, and the main office in Hannamdong. There is also an international reservation line (tel: 02-752-1851).

WHERE TO STAY

ACCOMMODATIONS

Six kinds of accommodation are open to the visiting foreigner:

Hotels: for all the comforts, conveniences, and privacy of home, nothing beats western-style hotels—which range in standard and price.

Yogwan: Korean guests might request: *pori ch'a* (barley tea), *Yo* and *ibul* (mattress and blanket, respectively, *pegae* (pillow), *ondol* (heated floor), and inexpensive home-cooked Korean meals. Some inns prepare a communal hot bath. Prices range from w5000 onwards for single occupancy.

Yoinsuk: The *yoinsuk*, another type of Korean inn, offers lodging in a private compound and isn't as consistently clean, convenient, nor as appealing as the *yogwan*. But the room rates are usually lower. Accommodation is native all the way.

Hasuk Chip: The *hasuk chip* (boarding house) has its place among students, working bachelors, and itinerants. Rooms are rented by the month, usually to long-term residents. Rent includes very simple home-cooked meals.

Setbang: For the working foreigner, the *setbang*, a rented room in a local home is yet another option. Except for the fact that he happens to share the same roof with others, the tenant is generally on his own.

Youth Hostels: A chain of youth hostels has been established in many of the provinces, and such facilities are open to international members. Membership is open at any of their branches. Some of the hostels, such as the Seoul Bando Youth Hostel and the Puyo Youth Hostel, are a combination of hostel-hotel, with communal rooms as well as plush, private rooms and suites.

HOTELS

(*denotes deluxe hotel)

Seoul Deluxe:

Chosun Hotel	771-05
Hilton Hotel	753-7788
Hotel Lotte	771-10
Hotel Shilla	233-3131
Hyatt Regency Seoul	798-0061
Seoul Plaza Hotel	771-22
Sheraton Walker Hill Hotel	453-0121

Seoul First Class:

Ambassador Hotel	275-1101
Hotel Seoul Garden	713-9441
King Sejong Hotel	776-4011/9
Korean Hotel	720-8611
New Seoul Hotel	735-9071/9
Pacific Hotel	777-7811/9
President Hotel	753-3131/9
Seoul Palace Hotel	532-0101
Seoul Royal Hotel	771-45
Seoulin Hotel	722-0181/8
Tower Hotel	253-9181/9
Yoido Hotel	782-0121/5

Seoul Second Class:

Astoria Hotel	276-7111/16

Bukak Park Hotel	734-7102/8
Central Hotel	265-4121/9
Empire Hotel	777-5511/9
Hamilton Hotel	794-0171/9
Metro Hotel	776-6781/8
New Kukje Hotel	732-0161/9
New Naija Hotel	723-9011/5
New Oriental Hotel	753-0701/6
Savoy Hotel	776-2641/51
Seoul Prince Hotel	752-7111/9
Seoul Rex Hotel	752-3191/4
Seoul Tourist Hotel	725-9001
Dehwa Tourist Hotel	265-9181/9

Seoul Third Class:

Academy House	993-6181/5
Eastern Hotel	764-4101/10
Hankang Tourist Hotel	453-5411
New Town Hotel	777-4251/8
Hotel New Yongson	795-0052/8
Chongji Tourist Hotel	265-6131/3
YMCA Tourist Hotel	732-8291/8
Boolim Hotel	965-0021

Pusan: (prefix 051)

Ae-rin Hostel	27-222/7
Arirang Hotel	463-5001
Bando Hotel	44-0561
Crown Hotel	69-1241
Dong Yang Hotel	22-1205
Ferry Hotel	463-0881
Haeundae Glory Hotel	72-8181/5
Kukdong Hotel	72-0081
Kukje Hotel	642-1330
Moon Hwa Hotel	66-8001
Paradise Beach Hotel	72-1461
Phoenix Hotel	22-8061
Plaza Hotel	463-5011
Pusan Hotel	23-4301
Royal Hotel	23-1051
Shin Shin Hotel	88-0195
Sarabol Hotel	463-3511
Tai Yang Hotel	43-8801
Tong Hae Hotel	53-1121
Tower Hotel	243-1001
UN Hotel	26-5181

Taegu: (prefix 053)

Daegu Soosung Hotel	763-7311
Dongsan Tourist Hotel	253-7711/6
Dong In Hotel	46-7211
Hanil Hotel	423-5001
New Yongsan Hotel	752-5551
Royal Hotel	23-9862
Tourist Center Hotel	45-0872

Cheju-do:

Cheju Grand Hotel*	(0641) 7-21312
Cheju KAL Hotel*	(0641) 6151
Cheju Hyatt Hotel*	5-2001
Cheju New-Plaza Hotel	(0641) 7-6161
Cheju Royal Hotel	(0641) 7-4161
Free Port Hotel (Seohai)	7-4111/40
Hotel Paradise Jeju	2-3111
Hotel Paradise Sogwipo	2-2161/7
Sogwipo Lions Hotel	2-4141/4

FOOD DIGEST

WHAT TO EAT

Pul Koki Jip (Barbecue Meat Restaurant): Beef (*so-koki*) and pork (*toechi-koki*) and short ribs (*kal bi*) are marinated in soy sauce, sesame oil, garlic, green onions, and toasted sesame seeds, then charbroiled.

Saengson Hoe Jip (Raw Fish Restaurant): Fresh raw fish is served sliced with a soy sauce (*kanchang*) or red pepper sauce (*cho-chang*). Other kinds of fish dishes such as *maeun t'ang* (hot pepper soup of fish, soybean curd, egg, and vegetables) are served.

Samgyae T'ang Jip (Ginseng Chicken Dish Restaurant): Chicken stuffed with rice, white ginseng, and dried oriental dates are steamed and served hot. Deep-fried chicken and other chicken dishes are also served.

Mandoo Jip (Dumplings Restaurant): Meat, vegetables, and sometimes soybean curd are stuffed into a dumpling and steamed, fried or boiled in a broth. Chinese-style cookie pastries baked in the restaurant fill the display window.

Poonsik Jip (Noodles Restaurant): Noodle dishes are the specialty but so are easily prepared rice dishes. Some of the popular dishes are *Momil kooksoo*, buckwheat noodles served with a sweet radish sauce; *Naengmyon*, cold potato flour or buckwheat flour noodles topped with sliced meat, vegetables, a boiled egg, and a pepper relish sauce and ice; *K'ong kooksoo*, wheat noodles in fresh soymilk; *Odaeng kooksoo*, wheat noodles topped with oriental fishcake in a broth; *Ramyon*, instant noodles in instant broth; *Udong*, long, wide wheat noodles with onions, fried soybean curd, red pepper powder, and egg; *Pipim-pap*, rice topped with parboiled fern bracken, bluebell root, soysprouts, spinach, and a sunny-side-up egg, accompanied with a bowl of broth; and *Chap Chae*, rice vermicelli stir-fried with vegetables and meat slices.

Paekpan Jip (Steamed Rice Restaurant): A bowl of rice is served with a variety of *kimch'i*, *namul* (parboiled vegetables), fish, and soup (usually made of soybean paste—the basic Korean meal. Other simple dishes, such as *naengmyon* and *pipim-pap* are often on the menu. In the evening, the *paekpan jip* switches into a *makkolli* jip (see Drinking section).

Posin T'ang Jip: *Posin-hada* means to build up one's strength. *Posin t'ang* is dog meat soup, a delicacy to the people.

Other popular Korean dishes include:

Sinsullo: chopped vegetables, meat, quail egg, fish balls, and gingko nuts in a brazier.

Sollong t'ang: rice in a beef and bone stew.

Pindaettiok: the Korean bean flour and egg pancake, filled with different combinations of vegetables and meat.

Roadside Carts: Roadside canopied carts lit in the evening with kerosene tapers serve *soju* along with *anju* specialties that vary from steaming mussels and broiled clams to fried chicken and pork. Prices are reasonable, starting at w100 for a bowl of mussels, and the environment is cozy—warm and convivial. Some carts are set up at lunchtime, but most will begin business at nightfall.

Chinese Shantung restaurants are as popular as Korean restaurants. They are designated by a red or green door plaque draped with a red strip of cloth. Homemade wheat noodles with various sauces make for a slurpy meal, *Tchajangmyon* is a popular order: pork, seafood, and vegetable tidbits stir fried in a sweet-sour black bean sauce, and topped with a boiled egg. Larger Chinese restaurants have a more varied menu that includes delicacies such as sweet-sour fried fish and meat.

Japanese restaurants complete with *suchi* (layer-covered rice rolls), *sashimi* (raw fish), and *tempura* (deep-fried batter-covered fish and vegetables) bars are scattered all over Seoul, and are even more common in the southern port of Pusan.

DRINKING NOTES

Tearooms (Tabang): *Tabang* (or *tasil*) is one of the most common signs in any Korean town. Koreans go to the *tabang* for everything but tea (in fact, the tea is free) or coffee. It is where businessmen strike deals, where students practice English with "native speakers," where friends gather to gossip, joke, and listen to music, and where lovers tryst. It is also where the honk, grind and smoke of the city is rivaled—but nobody complains. A cup of thin coffee is but a token to hours of socializing. The *tabang* has become a vital institution in contemporary Korean culture; a meeting hall outside the home and office for young and old, male and female. And with eight million souls in the capital alone, there is always room for one more tearoom to open above, below, or next to all the others.

Unlike teahouses or coffeeshops elsewhere, the Korean *tabang* provides a personal delivery service: a girl dressed in a uniform will deliver a hot cup of coffee in a scarf-wrapped thermos bottle to customers who call in orders and clearly indicate their whereabouts.

THINGS TO DO

TOUR PACKAGES

KTB Tours: the Korea Tourist Bureau offers tours to Panmunjom, the Folk Village, Kyongju and Pusan, Kyongju, and around Seoul by day or night.

Reservation counters can be found at the Hotel Lotte (tel: 778-0150), the Chosun Hotel (tel: 755-0207), the Hyatt (tel: 798-0681), the Shilla (tel: 295-3731), Hotel Koreana (tel: 724-2930), the Hilton (tel: 754-7380), the Ambassador (tel: 269-5675), and Sheraton Walker-Hill (tel: 444-3865). The main office number in Kangnamgu is (tel: 585-1191).

Tours to Panmunjom must be reserved 48 hours in advance with full name, nationality and passport number.

The trip, including lunch and a "briefing," takes eight hours and kids under 10 years of age are not admitted. Travelers must wear good clothes and pointing at the DMZ or speaking with north Korean officers at the DMZ is strictly forbidden. Buses leave Monday through Friday from the Lotte Hotel, but guests registered at the Chosun can be picked up there as well.

NIGHTLIFE

Makkolli Jip: The common bar or pub is a simple cafe which serves a variety of refined rice wines and beer. *Anju* (hors d'oevres) are served at an additional cost in most places. The cheapest liquor is *soju* (sweet potato wine). *Makkolli* (rice wine), however, is the most popular people's drink and is poured from a teapot or unique clear plastic *makkolli* bottle. Other expensive grades of booze such as *popchu* (popular in Kyongju) and *ch'ungchong* (the drink of ch'onju) are also available in some Seoul pubs.

Beer Halls: Crown and OB (Oriental brewery) *maekchu* are the only beers brewed locally. They come either bottled (*pyong*) or draft (*saeng*). Because of a high tax on beer, beer halls are more expensive drinking joints than *makkolli jip*. *Auju*, too, are comparably pricier but are nevertheless customarily ordered.

Cabarets: Often located in narrow alleyways in Mugyodong and Myong-dong in Seoul, cabarets are easy to notice because of the loud band music, neon signs and/or bow-tied doormen attempting to lure in passers-by. Dance hostesses inside do their part and expect a tip of at least w5,000 for their efforts. Highballs and beer are served. Patronize these *jip* with caution or with a good Korean friend. Closing time is usually 11 p.m. Salons are exclusive cabarets in a tidier setting (which customers pay for).

Nightclubs and Discos: Major western-style hotels have their own nite-clubs and discotheques. Drinks are taxed high in hotels. In Seoul there are a few disco-nightclubs in Myong-dong and It'aewon. Some are taxed high; e.g. a w3,000 bottle of beer is cheap. It'aewon discos cater mostly to Gls from the nearby U.S. 8th Army

Compound. Blues, jazz and rock music are spun.

Casinos: Blackjack, anyone? There are casinos in five hotels where one can gamble at roulette, poker, baccarat, craps, dice, *tai-sai* and other games of chance. Casino business hours differ from hotel to hotel. These gaming parlors are located at the following places:

Sheraton Walker Hill (Seoul)
Kwangchang-dong
Tel: 453-0121

Olympos (Inch'on)
Hang-dong
Tel: (032) 762-5181

Haeundae (Pus'an)
Tongnae-ke
Tel: (051) 72-0081

Song Ri San
198 Sanae-ri Naesonghi-myon
Tel: (0433) 2091

Cheju KAL (Cheju-do)
Ido l-ka-dong
Tel: (064) 53-6153

Cheju Hyatt
Sogwipo
Tel: (064) 32-2001

SHOPPING

WHAT TO BUY

Korea's unique arts and crafts and the towns which traditionally produce the best of particular products are:

Bamboo craft	Tamyang
Hemp cloth	Hansan, Andong
Lacquerware	Wonju
Oriental paper	Chongju
Pottery	Ich'on
Porcelain	Ansong
Rushcraft	Kanghwa City
Silk	Ch'unch'on, Kanghwa City
Brassware	Ansong, Taegu

SHOPPING AREAS

Popular merchandise and where to shop for them in Seoul include:

Brassware
It'aewon

Antiques
Ahyon-dong, Insa-dong Chugang Sijang (Central market). It'aewon

Boutique goods
Myong-dong, Idac-ap

Calligraphy paint brushes
Insa-dong, Kyonji-dong

Silk Brocade
Tongdae-mun Sijang (2nd floor), Chong-no 2-ka, Myong-dong (K'o Silk Shop)

Oriental paper
Insa-dong, Kyongji-dong

Korean Costumes
Tongdae-mun Sijang, and most other marketplaces

Topaz, "smokey topaz," amethyst, jade
underground arcades

Sweatsuits and athletic shoes and gear
It'aewon, Namdae-mum Sijang (across the Tokyo Hotel)

Korean cushions and blankets
Insa-dong, marketplaces

Custom-tailored men's suits
Hotels, Myong-dong

Name seals (custom-made name seals in stylistic characters carved of hard wood, stone, etc.)
along the busy streets

Korean herbal medicine
Chong-no 5-ka, Chong-no 6-ka

One needn't even go outside of Seoul to find these things. Huge marketplaces and alleys unfold bounteous displays that exhaust most shoppers. Department stores help narrow down the choices somewhat. Major Seoul shopping areas outside central city hotels are:

Lotte
Namdaemun 2-ga
Tel: 771-25

Shinsegye
Chungmuro 1-ga
Tel: 754-1234

Midopa
Namdaemun 2-ga
Tel: 754-2222

Saerona
Namchange-dong
Tel: 778-8171

New Core
Panpodong
Tel: 533-1001

Youngdong
Nonhyundong
Tel: 544-3000

UNDERGROUND ARCADES

Specialty shops can be found in underground shopping malls. Don't let the price tags intimidate you from bargaining. The larger more centrally located arcades are:

Namdaemun Arcade
Myong-dong Arcade
Sogong Arcade
Hangram Arcade
Ulchi-ro Arcade
Lotte Center 1st Avenue Arcade
Arcade Bando-Chosun

MARKETPLACES

Seoul marketplaces run on for blocks. Anyone who has anything to sell is there—from the button merchant to the antique dealer, rice cake *ajumoni*, and including *chige* (A-frame), bicycle and Kimaster delivery men. And haggling shoppers.

The distinguishing feature of Korean markets, however, is that shops with the same goods tend to group together—even set up the same way. Merchants say they are not hurt by competition caused by the close proximity; instead, the area becomes known for specializing in, say, second-hand books, sinks or antiques. Most things can be found at all of the markets.

SPORTS

Volleyball, soccer, basketball, tennis, table tennis, baseball, swimming, shooting, wrestling, gymnastics, and track and field are some of the western sports that have been integrated with Korean sports and are enthusiastically supported. Korea first participated in the World Olympic Games in 1946 in London. These days, athletes train at an indoor 18-acre camp at T'aenung on the eastern outskirts of Seoul. Sports facilities at T'aenung include an indoor swimming pool, shooting range, and gymnasiums for wrestling, boxing and weight-lifting. All kinds of sports events take place at the Olympic Sports Complex in Chamsil which was built for the 1988 Seoul Olympics. The stadium here has a seating capacity of 100,000 and there are facilities for a wide range of games.

MARTIAL ARTS

Other sports which draw wide attention and participation by visitors are martial arts. *T'aekwon-do*, literally the way of combat kicking and punching is a martial art exercise that has been developing in Korea for more than 2,000 years. It focuses on the combined strengths of body, mind, and spirit in devastating fist and foot blows. This empty hand-fighting technique was originally learned from China during the T'ang dynasty and has been developed since the Three Kingdoms Period (post 650 AD) into the form in which it is practiced today.

The National T'aekwon-do Association has a membership of 80 nations. In Korea, students train at some 1,100 centers. The World T'aekwon-do Federation (tel: 566-2505) is headquartered at Kukki-won, the main t'aekwon-do practice gymnasium in the southern outskirts of Seoul. Regular exhibitions are staged there for tourists.

Yusul ("soft art"), another martial art, was introduced from China to the Korea Royal court in 1150, but declined in popularity by the 17th Century. It was a characteristically passive defense which consisted of throwing, choking or blocking an aggressor. *Yusul* was taught to the Japanese, who called it *judo* and was later reintroduced to Korea during the Japanese Occupation when it was restyled and called *yudo*. It is now a compulsory martial art for Korean policemen. There are many national *yudo* centers, including a *yudo* college in Seoul.

Ssirum, Korean wrestling was introduced by the Mongol invaders during the Koryo Period. Once a form of self-defense, *ssirum* today is a simple folk sport for students and villages. Contestants hold each other around the back and wrap a cloth strip around their opponent's thigh and try to throw each other down using leg, hand, and body maneuvers. *Ssirum* matches are held during Tano and Ch'usok (spring and autumn festivals, respectively). Western wrestling is taking a firm hold on Koreans, since their enthusiasm was fueled by a major victory in the 1976 Montreal Olympics (in the featherweight freestyle event).

LANGUAGE

Korean *han'gul* is romanized in two ways: by the Ministry of Education system and by the McCune-Reischauer system, an internationally recognized romanization scheme. Both romanizations are used in literature, maps, and signs, which can confuse those unacquainted with the language. Learning the Korean alphabet, which is simple, would prove most beneficial, especially for the lone traveler.

Provided below are commonly used questions and statements romanized according to the McCune-Reischauer system. No matter what village, town or city in Korea you visit, you should be able to survive with the following common questions and statements. At least this simple lesson will lead you to a taxi, bus or train station, and then to food, shelter and a hot bath.

NUMERAL SYSTEM

The following is a list of basic numbers and their Korean pronunciation:

1	*Il*
2	*Ed*
3	*Sam*
4	*Sa*
5	*O*
6	*Yuk*
7	*Ch'il*
8	*P'al*
9	*Ku*
10	*Sip*
11	*Sip-il*
20	*Ee-sip*
30	*Sam-sip*
40	*Sa-sip*
50	*O-sip*
60	*Yuk-sip*
70	*Ch'il-sip*
80	*P'al-sip*
90	*Ku-sip*
100	*Paek*
200	*Ee-paek*
300	*Sam-paek*
567	*O-paek yuk-sip ch'il*
1,000	*Ch'on*
2,000	*Ee-ch'on*
4,075	*Sa-ch'on cho'il-sip o*
10,000	*Man*
13,900	*Man Sam-ch'on ku-back*

PHRASES

the airport
Konghwang

the subway
chi-hach'o

the taxi
taeksi

Seoul train station
Seoul yok

express bus terminal
Kosok t' ominal

the ticket office
p' yo p' a-nun kos-i

entrance
ipku

exit
ch' ulku

the public bathhouse or private bathroom
mogyok t' ang

the restroom
hwajang-sil

the restaurant
sik-tang, umsik-chom

the tea or coffee house
tabang

the bank
unbaeng

the hotel
hotel

a good Korean inn
cho-un yogwan

the post office
uch' e-guk

the embassy
tasea-kwan

International Telecommunication Office
Kukche-Chonsin-chonhwakuk

Please bring me some ____
____*chom katta ju-seyo.*

beer
maekchu

Cold drinking water
naeng su

hot water (for bathing)
ttuga-un mul

barley tea
pori ch'a

How many kilometers is it from here?
Yogi-so myot kilo im-nikka?

How long does it take to go there?
Olmana Killimnikka?

It takes _________.
_____ *kollimnida.*

30 minutes
samsip-pun

1 hour
han si-gan

Please call a taxi for me.
Taeksi jom pullo ju-seyo.

Just a moment, please.
Cham-kkan man kitari-seyo.

Please go straight.
Ttok paro ka-seyo.

Please stop here.
Sewo ju-seyo.

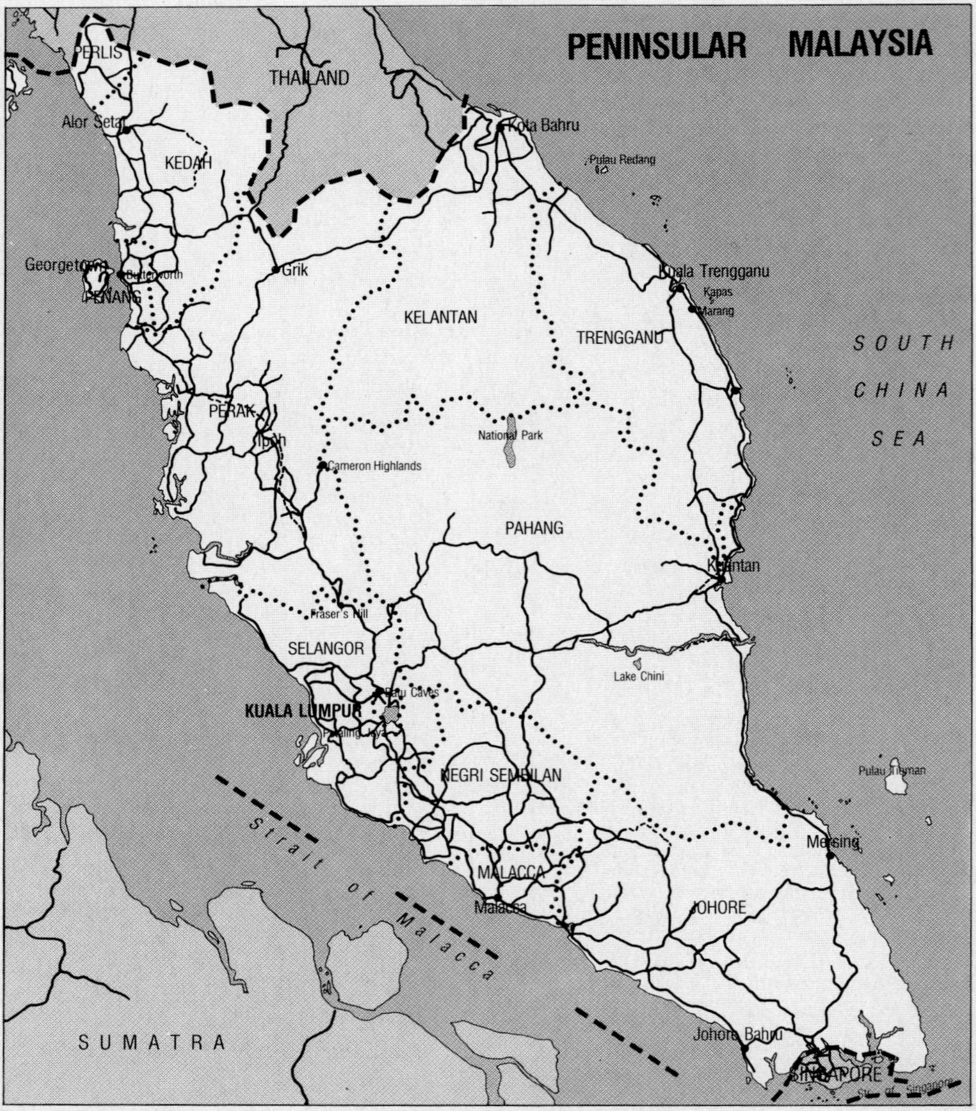

PENINSULAR MALAYSIA
PERLIS
THAILAND
Alor Setar
Kota Bahru
Pulau Redang
KEDAH
Georgetown
Butterworth
PENANG
Grik
Kuala Trengganu
Kapas
Marang
KELANTAN
TRENGGANU
SOUTH CHINA SEA
PERAK
Ipoh
National Park
Cameron Highlands
PAHANG
Kuantan
Fraser's Hill
SELANGOR
Lake Chini
Batu Caves
KUALA LUMPUR
Petaling Jaya
Pulau Tioman
NEGRI SEMBILAN
Strait of Malacca
Mersing
MALACCA
Malacca
JOHORE
SUMATRA
Johore Bahru
SINGAPORE
Strait of Singapore

EAST MALAYSIA
Kota Kinabalu (Jesselton)
Mount Kinabalu
Tanjong Aru
Sepilok Sanctuary
Sandakan
Labuan (Victoria)
Bandar Seri Begawan
BRUNEI
SABAH
Miri
Niah
Niah Caves
Bintulu
MALAYSIA
SARAWAK
Sibu
Bako National Park
Kuching
MALAYSIA

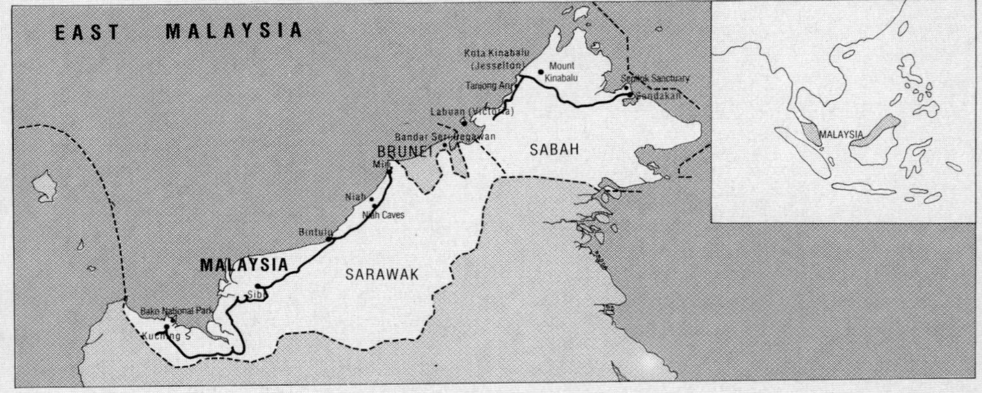

GETTING THERE

BY AIR

Few first sights in Malaysia can compete with the elegant M$52 million international airport that greets air passengers at Kuala Lumpur. Its bold design came as such a novelty to the sleepy landscape of Subang, 14 miles (22 km) from the city center, that several myopic citizens ran into trouble. "The first victim," reported a newspaper several days after the official opening in 1965, "was an airport porter who walked right into a glass pane at the north arrival hall. He injured his nose but did not break the pane which is quite strong and thick."

Kuala Lumpur's airport serves about 20 international airlines linking key cities of the world to Malaysia and providing the country with more than 90 percent of her visitors. Nearest international connections are with Singapore, a pleasant 35-minute flight away, and with Bangkok, an hour and 20 minutes away. Malaysia's capital is also accessible by air from Sabah and Sarawak or Penang Island to the north.

BY SEA

Sailors first glimpse Malaysia from bustling Port Klang (previously called Port Swettenham), 26 miles (42 km) west of Kuala Lumpur, or from the historic port of Penang, an ancient sanctuary for those once escaping the wrath of mainland lords. A number of cargo-cum-passenger ships and cruise liners call regularly at both ports.

BY LAND

Train tracks have a legacy in Malaysian lore. An inscription along the railway 3 miles (5 km) from Telok Anson reads: "There is buried here a wild elephant who in defense of his herd charged and derailed a train on the 17th day of September 1894." Though elephants have ceased being so chivalrous, smooth tracks still cut through the jungles roamed by wildlife, making train travel a chance to peek into the forested hinterland without having to slow down.

The more casual traveler can pick up a "shared" taxi at Johore Bahru, just across the causeway from Singapore, and settle down to a six-hour drive to Kuala Lumpur, without spending more than M$20. The secret of the bargain is that four or five passengers share one taxi. Bus fares are more reasonable on the air-conditioned express to Kuala Lumpur departing Singapore daily from the New Bridge Road fringe car park at 9 a.m. for the eight-hour ride. They also do a service up the East Coast.

TRAVEL ESSENTIALS

VISAS & PASSPORTS

Valid passports and a health certificate of vaccination against yellow fever are required, if traveling from an infected area. Citizens of countries enjoying diplomatic relations with Malaysia do not need a visa for a 14-day stay, which may be extended up to a three months' visit. However, this courtesy does not apply to citizens of communist countries, Israel, or South Africa, who must have visas to enter Malaysia.

MONEY MATTERS

The Malaysian dollar is a sound currency which has been in circulation since 1957, and at time of press, it is valued at around US$0.37. Singapore and Brunei dollars are of somewhat greater value, and no longer circulate freely in Malaysia. The importation of traveler's checks and letters of credit is unlimited. Visitors are allowed to bring in or take out with them any amount of Malaysian currency. It is much easier to take out cash if it has been declared upon arrival. Malaysians call their dollar the *ringgit*.

Banks offer better rates, and so do money changers with offices in downtown shop houses. If you are not is a rush, avoid changing money in the arcades of luxury hotels, since many of these shops levy a service charge by offering lower exchange rates: usually two to four percent. Deal directly with a bank or a licensed money changer and have plenty of local currency on hand when traveling to small towns and in rural areas.

In the more flashy, chic quarters of the larger towns—in department stores, shops, first-class restaurants and hotels—traveler's checks change hands easily. Bring your passport along when cashing traveler's checks: a formality which must be observed before heading off the beaten track where such checks are unacceptable. Established credit cards—Diner's Club, American Express, Carte Blanche—are honored in the major cities. Several hotel chains maintain their own credit card system. But when traveling through Malaysia, nothing could be better than the coin of the realm.

HEALTH

Travelers have few worries in a country the health standards of which are ranked among the highest in Asia.

Water is generally safe for drinking, but it is safest to drink boiled water, tea, coffee, or bottled beverages. Coffee shops in small towns sell fresh fruits and bottled drinks. Fresh hot food, cooked on the spot, has made *nasi goreng* (fried rice) and *mee goreng* (fried noodles) the local equivalents of hot dogs and meat pie.

WHAT TO WEAR

Light, cool, comfortable clothes, for both men and women, fare well in Malaysia where informal styles prevail throughout the year. *Batik* cotton fashions, on sale everywhere, are an easy "in" to local color. Well-worn airy shoes or sandals are a favor to the feet. For some formal occasions, men may be requested to dine in suits and ties; but sport shirts are otherwise the ubiquitous Malaysian style for anything from cocktails to floor shows. Ladies are at liberty to take any hint from Vogue's summer pages, though when visiting mosques and outlaying Malay villages, women should dress modestly. Shorts, tiny T-shirts and mini-skirts have yet to win acceptance in Asian towns and villages.

CUSTOMS

Import duties seldom affect the average traveler, who may bring in 250 grams of tobacco or cigars, or 200 cigarettes and one quart bottle of liquor duty free. Used portable articles are normally exempted from import tax. Narcotics, pornography, daggers, and walkie-talkies are strictly prohibited. Prominent "Death to drug traffickers" signs are everywhere.

GETTING ACQUAINTED

GOVERNMENT & ECONOMY

Malaysia is the official name of the former British colony of Malaya.

Independent since 1957, the Malaysian government is regulated by the Parliament comprising the Yang di-Pertuan Agong (King or Supreme Sovereign) and two Houses: the House of Representatives and the Senate. The executive functions of the government are carried out by the Cabinet, led by Datuk Seri Mahathir Mohamad who became Prime Minister in 1981.

The population of approximately 14.9 million comprises Malays (54 percent), Chinese (35 percent), and Indians and Pakistanis (10 percent), spread over 13 states. The capital city of Kuala Lumpur has approximately one million people.

Tin and rubber are the major export items, supplying 35 percent and 40 percent of the world's total output, respectively. Its major trading partners are Japan and the United States.

CLIMATE

A tropical sun and clouds laden with the makings of a sudden downpour compete for the skies of Malaysia, with the odds on the sun. Malaysia's seasons follow the monsoon winds, which splash rains inland from September to December on the West Coast of Peninsular Malaysia, only to be overtaken by sunshine within the hour. Rains arrive later on the East Coast of Peninsular Malaysia and in Sabah and Sarawak, where umbrellas sell well from October to February. Malaysia's weather, however, is generally warm, humid, and sunny all the year round. The highlands, both during the day and at night, and the lowlands in the evening are comfortably cooler, which may explain why Malaysia's night-life is liveliest outdoors.

BUSINESS HOURS

In an Islamic nation with a British colonial history, weekly holidays vary. In the former Federated States which were united under the British—Selangor, Malacca, Penang, Perak, Pahang and Negri Sembilan—there is a half-day holiday on Saturday and a full-day holiday on Sunday. The former Unfederated States, which remained semi-autonomous under British rule—Johore, Kedah, Perlis, Trengganu, and Kelantan—retain the traditional half-day holiday on Thursday and full-day holiday on Friday. Saturday and Sunday are treated as weekdays.

In all government institutions, the workday begins at 8:15 a.m. and ends at 4:15 p.m., with time off on Fridays from noon to 2:30 p.m. for communal *Jumaat* prayers at the mosques. Most private business stick to the nine-to-five routine. Shops start to close at 6 p.m. Large department stores keep their cash registers ringing past 9 p.m.

GETTING AROUND

DOMESTIC TRAVEL

By Air: Since Malaysian Airline System (MAS) first took to the skies in 1972 as the national flag carrier, it has come a long way in providing services not only to international cities but also between cities within Malaysia. Its fleet flies from Kuala Lumpur to Alor Star, Penang, Kota Bharu, Kuala Trengganu, Kuantan, Ipoh, Malacca, Johore Bahru, Kota Kinabalu, Kuching and vice-versa. In Sabah and Sarawak, internal air transport is just as efficient and regular too. Daily scheduled return flights connect towns like Kota Kinabalu with Labuan, Lahad Datu, Sandakan, Tawau, Bintulu, Kuching, Miri, Semporna, Tomanggong, Pamol, Kudat, Keningau, Ranau, Long Semadoh, Lawas, Limbang, Bario, Long Seridan, Marudi, Mukah Sibu, Kapit, Belaga, Simanggang, Bakalalan, Long Sukang and Long Lellang. Special economy tourist flights are also available from Kuala Lumpur to Penang, Kota Kinabalu, Kuching, Johore Bahru and Kota Bharu; and from these towns back to Kuala Lumpur.

A visitor must bear in mind, however, the visit passes issued for entry into the Malay Peninsula do not automatically entitle the holder entry into Sabah and/or Sarawak. A different pass must be obtained before setting out.

BY RAIL

The main railway line runs right from Singapore in the south to Thailand in the north, passing through the entire Malay Peninsula with stations at major principal cities and towns such as Johore Bahru, Kuala Lumpur, Gemas, Segamat, Ipoh and Butterworth. Another line branches off from this main one at Gemas to run northeast to Tumpat on the east coast. On these two lines, more than a dozen trains run throughout the day and into the night. Passengers can choose from air-conditioned first-class coaches in the day trains and first-class cabins with single or double berths in the night trains. For the casual traveler, sleeping berths are available in the second-class and sleeperettes in the third-class coaches.

The Malayan Railway—or Keretapi Tanah Melayu, as it is called—is known for its punctuality. Many tourists have touted it as one of the few in Asia which keeps to published times of arrivals.

WATER TRANSPORT

Traditionally, transport in Malaysia, particularly in the west, was by water. River transport, however, is no longer so important as a means of getting around within the country.

Several ferry services still exist, however. They cater to both passengers and motor vehicles. The most important service operates between Penang Island and Butterworth on the mainland.

Other services include that from Kuala Perlis to Pulau Langkawi in Malaysia's extreme northwest; from Lumut to Pangkor Island; and a longboat service from Labuan to Menumbuk in Sabah. Longboats have a capacity for 12 passengers and they depart only when there are sufficient passengers.

PUBLIC TRANSPORT

Buses: Most of the principal cities have their own regular scheduled bus services. Inter-state long-distance travel by bus is common, as it is reliable and relatively cheap.

The MARA Express has regular services connecting Kuala Lumpur and Singapore in about seven hours for M$16 (air-conditioned) or M$12 (non air-conditioned).

Taxis: Taxis remain one of the more popular and cheap means of transport, especially on a shared basis. You can hail them by the roadside, hire them from authorized taxi stands, or book them by telephone calls. In the latter case, the mileage is calculated from the stand or garage from which the vehicle is hired.

Trishaws: This is the most novel mode of transport recommended for short trips.

Except in Penang, where passengers are seated on a sun-hooded carriage in front of the cyclist or pedaler, a trishaw is a bicycle with a side carriage for the passengers.

PRIVATE TRANSPORT

Rent-a-car: You'd rather drive yourself around? You may, if you possess a valid international driving licence (a foreign licence has to be appropriately endorsed by the Ministry of Road Transport). You must be at least 23 years old but not more than 60.

Most of the international rent-a-car agencies have offices here. Rental cost is calculated on a per-day or per-week basis; it ranges from M$34 to M$165 per day and from M$204 to M$900 per week. Collection and delivery service is usually free if within city limits. Some firms levy a repositioning charge if you wish to "rent it here, leave it there." Motorcycles can also be rented from some of these agencies.

Motoring Advisories: Malaysia's road system is extensive and has some of the finest metal-surfaced rubberized highways in Southeast Asia, covering a total distance of 18,560 miles (29, 934 km). The main trunk road in West Malaysia runs northwards from Singapore to the Thai border. The East-West Highway is a recently completed project which connects Butterworth in Penang to Kota Bharu in Kelantan.

During the monsoon season from December to January, heavy rains may make road travel between Kuala Trengganu and Kota Bharu in the northeast difficult.

The road network in East Malaysia (Sabah and Sarawak) covers some 2,678 miles (4,320 km) of metal-surfaced roads. These roads are found mostly along the coastline and connect the major towns.

WHERE TO STAY

ACCOMMODATIONS

One may sleep in Malaysia in numerous styles: enamored by the old-fashioned elegance of a colonial lodge; tucked in a sleeping bag in an alpine mountain hut; soothed by Chinese singsong in a tiny hotel in midtown; or serenaded by the crickets outside the family guestroom of a Dayak longhouse in Sarawak.

Accommodations leave themselves wide open to personal preference. Most Malaysian small towns do not offer the cosmopolitan facilities of a worldwide hotel chain, but they do provide the personal touch, simplicity, and cleanliness of a wayside inn. Nearly every prominent city in the country has a comfortable Government Rest House offering convenient accommodation to visitors traveling through rural Malaysia. A typical urban street is dotted with small budget hotels renting simply furnished rooms for around M$10 to M$20.

KELANTAN

Hotel Perdana
Jln. Mahmud.
Tel: 09-785000.

Pantai Cinta Berahi Resort
Pantai Cinta Berahi.
Tel: 09-781307.

Temenggong Hotel
Jln. Tok Hakim.
Tel: 09-783130.

KUALA LUMPUR

Dashrun Hotel
285, Jln. Tuanku Abdul Rahman, K.L.
Tel: 03-292-9314, 292-9271

Equatorial Hotel
Jln. Sultan Ismail, K.L.
Tel: 03-261-7777.

Federal Hotel
Jln. Bukit Bintang, K.L.
Tel: 03-248-9166.

Fortuna Hotel
Jln. Berangan, K.L.
Tel: 03-241-9166.

Furama Hotel
Jln. Sultan, K.L.
Tel: 03-230-1777.

Grand Central Hotel
Jln. Raja Laut, K.L.
Tel: 03-441-3021.

Holiday Inn On The Park K.L.
P O Box 10983,
Jalan Pinang 50732 K.L.
Tel: 03-248-1066

Hotel Grand Pacific
Jln. Tun Ismail/Jln. Ipoh, K.L.
Tel: 03-442-2177.

Hotel Malaya
Jln. Hang Lekir, K.L.
Tel: 03-232-7722.

Kuala Lumpur Hilton Hotel
Jln. Sultan Ismail, K.L.
Tel: 03-242-2122.

Kuala Lumpur International Hotel
Jln. Raja Muda, K.L.
Tel: 03-292-9133.

Kuala Lumpur Mandarin Hotel
Jln. Sultan, K.L.
Tel: 03-230-3000.

Kuala Lumpur Merlin Hotel
Jln. Sultan Ismail, K.L.
Tel: 03-248-0033.

Malaysia Hotel
Jln. Bukit Bintang, K.L.
Tel: 03-242-8033.

Ming Court Hotel
Jln. Ampang, K.L.
Tel: 03-261-8888.

Mirama Hotel
Jln. Birch (Maharajalela), K.L.
Tel: 03-2489122.

Pan Pacific Kuala Lumpur
Jln. Putra, K.L.
Tel: 03-339-6322.

Plaza Hotel
Jln. Raja Laut, K.L.
Tel: 03-298-2255.

Shangri-La Hotel
Jln. Sultan Ismail, K.L.
Tel: 03-232-2388.

Shiraz Hotel
1 & 3 Jln. Medan Tuanku, K.L.
Tel: 03-292-0159.

Hotel South East Asia
Jln. Haji Hussein, K.L.
Tel: 03-292-6077.

Sungei Wang Hotel
Jln. Bukit Bintang, K.L.
Tel: 03-248-5255.

The Lodge
Jln. Sultan Ismail, K.L.
Tel: 03-242-0122.

The Regent of Kuala Lumpur
Jln. Sultan Ismail, K.L.
Tel: 03-242-5588.

Wisma Belia
40 Jln. Lornie, K.L.
Tel: 03-232-6803.

YMCA
Jln. Kandang Kerbau,
Brickfields, K.L.
Tel: 03-274-1439.

Jln. Davidson, K.L.
Tel: 03-298-2177.

MALACCA

Hotel Admiral
Jln. Mata Kuching.
Tel: 06-226822.

Malacca Straits Inn
Jln. Bandar Hilir.
Tel: 06-221101.

Malacca Village Resort
Ayer Keroh.
Tel: 06-323600.

Merlin Inn Malacca
Bangunan Woo Hoe Kan,
Jln. Munshi Abdullah.
Tel: 06-240777.

Ramada Renaissance Hotel
Jln. Bendahara.
Tel: 06-248888.

Regal Hotel
Jln. Munshi Abdullah.
Tel: 06-222433.

Shah's Beach Hotel
Tanjung Kling.
Tel: 06-226222.

PAHANG

Club Mediterranee
Cherating.
Tel: 09-591131.

Fosters Lakehouse
Ringlet, Cameron Highlands.
Tel: 05-996152.

Fraser's Hill Development Corp.
Holiday Bungalows
Fraser's Hill.
Tel: 093-382201.

Genting Hotel
Genting Highlands Resort.
Tel: 03-211-1118.

Highlands Hotel
Genting Highlands Resort.
Tel: 03-211-2812.

Hotel Samudra
Teluk Cempedak, Kuantan.
Tel: 09-21711.

Hyatt Kuantan
Teluk Cempedak, Kuantan.
Tel: 09-25211.

Merlin Hotel
Fraser's Hill.
Tel: 09-382300.

Merlin Hotel
Tanah Rata, Cameron Highlands.
Tel: 05-941205.

Merlin Hotel
Teluk Cempedak, Kuantan.
Tel: 09-522388.

Pelangi Hotel
Genting Highlands Resort.
Tel: 03-211-3813.

Samudra Hotel
Jln. Besar, Kuantan.
Tel: 09-522688.

Strawberry Park
Tanah Rata, Cameron Highlands.
Tel: 05-941166.

Tioman Island Resort
Tioman Island.
Tel: 09-445444.

Ye Olde Smokehouse Hotel
Brinchang, Tanah Rata,
Cameron Highlands.
Tel: 05-941214.

PENANG

Casuarina Beach Hotel
Batu Ferringhi.
Tel: 04-811711.

Continental Hotel
Jln. Penang.
Tel: 04-26381.

E & O Hotel
Farquhar Street.
Tel: 04-375322.

Garden Inn
Jln. Anson.
Tel: 04-363655.

Golden City Hotel
Lorong Kinta.
Tel: 04-27281.

Golden Sands Beach Resort
Batu Ferringhi.
Tel: 04-811911.

Holiday Inn Hotel
Batu Ferringhi.
Tel: 04-811601.

Merlin Hotel Penang
Jln. Burmah/Anson.
Tel: 04-376166.

Ming Court Hotel
MacAlister Road.
Tel: 04-26131.

YMCA
211, Jln. MacAlister.
Tel: 04-362211.

SABAH

Asia Hotel
Jln. Bandaran Berjaya,
Kota Kinabalu.
Tel: 088-53533.

Central Hotel
Jln. Tugu, Kota Kinabalu.
Tel: 088-53522.

Hotel Capital
Jln. Hj Saman, Kota Kinabalu.
Tel: 088-53433.

Hotel Perkasa Kundasang
Renau, Tawau.
Tel: 087-735811.

Hotel Shangri-La
Bandaran Berjaya, Kota Kinabalu.
Tel: 088-212800.

Hyatt Kinabalu International Hotel
Jln. Datuk Salleh Sulong,
Kota Kinabalu.
Tel: 088-219888.

SARAWAK

Aurora Hotel
McDougall Road.
Tel: 082-20281.

Borneo Hotel
Jln. Tabuan.
Tel: 082-244121.

Gloria Hotel
27, Brooke Road, Miri.
Tel: 085-36499/34773.

Government Rest House
Crookshank Road.
Tel: 082-242042.

Holiday Beach Hotel
Jln. Tanjung Batu.
Tel: 086-31622.

Holiday Inn Hotel
Jalan Tunku Abdul Rahman,
93100 Kuching.
Tel: 082-423111.

Sarawak Hotel
34, Cross Road, Sibu.
Tel: 084-33455.

SELANGOR

Dayang Hotel
Jln. Sultan, P.J.
Tel: 03-755-5011.

Merlin Subang Hotel
Jln. SS12/7, Subang Jaya.
Tel: 03-733-5211.

Petaling Jaya Hilton Hotel
Jln. Barat, P.J.
Tel: 03-755-9122.

Subang International Airtel
Subang Airport, Subang.
Tel: 03-774-2122.

TRENGGANU

Hotel Warisan
Jln. Paya Bunga.
Tel: 09-622688.

Pantai Primula Hotel
Jln. Persinggahan.
Tel: 09-622100.

Tanjung Jara Beach Hotel
Dungun.
Tel: 09-841801.

FOOD DIGEST

WHAT TO EAT

That Malaysia is a gourmet's delight is a threadbare statement. Variety begins not only with the different types of foods available but also with the flexibility in dining environments. Flexibility stretches from eating in a plush restaurant with a formal setting and attentive waiters, to the open-air roadside stalls.

During your stay, you should try to eat at these stalls, which are *the* place to try local specialties in home-cooked styles. The most hygienic of travelers is assured that it is perfectly safe to eat here, even though he may imagine his bowl of noodles being peppered by dust as cars whiz past.

The different peoples that comprise Malaysia's multi-racial population provide the country with enough tastes to please every palate. Of the different types of foods available, the most popular and unique are Malay, Chinese and Indian.

MALAY FOOD

Malay food is generally rich and spicy. Although each state has its distinctive style of preparation and taste, ingredients are common to all.

White steamed rice (*nasi*) is the staple grain. Ample use is made of seafood, chicken and meat. Coconut forms a basis for many dishes. The juice is refined drink and the meat is usually grated and squeezed to obtain coconut milk (*santan*). This gives a dish its taste and texture.

Perhaps the best known of Malay dishes is *satay*, slivers of barbecued beef or chicken dipped in hot peanut sauce. It is best eaten along with sliced cucumbers, onions and *ketupat* (steamed rice wrapped in coconut leaves).

Nasi padang is the best option for a filling meal of rice with a variety of curry dishes. Dishes are usually arranged on display at the stalls—there will be fish, beef and vegetable curries, among others—and customers select their meal from these.

The fingers of the diner's right hand are used to knead rice and spices before tucking them into this mouth. Nowadays a fork and spoon are common, though it is generally agreed that manual eating brings out the food's fullest flavor.

Other typical dishes worth trying include *tahu goreng*, fried cubes of soya bean curd and fresh sprouts with a spicy peanut dressing; *gado gado*, a salad of delicately steamed of raw vegetables, *laksa*, another type of spicy soup made of fine noodles and fish stock; *mee rebus*, boiled noodles; and *mee siam*, Thai-style noodles.

Of note is the local dessert *gula melaka*, made by topping sago with coconut milk and a syrup made of palm sugar—a guaranteed mouth-watering dish for the sweet tooth.

CHINESE FOOD

Chinese foods are found in abundance in Malaysia. You will do well to taste Teochew porridge, Hainanese chicken rice (rice cooked in chicken stock and served with delicately steamed chicken pieces), Hakka *yong tau foo* (beancurd stuffed with meat), Hokkien fried *mee* (noodles fried with pieces of meat, prawn and cuttlefish) and Chinese *laksa* (which differs from the Malay version).

INDIAN FOOD

Indian cooking is characterized by its complex and generous use of spices. With the exception of restaurants in big hotels which might modify their Indian dishes to cater to unaccustomed palates, Indian food here is just like what you would find in India. The crowning dish, most would agree, is the *nasi briyani*, a mixture of saffron and rose-water with rice steamed in milk and meat stock. An artificial yellow coloring gives this dish its other name, "yellow rice." For a greater variety of dishes at one sitting, one should try rice with various vegetables and meats.

Alternatively, these dishes can be eaten with *chapati*, an unleavened pancake, or *paratha*, a white flour dough. The Indian *rojak*—a selection of different foods like potatoes, eggs, cuttlefish, prawns and fish cake—is best eaten by dipping into a hot sweet-sour gravy.

At an outdoor eating place, one can usually eat both Chinese and Malay foods at the same meal, as stalls selling different types of food are usually neighbors.

But remember not to mix the cutlery from a Muslim stall with that of a Chinese. For example, do not use the fork from the *mee rebus* stall to eat your Chinese *laksa*.

Muslims consider pork an unclean food, and never will use it in their cooking. Chinese, on the other hand, use it in most of their dishes.

FRUITS OF THE LAND

Malaysia is a veritable Garden of Eden of fruits all the year round, but besides the all-time tropical favorites such as golden pineapples, rosy papaya, juicy water-melon and all sorts and sizes of bananas, there's a host of others your may not have seen before. Many are seasonal—all are delicious.

Durian is king of fruits to the Malaysian. Once you get pass the powerful smell, the taste is indescribably delicious. No two durians taste alike but some claim it is best likened to fruity-creamy-caramel.

Rambutans have marvelous hairy red-tinged-with-gold skins. The flesh is rather like lychees, juicy and sugar-sweet.

Mango comes long or rounded, green or yellow, and the golden flesh inside is soft, sweet and luscious.

Mangosteen is purple on the outside, white, sweet and juicy inside. The mangosteen ripens at the same time as the durian and they go well together. The Chinese believe that the "heatiness" or the durian is balanced by the "coolness" of the mangosteen.

Nangka or **Jackfruit** is the huge green fruit which you can often see on trees in the villages covered with sacks or paper bags to protect them from birds. The pulp is juicy and chewy at the same time. It can be eaten both raw and cooked and even the seeds are edible.

Starfruit, yellow and shiny, is a good thirst quencher. Cut it horizontally into star-shaped wedges and dip it in salt.

Pomelo looks and tastes like a sweet, overgrown, slightly dry grapefruit.

Buah Duku. To open a duku, just squeeze gently. The flesh is sweet and with a sour tinge. You'll probably eat dozens of dukus at one time, but watch out for the hard greenish center which can be bitter.

Buah Susu, literally translated "milk fruit," is better known as passion-fruit. There are many different varieties, all equally delicious. Crisp-skinned and orange from Indonesia, purple from Australia and California, but the local ones have soft, velvety yellow skins. The grey seeds inside are sweet and juicy.

SHOPPING

WHAT TO BUY

Where to buy? At modern multi-story shopping complexes, night markets (*pasar malam*), bazaars, fairs, sidewalk stalls, night-time lantern markets, special Saturday night markets, cottage industries where visitors buy handicrafts direct from the craftsmen, duty-free shops... the list goes on and on. There is certainly no shortage of places to shop.

But it is usually unwise to shop at a place you have been taken by a taxi driver or an unlicensed tourist guide: part of the price you pay for an article could well be the commission for you "guide."

It might be safer merely to wander around and choose a shop with window-shopping appeal.

BATIKS

Although *batik* printing did not originate here—it was first introduced from Indonesia some centuries ago—it has always been popular in Malaysia, especially in the state of Kelantan.

Nowadays, a great part of the industry has moved into sophisticated art salons and boutiques in Kuala Lumpur.

Batik printing is an art of fabric printing using wax-resistant dyes. A pattern is drawn on virgin fabric (once invariably cotton but now any material). Molten wax is applied to certain areas of the motif to protect them from contact with the dye.

After the first dyeing, the wax is boiled away. The process is repeated according to the number of colors desired. The result is dazzling prints with pure rich color and attractive designs.

Prices range widely depending on the type of material used, the exclusiveness of the design, and the number of colors used.

KAIN SONGKET

This is another kind of cloth which is distinctively Malay. It is a very luxurious materials—handwoven silk with gold or silver threads.

Often made into shawls or evening dresses, it can cost as much as M$500 a piece if rated first-class in terms of design, workmanship and material.

SILVERWORK

This is another cottage industry of Malaysia. Silver is daintily and delicately crafted into items like brooches, pendants, belts, jewelry boxes, bowls and rings by skilled artists.

In some places, visitors can watch these artists at their work. Kampong Sireh, a suburb of Kota Bharu, is one such place where it is possible to buy wares at factory prices and to have pieces made to order.

There is a large handicraft center in Kuala Lumpur (near the Tourist Information Office in Jalan Tun Perak) where a good range of jewelry and other items can be purchased.

PEWTERWARE

Products made from this 97 percent Straits-refined tin are widely regarded as good buys.

Vases, beer mugs, water jugs, trays and coffee/tea sets are some of the items into which the metal can be fashioned. It was in the factory at 231 Jalan Tunku Abdul Rahman, Kuala Lumpur, that *Selangor Pewter* made its debut as the world's finest pewter manufacturer.

KITES & TOPS

Kite flying and top spinning have been popular pastimes in Malaysia for as long as one can remember. Hence, here in Malaysia are some of the most skilled makers of kites and tops.

Even if you don't care tuppence for any of these two sports, you may purchase them for decorative and ornamental purposes from handicraft centers both on the east coast and in Kuala Lumpur. A large kite, for example, might be a good substitute for that conventional poster in your living room.

LANGUAGE

In Kuala Lumpur, chances are that the taxi driver knows a smattering of four languages. Among Malaysia's urban population, people shift tongues with neighborhoods. Malay is the national language, used officially in all government departments. English is widely spoken by people from all walks of life, along with the clicking sounds of Tamil, brought from South India, and a half dozen Chinese dialects—Cantonese and Hokkien predominating in the towns. A traveler can step into the most unlikely small town coffee shop and encounter a shopkeeper with a Senior Cambridge Certificate. Almost every village, however small, harbors a linguist. One way to find out who he or she is is to enter the nearest snack bar, order a soft drink and wait for the word to get around that a *turis* or *tamu* (guest) is in town. Eventually, the local translator will appear.

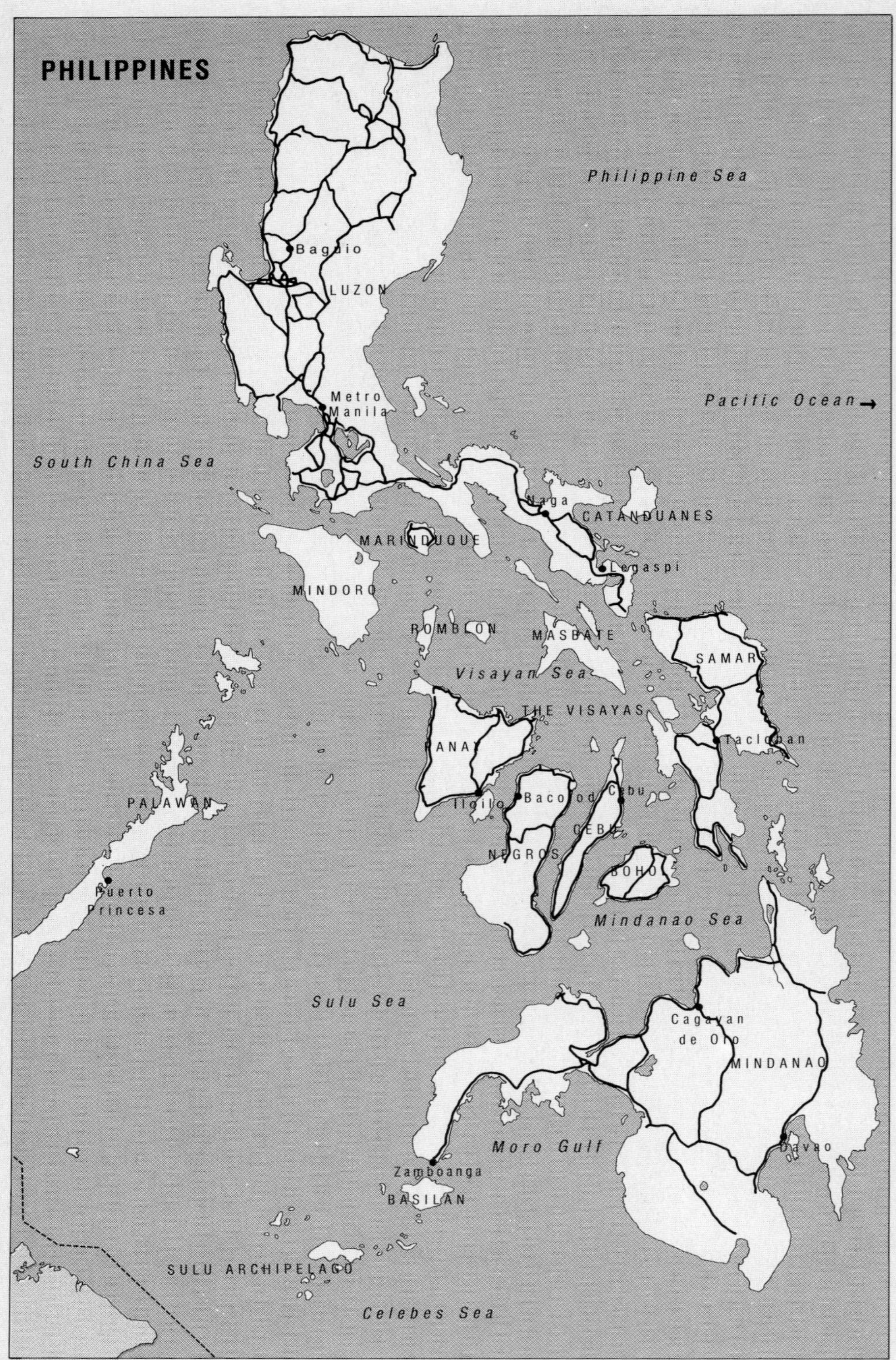
PHILIPPINES
Philippine Sea
Baguio
LUZON
Pacific Ocean
Metro
Manila
South China Sea
Naga
CATANDUANES
MARINDUQUE
Legaspi
MINDORO
ROMBLON
MASBATE
SAMAR
Visayan Sea
THE VISAYAS
PANAY
Tacloban
Iloilo
Bacolod
Cebu
PALAWAN
CEBU
NEGROS
BOHOL
Puerto
Princesa
Mindanao Sea
Sulu Sea
Cagayan
de Oro
MINDANAO
Moro Gulf
Davao
Zamboanga
BASILAN
SULU ARCHIPELAGO
Celebes Sea

GETTING THERE

BY AIR

The majority of visitors arrive and depart from Manila by air. Some 150 international flights arrive in Manila weekly. Manila International Airport and Domestic Terminal are centrally located. Mactan International Airport off Cebu in the South and Laoag International Airport in Ilocos Norte in the North also accommodate international flights.

BY SEA

Freighters and cruise ships take advantage of the excellent harbor of Manila Bay, although most travelers prefer to arrive by air. The government is adamant about protecting tourists from endangering themselves by traveling on small craft between East Malaysia (Borneo) and the country's southernmost islands. Muslim rebels and continuing piracy make this exotic route unadvisable.

TRAVEL ESSENTIALS

VISAS & PASSPORTS

All visitors to the Philippines must have valid passports. Citizens of countries with which the Philippines has diplomatic relations, who are staying in the country for not more than 21 days, do not need a visa provided they have tickets for their onward or return journeys. Visas may be obtained from Philippine diplomatic and consular offices abroad.

MONEY MATTERS

The monetary unit of the Philippines is the *peso* (P). There are 100 *centavos* to a peso. At time of press, the exchange rate fluctuates around 22 to a U.S. dollar. The U.S. dollar, pound sterling, Swiss franc, Deutsche mark, Canadian dollar, Italian lira, Australian dollar and the Japanese yen are all easily convertible. Outside Manila, generally, the U.S. dollar is widely acceptable after the peso. Traveler's checks can be easily cashed, and major credit cards are accepted.

HEALTH

Yellow fever vaccination is required upon arrival of visitors from infected areas, except for children under one year of age, who are, however, subject to isolation when it is necessary.

WHAT TO WEAR

Light and loose clothes are most practical. Pack a sweater though if you intend to go to the mountains. At formal gatherings Filipino men mostly wear the *barong Tagalog* (Tagalog shirt). This is long shirt with side slits, worn untucked. Traditionally it is made in white or pastels out of a very fine silk called *jusi*. The shirt is so transparent that a white T-shirt is always worn underneath. Filipino women often wear the *terno* for formal occasions. This is a long gown with huge "butterfly" sleeves and elaborate embroidery on the skirt and bodice. When visiting churches and mosques, remember that short shorts and any excessive or provocative dress is inappropriate.

CUSTOMS

Tourists may bring in the following items free of duty: (1) Personal effects: A reasonable amount of clothing for personal use; a small quantity of perfume; (2) Tobacco and alcoholic beverages: 400 sticks of cigarettes or two tins of smoking tobacco; two bottles of alcoholic beverages of not more than one liter each. Departures involve an airport tax of P200 (US $10).

GETTING ACQUAINTED

TIME ZONES

The Philippines is 8 hours ahead of Greenwich Mean Time. All year round sunrise is about 6 a.m. and sunset about 6 p.m. give or take 30 minutes.

CLIMATE

The best months to travel to the Philippines are from December to May during the dry season. From June to November is the season of the southwest monsoon, which brings sultry wet weather. Typhoons or tropical revolving storms usually take their toll around this period. On the average, the temperature hovers around 80°F (21°C). January is the coldest month with 78°F; (25.5°C) the hottest is May with 83°F; (28°C) Humidity is high, ranging from 71 percent in March to 85 percent in September.

BUSINESS HOURS

Shops open from 9 a.m to about 7 p.m. Mondays to Saturdays. In Manila many shops catering to tourists stay open on Sundays. The Philippine attitude of *bahala' na* (whatever happens) prevails outside Manila so shops don't usually stick to rigid schedules. Government and business hours are from 8 a.m. to 5 p.m, Monday to Friday with a lunch break from noon to 1 p.m. Banks are open from 9 a.m. to 4 p.m. Monday to Friday.

LANGUAGE

Most Filipinos are bilingual, with English still the basic language in business, government, schools and everyday communications. Pilipino, based on the Tagalog dialect, is the national language. There are 111 dialects and 87 languages spoken in the archipelago. Aside from English, Spanish is spoken fluently by a number of Filipinos.

Mabuhay, the first Pilipino word most tourists encounter, means "welcome" as well as "long live." *Po* and *ho* are traditional expressions of respect still in everyday use, specially when addressing elders. *Salamat*, meaning "thank you", is one of the most useful words you will ever need to learn. Try it and watch the smiles break out on the faces of your new Filipino friends.

GETTING AROUND

DOMESTIC TRAVEL

By Air: Transportation around the archipelago emanates from the country's hub, Manila. Flying is quick and cheap and Philippine Airlines, Aerolift and Pacific Airways Corporation, the country's domestic carriers cover the country with their routes. For those with time to spare transportation possibilities include bus, train, car and boat travel.

Philippine Airlines is the major domestic (and international) carrier operating to over 40 domestic points. Up-and-coming airlines competing with the flag carrier include Aerolift, (Daet, Cebu, Boracay, Bohol, Dipolog, Lubang and Busuanga) and Pacific Airways Corporation (Lubang, Boracay and Busuanga). Listed below are the telephone numbers of the three airlines.

Aerolift
Tel: 817-23-61

Pacific Airways Corporation
Tel: 832-27-31

Philippine Airlines
Tel: 832-09-91

WATER TRANSPORT

Manila and Cebu are the two centers of shipping. Be advised that inter-island boat travel will only suit those prepared to "rough it". The effort is rewarding however, as some of the ports served by the steamers have hardly changed in decades – and the bonus is that seemingly half the local populace greets arriving boats down at the wharf. Tickets on major lines (e.g. Manila-Cebu) can be booked through travel agencies. Again, the low fares are a pleasant surprise.

PUBLIC TRANSPORT

In Metro Manila, the bus and jeepney rates are P1 for the first 4 kilometers plus 25 centavos for every kilometer thereafter.

Tricycles (motorcycle with a side-car attached) are sometimes available for short trips on the side streets.

There are also air-conditioned Love Buses with terminals in Escolta in Binondo, Manila, The Center Makati and Ali Mall in Cubao, Quezon City. Rates are P8.

Taxi fare is P2 at flagdown for the first 500 meters and P1 for every 250 meters thereafter. Taxis can be found almost everywhere, especially near hotels, shopping centers and cinemas. Always have small change available and pay in pesos.

Metrorail, the overhead railway system, charges a flat rate of P3.50 at any point along Taft and Rizal Avenue, from Baclaran to Monumento in Caloocan City.

The Pasig River ferry operates from Lawton near the Central Post Office to Guadalupe near Makati. The fare is P9.50 one way.

TRAINS

Train travel is only for the very brave with lots of time to spare. Only one line operates out of Manila. The train from Manila's Tutuban Station in Tondo runs south to Legaspi City from where you can visit Mayon Volcano in the Bicol region.

BUSES

The central Luzon region near Manila and areas surrounding provincial capitals have a reasonable road system. Dozens of bus companies operate services to the main tourist centers of Luzon and fares are low by Western standards, e.g. The 5-hour journey from Manila to Baguio costs less than P100.

PRIVATE TRANSPORT

You can rent station wagons, bantams, coasters, buses, jeepneys and air-conditioned limousines. Cars may be rented with or without a driver. Charges vary according to type of vehicle.

Hourly rates are available, charges at one sixth the daily rate. In excess of 6 hours, daily rates apply. A valid foreign or international driver's license is acceptable.

CAR RENTAL AGENCIES

Avis Rent-A-Car
G & S Transport Corp.
311 P. Casal Street,
San Miguel, Manila
Tel: 742-08-87

Hertz Rent-A-Car
China Banking Corp. Building
Paseo de Roxas corner Villar Street
Makati, Metro Manila
Tel: 832-53-25

J Rent-A-Car
1573 Yakal Street
Sta. Cruz, Manila
Tel: 26-47-32

WHERE TO STAY

The Philippines offers a wide range of accommodation to suit every budget from beach resorts and pension houses to apartments and luxury hotels.

Manila boasts 10 de luxe hotels. The city has been well organized for tourism and conventions. The Department of Tourism and the Philippine Convention and Visitor's

Bureau have an excellent network of promotion offices all over the world to provide information and in some cases even make hotel reservations. For detailed information and rates contact the Tourist Information Center, Department of Tourism, 2nd floor, T.M. Kalaw Street, Rizal Park, Manila, tel: 50-17-03.

HOTELS

MANILA

DE LUXE CATEGORY

Century Park Sheraton
Vito Cruz, Manila
Tel: 522-10-11

Hotel Intercontinental
Makati Commercial Center
Makati, Metro Manila
Tel: 815-97-11

Hotel Nikko Manila Garden
Makati Commercial Center
Makati, Metro Manila
Tel: 810-41-01

Hyatt Regency
2702 Roxas Boulevard
Pasay City
Tel: 831-26-11

The Mandarin Oriental Manila
Paseo de Roxas Triangle
Makati, Metro Manila
Tel: 816-36-01

Manila Hotel
Rizal Park, Manila
Tel: 47-00-11

The Manila Midtown Hotel
P. Gil corner Adriatico streets
Ermita, Manila
Tel: 59-39-11

Manila Peninsula
Ayala Avenue corner Makati Avenue
Makati, Metro Manila
Tel: 819-34-56

The Philippine Plaza
Cultural Center Complex
Roxas Boulevard, Manila
Tel: 832-07-01

Silahis International
1990 Roxas Boulevard
Ermita, Manila
Tel: 57-38-11

FIRST CLASS CATEGORY

Admiral Hotel
2138 Roxas Boulevard
Ermita, Manila
Tel: 57-20-81

Ambassador Hotel
2021 A. Mabini Street
Malate, Manila
Tel: 50-66-11

Holiday Inn Manila
3001 Roxas Boulevard
Ermita, Manila
Tel: 59-79-61

Manila Pavilion Hotel
Maria Orosa Street, corner U.N. Avenue
Ermita, Manila
Tel: 57-37-11

Philippine Village Hotel
MIA Road
Pasay City, Metro Manila
Tel: 833-80-81

STANDARD CATEGORY

Aloha Hotel
2150 Roxas Boulevard
Manila
Tel: 59-90-61

Hotel La Corona
439 Arquiza Street, M.H. del Pilar
Ermita, Manila
Tel: 59-26-12

Hotel Soriente
1123 Bocobo Flores Street
Ermita, Manila
Tel: 59-91-03

Rothman Inn Hotel
1633 M. Adriatico Street
Ermita, Manila
Tel: 521-92-51

Sundowner Hotel
1430 A. Mabini Street
Ermita, Manila
Tel: 521-29-41

ECONOMY CATEGORY

Bayview Prince Hotel
Roxas Boulevard, Ermita, Manila
Tel: 50-30-61

Hotel Aurelo
Roxas Boulevard corner Padre Faura Street
Ermita, Manila
Tel: 50-90-61

Hotel Las Palmas
1616 A. Mabini Street
Malate, Manila
Tel: 50-66-61

Hotel MacArthur
2120 A. Mabini Street
Malate, Manila
Tel: 521-39-11

Iseya Hotel
1241 M.H. del Pilar Street
Ermita, Manila
Tel: 59-20-16

BAGUIO CITY

Baguio Park Hotel
Harrison Road
Tel: 442-56-56

Hotel Monticello
Maryheights, Kennon Road
Tel: 442-65-66

Hotel Nevada
Loakan Road
Tel: 442-24-00

BACOLOD CITY

Bascon Hotel
Gonzaga Street
Tel: 231-41

Sea Breeze Hotel
St. Juan Street
Tel: 245-71

Sugarland Hotel
Singcang
Tel: 224-62

CEBU CITY

Cebu Plaza Hotel
Lahug
Tel: 924-31

Magellan International
Corordo Avenue, Lahug
Tel: 746-21

Montebello Villa International
Banilad
Tel: 8507

Rajah Hotel
Fuente Osmeña
Tel: 962-31

Sky View
Corner Plaridel and Juan Luna streets
Luym Building
Tel: 730-51

ILOILO

Amigo Terrace Hotel
Iznart-Delgado streets, Iloilo City
Tel: 748-10

Del Rio Hotel
M.H. Del Pilar Street, Molo, Iloilo City
Tel: 755-85

Isla Naburot
Iloila
Tel: 761-12

Sarabia Manor Hotel
Gen. Luna Street, Iloila City
Tel: 727-31

Sicogon Resort
Carles, Iloilo
Tel: 792-91

FOOD DIGEST

WHAT TO EAT

Nowhere else is the Philippines' long history of outside influences more evident than in its food...the experience of a lifetime. Philippine cuisine, an intriguing blend of Spanish, Malay and Chinese influences, is noted for the use of fruits, local spices and seafoods. Food to the Filipino is an integral part of local art and culture, and the result is a tribute to the Pinoy's ingenuity in concocting culinary treats from eastern and western ingredients.

Filipinos eat rice three times a day, morning, noon and night. It is a 'must' to sample a Filipino breakfast of fried rice, *longaniza* (native sausage) and fish, which is normally salted and dried accompanied by tomatoes and *patis* (fish sauce) on the side.

When ordering it's best to watch the Filipinos. Even before the food arrives, sauce dishes are brought in and people automatically reach for the vinegar bottle with hot chili, or the soy sauce which they mix with *kalamansi* (small lemons). Grilled items are good with crushed garlic, vinegar and chili. It's a good idea to start a meal with *sinigang*, a clear broth slightly soured with small nature fruit and prepared with *bangus* (milkfish) or shrimp.

Some typical Philippine dishes worth trying are *tinola* which is made with chicken and *pancit molo* which is dumpling of pork, chicken and mushrooms cooked in chicken or meat broth. *Adobo* is pork in small pieces, cooked for a long time in vinegar with other ingredients such as chicken, garlic and spices and then served with rice.

A typical feast dish, *lechon* is suckling pig stuffed with tamarind leaves and roasted on lighted coals until the skin is crackling and the meat tender. It is generally served with liver sauce. *Sinanglay*, another festive dish, is fish or piquant crabs with hot pepper wrapped in leaves of Chinese cabbage, and then cooked in coconut milk.

Other Filipino favorites include *lumpia* – a salad of heart-of-palm and small pieces of pork and shrimp wrapped in a crepe and served with garlic and soya sauce and *kare-kare* which is a rich of oxtail, knuckles and tripe, stewed with vegetables in peanut sauce and served with *bagoong*, an anchovy based sauce.

Puddings are generally made with coconut rice or coconut milk. Among the most famous is *bibingka*, which consists of ground rice, sugar and coconut milk, baked in a clay oven and topped with fresh and salted duck eggs. *Guinatan* is a coco-pudding which is served with lashings or coconut cream. Ice creams are made in several fruit flavors such as *nangka* (jackfruit), ube and mango as well as the more usual vanilla, chocolate and strawberry.

THINGS TO DO

First and foremost the Philippines is renowned for its beaches. Choose from Boracay, Cebu, Puerto Galera, Camiguin, Bauang La Union, Sicogon, Batangas, Laoag and hundreds more. If you tire of sun and sand try heading for the hills of Baguio and the fabled rice terraces of Banaue visiting Bontoc and Sagada en route.

Visitors looking for something different might consider climbing Davao's Mt. Apo, diving in Palawan, golfing in Batangas, walking on Camiguin, visiting the tribal people in Zamboanga and Sulu or fiesta hopping around the islands.

Having "done" Manila, anyone with time to spare would do well to check out the following day trips, if day trips are your thing: Corregidor, Tagaytay and Taal Volcano, Villa Escudero, Sarao Jeepney Factory, Las Piñas Bamboo Organ, Hidden Valley Springs, Pagsanjan Falls and Batangas Philippine Experience.

TOUR GUIDES

For official tour guides, registered with the Department of Tourism telephone Manila: 50-17-03.

Anscor Travel Corporation
Regina Building
Makati, Metro Manila
Tel: 815-01-81

Baron Travel Corporation
Pacific Bank Building
Ayala Avenue
Makati, Metro Manila
Tel: 817-66-96

Far Travel Inc.
Asian Plaza I Building
Makati, Metro Manila
Tel: 815-14-25

Philippine Experience
Pacific Contact
Negros Navigation Building
Pasay Road
Makati, Metro Manila
Tel: 86-37-60

Rajah Tours Phil., Inc.
New Physician's Tower
United Nations Avenue
Ermita, Manila
Tel: 522-05-41

Sarkies Tours Phils., Inc.
J.P. Laurel Building
M.H. del Pilar Street
Ermita, Manila
Tel: 59-76-58

Southeast (Phil) Travel Center
451 Pedro Gil
Ermita, Manila
Tel: 50-66-01

Sundowner Travel Center
1430 A. Mabini
Ermita, Manila
Tel: 521-26-02

SHOPPING

WHAT TO BUY

The Philippines is an old Asian shopping emporium, dating back to the days when its coastal towns sold pearls, beeswax and tortoise shell to trading vessels all the way from Arabia. Today, the emphasis is on handicraft, woodcarving and the gifts of the sea. Almost all major cities are worth a shopping trip but a limited schedule that takes you to Manila, Cebu, Baguio and Zamboanga yields sufficient reward.

BASKETS

Philippine baskets are now found in many fashion capitals of the world, thanks to enterprising Pinoys who have at last seen their export potential after years of having taking them for granted. With all of their varying regional designs and recent streamlining, Philippine baskets are both the scholar's and the plain old shopper's delight. Made out of a range of natural fibers from the bamboo, the rattan vine, the nipa bush and various palms, these baskets come in a whole range of sizes and purposes, both functional and decorative.

They are all over the tourist shops but a special joy accompanies seeing them in bazaar-like display under the Quiapo Bridge, in the heart of Metro Manila. The Baguio market up in the mountain province is also worth a visit because it is where the antique designs of the mountain province converge with baskets from all over the Philippines, from Bicol through the Visayas and Mindanao.

Note also that there is a special line of baskets that have lately caused collection fever among the more knowledgeable Philippine-watchers. These are the smoked fish traps and locust baskets, as well as the lunch containers bought off the huts of Northern

Luzon where they are considered family heirlooms. So popular are these antique baskets that a line of endeavor has sprung up in the north – "cooking" new baskets woven in the old design to look as though they have stood beside a smokey Igorot hearth for decades.

MATS

First cousin to the baskets, Philippine mats are fascinating bits of local color recruited to line the walls of hotels. They range from the natural-colored *pandan* mats of most of Luzon to the playfully designed ones of Leyte and Samar in the Visayas and the dramatic geometries of Basilan and Sulu in Mindanao. What you find in Manila can be severely limited, with the exception of the Quiapo Bridge market, but finding yourself in Cebu, Davao or Zamboanga is the perfect opportunity to stock up on these inexpensive bits of folk art.

HANDICRAFTS

Abaca hats, placemats, coasters, bamboo trays, shell windchimes, ceramic pots and gewgaws are all over the tourist shops around the airport, Makati commercial center and the Ermita tourist belt. The macrame fever is also in full blush in these places, in shirts, blouses, bags and dresses, planters and wall hangings.

EMBROIDERY

Very few guests, in the country for the first time, resist the attractions of Philippine embroidery. The *barong tagalog* is now internationally famous and has many versions from the thousand-peso Pierre Cardin type to the humbler *polo barongs* (short-sleeved) much beloved by casual tourists. Depending on your tastes, you can choose the translucent pineapple fiber, *jusi*, for your material with the finest hand-embroidery or the less expensive ramie with machine-embroidery (though you sometimes can hardly tell). Go to the better known houses.

There is no lack of embroidered clothes for women, either – the *barong* dress shaped like the *barong tagalog* but longer, the embroidered kaftans and jelabas with matching scarves, bags and handkerchiefs.

JEWELRY

The most typically Philippine lines are shell and silver jewelry. Mother-of-pearl is perhaps the most popular, although coral and tortoise shell are also coming into their own. The best silver jewelry is to be found in Baguio where the guild-like training from St. Louis University has today engendered much fine craftmanship.

You can also find many examples of wood and vine jewelry in the specialty shops of Ermita and Makati, as well as beadwork from the tribes, notably the necklaces, earrings and ornamental hair pieces of the T'boli, the Mangyan and the Igorot tribes.

ANTIQUES

The first smiths of the Philippines are recorded in Mindanao. To this day, they continue to manufacture gongs, jewel boxes, betel nut boxes, brass beds and cannon replicas. They're all over the tourist belt but if someone tries to sell you an "antique", check it out first with a knowledgeable shopping guide. There are also ceremonial canopies embroidered and sequined to celebrate royal Muslim weddings and feasts in these shops, they make lovely buys.

WOODCARVING

Giant hardwood carvings of the Igorot tribesman and his woman were among the first items of Filipiniana brought home by the Americans. What they did not see were other more fascinating things like the rice granary god carvings and the animal totems from Palawan that can now be found in the Ermita tourist belt.

SPORTS

Golf: For most visitors to the Philippines, golf is a big attraction because the country has some of the finest courses in the world – including several championship courses. Teeing off amid lush tropical vegetation and water-laced inland resorts gives any golfer maximum enjoyment of the game. Also, because of the climate, golf is an ideal all-year-round sport.

To date there are more than 50 golf courses in the archipelago. Most are in Luzon, although there are some fine courses in the large cities of the Visayas and Mindanao. From its humble beginnings of a few thousand golfers in the 1920s, Philippine golf has become an increasingly popular sport with the advent of international golf tournaments and the development of well-appointed country clubs.

Green fees vary from links to links and are often slightly higher on weekends. Green fees vary from P100-500 plus rentals. Caddies, carts, golf clubs and shoes are available for hire on an hourly basis.

SKIN-DIVING

The archipelago is a skin-diver's paradise. In general the islands offer steep drop-offs, huge coral heads, large and small inlets, warm waters and fairly easy to obtain diving gear. Underwater photographers will have a heyday among the multicolored feather star, colorful coral gardens, clouds of tropical aquarium fish and schools of pelagic jacks.

Submarine cliff *aficionados* can experience the pulse-pounding thrill of swimming with schools of 30-pound garoupas, napoleon wrass and snappers, or witness the sinuous grace of a shark and the capacity of a 5-foot barracuda.

The best diving season in the Philippines is March, April, May and early June. During this period, seas all around are calm, rainfall is rare and waters are crystal clear.

Areas worth trying in Luzon include Balayan and Batangas Bays close by Punta Baluarte resort, Caban and Layag Layag, both on a small island and Devil point on Maricaban Island.

Cebu, too, offers both excellent diving close to shore and further offshore is the Hilurangan Channel between Cebu Island and Bohol to the south. There are many diver's guides on the subject including *Diver's Guide to the Philippines* by David Smith, Michael Westlake and Portfirio Castañeda (Unicorn Books Ltd.). The Department of Tourism can provide you with detailed information.

HORSE RACING

Horse racing is held generally on Tuesdays, Wednesdays, Saturdays and Sundays at San Lazaro Hippodrome and Santa Ana Race Track. Betting on horses is a big-time operation. Major races include the Gran Copa, National Grand Derby, the Founder's Cup and the Presidential Cup.

GETTING THERE

BY AIR

The smooth descent over Singapore's harbor and city—a shoreline in business by day, an illuminated city planner's outline by night—is well worth a window seat on the nearest side.

Even before landing, you will see the airport's magnificent 257-foot (78-meter) tall control tower. Singapore's **Changi International Airport** projects an aura of grandeur. In addition to the national carrier, Singapore Airlines, it is the touchdown for 48 international airlines with more than 1,500 flights a week. Since it opened in 1981, Asia's largest and most modern airport has provided for more than 40 aircraft movements every hour, facilities to handle more than 500,000 tons of cargo and 12.5 million passengers every year and car park capacity for 2,138 vehicles.

A second terminal, already completed, will double Changi's capacity enabling it to cope with 24 million passengers. The two terminals will be linked by the "sky train", an automated miniature rapid transit train system with a track length of 600 meters. It will be the first of its kind outside the USA and UK.

In keeping with its announced image of a "City within an Airport" the new terminal will have, among other facilities, a business center, a health center with gymnasium and sauna, day rooms with en suite facilities, medical center, exhibition centers, a 200-seat auditorium and a supermarket.

BY SEA

Sailors enter Singapore as did the ancients: through waterways which weave among tiny offshore islands once called the Dragon Teeth Straits.

From the early Chinese junks that braved the seas to trade dried fruits, sugar candy, tea or paper umbrellas, to steady tankers listing under the weight of the island's refined oil, the port of Singapore has been the hub of navigation on the eastern seas.

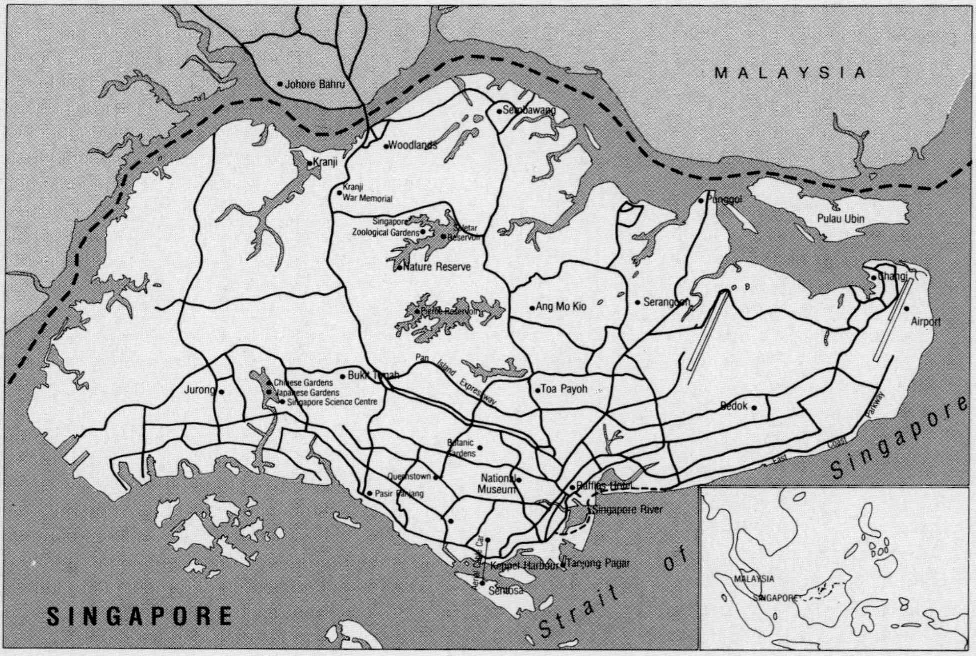

Three hundred shipping lines flying the flags of some 80 countries and serving 300 other ports call regularly. In fact, a ship arrives at and leaves the port every 10 minutes. Along with major ports like Rotterdam and Yokohama, Singapore is rated one of the busiest in the world.

Passenger lines serve Singapore annually from Australia, Europe, North America, India and Hong Kong. Entry formalities comply with standard immigration laws, and for quick orientations, the Tourist Promotion Board is on hand to greet arrivals with a mobile information service on the sights of the town.

BY LAND

Singapore, surrounded by waters on all sides, is connected by road and rail with the Malay Peninsula by the Causeway.

The railway takes travelers to Singapore from Bangkok en route Haadyai, Butterworth and Kuala Lumpur. The International Express departs from Bangkok Monday, Wednesday and Saturday at 4:10 p.m., stopping at Haadyai at 10:28 a.m. the next day and arrives at Butterworth at 6:45 p.m. From Butterworth, the Express Rakyat departs at 8:15 a.m. and arrives Kuala Lumpur at 2:35 p.m. The last link to Singapore is also provided by the Express Rakyat which departs from Kuala Lumpur at 3:05 p.m. and arrives Singapore at 9:35 p.m.

The fare for an air-conditioned coach from Butterworth to Singapore is S$50 and S$30 for one without air-conditioning.

Six other daily services run from Singapore to Malaysia. The morning trains depart at 6:30 a.m. and 7:30 a.m. The afternoon service leaves Singapore at 3 p.m. while the evening trains leave at 8 p.m., 8:30 p.m. and 10 p.m. For detailed fares and schedules, call the railway station on Keppel Road (tel: 222-5165). Reservations are accepted with advance payment, though arriving early for your train is advisable.

TRAVEL ESSENTIALS

VISAS & PASSPORTS

Visitors entering Singapore must posses valid national passports or internationally recognized travel documents. A certificate of vaccination against smallpox is necessary only for those coming from infected countries within the preceding 14 days. Visas are not necessary for a stay up to fourteen days, provided the visitor has confirmed onward passage and adequate finances. Collective passports or travel documents are permitted for group travel in tours of five to twenty people. However, these regulations do not apply to nationals from communist countries, Taiwan and South Africa who need visas to enter Singapore.

Tourist visas are usually issued and extended up to a maximum of three months at the Immigration Office, Pidemco Center (for enquiries, phone: 532-2877).

MONEY MATTERS

Singapore issued its own currency in 1957, choosing native orchids to adorn its dollar. In 1976, a second generation of currency was issued, depicting birds of the region perched above the island's buildings and industries. A third series depicting a variety of sailing vessels is now in circulation. The Singapore dollar was valued at approximately 1.87 to the U.S dollar or 3.17 to the British pound sterling at the time of going to press. Brunei dollars are roughly equivalent to the Singapore dollar. Singapore currently has two sets of coins in circulation. The newer 10, 20 and 50 cents are smaller in size than the old ones. Malaysian dollars are about 30 percent lower in value and no longer circulate freely. There is no limit on the amount of Singapore and foreign notes, traveler's checks and letters of credit brought into or out of the country.

Make no haste to change big money at luxurious hotels. Singapore's ubiquitous money-changers of Change Alley, Raffles Place and most shopping complexes are government licensed and reliable. Often they give better rates than those of leading hotels which deduct a service charge of 5 to 10 cents Singapore currency on each U.S. dollar. Currency exchange rates at banks fluctuate each day, but only very slightly. Traveler's checks generally get a better rate of exchange than cash. It's best to deal directly with any bank or licensed money-changer. Banking hours are Monday through Friday 10 a.m.–3 p.m. and Saturday 9:30 a.m.–11:30 a.m.

If you wish to deal with banks for your traveler's checks and other foreign currency transactions, it is advisable to do so on weekdays. Although most banks welcome such transactions, some do not handle them on Saturdays while others conduct them in small amounts only, based on Friday's rate.

Credit cards commonly accepted are American Express, Diner's Club, Carte Blanche. Asia Card, Master Charge Card and those of international hotel chains and airlines.

HEALTH

Inevitably the third word belonging to Singapore after "clean" and "green" is "healthy." Travelers have no worries in a place where one can drink water straight from the tap and consume food by the streetside. They can even participate in the hygiene campaigns like "Keep Singapore Pollution Free." The Republic lives up to this comforting reputation with efficient, contemporary medical facilities in numerous hospitals and clinics throughout the island. The closest anyone can come to a physical ailment originating in Singapore is over-eating and there is a quick cure for this; shopping on foot for a few hours.

WHAT TO WEAR

The daytime trend is pure casual comfort. Light summer fashions, easy to move in, are the right choice for a full day out in town. Wear a white shirt and tie for office calls. Evening dress is a more subtle combination of fads and formality. Only few very plush nightclubs and very exclusive restaurants favor the traditional jacket and tie. Most hotels, restaurants, coffee houses and discos accept more casual wear of shirt-and-tie (or even shirts without ties) for men and pleasant dress suits for the ladies. However, jeans-and-tee shirts is a taboo at most discos. To avoid embarrassment, visitors are advised to call in advance to check an establishment's dress policy.

CUSTOMS

Singapore essentially remains a free port. Personal effects (including cameras and radios), 1 liter spirits, 1 liter malt liquor or 1 liter wine and 200 cigarettes of 50 cigars or 250 grams tobacco may be brought in duty-free. Narcotics are strictly forbidden as are firearms and weapons, subject to licensing.

GETTING ACQUAINTED

GEOGRAPHY

Singapore, at the tip of the Malay Peninsula is about north of the equator and has an area of 250 square-miles (620 square-km). The Republic city-state consists of Singapore island and 57 other islets of which fewer than half are inhabited. The Government, not to be deterred by the limited land space, is constantly clearing swamps and jungles and reclaiming land from the surroundings waters.

About two-thirds of the island is less then 50 feet (15 meters) high and the highest point (Bukit Timah or "Tin Hill") stands at 585 feet (177 meters).

TIME ZONES

Singapore Standard Time is eight hours ahead of Greenwich Meridian Time. Aside from time variations made in certain countries during specific seasons, international time differences are staggered as follows:

Singapore	noon today
Hong Kong	noon today
Bangkok	11 a.m. today
New Delhi	9:30 a.m. today
Bonn	5 a.m. today
Paris	5 a.m. today
London	4 a.m. today
New York	11 p.m. yesterday
San Francisco	8 p.m. yesterday
Hawaii	6 p.m. yesterday
Sydney	2 p.m. today
Tokyo	1 p.m. today

CLIMATE

Conversations jump from rain to shine. Shine wins out on most occasions since the climate is equally warm and sunny the year round. Temperatures teeter between 87°F (30.6°C) at noon and 75°F (23.8°C) at night, the daytime heat cooled with sea winds and ample air-conditioning.

Asia's subtle seasons follow the monsoons, and from November to January high winds turn a bucket over Singapore. For ten minutes the city comes to a standstill under hawker stalls, arcades and umbrellas. Then as suddenly as they come, the rains vanish, leaving the pavements wet-washed, the lawns refreshed, and the umbrellas behind for sunshades.

CULTURE & CUSTOMS

The customs, religions and languages of nearly every nation in the world have converged in Singapore during some time in its history. Adjectives beginning with "multi" are common sounds on the Singapore scene, and a cosmopolitan tolerance is part of the city's character.

With everyday etiquette relaxed and straight-forward, visitors behaving courteously stand little chance of unintentionally giving offense.

Some ceremonies and special occasions, however, recall inherited traditions where a familiarity with certain customs sets everyone at ease.

TEMPLES & MOSQUES

Removing one's shoes before entering a mosque or an Indian temple has been an unspoken tradition for centuries. Within, devotees do not smoke, though neither of these customs generally applies to Chinese temples where more informal styles prevail. Visitors are most welcome to look around at their leisure and are invited to stay during religious rituals. While people pray, it is understood that those not participating in the service will quietly stand aside.

A polite gesture would be to ask permission before taking photographs; the request is seldom, if ever refused. Moderate clothing rather than brief skirts or shorts, is appropriate for a visit.

Most temples and mosques have a donation box for funds to help maintain the building. Contributing a few coins before leaving is customary.

PRIVATE HOMES

The hospitality of a Singaporean friend is a good feeling. In private homes, visitors are received as honored guests. Without hesitating, the hostess prepares some drinks, the best of whatever is available in the house whether it be rare imported tea or an iced soft drink. Wives pride themselves in serving good food at anytime a guest arrives, and when returning the visit they bring a small gift of fruit or cakes, as is the custom. Though not everything served is expected to be eaten, nothing pleases a hostess more than knowing her guests enjoy her cooking.

All Malays, Indians and Chinese remove their shoes at the door to keep the house free from dust outside. No host would insist his visitors do so, but it is the polite way to enter a home.

SHARING A MEAL

As every taste has its flavor, every food has its style. Chinese cooking is eaten with chopsticks. Most Malay and Indian cooking are eaten with the right hand (never the left) and Indonesian and Thai cooking with a large spoon and fork. A gourmet would no more eat a Chinese meal with knife and fork than a filet mignon with chopsticks.

Yet, enjoying Asian styles of dining begins only with a first try. Asian meals are usually served in large bowls placed in the center of the table, with each diner helping himself to a little from each bowl.

Piling up your plate with food is not only impolite but unwise. With more dishes to follow, by taking a little you can always help yourself to more. Local people are inwardly pleased if you join them in their styles of dining, for a simple reason: they know it tastes better that way.

WEDDINGS

A gift of money—S$40 would be an acceptable sum—is customary at weddings of all races. The gift is generally used as a contribution to the cost of the wedding banquet, often a lavish affair with many guests invited. The money should be placed inside an envelope with your name written on the back, and given to the bride or groom. Chinese present gifts of money in an *ang pow*, a small red envelope obtained at banks or stationers. Traditionally an even number of notes or coins is considered lucky.

TIPPING

Smiles follow tips everywhere, Singapore is no exception especially in the fashionable accessories of an affluent society like nightclubs, friendly bars and expensive restaurants. Here the magic number is 10 percent. Leading hotels are kind enough to do the tipping for you by adding a 10 percent service charge to every bill; a second time around is not necessary though neither is it refused. Bellboys and porters receive from $1 upwards (Singapore currency) depending upon the complexity of the errand. Yet, beyond the international thoroughfares, tipping is exceptional. In small local restaurants, food stalls and taxis, the bill includes the service, and with thank you (*terima kaseh* in Malay), simply a smile will do.

ON THE ROAD

When driving, be sure to put on the seat belt unless you want to enrich the Singapore economy by S$50. This ruling, implemented to reduce risks of car accidents, also applies to frontseat passengers of private cars and taxis.

On-duty polite patrols never hesitate to issue tickets when warranted, and they always have a good reason for doing so—exceeding speed limits, failing to give way, failing to obey road signs, etc.

Pedestrians are expected to use a designated crossing if one is available within 50 meters on either side. Designated crossing are zebra crossings, overhead bridges, underpasses, traffic light junctions fitted with green man and red man lights, and yellow parallel lines at intersections.

LITTERING

Singapore has something else to boast about. It is clean and green. Much pain has been taken by the Government not only to keep it that way but also to inculcate civic-conscious habits in its citizens. Litter bins dotting the island at short distance intervals make it inexcusable to drop a litter (be it a bus ticket, a cigarette butt, or a sweet wrapper) anywhere else and if you do, it's a fine of up to S$500.

SMOKING

For health reasons, smoking is discouraged, though not banned. In some public places like cinemas, theaters, libraries, lifts, public buses and the government offices, smoking is prohibited and the offense carries at fine of up to S$500. Signboards that serve as reminders are on display in such places.

GETTING AROUND

FROM THE AIRPORT

The airport is linked to the city center by the East Coast Parkway (20 minutes traveling time) and to the rest of Singapore by the Pan-Island Expressway.

There are three types of transport from the airport—private car, taxi or public bus. The inclined travelators in the Arrival Hall descend to a short tunnel that leads to the Passenger Crescent (the curbside for private cars) and the Arrival Crescent (the pick-up point for taxis). A surcharge, S$3 more than the fare shown on the taxi meter, is charged if you board the taxi at the airport. A 50 percent surcharge of the metered fare must be paid by the passenger if the taxi ride begins between 12 p.m. and 6 a.m. A number of public shuttle bus services run between the airport and nearby bus interchanges. For service numbers and routes, check the basement passenger terminal.

BUSES

Nearly 250 bus services ply the paved roads of Singapore today, connecting every corner of the island. Bus rides in Singapore, though more crowded and slower than taxis are less expensive, and more exciting; absorbing the local travelers, minitowns and marketplaces with all the immediacy it takes to turn an experience into a memory.

Buses (of two kinds here: single-levels and double-deckers) run from 6.15 a.m. to 11.30 p.m. on the average, with an extension of about a half hour for both starting and ending times on weekends and public holidays. Fares are cheap (minimum 50 cents, maximum 90 cents), and the amount payable is structured according to fare stages (half-a-mile is equivalent to one fare stage). You pay 50 cents if traveling over four or less fare stages: 60 cents for five to seven stages: 70 cents for eight to 10 stages; 80 cents for 11 to 13 stages; and 90 cents for 14 or more stages. Too much to remember? Then just have some change ready and ask the bus driver after boarding. Most buses are one-man-operated (OMO sign displayed on the front of the bus) and have no conductor.

An especially helpful source, available at most bookstores and newsstands at S$1, is the **Bus Guide**. This booklet gives complete details of all bus routes including a section on bus services to major places of interest in Singapore for the benefit of tourists. Or all Singapore Bus Service, Tel: 2848866 during office hours.

MASS RAPID TRANSIT

The Singapore government spent an estimated S$5 billion, for the Mass Rapid Transit (MRT) railway system project. It is Singapore's biggest single investment.

This decision was not made overnight; the first feasibility study was made more than a decade ago in 1972. Studies have shown that daily passenger travels within the country have increased so much that alternative means of mass transportation have to be sought. Construction began in October 1983, and when the entire project is completed in 1992, the MRT is expected to carry about 600,000 passengers daily.

The MRT system when fully operational will then have 41 stations spread over the island, and 66 air-conditioned trains running over a north-south and east-west line. The six-car train will then be able to take 1,800 passengers.

Fare collection is automatic: magnetically coded cards costs between 50 cents to $1.40. Stored value cards are valued at $10.

Depending on the station the first train rolls out between 6 a.m. and 6:40 a.m. Mondays to Saturdays, and between 6:45 a.m. to 7:25 a.m. on Sundays and public holidays. The last trains are between 11 p.m. and midnight, and 15 minutes earlier on Sundays and public holidays.

TAXIS

One of the rarest sights in Singapore is a main street without a taxi. Taxis are everywhere, everyone uses them. It is fast, easy and comfortable. The vehicles are clean and kept in tip-top condition (the cleanest taxi gets a prize in Singapore). Black and yellow, solid blue, green and white or red and white—all with "SH" on their licence plates—taxis run by meter. Each taxi is allowed a maximum of four passengers. The fare starts from $2.20.

Most taxi stands are found just outside shopping centers and other public buildings. You may join the queue at these or you may hail one from any curbside (except those market with double yellow lines).

In the early morning hours (12 a.m.–6 a.m.) sleepless drivers charge a midnight surcharge of 50 percent of the metered fare. The stories about the day the old meter broke down are never told now, but if the driver insists his meter is not working, catch another taxi.

Designed to alleviate traffic congestion, the Central Business District is a restricted zone for vehicles without an area license during the peak hours of 7:30 a.m. to 10:15 a.m. and 4 p.m. to 6:30 p.m. Monday to Saturday. Daily area license (S$3 per vehicle) are payable by the passenger.

Other surcharges payable, above the metered fare, at different times and for different reasons include S$3 per taxi for trips originating from the Changi airport, a S$1 for a trip from the restricted zone during 4 p.m. to 7 p.m. on weekdays and 12 p.m. to 3 p.m. on Saturday; S$2 for a trip engaged through a telephone call to a taxi stand and S$3 for taxi booking made at least half an hour in advance.

Most drivers speak or understand English. Still, it is better to be sure he knows exactly where you want to go before starting. Tipping is purely optional and discouraged by the government.

Taxis on radio call are available at Tel: 452-5555, 533-9009 and 250-0700 day and night.

TRISHAWS

A direct descendent of the historical rickshaw—covered carriage pulled by man on foot—is the trishaw, a bicycle with a sidecar. This is somewhat a vanishing mode of transport among locals due to its slow speed, its lack of sophistication and the unending hassle over the fare with the rider who is often a stubborn grumpy man in his 60s.

However, it is fast becoming a hot favorite among visitors. Its selling point lies in the fact that it goes at a speed slow enough for its passenger to absorb what goes on around but fast enough to cover most of the picturesque sights of downtown within an hour. Full information of itinerarized trishaw tours at stand and prices is available at your hotel's tour desk.

A word of caution: for a ride by a freelance rider be sure you agree upon a fare before getting on. Licensed riders are distinguished from these by colored control badges.

RENT-A-CAR

In the free spirit of independent travel on and off the main roads of Singapore, rent-a-car services provide the wheels if you provide the valid driver's license. Self-drive cars cost from S$60 to $350 a day plus mileage, depending on the size and comfort of your limousine. Contact any of the many companies renting cars through your hotel or the Yellow Pages—they will be the first to remind riders to bring along their passports.

Where to Stay

HOTELS

As the island country with its abundant attractions continues to draw crowds, the accommodation sector is experiencing a boom which seems to live on and on and on...

In one month least one hotel somewhere on the island is being renovated, while another is under-going expansion and still another is computerizing its operations. Such keen competition among the hoteliers spells two words: variety and quality. Variety ranges from the deluxe that makes living like a king a slice-life (spending like one too, of course) to low-budget guest houses for those whose only concern is for a roof above.

Amara
165 Tanjong Pagar Rd. S.0207.
Tel: 224-4488.
349 rooms; 8 restaurants serving local, European and Chinese food; bar; club; ballroom. Other facilities; conference room; banquet room; hairdresser; pool; health center; sports facilities; TV and IDD.

ANA
Nassim Hill, S.1025.
Tel: 732-1222.
462 rooms, restaurants serving local, European and Japanese food; bar and club. Other facilities: conference room; banquet room; pool; health center; hairdresser; doctor; TV and IDD. Rates: S: S$180-200; T: S$200-240; Suite: S$260-1000.

Apollo
405 Havelock Rd., S.0316.
Tel: 733-2081.
332 rooms; restaurants serving local, Japanese and Chinese food; bar; club. Other facilities: conference room; banquet room; TV and IDD. Rates: S: S$120-140; T: S$160-180; Suite: S$280.

Asia
37 Scotts Rd., S.0922.
Tel: 737-8388.
146 rooms; restaurants serving local and European food; bar. Other facilities; conference room; banquet room; gardens and TV. Rates: S: S$120-140; T: S$140-155.

Boulevard
200 Orchard Blvd., S.1024.
Tel: 737-2911.
529 rooms; restaurants serving local, European, Japanese and Indian food; bar. Other facilities: conference room; pool; health center; hairdresser; TV and IDD. Rates: S: S$155-230; T: 185-260; Suite: S$300-650.

Cairnhill
19 Cairnhill Circle, S.0922.
Tel: 734-6622.
220 rooms; restaurants serving Chinese food; bar. Other facilities conference room; hairdresser; pool; health center; TV and IDD. Rates: S: S$145-164; T: S$165-185; Suite: S$250.

Cockpit
6 Oxley Rise, S.0923.
Tel: 737-9111.
182 rooms; restaurants serving Chinese food; bar. Other facilities: conference room and TV. Rates: S: S$130; T: S$150; Suite: S$250.

Crown Prince
271 Orchard Rd., S.0923
Tel: 732-1111.
303 rooms; restaurants serving local, European, Japanese and Chinese food. Other facilities: pool, TV. Rates: S: S$180-220; T: S$210-250; Suite: S$530-1200.

Dai Ichi
81 Anson Rd. S.0207.
Tel: 224-1133.
420 rooms; restaurants serving Western, Japanese and Chinese food. Other facilities: shops: pool; health center. Rates: S: S$120; T: S$150; Suite: S$270-350.

Duke
42 Meyer Rd., S.1543.
Tel: 345-3311.
170 rooms; restaurants serving Chinese

food. Other facilities: conference room; banquet room; pool and TV. Rates: S: S$80; T: S$90; Suite: S$130.

Dynasty
320 Orchard Rd., S.0923.
Tel: 734-9900.
400 rooms; restaurants serving local, European and Chinese food, bar; ballroom. Other facilities: conference room; hairdresser; pool; health center; TV and IDD. Rates: S: S$190-300; T: S$220-300; Suite: S$500-2200.

Excelsior
5 Coleman St. S.0617.
Tel: 338-7733.
300 rooms; restaurants serving local, European, Japanese and Chinese food; bar. Other facilities: conference room; banquet room; shops; hairdresser; doctor; pool; health center; TV and IDD. Rates: S: S$140; T: S$155; Suite: S$300-1080.

Furama
10 Eu Tong Sen St., S.0105.
Tel: 533-3888.
354 rooms; restaurants serving local, European, Japanese and Chinese food; bar. Other facilities: conference room; banquet room; shops; hairdresser; pool; health center; TV and IDD. Rates: S: S$150-170; T: S$170-190; Suite:S $350.

Garden
14 Balmoral Rd., S.1025.
Tel: 235-3344.
216 rooms; restaurants serving local, European and Chinese food; bar. Other facilities: conference room; banquet room; hairdresser; pool; health center; TV and IDD. Rates: S: S$120; T: S$140; Suite: S$250.

Grand Central
22 Cavenagh Rd., S.0922.
Tel: 737-9944.
365 rooms; restaurants serving local, European and Chinese food; bar; club. Other facilities: conference room; banquet room; hairdresser; pool; TV and IDD. Rates: S: S$125-165; T: S$150-190: Suite: S$270.

Hilton
581 Orchard Rd., S.0923.
Tel: 737-2233.
435 rooms; restaurants serving local, European and Chinese food; bar; ballroom. Other facilities: conference room; banquet room; shops hairdresser; doctor; pool; health center; TV and IDD. Rates: S: S$160-210; T: S$185-240; Suite: S$320-1250.

Holiday Inn Park View
11 Cavenagh Rd. S.0922.
Tel: 733-8333.
350 rooms; restaurants serving European, Chinese and Indian food; bar; ballroom. Other facilities: conference room; banquet room; shops; pool; health center; sports facilities; garden; TV and IDD. Rates: S: S$190-200; T: S$220-290; Suite: S$300-800.

Hyatt
10 Scotts Rd., S.0922.
Tel: 733-1188.
791 rooms + 352-room extension; restaurants serving local and European food; bar. Other facilities: conference room; banquet room; hairdresser; pool; health center; TV and IDD. Rates: S: S$190-290; T: S$220-320; Suite: S$600-2500.

Mandarin
333 Orchard Rd., S.0923.
Tel: 737-4411.
1,200 rooms; restaurants serving local, European; Chinese and Japanese food; bar; club; ballroom. Other facilities: conference room; banquet room; shops; hairdresser; doctor; pool; health center; sports facilities; TV and IDD. Rates: S/T S$180-195; Suite: S$250-900.

Marco Polo
247 Tanglin Rd., S.1024.
Tel: 474-7141.
603 rooms; restaurants serving local, European food; bar; club. Other facilities: conference room; banquet room; hairdresser; pool; health center; sports facilities; TV and IDD. Rates: S: S$180-280; T: S$210-280; Suite: S$320-1200.

Marina Mandarin
6 Raffles Blvd. S.0103.
Tel: 338-3388.

557 rooms; 4 restaurants serving local, European and Chinese food; bar; club; ballroom. Other facilities: conference room; banquet room; shops; hairdresser doctor; pool; health center; sports facilities; TV and IDD.

Meridien
100 Orchard Rd., S.0923.
Tel: 733-8855.
419 rooms; restaurants serving local, European and Chinese food; bar; ballroom. Other facilities: conference room; banquet room; shops; hairdresser; doctor; pool; health center; TV and IDD. Rates: S: S$190-245; T: S$210-280; Suite: S$300-1200.

Meridien Changi
1 Netheravon Rd.,
Upper Changi Rd., S.1750.
Tel: 545-6632.
280 rooms; restaurants serving local, European and Chinese food; bar; ballroom. Other facilities: conference room; banquet room; hairdresser; doctor; pool; health center; sports facilities; TV and IDD. Rates: S: S$165-220; T: S$185-255; Suite: S$300-1200.

Ming Court
1 Tanglin Rd., S.1024.
Tel: 737-1133.
300 rooms; restaurants serving local, European and Chinese food; bar. Other facilities: hairdresser; doctor; pool; health center; sports facilities; TV and IDD. Rates: S: S$200; T: S$225; Suite: S$300.

Miramar
401 Havelock Rd., S.0316.
Tel: 733-0222.
346 rooms; restaurants serving local, European and Chinese food; bar. Other facilities: conference room; banquet room; hairdresser; doctor; pool; health center; TV and IDD. Rates: S$115; T: S$135; Suite: S$300.

Negara
15 Claymore Rd., S.0922.
Tel: 737-0811.
104 rooms; restaurants serving local and European food; bar. Other facilities: pool. Rates: S: S$90-140; T: S$110-160; Suite: S$205.

New Park
181 Kitchener Rd., S.0820.
Tel: 295-0122.
525 rooms; restaurants serving local, European and Chinese food; bar. Other facilities: conference room; banquet room; shops; hairdresser; health center and TV.

Novotel Orchid Inn
214 Dunearn RD., S.1129.
Tel: 250-3322.
473 rooms; restaurants serving local and European food; bar. Other facilities: conference room; banquet room; hairdresser; pool; health center; gardens; TV and IDD. Rates: S: S$140, T: S$160; Suite: S$250.

Oberoi Imperial
1 Jln Rumbia, S.0923.
Tel: 737-1666.
600 rooms; restaurants serving local, European, Chinese and Indian food; bar; ballroom. Other facilities: conference room; banquet room; shops; hairdresser; doctor; pool; health center; and TV. Rates: S: S$165-195; T: S$185-215; Suite: S$330.

Orchard
442 Orchard Rd., S.0923.
Tel: 734-7766. 350 rooms; restaurants serving European food; bar; ballroom. Other facilities: conference room; banquet room, hairdresser; pool; TV and IDD.
Rates: S: S$170-185; T: S$190-210; Suite: S$395-1000.

Pan Pacific
7 Raffles Blvd. S.0103.
Tel: 336-8111
800 rooms. 9 restaurants serving local, European, Japanese, Chinese and Polynesian food; bar; ballroom. Other facilities: conference room; banquet room; hairdresser; doctor; pool; health center; sports facilities; TV and IDD.

Paramount
25 Marine Parade Rd., S.1544.
Tel: 344-5577.
250 rooms; restaurant serving local, European and Chinese food; bar. Other facilities: conference room; banquet room; shops; hairdresser; pool; health center; TV and IDD. Rates: S$120-130; T:S$135-165; Suite: S$220-345.

Plaza
7500A, Beach Rd., S.0719.
Tel: 298-0011.
355 rooms; restaurants serving local and European food; bar; club. Other facilities: conference room; banquet room; shops; hairdresser; doctor; pool; health center; shops facilities and TV. Rates: S: S$130-160; T: 150-180.

Peninsula
3 Coleman St., S.0617.
Tel: 337-8091.
315 rooms; restaurants serving local and European food; bar; club. Other facilities: conference room; banquet room; shops; hairdresser; pool; health center and TV. Rates: S: S$125-140; T: S$140-155; Suite: S$280.

Phoenix
Orchard Rd/Somerset Rd., S.0923.
Tel: 737-8666.
300 rooms; restaurants serving local, European and Chinese food; bar. Other facilities; conference room; banquet room; hairdresser; doctor TV and IDD. Rates: S: S$132-154; T: S$154-176; Suite: S$210-250.

Raffles
This historical landmark in currently closed for restoration. When it is reopened at the beginning of 1991, Raffles will have all the state of the art facilities which will all be carefully hidden behind a 20th century facade. Thus, guests will be met at the Changi Airport by vintage automobiles. The new Raffles will consist of suites only—104 of them.

Regent
1 Cuscaden Rd., S.1024.
Tel: 733-8888.
442 rooms; restaurants serving local, European and Chinese food; bar; ballroom. Other facilities: shops; hairdresser; doctor; pool; health center; TV and IDD. Rates: S: S$210; T: S$250; Suite: S$500.

River View
382 Havelock Rd., S.0316.
Tel: 732-9922.
483 rooms; restaurants serving local, European, Japanese and Chinese food; bar; club. Other facilities: conference room; banquet room; doctor; pool; health center; gardens; TV and IDD. Rates: S: S$160-170; T: S$180-190; Suite: S$400.

Royal Holiday Inn
25 Scotts Rd., S.0922.
Tel: 737-7966.
600 rooms; restaurants serving local, European and Chinese food; bar; ballroom. Other facilities: conference room; banquet room; shops; hairdresser; pool; health center; sports facilities. Rates: S: S$175; T: S$205; Suite: S$380.

Shangri La
22 Orange Grove Rd., S.1025.
Tel: 737-3644.
810 rooms; restaurants serving local. European, Japanese and Chinese food; bar; ballroom. Other facilities: conference room; banquet room; shops; hairdresser; doctor; pool; health center; sports facilities; gardens; TV and IDD. Rates: S: S$180-355; T: S$215-370; Suite: S$470-2175.

Sheraton-Towers
39 Scotts Rd., S.0922.
Tel: 732-0022.
412 rooms; 3 restaurants serving European and Chinese food; bar; club; ballroom. Other facilities: conference room; banquet room; hairdresser; doctor; pool; health center; TV and IDD. Rates: S/T: S$180-250; Suite: S$350-1000.

Tai-pan Ramada
101 Victoria St., S.0718.
Tel: 336-0811.
500 rooms; restaurants serving local, European. Japanese, Chinese and Thai food; bar; ballroom. Other facilities: conference room; banquet room; hairdresser; doctor; pool; health center; TV and IDD. Rates: S: S$140-180; T: S$160-200; Suite: S$240-1000.

Westin Plaza
2, Stamford Rd., S.0617.
Tel: 338-8585.
796 rooms; 11 restaurants serving local, European; Japanese and Chinese food; bar; ballroom. Other facilities: conference room; banquet room; hairdresser; doctor; pool; health center; shops facilities; TV and IDD.

Westin Stamford
2 Stamford Rd.,
Tel: 338-8585.
1,253 rooms; 11 restaurants serving local, European, Japanese and Chinese food; bar; ballroom. Other facilities: conference room; banquet room; shops; hairdresser; doctor; pool; health center; sports facilities; TV and IDD.

York
21 Mt. Elizabeth, S.0922.
Tel: 737-0511.
400 rooms, restaurants serving local, European and Chinese food; bar; ballroom. Other facilities: conference room, banquet room; shops hairdresser; pool; health center; TV and IDD. Rates: S: S$150-220; T: S$165-2220; Suite: S$220-320.

ECONOMY HOTELS

Air View
10 Peck Seah St., S.0207.
Tel: 225-7788.
28 rooms; restaurant serving Chinese food. Rates: S: S$41; T: S$45.

Bencoolen
47 Bencoolen St., S.0718.
Tel: 336-0822.
69 rooms; restaurant serving local and European food; bar. Rates: S: S$58-66; T: S$68-76; Suite: S$85-105.

Broadway
195 Serangoon Rd., S.0821.
Tel: 292-4661.
63 rooms; restaurant serving local and European and Chinese food; TV. Rates: S: S$70-80; T: S$80-90.

Grand
25 Still Rd. South, S.1542.
Tel: 345-5261.
25 rooms; TV. Rates: T:S$70-80.

Great Southern
36-42. A/B Eu Tong Sen St., S.0105.
Tel: 533-3223.
38 rooms. Rates: S:S$28; T: S$48-52.

Mitre
145 Killiney Rd., S.0923.
Tel: 737-3811.
19 rooms, restaurant serving local and European food; bar. Rates: S: S$44; T: S$56.

New Seventh Storey
229 Rochor Rd., S.0718.
Tel: 337-0251.
38 rooms; restaurant serving European, Japanese and Chinese food; bar and TV. Rates: S: S$59; T: S$75.

Mayfair
40 Armenian St., S.0617.
Tel: 337-4542.
27 rooms, restaurant serving Chinese food. Rates: S: S$54; T: S$63.

Strand
21 Bencoolen St. S.0718.
Tel: 338-1866.
130 rooms. Rates: S/T: S$54.

Supreme
15 Kramat Rd., S.0922.
Tel: 737-8333.
100 rooms; restaurant serving local, European and Chinese food; TV. Rates: S: S$75; T: S$85; Suite: S$125.

CULTURE PLUS

MUSEUMS

The National Museum, founded as early as 1823, had skeletons of a Sumatran rhinoceros, a horse and a tiger in its possession by 1877. Relics of Old Singapura's enigmatical past, like the cryptic "Singapore Stone" said to have been heaved into the river by a Malay strongman to prove his prowess to the king, survive in indecipherable fragments. The famous jewels of Majapahit—armlets of pale gold, six rings set with eleven inferior diamonds, and an odd jeweled clasp—are Singapore's opulent if slender link with the 14th century; not to mention a medieval Persian spittoon spotted on top of a junk heap by a Chinese collector in 1942.

The museum has its wealth stored in *kris* daggers, spears, idols, masks, belts of beads and betelnut boxes collected some years ago from the region's rarer civilizations. A walk through its galleries adds a hidden dimension of Asian history to the city's commercial sky-lines.

The National University of Singapore's Art Collection, housed in a separate wing, specializes in the pottery and porcelain of China illustrating 4,000 years of its manufacture. Collections also include a selection of ancient Indian sculpture and ancient Asiatic fabrics.

The National Museum is open from 9 a.m. to 5.30 p.m. (closed on Monday), including Sundays and public holidays. The National Art Gallery is in the same building. The gallery was opened in 1976 and displays the National Permanent Collection of Art as well as various local and international art exhibitions. Open from 9 a.m. to 5.30 p.m.

A group of volunteer guides called the "Friends of the Museum," conduct free tours around the National Museum everyday at 11 a.m., except Saturdays, Sundays and public holidays. Tel: 337-6077.

THEATERS

If you have seen a postcard depicting the statue of Sir Stamford Raffles standing in Empress Place, you'll probably have noticed a white building in its background. That white building is the **Victoria Theater**, the oldest theater in Singapore, and it was originally conceived far back in 1854 as the Settlement's Town Hall, a place of meeting and social reunion, theatrical performances, balls and concerts.

To amateurs accustomed to haphazard schedules in vacant assembly rooms, Town Hall was a godsend. As Singapore's first permanent theater, it delighted audiences on Opening Night 1860 with a performance of "A Storm in a Teacup." It has since been rebuilt and renovated several times, often in the throes of opposition to new-fangled change, yet still retains the tradition of an older style. French cellists say the acoustics are excellent. The newly-constructed **National Theater** is in Kallang and is used for live performances.

FESTIVALS OF ARTS

Public opinion has it that Singapore is a cultural desert and its citizens are often accused of being unappreciative of the arts. Rightly or wrongly, the government saw the need to organize an arts festival, aimed at creating an awareness of the arts among Singaporeans.

The Singapore Festival of Arts, a local premier cultural event, has a relatively short history—the first festival was held in 1977 followed subsequently by one in 1978, another in 1980 and the fourth one in 1982. Each of these grows in aspiration and scale as compared to its predecessors.

The 1990 event, spread over nine days in December, comprised performances by some 700 artists of 18 troupes from Singapore as well as nine other Western and Asian countries. A rare treat for lovers of drama, dance and music; programs featured ranged from modern ballets, classical Indian dances, traditional Javanese and Japanese dances to Chinese Orchestra, the Beijing Opera, the Zegreb Soloists from Yugoslavia and semi-local dramas. In conjunction too, art exhibitions displaying works of local and foreign artists were held and award-winning movies from all over the world were screened.

Having received good response, the Festival will be continued biennially.

LIBRARIES

More than a few books on Singapore have been put together upstairs in the Reference Room of the **National Library** where the Republic's archives and valuable South East Asia collection are readily available to the public. Librarians are quick and knowledgeable when it comes to finely specific subjects; they also point out significant works on Singapore in general.

The lending library downstairs is particularly good and open to all. Visitors may check out books by registering with the library and making a S$10 deposit, which is returned whenever you withdraw your borrowing privileges. (Bring your passport along as identification.) The Library, next to the museum on Stamford Road, is open Monday to Saturday from 8:30 a.m. to 8 p.m.

At present, there are five branch libraries in the residential areas of Toa Payoh, Marine Parade, Queenstown, Bukit Merah and Jurong East with more to open soon.

Besides lending books and serving as a reference source, the library and its branches feature programs like talks, forums, workshops, cultural shows, exhibitions and storytelling sessions. Check your morning papers for details or call tel: 337-7355.

SHOPPING

Those seeking out shopping venues in Singapore will find that the problem isn't where to go but rather which to go. Turn the corner of any street and chances are that you'll find a departmental store or at least a shopping center, a plaza, an emporium, some tiny shops along the footway of a row of shop-houses, or a vendor with his merchandise sprawled out on a mat.

Singapore owes its deserving title of "Shoppers' Paradise" to two main facts. One, there is no import duty or sales tax on most items which makes it cheaper to buy them here than back home; and two, there is a wide variety of products here brought by exporters from all over who find Singapore a ready market due to its free trade policy. One scene, typical of Singapore, continues to mesmerize visitors: a brightly lit space that may or may not be enclosed occupied by vendors who take pride in their items which not only fill the shelves to the edges but spill out onto portable shelves or display stands placed just outside the shops.

The Yellow Pages is an extremely good aid for singling out specific shops to obtain your purchases. But for those who have to stretch precious time, it is advisable to shop at areas where you can find all your wants. Highly recommended areas are **Orchard/ Tanglin, Chinatown/People's Park complexes, Change Alley/The Arcade** and **Arab Street/Beach Road**.

Wherever you shop, obey the two golden rules: bargain (except in departmental stores and other fixed prices shops); and do not buy at the first shop but compare prices.

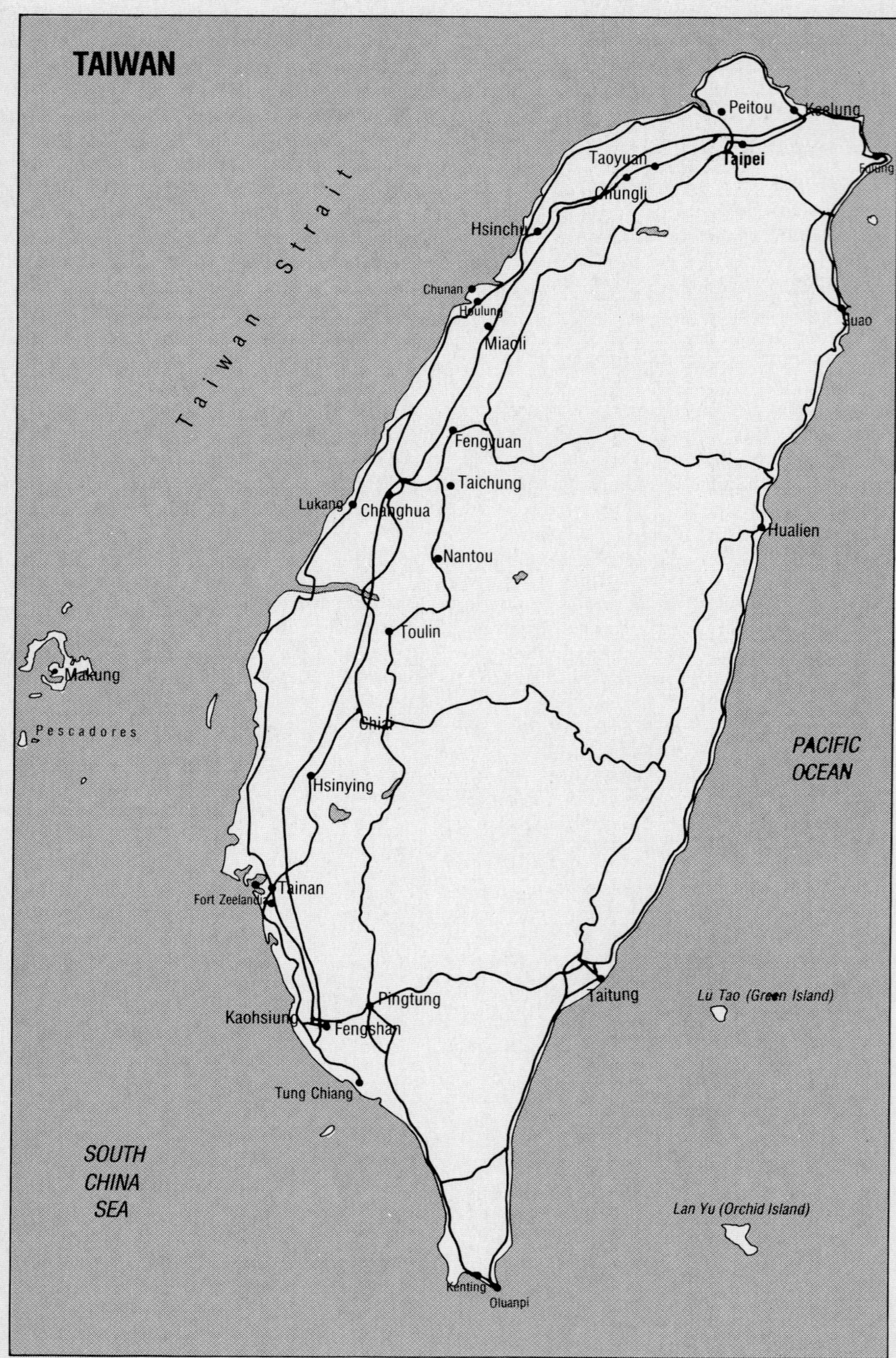
TAIWAN
Peitou
Keelung
Taoyuan
Taipei
Fulung
Chungli
Hsinchu
Taiwan Strait
Chunan
Houlung
Suao
Miaoli
Fengyuan
Taichung
Lukang
Changhua
Hualien
Nantou
Toulin
Makung
Chiai
Pescadores
PACIFIC
OCEAN
Hsinying
Tainan
Fort Zeelandia
Taitung
Lu Tao (Green Island)
Pingtung
Kaohsiung
Fengshan
Tung Chiang
SOUTH
CHINA
SEA
Lan Yu (Orchid Island)
Kenting
Oluanpi

GETTING THERE

BY AIR

Taiwan lies along one of the busiest air routes in Asia, and stopovers there may be included on any round-the-world or regional air tickets at no extra cost. Sixteen international airlines currently provide regular, scheduled air services to Taiwan:

Almost all international air traffic to and from Taiwan goes through the Chiang Kai-shek International Airport in Taoyuan, about 45 minutes from downtown Taipei. This is one of the safest, most well-designed airports in the Orient, fully equipped with the latest technology and passenger facilities to accommodate five million passengers and 400,000 metric tons of cargo annually. While you are here, it makes sense to visit the adjoining three-story Chung Cheng Aviation Museum. More than just a museum which exhibits models of aircraft (about 700 of those), it offers facilities for visitors to test their flying skills or experience the sensation of flying. Also housed within its premises are dioramas and close-circuit TV displays which trace aviation history from time of Icarus' plight to modern day space inquiries. The building is Asia's version of the National Aviation Museum in Washington, D.C.

At Kaohsiung in the south, Taiwan's other international airport, regular air services connect the island to Tokyo, Osaka, and Seoul. This route is served by China Airlines, Japan Asia Airways, and Singapore Airlines.

BY SEA

Of the five international sea ports in Taiwan (Keelung, Taichung, Kaohsiung, Suao and Hualien), the Kaohsiung and Keelung harbors are two of the largest and busiest at which a number of luxury sea liners call.

The Arimura Line of Okinawa operates a regular passenger ferry between Keelung and Okinawa. The ferry leaves Keelung on Monday at 8 a.m. and arrives in Okinawa on Tuesday at 7 a.m. The return trip departs Okinawa on Friday at 7 p.m. and arrives in Keelung on Saturday at 4 p.m. One-way fares for this trip are US$100 for Deluxe Class, US$85 for First-Class, and US$71 for Economy-Class. For further information and reservations contact Yung-An Maritime Co., Tel. 771-5911/8

TRAVEL ESSENTIALS

VISAS & PASSPORTS

Visas for travel to Taiwan may be obtained at the various ROC embassies, consulates, and representative offices around the world. Refer to the section on "Useful Addresses" for a listing of the overseas ROC embassies and consulates which represent Taiwan affairs in foreign countries.

The ROC government has replaced the various types of visa it used to issue to foreign visitors by one single visitor visa. When applying for a visitor visa, a completed application form, incoming and outgoing travel tickets (or a letter from your travel agent), three photos, and documents stating the purpose of visit other than sightseeing or transit are required.

Visitor visas are valid for 60 days (unless restricted to two weeks) and may be extended twice for 60 days each for a total of six months stay in Taiwan. All holders of visitor visas may not work in Taiwan without authorization.

Visitors from countries without ROC embassies or consulates such as Australia and Germany may approach the Taiwanese trade representatives and non-government agencies in their respective countries for letters of recommendation. These letters of recommendation may then be exchanged for visitor visas at any ROC embassy or consular office en route to Taiwan or on arrival at Chiang Kai-shek International Airport, the Kaoshiung International Airport, the Keelung International Seaport or the Kaoshiung International Seaport.

MONEY MATTERS

Since the island-wide coinage change in 1981, more than 800 million new coins in denominations of 50 cents, NT$1, NT$5, and NT$10 (totalling to over NT$2.6 billion) have been reminted. Except for the 50-cent coin which has a plum blossom on it, all the others bear the profile of Chiang Kai-shek. Bills come in units of NT$10, NT$50, NT$500, and NT$1,000.

Foreign currencies can be easily exchanged for the local and vice versa at banks, hotels, most shops and all authorized money dealers. However be sure to obtain receipts of all such transactions. You will find them saving you a lot of hassle with the customs authorities when you try to reconvert unused New Taiwan dollars upon departure.

Traveler's checks are also widely accepted at most hotels and other tourist-oriented establishments. This also applies to major credit cards such as American Express, Visa, Master Charge, Diner's Club, but the same cannot be said of personal checks which are difficult to cash, unless you are willing to wait for two or three weeks while they clear.

HEALTH

Effective cholera and yellow fever inoculation certificates are required for passengers coming from certain countries or have stayed more than five days in infected areas. For certificates to be effective, they must be issued at least seven days prior to but not more than six months before arrival. Otherwise, health certificates are not normally required.

WHAT TO WEAR

During the hot season, appropriate clothing for Taiwan should include light cotton shirts and blouses, loose cotton skirts and trousers, casual sportswear, and comfortable walking shoes. Men need not wear jackets and ties, for even during office hours most Chinese businessmen prefer to wear leisure suits and open-collars to beat the heat in summer. You may want to bring along a light weight jacket or dress for formal banquets and receptions, but otherwise such clothing is not necessary.

During the cold season, be sure to bring along some comfortable woolens to help protect you from the bone-chilling, moisture-laden airs of winter in Taiwan. Sweaters, woolen jackets and dresses, warm pants and socks will all come in handy during Taiwan winters, especially in Taipei. People in Taiwan tend to dress a bit more formally on winter evenings than in summer.

During both seasons it is advisable to bring along some sort of rain gear, such as raincoats or umbrellas. As they say, "Taiwan's climate is like the mood of a woman," and it can burst out in thunderstorms at any moment without forewarning.

EXTENSION OF STAY

To extend a tourist visa in Taipei, you must visit the Foreign Affairs Office of the Taipei Municipal Police Administration. It is located at the back of the Police Headquarters building on the corner of Wu-Chang Street and Chung-Hwa Road near the China Bazaar.

Be sure to apply for extensions at least one to two days before your visa expires. For further information, call the Foreign Affairs Police at 361-0159 or 311-9940.

ON DEPARTURE

All outbound passengers must pay an exit airport tax of NT$300. You must present the receipt when checking in.

GETTING ACQUAINTED

CLIMATE

Overlying the tropics and sub-tropics zones, Taiwan sports the tropical climate in the southern and western flatlands and the subtropical climate in the north and the mountainous regions. Its location also subjects it to annual typhoons which pass through between the months of July and October, but most of these cause little more than strong winds and heavy rains over the island.

Taiwan's climate does not have four distinct seasons, but two: a hot season which lasts from May till October and a cold from December to March. The island remains excessively humid throughout the year and receives abundant rainfall: with the east (upland) receiving more than the west (lowlands). Except in the northern region where rainfall is more even, mean annual rainfall in other parts of the island range from 102 to 200 inches.

Temperature falls with altitude; snow falls on the summits of the Central Range in the cold season while lowland Taiwan remains frost free.

The most pleasant times of the year for travel in Taiwan are March through May and September through November, especially in Taipei.

CULTURE & CUSTOMS

The Chinese, like the Koreans and Japanese, used to bow low and clasp their hands together when being introduced to someone new, but today the Western handshake has displaced that ancient custom.

Nevertheless, the Chinese still shy away from overly boisterous greetings in public, such as hugs, kisses and resounding slaps on the back. A firm handshake, friendly smile, and slight nod of the head are the most appropriate gestures of greeting.

In Chinese, a person's family surname precedes both is his given personal names and his formal titles. For example, in the name "Li Wu-ping," *Li* is the surname and *Wu-ping* are the personal names. In the term "*Li jing-li*," Li is the surname and *jing-li* ("manager") is the title. Most Chinese names consist of the three characters—one surname and two personal names—but may use only two.

The majority of Chinese family names come from the "Old Hundred Names" (*Lao-Bai-Hsing*) first formulated over 3,000 years ago in feudal China. Among the most common are Li, Wang, Chen, Hwang, Chang, Yang, Liang, and Sun.

During formal introductions, the Chinese today usually exchange name cards, which has become the tradition throughout the Far East. In fact, many people don't even listen to oral introduction, but wait instead to read the person's card. It's a good idea to have some personal name cards printed up before traveling anywhere in the Orient. As the Chinese says,"When entering a new land, follow the local customs."

Some of the most common titles used in Chinese during introductions are:

Hsien-sheng
"Mister," as in "Li hsien-sheng"

Tai-tai
"Mrs.," as in "Li tai-tai"

Hsiao-jye
"Miss," as in "Wang hsiao-jye"

Fu-ren
"Madame," as in "Chiang fu-ren"

Lao-ban
"Boss," as in "Chen lao-ban"

Jing-Li
"Manager," as in "Liang jing-li"

The Chinese term *ching-keh* literally means "inviting guests" and refers to the grand Chinese tradition of entertaining friends and associates which lavish generosity, usually at banquets. The Chinese are perplexed when they see Westerners call for their bills at restaurants, then pull out pocket calculators and proceed to figure out precisely how much each person at the table must contribute, right down to the last dime. The Chinese, on the contrary, almost get into fist fights while arguing for the privilege of paying the bill for the whole table. To the Chinese, "inviting guests" out for dinner and drinks is a delightful way to repay friends for favors or to cultivate new business relationships, and they do so often. For one thing, this is the type of gift which the giver may always share with the recipients. For another, the very moment you've paid a hefty dinner bill, everyone at the table is immediately obligated to invite you out as their guest sometime in the near future. This way, although the bill is high when it's your turn to "*ching-keh*," you only end up paying for one out of 12 banquets. In the final analysis, it all balances out, and everyone takes turns earning the "big face" that comes with being a generous host.

When toasted at dinner parties, it is well-mannered to raise your wine cup with both hands: one holding it and the other touching the base. The host would take his seat opposite (not beside) his guest-of-honor and it is fitting to have his back to the door and his guest-of-honor's facing it.

Tea served at the end of a meal is your host's polite insinuation that the party is over and that it is time for you to leave. So don't overstay your welcome even though your host may insist. What is mere courtesy to the Chinese is often regarded as hypocrisy to Westerners. For example, even though it is late and the host would love to call it a day, he will gently persuade his guest to stay longer. In this case, it is up to the guest to detect from the host's tone what's the best thing to do. But this requires skill and good cultural sense. An experienced traveler once ventured, "The rule of the thumb is to do the exact opposite that your Chinese friend suggests." Try it if you must but with discretion, please.

TIPPING

Generally speaking, heavy tipping is not expected in Taiwan, although token gratuities are always appreciated. Hotels and restaurants automatically add 10 percent service charge to your bills but his money rarely gets distributed among the staff, so a small cash tip of five to 10 percent is always welcomed in restaurants.

Taiwan taxi drives do not get upset if you do not tip them, but is customary to let them "keep the change" in small coins when paying the fare. Taxis still cost for less in Taipei then most places but the cost of gas and maintenance here is quite high, so drivers appreciate even the smallest tips.

The only places in Taiwan where heavy tips are routinely expected are in winehouses and dance-halls, where big tipping wins you "big face" and big favors from the ladies.

GETTING AROUND

FROM THE AIRPORT

The are two types of shuttle buses which operate daily service between the old Sung-Shan domestic airport in downtown Taipei and the new Chiang Kai-shek International Airport in Taoyuan.

The public Express Bus Line costs NT$32 one-way, but it has very little luggage space. It runs every 15 minutes in both directions between 6:30 a.m. and 10:40 p.m. The private Chung-Hsin Line costs NT$72 one-way, and it has ample space for luggage. It runs in both directions every five to 10 minutes between 6:20 a.m. and 8 p.m., then reduces frequency to every 15 minutes until the last bus departs at 10:30 p.m.

From the domestic Taipei Airport bus terminal you are only 10 minutes by cab from most major downtown hotels, many of which operate their own private airport shuttles. For further information on airport shuttles call 771-1330.

DOMESTIC TRAVEL

By Air: Regular scheduled domestic air service in Taiwan is provided by the international flag-carrier China Airlines and by Far East Air Transport (FAT), the main domestic carrier. These two airlines operate a total of 24 runs a day between Taipei and Kaoshiung (a 40-minute flight), 18 between Taipei and Hualien (30-minute), six between Taipei and Pescadores (40-minutes), for between Taipei and Tainan (40-minute), and four between Taipei and Taitung (40-minute). In addition, they schedule flights which connect various cities in the South with each other and with the Pescadores. As of 1990, the one way airfare between Taipei and Kaohsiung was set at NT$1,052, Taipei and Hualien at NT$750, Taipei and Tainan at NT$928, and Taipei and Pescadores at NT$967.

In addition to the above, Taiwan Aviation Corporation (TAC) operates special flights from Taitung to Orchid Island and Green Island, and occasionally from Kaohsiung out to some of the smaller outer islands. Great China Airlines (GCA) operates a helicopter service from Taichung to Sun Moon Lake, Mt. Ali (more commonly known as Alishan), and Pear Mountain in central Taiwan. Yung-Sing Airlines (YSL) schedules flights from Kaohsiung to the Pescadores and other islands, and from Taitung to Orchid island and Green Island.

Strict security measures are enforced on all domestic flights within Taiwan, and foreign passengers are required to show their passports prior to boarding, so don't leave yours behind in Taipei when traveling down-island by air. For bookings and other information, you may call your travel agent or the carriers directly.

Highway Express Buses: A special fleet of deluxe highway express buses serves the Taipei/Kaohsiung and Taichung/Kaohsiung routes, using the new North/South Expressway.

The one-way fare between Taipei and Kaohsiung is NT$414, and reserved-seat tickets from this route may be purchased up two days in advance. These buses depart both Taipei and Kaohsiung every 20 minutes between 7 a.m. and midnight.

Railway: The Chinese Railway Administration maintains an extensive railroad network which connects various points of the island with Taipei and other major cities. Passenger carriages are impeccably clean and comfortable, and service includes such local amenities as complimentary cups of fragrant Taiwan tea kept hot throughout your journey with regular infusions of water, newspapers and magazines, and towels to refresh your face and hands.

Reservation for first-class express trains in Taiwan must be made at least one but no more than two days prior to scheduled departures. However, although you may purchase round-trip tickets in advance, reservations for return trips must be made upon arrival at your destination, also one to two days in advance. Even for local trains, it is highly advisable to purchase your tickets at least several hours, and preferably a full day, prior to departure. In Taipei, advance train tickets may be purchased directly at the Central Railway Station by lining up before the appropriate window. Most hotels and travel agencies will also arrange advance train reservations on your behalf. To make first-class express train reservations by phone, call the following numbers:

Taipei; 312-2255 or 551-1131, ext. 2460
Taichung; 228-9608/9 ext. 246 or 346
Kaohsiung; 221-4821/221-2376, ext. 253

WATER TRANSPORT

The Taiwan Car Ferry Co. operates daily service between Keelung and the scenic east coast town of Hualien. It departs daily from Keelung at 9 a.m. and arrives in Hualien at 3 p.m. Return trips depart Hualien nightly at 10:30 p.m. and arrive back in Keelung the following morning at 6 a.m. The one-way fare is NT$350 per person, but special First-Class cabins (two beds plus TV) for two are available for about NT$600. Tickets are sold at 108 Chung-Shan North Road. Sec. 2. and at Peir 2. 16 Kang-Hsi Street in Keelung. For further information and reservations in Taipei contact Taiwan Car Ferry Co., Tel. 522-1215/7.

PUBLIC TRANSPORT

Buses: One of the first things you'll notice in Taipei is the incredible number of public buses on the streets. For budget-minded travelers, buses provide frequent and a very inexpensive means of transportation to any point within or without the city limits. However, unless you are endowed with an extra measure of Oriental patience, it is advisable to avoid the buses during heavy rush hours, which fall between 7.30 a.m.-9.30 a.m. and 5 p.m.-7 p.m. During these hours, passengers on buses are packed in like sardines and traffic moves at a snail's pace. Outside these hours, buses provide a convenient and inexpensive mode of inter-city transport.

There are two types of city buses: regular and air-conditioned. The regular bus costs NT$6 per ride, and the air-conditioned coach costs NT$8. Tickets and tokens should be purchased in advance at the little kiosks which you'll find at all bus-stops.

City bus service runs continuously from about 6 a.m. until 11.30 p.m. In order to signal the driver to stop at an upcoming station, simply pull the bellcord. There are so many buses and bus-routes within metropolitan Taipei that it is best to ask a hotel clerk or local acquaintance for directions before venturing out on your own. All buses are designated by code numbers, which indicate their routes and final destinations.

TAXIS

Sometimes it seem as if there are as many taxis in Taipei as people. Usually all you have to do to get a cab in Taipei is stand on the curb and wave your arm in the street: within moments a taxi will glide to a halt by your feet and the door will automatically swing open as the driver pulls a lever inside.

All taxi fares are calculated according to the meter. The basic fare has risen since 1988, and a further charge is added for each additional half kilometer. Taxis in Taiwan do not expect heavy tips, but they appreciate it if you let them "keep the change" in small coins. Due to the distance and long waits between fares at the CKS International Airport in Taoyuan, taxis are permitted to charge an additional 50 percent of the amount on the meter when running passengers between the airport and town. Currently, this comes to about NT$850 (US$22) one-way. In small towns and villages down-island, taxis usually charge a set fee of about NT$40 to take you anywhere within town. If you wish to retain a taxi for a full-day, or for a long, round-trip excursion to a specific destination, ask a hotel clerk or local acquaintance to negotiate either a set fee for the whole day or a discount on the meter fare.

Be forewarned: although Taiwan's taxi drivers are almost uniformly friendly and polite, they tend to drive like maniacs. Many tourists have their wits scared out as their taxi drivers weave carelessly between speeding buses and trucks, narrowly missing pedestrians, run through red lights, careen through swarms of buzzing motorcycles, and screech blindly around corners. Unfortunately, this sort of driving is the rule rather than the exception in Taiwan, and very little can be done about it. Should you get a particularly reckless driver, have him pull over immediately, pay him the fare on the meter (with no tip!), and hail another cab. There is never a shortage of cabs anywhere in Taipei, day or night rain or shine.

Very few taxi drivers in Taiwan speak or read English sufficiently well to follow directions given in English. So it's always a good idea to have your destination written out in Chinese before venturing out by cab.

WHERE TO STAY

HOTELS

Ever since the 1978 big boom in new hotel construction, the quality of hotel accommodations in Taiwan has been steadily improving. Today, travelers in Taiwan have a wide range of styles and prices to choose from when selecting a hotel, especially in Taipei.

There are 104 tourist hotels operating on the island, with a total of more than 19,800 rooms available. Rates range from NT$400-6,600 for singles, NT$550-6,600 for doubles, and NT$1,500 up for suites. Note that ten percent service charge is added to all hotel bills.

Chinese hotels are renowned for attentive,

gracious service rendered with a spirit of pride and a genuine desire to please. Visitors are treated as personal guests rather then anonymous patrons, and hospitality is approached more as an art than as an industry. However, Western travelers occasionally encounter frustrations. One reason is the ever-present language barrier: though uniformly trained in English, most Chinese hotel staff understand very little; yet to avoid "losing face" by admitting they don't understand your request, they'll sometimes nod and pretend to understand, then promptly forget about it. Another reason is cultural: Chinese priorities often differ from Western's, and what seems of vital importance to you may seem trivial to the Chinese. Nevertheless, minor professional shortcomings in Taiwan's hotel industry are far outweighed by its notable strengths; its warmth, friendliness, and courtesy.

Tourist hotels in Taiwan are ranked in two categories: International Tourist and Regular Tourist. The former offers greater luxury and more varied facilities, while the latter offers lower rates and simpler services.

TAIPEI

Hilton International Taipei
38 Chung-Hsiao W. Rd., Sec. 1;
Cable: HILTESL;
Telex: 11699, 22513;
Tel: 311-5151.
Directly across from Central Rail Station; 413 rooms; polished, professional service in all departments; award-winning food & beverage facilities; lively disco; sauna.

The Ritz
155 Min-Chuan E. Rd.;
Cable: THERITZ;
Telex: 27345;
Tel: 597-1234.
Located in northeast Taipei, near the nightlife area; 283 rooms; small hotel with personalized service; "art-deco" decor; good European food and beverage facilities.

Lai-Lai Sheraton
12 Chung-Hsiao E. Rd.; Sec. 1;
Cable: SHANGTEL;
Telex: 23939;
Tel: 321-5511.
Located three blocks from Hilton; 705 rooms; large hotel with many facilities including disco-club, health-club, and several restaurants.

Asia World Plaza Hotel
100 Tun Hwa North Road;
Cable: ASIA WRDHTl;
Telex: 26299 ASIA WRD;
Tel: 715-0077
Located in the heart of the business district; 720 rooms; huge hotel with 57 bars and restaurants, cinemas, theater restaurant, fitness center, underground parking, convention facilities, a department store, shopping mall with 500 boutiques and all major hotel amenities.

Howard Plaza
160 Jen Ai Rd., Sec. 3
Telex: 10702 HOPLATEL TAIPEI;
Tel: 700-2323.
Central downtown location within walking distance of shopping and entertainment district; 606 rooms; elegant decor; continental ambience.

The Grand Hotel
1 Chung-Shan N. Rd., Sec. 4;
Cable: GRANDHOTEL;
Telex: 11647;
Tel: 596-5565.
Located on top of Round Hill overlooking the city; 530 rooms; classic Chinese palace architecture; exquisite traditional ambience; extensive gardens and private recreation club.

The President Hotel
9 Teh-Hui St.;
Cable: PRESDENT;
Telex: 11269;
Tel: 595-1251.
Located amid the most lively nightlife area; 469 rooms; popular among businessmen; quick access to highway.

The Ambassador
63 Chung-Shan N. Rd., Sec. 2;
Cable: AMBASATEL;
Telex: 11255, 11184;
Tel: 551-1111.
Located along Chung-Shan N. Rd, close to shopping area; 481 rooms; indoor swimming pool; roof-top bar lounge with superb views; convenient access to shops.

The Imperial
600 Lin-Sen N. Rd.,
Cable: IMPTEL;
Telex: 11382, 11730,
Tel: 596-5111, 596-3333.
Located near President Hotel; 336 rooms; convenient access to nightlife district; disco club; sauna.

Brother Hotel
255 Nanking E. Rd., Sec. 3;
Cable: BROTHERTEL;
Telex: 25977;
Tel: 712-3456.
Located in east Taipei; 282 rooms; excellent Cantonese "dim-sum" restaurants, rooftop lounge, well-maintained rooms.

HOSTELS

If you're willing to sleep in dormitories, eat in cafeterias, and travel exclusively by bus, then you can actually tour Taiwan for as little as US$10 per day by utilizing facilities operated by the China Youth Corps (CYC). CYC operates a series of Youth Activity Centers and Youth Hostels around the island, and budget-minded travelers may avail themselves of these inexpensive facilities. Information and reservations for the 15 hotels and eight activity centers sponsored by CYC headquarters at 2199 Sung-Kiang Road, Taipei, Tel: 543-5858.

Due to the popularity of these facilities, groups and individuals from overseas who wish to use them should make reservations well in advance. They usually remain fully booked from July through September and from January through February.

If you have not made prior arrangements and wish to "play it by ear" as you go, then at least be sure to call ahead to your next intended stop to make sure hostel accommodations are available.

Rates for room and board vary at different centers, but on the average three meals a day can be had for about NT$30-50, dormitory accommodations for NT$60 a night. Most of these establishments also offer private individual rooms at higher rates, and some even have spacious bungalows for families or small groups.

CULTURE PLUS

MUSEUMS

The rich and colorful history of the Chinese together with the pride they take in knowing and preserving their cultural roots have spawned many museums in Taiwan devoted to the procurement, care study and display of objects of lasting value and interest. In Taipei alone, there are about a dozen such institutions, with the world-renowned **National Palace Museum** as the largest of them all. Itself a monument with 18 years of history behind it, the museum is home to some 620,250 priceless relics of bronze, porcelain, jade, lacquer, enamelware, paintings, portraits, tapestry and embroidery, rare books and documents. The museum is open daily throughout the year and admission charge is a mere NT$30 per person.

Just close by is the **Chinese Culture and Movie Center** whose main attractions are a wax museum and a "Middle Kingdom Village." The former displays wax models dressed in authentic Chinese costumes worn through the ages while the latter contains palaces, houses and inns architecturally similar to those found in the old Chinese Imperial and early Republican times. Many movie-makers have used this village as a shooting location and that probably explains why Chinese movie fans have found the setting in the background familiar in different movies. Admission into the center costs NT$30 and an additional NT$15 for each child you have with you.

Second in magnificence to the Palace Museum is the **National Museum of History** within which are exhibits reflecting more than 4,000 year of Chinese culture. The treasures found in this institution are not to be named nor listed; they have to be seen to be appreciated. Initially set up with public funds, the collection housed is being continuously enlarged by private individuals, mainly civic-conscious Chinese. Open daily, admission charge is NT$10.

In addition to these are special museums like the **Postal Museum**, the **Children's Museum**, the **Butterfly Museum**, etc. Do not be deceived for although the names speak for themselves, visits to them while downtown are worthwhile.

CHINESE OPERA

Taiwan is one of the best places in the world to attend the opera, Chinese style. From the bizarre melodies mouthed by magnificently-costumed performers to the exotic orchestral accompaniment to the astounding acrobatics and martial arts displays of the performers, a night watching a Peking Opera will surely prove entertaining as well as educational.

For a preliminary taste of Peking or Taiwan opera, try the television set. Live performances are broadcast almost every day. In the back alleys of Taipei and outside the big city, keep your eyes open for the traveling opera companies that set up and perform for several days.

DANCE

There is a limited amount of traditional folk dancing in Taiwan, most performed by minority groups. Snippets of aboriginal dance can be viewed at the various aborigine tourism centers around the island. Other forms of dance are performed as part of the Chinese culture show staged daily at 10:30 a.m., 2 p.m. and 4 p.m. in the first briefing room on the third floor of the **Dr. Sun Yat-sen** Memorial Hall.

On the other hand, modern dance has gained in popularity in Taiwan in the past decade. The Cloud Gate Dance Ensemble, led by Lin Hwaimin, has spearheaded the movement. It combines both Chinese and Western techniques and ideas choreographed to the music of contemporary Chinese composers. The group, internationally-acclaimed during a tour of Europe in 1981, holds regular performances in Taipei. Consult your hotel or the Taiwan Visitors Association (Tel: 594-211/4) for the schedules of the Cloud Gate ensemble.

MUSIC

Taiwan has produced numerous musicians of world class. Western classical music is regularly performed at various venues in Taipei by the Taiwan Provincial Symphony Orchestra and the Taipei Municipal Symphony Orchestra. Consult your hotel information desk or such organizations as the National Music Council and the Chinese Classical Music Association for information on scheduled performances. Traditional Chinese music has its roots in both special temple rituals and folk music.

HANDICRAFT CENTERS

If people were classified according to how good they are with their hands, you will definitely find the Taiwanese ranked among the top.

The Taiwanese take great in the things they can make with their hands; from lanterns and toys, handbags and baskets, bamboo and rattan crafts, rugs and carpets, to knitwear and embroideries, and so the list goes on. The government **Handicraft Exhibition Hall** opened for public viewing in June 1977. Exhibits number more than 1,500 and are from all parts of Taiwan, some produced by cottage industry and others by regular plants. The Hall, in Tsaotun, is situated on the highway running from Taichung to the Sun Moon Lake and the Chitou Forest Recreation Area. Open daily except Mondays, national and public holidays from 9 a.m. to noon and from 1 p.m. to 5 p.m., the hall is well worth a visit.

While in Tsaotun, also call at the **Taiwan Provincial Handicraft Institute** also operated by the Taiwan provincial Government within which you will find a factory, a kiln and a research laboratory.

In Taipei, an excellent selection of local handicrafts are on display for sale at the Chinese Handicraft Mart at #1 Hsu Chou Street, Tel, 321-7233. This is a good place to do your souvenir and gift shopping all in one trip.

SPORTS

In recent years, sports activities have enjoyed increasing popularity in Taiwan, which hosts frequent international sports events and regularly sends teams to compete abroad. In international competitions, Taiwan's athletes have scored major victories in golf, soccer, and the martial arts, and Taiwan's hard-slugging Little League baseball teams have repeatedly made world headlines during the past decade by winning six world championships. Taiwan proudly boasts two Olympic Medalists: decathlon star C. K. Yang, Taiwan's "Man of Iron;" and runner Chi Chang, "Asia's Flying Antelope." The sports most easily accessible to tourists in Taiwan are golf, tennis, and swimming.

GOLF

Golf is the oldest organized sport in Taiwan, and all 17 of Taiwan's golf clubs, nine of which are close to Taipei, are open to foreign visitors for guest memberships. The clubs are open all year round. The oldest club on the island is the **Taiwan Golf and Country Club** in Tan-Shui, which was built by the Japanese in 1919. The **Hualien Golf Club** dates back to 1928. Taiwan's avid golfers garner frequent victories in competitions on the Asia Circuit.

TENNIS

Tennis has been the fastest growing sport in Taiwan in recent years, and hundreds of new courts have been laid out around the island to meet the demand for tennis facilities. In Taipei, you'll find excellent facilities for tennis at public courts, private clubs, and several hotels.

SWIMMING

In addition to public beaches, there are numerous swimming pools at various hotels, clubs and resorts around the island. Guests of the Grand Hotel have free access to the Olympic-sized pool at the adjacent **Yuan-Shan Club**, which is otherwise open only to members and their guests. For a nominal fee, you may enjoy a swim surrounded by green mountains at the **China Hotel** on Yangming Mountain. For a nominal fee, visitors may also use the outdoor pool at the **Mandarin Hotel** and the indoor pool at the **Ambassador Hotel**. The **American Club** and the **Yangming Mountain Country Club** both have large pools, but you must be accompanied by a member to use them.

MARTIAL ARTS

Traditionally, the Chinese have kept in shape by practicing various ancient forms of martial arts exercises, and in recent years these traditional forms have made in a major comeback in Taipei.

Every morning at dawn thousands of people pour into the parks and streets of Taipei to practice **tai-chi, martial arts, yoga, sword dances,** or simple **aerobics**. Visitors may also get a good work-out each morning by simply joining whatever group interests them and mimicking their gentle movements.

The four most popular places in Taipei for early morning exercise sessions are **New Taipei Park** (near the Hilton), the landscaped grounds of the **Chiang Kai-shek Memorial Hall**, the compound of the **Sun Yat-sen Memorial Hall**, and the hills around the Grand Hotel. The reason that these exercise sessions always take place at the crack of dawn is that the Chinese believe the air is most densely impregnated with *chi* ("vital energy") at that time.

MOUNTAIN CLIMBING

Two-thirds of Taiwan is covered with lush evergreen mountains, and these rank among Taiwan's greatest attractions for mountain-climbers and trekkers. The two favorite climbs are to the 13,114-foot peak of **Jade Mountain** (Mt. Morrison), which is the highest in Taiwan and all Northeast Asia, and to the 12,743-foot summit of **Snow Mountain** (Mt. Sylvia), which is Taiwan's second highest peak.

Climbers bound for Jade Mountain usually take the express train down to Chiayi, then switch to the alpine diesel train for the ride up to the Alishan Forest Recreation Area. From there they proceed 12 miles up to Tungpu base-camp, where there is a hostel. The next morning they make the ascent up Jade Mountain where there is a second hostel located just 2,287 feet below the summit. You should allow four days for the trip from the Alishan Area to the summit of Jade Mountain and back.

Snow Mountain is located north of Pear Mountain (Li-Shan), midway along the spectacular East-West Cross-Island Highway. You can get to Pear Mountain by driving in either from Taichung or Hualien. From there, a bus takes you to Mt. Huan in the foothills of Snow Mountain, and a car carries you on up to the Wuling Farm at 5,777 feet altitude, where simple lodgings are available overnight.

Climbers commence their ascent of Snow Mountain the following morning and should allow four days for the trip from Pear Mountain up to the summit of Snow Mountain and back.

For less formidable climbs, there are many scenic mountains located between Taipei and the northern coastline which require no prior arrangements nor police permits. **Seven Stars Mountain** at 3,675 feet, is the tallest of these gentle northern peaks.

SKIING

For two months each year (January and February) enough snow falls on the slopes of Mt. Ho-Huan ("Harmonious Happiness Mountain") to permit skiing.

Rising to an altitude of 11,208 feet in central Taiwan, Mt. Ho-Huan is easily reached by taking the Tayuling-Wushe branch of the East-West Cross-Island Highway. Its amenities include the cosy Pine-Snow Hostel, which accommodates 150 persons, a 400-meter ski-lift, ski instructors, and fabulous alpine scenery which is well worth viewing even if you do not ski.

Since temperatures there never rise above 60°F (14°C), **Harmonious Happiness Mountain** also makes an excellent summer resort, especially for hiking and mineral baths.

SCUBA & SKIN DIVING

An entirely new kingdom of colorful sea-life unfolds for divers who plunge into the blue waters off Taiwan's coral coasts. Indeed, enormous colonies of live coral form one of the island's greatest underwater attractions, with colors in every conceivable shade of pink to purple.

An astonishing variety of tropical and semi-tropical fish and molluscs; exquisitely shaped and colored conch, cone, cowrie, and other shells; brightly-plumbed sea lilies; and other exotic underwater life inhabit these vast coral communities in Taiwan's off-shore waters.

The most spectacular diving in Taiwan is found near Oluanpi at the southernmost tip of the island. The rocky, shallow shoreline here also permits excellent snorkeling. In the north, divers like to explore the underwater coral kingdoms off the coast of Yeh-Liu, which is famous for the bizarre formations of coral-rock protruding from the seaside promontory.

LANGUAGE

Grammatically, spoken Chinese is so simple and direct that it makes other languages seem cumbersome, archaic, and unnecessarily complex by comparison. There are no conjugations, declensions, gender distinctions, tense changes, or other complicated grammatical rules to memorize. The spoken language consists of simple sounds strung together in simple sentence patterns, with the basic "subject/verb/object" construction common to most Western languages. Tones, while foreign to Western tongues, come naturally with usage and are not that difficult to master.

Even within China, the various provinces give different tonal inflections to the various sounds. Proper word-order and correct context are all you need to know about Chinese grammar.

In Taiwan, the Mandarin dialect (known as *gouyu*, "National Language") has been declared the official *lingua franca* by the government. Mandarin, which is based upon the pronunciations which prevailed in the old imperial capital of Peking, is by far the most melodious dialect of China.

In addition to Mandarin, there is a local dialect called "Taiwanese" which is derived from China's Fukien Province, ancestral home of the vast majority of Taiwan's Chinese populace. Taiwanese is commonly spoken among local people, especially in the rural regions, and one of Taiwan's major television stations broadcasts programs in that dialect for their benefit.

The older generation still speaks some Japanese—a remnant influence of Japan's colonial occupation—and younger people tend to understand at least some basic English. But though English is a required subject for all Chinese students in Taiwan throughout middle and high school, it is spoken fluently by very few.

It helps immensely to learn a little spoken Chinese before traveling in Taiwan. Not only will it help you get around, it will also give you "big face" among the Chinese, who are always surprised and flattered to find a foreigner who has bothered to learn a bit of their language.

GREETINGS & ADDRESS

Hello; how are you?	*Nee how-ma?*
Fine; very good	*Hun-how*
Not so good	*Boo-how*
Goodbye	*D-zai-jyen*
See you tomorrow	*Ming-tyen jyen*
Good morning	*Dzao-an*
Good evening	*Wan-an*
You; you (plural)	*Nee; nee-men*
I; we	*Wo; wo-men*
He; she, it; they	*Ta; ta-men*
Who?	*Shay?*
Mr. Lee	*Lee syen-sheng*
Miss Lee	*Lee shiao-jyeh*
Mrs. Lee	*Lee tai-tai*
Thank you	*Shyieh-shyieh*
You're welcome	*Boo keh-chee*

TIME & PLACE

Where?	*Nah-lee?*
What time?	*Jee dyen joong?*
What day? (of the week)	*Lee-bai jee?*
Today	*Jin-tyen*
Tomorrow	*Ming-tyen*
Yesterday	*Dzuo-tyen*
One o'clock	*Ee dyen-jongg*
Two o'clock	*Liang dyen-joong*
Very far	*Hun yuan*
Very close	*Hun jin*

FOOD & BEVERAGE

Restaurant	*Tsan-ting*
Bar	*jiou-bah*
Let's eat; to eat	*Chir-fan*
Let's drink; to drink	*Huh-jiou*
Ice	*Bing*
Beer; cold	*Pee-jiou; bing pee-jiou*
Water; cold	*Shway: bing-shway*
Soup	*Tang*
Fruit	*Shway-gwo*
Tea	*Cha*
Coffee	*Ka-fay*

Hot	*Reh*
cold	*Lung*
Sugar	*Tang*
A little bit	*Ee-dyen*
A little bit more	*Dwo-ee-dyen*
A little bit less	*Shao-ee-dyen*
Bottoms up!	*Gahn-bay!*
Settle the bill	*Swan-jang*
Let me	*Wo ching-keh*

HOTEL & TRANSPORTATION

Hotel	*fan-dyen*
Room	*fang-jyen*
Airport	*fay-jee-chung*
Bus	*Goong-goong chee-chuh*
Taxi	*Jee-cheng-chuh*
Telephone	*Dyen-hwah*
Telegram	*Dyen-bao*
Airplane	*Fay-jee*
Train	*Hwo-chuh*
Reservations	*Ding-way*
Key	*Yao-shir*
Clothing	*Ee-fu*
Luggage	*Shing-lee*

SHOPPING

How much?	*dwo-shao*
Too expensive	*Tai-gway*
Make it a bit cheaper	*Swan pyen-ee-ee-dyen*
Money	*Chyen*
Credit card	*Shin-yoong kah*
Old	*Lao*
New	*Shin*
Big	*Dah*
Small	*Syiao*
Antique	*Goo-doong*
Red	*Hoong*
Green	*Lyu*
Yellow	*Hwang*
Black	*Hay*
White	*Bai*
Blue	*Lan*
Gold	*Jin*
Jade	*Yu*
Wood	*Mu*
Proprietor; shop-owner	*Lao-ban*
Wrap it up	*Bao-chee-lai*

BASIC SENTENCE PATTERNS

I want...	*Wo yao...*
I don't want...	*Wo boo-yao...*
e.g I want cigarettes	*Wo yao syahng-yen*
Where is...	*dzai nah-lee?*
e.g. Where is the restaurant?	*Tsan-ting dzai nah-lee?*
Do you have... beer?	*Nee yio may-yio... pee-jiou?*
I like...	*Wo shee-hwan...*
I don't like	*Wo boo-shee hwan...*
e.g. I like you.	*Wo shee-hwan nee.*
I wish to go...	*Wo yao choo...*
e.g. I wish to go to the hotel.	*Wo yao choo fan-dyen.*

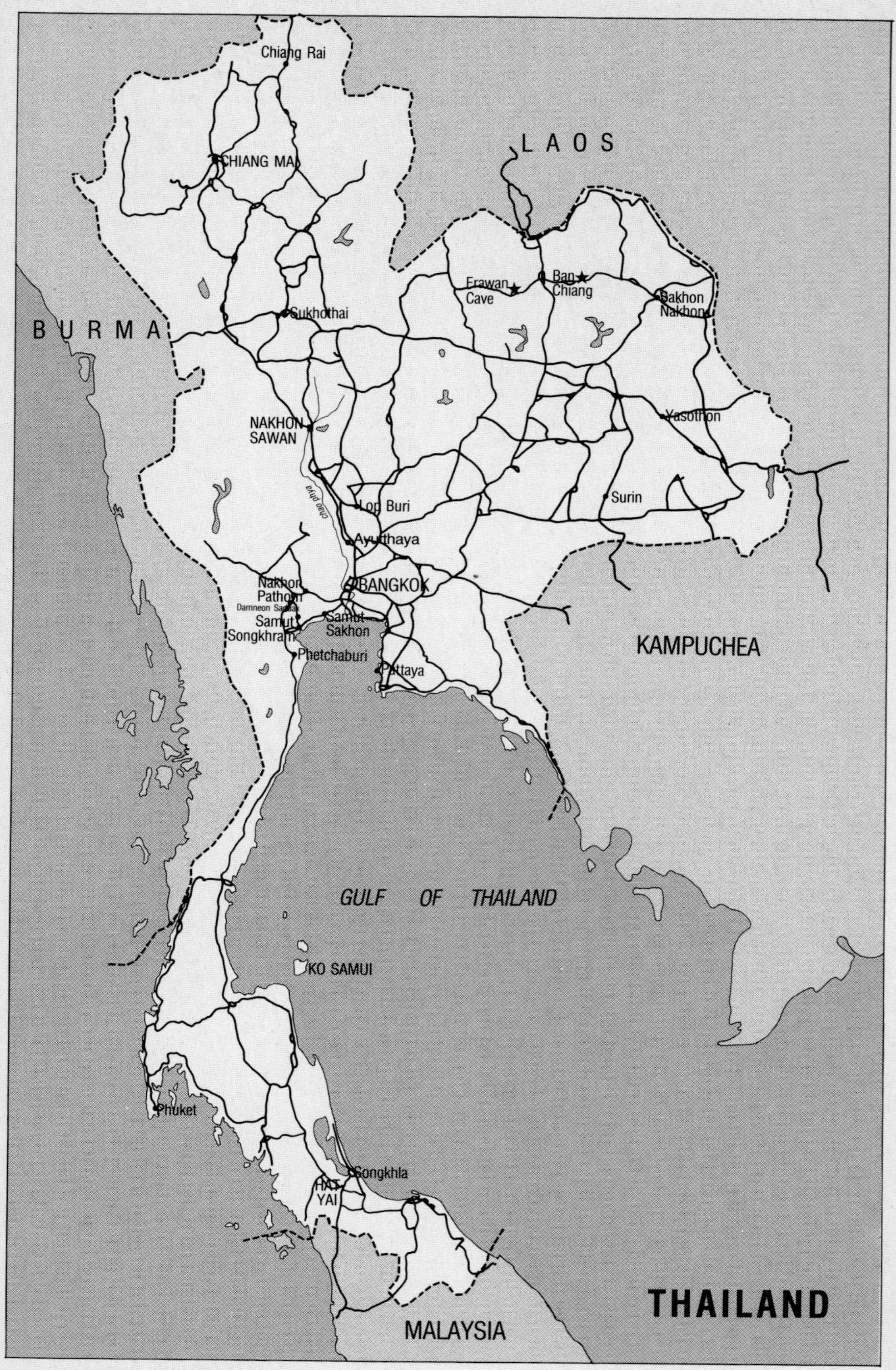
Chiang Rai
LAOS
CHIANG MAI
BURMA
Sukhothai
Erawan Cave
Ban Chiang
Sakhon Nakhon
NAKHON SAWAN
Yasothon
Lop Buri
Surin
Ayutthaya
BANGKOK
Nakhon Pathom
Samut Songkhram
Samut Sakhon
Phetchaburi
Pattaya
KAMPUCHEA
GULF OF THAILAND
KO SAMUI
Phuket
Songkhla
HAT YAI
THAILAND
MALAYSIA

GETTING THERE

BY AIR

More than 35 international airlines call at Bangkok's Don Muang International Airport whose customs clearance and passport checks are relatively fast. A new international passenger terminal completed in 1988 will further speed arrivals and departures. Remember that Bangkok airport tax for outgoing passengers on international routes is 150 *baht* per person.

Although nearly all air passengers arrive and depart from Bangkok, there are international airports at Chiang Mai, Phuket and Hat Yai.

BY SEA

From Europe, companies such as Ben Line Steamers, Polish Ocean Lines and Nedloyd ship out to Bangkok. From the United States, Pacific Far East Line, American President Lines and State Lines go to Bangkok. There are also many ships sailing regularly from Japan, Hong Kong and Singapore. Inquire with local travel agents agents for schedules and fares.

BY RAIL

Except when it rains so hard that railroad tracks are submerged. Thai trains are reliable. You can get first-class, air-conditioned sleepers going anywhere within the country for less than 500 *baht* (US$22.) There is daily railroad service between Singapore, Malaysia and Thailand.

BY ROAD

Roads in Thailand are excellent. Roads are being improved and extended into the more remote provinces, but apart from the southern road links with Malaysia, Thailand is virtually road-locked. At present there is no road access to and from Burma, a missing link in the Asian Highway that stretches from Turkey to Singapore.

There are three main roads crossing the Thai-Malaysian border in the south. Inexpensive taxis and minibuses ply the routes between major towns. Malaysia closes its border at 6 p.m. daily, so plan your itinerary in accordance.

In case you are driving yourself or renting a car, Malaysia prohibits any vehicle from Thailand that does not have an insurance policy. Most cars in Thailand do not.

TRAVEL ESSENTIALS

VISAS & PASSPORTS

All foreign nationals can stay in Thailand for up to 15 days without a visa. For a longer stay a visa must be obtained from Thai embassies or consulates abroad. Tourist visas cost US$5; applications must be accompanied by three passport sized photos. Visas are granted for a period of 60 days, with a possible extension of another 60 days upon request. However, getting an extension is such a hassle that visitors tend to sidestep requirements (which include presenting a resident sponsor with a guarantee-bond of US$250) by simply leaving the country and obtaining another tourist visa.

A person who wishes to leave Thailand and return before expiry of this tourist visa must first obtain a re-entry visa. This can be done Mondays to Friday from 8:30 a.m. to 3:30 p.m. at the Immigration Division, Soi Suan Plu, South Sathorn road (Tel: 286-9222); or Saturday, Sunday and government holidays between 8:30 a.m. and 2:30 p.m. at the Tourism Authority of Thailand, Rajdamnoen Avenue. Cost of a re-entry visa is 500 *baht*, and it must be accompanied by one photo.

A visa is valid for one entry within 60 days

THE PROBLEMS OF A

HEAVY TRAFFIC.

You'll come across massive Thai jumbos at work and play in their natural habitat. In Thailand, elephants are part of everyday rural life.

FALLING MASONRY.

A visit to the ruined cities of Sukhothai or Ayutthaya will remind you of the country's long and event-filled history.

EYESTRAIN.

A problem everyone seems to enjoy. The beauty of our exotic land is only matched by the beauty and gentle nature of the Thai people.

GETTING LOST.

From the palm-fringed beaches of Phuket to the highlands of Chiang Mai there are numerous places to get away from it all.

MNC&H/THA/8652P

OLIDAY IN THAILAND.

GETTING TRAPPED.

In bunkers mostly. The fairways, superb club houses and helpful caddies make a golf trap for players of all standards.

HIGH DRAMA.

A performance of the 'Khon' drama, with gods and demons acting out a never-ending battle between good and evil, should not be missed.

EXCESS BAGGAGE.

Thai food is so delicious you'll want to eat more and more of it. Of course, on Thai there's no charge for extra kilos in this area.

MISSING YOUR FLIGHT.

In Thailand, this isn't a problem. Talk to us or your local travel agent about Royal Orchid Holidays in Thailand.

Thai
We reach for the sky.

from the date of issue. Should the holder of the visa be unable to enter Thailand within this period, Thai embassies or consulates generally will extend the visa for a period not exceeding the period of validity of the applicant's passport, nor exceeding a period of six months.

MONEY MATTERS

The unit of currency in Thailand is the *baht* (pronounced "baad"). One US dollar is equivalent to 25.4 *baht* (at time of press). One baht is divided into one hundred *satang*. Coins are valued at 25 *satang* (smaller gold coin), 50 *satang* (bigger gold coin), one *baht* (smaller nickel coin) and five *baht* (bigger nickel coin). The 25-*satang* coin is commonly called a *salehng*. Paper notes are valued at 10 (brown color), 20 (green), 50 (blue), 100 (red) and 500 (purple)*baht*.

If you have traveler's checks in America dollars, they can be cashed at banks in all provincial capital; so there is no need to carry unmanageable amounts of baht notes with you outside of Bangkok. Traveler's checks in other currencies, however, are best cashed in Bangkok. As a rule, hotel exchange rates are poorer than those offered by banks and authorized money changers.

Keep in mind that most hotels do not accept personal checks.

HEALTH

Incoming visitors need an International Certificate of Health, showing a small pox vaccination within the last three years, if arriving from an infected area. Yellow fever inoculations are required by persons coming from or going to contaminated areas; children less than a year old are exempted.

HYGIENE

In a country where people are as personally neat and cleanliness-conscious as the Thais, there are relatively few health hazards stemming directly from poor sanitation.

Tap water in Bangkok is considered relatively safe, but to be doubly sure, drink purified bottled water.

Travelers who have never reckoned with the tropical sun should keep in mind that noon is not the wisest time to sunbathe; you will earn a burn in just 15 minutes. If you are out touring, exposed to the elements, wear a straw hat or carry a paper parasol.

WHAT TO WEAR

Light and loose clothes are best suited to Thailand's climate. For the hot season, pack clothes that provide adequate protection from the direct sun—cotton is best, and umbrellas and sunglasses are highly recommended. For the rainy season, it is wise to carry clothes that dry quickly after a sudden downpour. For the four months from November to February, warmer clothes (at least sweater and warm socks for the chilly nights) are necessary in the North and other hilly regions, as there is no central heating or even household fireplaces.

Bangkok is highly westernized in its business and social dress, with provincial centers following suit. Certain restaurants require jackets and ties for dinner. At traditional ceremonies and formal gatherings, however, Thai women often prefer to don their ethnic silk costumes.

CUSTOMS

As with most countries, Thailand prohibits visitors bringing in illicit narcotic drugs and explicit pornography. Firearms require a permit from the Police Department. Goods that may be imported duty-free include 200 cigarettes, one liter of wine or spirits, a camera with five rolls of film, and a reasonable amount of personal effects.

Visitors are permitted to bring in any amount of foreign currency for personal use but must fill in a currency declaration form for larger sums. No one can bring in or take out of Thailand more than 500 *baht*. Holders of family passports are permitted to export 1,000 *baht*.

Getting Acquainted

GOVERNMENT & ECONOMY

Thailand is a constitutional monarchy. The head-of-state since 1946 has been King Bhumipol Adulyadej.

Almost 50 million persons make their homes in Thailand: nearly five million of them live in Bangkok. Rice is the major export crop. Nearly three million tons is exported annually, ranking second in the world. Thailand is the world's largest exporter of tapioca, second largest of rubber, and the fifth largest producer of tin. Teak, sugar cane, maize, tobacco and cotton are other important export crops. And fisheries rank high in the economy.

The gross national produce (1988) is US$57.2 billion. The per capital income (1988) is US$1,039.

GEOGRAPHY

Although Thailand is situated well within the tropics, there is a wide climatic range depending on the time of year and the part of the country. The Central Plains (including Bangkok), the hilly North, and the arid, flat Northeast share the same seasonal patterns. The so-called hot season spans March, April and May, although many foreign residents argue that it is hot throughout the year when it is not raining. Daytime temperatures in the hot season are in the 86°F(30°C) range and can reach 104°F (40°C), especially in the Northeast.

In June, the southwest Monsoon ushers in the rainy season with slightly lower temperatures but higher humidity. In Thailand, the monsoon season amounts to five months of unpredictable weather. Some days bring erratic rainstorms while others are clear and sunny. November ushers in the cool season, particularly in the North where night temperatures can drop to 8°C (46°F). Bring a sweater or jacket if traveling there between November and February.

The long isthmus in South Thailand, which straddles the Gulf of Thailand and the Indian Ocean, has a climate similar to that of Malaysia—subtle seasonal variations with the weather generally warm, humid, and sunny year-round. Rain is possible almost any time.

CULTURE & CUSTOMS

Some customs are important to keep in mind during a visit to Thailand. The Thais are far too genial and easy going to expect a *farang* ("foreigner") to observe all their ways, but here, as anywhere, it helps to have a few general ideas about the *dos* and *don't* of polite society.

Perhaps the one area (besides showing proper respect for the monarchy) where they *can* be sticky is regarding behavior in a temple. Visitors are required to remove their shoes before entering the building containing the principal Buddha image, which is the one where people will be sitting about the floor paying homage to the Buddha. Women are not allowed in the monks' quarters, nor should they hand anything directly to a monk. (Should the occasion arise when a woman *has* to give something to a monk and no man is around to perform the service, she places the object on a table or on the ground and then the monk is free to pick it up for himself.) What few unpleasant incidents there have been involving foreigners in *wats* have arisen because the Thais felt some deliberate insult had been given to their religion. One, a few years ago, came about when some visitors to the ruins of Sukhothai were photographed sitting on the head of a huge Buddha image—a double insult actually, since the head is considered the most sacred part of the body. Another resulted from a singularly insensitive team of fashion models who not only posed provocatively but even changed their clothes in the compound of Wat Phra Kaew.

GREETINGS

When Thais meet one another, they do not usually shake hands. The customary greeting is the *wai*, with the hands raised as if in prayer. Traditionally, the higher the hands are held the more respectful is the *wai*, so that by observing two people you can tell theoretically their respective ranks. But rank is a complicated matter in Thailand, involving, as it does, such things as age, occupation, and social position. For an outsider, it is enough to make the gesture.

As the feet are the lowest part of the body, it is considered rude in Thailand to point your feet at anybody, especially if the gesture is deliberate. Most Thais strive mightily to avoid doing so even accidentally, and as a result you seldom see people with their legs crossed, or if they are, they tend to keep the toes pointed carefully toward the floor.

DRESS

Thais are extremely neat in their appearance, and even in a slum it is rare to see anyone who is really dirty or unkempt; mechanics, covered with grease and grime at the end of the day, emerge from their evening bath as spotless as if they had never come within reach of an engine. (All Thais bathe at least once a day and usually twice.) To say that someone is *mai rieb-roi* ("not neat") is almost as serious as saying that he is *mai suparb* ("not polite"), and very often it is the same thing; disorderliness can be regarded as rude in certain circumstances. Although among some younger, westernized Thais—the kind you see roaming about Bangkok shopping centers—it is considered smart (*sa-mart*) to dress in the loose, semi-hippie garb of Western teenagers, to the great majority of the population it is simply *mai rieb-roi*. Similarly, to conservative Thais, there are polite and impolite colors—a brightly colored dress is acceptable on a young girl but not on an older woman, who ought to wear somber shades or pastels. (There are even certain colors for certain days; Sunday, for example, is the only day on which almost anyone can wear red without being considered *mai-suparb* in the extreme.) As a general rule, of course, foreign visitors are not included in all these strictures, and as long as you look reasonably presentable (even in a *mai-suparb* color) you are not likely to get a second look on the street. It *is* frowned upon, however, for a woman to wear shorts in public particularly in a temple, or to show too much of the rest of her body either for that matter.

PUBLIC BEHAVIOR

It is common to see two Thai men holding hands as they walk along the street—a sign, incidentally, of simple friendship; nothing else—but very rare to see a man and woman doing it, for public displays of affection between the sexes is an old and strong taboo. During the Vietnam war, when Bangkok was a major rest and recreation center for thousands of American servicemen, one of the most frequent criticisms leveled at them was their public behavior with bar girls, innocent though most of it was by American standards. The experience has left many well-bred Thai girls wary about even being seen with a *farang* for fear she will be held in contempt by others.

SURNAMES

Surnames are a relatively recent innovation in Thailand, having been introduced only fifty-odd years ago during the reign of King Rama VI. Before that, people were called simply by a single name, followed by an explanation, if necessary, such as "son of..." or "from the town of..." Even today the average Thai last name is usually so long and complex that it is seldom used; thus Mr. Kraisri Nimmanahsominda is called, simply, Mr. Kraisri *Khun*, in Thai is the equivalent of either Mr. or Miss or Mrs., and is used for both men and women. You may encounter titles of Thai royalty, which in descending order are *Mom Chao* (M.C.), *Mom Rajawong* (M.R.), *Mom Luang* (M.L.).

Getting Around

FROM THE AIRPORT

From Don Muang Airport to Bangkok 14 miles (22 km south), air-conditioned sedans offer 24-hour service, while buses leave every half-hour. Tickets cost 300 *baht* and 100 *baht* respectively.

Public taxis are not metered. Be sure you first agree on a fare, normally between 180 and 200 *baht*. Bus fares are 3.50 *baht* for a regular bus and 15 *baht* for an air-conditioned bus. Pick-up points for public taxis and buses are just outside the airport gate.

Across the highway, is the Don Muang Railway Station. A train ride to Bangkok costs 4 baht. However, this is recommended only for visitors with light luggage.

DOMESTIC AIR TRAVEL

Thai Airways (do not confuse it with Thai International) links major cities throughout the country with its fleet of Boeing 737s. In the North, it flies daily to Chiang Mai, with less frequent stops at Phitsanulok, Phrae, Nan, Lampang, Chiang Rai and Mae Hongson. In the Northeast, there are daily flights Ubon Rajthani, and other stops in Udon, Nakhon Phanom, Khon Kaen and Loei. The south-bound schedule includes the island resort of Phuket, as well as Haadyai, Trang and Pattani.

Thai Airways also has regular flights to Penang and Kuala Lumpur in Malaysia, and weekly flights to Hanoi, Vietnam. For reservations call 281-1633 in Bangkok.

WATER TRANSPORT

Thailand has an estimated three million kilometers of navigable waterways. Most visitors limit their water travel to trips around Bangkok, or possibly the daily launch to Ayuthaya on the Oriental Queen. Cost of that excursion is 650 *baht* including lunch. Hotels in Bangkok and all provincial capitals can arrange localized excursions.

The Thai Navigation Company has three passenger-cargo ships that travel south from Bangkok, down the Gulf of Siam and South China Sea, to Koh Samui, Songkhla, Pattani and Narathivat. Departures are Wednesday and Saturday. Full nine-day cruise rates average about 1,000 *baht*.

TRAIN TRANSPORT

Thai trains are comfortable and reliable, though they are crowded all year round. The State Railway of Thailand runs international express, express, rapid, ordinary and diesel railcar services in three passenger classes over an extensive and well-maintained network. Costs are very reasonable.

You can choose from third-class situps, second-class air-conditioned situps (with reclining chairs), second-class sleepers, and first-class air-conditioned compartments. For information and reservations call the Bangkok Railway Terminus at 233-7010, or Hua Lampong Station at 223-3762.

PUBLIC TRANSPORT

Air-conditioned coaches and ordinary buses run from Bangkok to every town in Thailand. All told, 2,744 buses are operated by the state Transport Company over 134 routes to all 72 provinces; and another 2,246 buses operation on 147 routes within or between the provinces. In Bangkok, there are three major bus terminals:

Northern and Northeastern routes: Taladmochit, on Paholyothin Road, tel: 282-6660.

Eastern route: Ekamai on Kukhumvit Road, tel: 392-2520. This is the route that goes to Pattaya and points beyond.

Southern route: Sam Yaek Fai Chai on Charansanitwongse Road in Thonburi, tel: 411-1337.

There are also numerous private buses and coaches that ply routes between major cities. Check with local agencies for schedules and fares.

PRIVATE TRANSPORT

It is possible to rent cars with major agencies in Bangkok. Indeed, there are 27,400 miles (43,840 km) of national and provincial highways in Thailand, and another 7,500 miles (12,000 km) under construction. But most signs are in the Thai language only; driving can be hazardous for the uninitiated; and other forms of transportation are universally recommended to visitors. Chauffeur-driven rentals are usually best.

TRANSPORTATION IN BANGKOK

Buses: The Bangkok Metropolitan Transit Authority (BMTA) runs blue and white city buses. Route numbers in front and on the back, can be checked against maps sold in most bookstores.

The buses are usually very crowded during the rush hours in the morning and afternoon, but are relatively vacant at other times during the day. Bus fares start at 1.50 *baht* for the first 10 kilometers, with an additional one *baht* for the next 10 kilometers.

Air-conditioned buses, also run by the BMTA, link major places in Bangkok. They are quite comfortable and not so crowded. Fares start at five *baht* for the first eight kilometers and two baht for each additional kilometer.

Taxis: All taxis are air-conditioned. Bargaining is essential, as taxis do not have meters. Many drivers do not speak English, so have your hotel desk write your destination in Thai and suggest the approximate fare. Short trips usually are a minimum of 30 *baht*; a trip from the Grand Palace to the major hotel districts should be 50 to 60 *baht*.

Pedicabs: Commonly known as *sam-lor* or *tuk-tuk*, they consist of a motor-scooter around which a two-seat carriage has been built. They are worth trying for short trips. Prices start at 10 *baht*; again, bargaining is essential.

Boats: Numerous ferries and express boats ply the Chao Phya river and major klongs. In addition, several day and night cruises can be booked through major hotels. Going rate for renting private jetboats along the river bank is about 300 *baht* per hour, regardless of the number of passengers.

WHERE TO STAY

HOTELS

There is no telling just how many hotels there are in Thailand. They exist all over the country and their standards range from deluxe international inns to small, simple establishments which cater to on-the-move hitchhikers.

Fluctuations in exchange rates and rampant inflation make it virtually impossible to pinpoint hotel rates. As a general rule, rates are highest in luxury hotels found in resort cities and provinces like Bangkok, Chiang Mai and Pattaya. It is always advisable to call ahead or check with a travel agent about the latest prices. Most lodgings add a 10½ percent hotel tax and a 10 percent service charge.

You may rest assured that finding a hotel that suits your needs and budget is never a task. The list in the back will give an idea of what is available in Bangkok.

BANGKOK

Airport Hotel
333, Chert Wudthakas Road,
Don Muang
Tel: 566-1020.

300 rooms overlooking tropical gardens and a pool. 24-hour coffeeshop, 3 restaurants, and video lounge. Connected to the airport by skybridge and also by bus shuttle services.

Ambassador
Soi 11 Sukhumvit Road
Tel: 251-5141.

Has Western, Japanese, Chinese, Thai and seafood restaurants, 3 bars and 2 coffee houses; 24-hour room service and basement nightclub. In the center of the commercial and entertainment districts.

Asia
296 Phya Thai Road
Tel: 281-1433.
Easy access to town, poolside snacks. European-Chinese-Japanese cuisines.

Bangkok Center
382 Rama IV Road
Tel: 235-1780.
Situated near the Chinatown district just across the road from Hua Lampong railway station Coffee shop and restaurants.

Bangkok Palace
City Square, Petchburi Road
Tel: 251-8874.
Swimming pool, two restaurants, coffee shop. In the heart of Bangkok. Walking distance from the Rajdamri shopping arcade.

Century
9 Rajprarob Road
Tel: 252-9755.
European-Chinese-Japanese cuisines. Friendly atmosphere.

Continental
971 Phaholyothin Road
Tel: 278-1596.
European, Oriental and Thai cuisines and all the usual amenities.

Dorchester
21 Soi Kotoey, Pratipat
Tel: 279-2641.
Restaurant, coffee shop, swimming pool and shopping arcade.

Dusit Thani
946 Rama IV Road,
Saladang Circle
Tel: 233-1130.
One of Bangkok's top hotels. Several restaurants and varied cuisines. Has discotheque and sauna in addition to all the standard amenities. Located in business and entertainment area.

Erawan
494 Rajdamri Road
Tel: 252-9100.
One of Thailand's distinguished hotels, it has a tropical garden and Continental restaurant, post and travel offices and a full range of other services.

Federal
27 Sukhumvit Road (Soi 11)
Tel: 252-5143.
Centrally situated in a residential area with all facilities.

First
2 Petchburi Road
Tel: 252-5010.
European, Chinese and Thai cuisines and round-the-clock coffee shop. Features a nightclub and "sightseeing" counter. Conveniently situated in center of movie district.

Florida
43 Phya Thai Square
Tel: 245-3221.
Undistinguished but pleasant and homely. Features all the usual amenities in addition to being close to a delightful Laotian nightclub.

Fortuna
19 Sukhumvit Road (Soi 5)
Tel: 251-5121.
Situated in the center of the bar district and somewhat unprepossessing but boasts all the standard amenities.

Golden Dragon Hotel
20/21 Ngarmvongwan Road
Tel: 588-4751.
Restaurant and coffee shop. Swimming pool. Fifteen minutes from the airport.

Grace
12 Sukhumvit Road (Soi 3)
Nana North
Tel: 252-9170.
In the center of the bar district and known for its exotic coffee shop. Provides all the facilities.

Hilton International Bangkok
Nai Lert Park,
North Wireless Road
Tel: 252-3622, 252-7380.
400 luxurious rooms and suites with private balconies. Swimming pool, poolside bar, 4 restaurants, health club, tennis and squash courts.

Impala
Wireless Road
Tel: 391-0038

Pleasant and luxuriously appointed, has shopping arcade and spacious garden.

Indra Regent
Rajprarob Road
Tel: 251-1111.
One of the larger international-type hotels with European, Chinese, Thai cuisines and a splendid coffee shop.

Mandarin
662 Rama IV Road
Tel: 233-4980.
Conveniently located near the railway station. All standard amenities which includes European, Chinese, Japanese and Thai cuisines.

Manhattan
Soi 15, Sukhumbit Road
Tel: 252-7141.
European, Chinese, Japanese, Korean and Thai cuisines. Round-the-clock coffee service, beer garden and a friendly atmosphere.

Miramar
777 Mahachai Road (Samyod Road)
Tel: 222-1711.
Bar, restaurant and coffee shop, 2 conference rooms, travel agency and money changer. Located in Chinatown and business center of Bangkok.

Montien
54 Suriwongse Road.
Tel: 234-8060.
High class hotel with luxury apartments; situated in the center of the entertainment district.

Morakot
2802, New Petchburi Road
Tel: 314-0761.
Facilities include dining room, bar, coffee shop, swimming pool, travel agency and shopping arcade.

Naral
222 Silom Road
Tel: 233-3350.
Top international standard hotel. Boasts a revolving roof-restaurant, European and Asian cuisines, German beer cellar and Italian coffee shop.

Oriental
48 Oriental Avenue, New Road
Tel: 234-8620.
Picturesque top-class hotel with a historic past associated with personages like Joseph Conrad and Somerset Maugham. Special appeal is its site overlooking the Chao Phya river.

Park
6 Sukhumvit Road (Soi 7)
Tel: 252-5110.
Restaurant serving European and Chinese food. Bar, money changer and the usual amenities.

Peninsula
295/3 Suriwongse Road
Tel: 234-3910.
Medium-type hotel with all the standard facilities.

President
135/26 Gaysorn Road
Tel: 252-9880.
International standard hotel. Conveniently situated in the center of town. Has all facilities with European and Thai cuisines.

Prince
1537/1 New Petchburi Road
Tel: 251-3318.
Somewhat far from town but has all facilities and reasonable rates.

Princess
Charoen Krung Road
Tel: 234-2951.
Medium-type hotel withall the standard facilities.

Rajah
Sukhumvit Road (Soi 4)
Tel: 252-5102.
All facilities with European, Chinese and Thai cuisines.

Ramada
1169 New Road
Tel:234-8971.
Dining room, nightclub cocktail lounge, coffee shop and tea lounge.

Reno
40 Soi Kasemsan 1,
Rama I Road
Tel: 252-6121.
Restaurant, swimming pool.

FOOD DIGEST

WHAT TO EAT

The problem of eating in Bangkok, as one gourmet has observed, is not so much where as what.

The city probably has a more diversified selection of restaurants than any other capital in Asia, with the possible exception of Tokyo, with a range running from cheeseburgers to *sukiyaki* and almost everything in between.

Within a relatively small area you can eat Mexican, French, German, Italian, Scandinavian, Hungarian, Japanese, Vietnamese, Korean, English, American, Laotian, Filipino, Indian, Indonesian, Swiss, Burmese and Austrian—and not, in most cases, vague approximations but the real thing, prepared by cooks from the country in question.

Half a dozen provinces of China are represented, from bland Cantonese to spicy Szechuanese, offering not only such splendors as Peking Duck but esoteric oddities like duck tongues and chicken breast stuffed with bird's nest.

You can dine on Central, Northern, Southern, and Northeastern Thai food, either in fairly basic surrounding or in lavish, air-conditioned comfort while watching a show of folk and classical dancing.

Your hotel bookshop will probably have a number of restaurant guides to help you make a choice; one that is recommended is *Eating Out In Bangkok* by Harry Rolnick, a highly personal but dependable compilation by a long-time resident of Bangkok.

Except for weekends, reservations are usually unnecessary, even at the fanciest restaurants; only one hotel restaurant requires a jacket and tie.

ROADSIDE KITCHENS

Inveterate snackers, Thais like to eat when the mood strikes them, at almost any hour of the day or night. Their philosophy regarding food is, quite simply "Eat when you are hungry." Wherever you go in Thailand you will see them around a noodle vendor's bicycle or at one of the temporary sidewalk stalls that spring up as if by magic wherever people are likely to be working or passing by—eating a bowl of rice noodles garnished with a bit of fried meat and coriander, a delicate little pancake folded around a sugary sweet, or a deep-fried banana fritter.

These portable kitchens, using only the basics in equipment—usually only a brazier of charcoal and a few pots and pans—turn out culinary delights remarkably complex by any standards.

NIGHTLIFE

The nighttime world of Thailand needs no introduction. Night life is as important to Bangkok visitors as sandy beaches are to Hawaii or cherry blossoms to Japan.

Thai nightlife is centered around nightclubs, bars, massage parlors and—more recently—discotheques, all of which exist in almost all corners of the country.

Musical entertainment, provided by pop groups or solo vocalists, is available at the larger hotels. It is difficult to know just what is featured since hotels rotate their acts. Call to check first.

For a cheaper way to enjoy an evening drink and perhaps a meal with musical accompaniment, there are many open-air restaurants around Bangkok—especially along Lard Prao Road—where live bands play music of Thai modern genre and (occasionally) Western.

If your idea of a well-spent evening is jiving to the latest sounds, drinking and chatting with beautiful hostesses, visit any of the bars and nightclubs on Patpong Road or Soi Cowboy (off Soi 21, Sukhumvit Road). These bars are famous for their open and friendly bargirls. Most of them also stage floor shows, with the first show starting about 10 p.m.

Fancy trying Bangkok's famed massage parlors? Try those along Patong II Road (the small road parallel to the main Patpong Road) or on Petchburi Road. A massage will cost from 120 *baht* per hour upwards although much depends on the class of establishment... and how elaborate a massage you require.

SHOPPING

WHAT TO BUY

Shopping is a pleasure, not only because of the variety of things to buy also, nowadays, because of the ubiquity of Bangkok's air-conditioned shopping centers where it is possible to get a good deal of your buying done without being laid out by the heat.

The following are some of the things Thailand is noted for, both the quality and the price in most cases, being superior to anywhere else.

THAI FABRICS

Thai silk is too well known to need any introduction; suffice to say that is here, in quantity, in assorted weights, in meters, or made up into clothes and other items. It may, however, be useful to note that the quality of silk is not always uniform, and in some shops that offer suspiciously good bargains, the cloth may have been cleverly interwoven with rayon or some other synthetic; stick to the better-known shops unless you are good at telling.

Handwoven Thai cotton is less famous and unjustly so, for it is a soft but durable material that is wonderful for dresses, upholstery, and other uses. In many shops you can get the cotton in the same colors and prints as the silk at around 40 to 50 *baht* a meter.

JEWELRY

Gold in Thailand is considerably cheaper than in Europe or the United States, and the craft of making modern jewelry—as distinct from the traditional Thai designs—has progressed to the point where many tourists now rank Bangkok ahead of Hong Kong.

Best buy among native stones is the sapphire, blue or black, star or plain: also you can sometimes find good rubies from Cambodia and Burma.

Most stones are less expensive than in the West. For something different, look at the Thai princess ring, which has nine tiers set with nine different precious and semi-precious stones.

HANDICRAFTS

If you are going to Chiang Mai, where most of the Thai handicrafts come from, wait and buy them there.

Otherwise, look for the hill tribe embroidery, laquerware, painted umbrellas, wood carvings, basketwork, and delightful fish mobiles made of woven bamboo which Thai mothers hang over cribs as pacifiers.

The government-sponsored Narayana Phand, on Larn Luang Road in Bangkok is a good place to buy most of these.

CELADON

This was originally made in Thailand during the Sukhothai period, died out, and was revived about 20 years ago. Vases and lamp bases are good buys; complete dinner sets are also available as well as a variety of souvenir pieces.

DOLLS

For collectors, there is wide selection in a classical dance costumes or depicting the various hill tribes of the North.

BRONZEWARE

Long one of the most popular buys with tourists, bronzeware now comes in plain, modern designs as well as the traditional Thai ones.

You can get everything in it from complete cutlery sets to salad bowls; look also for bronze temple bells to hang on a terrace or patio. At several shops you can get bronzeware that has been siliconized so that it will not tarnish.

SPIRIT HOUSES

There are some charming ones in the shape of little Thai-style houses which are not too bulky to send or carry.

ANTIQUES

Best buys are Chinese porcelains and furniture, carvings from Thai temples. Sawankhalok (a porcelain made near Sukhothai in the 14th century), old Thai paintings, silver betel-nut boxes, Burmese tapestries and wooden figures. Fakes abound, especially in Buddha images, so know what you are doing or go to the best shops.

For most Buddhist art of Thailand, a permit is required from the Fine Arts Department before the pieces can be taken out of the country. The good shops will take care of this complicated job for you.

SHOPPING AREAS

The Central Department Store, with its five branches in Silom, Chidlom, Wangburapa, Ladya and Ladpraw, is the best place for a visitor who does not have enough time to go around the country to shop for gifts from various provinces. It also has goods from all over the globe. (Prices are fixed;credit cards and personal checks are accepted.)

Thai Daimaru has two branches; one in Rajdamri Arcade on Rajdamri Road and the other at Phra Kanong on Sukhumvit Road. It sells mostly imported goods from Japan. (Prices are fixed; credit cards and checks are accepted.) **The Mall Shopping Center** on Rajdamri Road offers for sale goods from all around the world at fixed prices. **Robinson Department Store** has three branches; Rajdamri, Victory Monument and Stam Square. You will find a good range of ready made clothes here at fixed prices.

Those who like bargaining will find small or big shops on almost every street of Bangkok offering everything from rubber bands to jewelry. A few big shops accept credit cards and checks but most prefer cash.

ART/PHOTO CREDITS

Photographs	
313	**Apa Photo Agency**
46/47	**Borget, Auguste/Hong Kong Museum of Art Collection**
114	**Bruchmann, Peter**
94	**Compost, Alain**
80	**Courtesy of Archives of the Royal Tropical Institue, Amsterdam**
194	**Courtesy of Muzium Negara**
122/123, 142	**Courtesy of Tokyo National Museum**
71, 77	**Cranbourne, Ray**
137	**Dorel, René**
52, 61, 64, 66, 73, 149, 162, 173, 180, 183, 184, 221, 234, 258, 274, 285, 303, 311	**Evrard, Alain**
148	**Friedrich, Peter**
267	**Gocher, Jill**
32, 35, 75, 95, 216/217, 256/257, 259, 260	**Gottschalk, Manfred**
150	**Grazer, Allen F.**
282	**Guether, Heidrun**
Cover	**Hahn, Werner**
57, 63, 68, 72, 97, 120, 128/129, 131, 143, 144, 146, 147, 154, 156, 168/169, 171, 202, 228, 242, 268, 280/281, 284, 286, 290, 306, 312	**Heaton, D & J**
15, 109	**Hesselyn, Brent**
177	**Hetier, Michel**
3, 5, 10, 11, 12, 14, 16, 17, 69, 83, 86, 87, 96, 98, 100, 101, 102, 103, 106, 107, 108, 110, 111, 112, 113, 126, 127, 136, 140, 145, 152, 188/189, 193, 203, 213, 215, 218, 226, 227, 237, 238, 239, 241, 243, 245, 263, 296/297, 302, 310, 317, 319	**Höfer, Hans**
298, 308, 309, 316	**Invernizzi, Luca**
18, 248/249, 261	**Jezierski, Ingo**
201	**Joyce, Tony**
22, 26, 34, 38, 43, 45	**Klein, Wilhelm**
48, 54/55, 58, 62, 118/119, 130, 159, 304/305, 315	**Kugler, Jean**
211	**Lat**
65, 67, 85, 99, 236	**Lawrence, Max**
167, 170, 178, 182, 185, 196/197	**Lawson, Lyle**
190, 198, 208, 209, 210, 212, 246/247, 250, 253	**Little, Philip**
6, 7, 13, 50, 53, 56, 59, 70, 91, 200, 204, 214, 252	**Lloyd, R. Ian**
8/9, 164, 166, 172, 176, 179, 181, 187, 220, 224, 225, 229, 231	**Lueras Leonard**
33, 40, 78/79, 82, 84, 90, 115, 117, 233, 269	**Müller, Kal**
138, 314	**Nakayama, Ben**
139, 206	**Oey, Eric**
20/21	**Pfannmüller, Günter**
235, 264	**Reichelt, G. P.**
92, 93, 133, 134, 157, 174, 175, 265, 292, 293	**Riel, Paul Van**
272/273	**Rocovits, Dan**
30, 36/37, 39, 41	**Rubenstein, Bill**
60, 278, 279	**Ryan, David**
207, 271, 277	**Salmoiraghi, Frank**
88/89	**Schoellhammer, Thomas**
222, 230, 232, 240, 262, 320	**Seitz, Blair**
266	**Stroheim, Paul Von**
24, 25, 51, 124, 125, 132, 141, 165, 192, 276, 300, 301	**'Wah'**
28/29, 31, 42, 104, 195, 199, 283, 291, 295, 307	**Wassman, Bill**
135, 151, 155, 160/161, 287	**Wheeler, Nik**
223	**Yamsuan, Noli, Jr.**
254/255	**Yap, Rendo**

INDEX

A

B

C

D

E

F

G

H

I

J

K

L

M

N

O

P

Q

R

S

T

U

V

W

Y

Z